MEN OF ARMOR:
THE HISTORY OF B COMPANY, 756TH TANK BATTALION IN WORLD WAR II

MEN OF ARMOR: THE HISTORY OF B COMPANY, 756TH TANK BATTALION IN WORLD WAR II

Part II: Cassino and Rome

JEFF DANBY

CASEMATE
Philadelphia & Oxford

Published in the United States of America and Great Britain in 2022 by
CASEMATE PUBLISHERS
1950 Lawrence Road, Havertown, PA 19083, USA
and
The Old Music Hall, 106–108 Cowley Road, Oxford OX4 1JE, UK

Hardback Edition: ISBN 978-1-63624-015-2
Digital Edition: ISBN 978-1-63624-016-9

A CIP record for this book is available from the British Library

Printed and bound in the United Kingdom by TJ Books

Typeset in India by Lapiz Digital Services, Chennai.

For a complete list of Casemate titles, please contact:

CASEMATE PUBLISHERS (US)
Telephone (610) 853-9131
Fax (610) 853-9146
Email: casemate@casematepublishers.com
www.casematepublishers.com

CASEMATE PUBLISHERS (UK)
Telephone (01865) 241249
Email: casemate-uk@casematepublishers.co.uk
www.casematepublishers.co.uk

Front cover: National Archives, SC 190187.

To all the fine men who served in
B Company of the 756th Tank Battalion
During World War II,
Especially those forty-seven tankers
Who made the ultimate sacrifice.

"To survive you often have to fight, and to fight you have to dirty yourself."
—George Orwell

"Never tell people how to do things.
Tell them what to do and they will surprise you with their ingenuity."
—General George S. Patton

"In war, only the simple succeeds."
—Field Marshal Paul von Hindenburg

"The tragedy of war is that it uses man's best to do man's worst."
—Henry Fosdick

"Next time you invade Italy, don't start at the bottom."
—General Fridolin von Senger und Etterlin

Contents

List of Maps

BASIC MILITARY MAP SYMBOLS

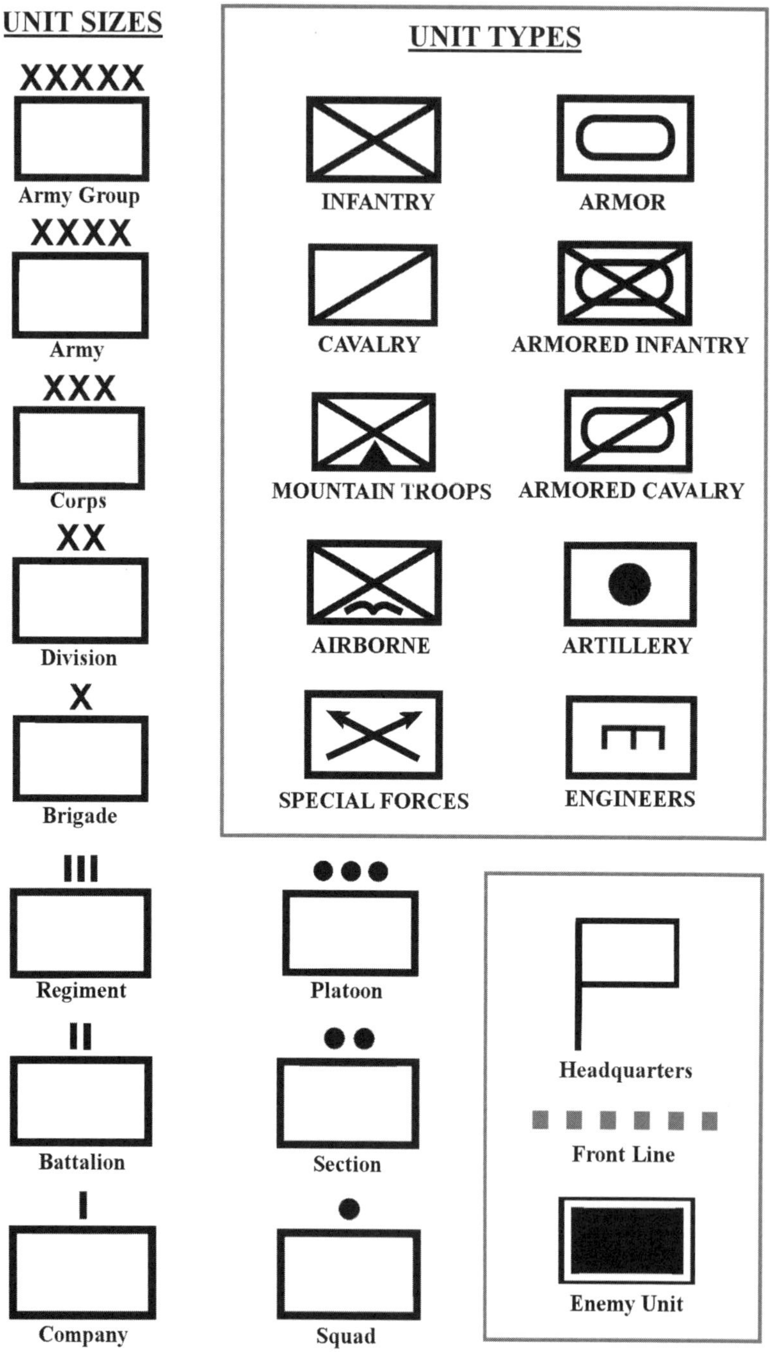

Nearly two-and-a-half years have passed since the 756th Tank Battalion's formation at Fort Lewis, Washington, in June 1941. The U.S. Army lacked tanks at the time, so novice crews rehearsed field tactics by carting around lumber frames—much to the amusement of passing infantrymen. In the following months, a smattering of outdated "combat cars" arrived in dribs and drabs, but after the attack on Pearl Harbor, the "tankers" received a full complement of light tanks and training commenced in earnest. The battalion battled the French briefly at Casablanca during Operation Torch *and observed the epic destruction of the famed Afrika Korps in Tunisia before joining Operation* Avalanche *and pursuing German forces up the boot of Italy in the fall of 1943. After upgrading to M4 "Sherman" medium tanks that December, the battalion was attached to the 34th "Red Bull" Infantry Division and tasked with taking Cassino, Italy. Braving flooded fields, thick mud, and withering enemy fire, the tankers crossed Rapido River and established a firm bridgehead by 29 January 1944. This accomplishment, however, was costly. Several tanks were lost, with crews either killed or captured—including popular B Company commander, Captain Charles M. Wilkinson. Command fell upon the shoulders of 1st Lieutenant David D. Redle who must now lead his surviving crews on to their next objective: the ruined town of Cassino itself—a crumbling hellscape bristling with German defenders and patrolled by deadly anti-tank assault guns. The mission is daunting. Privately, Lt Redle does not expect to survive.*

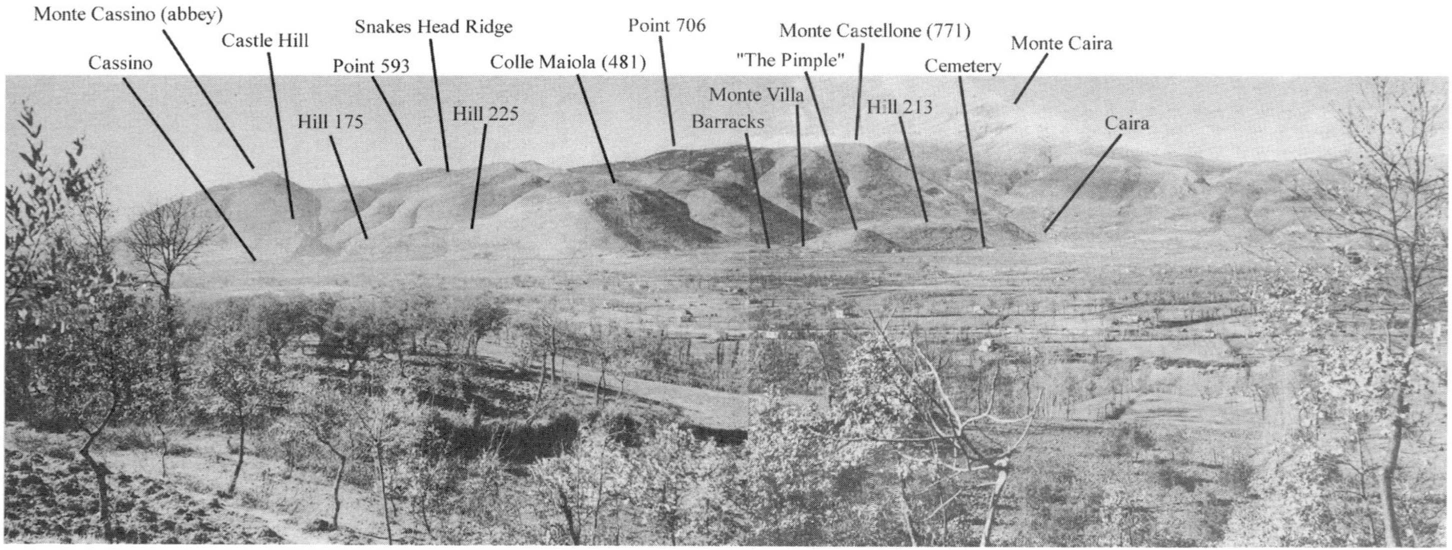

View of Cassino to the West from San Michele. (U.S. Army)

ITALY - 1944
0 10 20 30 40 50 60 70 80 90 100
200
SCALE in MILES
FRANCE
Milan
Verona
Venice
Trieste
Po River
Genoa
Pola
YUGOSLAVIA
Bologne
La Spezia
Rimini
Nice
Pisa
Florence
Arno River
Zara
Ancona
ITALY
ADRIATIC SEA
CORSICA
ELBA
Pescara
Civitavecchia
Tiber River
Rome
TYRRHENIAN SEA
Anzio
Cassino
Foggia
Volturno River
Gaeta
Capua
Bari
Naples
Monte Vesuvius
SARDINIA
Eboli
Sorrento
Salerno
Taranto
Sapri
Gulf of Taranto
Belvedere
Palermo
Scilla
Messina
Strait of Messina
SICILY
Bizerte
N
W
E
S
TUNISIA
Tunis
PANTELLERIA

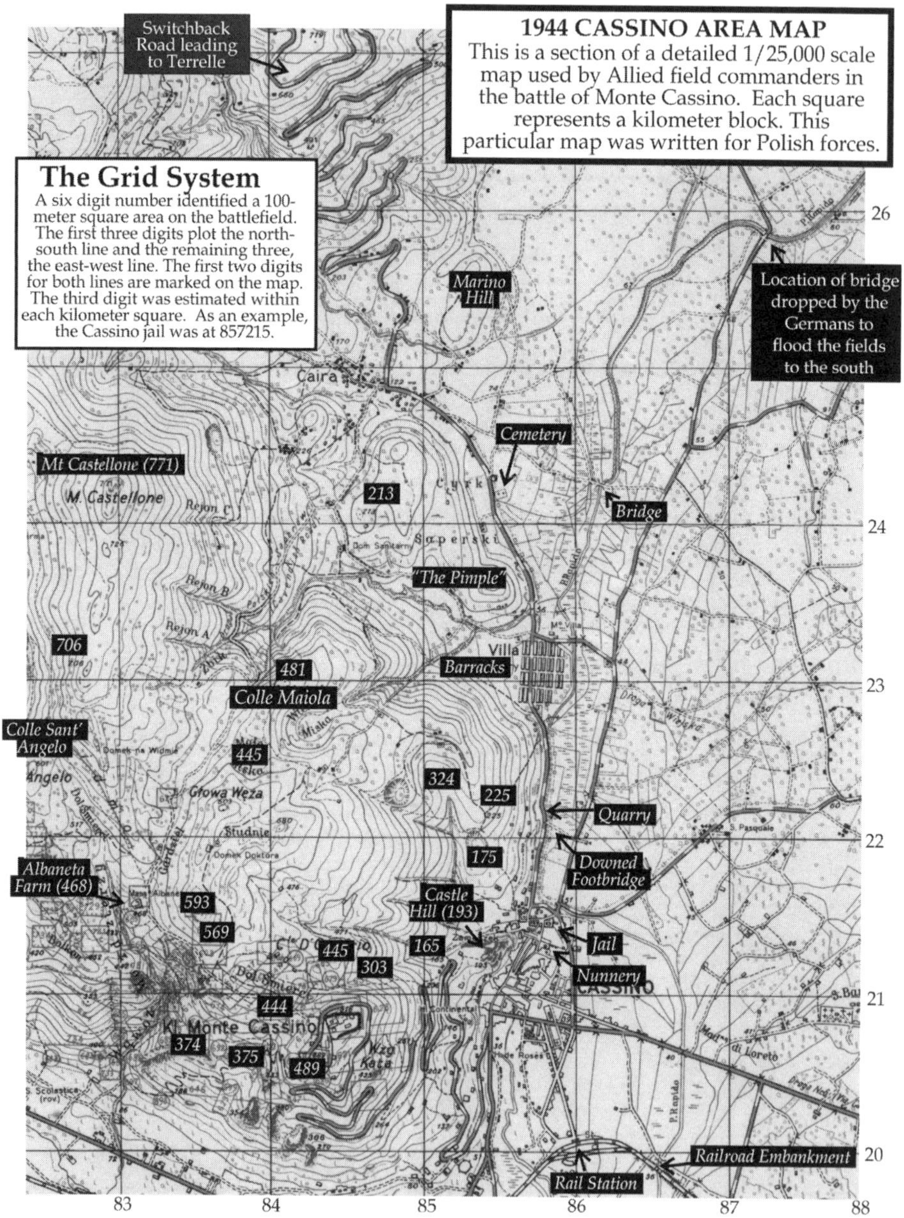

1944 CASSINO AREA MAP
This is a section of a detailed 1/25,000 scale map used by Allied field commanders in the battle of Monte Cassino. Each square represents a kilometer block. This particular map was written for Polish forces.
The Grid System
A six digit number identified a 100-meter square area on the battlefield. The first three digits plot the north-south line and the remaining three, the east-west line. The first two digits for both lines are marked on the map. The third digit was estimated within each kilometer square. As an example, the Cassino jail was at 857215.
Switchback Road leading to Terrelle
Location of bridge dropped by the Germans to flood the fields to the south
Marino Hill
Caira
Cemetery
Mt Castellone (771)
M. Castellone
213
Bridge
'The Pimple'
706
481
Barracks
Villa
Colle Maiola
Colle Sant' Angelo
445
324
225
Quarry
175
Downed Footbridge
Albaneta Farm (468)
593
569
Castle Hill (193)
165
445
303
Jail
Nunnery
CASSINO
444
Kl. Monte Cassino
374
375
489
Railroad Embankment
Rail Station
26
24
23
22
21
20
83
84
85
86
87
88

CHAPTER ONE

Cassino, First Attack: 2 February 1944

M4 "Sherman" medium tank (1942)

In the chilly midnight gloom of 2 February, the weary men of I Company of the 133rd Infantry Regiment solidified their gains along the barracks' southern edge and stole a few hours of slumber ahead of the next attack. At 0430, L Company snuck across the river to assume positions along I Company's right flank.[1] K Company remained on the east side of the river, but fanned out to cover the entire riverbank section assigned to the battalion. To K's south, A Company troops posted along the river reported hearing German trucks and men moving about inside the north end of Cassino.[2] Three vehicles of some sort were also heard rumbling down the narrow road leading from the barracks into town, but it was too dark to identify them.[3]

With the glimmering of dawn, a lone German rifleman sitting high on Hill 225 fired sporadically down into the barracks. From so far away, his scattered shots only pinged off the cement columns nearby, creating more nuisance than threat.[4] A thin fog again blanketed the valley, helping to shroud the Americans organizing below.[5] No doubt, countless sets of German eyes strained to pierce through that same swirling haze from hidden positions spread across the adjacent hillside.

Suddenly, 34th Infantry Division artillery batteries pummeled the north end of Cassino—shattering stone walls and churning up gray columns of dust. The Allies felt confident the town had been long since cleared of all townspeople, but one veteran American infantry officer wasn't entirely convinced: "We always find some old woman who stayed behind to feed their cats,"[6] he remarked warily to a reporter.

The fierce, ground-shaking barrage lasted several minutes before ending abruptly—a hellish reveille meant to fray the nerves of German defenders burrowed among the town's foundations. Thereafter, those same terrifying batteries would be unleashed only at the direct request of the advancing infantry.[7] During this time, the tanks of 1st Lieutenant (1st Lt) Dale F. Pride's 2nd platoon of A Company, 760th

Tank Battalion, drew back to Hill 213 for rest and resupply, and the crews' two-day attachment with the 133rd shifted over to the control of the 756th Tank Battalion.[8]

The 34th Division had, again, drawn back the battle bow and prepared to spring forth. The next attack would commence at 0730 hours as two coordinated prongs, designed to envelop and overwhelm Cassino over the highlands above and through the valley below.[9] During the night, elements of the 142nd Infantry Regiment successfully relieved 2nd Battalion, 135th Infantry Regiment, lynchpin positions roughly a mile southeast of Monte Castellone on Hill 445[10]—freeing more troops for the mountain attack. The 135th was instructed to jump off at 0700 hours and advance south on a parallel no further than Hill 225 in order to maintain pace with the valley attack. At 0730, the 133rd Regiment and the 756th Tank Battalion would press forward along the river road toward town.[11] If all went as planned, the 135th would seize Colle S'Angelo, Hill 706, Massa Albaneta, and storm the south and southeastern slopes of Monastery Hill by the end of the day.[12] At the same time, the Allies hoped the 133rd and tanks might roll all the way through Cassino to seize the rail station at the southernmost edge of town.[13] The attack planners had every reason to feel optimistic. The previous day's reports from 135th patrols scouting the highlands were encouraging, and additional observations from French forces and Task Force Butler further north suggested German forces may have retreated as far west as Monte Caira.[14]

***

As dawn broke on 2 February, 1st Lt David D. Redle's composite column of eleven rumbling B and C Company M4 mediums slowly emerged from beyond The Pimple, crossed the narrow bridge, and passed the ruined tanks once commanded by Lt Wayne B. Henry and Captain Charles M. Wilkinson before weaving down the narrow, rubble-strewn street and cutting through shattered rows of barracks.[15] Masses of twisted rebar columns, wood beams, and concrete foundations still smoldered in places. Groggy infantrymen congregated wherever cover could be found, loading weapons, packing spare ammo magazines, and grumbling obscenities amongst themselves. Somewhere on the misty hillside further south, a German machine gun (MG) burped a rude salutation in short, uneven bursts.[16] Redle conferred briefly with I Company commander Captain Wayne Fraizer over a combined course of action.[17] Because the roadway heading into town was so narrow, the infantry could not advance as two companies moving abreast—the tactically preferred method. Instead, I Company and the tanks would snake together as a long thin column down the sliver of road on the left, while L Company shadowed their progress by crawling along the steep hillside along the column's immediate right.[18]

Though only twenty-two years of age, Fraizer was already a proven, experienced combat veteran.[19] The Jamestown, New York, native had guided his I Company men through similar tactical challenges and many tough battles over the past three months.[20] Despite the current terrain restrictions, Fraizer felt confident the combined firepower of Redle's tanks and the pluck of his infantrymen would carry the day.[21] Working in their favor was the fact the German hillside bunker positions had been built with fields of fire limited only to the terrain beyond the river, and Fraizer's men and Redle's tanks would be striking each of these positions, one at a time, from the side. To give the attack some semblance of breadth, Redle instructed four 2nd Platoon, C Company, tanks trailing him to take the first suitable grade down into the drained riverbed running adjacent to the roadway. If the wet gravel could support the tanks' weight, not only could those tanks advance in favorable defilade along the six-foot-deep channel,[22] but the two lead tanks to both columns could support each other should any threat arise ahead.[23]

Due to attrition suffered after two continuous weeks of combat, the numerical strength of Captain Fraizer's company fell from the standard 180 men to only 120. Despite losing what amounted to an entire platoon's worth of firepower, Fraizer's men remained remarkably buoyant about their prospects. Many fully expected to storm through an empty town. In his last-minute verbal instructions, however, Fraizer cautioned his men against careless behavior and to stay especially alert for wired booby traps—particularly those planted near "souvenir"-worthy items. Retreating Germans knew many Americans salivated at the sight of enemy helmets, pistols, insignia, etc., and didn't hesitate to turn this form of kleptomania to their advantage. At the end of Fraizer's pep talk, a long curtain of smoke arose along the north edge of Cassino, as if on cue. The optimists of I Company interpreted this unexpected appearance as further evidence of German withdrawal, but the pessimists countered that the same screening smoke could also signal an enemy merely repositioning their defenses.[24]

At 0730, as the tanks and infantry rolled southward, beyond the barracks, American artillery smoke canisters howled in from overhead, bouncing and bursting all over the area. One white-hot phosphorous shell struck the ground near the rear deck of Redle's lead tank. The heat flared with such intensity the young tank commander had to duck down inside his turret to avoid getting baked.[25] No one had ordered smoke to fall at this location. The advance halted momentarily as the infantry scrambled for cover and confusion rippled along the column. After several quick and brusque phone calls, the culprit was identified as the 151st Field Artillery, who had misinterpreted the drop instructions. The trajectory was promptly shifted to fall several hundred yards further south to provide an appropriate screen shielding the column's departure from the barracks.[26] Once the advance resumed, one German MG further ahead foolishly sprayed measured bursts toward the approaching force—only to be unceremoniously silenced by one of the lead tanks.[27]

For the next hour, Redle's M4s and Fraizer's men probed judiciously southward a full 200 yards without encountering much resistance.[28] In the meantime, L Company gathered in the barracks' north section and prepared to shadow along the hillside. At 0828, a hitherto unknown bunker housing two or three German machine guns opened fire from the southwest corner of the barracks, killing two L Company men outright and scattering their stunned comrades. The ambush was pure suicide. The M4s holding the rear of Redle's column promptly turned their turrets around and blasted the MG crews into oblivion. To be sure of no repeats, Lt Redle ordered the rearmost tank commanded by Corporal (Cpl) Harold M. Behymer to stay back and assist the infantry in mopping-up operations before rejoining the column.[29] After a delay lasting only a few moments, L Company resumed preparations.[30]

By 0930, Redle's column had progressed a full 500 yards south of their departure point. The road remained very narrow—barely wide enough to accommodate a single M4[31]—but four of Redle's accompanying tanks were able to dip down into the drained river channel and maintain pace to the left of the others. German resistance along the steep hill increased here and there—only to be silenced methodically by tank gunners or bounding infantry teams chucking grenades. Other times, pockets of prisoners emerged from holes waving white flags.[32] Still, the overall response had been far weaker than Redle expected. Up to this point, the column's advance had been shielded from the view of Cassino behind Hill 225's steep slope—which probably explained the Germans' subdued reaction thus far.[33] Anyone observing from town wasn't about to prematurely reveal their gun positions or waste ammunition firing at targets they couldn't see or had no chance of hitting.

This particular spot in the road had been anticipated and discussed during the battalion planning meeting the night before. It represented an emergence point—the first few yards of roadway visible from Cassino and the likely focus for any anti-tank (AT) guns hidden there—so Redle halted the column and contacted the 756th Tank Battalion commander, Lieutenant Colonel (Lt Col) Harry W. Sweeting, via radio to coordinate the next phase of movement. The 81mm mortar and 105mm assault gun platoons of the 756th had the responsibility of dropping and maintaining a smokescreen 300 yards ahead of the advance.[34] From this point forward, the tanks would scout ahead to draw fire and neutralize any German MG positions encountered along the way. The infantry would follow—but only at a safe distance to the rear.

Redle's tank edged past the road bend to test the German response. Immediately, an AT gun hidden deep among the buildings of town opened fire on him. A split second later, a high-velocity armor piercing (AP) round glanced off the bottom edge of the M4's lower front plate with a deafening clang, gouging out an inch-and-a-half furrow of gleaming steel. Redle's crew, already keyed up on adrenaline, sat stunned for a second or two, regaining their wits.[35] Fortunately, the shot failed to penetrate the final drive housing behind which bow gunner Private First Class (Pfc) David J. Orris and driver Technician 5th Class (T/5) Arne Strand were seated.[36] While smoke canisters fell down along the road ahead and burst to form an enormous white curtain, Strand gunned the M4 forward beyond the registration point. This time, the German gun remained mercifully silent.

Over the next forty-five minutes, Redle's tank force inched along the road and nearby river channel with scattered infantry trailing a few dozen yards to the rear. All the while, Redle kept a wary eye toward Cassino—in case the wall of smoke swirling ahead split open to allow the German AT gun to see them again. Along the way, the tanks tangled with several new German MG positions and pillboxes—some cleverly burrowed behind terraced walls or inside reinforced rooms of expropriated hillside homes.[37] A few were located right next to the road, and Redle's tanks could not fire high explosives (HE) into them for fear of wounding themselves or their supporting infantry. Instead, AP rounds were fired point-blank into these positions.[38] In the meantime, infantrymen progressing along the hillside to the rear neutralized bypassed bunkers under the tried and true "draw attention and flank" method. A BAR (Browning Automatic Rifle) man or trailing tank gunner would spray MG fire onto the target as several riflemen clambered over adjacent rocks to a point where they could fire into the rear entrance—usually only a small hole. If the Germans inside couldn't be coaxed into surrender, grenades were carefully tossed to carom off adjacent rocks and explode inside.[39] The work was slow, exacting, and dangerous, but paid steady dividends.

After advancing another 500 yards, scraping past high stone retaining walls and vertical slabs of granite, Redle's column approached a flat quarry area cut like a scallop shell into the steep hillside. Suddenly, several large explosions rocked along the right side of Redle's tank. Redle reflexively ducked his head inside the turret, then popped up quickly to see if any trailing infantrymen had been hit. No one was hurt, but he glanced back in time to see a series of grenades tossed hastily from a hidden pillbox his tank had just passed.[40] Several more explosions buffeted over the rear deck, causing little damage but producing thick clouds of billowing black smoke.

With the hull pressed so closely against the granite slope, the main gun could not be traversed rearward, so Redle quickly surveyed his surroundings again to make certain no American infantry were nearby and then ordered Strand to back up. Once the tank reversed about a dozen yards, Cpl Alexander L. Huffman, the loader, slammed an HE round into the gun breech and gunner Sergeant (Sgt) Eugene Wunderlich promptly blasted the bunker at point-blank range.[41] A terrific explosion followed—spraying pulverized rock across the rocking bow. The violent blast, however, failed to pierce the wall or convince the Germans inside to quit. More "potato masher" grenades tumbled out at a frantic pace. Wunderlich called upon Huffman to seat a concrete piercing shell and then fired again into the stubborn bunker.[42] This time, the dissipating dust revealed a pair of white long johns waving back and forth from the end of a rifle barrel. Fourteen shell-shocked PWs (Prisoners of War) emerged with hands thrust high into the air, and Fraizer's men poured in swiftly from the rear to process them.[43]

The incident left Redle fearful his column had bypassed similarly hidden bunkers, and so he ordered all tanks to his rear to back up a few hundred yards and assist the infantrymen clearing out the ridge. By now, Fraizer's company had become fully consumed with locating and eliminating German pillboxes and dugouts constructed at various elevations. The task was daunting. Many bunkers had been built to accommodate up to eight men and reinforced with stone, timber, and even concrete.[44] To avoid any friendly fire accidents, Redle insisted his tankers fire only AP rounds from their main guns and to only rake targets with careful, measured bursts of .30-caliber MG spray. In time, these painstaking efforts convinced several more pockets of defenders to emerge from their besieged hollows and exit the war as prisoners.[45]

Once the infantry had finally caught up to his position, Redle directed Strand to ease forward again. Along the ridge just above the quarry, Wunderlich perceived a small, odd-looking grassy knob and decided to fire HE onto the spot. The resulting blast peeled back a large chunk of soil to reveal a sinister looking plate of blackened steel. Wunderlich followed with an AP round zeroed into the same spot. The infantry closed in moments later and extricated two wounded machine gunners. As Redle's tank resumed forward, an admiring infantryman working along the ridgeline shouted down how Wunderlich's expert marksmanship had severed the German pillbox's MG barrel in two.[46]

Next, Redle called for a new drop of 756th mortar smoke and successfully advanced another 100 yards beyond the quarry. Upon encountering an anti-tank ditch the Germans had blown across the middle of the road, however, he was finally forced to halt.[47]

The crescent-shaped quarry was tucked conveniently away from the eyes and guns of Cassino. With dimensions approximately 200 feet long and fifty feet wide, the flat space provided the perfect staging ground for any future attacks toward town. It was also one of only two locations along the long road winding down from the barracks wide enough to allow two tanks to pass.[48] Without a doubt, this sheltered stone cove had to be secured. The high cliff at the quarry's center rose approximately sixty feet above grade, and the Germans had excavated a series of MG nests along the edge. To take them out, Fraizer's infantrymen scaled the steep slope, flanked each position individually, and tossed hand grenades into their rear "rat hole" entrances. Fraizer had finished neutralizing one nest and was clambering across the open rock toward another when a bullet pierced his foot. Although his wound was not serious, the young captain had to be helped back to the 3rd Battalion command post (CP) and command transferred temporarily to I Company executive officer (XO), Lt William Higgins.[49] As Higgins took a few moments to reorganize the company, his weary men wolfed down some cold C rations to restore their flagging energy.[50]

In the meantime, L Company edged closer along the ridgeline behind I Company's positions, neutralizing more elevated bunkers while processing prisoners bypassed earlier during the road column's advance. At one point, a German MG position was identified further up the ridge, and the infantry called for Redle's tanks below to train their 75mm guns upon the spot. "Come out of there you sons of bitches!" an infantryman hollered up the barren hill. To everyone's shock a reply echoed back in perfect English: "Just a moment, please, we'll be right down!" A few seconds later, a German officer and three enlisted men emerged with their hands up.[51] By late morning, a total of twenty-seven Germans had given up the fight.[52] At 1030, Major Warren C. Chapman, 3rd Battalion, 133rd, commander, felt secure enough in his battalion's progress to order K Company to vacate their east bank riverside positions and cross over to the barracks. This repositioning was set for 1130, after which, K Company would follow I and L Companies and assist in mopping-up operations.[53]

With the quarry area now relatively secure, Higgins met with Redle to plan a resumption of the attack.[54] Redle told Higgins of the German anti-tank ditch in the road approximately 300 yards north of town. At first, Higgins proposed that his infantry should advance alone—but after further discussion, the two officers decided to proceed together. Once the obstacle was reached, Higgins's men would attempt to fill the ditch as Redle's tanks idled nearby and provided fire protection.

As soon as the tanks and infantry began moving, the Germans holding the southern slope responded with withering rifle and mortar fire.[55] When the column reached the ditch, Higgins's men were forced to duck and dart while tossing chunks of rock and rolling larger stones into the hole—but Redle's tanks were able to discharge adequate suppressive MG fire in support of the effort.[56] Through careful coordination, hustle, and toil, the ditch's edge closest to the hill was finally packed high enough to allow vehicular passage. The right track to each tank, however, still had to claw up several feet of hillslope to skirt by. A dead German lay just beyond the pit, and the tank drivers were given no choice but to crush the unlucky man's corpse.[57]

At the same time, the M4s of 2nd Lieutenant (2nd Lt) Howard F. Michael's 2nd Platoon, C Company, advanced along the riverbed just beyond the southern edge of the quarry, but halted after reaching a downed cement footbridge, axed tree logs, and other debris piled crossways by the Germans to form a tank barricade.[58]

At 1040, someone in the 133rd Regiment headquarters (HQ) prematurely informed the 34th Division HQ that the "tanks broke through" and were "now at the north edge of Cassino."[59] Based on this report, the 1st Battalion, 133rd, waiting along the east river bank north of town prepared to join the attack at two preplanned river crossing sites.[60] The news shot through the upper command structure like lighting. Twenty minutes later, the II Corps phoned 34th Operations, wanting to know if American troops had, indeed, breached Cassino. This time, the 34th hedged: "Will call you back in half an hour with all the details."[61]

At 1100, not long after Redle's tank skirted beyond the anti-tank ditch, a high-velocity German gun fired from inside the smoky veil shrouding Cassino.[62] Redle's eyes registered the telltale flash dead ahead. A split second later, a hot AT round roared past his head with a hellish snarl—leaving him temporarily deaf in his left ear.[63] Redle ordered his crew to back up immediately while returning blind fire. At the same time, he switched on his radio mic to tell Sweeting the German gun was positioned at the entrance of town, 300 yards forward on the main road.[64] Sweeting directed the mortar platoon to drop heavier smoke and requested his artillery liaison officer to arrange a strike upon the position.[65] In the meantime, Redle ordered the entire road column to back-up to the quarry for protection.

At 1120, Redle radioed Sweeting again and requested the smoke be lifted so his crews could determine if the artillery strike was successful. If not, they would attempt to locate the gun themselves and knock it out.[66] Sweeting agreed to the plan and called for the artillery halt, but the bombardment persisted, nonetheless, until 1135.[67] In the meantime, Redle's tanks re-emerged from the quarry area with Higgins's infantrymen skulking along the road's edge ahead to see if they, too, could help spot the deadly guns.[68] At this point, Redle's crews suspected the Germans had hidden several of them in the north section of town.[69] Some were, undoubtedly, the same self-propelled (SP) guns that had escaped the barracks the night before.

Redle's M4s crept ahead at a snail's pace—but only the lead tank was in any position to fire directly into town. All four of Lt Michael's tanks halted in column nearby, behind the riverbed obstruction, benefited from better defilade positions,[70] but only Sgt James M. Riley's tank had a clear shot forward as well.[71]

As noon approached, the smoke and dust dissipated to reveal a ghostly outline of the north edge of town. After a few minutes, flat gray shapes resolved into ruined buildings and rubble piles. To the left loomed a large three-storey concrete-and-stone jail adjoined by a small chapel called the Chiesa Santa Maria Annunziata.[72] A slender bell spire rose above the shattered roofline at the far end. Remarkably, the tower's delicate dome cap was still intact. Pale-yellow stone apartments, homes, and shops lay clustered tightly from the jail all the way over to the main road on the right. Many suffered blast damage sustained after receiving direct artillery hits: roofs were caved in, windows blown out, and walls had partially collapsed into cascading mounds of shattered stone and broken furniture. The town's northern edge was boxed above a protective flood wall built of fieldstone. This six- to ten-foot-high wall lined the sunken riverbed and buttressed the raised road leading down into town. A short distance beyond the town's entrance, the wall swung sharply to the left, but the road continued southward into a small plaza. The river wall effectively formed a moat and the narrow blacktop road—the only way into town from the north—represented a tight bottleneck. The Germans knew how to choose a defensive position.

The moments ticked away as slow torture—marked with sporadic, nervous chatter of small arms exchanged between both infantries from a distance. The townscape haze dissolved further to reveal even finer details: blown gaping windows, darkened doorways, sharp corners, and forbidding alleyways. Any one of such places could conceal a deadly AT gun. Suddenly, the cool air cracked with the thunderous growl of a flat trajectory slug whooshing past the quarry, and then disappearing somewhere beyond the barracks. Several more rounds followed in quick succession—narrowly missing the lead M4s on the road and in the riverbed—but this time, no barrel flashes could be perceived in town. With steely nerves, the lead tank crews returned fire and strained to see the response. A few moments later, another volley of AT rounds screamed through, but failed again to strike their intended targets—either sailing harmlessly overhead or fragmenting into sparkling flashes of molten steel against the nearby granite. It seemed a second German AT gun had joined the fray—yet no one could detect the gun flash from either source. Evidently, the Germans had shifted their defenses after Sweeting's artillery strike to better hide their gun positions. Several American tank commanders dismounted with binoculars in hand and climbed partway up the granite cliff in hopes of gaining a better view. All the while, the two lead tanks continued firing into town while bravely staring down the inevitable response. This nerve-wracking, high-stakes, high-caliber gunfight lasted another forty-five minutes without anyone scoring a hit.[73]

German MGs began chattering away with newfound confidence from the jail and other hidden locations around town, pinning Higgins's infantry against the slope and halting their forward progress.[74] At 1225, the German AT guns fired again. This time, a round struck Sgt Riley's tank positioned down in the riverbed. The crew threw open the hatches and abandoned in haste, but Riley returned with his driver a few minutes later to survey the damage. The tank hadn't caught fire, so Riley summoned the rest of the crew back to their posts to resume battle. A few moments later, another round skimmed across the turret's top, blowing the commander's hatch completely from its hinges and peppering Riley's face and neck with shrapnel. Though bleeding and wracked with pain, the enraged sergeant refused evacuation and continued the fight alongside his determined crew.[75]

Another snarling German AT round came within an inch of decapitating Lt Michael, who commanded the third tank in the riverbed—leaving him severely concussed with a ruptured eardrum and in need of evacuation.[76] The AT gun crews had managed to find a way to zero in upon the M4 turrets positioned along the riverbed and very nearly killed two commanders in the space of only a few minutes. Because no one could locate the well-camouflaged guns, Sweeting reluctantly ordered Redle to pull back the column.[77] The tanks on the road retreated to the safety of the quarry, and the C Company tanks in the river channel pulled far enough back to escape the view of town. During the move, however, one C Company tank threw a track in the wet gravel and had to be temporarily abandoned.[78] Besides Lt Michael and Sgt Riley, two other C Company men were also wounded during the standoff: Pfc Rocco Peluso suffered scalp wounds but remained on duty. Pfc Walter Burg's injuries, however, required his evacuation.[79]

Despite the loss of tank support, Higgins's I Company infantrymen continued to press forth courageously along the narrow road toward town. They hoped to locate the AT guns before nightfall, pick off their infantry protection, and kill the crews with hand grenades. The sun blazed high in the clear afternoon sky and temperatures fluctuated in the low forties—but the ever-present haze of battle hovered just above ground in the stagnant air.[80] Higgins's men needed a lucky break to even locate the guns. In the meantime, Redle and his frustrated tank commanders—reduced to unhappy bystanders stalled about the quarry—scanned Cassino obsessively through field glasses.[81] The effort, however, seemed pointless. The same smog shielding the advance of Higgins's men also concealed the AT gun positions in town. Every so often, one would fire off a defiant round in the direction of the barracks—and still not reveal its location.[82]

While Higgins's men stalked ahead in measured bounds, the 133rd Cannon Company's 75mm pack howitzers positioned across the river laid a fresh blanket of smoke just ahead of the advance.[83] By 1530, Higgins's men had covered a full 300 yards to breach the outskirts of Cassino.[84] The encroachment, however, was countered by the heavy bite of German small arms (S/A) fire raining down from homes and apartments lining the steep hillside. With afternoon slipping quickly away, Higgins gave up hope his men could neutralize the German AT guns with the help of the sun. Any attempt would have to wait until after nightfall.[85] Higgins was also unsure of how far the 135th had progressed in the highlands nearby and voiced concerns to 3rd Battalion HQ over the vulnerability of his right flank. His men had gained a lot of ground throughout the day, and he wanted assurances he had not led them out on a limb. To protect those gains, guards had to be posted along the way and Higgins counted only thirty-eight men available to continue forward.[86] After securing point positions on the roadway near the town's entrance, Higgins was called back to the 3rd Battalion CP in the barracks area to confer with Major Chapman over his company's next move. While departing, the young lieutenant told his NCOs (non-commissioned officers) to hold steady until his return.[87]

The tactical situation on the high ground right of the 133rd proved fluid, confusing, and disappointing. Only one battalion from the 142nd Regiment arrived in relief, when all three were sorely needed to assure a proper execution of the 135th's attack upon the abbey. The other two 142nd battalions still lagged somewhere to the north. The 135th's 1st and 2nd Battalions jumped off as planned at 0700 hours, but encountered heavy resistance almost immediately. What started as dismal progress ground to a complete halt under intense German shelling, and the identification of battle lines became nearly impossible for those trapped in the chaotic crossfire.[88] Which side controlled what rock pile, crevice, or ravine at any given moment was often anyone's guess. Worse, the Germans mounted a shockingly energetic counterattack on the 135th's right flank—storming up the backside of Monte Castellone and retaking the summit.[89] By late afternoon, the 3rd Battalion, 135th, recaptured the peak, but only after an unexpected and heavy expenditure in lives, ammunition, and time.[90]

All day long, 34th Division commanding general Major General (Maj Gen) Charles W. Ryder pressured his 135th commanders to maintain a parallel pace with the 133rd's more successful drive on Cassino,[91] but supplies of all types dwindled at an alarming rate in the highland struggle.[92] On account of poor road conditions, only big, powerful 6x6 supply trucks lumbering in through the Mignano Gap could handle the torturous trek all the way to Caira.[93] Anything lighter mired in the muddy Rapido River approaches. To the west of Caira, the 135th hadn't yet established the supply routes necessary to keep their troops properly armed and provisioned for the mountain fight. No truck could negotiate the rocky narrow footpaths snaking up through the area. For the moment, the only method of transport was by foot—which delivered just a fraction of what was needed.[94] Only highly trained mule trains plodding back and forth on a tight schedule could satisfy the 135th infantry's insatiable demands for ammunition, water, and food. Until those teams and their skinners could be secured, the II Corps called forward a company of Italian troops to porter supplies as a temporary measure.[95]

The 168th Infantry Regiment resting in reserve on Hill 213 was available,[96] but Ryder was not inclined to throw more troops into the mountains until reliable supply routes could be established first.[97] To do so would only compound an already challenging logistical problem. Nevertheless, Ryder voiced his concerns about pockets of Germans spread across Colle Maiola—especially those overlooking the barracks from a hill point called "324," and requested the 135th send troops over to those positions.[98]

Up to that point, the 133rd Regiment had captured forty-five Germans during the day. Most prisoners reported assignments with the 132nd Grenadier Regiment (44th Infantry Division) or the 211th Grenadier Regiment (71st Infantry Division). At 1706, nine more surrendered from a bunker position inside a house roughly 200 yards up the slope of Hill 225, directly overlooking the quarry.[99] Four days earlier, the 168th Regiment had painstakingly captured hidden bunkers full of Germans everywhere on Hill 213 and The Pimple. The men of the 133rd encountered similar installations all over Hill 225—and yet only a fraction of the half-mile long ridge had been cleared.

***

At 1630, the 756th Tank Battalion S-3 (operations officer), Captain Edwin Y. Arnold, contacted Redle at the quarry and told him to prepare for a tank/infantry attack on town.[100] A short time later, Sweeting's voice crackled over Redle's headset informing him of a sustained divisional artillery bombardment commencing at 1700 and rolling through the north section of Cassino. The barrage was designed to suppress German AT gun fire and allow the ground attack to breach town. The new orders baffled Redle as he knew the infantry officers had been called back only a few moments earlier to a battalion CP meeting and couldn't have returned from the barracks area so soon—nor could the scattered troops organize with only a half hour of lead time. Redle asked an infantry sergeant left in charge of the quarry guard if he had also received new attack orders. The young NCO reported his only instructions were to stand pat—and gruffly added that he wasn't about to send anyone anywhere until his superior officers told him to do so. The sergeant's leathery resolve convinced Redle that Sweeting was operating under false assumptions—and yet he couldn't directly tell his commanding officer (CO) of the infantry's unpreparedness for fear the Germans were monitoring his radio band.[101] Redle chose, instead, to stall for time—telling Sweeting he needed a few more minutes to iron out the particulars. The delay, he hoped, might be enough to allow for an early return of the infantry officers or for Sweeting to consult others over secure CP phone lines and alter the plan.[102] In no way could Redle send tanks into town without infantry support. Once the covering artillery fire fell silent, his crews would be picked off like sitting ducks.

Sweeting radioed back several more times to inquire on the progress—growing more and more irritated with Redle's excuses. Finally, as the artillery began bursting across Cassino at precisely 1700, a now livid Sweeting hailed Redle one final time with a direct order: "Commit your reserve tanks from C Company!"[103]

A third voice burst in over the radio. It was 2nd Lt James W. Granberry, commanding the 3rd Platoon of C Company, and anchoring the rear of Redle's tank column throughout the day: "Don't worry, I'm on my way!" the platoon leader eagerly assured Sweeting.

Redle instructed Granberry to stop by the quarry to meet in person before proceeding, but the platoon leader failed to respond. Because of some technical glitch, Redle could hear the lieutenant's voice but not vice versa. Moments later, the four-tank column thundered past the quarry with Granberry waving confidently to Redle before disappearing beyond the hill slope. No infantry accompanied them. Sweeting had just ordered four tanks to enter Cassino alone and Redle was completely powerless to intervene without risking a court martial.[104] He hoped, somehow, the infantry positioned closest to town received orders to join Granberry's attack.

The 34th Division's artillerymen threw down another fearsome spectacle—proving again, it was far more preferrable to suffer under a German barrage than an American one. Countless flashes erupted into tall, splendid plumes of plaster, whirling stone, and tumbling timbers; and the valley reverberated under a rolling, ceaseless thunder. Cassino shuddered from the assault before disappearing wearily beneath another broad cloak of swelling smoke and dust. Granberry's tank column rolled down the narrow road unopposed. As they neared the village limits, the hellish barrage lifted—the way Sweeting had informed Redle it would occur earlier.[105] The halt also served as the signal for Granberry to storm town, and so his four M4s roared in single file past the few dozen men Higgins left stationed in the first few houses at the town's entrance—leaving exhaust fumes wafting before astonished faces. No one expected tank support this soon. No one had orders to follow, and so no one did.

Granberry's crews rolled into a ghostly town swathed in thick acrid haze left over from the intense artillery assault, taking great care to avoid overturning into the dry riverbed immediately to the left. On the right the silent silhouettes of terraced homes, stone garden walls, and a long two-storey apartment building built along the steep slope slipped by. They reached a three-way intersection—with a narrow, raised road to the left following the river behind a block of tightly packed homes, meandering in the direction of the jail and chapel. Approximately fifty yards ahead lay a small bridge spanning a spillway and abutted closely with three-storey stone buildings. Beyond lay more buildings and a small "town square" on the right. Aside from the occasional crack of S/A fire echoing down the tight, empty streets, not a hint of opposition could be detected. Strangest of all, the AT guns remained absolutely silent. Granberry probed ahead guardedly to the small bridge, and then stopped, waited, and observed. His platoon halted behind him—spread out in twenty-five-yard intervals and prepared to fire at anything that moved. After a few moments, a few salvos of artillery rounds whooshed overhead and burst deeper into town, but other than that, nothing seemed amiss.

At 1740, Granberry's voice crackled across the battalion radio band reporting he had breached town without resistance. He also commented that the artillery falling further ahead seemed to originate from Allied batteries. Redle chimed in, cautioning the platoon leader to organize his position defensively and await infantry support.[106] Again, Granberry gave no response. Evidently, Redle's voice still wasn't reaching him. Captain Arnold suggested to Sweeting that more tanks should be sent to solidify Granberry's gains, but the battalion CO decided to instead pressure the 133rd's liaison officer assigned to his CP to rush in their troops.[107] As a precaution, Sweeting requested the 34th Division artillery shift their fire away from the north quarter of town.[108]

In the meantime, Lt Higgins and Captain Fraizer, now hobbling upon a bandaged foot, reached the outskirts of town and hastily organized the riflemen posted near the town's entrance. Tagging along was Tom Treanor, the fearless *Los Angeles Times* war correspondent.[109] At 1800, when a small group of infantrymen set out toward Granberry's tanks, German S/A opposition kicked up considerably. Clearly, the town had not been abandoned as hoped. A few Germans, at the very least, stayed behind to fight. Fifteen minutes later, Fraizer reported his men making steady progress against more subdued opposition gunfire.[110] Colonel Mark M. Boatner, commanding the 168th and monitoring Fraizer's phone report, counselled against overconfidence by remarking to 133rd CO, Colonel Carley L. Marshall, that the fortifications his men encountered earlier on Hill 213 were "astounding" and how "[Fraizer's men] can expect more of the same in Cassino."[111] Marshall, however, was more concerned over the potential for a German counterattack streaming down from the highlands: "I hope the 135th Infantry can help us out on our right flank," he replied.[112] Marshall also feared the division's ongoing artillery operations were still dispatching rounds dangerously close to his men and complained immediately to Ryder's HQ about it. The barrage promptly halted and the batteries were instructed not to resume until cleared first by either Marshall or Lt Col Sweeting.[113]

The artillerymen didn't have to wait long for those instructions. At 1820, the 756th Tank Battalion requested a smoke drop to cover Fraizer's men as they advanced toward Granberry's tanks.[114] With the sun fading fast behind the western mountains, the situation turned alarming. After dark, four isolated tanks were completely vulnerable to attack. Granberry radioed to assure everyone that his crews were in good shape and patiently waiting the infantry's arrival.[115] In the meantime, Fraizer's men darted cautiously from point to point through deepening shadows and eerie street silence toward Granberry's position. They dared not risk moving out in the open for fear of getting cut down.

Without warning, all hell broke loose.[116] From somewhere to the left, deep in the dwindling twilight of town, a dreaded German SP gun fired—piercing the last tank in Granberry's column with a sickening metallic thud. The panicked crewmen tumbled out of hatches and scrambled for whatever cover they could find nearby. A second AT gun hidden much deeper among the alleyways dead ahead also started firing toward the rear of the tank column. At the same time, German MGs concealed in nearby buildings joined the fracas—forcing Fraizer's men to halt in place and squeeze tightly against stone walls and rubble piles. Granberry's three remaining tanks, now trapped ahead and alone, returned fire blindly but found little room to maneuver. To escape the steady wrath of the AT gun, Granberry led his crews further ahead where they could finally turn right for protection inside the small civic square.[117]

At 1840, Granberry reported the loss of his rear tank and grim news of German infantrymen engaging them directly in the darkness.[118] Surprised by the sudden turn of events, Sweeting ordered the lieutenant to immediately pull his remaining tanks from town—without realizing all three had been cleverly trapped. Because of the earlier radio trouble, no one was even sure if Granberry heard Sweeting's order at all. Redle, convinced Granberry's receiver was dead, decided the only remaining option was to attempt a rescue.[119]

Redle ordered his crew and those of Cpl Behymer's tank to mount up immediately.[120] Nearby infantry volunteered for the ad hoc effort. After warming the cold radial engines for a minute or two, the small two-tank rescue section stormed out of the quarry and turned down the road with a fearless contingent of riflemen clinging to the bouncing decks. Ahead lay a smoky, otherworldly townscape illuminated with piercingly bright German flares drifting high in a deep indigo sky as unseen sporadic gunfire crackled below. Granberry radioed that a second tank from his platoon had become immobilized. For the umpteenth time, Redle tried hailing him, without drawing an answer.

Redle's tank pulled tightly behind the knocked-out tank at the end of Granberry's column and halted. Cpl Behymer shuddered to a stop a few dozen yards behind him. While the accompanying infantry slid off the decks to take defensive positions nearby, a few of Fraizer's men darted up to help bolster the effort. The way through was completely blocked, with no space on either side to squeeze by. The stricken tank hadn't burned, so Redle dashed down from his commander's hatch and scrambled up the rear deck of the derelict tank. He found no one inside and saw no sign of Granberry's three remaining tanks anywhere along the road ahead.[121]

The arrival of these new Americans drew swift German wrath. AT gun fire burst off nearby houses and MG tracer fire flooded the narrow roadway. As Redle scrambled back inside his turret to coordinate counter fire, fierce red streaks of flame screamed past his head from another unseen German AT gun ahead to the left.[122] One snarling round struck the corner of a house to his right—collapsing a large section of wall over the top of Redle's tank. The company commander ducked and emerged unhurt from his hatch—finding large, heavy stones scattered across the turret and back deck.[123] The tank gunners and Fraizer's riflemen returned blind fire but were clearly bottlenecked and overmatched by the German response.[124] After enduring a ten minute firestorm, Sweeting's voice finally broke in over the radio instructing Redle to withdraw his two-tank section all the way back to the barracks for the evening.[125] Sadly, this meant Granberry's crews would be abandoned until morning. As Redle's drivers opened the engine throttles and reversed out, the infantry followed—at one point, breaking into a breathless run for safer ground to the rear.[126]

Meanwhile, rumors spread like lightning through 756th Tank Battalion ranks that Lt Redle and crew were also missing in action. Upon hearing this, some B Company men broke down emotionally.[127] Redle and crew were safe, of course—but only after dodging several heart-stopping brushes with death throughout the day. As a result, all five men returned to camp as different souls. They learned they could trust one another with their very lives while under fire—a sacred bond that could never be forged through training alone. The experience, however, left each man struggling privately with dire thoughts over his own mortality. The clearing of shattered stones from the back deck, the running of fingers over the near-fatal hull gouge along the differential housing, and the inspection of countless chip marks and lead splatter left from MG fire raking across the hull, led each man to wonder how many more such missions he could survive.[128] The now battle-tested tankers could only restock their M4 and wait until the next day to find out.

Privately, Redle concluded he would not survive the battle for Cassino. His assumption was not fatalistic, but realistic—based upon mathematical odds and not emotion. Had that one AT shot been three inches to the right, he would have been decapitated. Had the other round struck three inches higher, his driver would have been killed and the tank likely burned. Had the wall fallen three more inches to the left, his skull would have been crushed. Each near miss was akin to a coin flip turning up "heads" in his favor. Winning streaks like this didn't last forever. For

Redle, the realization was strangely liberating. Rather than fret over his own mortality, the young lieutenant felt free to fully concentrate on his job.[129] Nevertheless, he continued to pray often and fervently for his own safety and that of his men. Redle never wavered once in his Catholic faith.[130]

***

Granberry's tankers earned the honor of becoming the very first Allied forces to enter Cassino, but the accolade proved an empty one.[131] Lt Col Sweeting's roll-of-the-dice orders sent four of his tank crews into a disastrous German ambush. Five days earlier, that same audacity secured a permanent Allied bridgehead across the Rapido. Yes, the tanks did lead the charge at the time and the infantry followed soon after—but Sweeting had exploited river-channel defilade brilliantly and used the element of surprise to his fullest advantage. He also attacked in one broad wave involving more than twenty tanks. Aside from the audacity element, Granberry's mission contained none of the other ingredients necessary for success. Surprisingly, Maj Gen Ryder didn't blame Sweeting for this error in judgment. He blamed, instead, his infantry officers for not maintaining pace with Sweeting's initiative. When the general first heard word of Sweeting's tanks alone in town and pinned down by SP gunfire, he demanded to know why the infantry wasn't with them. "Colonel Marshall is trying to reorganize the force to take them in there," he was assured. So displeased was Ryder with that tepid response he told Colonel Marshall to personally lead the troops to be assured they reached Granberry.[132] Sweeting's aggressiveness may have earned Ryder's confidence and praise, but the officers and men of the 756th were not so keen to find themselves playing the roles of expendable chess pieces. Grumblings of discontent circulated around the battalion—exceeding the daily bitching typical of combat troops.[133]

***

Granberry and his men suffered the grave consequences to Sweeting's crapshoot. Adding salt to those wounds was the knowledge that those hidden German SP guns prowling about and wreaking havoc in the north quarter of town were the same ones that had escaped the barracks the night before—and their crews were extremely crafty. One AT gun crew, under the command of *Oberleutnant* Edwin Metzger waited patiently for all four of Granberry's M4s to pass before knocking out the last one—entrapping the rest.[134] Deprived of infantry support and the only avenue of retreat, Granberry's three surviving tanks were forced forward to avoid further wrath from Metzger's guns. This put them in the line of fire of another very persistent AT gun hidden further up the road. Fortunately, that AT gun was of an older design and smaller caliber. Three of its shots hit squarely upon the sloped frontal plate of the second tank commanded by Sgt James T. Vaughn, but failed to penetrate and caromed off instead into the dwindling twilight. After crossing the small bridge, Granberry and Vaughn hurried for the dark safety of the town square,[135] but before Vaughn's tank could turn right, the AT gun fired again, striking his turret ring and freezing the main gun in place.[136] The third tank became hung up on the small bridge and couldn't break free. That crew abandoned their hopeless situation and managed to sneak back to the 133rd Infantry positions.[137]

German grenadiers emerged from nearby bunkers and threatened to kill Granberry's crew with magnetic mines, hand grenades, and machine pistols.[138] To prove their seriousness, they lobbed a white smoke grenade onto the turret—causing flash burns to the lieutenant's face. Granberry finally relented and surrendered his tank and crew.[139] The wounded lieutenant was then marched ahead of another group of Germans over to Vaughn's tank to convince his crew into surrendering as well.

"Vaughn, it's me! Give up and save the crew! Yours is the last tank!" Granberry yelled.[140]

After a few seconds, Vaughn and his crew emerged with hands high and the two captured crews were escorted over to the jail building.[141] Before the arrival of dawn, the Germans recovered both tanks and drove them south out of town. They failed to free the third tank rolled partway over into the spillway, and so they draped a German flag across the hull with every intention of salvaging it later.[142] The fourth tank in Granberry's column, disabled earlier near the entrance of town, was inspected by the Germans but found undrivable. To prevent American recovery, the interior was scorched with explosives.[143]

Once contact was lost with Granberry and Redle's tanks were forced to withdraw, Sweeting instructed Captain Arnold to continue monitoring the battalion radio—just in case the missing lieutenant miraculously called in again. Sweeting learned from his bitter lesson, nonetheless, and specifically instructed Arnold *not* to send in more tanks unless the infantry also advanced. The infantry, however, had no plans to attack the town for the rest of the night.[144] Allied artillery kept falling over the north end of town, but purposefully avoided the town square, as the area was Granberry's last known position.[145] If any silver lining could be recovered from the situation, it lay in the impressive haul of prisoners and enemy equipment captured during the day. The barracks area and Hill 225 yielded thirty rifles, six heavy MGs, ten light MGs, three machine pistols, one 50mm mortar, 3,000 hand grenades, 150,000 rounds of MG ammo, 5,000 rounds of rifle ammo, as well as large stockpiles of food, clothing, and personal equipment.[146] An abandoned German *Sturmgeschütz* III was also found hidden within the walls of one of the ruined barracks. Large rocks had been piled eight to ten feet around it as added protection.[147] By the end of the day, the tally of German prisoners had swelled to 150, and 133rd infantrymen weren't even close to clearing out the rest of Hill 225.[148]

After nightfall, the 135th Regiment, fighting in the nearby highlands, still hadn't dispatched anyone over to Hill 324—after promising Ryder they would do so earlier. Colonel Marshall was frustrated over the delay because the Germans holding the point could observe much of his troops' activity in the ruined barracks below. He became tired of waiting and decided to dispatch a platoon from the 3rd Battalion, 133rd, to attempt a nighttime capture of the spot. At 2025, the platoon reported taking the position but complained bitterly of German sniping "pretty bad down below"—making their stay unbearable. Marshall seized upon these details to pressure the 34th HQ into sending the promised troops over from the 135th—reminding the operations (G-3) staff that *he* somehow found a way to spare the scarce men even though they were needed "very badly" on Hill 225. The ploy worked, and an embarrassed 135th staff promised to send a relief unit immediately.[149] Finally, at 2234, C Company, 135th arrived at Hill 324 to relieve Marshall's men.[150]

In fairness, the 135th Regiment's logistical problems had worsened due to the relief delays. The 1st Battalion, 142nd, arrived late to take over 3rd Battalion, 135th, positions in the mid-afternoon.[151] This swap was supposed to have taken place the night before. Had those troops appeared a few hours earlier, the German counterattack on Monte Castellone would have been more easily repelled. As a result, the 3rd Battalion, 135th, lost a full afternoon retaking the summit instead of attacking south. By 1800, the mountaintop was finally secured—and the 3rd Battalion had to reorganize and resupply for a dawn attack planned for the following day.[152] The 1st and 2nd Battalions of the 135th also suffered a wasted day. German resistance stymied the advance of both battalions well into the night. In fact, in order to send troops over to Hill 324 to relieve Marshall's men, C Company, 135th had to be pulled straight out of a firefight.[153] Finally, because of dwindling supplies and ammunition, the 135th was forced to suspend offensive operations altogether until morning.[154]

The 133rd was in far better shape, both logistically and tactically. The capture of Hill 324 and the steady progress made clearing Hill 225 freed the regiment to prepare for a second, more robust, attack on Cassino. The 3rd Battalion consolidated positions both near the quarry and closer to town. The remainder of the 1st Battalion gathered directly across the river from 3rd Battalion positions and prepared to strike town from the northeast.[155] C Company, 133rd, would lead that attack.[156] The 100th (Nisei) battalion, still being reconstituted, would also lend support wherever needed.[157] Tanks from the 753rd and 760th Tank Battalions of the 1st Tank Group positioned several hundred yards east of the river prepared to storm Cassino—once the infantry of the 133rd established a firm bridgehead in town.[158] Engineering teams were dispatched to blow river abutments to create a tank path[159] and another team prepared a bridge crossing at Highway 6.[160] In all, four converging tank attack routes were to be employed.[161] To screen the attack, smoke candles were placed all along the Rapido—set to be ignited on Maj Gen Ryder's orders and kept burning continuously throughout the day.[162] Plans were also made to shift one battalion from the 168th Regiment in support of the tank attack from the east.[163] The 1st Tank Group assured Maj Gen Ryder and II Corps commander Maj Gen Geoffrey Keyes that they were ready to attack *en masse*—if the engineers could, in fact, deliver on the tank crossings.[164] The Rapido River represented, yet again, a wildcard to the plans.

The other wildcard lay with the actions of the German SP guns lurking about the north section of town. The infantry carried the responsibility of spotting them ahead of the tank attack.[165] These guns were too dangerous to send tanks in blindly seeking them out. During the past twenty-four hours, German AT gun crews had been responsible for knocking out one M4, damaging two others, and capturing three more—all without suffering a single loss.[166] This math was unsustainable.

Late that evening, Sweeting reported at Colonel Marshall's farmhouse CP back across the river to coordinate strategy for the morning attack.[167] The two officers shuffled maps and onionskin overlays across a plain table in an austere room behind windows covered in thick blankets to prevent light leaks. Marshall's staff shared the old stone farmhouse with a devout Catholic family who maintained a blessed shrine to the Virgin Mary and prayed the Rosary in Italian several times each day. Marshall and his men always showed proper courtesy to the homeowners and vice versa.[168] As the family prayed fervently in an adjacent room, the American officers concluded plans to return Cassino to their rightful owners. This time, everyone clearly understood the infantry would lead and the tanks would follow—but only on the infantry's orders. No assumptions, no misunderstandings, and no crapshoots ....

While expectations soared for a successful attack led by the 133rd Infantry Regiment, the challenge of destroying those elusive German SP guns kept Sweeting awake all night.[169]

German "Tank Kill" badge

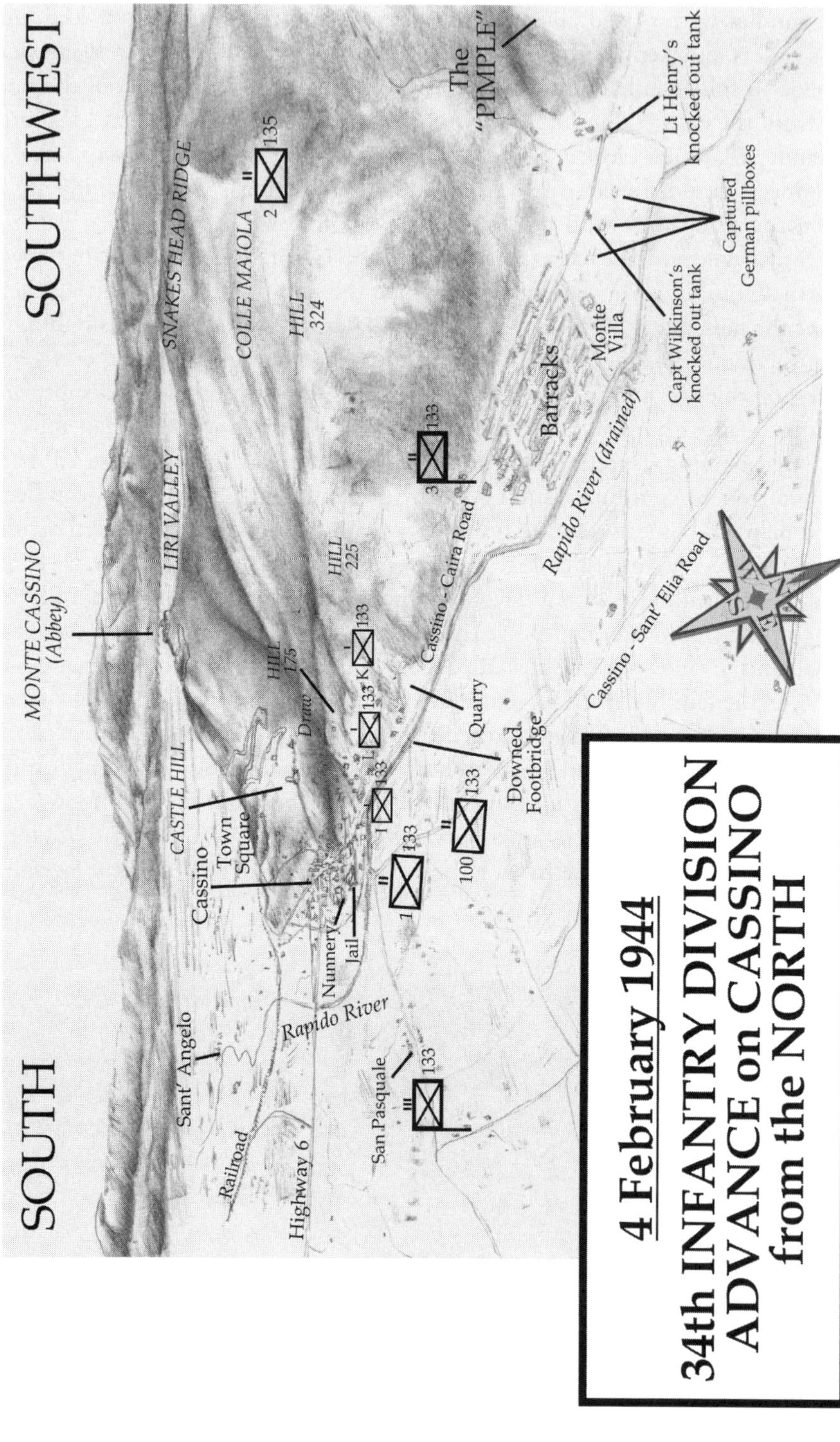

4 February 1944
34th INFANTRY DIVISION
ADVANCE on CASSINO
from the NORTH
SOUTH
SOUTHWEST
MONTE CASSINO
(Abbey)
LIRI VALLEY
SNAKES HEAD RIDGE
COLLE MAIOLA
HILL 324
HILL 225
HILL 175
CASTLE HILL
Draw
The "PIMPLE"
Cassino
Town Square
Nunnery
Jail
Sant' Angelo
Rapido River
Railroad
Highway 6
San Pasquale
Cassino - Caira Road
Quarry
Downed Footbridge
Barracks
Monte Villa
Rapido River (drained)
Cassino - Sant' Elia Road
Lt Henry's knocked out tank
Captured German pillboxes
Capt Wilkinson's knocked out tank
2 135
3 133
1 133
K 133
L 133
100 133
III 133

CHAPTER TWO

Cassino, Second Attack: 3 February 1944 to 5 February 1944

The dark early morning hours of 3 February brought no tranquility, and the raucous sounds of combat raged as if the sun had never descended. Both the 135th and 133rd Infantry Regiments had tried using the night to reposition troops ahead of the planned dawn attack, but the defenders had made the process a holy hell. In the frigid highlands, German marking flares blazed continuously overhead as their artillery shells rained down in furious rage—bursting rocks, showering gravel, and clattering shrapnel across windswept granite and stark crevices. The bombardment fell far heavier than usual. Even as far north as Caira and Hill 213, the 168th reported German artillery falling on their positions at a rate of "four times as much as usual."[1] Ryder could do little else except call for more vigorous counterbattery response from his own artillery units.[2] At 0405, the 135th tried sneaking men east of Hill 475, but failed and drew forceful S/A and MG fire.[3] The Germans, it seemed, weren't sleeping anywhere.

Meanwhile, along the north edge of Cassino, relentless German mortar and artillery burst upon 133rd positions as well. At 0125, a series of explosions rocked the town's center, and a large fire was seen raging for a while.[4] No one was sure if American artillery scored the hit or the Germans accidentally ignited one of their own ammo stores. Whatever the cause, the incident had no effect on the ferocity of battle. At 0259 hours, the 3rd Battalion, 133rd, reported sluggish progress repositioning men near the town's north entrance. Withering small arms fire emanating from the hillside, especially, hampered their movement. German artillery and mortar fire fell so heavily along the river that C Company could not cross and join the 3rd Battalion as planned.[5] The Germans also began dropping smoke west of Hill 225 near a section south of point 324—for reasons unknown.[6] If any positive news came during the night, it was the engineer reports claiming that a bridge east of Cassino had been repaired and readied for tanks.[7]

After sundown, Lt Redle withdrew his tanks all the way back to The Pimple area for resupply. Redle's company, still holding at two platoons in strength, was not slated to support the infantry's morning attack. If any tanks were called forward, C Company, 760th, crews waiting in reserve the past two days near Caira would respond.[8] Nevertheless, Redle was told to be prepared to commit two or three of his best tanks and crews if the infantry asked for additional tank support.

Prior to dawn, Redle accompanied Captain Arnold and 1st Lt Frederick L. Nelson, company commander of C Company, 760th, to the quarry area to check on the infantry's progress. After an hour, the three officers returned to The Pimple,[9] and learned that the 756th Tank Battalion XO, Major Welborn G. Dolvin, was bringing over the day's tactical plans.[10] This time, Sweeting chose to stay with Colonel Marshall at the 133rd CP during operations—to eliminate any miscommunications as had happened the day prior.

At the same time, the 3rd Battalion, 133rd, attacked the north end of town. By 0615, I Company captured two prisoners and battled past heavy MG fire to gain sight of the town square. Ahead, they could see the third tank of Granberry's ill-fated platoon tilted partway off the spillway bridge with a swastika flag draped over the deck. No one was around it. Unbelievably, the engine was still running.[11]

Three hundred yards to their left, C Company, 133rd, finally cracked into the northeast edge of town—working one platoon across the Rapido at first, followed by the rest of the company.[12] By 0725, C Company reported taking eleven prisoners without any losses—despite crossing through a heavy gauntlet of small arms fire. After securing several outermost buildings—including an abandoned police barracks and telephone exchange—the sinister sounds of German tracked vehicles were heard creaking and clanking in the nearby smoke. Then, C Company's point men caught a glimpse of a German SP gun emerging in a hazy alleyway and peppered the squat hull with bullets. One lucky slug shattered the driver's prism. Blinded, the crew threw open the hatches to escape, but were shot as they fled.[13] At 0740, a second German SP gun was seen briefly east of the jail—shifting to and fro like a fuming rhino.[14] Fifteen minutes later, spotters from the 151st Field Artillery witnessed four German Mark IV tanks thundering through the southern sections of town.[15] Cassino seemed to be crawling with German armor.

At 0820, Sweeting met with Colonel Marshall at his farmhouse CP east of the Rapido to discuss these new reports describing Cassino as "stuffed full of SPs."[16] Neither officer had expected so many. During the meeting, alarmed C Company officers called in and described hearing several more German tanks moving closer to their positions along the northeastern edge of town. The two colonels agreed a second wave of attacking infantry with close tank support was needed to drive the SPs out. This new challenge injected a shot of energy into Sweeting—who still smarted over the loss of Granberry's platoon the night before. Ever since their capture, the Germans had been using the radios from Granberry's tanks to verbally taunt and confuse the other tank crews of his battalion.[17] Sweeting wanted revenge.

By 0900, Sweeting bounded into his battalion CP to flesh out the new attack details alongside Major Dolvin.[18] As the two plotted hastily, three German SP guns with supporting infantry counterattacked C Company positions in town. In only a few short minutes, the 1st Battalion, 133rd, was stripped completely of all morning gains and sent scurrying back across the river.[19] The tank destroyers (TDs) supporting the infantry from hidden positions further east proved completely ineffective in halting the rout.[20] These tank-killing guns sat too far off in the distance and the German SP crews skillfully avoided those sections of town covered by their narrow line-of-fire.

The turn of events proved so disheartening that, by 1010, the 34th Division operations staff began inquiring with other Fifth Army units on the availability of flame throwers.[21] One cache was located with a chemical maintenance outfit in Capua—forty miles to the south—and the unit promised to ready eight flame throwers by 1600. A group of engineers was dispatched to fetch them.[22] Each one of these terrifying weapons featured an impressive searing range of seventy-five yards on a full minute of charge. The only problem was that no infantryman in the 34th Division knew how to operate them.[23]

Not all the morning news was bad. L Company, 133rd, continued making steady progress in the capture of Hill 175. This ridgeline extended a few hundred yards downrange of the quarry and offered a full view of the north section of town. The Germans had been using numerous positions built into the terraces and stone homes along that same slope to send heavy streams of MG fire down upon the approaching Americans.[24] Now, each of those nests was being systematically silenced by nimble L Company infantrymen. The company commander, 1st Lt Dennis F. Neal, was a veteran of many battles dating all way the back to the North Africa campaign. Not only was he a calm and deeply religious 26-year-old with steady nerves and an unbreakable smile, but a masterful tactician as well.[25] Although Neal's company had been hollowed down to only two effective rifle platoons,[26] he brilliantly organized his remnants into one sweeping pincer wave moving across the hillside in such a way that his attacking force appeared much larger—causing many German defenders to lose their fighting nerve and abandon the area.[27] The remaining holdouts were vanquished one at a time by first dropping smoke from 133rd Cannon Company howitzers with pinpoint accuracy, and then flanking each position with overwhelming troop numbers.[28]

***

While Neal's men cleared the hill in systematic fashion, K Company, under the command of 1st Lt Horatio Nelson Long, made contact with elements of the 135th Regiment high upon Colle Maiola.[29] This rendezvous closed an operational gap between both regiments and brought a sigh of relief to Colonel Marshall—who had been troubled for some time over thoughts of Germans counterattacking his regiment's exposed right flank.

Mopping-up operations began winding down on Hill 215 north of the quarry. Although most German bunkers had been cleared, Chapman's troops still scoured across the rocks, through the ruined homes, and among the stunted olive trees and cacti growing along the steep hillside—in search of stragglers, dangers, and treasures. German helmets, canteens, mess kits, gas masks, and empty cartridges and canisters of all types littered the slope in many places. Candles, a prized scarcity for both sides, were promptly pocketed wherever found. German canned butter rations, also highly valued, quickly disappeared into backpacks. Canned potatoes, though, were too greasy for the American palate and usually passed over.[30]

One 3rd Battalion, 133rd, detail investigated a hillside cluster of three ruined homes. The furthest up the slope—little more than a shanty—had suffered a direct artillery blast. The lone occupant, an Italian woman, lay dead inside—horribly dismembered. Inside a second home, further downhill, was another dead civilian woman felled by shrapnel. She appeared to have been deceased for at least two days. Nearer to the road and behind a third ruined home, the Americans discovered a makeshift shelter fashioned of planks and stones piled against the back wall. The poor craftsmanship was obviously not German. Inside, the Americans discovered two frightened, emaciated boys—still alive, staring back with dazed but curious brown eyes. Both were shoeless and nearly naked save for frumpy, faded overcoats many sizes too large draped around their boney shoulders. An Italian-speaking sergeant was called over and learned the boys' names were Francesco Truppo and Raphale Dolsinlo. Each claimed to be thirteen years old, but neither looked it. Both were orphans. Francesco said his mother was the dead woman in the middle home and the Germans had taken his father away. Raphale said his mother died earlier in Naples. Neither knew the identity of the other woman in the ruined shanty. The boys had been subsisting off livestock corn they gnawed uncooked off the cob. Both were given C-ration cans of meat and beans and the gesture seemed to relax them a bit. Later, when a team of litter bearers came through carrying a wounded man, the two orphans were sent along to receive better care from the rear echelon.[31]

***

The Germans in the highlands to the west continued making trouble for the 135th Regiment. That same morning, the 3rd Battalion, 135th, successfully advanced down from Monte Castellone to occupy Point 706 approximately three-quarters of a mile south.[32] Point 706 sat two miles west of 133rd positions on a parallel roughly in line with the barracks. At the same time, the 2nd Battalion, 135th, on Colle Maiola moved south of Point 481 toward Snakeshead Ridge—rising a half-mile in the southwest on a parallel with the quarry in the 133rd area. In the swirling mists of another bone-chilling morning, the Germans counterattacked eastward with astonishing strength—storming somewhere between 200 to 300 troops. The attackers were eventually driven back, but the Americans thinly dispersed across the barren hillcrests were left nervous and edgy thereafter,[33] and the 2nd Battalion, 135th, was forced again to ration dwindling ammunition for fear of future incursions.[34] Wary American commanders inquiring on the progress of the 2nd Battalion, 142nd, were told their relief was not expected to arrive until much later in the day. The French still needed the help.[35]

Meanwhile, back at the 756th Tank Battalion CP near San Michele, Sweeting and Dolvin's attack planning concluded. This time Dolvin would lead the charge into Cassino. The infantry and tanks would strike together from the barracks beginning at 1530 hours. Artillery salvos were arranged to fall in seven rolling waves 200 yards ahead of the advance. Company C of the 760th would attack in column along the road, while the tanks of B Company, 756th, shadowed in support positions nearby along the drained river and stationary A Company, 756th, tanks provided more distant fire support from the east across the river. Sweeting would remain at the battalion CP to coordinate artillery and mortar support while maintaining close contact with Dolvin.[36] Sweeting hoped this combined arms approach would finally flush the German SPs into the open where his tanks could "snipe them out of edge of town, make them back up and then shell and smoke them in order to get into town." [37] In other words, the plan was another crapshoot. This time, at least, all details had been coordinated ahead of time with Colonel Marshall's infantry.

***

At 1230, Major Dolvin arrived at the 3rd Battalion, 133rd, CP just south of the barracks.[38] In cool forty-degree temperatures under partly cloudy skies providing fair visibility,[39] the 27-year-old 756th Tank Battalion XO conferred with Major Chapman of the 133rd, Captain Arnold, Lt Redle, and Lt Nelson over the plans. He learned none of the infantry had stayed in town the prior night, but did maintain positions along the northern outskirts.[40] While the officers conferred, Dolvin's tanks were topped off with ammo and fuel and then gathered to roll southward from the quarry.[41] At that same moment, an Allied plane swooped in low from the north and roared along the riverbed—strafing 100th (Nisei) Battalion positions along the eastern side before disappearing southward.[42] The incident felt like a bad omen. Then, at 1325, roughly a dozen German ME-109 and FW-190 planes buzzed in from the south near Monte Trocchio, but were driven off by Allied AA units before any could deliver damage.[43]

The 133rd arranged for a coordinated artillery bombardment on the last known locations of the German SP guns,[44] and the TDs hidden across the river were told to "snipe" any SPs attempting to retreat from town.[45] When 1530 arrived, the 133rd was not quite ready to jump off.[46] The K Company contact patrol sent up into 135th territory had just returned. L Company tangled with a few remaining pockets of resistance on Hills 225 and 175,[47] and I Company, positioned at the north edge of town, was still receiving supplies. Potable water remained scarce, but a shipment of canned C-rations and prepackaged K-rations did arrive—and the thirsty, hungry, and tired men gorged themselves on yet another round of the monotonous fare—their sole sustenance for days on end now.[48] As a final preparatory move, one reserve platoon from K Company marched to the quarry area to augment the coming tank attack.[49]

At 1555, the American artillery assault on Cassino commenced with the usual thunder and fury.[50] While shock waves buffeted through the north quarter of town, a steady, pelting rain of shrapnel and rock fragments fell all over the slope of Hill 175 and the baseline road. To escape the deadly hail, Fraizer's men huddled beneath any available cover near the town's entrance and waited as more shells screamed overhead and burst among the crumbling buildings and alleyways 200 yards south.[51] All at once, the fury ended. After a few moments of relative peace, white phosphorous smoke rounds blossomed like cottony flowers among the ruins—and then billowed together rapidly to form a swirling blanket, broad and thick enough to make the entire town disappear.[52]

At the quarry, Major Dolvin called together the tank officers and Staff Sergeant (S/Sgt) Oric Johannesen near his tank for last-minute instructions. Johannesen was instructed to lead his tank in the point position along the riverbed and proceed around the bend first. His mission was to draw fire to allow the other tanks to locate the AT gun positions and neutralize them. Johannesen had just played this same high-stakes game of "chicken" the day before. Alarmed over being asked to gamble his life again, the blond staff sergeant suggested, in fairness, someone else should take the turn.

"You are it!" Dolvin ordered, impatiently.

The meeting adjourned and the commanders dropped inside their turret hatches and fired up their engines.[53]

Dolvin's tanks trundled out of the quarry and pivoted south down the narrow road leading to town with K Company platoon riflemen serving as escorts.[54] Dolvin's M4 assumed the lead with 1st Lt Leo J. Trahan's 2nd Platoon of C Company, 760th, following immediately behind him.[55] In the drained riverbed to Dolvin's left, Lt Redle commanded a composite platoon of B and C Company, 756th, tanks restocked after battling the day before.[56] As ordered, S/Sgt Johannesen's tank led the river column. As Dolvin's tanks rolled forward slowly, Redle's crews mirrored the pace.[57]

At 1630, Dolvin radioed to Sweeting that he had reached the same blown culvert encountered by Redle's tanks the previous day. Dolvin's column idled while infantrymen packed the pit with added rubble to provide a more substantial foundation. After ten minutes of effort, Dolvin's column resumed the advance.[58]

The Germans responded by marking Hill 213 and a house by the cemetery with artillery smoke. Twenty-eight rounds of high velocity, flat trajectory fire soon followed in rapid succession—screaming down from the north and rocking the hillside under a chain of explosions.[59] Two minutes later, the 13th Field Artillery Battalion gained a fix on the source and pounded back in counterbattery.[60]

By 1645, Dolvin's force had probed ahead another 100 yards south of the blown culvert but halted to request a cease in artillery fire.[61] At this point, the smoke cover had grown so vast that clouds rolled by the 133rd CP two miles to the northeast. Dolvin's tankers had to see the town in order to proceed and fire effectively. As the crews waited for the thick white phosphorus shroud to dissipate, 1st Battalion, 133rd, riflemen crept back toward the river in hopes of recapturing the northeast part of town.[62] For the next twenty minutes, the infantry and tankers watched the battered town emerge from thinning mists, waiting for a response—and yet nothing happened. The Germans sat stone silent. Dolvin cautiously edged his road column forward along the narrow road. Johannesen and Redle followed—matching the major's slow progress in fits and starts in the riverbed nearby. Gray, blocky structures of Cassino resolved into finer features. More roofs had been blown open. More walls had collapsed. More fires smoldered here and there. And still, nothing happened.

Finally, at 1710, the loud crack from a high velocity cannon in town shattered the calm—hurling a nine-pound slug 3,000 feet per second up the road, well ahead of its own sound wave.[63] The rifling shot howled past the turret of S/Sgt Johannesen's tank. For several seconds, Technician 4th Class (T/4) Bert L. Bulen, Johannesen's gunner, stared blankly into his gun scope—too petrified to look up for fear his tank commander had been decapitated.[64] But when he felt Johannesen fidget behind him and heard the staff sergeant speak again through the intercom, the 23-year-old Oklahoman breathed a heavy sigh of relief.[65]

Seconds later, another projectile snarled from town. This one pierced steel with a sharp bang—burrowing into the final drive housing of Dolvin's lead tank, and shredding both the transmission and driver's legs with spalls of molten steel.[66] With his tank now knocked dead upon the roadway, Dolvin sprang from his commander's hatch with his headset still on and disconnected wire trailing, scrambled down the left side and leapt onto the rear deck of Redle's tank parked in the river channel only fifteen feet away.[67] At the same time, his tankless crew helped the wounded driver escape while the interior smoldered, popped, and sparked. At once, the major pressed up tight against the back of Redle's turret and handed over his headphone jack. Once the headset was connected to the radio receiver inside, Redle gave Dolvin his own microphone.[68] Clearly, the German SP guns hadn't gone anywhere, and Dolvin feared they were about to claim more victims. He ordered Sgt Johannesen's and Lt Redle's tank drivers in the riverbed to back up far enough to get out of the line of fire.[69] In the meantime, Lt Trahan's idling roadway tanks, somewhat screened and protected by Dolvin's disabled tank, waited in place.

Sweeting, monitoring Dolvin's radio instructions, burst in over the battalion band:

"What's holding you up?" The battalion commander asked incredulously.

Dolvin paused for a second to survey his surroundings with eyes wide in feigned wonder. Then he lifted the hand mic and replied in his slow Georgia drawl:

"I don't know, Colonel, but I think it's *Germans*!"[70]

Allied artillery and smoke began falling across town again, and Dolvin pleaded for more infantry support.[71] While the town quaked and vanished behind a new cloak of smoke, Dolvin jumped down from Redle's tank, clambered up the muddy riverbank to gain the rear deck of Lt Trahan's tank holding the third spot in the column. Taking charge of Trahan's hand mic this time, Dolvin ordered the lieutenant's four-tank platoon to edge forward and test the clearance between his own smoldering tank and the steep hillslope. The major's hunch was correct. One by one, each tank scraped by and headed in column directly for the swirling phosphorus cloud, with Dolvin stooped behind Trahan's turret directing the revived attack. Along the way, infantrymen emerged from places of cover to either pile atop the rear decks or crouch alongside the creeping hulls.[72]

After five minutes, Trahan's tanks breached the entrance of town, pulling along an entourage now swelled to roughly fifty of Fraizer's infantrymen.[73] The column pierced the swirling haze and German MG fire sputtered in protest—raking erratic bursts over hulls, causing riflemen and BAR men to cuss and press tightly against turrets and rear decks. The four tanks moved haltingly ahead, but returned fire with liberal abandon—spitting MG fire into windows and doorways and blowing out entire rooms with devastating flashes from their main guns.[74] Through it all, however, the German SP gun stayed conspicuously silent.

The foggy combat conditions didn't faze Trahan's crews. They had experienced the same conditions a few days earlier during the stunning capture of Caira. Their attack method was simple and direct: any location suspected of harboring a German observer or MG nest was blasted without mercy.[75] As a consequence, the German MG fire abated momentarily, allowing the infantry to storm a tight row of houses near the roadside. Utilizing tried-and-true squad level tactics, a three-man or four-man team approached a target home and tossed grenades into the lower windows. Upon detonation, the team rushed in to secure the lower floor. Their squad mates positioned outside then fired rifle grenades into the upper storey—forcing any Germans hiding above to flee down to the lower floor where they were either captured or killed.[76]

Trahan's lead tank was forced to halt at a new anti-tank ditch the Germans had blown in the road just beyond the first intersection. Another series of smoke shells were dropped to provide cover for the bounding infantrymen carting rocks and debris to fill the pit.[77] As the Americans darted back and forth dumping fill, blind automatic fire from both sides sprayed wildly through the mists.[78] At that same moment, several hundred yards further east, German mortar and artillery rounds burst as splattering plumes of muddy soil along the Rapido. The Germans seemed to know exactly where the next phase of attack would commence. The 1st Battalion, 133rd, infantrymen who were hunkered along the riverbanks withstood the withering assault and continued amassing under fire. Nevertheless, as a precaution, 100th Battalion troops were moved in behind to bolster their rear positions.[79]

At 1730, hitherto silent German MG nests concealed along the southern face of Hill 175 gushed at once, showering streams of deadly tracer fire down upon Trahan's four tanks. The lead storm rained with such ferocity that the supporting infantrymen scurrying for cover feared the beginnings of a counterattack.[80] At the time, Lt Higgins had been establishing his forward CP inside a crumbling home on the edge of town when the violent ruckus erupted. He instinctively grabbed for his field phone to beg for reinforcements—only to find the line had been severed. Next, he dispatched a sergeant to the rear with the same request, but the man returned a short time later saying no reinforcements were available. In desperation, Higgins pulled several nearby MG crews from the hillside and hastily repositioned them on the road ahead.[81] The move left his right flank dangerously vulnerable, but the young lieutenant saw no better option.

Several hundred yards further north, Major Chapman bolted out from the interior of his forward CP on the slope of Hill 175 toward the first sounds of trouble. A side terrace to the crumbling two-storey stone home provided the perfect vantage point from where he could study the situation and direct an array of M Company heavy MG crews positioned nearby.[82] L Company had cleared much of the eastern face of Hill 175, but the south side remained solidly under German control.

"It's getting hot. Jerry is counterattacking on the far side of the hill. I'm short of men," the major exclaimed in passing to reporter Tom Treanor—who happened to be visiting Chapman's CP that very moment.[83]

Fearing the enemy might storm over the hillcrest at any moment, Chapman hastily ordered all his HQ staff members, radiomen, and clerks to grab their M-1 Carbines and scurry up the stepped hill to shore up his right flank.[84] He then raced among the nearby terraces, barking out instructions to each of his MG crews.[85]

The German onslaught of MG, mortar, and artillery fire continued—but the SP guns remained conspicuously absent from the fray. A somber Dolvin radioed Sweeting to report the infantry buckling under the pressure and gave his grave assessment that the position wouldn't hold without reinforcements. Ten minutes later, Dolvin radioed again, saying the situation had only worsened and asking for the authority to withdraw the tanks.[86] Sweeting reluctantly agreed to the request—but only "if conditions warrant."[87]

Dusk fell rapidly and the enemy assault-by-fire showed no signs of dwindling. The young major knew the Germans hidden in town would soon gain the upper hand against his vulnerable tanks. At 1752, with loath resignation, Dolvin clicked on Lt Trahan's hand mic and ordered the withdrawal of the platoon.[88] As the four tanks began reversing out of their tight positions along the narrow road, one German SP gun made a dreadful return. From somewhere deep inside the hazy curtain to the south, a bright green streak of light flashed through at head level—narrowly missing the tanks before disappearing north beyond the barracks with a deafening thunderclap.[89] Several more streaks howled through in quick succession. One narrowly missed Dolvin's helmet—singeing his face as it rocketed by. The stunned major ordered the driver to reverse, but the next round struck iron—jolting Lt Trahan's M4 with a ghastly metallic thud.[90] For a few seconds, the stricken tank only smoked heavily—but then a fiery inferno erupted all at once throughout the crew compartment. Dolvin, Trahan, and two crewmen barely escaped with their lives. Two others, however, perished in flames now jetting out the hatches like roaring blowtorches. Inside the raging cauldron, ammunition sizzled and popped, and the chassis soon shuddered from the irregular bursting of 75mm shells—sending ruptured casings hissing and whirling skyward.[91] The four survivors found cover a safe distance away, but Trahan was bleeding heavily from the face—shot, somehow, during the mad escape.[92] The gunner, Cpl John P. Isabella, also suffered from agonizing facial burns and shrapnel wounds to his hand.[93]

For a few moments, chaos reigned among the three other tanks as Dolvin raced around trying to restore order.[94] Two M4s were trapped forward of Trahan's burning hulk and their supporting infantry hesitated between staying to protect them or beating a retreat. With heavy bullet fire still raining down upon them from the south face of Hill 175, neither option held appeal. Colonel Marshall and Lt Col Sweeting compounded the confusion by hastily conferring and rescinding the withdrawal order—at the very instant Trahan's tank erupted into flames.[95]

A solitary American soldier trotted out of town and burst into the I Company CP 600 yards away. Captain Fraizer turned and immediately confronted the breathless infantryman:

"Why did you come out?"

"All the tanks are knocked out. Everyone is coming out," he answered while sucking air.

Three more gasping soldiers emerged in the doorway.

"Goddamnit!" the hobbling captain howled, "I told 'em to get in those houses and stay in 'em!"

Fraizer promptly sent all of them back into town.[96]

From a shattered stone cubby hole of a CP near Trahan's burning tank, Lt Higgins calmed his remaining men and had them reposition along the narrow city street.[97] With dusk hanging heavy, Higgins's next challenge was to organize the rest of his meager forces and ride out the night. Tank commander Sgt Lester Fenner tried shifting his M4 into a better defilade position, but the street proved too narrow and too heavily rubble strewn to properly pivot. One tread clipped the edge of a deep shell crater and promptly bogged. The more Fenner's driver tried pulling away from the crumbling rim the more the tank tilted. Unnerved by the relentless pinging of S/A fire off the hull and fearful the hidden SP gun would claim them next, the panicked crew abandoned their immovable M4 and bolted for nearby protection in a ruined house occupied by Higgins's infantry.[98] Under Dolvin's direction, the two remaining tanks repositioned defensively in time for the anxious crews to watch the last glimmers of sunlight disappear behind Monastery Hill.[99]

Since the Americans' arrival at Cassino, the Germans had shown an uncanny knack for striking at the worst possible time. Speculative suspicions began circulating of enemy observers, immune to retaliation, watching the Allies' every move from behind the high dark windows of the pristine abbey less than a mile away. Certainly, the Germans could observe troop movements just as effectively from the tall stone tower on nearby "Castle Hill," but the old yellow castle was subject to Allied artillery. The old monastery, however, was strictly off limits to Allied fire, and the rumor took root because few believed the Germans would actually honor the abbey's neutrality.

At 1810, a false report spread among 34th Division HQ staff that three of Trahan's four tanks had been knocked out.[100] In reality, Major Dolvin felt confident enough in the configuration of local defenses to begin walking back to the quarry for more help. His progress was slowed, however, when he stopped to support a wounded tank crewman with a broken leg along the way.[101] Twenty minutes later, the major finally arrived at Captain Fraizer's CP. He promptly phoned Sweeting and reported three tanks in town "holding O.K."—thus dispelling the rumors of another disaster.[102] Then, Dolvin departed for the 3rd Battalion CP near the barracks to meet with Major Chapman.[103] Sweeting feared the Germans would use the cloak of darkness to capture Trahan's three tanks the way they ensnared Granberry's platoon the prior evening. To assuage these concerns, the infantry promised Sweeting they would send more troops to town as soon as possible, but cautioned that the three tanks currently in place would eventually need to move forward to create vehicular passage for more to enter from the north and the east.[104]

Around the same time, I Company sergeant Adrian Van Steenbergen bolted into the I Company CP with an urgent plea from Lt Higgins to send reinforcements. It was a case of borrowing from Peter to pay Paul. Nevertheless, Captain Fraizer cobbled together a small contingent by drawing from his meager defenses positioned along the nearby hill. Within the hour, Van Steenbergen led this ad hoc platoon back into town—with reporter Treanor tagging along audaciously. The men arrived at a nocturnal hellscape. Trahan's tank continued burning violently between the tight road and a shattered apartment building. Every so often, a scorched shell inside burst in a brilliant white flash—ejecting shrieking metal fragments out of the hatches in all directions.[105] To avoid the bite of shrapnel, the sergeant directed his men to track tightly along a stone terrace a safe distance away. The grime on their passing faces reflected the angry red light of the flickering flames.[106]

Colonel Marshall, recognizing his regiment was most vulnerable on the right flank, also feared a nighttime counterattack. To lessen the threat, the Germans holding the south face of Hill 175 had to be driven out, but Marshall lacked the immediate means to do so. L Company and one platoon from K Company were spread too thinly along the eastern face of Hill 175 and still too heavily involved in clearing the remaining resistance to even consider putting on the job.[107] One heavy weapons platoon (.30-caliber heavy MG crews) from M Company had been repositioned forward to buttress the toehold in the north edge of town held by I Company and the K Company platoon, but planned-for 1st Battalion reinforcements remained stymied along the east bank of the river. Any movement drew withering German artillery and mortar fire, with the heaviest rounds howling down from the north.[108] Whatever counterbattery response the division's artillery had employed wasn't working. Marshall concluded his best choice was to consolidate. Toward that end, he ordered 133rd Cannon Company crews to drop smoke behind 3rd and 1st Battalion positions to allow the 100th Battalion to form a wider and tighter ellipse behind 1st Battalion positions.[109] The 2nd Chemical Mortar Battalion, attached to the 34th Division, offered to drop supplementary smoke on Hill 175, but Marshall declined out of safety concerns for his men still clearing the ridgeline.[110]

The 34th Division HQ informed Marshall of the acquisition of eight flame throwers and promised to deliver them as soon as possible.[111] The problem now was operators. Even the engineers sent to Capua to obtain the fearsome weapons did not how to use them, so a call went out to the 36th ("Texas") Infantry Division to learn if they had anyone trained to operate them.[112]

Later that evening in Cassino, tank commander S/Sgt Pinckney D. Upchurch realized that Sgt Fenner's tank, though abandoned, was still operational. He sent over two of his own crewmembers, Pfc Lawrence J. Chapman and Private (Pvt) Frank J. Costanza, to man the immobilized tank's main gun.[113] During a lull in combat, Upchurch dropped to the ground from his turret to consult with Lt Higgins in his CP nearby—only to discover Tom Treanor crouched near his tank treads with a pad of paper and pencil in hand. The courage of the war correspondent stunned Upchurch momentarily, but he answered several of Treanor's questions before the two scurried off in the direction of Higgins's CP.[114]

By 2250, the 133rd showed slow-but-steady progress solidifying their positions. Despite the heavy German artillery and mortar fire, both B and C Companies of the 1st Battalion finally crossed the Rapido to gain an edge into the northeastern part of town. A Company was in the process of joining,[115] while the 100th Battalion pressed in behind to assume the vacated positions along the eastern edge of the river.[116] I Company and K Company Weapons Platoon held firm at the north edge of town, occupying a scant five houses near Trahan's three tanks.[117] One section of MGs from M Company also supported them. Further northwest, L Company continued clearing out pockets of scattered resistance on the eastern slopes of Hill 175, as K Company and the remaining heavy MG crews of M Company maintained defensive positions along Hill 225 on the battalion's rear right flank. The day's modest gains had required the combined efforts of the entire division. Nearly 10,000 rounds of artillery had been expended by 34th Division batteries in the prior twenty-four hours in support of the infantry's efforts.[118]

As midnight neared, ammunition and supplies were carried in from the barracks on foot and dropped off just short of town. At the same time, thirty-six more German prisoners were processed.[119] The eight flame throwers began the long transit from Capua—but more critically, two towed AT guns had been wheeled into the north edge of town to help shield Fraizer's men from the SP guns.[120] The Germans, realizing the Americans had succeeded in reinforcing their positions, set off dynamite charges and dropped the small bridge into the spillway near the town square. Before doing so, however, they finally freed the tilting M4 from the bridge's edge and drove off with a third prize from Lt Granberry's ill-fated platoon.[121]

To better assist the walking wounded, the 3rd Battalion, 133rd, Aid Station relocated from across the river into a cleared bunker near the barracks. Nearly every infantryman gritted through with a minor wound or injury of some kind. Others bore more serious wounds or injuries sustained from multiple incidents. Under normal circumstances, men shot in the limbs, like Captain Fraizer, would have been evacuated. But the want of troops was so dire, that even those in need of surgery were simply treated with sulfa, patched with bandages, and dispatched back to their units. If a man could still hobble about and fire a rifle, he was considered battle-worthy and the doctors were under strict orders not to send anyone on to a hospital unless absolutely necessary.[122]

During the night, the 34th Division engineers redoubled their efforts to repair destroyed bridges east of town in hopes of opening ways for the 753rd Tank Battalion to also move into Cassino. These included not just the larger bridges that once spanned the Rapido, but several smaller ones the Germans had demolished at critical creeks and irrigation canals along the approaches.[123] As usual, repair progress was greatly impeded by the periodic bursting of preregistered German artillery and mortar fire.

Around midnight, Sweeting met with Colonel Marshall at the 133rd CP and the two commanders agreed to refrain from any major attacks the following day in order to consolidate gains in the north quarter of town. Sweeting pledged to reinforce the three tanks still operating in town,[124] but Maj Gen Ryder had given explicit orders not to attempt to do so during the night.[125] Therefore, Sweeting alerted his tankers to prepare to move at first light.[126]

***

As usual, the 756th tank crews used the cover of night to resupply and maintain their vehicles, and, as usual, found little time for sleep. The men had grown so accustomed to the laborious routine that few words needed to be exchanged as they went about their business. Several more tankers had been lost during the day—two from C Company were killed and two others wounded and evacuated. Two men from HQ Company were also wounded and evacuated.[127] An emotional numbness had taken root and men were missed simply because they weren't there to do their jobs.

Several T2 recovery vehicle crews were dispatched across the Rapido river ford north of Caira bridge to salvage what they could of the four A Company tanks knocked out the week prior. While dodging the irregular bouts of German mortar and artillery fire bursting about the fields east of the cemetery, the crews inspected two of the tanks, but found them completely charred and unrecoverable. Captain French G. Lewis's M4, however, showed two AT holes to the turret, but appeared otherwise undamaged. Inside, the captain's bloody coat still lay draped over his seat as though he had stepped out momentarily, but the decaying body of Pvt Edward J. Dudzinski crumpled against the basket mesh on the floor testified otherwise. Brown, crusted blood stains and grayed flesh bits were splattered everywhere, and a vomit-inducing stench of death filled the interior. T/4 Cullen Ward slipped down into the driver's seat and found the engine turned over with little effort. He asked his partner, T/4 Howard Bowers, who had squeezed down the bow gunner's hatch nearby, to take over the controls, but the young man was so spooked by the dead crewman that he sat paralyzed in his seat.[128] Ward simply shrugged, threw Lewis's tank into gear, and followed one of the T2s back toward the river. As they approached the ford, the Germans lashed at them with another volley of artillery. One blast pitched Ward forward against the driver's hatch so violently, he was temporarily knocked unconscious. He awoke to find all his front teeth missing and a numbed mouth bleeding like an open spigot. Bowers's helmet had been pierced through from a sizeable piece of shrapnel. By sheer miracle, the sizzling fragment missed his head, and tumbled down inside his coveralls—causing Bowers to whoop, gyrate, and bang about the tank interior in a frantic attempt to shake it down past his tender nether regions. Eventually, the hot shard slipped down into Bower's pant leg and the poor kid resorted to ripping off his boot to finally find relief.[129] For Ward, the real tragedy of the whole incident was that it hurt so much to laugh so hard.

***

In the early morning hours of 4 February, the 1st Tank Group alerted the 34th Division HQ of thirty enemy tanks spotted near Piedimonte San Germano—only five miles due west of Cassino.

"We may have a good fight on our hands in the morning," an austere voice on the other end of the phone line concluded ominously.[130]

Furnished with this alarming intelligence, the 133rd continued shoring up positions along the north edge of town—positioning the two towed 37mm AT guns, in particular, a little deeper inside town. L and K Companies moved higher and closer to the southern face of Hill 175—preparing for a new attack that would hopefully take them all the way to Castle Hill.[131] By 0300, all three 1st Battalion, 133rd, rifle companies had successfully crossed the Rapido, but had yet to make contact with the 3rd Battalion further west. The 1st Battalion had only four M-10

TDs assisting them—but from a great distance to their rear, and no AT guns or close tank support to speak of on their side of the river. Recognizing this vulnerability, 1st Battalion HQ inquired about the availability of the new flame throwers and were told the 3rd Battalion had received them and would send some over.[132]

Meanwhile, east of Cassino, the engineers working at the Rapido near the downed Highway 6 bridge requested an M4 tank to test their bypass handiwork. The 753rd Tank Battalion sent one forward—but the crew was forced to halt after drawing heavy German fire of all types. A sustained barrage of suppressive fire from division artillery was arranged to get them moving again.[133] The tank reached the riverbank—only to discover just the near side had been blasted down to form a ramp. The far bank still sat nearly vertical at over seven feet high and was "absolutely impossible" to climb. How anyone could think a tank could scale such a tall obstacle was unfathomable. The engineers were told to return and blast down the opposite bank.[134] Obviously, no tanks would be crossing into Cassino from the east before morning.

***

The dawn brought intermittent rain showers and poor visibility.[135] The II Corps were so troubled by earlier sightings of German armor at Piedimonte they ordered the 34th and 36th Division to refrain from using any smoke in the valley outside of Cassino. The II Corps also told the 1st Tank Group to delay a planned eastern attack on town—preferring, instead, to retain as many Allied tanks available as possible should swarms of panzers suddenly emerge from the Liri Valley. This meant 1st Battalion, 133rd, infantrymen had to plan their next attack without the close armor support they had been promised. This, after clawing their way across the Rapido for a second time. In the meantime, the tanks of the 753rd Tank Battalion remained on standby several thousand yards further east, waiting to "fire at any target that appears" in the Liri Valley.[136]

The three operational tanks of Trahan's platoon survived the long night at the town's north edge.[137] As fatigued infantrymen ventured out guardedly in the bitter early morning cold through courtyards and alleyways nearby, the crews laid down bursts of suppressive fire from their coaxial MGs and main guns. Sgt Fenner's tank still hanging askew along the crater's edge, however, became unmanageable. Every time the two-man substitute crew traversed the turret or fired the main gun, the hull tilted further and further to one side. Fearing the tank would soon tumble completely over, Pfc Chapman and Pvt Costanza dismounted and scrambled back to their own tank commanded by Sgt Upchurch.[138]

Sweeting had promised Marshall help. At dawn, two tanks from the 2nd Platoon of A Company, 760th, arrived to shore up Upchurch's position.[139] The lead tank, commanded by 1st Lt Dale Pride,[140] a 27-year-old Missouri farmer,[141] barely squeezed past Trahan's charred wreck, still smoldering a few yards west of the canalized river.

Once the second tank successfully followed, both lurched forward beyond Upchurch's position to help escort the infantry probing deeper toward the town square.[142] At 0840, 3rd Battalion infantrymen, perhaps feeling isolated, reported they still hadn't made contact with the 1st Battalion operating someplace on their left and weren't exactly sure where they were. An enemy tank of some sort appeared briefly on a segment of high winding road leading up to Castle Hill in the southwest. The tip was passed along to the artillery.[143] To conceal Pride's tanks and the handful of infantrymen closing in upon the town square, Colonel Marshall requested a smoke drop over the south section of Cassino.[144] At the same time, five B Company, 756th, tanks supported the effort from defilade positions 600 yards to the north. S/Sgt Johannesen and Sgt Roland L. Buys blasted away at targets in town from tucked locations along the quarry wall, while Sgt Charles Graffagnini and 2nd Lt John J. Czajkowski—since returned with a bandaged hand—dispatched more direct fire from the roadway nearby.[145]

Higgins's men resumed the hazardous work of house-to-house fighting in the north quarter of Cassino. One block of tightly packed homes along the left side of the road between the first alleyway road and spillway bridge proved especially challenging.[146] Close tank support was impossible here because the gaps between many homes were too narrow to allow vehicular passage. The rubble from previous artillery strikes had also blocked many approaches. Support walls and even entire buildings had been reduced to varied stages of collapse.[147] Worst of all, every debris-strewn courtyard seemed to be well covered by German crossfire emanating from multiple angles. Great skill and planning had gone into creating such defenses, and overcoming each position was like trying to capture a fort inside a puzzle. Every interlocking German gun position had to first be identified. Then each spot had to be neutralized, one after the other, by employing clockwork squad coordination: a grenade tossed through a window and a door kicked down right after the blast, followed by liberal bursts from Tommy guns. Any Germans found still alive in a room were usually too dazed to fight and surrendered willingly.[148] This dangerous and tedious process had to be repeated over and over again and proved the only dependable way to untangle and subdue a German "kill zone"—and after every encounter, the infantry adapted and improved upon their methods. Rifles and mortars proved useless in such house-clearing situations and were set aside. Hand grenades, wired explosives bundles, and fully automatic weapons such as Tommy guns, BARs, and light .30-caliber and heavy .50-caliber MGs yielded the best results.[149] Once a house was completely cleared, two men stayed behind as guards—to prevent the Germans from sneaking right back in and retaking the position.[150] This meant as the day progressed, fewer and fewer men remained to carry the attack forward—and Higgins's company was already woefully depleted.

Eventually, a small spearhead of riflemen reached the narrow roadway bordering the canalized spillway running down from the hills.[151] Under a dreary light drizzle,[152] this remnant attack force, comprised of only six men, crossed the downed bridge and took control of two large buildings at the north edge of the square. With this final triumph, the 3rd Battalion's north quarter holdings had been expanded a full 100 yards deeper inside the town.[153]

In the meantime, the Germans launched a surprise counterattack upon 1st Battalion positions a few hundred yards to the east.[154] At least three German tanks positioned near the jail joined in the assault—although up to six German tanks or SP guns were believed to be prowling about the area. At one point, three SP guns were spotted huddled and firing from along the western wall of the jail, but only mortar fire could reach them in such a tight area. Sweeting directed the battalion mortar platoon to lob HE rounds upon them, in hopes of breaking their resolve and driving them away. The small explosions failed to dislodge them. Next, he ordered his mortar crews to drop white hot phosphorous atop their hulls. This time, when the smoke lifted, the three SP guns were gone.[155] The effort, however, was too little and too late. By noon, the withering SP fire had forced all three companies of the 1st Battalion back across the Rapido—all the way to a streambed 100 yards further east.[156] TD fire from afar, again, proved completely ineffective in supporting the common infantryman, and not a single SP gun had been "sniped."

All afternoon, a cold steady rain fell over the battlefield—creating dangerously slick ground conditions in addition to keeping everyone soaked and miserable.[157] Combat operations slowed to a point where both sides seemed content with exchanging artillery, mortar, and small arms fire from a distance. The German tanks seen earlier near Piedimonte had yet to show, so nobody dared let down their guard.

S/Sgt James "Red" L. Harris, a red-headed, freckle-faced platoon leader in A Company, 756th, scanned the misty town through his twenty-power artillery scope from a concealed tank position roughly 1,000 yards northeast of town—wiping the lens regularly to clear away beading droplets. For several days, Harris had been using the scope quite effectively to direct fire support operations for his tank crews dug-in and camouflaged nearby. During the afternoon, the 27-year-old staff sergeant watched a German ambulance drive up from the south and pull to a stop next to a building in town. To his shock, crates of ammunition were being unloaded from the rear—a clear violation of Geneva Convention rules. Redle, listening in to the battalion radio band, heard Harris describe the unfolding scene to his gunners in a manner similar to a baseball play-by-play radio announcer: the unloading had finished. The rear doors were closed. The driver climbed back inside. "OK, hold it," Harris paused between his slow Texas drawl delivery, "another guy is getting in …." He then gave the fire order, and the ambulance was obliterated.[158]

Colonel Marshall gave up trying to inject the 1st Battalion into town from the east. Without close tank support, a third attempt was also likely to fail. He instead ordered the 1st Battalion to shift to the rear of the 3rd Battalion positions after dusk and relieve L and K Companies on Hill 225 and Hill 175. By 1900, this move was completed and A and C Companies assumed the right flank of the 3rd

Battalion—finally freeing L Company to shore up I Company positions in town.[159] At the same time, I Company reported their men were situated well in the northwest part of town and riding out the rain storm.[160] Twelve Germans were taken prisoner during morning consolidation operations,[161] yet American casualties had been surprisingly light. The four supporting tanks and two towed AT guns also reported ending the day in "good shape," and plans were underway for a more ambitious and coordinated attack involving the 1st Battalion the next morning. Because the wet weather had also dampened combat activity, ammunition stocks held up better than expected,[162] but after dark, additional supplies were still carried down from the barracks on foot.[163]

***

At the close of day, the 756th Tank Battalion reported thirty-nine tanks as operationally fit with thirty others still under repair. A total of fifteen had been lost to date. The attached C Company, 760th, and 2nd Platoon of A Company, 760th, reported twelve operationally fit tanks with four under repair and five lost.[164] The tanks situated west of the Rapido and closest to the action were dispersed as follows: four C Company, 760th, tanks held point positions in the northwest part of Cassino; B Company (reconstituted with only two platoons), one platoon each from Company A and C Company, 756th, and the remainder of C Company, 760th, sat tucked behind The Pimple north of the barracks, receiving supplies. Due to the harassing, unpredictable, and intermittent blasting of German artillery shells, all crews slept inside cold, cramped tank interiors—usually propped up in uncomfortable seated positions. For a full week now, the tanker's battle station also served as his bed.[165] Life was dirty, smelly, itchy, and completely devoid of privacy. The same grimy socks, undergarments, coveralls, and winter jackets were worn day in and day out. Shaving or even washcloth bathing of the face or hands was impossible for most.[166] Young men, who came to detest the triviality of equipment inspections and boredom of bivouac life and once pined for the excitement and "glamour" of combat, now realized they had been sent on a camping trip in hell.

The 756th Tank Battalion CP continued operating one-and-a-half miles west near San Michele—but the staff prepared to move across the Rapido into Caira that very night. Service elements remained near San Pietro, where they could safely function beyond the range of most German artillery cannon.[167] Supplying and maintaining armor in combat was a round-the-clock challenge—especially for the service crews toiling away nine miles from the front. Many now suffered from the debilitating effects of chronic sleep deprivation.

Throughout the day, Lt Col Sweeting had been consumed with the task of knocking out the German SP guns infesting northern Cassino. During the morning, he directed fire from his battalion mortar platoon and on-call 34th Division artillery batteries upon any suspected gun positions.[168] At noon, he repositioned a platoon of TDs from C Company, 776th, in the barracks area, where he hoped a closer firing platform would improve the crews' odds for success.[169] Although the four TDs fired a total of seventy-five HE rounds at suspected German SP and AT gun positions in town over the course of the afternoon, they failed to register a single kill.[170]

At 1600 hours, Sweeting met with Colonel Marshall and the CO of the 235th Engineer Battalion in the 133rd CP. There, Sweeting unveiled his latest imaginative idea: sneak two towed 57mm guns from the 133rd Regiment AT Platoon to the top of Hill 175. He hoped when the SP guns appeared again in the town below, they could be ambushed and destroyed from above. The two other officers signed off on the idea, but told Sweeting his battalion would be responsible for moving the guns across the river.[171]

Sweeting's tankers were promised that once Cassino fell, all tanks under the command of the 1st Tank Group (the 753rd, 755th, 760th, and 756th Tank Battalions) would be pulled from combat for rest and reorganization.[172] If this announcement was meant to generate extra incentive to "fight harder," it failed. Everybody had already been giving their best efforts toward winning—yet remained frustrated over the results. When the 756th first arrived at the Rapido, Sweeting boasted openly on how he was not going to shave his face again until Cassino fell to the Allies. After two long, grueling weeks of battle, however, the lieutenant colonel showed up one morning clean shaven without saying a word. His dark thick beard had only become an embarrassing reminder of a very naïve and foolish boast.[173]

To defeat the Germans, the SP and AT gun crews had to be outsmarted. Unfortunately, it was difficult to determine exactly how many were stalking or positioned throughout the north end of town. Nine prisoners from the German 211th Grenadier Regiment told 34th Division intelligence interrogators of several more AT guns hidden deeper among the buildings.[174] Two other prisoners were SP gun crewmen captured during the previous week. One was *Oberwachtmeister* (1st Sgt) August Riedmaier, and the other was *Gefreiter* (Corporal) Walter Augustin. Both came from the 3rd Battery, 242nd *Sturmgeschütz-Abteilung* (Assault Gun Battalion)—the SP unit that had become the bane of the 34th Division and the 756th Tank Battalion. What the two enemy crewmen disclosed was instructive: they said the 242nd was first battle-hardened in Russia before moving to Arce, fifteen miles northwest of Cassino, in November 1943, and then the Gustav Line in mid-January. The 242nd was organized into three batteries consisting of three platoons with three SP guns each. Most were *Sturmgeschütz* III model assault guns equipped with long barreled 75mm guns tipped with muzzle brakes.

A fully tracked *Sturmgeschütz* III weighed twenty-one tons and fought with a crew of four. Each one, fully stocked, carried a total of eighty-four rounds of 75mm shells (fifty-five HE, twenty-one AP, and eight smoke). Protected by armor two inches thick at the front and one inch thick on the sides, the *Sturmgeschütz* III served as an effective infantry support anti-tank gun and proved a deadly tank killer while prowling the steppes of Russia. At eighteen feet long and nine-and-a-half feet wide, the hull had roughly the same dimensions as an American M4, but for one key feature: height. A *Sturmgeschütz* III stood only six-and-a-half feet tall—nearly three feet shorter than an M4 medium—making its squat profile much easier to conceal. Though it lacked a rotational turret, its 75mm main gun could still traverse twelve-and-a-half degrees to either side—a range more than adequate for any AT gun lying in ambush. The main gun also fired at a deadly 2,524 feet per second—roughly twenty-five percent faster than an M4's 75mm—making its AP round capable of penetrating over three-and-a-half inches of sloped armor from as far away as 3,280 feet.[175] Any unsuspecting M4 could easily be knocked out within that distance—a *Sturmgeschütz* III capability Sweeting's tankers had already discovered by spilling blood.

The prisoners also said their 1st Platoon had been assigned at Cervaro and that two of their three guns had been knocked out there. The 2nd Platoon had been positioned between the cemetery and Caira and lost all three of their guns in battle. Riedmaier, however, boasted of taking on ten American tanks and destroying four of them. He claimed he had been able to knock out so many because the Americans had advanced with their sides toward him instead of head on. Augustin also spoke of knocking out three tanks before his own SP gun was incapacitated from a direct hit. His platoon's last SP gun was destroyed by the crew when their position became untenable.[176] Without a doubt, the two captured 242nd SP commanders were experienced, cunning, and proud soldiers. Their confident attitudes demonstrated to the Americans that the remaining SP crews carrying on the fight in Cassino would not be easy to deceive or defeat.

Upon the arrival of night, Italian troops serving temporarily as 133rd Regiment litter bearers tried recovering more of the dead.[177] Many had been deceased for days—strewn about the fields and hillsides or partially entombed beneath building rubble. Despite the cold temperatures, the stench was pervasive and atrocious. Many corpses had since become disarticulated—reduced to rotting limbs or torsos blown about over and over again by exploding mines, mortar, and artillery. In just one 200 by fifty-yard area stretched north of the barracks along the Rapido, over ninety mutilated bodies had been recovered by Graves Registration. Many lacked dog tags and could not be easily identified.[178] Both the presence and condition of these remains had an adverse effect on the morale of the living—and yet only the most accessible victims could be recovered and taken away. Retrieving bodies trapped in unmarked minefields was too dangerous and simply not attempted.[179] Daylight ventures drew immediate German shelling, whereas approaches by night required a flashlight—which also attracted German wrath.[180] The unreachable departed fell into an administrative limbo—not yet "officially" dead or missing, and certainly not on duty either. Company 1st sergeants were reluctant to report a duty status change unless absolutely certain—for fear of embarrassment or disciplinary action. Strange things had happened in the past. Soldiers assumed dead or captured sometimes turned up alive and well a few days later. The tank drivers cutting through fields or trampling across rubble took great pains to avoid crushing corpses from either side—which often proved impossible. The unfortunate German *landser* killed on the road just south of the quarry had been crushed over by tank treads so many times that his pressed mass was no longer recognizable as a human being. He had become both unrecoverable and unidentifiable. He would never have a gravesite—forever "missing in action" to his comrades and a grieving family who would never know what became of him. Many souls lost in Cassino ended up like this man.

Two recently reclaimed bodies belonged to crewmen from B Company of the 756th Tank Battalion. The names of these men could now be released, at last, from administrative purgatory. Back in the States, the devastating, life-changing telegrams would be delivered by fresh-faced boys on bicycles. Knocks on doors were answered by apprehensive mothers, fathers, or wives. Trembling hands pulled free Western Union half-sheets from window envelopes to reveal bold lines of blue capitalized teletype. The lettering always began: "THE SECRETARY OF WAR DESIRES ME TO EXPRESS HIS DEEP REGRET …" and closed with "J A ULIO THE ADJUTANT GENERAL." A few days later, neighbors would notice the blue service star once proudly displayed in a living room window had been changed to gold. Hearts sank. Everybody dreaded the gold star.

Cpl Paul T. Tirpak's big body was pulled from Wilkinson's knocked out M4 north of the barracks. His B Company comrades hoped the brawny Clevelander had been taken prisoner along with the others. But now, his strapped and covered remains arrived at the battalion HQ in a stretcher atop the hood of the medics' jeep.[181] Because Tirpak's dog tags had been obliterated by the same *Panzerfaust* blast that had knocked out the tank, the battalion's communications officer, Captain Edwin B. Olson, and D Company's 1st Sergeant (1st Sgt), Arthur F. Richter, were asked to peel back the tarp and make a formal identification.[182] For two-and-a-half years, Tirpak had been the "older brother" to many enlisted men in B Company. Now this strong athletic man with an infectious, optimistic zeal for life, and a doting fiancée back home lay broken in two pieces. His entire chest and mid-section were gone—as if the war had purposefully and savagely targeted this man's giant heart.[183] Whenever spirits sagged among his tankmates, Tirpak would always proclaim brightly: "The war's going to end tomorrow and we'll be home the day after that!" In a sense, he was right—but not in the way he expected or in the condition anybody wanted to return home.

That same night, the tall, lanky frame of 2nd Lt Wayne B. Henry was also exhumed from a shallow gravel grave prepared by the Germans near the bridge north of the barracks.[184] Lt Redle was asked to identify the bullet-ridden lieutenant.[185] Word of these losses spread quickly among the ranks—and Tirpak and Henry landed the unlucky distinction as B Company's first confirmed combat deaths.[186]

***

The late-night hours of 4 February brought surprising calm. Weather forecasters, however, warned of heavy rainstorms arriving after midnight with winds whipping up to fifty miles per hour (MPH).[187] Both sides had grown weary after three straight days of fighting and seemed to stop all at once to draw a deep breath before the morning. The 100th Battalion holding the east side of Rapido received a few shells around 2222 hours.[188] The 135th also reported receiving a few stray shells, but this "harassment" turned out to be errant Allied rounds falling short of intended targets.[189]

During the previous twenty-four hours of combat, the 34th Division artillery expended another 10,000 rounds in and around Cassino. The 151st Field Artillery Battalion alone fired 4,568 rounds in direct support of the 133rd Regiment's consolidation efforts in the north section of town. Artillery was generally ineffective against the hardened concrete and steel bunkers built along the foundations of stone buildings, but the explosions did keep the Germans from climbing out of their holes, at least.[190] After four days of furious use, though, the fouled gun barrels to all the 155mm, 105mm, and 75mm cannon had to be cleaned and serviced to avoid exceeding their operational limits. The German artillerymen must have faced similar maintenance challenges, because a weird respite followed where few artillery rounds were exchanged from either side. This odd and unexpected combat lull extended all the way into French-held territory to the north.[191]

***

During the past two days, in the western highlands, the 135th Regiment made slow but steady progress southward toward the monastery.[192] Mule trains now operated regularly over the twisting, narrow, rocky pathways winding up from Caira. What supplies the plodding beasts could carry were enough, at least, to keep things moving. The entire 142nd Regiment finally relocated from the north—no longer serving as relief, but as partners with the 135th in a general push toward the Liri Valley. Maj Gen Ryder felt comfortable enough in their progress to order the 2nd and 3rd Battalions of the 168th off of Hill 213 to assume new reserve positions closer to the action. One battalion was sent to Colle Maiola immediately west of the barracks, and the other was placed on Hill 892 roughly a mile northwest of Caira.[193] Like their 133rd Regiment brethren in town below and to their right, the 135th, 142nd, and 168th Infantry Regiments drew up ambitious plans to strike at dawn. This time, the Americans hoped a combined attack by all regiments would generate enough momentum to carry them all the way to the monastery.

The Allied commanders from British General Sir Harold Alexander, commanding all Allied Forces in Italy, down to Maj Gen Keyes of the II Corps, sensed a breakthrough was imminent and redirected resources accordingly. The 36th Division, still positioned east of the Rapido near San Angelo, was told by the 56-year-old[194] Keyes to prepare for an attack into the Liri Valley via Highway 6 with the intent of taking Piedimonte San Germano, five miles west of Cassino.[195] General Alexander scrambled together a provisional corps comprised of the 2nd New Zealand Division and the British 4th Indian Infantry Division and assigned New Zealander WWI hero Lieutenant General (Lt Gen) Bernard C. Freyberg as commander. Once Cassino and the abbey fell, Alexander hoped Freyberg's two fresh divisions would pour into the Liri and pursue the retreating Germans far enough north to conjoin with the Anzio beachhead.[196] Again, all grand battle plans appeared stunningly successful on paper.

Maj Gen Ryder stayed far more cautious and focused upon his division's immediate goals. Except for two Nebelwerfer mortars (twelve rockets in total) firing off every hour or two during the night, the Germans remained remarkably quiet throughout the area.[197] Ryder, always leery of a counterattack, instructed the 133rd to use the lull to stock up on as much ammunition as possible.[198]

Sweeting arranged for M5 light tanks from D Company to tow the infantry's two 57mm guns across the Rapido. Just before midnight, the two small AT artillery pieces were unhitched near the barracks and turned over to Chapman's men.[199] In a cold, intermittent rain, a team of engineers and infantry winched, dragged, kicked, and cajoled one of the 2,100-pound guns all the way up the side of Hill 225 into a camouflaged position. By 0200 hours, the piece was in place. The other team labored until dawn but failed to get their gun in position—so they quit out of concerns the Germans would see them at daylight.[200] In the meantime, the 756th Tank Battalion's forward CP completed a move from San Michele to Caira.[201] An intermediate CP remained in San Michele to maintain general administration and coordinate the flow of battalion materials arriving from the rear supply CP at San Pietro.[202]

***

The dawn of 5 February broke, bringing cool, light fog under an overcast sky. The vacillating rains had ceased for the time being, but a gentle, capricious wind played cruel tricks with visibility—shifting the range from as far as two miles down to zero and back again in the span of only a few minutes.[203] The north area of Cassino sat eerily silent. All three rifle companies of the 3rd Battalion, 133rd, had been precisely positioned in town, properly stocked, and prepared to jump off at 0630 sharp.[204] To their right, on the south face of Hill 175, A Company shifted into a point position, with B Company echeloned slightly to their right, and C Company trailing both. All 1st Battalion troops had also been laden with extra ammo.[205]

At 0635, scouts from the 3rd Battalion, 133rd, set out west of the small bridge near the town square and followed the canalized spillway up into the fog-shrouded draw connecting Hill 175 to Castle Hill. They reported no enemy reaction.[206] At the same time, lead elements of the 1st Battalion crept off the crest of Hill 175 and swept stealthily around the top of the craggy draw toward Castle Hill.[207] Surprisingly, they also drew no fire. Evidently, the Germans had vacated the south face of Hill 175 sometime during the night. By 0735, the Germans holding Castle Hill detected the intrusion, and the familiar chatter of small arms echoed throughout the rocky ravine. Every so often, some larger gun cracked among the ruined buildings somewhere in the south—indicating German SPs still prowled about.[208] By 0810, the 1st Battalion reported establishing a firm "foothold" and were presently "sweeping around" the top of the draw toward Castle Hill. To avoid friendly fire mishaps, 135th infantrymen working the highlands to the right were alerted of these 1st Battalion, 133rd, intentions.[209]

By 0945, both attacking 133rd battalions reported encountering increased German small arms fire—emanating particularly from well-concealed positions around the base of the tall, thick stone tower rising atop Castle Hill. The 1st Battalion reached the edge of Castle Hill—an impressive 400-yard journey from their starting point—but progress had slowed under considerable resistance.[210] The four tanks in town tried moving west in support of the 1st Battalion but could find no clear pathway into the draw—so the crews continued assisting nearby 3rd Battalion infantrymen instead with house-to-house fighting.[211]

By 1000, the fog lifted considerably, and the air warmed to a more comfortable forty-five degrees. Then, a blue sky swiftly emerged with such shocking clarity that the majestic snowcapped crown of Monte Caira rising five miles away in the northwest seemed to hover only an arm's length away.[212] This dramatic improvement in visibility came as a double-edged sword—for what the American attackers could see, the Germans defenders could see as well.

During the highland attack, 135th Regiment riflemen crept to within 200 yards of the monastery. Further west, the 2nd Battalion, 135th, captured Hills 593 and 563 near Massa Albaneta.[213] The progress was dazzling, and the troops closing in upon Monastery Hill could now look down upon Cassino and observe much of what had been hidden before. Two tanks were seen parked near a mountain road bend southwest of the yellow castle. Clearly, this was not American armor perched so high in enemy-held territory. A cub spotter plane was launched to find out if more German panzers lurked even higher along the same switchback route leading up to the abbey.[214]

Noon passed, and German reaction grew more heated. The SP guns in town, especially, barked away with more irritated frequency. All of Redle's B Company tanks now provided rear fire support for Chapman's infantry probing deeper into town. From positions by the quarry and areas north around the barracks, Redle's M4s fired back in defiance.[215] Because of intense German mortar and S/A fire, the 1st Battalion's attack stalled among the ridges and gullies of the saddled draw between Hill 175 and Castle Hill. The fire, especially, pouring from the eastern slope of Monastery Hill pelted down upon their helmets like a hailstorm.[216] One particularly loathsome Nebelwerfer unit, concealed in a draw only a few dozen meters away from the abbey, emerged as the 1st Battalion's most galling bane. Artillery Cub planes circled about like khaki-colored kites in the blue skies high overhead trying to gain a fix on the elusive launcher's position—yet the deadly rockets kept screaming through and bursting among the frustrated Americans huddled among the ravines.[217] The two German tanks partially burrowed near the south side of the castle tower soon joined the fracas,[218] and the GIs pinned flat against the jagged rocks below wondered, again, if their every move was being carefully monitored by observers inside the unscathed abbey.

The frustration extended eastward, where the German SP guns continued prowling the north alleyways of Cassino, harassing American infantry, and consuming Sweeting's attention. All morning long and into the early afternoon, the animated battalion commander directed his assault guns, mortars, and attached TDs and 59th Artillery howitzers to fire anywhere he suspected the guns to be skulking—yet he saw no evidence of success.[219] At 1300, Sweeting escorted Arnold, Redle, plus all available platoon leaders and platoon sergeants of C Company, 760th, on a reconnaissance jaunt to the north outskirts of Cassino.[220] He showed the group all the places he suspected the SP guns to be operating, as well as the location of the destroyed bridge, and the infantry's chief objectives: namely, the town square to the right and jail to the left. The enemy's high ground advantages were discussed—particularly the yellow hilltop castle in the fore and monastery sitting much higher in the distance. To counter these advantages, Sweeting said he and Major Chapman would establish a joint CP in a ruined house low on Hill 175 near the town's north edge—providing a panoramic view of the battlefield.[221] From there, the two battalion commanders could closely coordinate the next attack.

Next, Sweeting did something very foolhardy and undisciplined—especially for a West Point-educated officer. As the group visited an infantry observation post (OP) position hidden near the quarry, Sweeting spotted several Germans moving along the hillside in the distance. He impulsively grabbed an infantryman's rifle and took several futile shots at the tiny gray figures. The Germans answered with a swift burst of MG fire. Fortunately, no one was hit by the retaliatory spray, but the long canvas skirt of Sweeting's overcoat was perforated with three fresh holes. Any bullet could have easily wounded or killed him—a discovery everyone else found alarming but Sweeting considered hysterically funny. The battalion commander's risky behavior not only revealed the OP's position unnecessarily to the enemy, but eroded the trust of his closest officers.[222]

At 1330, a surprise swarm of roughly two dozen German fighter-bombers raced swift and low on an attack line running from Cassino though Caira—dropping 500-pound bombs while screaming by. Six bombs exploded in Caira—mostly around the 133rd Regimental CP. One jeep was shredded and several men lay wounded.[223] The timing of the German strike seemed suspicious, because the 133rd had moved their CP into the location only a few hours earlier. Abbey observation was suspected.

By mid-afternoon, Sweeting and his reconnaissance team returned to the 3rd Battalion, 133rd, barracks CP after their lengthy survey of Cassino.[224] Sweeting proceeded on to Caira to meet with Colonel Marshall, and check on the relocation progress of his own CP.[225] Part of the 756th HQ had been established, but the six 105mm M7s of the Assault Gun Platoon weren't expected to cross the Rapido until early evening.[226]

At 1705, twenty-five more German FW-190 and ME-109 aircraft swooped in from the west and dropped another slew of tumbling bombs—this time striking 135th Regiment highland positions before targeting Cassino and the thin road leading down from the barracks.[227] Lt Redle had just eased down inside his commander's hatch and prepared to depart the quarry when the attack occurred. One plummeting bomb narrowly missed the rear deck of his tank and blew a cylindrical engine air cleaner completely off the hull.[228] In a flash, the incursion was over, and the rolling gray planes vanished behind the mountains. Five minutes passed and another wave of German fighter-bombers attempted an audacious raid straight down the Mignano Gap. Every anti-aircraft battery in the region responded and the overmatched planes swerved away to the east—still holding their undelivered payloads.[229]

***

With the sun setting low, the 1st Battalion sat pinned in the saddle between Hill 175 and Castle Hill, and the besieged men prepared to ride out their predicament through the night. Despite the afternoon's combat challenges, they had finally succeeded in establishing contact with 135th troops high to their right—thus closing a flank gap that had been nagging Colonel Marshall.[230]

In the meantime, the 3rd Battalion continued their slow, painstaking push into the north quarter of Cassino.[231] The better part of the day had been spent clearing just one small block of houses.[232] Battle lines were so fluid and compact, the Americans gaining one room often heard their Germans adversaries conversing in the next.[233] The deeper Chapman's men probed, the more elaborate they found defenses in well-fortified positions. Buried along many foundations were MG nests inside hardened concrete bunkers or thick portable steel casings built to withstand direct bomb blasts.[234] Other MG positions had been disguised as rubble piles.[235] The Germans also constructed barricades of sandbags, rubble, and loose stone funneled in a manner to herd unwary Americans into "kill zones"[236]—incorporating fields of MG fire arranged to overlap with one another.[237] To overcome such defenses, the 3rd Battalion expended grenades and TNT charges in enormous quantities.

On an average day of street fighting, Chapman's men easily tossed over 500 hand grenades.[238]

An M4's 75mm gun was the infantry's best weapon for neutralizing a troublesome German bunker. If an HE round failed to penetrate, then an AP round would be fired to open a hole in the concrete or steel exterior. Next, a follow-up round of HE was threaded through—often vaporizing the defenders inside. The M4's mobility, however, was severely limited—particularly in the densely packed and debris-strewn areas of Cassino. In those places the tanks couldn't go, the infantry discovered the bazooka was an extremely effective bunker-busting tool. Major Chapman approvingly called the simple weapon "the squad leader's 'direct fire artillery.'"[239] An M-1 bazooka was originally designed in 1942 to serve as an infantryman's last-ditch defense against a marauding enemy tank. Basically, the weapon functioned by inserting a small 2.36-inch diameter rocket into a simple 54-inch tube, then raising it to the shoulder and aiming toward a target. A finger trigger ignited the rocket propellant with an electrical spark. Each finned rocket weighed only 3.4 pounds but delivered a shaped explosive charge capable of penetrating up to five inches of steel.[240] Actual combat results against armor, however, proved disappointing. The weapon required an operator to stand or kneel out in the open within thirty yards of an enemy tank to have a fair chance of hitting it—a serious personal gamble in the thick of combat. If the operator was seen before he could fire, he was often killed. If he fired and missed, then he was most certainly killed.

In Sicily, the infantry discovered bazooka rockets worked wonders against static defensive emplacements and started experimenting with the weapon in street-fighting settings. At Cassino, Chapmen's men perfected a bazooka method that enabled them to completely circumvent German "kill zones" arrayed among the courtyards and alleyways.[241] Rather than engage such places directly on the outside, Chapman's men flanked them by blasting through the interior walls of nearby homes. Once they captured the room in one house, several bazookas were employed to blast a hole and gain entry into the next. The stone walls were so thick in most homes that it took, on average, nine or ten bazooka blasts to accomplish the task.[242] After a hole was made big enough for a man to enter, hand grenades were tossed into the other room, and an assault team stormed through while spraying suppressive bursts from their Tommy guns.[243] The tactic proved so successful that highest priority was given for the delivery of as many bazookas into Cassino as possible.[244] As a result of the bazooka's success, the flamethrower faded as an offensive option. The flamethrower was also an unattractive choice due to extreme hazards for the operator fighting in such close quarters.

The radio proved virtually worthless in the street fighting of Cassino. The 3rd Battalion, 133rd, was given SCR-536 "Walkie-Talkie" AM handhelds—which were already notoriously unreliable. Backpack-type SCR-300s proved more dependable, but the 3rd Battalion hadn't been issued any. To maintain vital communication links between the battalion CO, company commanders, platoon leaders, and outposts, phone lines were strung between CPs or old-fashioned message runners were dispatched on foot. Because phone connections were regularly severed by indiscriminate artillery and mortar blasts, or careless vehicular traffic, surly linemen had to constantly run about unspooling new lines while ducking sniper fire.[245]

Evening fell, and the hard slog of offensive operations eased. All four tanks stayed in town to protect the infantry while a team of engineers arrived under cover of darkness to devise ways of circumventing the blown spillway bridge near the town square.[246] The engineers hoped to construct some type of alternate span sturdy enough to allow tanks through.[247] At the same time, fresh supplies were carried down from the barracks to replenish the infantry and tanks in town. The four tank crews blew through 75mm HE rounds and .30-caliber ammo almost as quickly as the infantry tossed hand grenades. 1st Lt Nelson, the C Company, 760th, company commander, had the difficult task of making sure his tank crews received timely supplies and never exhausted their stocks.[248]

At 2100, the 1st Battalion remained hunkered upon the northern approaches of Castle Hill but had run short on their supplies.[249] The Germans knew. Twenty minutes later, *feldgrau* uniforms poured down in droves from the heights—driving the stunned Americans all the way back to Hill 175. This masterfully timed counterattack erased the 1st Battalion's gains for the entire day.[250] To shore up the 1st Battalion's eroded position on the right flank, Colonel Marshall hastily ordered the 100th Battalion to press in closer along Hill 175.[251] The 3rd Battalion positions further east were not targeted in this attack, but several tanks moved down to the quarry—just in case the Germans decided to strike again later that night.[252] All other tanks and crews not fighting in town or assigned stand-by duties at the quarry, returned to The Pimple area for another cycle of maintenance, resupply, and, hopefully, a sliver of rest.[253]

Each night, 1st Lt William F. Bouch, the 756th Tank Battalion's transportation officer in Service Company, delivered a fresh dossier of aerial photos to Lt Redle. Redle would then pull together his platoon leaders and sergeants to study the images under flashlight. This night began no differently. Redle, his crew, and a few other tank commanders huddled together closely to review Bouch's latest batch. Behind them, an infantry chow line formed at the northeastern base of The Pimple. For the most part, this small patch of land tucked behind the hill had been shielded from German artillery arcing in from the west. This time, however, the Germans surprised everybody with a barrage coming from the north. All at once, explosions buffeted the area. One round burst near Redle's congregation—knocking everyone to the ground. After several moments of sheer terror, the attack ceased and Redle scrambled to his feet, concussed but otherwise unhurt. Several of his men, however, lay sprawled and motionless. Sgt Gene Wunderlich suffered the brunt of the blast. His right leg was completely severed and the spray of shrapnel had exposed bones and severed arteries in all three of his remaining limbs.[254] Redle rushed to apply crude tourniquets before his gunner succumbed to shock and perished.[255] The work was adequate enough to stabilize Wunderlich until medics could arrive, but the man's ghostly white complexion made Redle fear his efforts weren't enough to save him.

Pfc David J. Orris, Redle's bow gunner, also lay dying nearby with his back split wide open. The Painesville, Ohio, kid had just celebrated his twenty-first birthday the day before.[256] S/Sgt Oric Johannesen lay stricken as well. A quarter-sized piece of shrapnel had entered his back and exited his chest before lodging in a pack of Camel cigarettes tucked inside his breast pocket.[257] Although both entry and exit wounds showed little blood and appeared relatively small, there was no way of telling how badly the tall blond's vital organs had been shredded on the inside. Usually, men suffering such torso wounds had only moments—perhaps hours at best—left to live. Johannesen's situation was especially distressing as the 26-year-old was a married father with an infant daughter.[258] Sgt Roland L. Buys, a 25-year-old tank commander from Heber City, Utah, also lay riddled with shrapnel.[259] All four victims were eventually evacuated, as were a large number of chow line infantrymen also wounded during the barrage.[260] Another B Company tank commander had been knocked unconscious, but regained his senses. As a precaution, he was examined closely for puncture wounds, and since none could be found he remained on duty.[261]

***

The Germans came tantalizingly close to conceding Cassino on the evening of 2 February—when Granberry's platoon first burst into town. The sudden appearance of American tanks had stunned the defenders enough to consider retreating southward. Sweeting's instincts were right, after all—even though the execution had been botched and uncoordinated. *If Marshall's infantry had escorted Granberry's tanks from the start, the German defenders had standing orders to withdraw.*[262] This astounding testimony was given by several different German prisoners to 34th Division intelligence (G-2) interrogators afterwards. But because Granberry's tanks were left unprotected and consequently captured, the original retreat order was canceled, and reinforcements were rushed forward to fortify the thinly held town. The next morning, the orders were amended to: "Hold at all costs."[263] Still, the prisoners reported low morale among their comrades, and specified the constant U.S. artillery pounding, in particular, as having taken a psychological toll.[264] Prisoner attitudes over the war's prospects ran the gamut. Many were ambivalent about the outcome and simply grateful to be out of it. Others insisted Germany had chosen the valiant and worthy path of saving the world from communism—but were losing the struggle.[265] Some prisoners were Polish nationals pressganged into the German Army and never wanted to be there in the first place.[266]

Surprisingly, many captives freely provided crucial details about the town's defenses—almost as a point of pride. Interrogators learned many bunkers had been constructed along the perimeter of town—inside the first few blocks of buildings.

Each site generally housed eight men.[267] The jail was identified as the CP location for the 6th and 7th Companies of the II Battalion, 211th Grenadier Regiment, and served as the command center coordinating all north end defenses of Cassino as well. The I Battalion, 211th, reportedly held the south section of town.[268] Because of dreadful battlefield attrition, many 211th companies were operating at only one-third combat strength.

The prisoners also said two AT guns had been positioned in the northern part of town—one along the main road and another approximately 300 yards further south near a church.[269] These details were seemingly outdated, though, as those guns had already been encountered and likely moved. Three or four SP guns were said to patrol the northern streets,[270] but seven more pieces of tracked armor had arrived in Cassino during the morning of 3 February. Two additional pieces were supposed to join later, but were delayed because of repairs.[271] Most were Mark III chassis type machines equipped with a long-barreled 75mm main gun and a single MG for protection. One captured SP crew member reported each of his assault guns carried forty-eight rounds of HE, thirty-eight rounds of shaped charge hollow nose (HLB—Hohlladung-B), ten rounds of PAK 39, ten rounds of PAK 4, three AT grenade charges, and four or five Teller mines. The same prisoner also detailed how SP gun crews usually delayed an attack until an American tank target was within 400 yards, and preferred holding fire until more than one tank appeared.[272] It was difficult to find any good news in this testimony.

Another prisoner said that the 15th Panzer Grenadier Division's primary responsibility was not to attack but defend the Liri Valley. He also revealed three more German tanks had been stationed behind the monastery and elite paratroopers had been rushed into the area during the night of 4 February.[273]

The information provided by the German prisoners, though stale in some cases, was still generally reliable. Fresh troops from the 3rd Battalion, 3rd Paratrooper Regiment, were, in fact, rushed in from the Adriatic coast. At that very moment, these tenacious *Fallschirmjäger* reinforcements were systematically rolling back 135th Regiment progress in the highlands.[274] The arrival of these elite German shock troops was an unwelcome development for the fatigued Americans. So much so, that at the close of the day, the 135th's morale was reported as only "fair."[275]

American morale down in the valley also wilted as a result of comrades lost and opportunities missed. Expectations began to sour. B Company of the 756th had a particularly rough day. The German artillery attack had claimed four tank crewmen—three were experienced tank commanders.[276] Lt Czajkowski also transferred to the hospital with an illness,[277] leaving Redle, again, with only one other officer—2nd Lt Howard M. Harley, commanding the 1st Platoon.[278] Because B Company lacked an XO, Redle sent Pfc Clyde W. Guild as his representative to CP meetings. Oftentimes, Guild was the only enlisted man among officers crowded around a planning table.[279] This officer shortage also forced Redle to call upon his most experienced sergeants to lead his platoons. S/Sgt James E. Haspel was given charge of the 2nd Platoon, while Sgt Haskell O. Oliver took over the 3rd platoon.[280]

The 34th Division missed a golden opportunity on 2 February to capture Cassino, and perhaps the abbey as well. Even so, all wars can be characterized as a succession of failures, one after the other—generating endless "what if" questions afterwards. Good leaders, smart soldiers, and seasoned combat veterans accept these conditions, adapt, and move on. Cassino wasn't going to succumb to waves of tanks emerging triumphantly from white phosphorus mists like Sweeting imagined, or before masterfully planned troop formations flanking the highlands under the inspirational orders of brilliant generals. Cassino's fate now fell squarely upon the shoulders of ordinary privates, sergeants, and junior officers thrust into a brutal and unforgiving slugfest. Not only was this a cruel close-quarters contest between common men, but a battle against physical exhaustion and those despairing mental demons that conspire to undermine every man's fortitude.

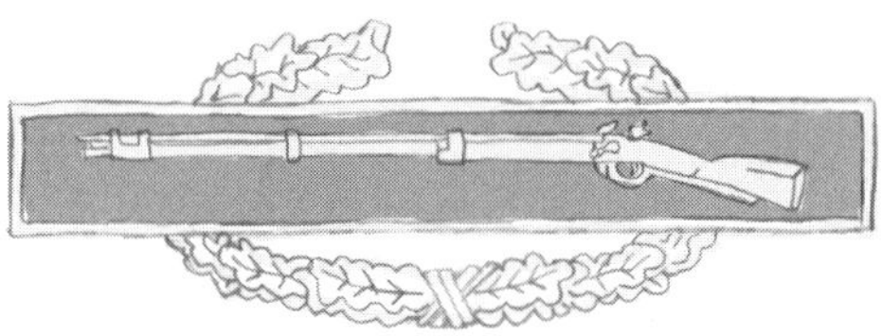

U.S. Army Combat Infantry badge

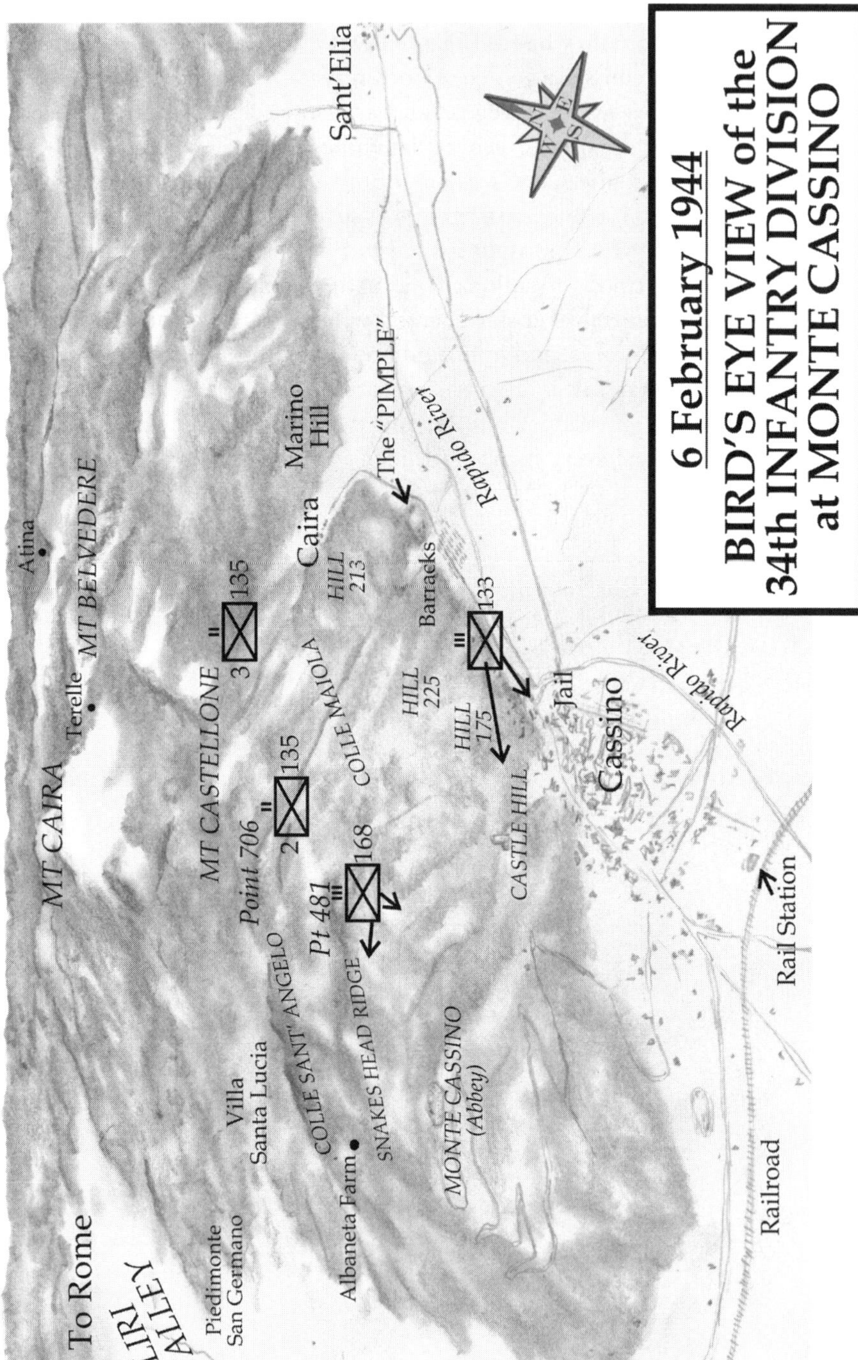
6 February 1944
BIRD'S EYE VIEW of the
34th INFANTRY DIVISION
at MONTE CASSINO
To Rome
LIRI VALLEY
Piedimonte San Germano
Albaneta Farm
Villa Santa Lucia
COLLE SANT' ANGELO
SNAKES HEAD RIDGE
MONTE CASSINO (Abbey)
Railroad
MT CAIRA
Point 706
Pt 481
2 135
168
MT CASTELLONE
COLLE MAIOLA
CASTLE HILL
Rail Station
Terelle
HILL 175
HILL 225
Cassino
Jail
Rapido River
3 135
MT BELVEDERE
HILL 213
Barracks
133
Atina
Caira
Marino Hill
The "PIMPLE"
Rapido River
Sant'Elia

CHAPTER THREE

The Big Push: 6 February 1944 to 8 February 1944

A stark and dazzling moon rose high over Cassino, spilling rich silvery light across the desolate townscape below.[1] As the night air hung stagnant and dank, artillery batteries on both sides maintained a peculiar reign of silence.[2] Midnight neared and the 3rd Battalion dispatched a reconnaissance patrol deeper into town, hoping the bountiful moonlight filtering through the ruins might finally reveal the whereabouts of those vexing German SP guns.[3] A small party departed at 2230 hours and crept like burglars beyond the main line of resistance—taking great pains to stay concealed within the stark shadows of broken walls and shattered alleyways. They progressed a full seventy-five yards southeast of the first road junction before finding they could probe no further without being seen—so they halted and listened for a while. Somewhere not too far away, enemy soldiers barked at each other in gruff, lively conversation. Further in the distance, the clanging of repairs on some armored vehicle could also be heard.[4] Nothing could be seen, however, so the patrol returned at 2345 without the Germans ever knowing of their intrusion.

At 0120, 6 February, the 135th Regiment HQ in Caira reported fifteen rounds of German 75mm artillery had just exploded in their area, with all shells whistling in from the north.[5] Over the next few hours, several more scattershot rounds burst here and there, but did little damage.[6] Every so often, a crack of small arms erupted somewhere in the night, as though something serious was about to start, but silence always followed.[7]

At 0415 hours, Colonel Marshall repositioned his 100th (Nisei) Battalion on Hill 213 to his regiment's rear[8] with orders to prepare for a second assault on Castle Hill.[9] In town, Lt Pride's two-tank section, plus the two surviving tanks from Lt Trahan's platoon under S/Sgt Upchurch's command, received long-awaited relief.[10] Upchurch's crews had been fighting non-stop for nearly sixty straight hours.[11] And after suffering for two days while holed up with nearby infantrymen, wounded C Company, 760th, tankers Lt Leo Trahan, Cpl John Isabella, and Pvt Carl Tedder were finally whisked away to an aid station.[12] The three relief tanks comprising 2nd Lt Eugene E. Gleissner's 3rd Platoon, C Company, 760th, assumed defensive positions near the ruined apartment building lining the west side of the road. Gleissner edged his tank into the point position furthest south and aimed the main gun deeper into town. Although Gleissner had been assured of the presence of many infantrymen positioned nearby and to his left, the lieutenant couldn't see a soul. These unnerving conditions made Gleissner's crews feel completely isolated.[13]

At daybreak, the Germans pummeled the north section of Cassino with startling ferocity. As thick waves of artillery rolled through—shattering roof remnants and showering the streets with torrents of debris—small arms of every type started popping away.[14] A clear morning sky provided superb visibility,[15] but the Americans couldn't pinpoint the origin of the artillery rounds and feared a brewing counterattack.[16] In the chaos, Gleissner's tank crew caught sight of a group of Germans scurrying from a building deeper in town and blasted them into oblivion.[17] On nearby Hill 175, the troops of the 1st Battalion, 133rd, hunkered down, preparing for the worst.

Captain Washington C. Carter, 3rd Battalion XO, commanded the meager forces clinging to the north edge of town. While Carter rode out the barrage inside his forward CP, Lt Vince Kelly, XO of K Company, phoned to warn of a German tank seen moving in the captain's direction. Carter immediately called the 3rd Battalion HQ near the barracks for the help of the TDs stationed nearby.[18] That same moment, Lt Gleissner saw the same German tank—a Mark IV—only fifty yards away to his ten o'clock, nosing around a shattered house. Gleissner barked out the location to his crew, but his flustered gunner couldn't locate the intruder in his sights. The German tank fired first, striking the M4's turret mantlet just above the gun barrel. The round failed to penetrate and spun skyward with a hellish howl. The violent jolt caused the main gun to prematurely fire and buffeted Gleissner's crew about the cold turret interior.[19] While the stunned tankers scrambled to regain their wits, one vigilant TD hidden back near the barracks returned fire and pierced the German tank's turret before its crew could fire a kill shot.[20] Survivors tried piling out of their stricken Mark IV, but nearby American infantrymen picked off each one before they could scamper away.

Gleissner's crew had been extremely fortunate. The Mark IV's glancing shot shook the tank so violently that many interior bolts had to be retightened later by hand.[21] The near miss, however, had splattered Gleissner's helmet and forehead with spalls of molten steel, leaving the lieutenant bleeding profusely. As a consequence, the platoon leader was evacuated immediately.[22]

At 0815, two separate waves of German planes—mixes of ME-109s and FW-190s—swarmed through the valley like angry bees. The first wave fumed in from the south, disgorging a string of anti-personnel and delayed-action bombs while skimming along the western edge of the Rapido. Moments later, a second wave screamed down from the north—releasing another tumbling chain of bombs along the same route. While explosions rocked the riverbed, the intruders tilted aloft and made an audacious escape.[23] Five minutes passed before a third wave appeared—this time as a roiling cloud in the southern skies. This newest swarm, comprising nineteen planes, swung eastward to threaten Allied positions on Monte Trocchio and along Highway 6.[24] The II Corps AA batteries struck first—transforming four German attackers into flaming comets and causing two others to swerve away trailing engine smoke.[25] At 0830, yet another wave, involving eighteen German planes, bombed Caira and the barracks north of Cassino.[26] This time, the 133rd Regiment CP suffered a direct hit—killing the S-3, Major William H. Blytt, and wounding several others.[27]

Lt Col Sweeting had just departed the 756th CP in Caira when the first bombs burst. He reached the 3rd Battalion, 133rd, CP near the barracks in time to hunker through the 0830 assault.[28] While the dust settled in the aftermath, he conferred briefly with Major Chapman and Colonel Marshall on the day's objectives—which centered, not surprisingly, on locating and destroying the SP guns ahead of the infantry's newest attack.[29] At 0900, Sweeting dashed down to the forward infantry OP near town to coordinate the latest SP hunt. All the firepower at his disposal—the 756th Tank Battalion's assault guns, mortars, tanks, TDs, and supporting artillery—waited patiently for his orders.[30] Sweeting's most current plan relied on the repositioning of the two towed 57mm AT guns to new locations atop Hill 175, much closer to town. The infantry, however, had trouble pushing the heavy wheels up the rocky slope and asked to swap guns for lighter mountain howitzers instead.[31] Sweeting insisted on keeping the 57mms and asked the engineers for assistance.[32] These guns were meant to play the hidden "aces" up Sweeting's sleeve.

At 1020 hours, eight more German planes stormed over the hillside and bombed the south edge of The Pimple before vanishing in a flash.[33] His patience now threadbare, Colonel Marshall phoned the division and requested for AA batteries to relocate into the area.[34] At noon, another wave of six to ten FW-190s struck Caira again and sped off.[35] Although these air attacks were exasperating for the Americans on the receiving end, German ground troops suffered far worse under much heavier Allied aerial and artillery bombardment. Apparently, the Luftwaffe was taking advantage of unusually clear skies to exact some small measure of revenge.[36] For the Americans, a more ominous incident occurred at 1150: a German tank was seen rolling through the eastern section of town just north of Highway 6.[37] Even more alarming, a German prisoner declared many more tanks from the 15th Panzer Grenadier Division were also moving toward town.[38]

The clear weather allowed American mortar and artillery to strike targets with greater frequency and precision—but because German defenses had been so well fortified, the results proved disappointing. The two German tanks positioned west of Castle Hill were dug in so effectively they could not be hit with artillery.[39] The 133rd Cannon Company tried lobbing dozens of 75mm howitzer rounds upon them, but gave up after realizing the effort was futile.[40] While the 1st Battalion consolidated positions on Hill 175 ahead of the planned 8 February attack on Castle Hill, one chattering German MG across the craggy draw grew particularly bothersome. All afternoon, Cannon Company tried killing the crew by hurling round after round at it, but the annoying MG could not be silenced.[41]

At 1230, divisional artillery HQ organized a time-on-target (TOT) attack on the yellow stone castle.[42] In this type of operation, several batteries coordinate their cannon fire to strike a target in a single instant. The hope was to collapse the entire structure under one colossal explosion. The timing worked, and a spectacular burst did indeed rock the hilltop—but when the dust cleared, the tall tower remained. At best, a few stones may have been shaken loose, and the German MGs and riflemen positioned in and around the castle resumed firing as though nothing had happened. Hoping to at least suppress that stubborn fire, Colonel Marshall ordered Cannon Company to keep blasting the castle until nightfall.[43] That same afternoon, the 100th Battalion, 133rd, was relieved by 142nd Regiment troops and pulled back to The Pimple to reorganize.[44]

In the meantime, tantalizing progress was made on the massif nearby. Earlier that day, elements of the 168th and the 2nd Battalion, 135th Regiment, attacked Monastery Hill. On separate occasions, two different platoons reached the high ramparts of the ancient building before being forced back by heavy S/A and MG fire. One platoon even succeeded in taking prisoners before withdrawing.[45] The two platoons discovered Germans dug in along the monastery's foundation—clearly within the buffer zone the Germans had marked earlier as "neutral."[46] Other active German positions were seen along the road leading up to the abbey's entrance. The 135th Regiment secured ground roughly 300 to 400 yards away, but could not close the distance gap due to heavy German fire emanating from those abbey base positions.[47] Sensing a breakthrough, Maj Gen Ryder requested permission from the II Corps to use mortar and artillery.[48] At 1405, Maj Gen Keyes granted the request but with very specific restrictions.[49] Fire could be placed on provable German resistance spots near the abbey but only with extreme care.[50] All rounds had to be closely observed and carefully adjusted at all times—and under no circumstances would the fire become indiscriminate or used for "razing."[51]

That same afternoon, the 3rd Battalion, 133rd, continued the painstaking work of clearing out the enemy from yet another block house row.[52] Because Cannon Company had been given the task of pounding the castle to allow the 1st Battalion to reorganize on Hill 175, the 3rd Battalion fought the entire day without any howitzers.[53] Instead, Chapman's men relied exclusively on the tanks and TDs for fire support.[54] The M4s were often called forward to blast holes through walls so the infantry could capture adjacent buildings. This tactic also effectively circumvented the courtyard lattice traps the Germans had set, hoping to goad unsuspecting Americans into MG crossfire.[55]

After Lt Gleissner was evacuated, command of the 3rd Platoon, C Company, 760th Tank Battalion fell to T/4 Wilber E. Stoppenhagen of Decatur, Indiana.[56] While assisting those 3rd Battalion wall blasting operations, Stoppenhagen's tank crew fired MGs periodically at German infantrymen darting back and forth across the road 100 yards away. At one point, a German MG responded in a fit of rage—pelting Stoppenhagen's turret with gusts of splattering lead. The startled sergeant yanked his turret hatches closed and continued directing fire from the tight interior—relying on his narrow periscope sights to locate targets. Eventually, the German MG's irregular spray shattered the periscope glass. Hoping to pinpoint the irritating source, Stoppenhagen cracked his turret hatch open and paused. The MG belched again. One slug perforated the sergeant's helmet—missing his skull by a mere fraction of an inch.[57] Stoppenhagen, however, did catch a glimpse of the gun's telltale flashes only thirty-five yards away—and his gunner promptly obliterated both MG and crew with a flash of HE.

By late afternoon, Stoppenhagen's tank's main gun had become so heavily fouled from overuse that a round lodged in the barrel. To clear the obstruction, Stoppenhagen instructed his gunner to traverse the turret rearward. He then climbed onto the back deck and rammed a cleaning rod down the gun tube. Some German rifleman sniped at him as he labored but missed with every shot. Over the next two hours, Stoppenhagen repeated this perilous five-minute procedure three more times—drawing the same unwelcome attention. But on each occasion, the sergeant successfully eluded the bullets and safely returned to his tank commander position.[58]

At 1800 hours, an order circulated among all American units positioned along the Rapido to clear out the riverbed.[59] A short time later, a jeep bounded down the dry channel from the barracks to a point just beyond the quarry and then backtracked, the occupants making absolutely certain the bed was free of all vehicles and men.[60] Shortly afterwards, the temporary dam created by the dropped bridge near Sant' Elia was blown open and the river resumed its natural course.[61]

The tanks of B Company and C Company, 756th, returned to the assembly area near Hill 213 for the evening. T/4 Stoppenhagen's platoon continued fighting in town, but the remaining tanks of C Company, 760th, also withdrew to Hill 213 for rest and resupply.[62] Throughout the day, most of the battalion's tanks ran fire support sorties back and forth from Hill 213 to the barracks area. There, the crews blasted at targets deeper in Cassino to help shield the infantry operating in the northern streets, with a lion's share of the shells directed toward breaking up any German attempts to shore up their own troop positions.[63] After the tanks expended their ammunition, they withdrew, resupplied, and returned to fire all over again. These trips became so routine, the tankers took to calling them "milk runs."[64] One platoon of A Company, 756th, tanks lent additional fire support from camouflaged positions across the river approximately a mile east of the barracks. These tanks did not withdraw when empty but remained in place. Ammunition, gasoline, and provisions were then trucked down to the crews after dark.[65]

Supplies were also delivered after nightfall to Stoppenhagen's three tanks in town. The 75mm rounds were dumped, still wrapped in packaging tubes, and the crews had to dismount to unpack them before restocking their interior storage racks—a dangerous process.[66] By 2100, the exercise seemed pointless once four relief tanks from C Company, 760th, began plodding the two-mile journey down from Hill 213.[67] Smoke shells fell about Cassino to hide the platoon's approach from German flares flickering overhead. Once the platoon rolled past the quarry, Allied artillery exploded deeper in town to help drown out the engine noise.[68] When the four tanks arrived, however, Stoppenhagen's tanks and exhausted crews were unable to withdraw past them and continued stocking up on supplies ahead of another long, sleepless evening.[69]

The infantry, of course, remained in place. Their supplies were also deposited in piles near the town's entrance and had to be further divided and dispersed stealthily among the squads hunkered about the ruins. Troops holding the vanguard generally operated in teams of four or five men. Sleep only came in two or three hour shifts under a rotating guard duty. To remain awake, the man on watch drowned himself in hot coffee, brewed over a tiny Coleman stove.[70]

***

6 February 1944 ended with no changes to the battle lines. Sweeting's tanks sat stalemated—basically strung out as a column restricted to the road running from Hill 213 down to the town's entrance, and unable to advance due to the shrewd German SP guns hidden in town. The infantry on both sides also remained deadlocked—inside the crumbling town and atop the rugged hills nearby. Although American forces perched on Monte Castellone could clearly see Highway 6 only a few miles to the west and southwest, this crucial Liri Valley objective lay frustratingly out of their reach.[71]

The day served chiefly for respite, regrouping, and reorganization—another long draw of the battle bow ahead of the next release. Preparations would continue through 7 February. Then, on the orders of Lt Gen Mark W. Clark, commanding the U.S. Fifth Army, the Americans would attack one final time.[72] General Alexander, commanding the Allied 15th Army Group controlling the U.S. Fifth Army, granted Clark until 12 February to take Cassino, but the British general also sensed that American troop morale was degrading at an alarming rate. He dispatched a close associate to investigate, and his suspicions were confirmed.[73] Still hopeful Clark would deliver, Alexander shifted the 2nd New Zealand and 4th Indian Divisions down from the British Eighth Army in the north. Should Cassino fall, fresh troops would be on hand to exploit the victory and pursue the retreating Germans through the Liri Valley.[74] Should Clark's attack fail, then those same British divisions would, instead, relieve the exhausted U.S. II Corps' 34th and 36th Infantry Divisions.

Lt Gen Mark Clark was a tall, lanky man, pulled in dozens of different directions by superiors and subordinates alike. His U.S. Fifth Army was comprised of American, British, French, and French North African colonial forces fighting across a war-ravaged, destitute country populated by displaced civilians administered by unreliable officials. Until recently, many Italians had been ardent fascists assisting the Germans. Clark was expected to maintain order in this multilingual setting while fighting a winning war against an extremely cunning and determined German army. Every decision, large or small, was fraught with political and military peril. After holding a modest rank of major during the Fall of France in 1940, the 1917 United States Military Academy (USMA) graduate skyrocketed up the command chain to become a lieutenant general by November 1942—the youngest in U.S. Army history.[75] At the time, Clark was only forty-six years old. Despite this young age, the upstate New Yorker was no stranger to danger. Shrapnel cut him down as a 22-year-old infantry captain fighting in World War I, leaving him seriously wounded.[76] Twenty-four years later, Maj Gen Clark was nearly captured while dispatched on a secret and dangerous behind-enemy-lines diplomatic mission negotiating the surrender of the North African French forces ahead of the Operation *Torch* landings. Clark now faced the greatest challenge of his career. With American prestige on the line, the 6'3" tall[77] hawk-nosed commander was resolved to avoid another U.S. Army operational embarrassment under the scolding eyes of British superiors—like those earlier debacles suffered in North Africa or, nearly so, on the beaches of Salerno. To improve his chances for a breakthrough, Clark repositioned the 36th Division to bolster the 34th Division's right flank and requested British X Corps forces to the south and Juin's French troops to the north attack simultaneously. All these units, however, had also been greatly depleted after weeks of ceaseless combat.[78]

In the meantime, Hitler ordered his Gustav Line forces to hold Cassino at all costs and challenged those occupying Rome to shove Anzio Allied troops into the sea. Field Marshal Albert Kesselring, the smiling optimist commanding all German forces in Italy, believed both goals were attainable. As a result, the Wehrmacht redoubled offensive efforts against the Anzio beachhead beginning 7 February.[79]

So many decisions in war are born out of fear. The Allied high command feared losing their Anzio toehold and becoming entrapped at Cassino the way the Russians had ensnared the Germans at Stalingrad twelve months earlier. With the passing of each cold, wet, and miserable day, the grind of the Italian campaign felt more and more like the static trench warfare of the previous war—a long, wasteful, and dreadful draw. Allied fears over this loss of momentum generated enormous pressures to disrupt the status quo, and the weight of those worries passed down from Alexander through Clark to Keyes and Ryder, growing heavier as those apprehensions fell. In turn, regimental and battalion commanders exhausted their creative energies devising hasty battle plans and issuing chancy orders that may or may not yield results.[80] In the end, however, it was the unwashed, sleep-deprived junior officers and NCOs who risked their lives on the battlefield trying to make those orders work. Oftentimes, those efforts were not enough.

***

Dawn broke on 7 February with high cloudy skies but clear ground visibility.[81] Temperatures dipped into the upper thirties and an easterly wind kicked though at a brisk twenty MPH.[82] During the previous night, the 3rd Battalion, 133rd Regiment, increased the number of reconnaissance patrols seeking out German SP guns and MG nests.[83] Just after midnight, one I Company patrol probed as far as a road junction 150 yards inside town. They retired, however, upon hearing the menacing sounds of hobnailed German boots pacing the darkened streets nearby. Later, L Company dispatched a patrol to the same area. Once they ventured beyond a disabled German tank, however, rifle shots cracked from a nearby basement window. The patrol tossed grenades toward the building's foundation to beat a hasty retreat. Around 0300 hours, another patrol was dispatched to the same place to gauge enemy strength. More rifle shots cracked from the same basement window and more grenades were tossed to cover a retreat. The patrol never did determine the number of Germans positioned there.[84]

It was not unusual for a night patrol to return with scant intelligence or nothing at all. The point of a recon mission was to learn something useful while dodging a fight and avoiding capture—all the better if the enemy never knew you were even there. The Germans, of course, sent out patrols of their own with similar objectives. This endless game of cloak and dagger was played by both sides. Sometimes, the Germans were fully aware of an American patrol in their midst—but allowed them to pass unchallenged. No infantryman worth his boots ever revealed his position without good reason. In keeping one's cover, it was better to let an enemy patrol stroll by obliviously and save the ambush for another day. On some occasions, one patrol might encounter an enemy patrol prowling the opposite way along the same narrow street. The two rival groups would often slide past each other with tense stares, racing hearts, and fidgeting fingers—only to disappear again into the deep, dark night. During those brief, strange encounters, nobody dared do anything "stupid."

On this particular night the 3rd Battalion's more aggressive patrolling concluded that no German vehicles, aside from the one disabled tank, lurked nearby.[85] Perhaps this "good news" would prove useful to the planners further up the command chain drafting the final attack orders.[86]

Prior to dawn, German artillery harassment had been mild. Around 0200, a few scattered "screaming meemies" burst amongst 135th Regiment positions in the highlands. A little later, approximately a dozen more rockets fell roughly 200 or 300 yards beyond 133rd positions. After that, a relative calm resumed.[87]

A light snow swirled as infantrymen of the 3rd Battalion, 133rd, set about the morning's business of patrolling the north section of town and clearing out scattered pockets of resistance.[88] The flurries dissipated by 1000, leaving behind a cold, biting wind but crystal-clear skies.[89] Colonel Marshall, 133rd CO, took the opportunity to carefully study the monastery through a pair of binoculars. In a middle row of windows on the eastern wall, he noticed a missing glass pane covered with a blanket. He studied the oddity suspiciously and saw what appeared to be a spotting scope poking from beneath one tucked corner. In an upper right window on the same side, he caught a glimpse of what appeared to be a second scope. He also saw German troops moving about the base of the abbey along the north side. Now angered, Marshall relayed his observations to the 34th Division HQ, forthrightly.[90]

To help thwart the next German aerial assault, the II Corps arranged for a battery from the 105th Anti-Aircraft AW (Automatic Weapons) Battalion to relocate closer to Cassino.[91] The 105th had originally been stationed east of Monte Trocchio. Tragically, on this particular day, German Luftwaffe pilots weren't the ones responsible for bombing Allied positions from the sky. At 1700, four American A-36 attack/bombers raced over II Corps positions toward Caira. A patrolling British Spitfire, mistaking the grouping for Messerschmitts, followed in hot pursuit—causing the A-36s to ditch their bombs in order to escape. The men from Battery A, 125th Field Artillery Battalion, were queued up near a kitchen truck below the spectacle, awaiting a hot meal. Two jettisoned bombs exploded among the GIs, killing the Battery CO, his XO, and eighteen others. Another twenty-five cannoneers lay wounded in the gory aftermath.[92] Ironically, had those planes been German, the artillerymen would have run for cover and survived.[93] Although an A-36's profile was similar to a Messerschmitt, the troops on the ground had no problem telling the difference. Two other dropped bombs exploded near the 753rd Tank Battalion CP, but fortunately nobody else was killed or wounded in the blunder.[94] An appalled II Corps staff demanded a full and immediate investigation into the incident.

German artillery fell heavily all afternoon. Some 300 shells exploded just along the narrow road leading from Caira down to Cassino.[95] Most came from light and medium caliber cannon firing from the southwest and the north.[96] Counterbattery observers witnessed telltale flashes at ten separate locations and returned fire upon eight of them. Despite unfavorable wind conditions, acoustic tracking methods also pinpointed the location of another German gun position.[97] The German batteries continued firing regardless. From 1630 to 1715, Caira rocked under one blast after another.[98] Soon after sundown, another violent gust of German shells exploded about Caira and surrounding highlands—cutting down 135th Regiment CO, Colonel Robert W. Ward, as he set out to survey battalion positions and deliver his finalized attack plans. The seriously wounded 38-year-old West Pointer was swiftly evacuated,[99] leaving his XO with hefty command responsibilities at a very critical time.[100]

American artillery responded vigorously—especially the 75mm howitzers of 133rd Cannon Company.[101] Castle Hill was pounded without pity all afternoon. One adjacent cave, in particular, received special attention. The 1st Platoon of Cannon Company fired 1,212 shells in all—besting their own 24-hour unit record by 100 rounds.[102] The thrashing persisted well into the night.[103] From concealed positions near the barracks, the TDs of the 776th Tank Destroyer Battalion lent their 3-inch guns to the effort, and finally destroyed a Nebelwerfer launcher concealed higher up the hillside.[104]

After dark, an exchange was arranged of the tanks positioned in town.[105] As with the previous night, smoke and artillery preceded the relief platoon's arrival—concealing the armor swap from prying German eyes and ears. When completed, Lt Pride's A Company, 760th, platoon assumed the positions vacated, finally, by T/4 Stoppenhagen's departing tanks.[106] This time, however, the Germans cleverly flipped the situation to their own advantage and used the commotion to reposition a hidden SP gun in the deep, dark recesses of town. Once the haze cleared, the stout gray gun achieved a sight line straight up the road. As 2200 hours neared, Lt Pride's four tank crews confidently settled into defensive positions along the north edge of town. Then, the skulking SP gun fired. A split second later, the chassis of Sgt Laurence Stander's tank shuddered with a sharp metallic thud. As the tank interior sparked and choked with smoke, the dazed driver and bow gunner threw open the front hatches and spilled unceremoniously onto the street below. Powered by a heavy jolt of adrenaline, Sgt Stander hoisted himself out of the turret and tumbled to the ground. His pants hung as tattered shreds, both legs mangled and bleeding profusely. Cpl Earl W. Shipman, the gunner, also maimed by shrapnel, barely trailed Stander to safety—clearing the turret as flames swirled out the hatches. Inside, Pvt Maurice A. Cail, the loader, lay crumpled in shock against the turret basket—too lacerated to save himself. For several frantic minutes, Sgt Stander tried rescuing his helpless crewmate, but the mounting flames and intense heat soon forced him away. As Pvt Cail perished in the ensuing conflagration, a severely burned and distraught Stander wept openly on the ground nearby, and the German SP gun slipped away unscathed into the gloom of the night.[107]

At 2100 hours, Lt Col Sweeting called all his company commanders together for a final battle briefing. The attack planned for the following morning was multi-phased and included several contingencies. Sweeting spread open a map showing the north section of town and explained each aspect in detail. Streets and key locations were identified with coded alphabet letters. Both C Company, 756th, and C Company, 760th, were given the responsibilities of directly supporting the infantry attack. C Company, 760th, would strike through the town square on the right and proceed down the main street of town (line "A-L-M-N") to point "O" at the southeast base of Castle Hill, approximately 500 yards inside of town. If all progressed as planned, the three-way intersection at "O" would serve as the halting point. C Company,

756th would strike on the left toward the jail ("B"), proceed south past the nunnery ("D") through two municipal squares ("G" and "H") until reaching a clock tower ("K"). Once there, they would outflank a German AT gun position identified at road intersection "P" southeast of the clock tower, knock it out, and wait. Lt Redle's B Company tanks would trail on the far left—shadowing the progress of C Company, 756th. If all went well, Redle's tanks would proceed down road "C–E" and attack key buildings at "I" and "F" in the eastern part of town before proceeding south and halting at road intersection "Q." Throughout the attack, A Company would provide fire support from across the river.

Sweeting readily admitted to his commanders that the plan was overly ambitious and even expressed his personal belief that the tanks would achieve little beyond limited infantry support. Ruined cities offered little room for tank maneuver, and the mounting piles of rubble choking off the narrow streets and alleyways gave Sweeting little confidence any armor could get through at all. Still, he hoped one or two tanks might find some way to aid the infantry as they progressed south. In truth, claustrophobic Cassino and the craggy massifs nearby were the milieu of foot soldiers. Tanks were never intended to conquer mountains or storm crumbling medieval valley towns.

Sweeting seemed more preoccupied over the whereabouts of the German SP guns. The hunt had become his consuming obsession. Too many of his tanks had fallen victim to their AT fire without them suffering the sting of reciprocal revenge. At last, Sweeting believed he had finally gained the upper hand in the deadly contest: a 57mm gun had been secretly repositioned atop Hill 175 that very morning.[108] A radio link was then established between that gun and the forward OP Sweeting shared with Major Chapman inside a house overlooking the town 400 yards south of the quarry.[109] Sweeting would observe and direct his tanks from this forward OP during the morning attack—essentially offering them as bait. The moment a German SP gun appeared, Sweeting would immediately alert the 57mm crew hidden above to fire the kill shot. The trap seemed foolproof.

Sweeting ordered the tanks to amass at the quarry before dawn. Captain Arnold would coordinate their entry into town when the infantry called them forward. Once the tankers found "good shooting light" around 0700, the attack would commence. Sweeting reminded his officers to "follow the infantry closely and supply fire at close ranges"—emphasizing the primacy of the troops on the ground calling the shots.[110]

Lt Gen Mark Clark hoped this final coordinated assault by Keyes's II Corps would generate the shock necessary to overrun the abbey and spill down into the Liri Valley beyond the massif.[111] Despite heavy attrition and mounting exhaustion, every unit was given a critical role in the plan. The 36th Division's reconstituted regiments would augment the attack through the highlands.[112] The 141st and 143rd Regiments had already relieved many hilltop positions held by the 34th Division—freeing those units to spearhead the offensive itself.[113] The 142nd Regiment was instructed to pass through those positions and seize Piedimonte San Germano to the west.[114] The 168th and 135th Regiments of the 34th Division were tasked with capturing Monte Cassino in the middle,[115] while the infantry of the 133rd and tanks of the 756th Tank Battalion swept through town along the eastern base.[116] If all three prongs of this attack succeeded, the 1st Tank Group—comprising all of the 753rd and two companies of the 760th Tank Battalion—would then be unleashed, cross the Rapido, and pour into the south section of town via Highway 6.[117] At the same time, the British X Corps to the south and French Expeditionary forces to the north would also strike—hopefully throwing the Germans off balance, eroding their confidence, and finally fracturing their defensive stance.[118]

Sweeting was right. The plan was extremely ambitious.

***

It was an unusually quiet evening in Cassino yet again.[119] For a third straight night, a cold bright moon rose over Monte Trocchio to the east—casting dramatic shadows across the streets of the ruined town. While the 100th Battalion, 133rd, moved to their final staging area on Hill 175,[120] the 3rd Battalion, 133rd, dispatched a series of patrols deep into the north section of town. The men were instructed to listen especially for the low idling growl of German tank engines,[121] and watch for any armor or MG crews on the move. Captain Washington C. Carter, battalion XO, awaited news from his forward CP in a ruined house near the town's edge.[122] After fifty quiet, anxious minutes, the burping staccato bursts of a German MG and the slower rat-tat-tats of several American Tommy guns reverberated among the buildings somewhere to the south. Somebody had been discovered. After several minutes, the wrathful exchange dwindled down to a few sporadic shots before halting altogether. Five more minutes passed when 2nd Lt Paul Riordan of L Company burst into the CP followed closely by a contingent of seven gasping enlisted men. "It took us fifty minutes to get out there and five minutes to get back," the young lieutenant remarked between halting breaths. His team had ventured past a burned-out tank up the road and advanced a full 500 yards into the city. While negotiating a narrow street between a white house and a steepled building, Riordan's men were surprised by the sudden appearance of several German riflemen. Somebody panicked and shots were exchanged. Then an MG hidden in a nearby basement opened fire. "We fired back, tossed a few grenades in the window and shagged our tails," Riordan recounted matter-of-factly. Fortunately, nobody from Riordan's patrol was killed or wounded during the startling encounter.[123]

A half hour later, the peace was shattered yet again by rifle shots, automatic fire, and the popping of grenades. After listening for a while, a puzzled Captain Carter remarked, "That's outgoing American fire." The signature sounds of German weapons were suspiciously missing. Lt Higgins theorized that perhaps the Germans were using American weapons—as they had deviously done a few months earlier against L Company at Oliveto. "They even knew what outfit we were," Higgins grumbled. "Once they hollered 'Hey L Company!' to the L Company boys. Then they threw potato mashers."

The two officers continued listening intently. Several more periods of silence followed—only to be broken by long successive bursts of American MG fire. Suddenly, Lt Sisco burst through the broken doorway of Carter's CP, griping bitterly how Lt Luther Spurlock's men had been firing on his patrol. Carter grabbed his field phone hastily. His heavy Alabama drawl reverberated along the long line strung over to Spurlock's position:

"Cut those damn sputter guns of yours. We've got patrols out!"

Spurlock vehemently denied his men had fired on Sisco's men at all. "We're just firing some more on that old hole," he defended.

The "hole" was a well-known and troublesome German bunker positioned nearby.

"Well quit firing on that old hole!" Carter fumed. "I'll send a tank up tomorrow to put its snout right down the hole!"[124]

After the animated phone exchange, Sisco reported to Carter that his men neither saw nor heard any German armor in the section of town they patrolled.[125] This news was rather disappointing.

A third patrol led by Lt Stanley Davis returned moments later. His four-man unit scouted to the northeast corner of the square along the base of Castle Hill, but after hearing German soldiers walking atop the tiled rooftops nearby, the team backtracked to avoid detection. They also saw no German armor.[126]

Disappointed over the weak haul of intelligence, and with the division's attack set to commence in only three hours, Captain Carter dispatched another series of patrols out into the streets and alleys. The first left at 0115, 8 February, but returned forty-five minutes later after tripping off a new round of enemy MG and rifle fire in the vicinity of the burned-out German tank.[127] A second patrol led by Lt Riordan scouted a known German MG position near another disabled German tank approximately 150 yards away. This time, Riordan's men stayed out of trouble, but returned saying the MG had moved and they saw no sign of armor activity.[128] Despite the best efforts of Carter's additional patrols, the German SP guns remained maddeningly elusive.

***

Meanwhile, in the highlands a mile to the west, the 168th and 135th Regiments prepared to strike at the appointed "H-Hour" of 0400. The 34th's attack plan called for the 135th to move upon Massa Albaneta on the right to protect the 168th's push toward the monastery on the left.[129] Frost-numbed hands checked and rechecked ammo, cold joints creaked as stiff bodies lifted from cramped positions of cover.

Weary, bloodshot eyes stared out from grimy, stubbled faces straining through the bleak fog that always seemed to swirl about the craggy granite in the predawn hours. A frozen finger was always hooked around the trigger.

Life on the massif had been absolutely brutal the past few days. The 141st and 143rd Regiments of the 36th Division had arrived in relief a few days earlier, but the rush to move them also left them unprepared to attack so soon.[130] Supply continued to be a supreme challenge.

The 168th's first attempt to take the abbey on 5 February stalled after absorbing intense German fire of all sorts. The men became pinned against the rocks and could not withdraw safely without inviting death—so they settled in place. The ground, however, was too hard to excavate foxholes, so makeshift protection had to be fashioned from loose stone. These walled structures still left the men vulnerable to overhead mortar and artillery fire. The unforgiving terrain was comprised of deep ravines, jagged slopes, and treacherous trails that severely restricted movement. In many places, the men could only pass through one soldier at a time—or at best in small groups—often crawling on raw knees to get from one place to another. The clash of frigid air and valley humidity in the high elevations produced freezing drizzle and often snow on a daily basis. These cold, soggy conditions day in and day out made for a miserable existence.[131]

Nobody moved unless they had to—especially during daylight hours.[132] No one dared crawl out into the open to answer the call of nature. Even those replaced by fresh troops were loath to relocate for fear of snipers. And the arriving replacements were often not high-quality troops. In many cases, non-combat servicemen had been pulled from kitchens, motor pools, or HQ clerical positions and expected to magically transform into combat infantrymen.[133] Although the new troops were cautioned sternly and repeatedly to hug the ground during artillery attacks, many could not resist the natural instinct to jump up and run when the artillery started bursting—and usually perished as a result.[134] Others, who heeded the warnings and squeezed against the cold rock, enduring one brutal German pummeling after another, went mad after experiencing several days of this.[135] The real war was always fought inside one's own mind.

As with Cassino below, German defensive positions spread over the highlands above were well selected, well constructed, and interwoven to provide each location with covering crossfire from several neighbors. German MG hilltop positions were often dynamited out of the rocky ground, then shielded on the sides with sandbags or steel, before being topped with a roof plate of armor. Larger bunkers were excavated much deeper into the granite and reinforced with logs and crushed gravel. German mortar positions were placed along the hillcrests, protected with logs, and concealed with camouflage. The spotters positioned in the foreground disguised themselves so cleverly that they proved almost impossible to detect. The only giveaway that might betray an observer's position was often only an eyehole-sized notch in a pile of rocks.[136]

Any suspected German redoubt had to be approached with great patience and care. Studious observation and complex tactical planning were required before an attack could be attempted, and overwhelming firepower was almost always necessary to assure a successful outcome. Oftentimes, the only option was to call upon American artillery.[137] As a result, the Germans rarely moved about openly during the day, and thus were not as vulnerable to artillery bursts. Those burrowed deep inside fortified bunkers were unaffected by even the occasional direct hit.[138]

***

For the past three days, the Americans had augmented positions and shifted troops around hoping to find some way of dislodging the Germans somewhere. The 168th Regiment relieved the 135th on the right flank to allow the 135th to test Snakeshead Ridge west of Monte Cassino.[139] The 142nd was relieved by the reconstituted-but-still-weakened 141st and 143rd Regiments in order to probe further westward toward Massa Manna.[140] Whenever the Americans seemed to make some headway, the Germans recovered quickly and counterattacked with zealous tenacity. In the end, little to no ground was ever gained. At times, combatants were separated by only a few yards, fighting harrowing life-or-death battles to win control of a mere pile of frigid rocks or an icy boulder.[141] Even at night, during those moments of relative "peace," both sides could often hear their adversaries' conversations hanging in the heavy cold air—redlining the stress levels of everyone.[142] The conditions smacked of stalemate.

American supply lines into the mountains were an ongoing logistical nightmare. The men holding the heights hadn't enjoyed a hot meal in ten days.[143] Everything—ammo, rations, supplies—had to be transported up by mule train.[144] Each mule could only carry 160 pounds of material and twenty of those pounds were dedicated to food and water just so the animal could survive the journey.[145] A mule train consisted of anywhere from a few individuals to several dozen animals, with seventy-five mules needed to supply just one battalion each day.[146] Every caravan set out from the relative safety of San Michele and trudged in single file through the sucking mud, then crossed the Rapido before passing through Caira and plodding up into the treacherous foothills. There, supplies of all kinds—including wearisome C and D rations and cold waterlogged bread—were unpacked.[147] Sick and wounded infantrymen were then strapped to litters atop the mules' backs and the caravan returned to start the cycle all over again.[148]

To avoid German observation, no journey could be made during the day. Each round trip began at dusk and took roughly fourteen hours to complete.[149] Naturally, German mortar crews made sure the long, narrow supply route was well registered so as to torment the trains without quarter. The sodden ground in the valley tended to absorb the shock of artillery and mortar explosions, but the jagged rocks in the highlands only amplified the effectiveness. Shards of hot, deadly steel spattered across wide areas only to ricochet, bounce, and spin repeatedly until fully spent of energy.[150] Invariably, these razor-sharp edges found warm flesh to pierce and both man and beast tumbled over dead into unrecoverable places along the trails. Out of practical necessity, their splayed corpses were left to rot in the gorges below and the dank air was always laden with the pervasive, nauseating, sewer smells of death.[151] The same blasts repeatedly severed phone wire strung along the same narrow pathways—and sleep-deprived wiremen with frozen fingers and bad attitudes toiled about constantly splicing communication lines back together.[152]

A favorite German mortar tactic "boxed in" a mule train by first blasting the front of the column before striking the rear. Consequently, nobody wanted to lead. Mules were not stupid animals. They, too, sensed the mortal danger, and balked stubbornly when forced ahead.[153] They also panicked at the sound of shellfire, and keeping them calm required the skills of seasoned mule skinners. Such tradesmen were difficult to find, and the Allies combed constantly through their ranks and across the Italian countryside for anyone with mule skinner experience.[154]

***

The critical 0400 "H-Hour" arrived as temperatures plunged to a frigid twenty-six degrees, and the grand attack commenced under cover of darkness.[155] The 135th Regiment jumped off first—edging stealthily over rugged terrain toward Hill 367 west of Monastery Hill.[156] A half-mile to their left, the 168th Regiment crept toward the silent abbey perched atop Hill 519.[157] A few quiet moments passed, but something alerted the Germans, and their guns erupted at once, sending a heavy hail of S/A, mortar, and artillery fire—mostly spitting from emplacements along the foot of the abbey and the long ridgeline to the west. The barrage was ruthless and unceasing, and after covering only a few hundred yards the American advance stalled completely.[158] Allied artillery was called in to pound German positions along the ridgeline.[159] This retaliation, just as ceaseless and brutal, continued well past daybreak.[160]

In the valley, the 133rd awaited word on the progress of the 135th and 168th while preparing to strike deeper into town. At 0510, the 1st and 100th (Nisei) Battalions of the 133rd began massing at their jump-off point south of the barracks. They were detected and fifty rounds of German medium artillery burst around them as they assembled.[161]

At 0600, Sweeting and Arnold conferred with Colonel Marshall at the 133rd CP in Caira for ten minutes over last-minute details. A half hour later, Sweeting raced down to the forward OP near town and settled in to direct his tanks.[162] The OP was shared with Major Chapman inside a roadside villa low on Hill 175, only a few dozen yards from town. All windows facing south were covered to prevent German observers from identifying the location. About a dozen heavy MGs and crews were positioned along the slope nearby, set to repulse any possible German intrusion.[163]

On the road nearby, thick, black smoke still billowed from Sgt Stander's charred tank. Every so often, a sizzling 75mm round ruptured with a bang inside the scalding hull—shaking loose mortar from adjacent buildings. Inside the crowded CP, nervous men fussed over radio and telephone equipment. Every fresh gust of American artillery rolling through town caused plaster to rain down from the ceiling and the men fiddled with the equipment all over again. Meanwhile, Lt Pride's three remaining tanks cranked their engines to steady growls while grimy infantrymen gathered in clusters along shattered walls.

Sweeting and Chapman believed they had crafted a sound attack plan and spent a few minutes reviewing the particulars together one final time. Observers had been placed at several key locations to the rear, watching for the appearance of the SP guns. The TD crews positioned near the barracks and across the river further to the northeast did the same.[164] An artillery liaison officer stood by both battalion commanders—always prepared to phone in hellfire from above, and the 57mm gun crew concealed atop Hill 175 were only a radio call away.

"Are you ready to get going with your infantry, Chapman?" Sweeting finally queried.

"Should be, sir," Chapman replied, "Jesus, I hope I never have another nut as tough as this to crack."[165]

The past ten days had been trying enough. Now both officers felt as though the entire weight of the Fifth Army had been suddenly thrust upon their shoulders.

***

A dull dawn glow filtered through partly cloudy skies and a dim gray haze hovered over the town.[166] Sporadic, pestering German S/A fire began raining down from the direction of the abbey onto 133rd positions below,[167] causing the hillside American MGs networked around the forward OP to respond sevenfold. Streaming bursts of red tracer-laced .30-caliber crisscrossed over the town square in search of any dark window, crack, or crevice the Germans were suspected of hiding in.[168] Every so often, the raucous, ungodly whoosh of an American 8-inch howitzer shell split the morning air, followed by a lifting blast that quaked the ground like gelatin. The awesome firepower of these enormous cannon was specially arranged with II Corps artillery.[169] The main target was the old jail only a few hundred yards away, and every incoming round seemed to hit the mark. The ear-splitting concussion of each 200-pound shell reverberated across the nearby granite like fractured bells from hell and sent tall pillars of dust billowing skyward like wrathful genies. With time, the torrid smoke dissipated into thick drifting haze.[170]

At 0645, the 168th holding Point 444 reported a few men had braved the heavy German crossfire to claw up the slope of Hill 489—only a few hundred yards southwest of the abbey.[171] This was a fragile achievement, but represented enough progress for the 133rd to commence their attack on the town.[172]

No one in town had seen any sign of the SP guns since the previous day, and Sweeting believed there was no better moment to strike. He turned to Chapman:

"Let's get them going. I'll move the tanks forward a block. Get your infantry started and I'll throw my tanks in there."[173]

At the same time, the 1st and 100th Battalions, 133rd, advanced toward the craggy ridges between Hills 165 and 193, but soon halted after attracting vigorous German S/A, mortar, MG, and artillery fire.[174] White phosphorus smoke cover was called upon to proceed further.

The tanks in Cassino jerked forward tentatively in fits and starts toward the town square.[175] As they trundled, an L Company infantry platoon led by 2nd Lt Paul F. Riordan crouched along their hulls. Sweeting watched through well-worn field glasses from an obscured window in the OP villa, scanning alternately to the left and right. The dust finally dissipated enough for him to catch sight of a gray pudgy *Sturmgeschütz* III looming on the western side of the square only 200 yards away. Then, as if sensing detection, the squat gun scurried like a startled cockroach over to the southeast corner. Stunned, Sweeting immediately grabbed his radio mic and warned Lt Pride and the other two tank commanders of the danger. At this point, however, Pride's crews had become preoccupied. German MGs had opened up on the infantry and the tanks were busy firing back.[176]

The AT liaison officer attempted alerting the 57mm crew atop Hill 175—but discovered a dead silent radio link. While the anxious officer fumbled with the controls, an exasperated Sweeting watched the ugly machine wriggle into an ambush position only 100 yards away from Pride's advancing column. He scanned eastward toward the nunnery building roughly 300 yards away, beyond the jail. A second *Sturmgeschütz* emerged from just beyond the convent's western wall. With cool cocksureness, the deadly tank killer rocketed over to the main street of town, spun toward Pride's tanks, and halted behind a slight rise in the narrow cobblestone street. His voice hoarse from a sudden surge of adrenaline, Sweeting alerted Pride's crews of this new intruder. Pride confirmed seeing the second SP gun roughly 150 yards to the south and fired several desperate AP rounds at it. The SP gun crew had preselected the spot with expert skill. The dip in the road left only the top few inches of gun exposed and Pride's slugs either whooshed over the target completely or struck the foreground cobblestone in a spray of sparks and skipped harmlessly overhead.

The SP gun returned fire, piercing Pride's tank with precision—killing the driver and another crewman instantly. Sweeting watched in horror as the three surviving crewmen bailed out and stumbled away. For good measure, the SP gun unleashed another round—and the smoking hulk exploded into an orange gush of flames. Without hesitating, the SP gun hurled several more high-velocity slugs toward a second M4 in the trapped column. It too shuddered violently after absorbing a direct hit, and another shocked crew threw open their hatches in panic.[177] Some crewmembers were on fire as they tumbled onto the street, and Riordan's infantry had to grab them, amid bullet fire, and roll them across the rubble in order to quench the flames.[178]

Now absolutely livid, Lt Col Sweeting swirled around to the AT liaison officer and screamed: "Get the anti-tank gun on them!"

"I can't reach them," the panicked officer spluttered.

"Have you taken that God damned thing apart and seen if the connections are OK?" Sweeting fumed.

"Yes, yes. It still won't work."[179]

Although parts of the town remained obscured by morning fog and yellow dust kicked up from battle, Sweeting was thoroughly convinced the 57mm AT crew on the nearby hill should have seen both guns and stood pondering momentarily why they hadn't fired. For a split second, he considered calling in a salvo of heavy artillery, but the proximity of American infantry gave him pause.[180] Instead, he gritted his jaw and watched helplessly as the triumphant German SP commander bounded out from his hatch and onto the narrow street. Using a series of quick hand signals, the confident figure guided his driver backing the twin tracks away from the road dip. A few seconds later, the fleet-footed commander and his ugly SP gun slithered behind a building and disappeared.

Everyone in the OP had become so transfixed watching the brief and shocking confrontation that they temporarily overlooked the first SP gun still lurking in the square. By now, its gun barrel had been raised and squared directly upon the OP. With a vivid flash, an explosive shell slammed into the rocky hill above the villa, shaking loose sheets of ceiling plaster and showering the roof with a cascade of broken stone. The sound was deafening. A second round erupted with another earsplitting jolt—narrowly missing the OP again, but shaking loose even more mortar and stone. An animated staff tried carrying about their duties, but the third shot completely rocked the house—causing everyone to dive for all available cover. Major Chapman crouched in a corner, reciting prayers.[181] War correspondent Tom Treanor leapt down a damaged stairwell in one bound. The blast had caused dust to spurt from every crack and those inside feared the entire floor might collapse.[182] For several anxious moments, Chapman's staff awaited the *coup de grâce*. It never came. For reasons unknown, the SP gun pivoted slightly and expended several more rounds trying to pick off MG hillside positions around the OP. Then, like a cat suddenly bored by the hunt, halted fire and retreated from the square. Then, it too disappeared into the maze of narrow streets further south.[183]

The OP staff regained their senses and found much of their equipment ruined. Treanor emerged from the stairwell unhurt but covered in dust and badly shaken emotionally.[184] Sweeting and Chapman resumed their hollering into any phone that still functioned. Chapman found one crucial line dead and bolted outdoors to personally splice the severed wires back together. He returned to call an artillery strike on the retreating SP guns,[185] even though the chances of actually hitting one were exceedingly slim.[186] For the umpteenth time, the SP guns succeeded in disrupting Allied plans while picking off American tanks, and escaping to fight another day. The pattern was beyond maddening.

While the OP was under attack, however, the L Company infantry pushed forward 100 yards inside of town. Using the supporting fire of the lone surviving tank from Lt Pride's platoon and under the inspired leadership of Lt Riordan, the infantry bounded over the debris-filled street to reach beyond another ring of intense German S/A and MG fire. During the maneuver, Riordan became separated in the rubble ahead of his men. He managed to shoot two Germans dead before one of their bullets slammed into his torso only two inches above the heart. Riordan's men quickly pulled their platoon leader to safety—but found him pale and barely breathing. Concerned for the safety of any stretcher bearers called forth, the 24-year-old Kansan refused evacuation and expired shortly afterwards.[187] The prior week, Riordan had singlehandedly neutralized several key German MGs during the capture of Hill 175.[188] For his actions both then and on this morning, the former Montgomery Ward shipping clerk was awarded the Medal of Honor, posthumously.[189] He left behind a grieving fiancée.[190]

As of 0735, L Company reported drawing only light sporadic S/A fire, but their forward positions were tenuous.[191] Intent on reinforcing those gains, Sweeting ordered Captain Arnold to rush forward the 1st Platoon, C Company, 756th.[192] Moments later, five tanks thundered past the OP toward town. Their triumphant arrival inspired the infantry to press another fifty yards further, but the lead tank screeched to a halt upon receiving several rounds of grazing German rifle grenade fire—all aimed at the tank commander's head.[193] Worse, the tankers discovered they couldn't advance beyond the blown spillway bridge at the northeast corner of the square.[194] The morning pounding from the 8-inch howitzers had also clogged the narrow road leading east toward the jail with thick piles of rubble—rendering the way impassible. The tanks had no other option but to pull back slightly from the grenade fire. As a consequence, Sweeting ordered the crews to turn west instead and support the infantry clearing buildings along the north edge of the square.[195] In the meantime, Lt Pride's surviving tankers and his platoon's only remaining tank withdrew to Hill 213. Many more days would pass before Pride's platoon could be reconstituted for battle.[196]

Next, several light tanks from the 1st Platoon of D Company, 756th, arrived at the town's entrance with instructions from Sweeting to settle in place and provide fire support to cover the infantry's advance along the square.[197] Lt Redle was alerted at the quarry to ready his tanks for a possible move along the eastern roadway leading to the jail in support of the C Company platoon. Any B Company move, however, would only occur under cover of smoke and once Sweeting gave the go ahead.[198] As of 0815, the 3rd Battalion secured ground roughly 150 yards inside town, but German resistance had only stiffened.[199] Fearful of congesting the cramped entrance of town with too many tanks, Sweeting decided against calling Redle's crews forward.

In the draw further west, the 1st and 100th Battalions made steady progress after an inauspicious start. At 0715, Cannon Company laid down a perfectly placed smokescreen enabling both battalions to revive the attack.[200] By 0735, the Nisei troops advanced a full 800 yards around the horseshoe draw and reached Hill 165—just 200 yards west of the castle tower.[201] One entire company even managed to occupy a section of Castle Hill (193) itself.[202] Surprisingly, the 100th Battalion encountered only a few bursts of mortar and no S/A fire whatsoever during their advance.[203] On Hill 165, however, the Nisei troops tangled for a full forty-five minutes with the two German SP guns burrowed along the switchback road behind the tower. By 0730, one gun had been completely destroyed by bazooka fire. At 0840, the second gun, hidden inside a house, was struck in the track and disabled.[204] At the same time, the 1st Battalion attacked the northwest slope of Hill 193 while braving heavy German mortar and MG fire.[205] Just then, moderate winds began swirling through rocky draw, wreaking havoc with the mortar smoke and complicating operations. The infantry could never be sure from one minute to the next if their precious cover might drift away completely, leaving them completely exposed.[206]

In the highlands west, the 135th Regiment reported fair progress as well. By 1055, dogged infantrymen had advanced as far as a rocky draw 300 yards east of the abbey. As they scurried, darted, and crept, German positions 300 yards southwest on Hills 375 and 374 were pounded beneath a heavy deluge of American mortar and artillery shells. The Germans retaliated by blasting the 135th OP on Hill 593 with steady mortar fire of their own.[207]

American 4.2-inch mortars were especially effective against enemy positions. The Germans dubbed this dreaded weapon "silent death" because each bursting 4.2-inch diameter round splintered into far finer fragments than those produced by the more common 81mm mortar. One tiny splinter could pass completely through a man—often shredding organs and major arteries without leaving much of an entrance wound.[208] A stricken soldier would often bleed internally, go into shock, and die long before his concerned comrades could ever find a skin mark on his body.

***

Because of the downed bridge and debris-filled roadway leading to the jail, Sweeting and Chapman decided to withdraw the tanks, consolidate the infantry's gains, and regroup for an afternoon attack. Chapman believed his men could clear the roadway in time and issued orders to do so.[209] To protect those efforts, Sweeting directed TD, mortar, and assault gun fire on any place he suspected the SP guns to have retreated.[210]

The tanks were withdrawn temporarily to the quarry. Sweeting set out from the OP on a quick foot reconnaissance—returning a short time later to confer with Captain Arnold and the 1st Platoon leader for C Company, 756th.[211] Their new plan dispatched the 1st Platoon to town in the early afternoon in support of the infantry. Once the roadway was clear, the attack would then hook left toward the jail.[212]

By midday, all three 133rd battalions had consolidated ground taken during the morning and prepared to strike again. At 1320, in brisk thirty-four-degree temperatures and good visibility, the tanks rolled back into town.[213] Upon arrival, the infantry immediately called forth the 75mm guns to neutralize several enemy strongpoints. On occasion, German snipers or rifle grenadiers targeted the heads of the tank commanders,[214] but missed. As both sides clashed, infantrymen scurried back and forth—clearing away loose stone and broken timbers from the narrow roadway. Before the hour passed, however, the tankers radioed they were already running low on ammunition. To maintain the momentum, Sweeting directed one tank section to support those infantrymen clashing among the buildings along the western edge of the square. The other section was ordered to withdraw immediately to the quarry for resupply. At the same time, the 2nd Platoon, C Company, 756th, moved into town to reinvigorate the fight.[215] Meanwhile, Lt Redle's B Company crews remained at the ready to exploit any breakthrough.[216]

The arrival of the 2nd platoon gave the infantry a much-needed boost. The roadway had been cleared well enough to allow an attack toward the jail, and the new offensive commenced at 1330. At the infantry's direction, the M4 guns blasted constantly and 75mm HE explosions blew out the interiors of nearby buildings.[217] At first, much attention was directed toward the square's southern edge, but efforts soon shifted to targets on the east side of town.[218] The steady pressure paid dividends. By 1445, lead elements of L Company seized another fifty yards of ruins—quickly closing in upon the jail.[219] To avoid any friendly fire casualties, the infantry kept a steady stream of runners huffing back and forth to the tankers. A tank commander only targeted those positions personally designated to him by the runner and then awaited further instructions from the next runner before firing again. The wait was never long and the system worked exceedingly well. Another signal the tankers used to indicate their guns had finished firing on a particular position was for the lead tank to dispatch four quick rounds into the target's doorway. The infantry then knew it was safe to immediately storm the building.[220]

Good communication bred trust. By mid-afternoon, tanks could fire repeatedly on the jail and nearby buildings without fear of hitting any infantrymen operating nearby—even as riflemen bounded, dropped, and rolled only a few dozen yards away. Such close supporting fire enabled the infantry to capture one key house directly across from the jail and clear even more rubble from the road.[221] Efforts soon shifted to the jail's western wall, a nearby courtyard, and an adjacent building. With clockwork efficiency, the tanks laid down a sustained barrage of suppressive fire—thus allowing the infantry to storm across the courtyard and seize a small portion of the jail. After this quick and stunning achievement, the tanks halted fire.[222]

At this point the tanks moved into positions near the northeast corner of a captured house only seventy-five yards away from the jail. They could not, however, close the distance. Heavy debris piles blocked the way. The two lead tanks tried mounting the rubble, but could not maneuver through. By 1515, the second tank began backing away. At that moment, a German rifle grenade burst at the turret ring—rattling the crew and igniting a small flash fire inside.[223] The crew quickly extinguished the blaze but discovered the turret had hopelessly jammed. At this point, they decided to abandon the tank. That very instant, the commander of the lead tank, S/Sgt Dennis W. Grigsby, slumped over dead from a clean shot to the head taken by a German sniper.[224] A split second later, another rifle grenade exploded against the gun barrel—rendering it inoperable as well. Because Grigsby's lead tank was now trapped ahead of the second immobilized tank, the surviving crew was forced to dismount and scramble for cover.[225]

When Sweeting heard of this development, he alerted the barracks TDs to cover the two remaining tanks working the east end of Cassino. The infantry phone lines happened to be out at that very moment, so Sweeting decided to hike down into Cassino and survey the situation firsthand.[226] While dodging bullets and ducking from wall to wall, the fearless lieutenant colonel queried his tank commanders and any available infantry officers on the tactical situation. He learned K Company had captured buildings north and east of the square as well as several others along the east side of the main road. He confirmed L Company occupied the key house directly across from the jail, an adjacent courtyard to the northwest, and a tiny section of the jail. L Company hoped to solidify their gains but couldn't reinforce the men inside the jail on account of an unlocatable sniper and MG fire.[227] Assured that the infantry and remaining tanks were, in fact, secure, and with no further attacks having been planned for the evening, Sweeting returned to the quarry.[228] There, he directed 2nd Lt Gordon E. Perkins, acting commander of C Company, to withdraw his tanks under the cover of darkness to the assembly area at Hill 213.[229]

As 1800 neared, the infantry continued strengthening their hard-won positions in town. The two disabled C Company tanks, however, particularly the one nearest the house across from the jail, completely blocked the roadway and hindered consolidation efforts. Both tanks had to be cleared.[230] The II Corps also feared this vulnerable state of affairs might invite a German air attack and sent an alert out to all AA units to remain vigilant.[231]

At 1800, Lt Col Sweeting visited the 133rd CP in Caira to coordinate the next day's actions with Colonel Marshall.[232] To better protect his troops, Marshall wanted to reposition the towed AT guns deeper in town during the night.[233] The two officers discussed ways of facilitating tank movement—such as the clearing of roads and filling of ditches. Sweeting was particularly concerned about the downed bridge near the square. His tanks could not penetrate deeper into town until the engineers either built another bridge or backfilled the location.[234] The engineers were also called upon to clear the heavier rubble away from both roads leading to the jail.[235]

The 133rd hadn't achieved any hoped-for "breakthrough," but the day's efforts and sacrifices did gain considerable ground. After dusk, contact patrols were dispatched to maintain communications between all three battalions and solidify the front line.[236] The 1st Battalion settled into defensive positions upon the northwest slopes of Hill 193,[237] while 100th Battalion held firm on Hill 165 nearby—after weathering a heavy spate of German MG fire mid-afternoon.[238] From time to time, the immobilized SP gun near the switchback road fired at them in defiance, but without consequence.[239] The 3rd Battalion continued consolidating positions near the jail to their best abilities, but the two knocked out M4s blocking the roadway and constant harassment from German snipers impeded the work. As a consequence, Colonel Marshall drew up no plans for any largescale attacks for the following day—preferring, instead to allow his troops more time to secure ground already taken. [240]

In the west, the 168th and 135th Infantry Regiments renewed the highland offensive at 1500 hours behind another crushing Allied artillery barrage.[241] As usual, German resistance was ferocious,[242] but the 168th did manage to crawl close enough to enemy positions on Hill 303 for the battle to degenerate into a frantic grenade tossing match.[243] The Americans reported encountering German paratroopers—fresh, disciplined, and extremely difficult to defeat.[244] K Company scrapped to within 200 yards of northwest corner of the abbey before being thrown back.[245] They discovered the monastery's perimeter sewn so thick with German pillboxes, MG, and 81mm mortar positions, that an approach proved impossible to sustain for very long.[246] The 2nd Battalion, 135th captured Hill 569, but a heavy counterattack pouring from the southwest threatened to dislodge them by nightfall.[247]

At 2000, Sweeting called his company commanders together to develop plans for the following day. His first order of business was the recovery of the two disabled M4s across from the jail. Until these were moved, no other tanks could get through. The officers decided to dispatch crews during the night in an attempt to restart the engines and retrieve both tanks.[248] Tank operations for 9 February would be limited to supporting the infantry as they cleared the jail and adjacent buildings, plus any remaining houses on the square. Sweeting relayed the news about the few American infantrymen infiltrating the jail, but gave his personal opinion they would not be able to remain there through the night and that the tank crews should be prepared to resume fire on the jail come daybreak.[249] "Milk runs" were assigned as follows: C Company, 760th, would remain in reserve. During the night, several tanks from D Company, 756th would infiltrate town and determine the best ways to remove the two disabled C Company, 756th, tanks near jail in addition to the three knocked-out M4s still partially blocking the main road.[250] In the morning, Redle's B Company crews would head to town and blast the jail and any other buildings on the square identified as problems by the infantry. A Company would continue to provide supporting fire from across the river. As always, Sweeting would direct all tank operations from the hillside OP.[251]

After nightfall, the 133rd continued reorganizing and resupplying as German artillery rained down upon them with disruptive irregularity. In case the German SP guns reemerged, two towed 37mm AT guns were repositioned deeper inside the town as foils.[252] One gun was wheeled inside the front bedroom of a crossroads home and pointed southward. Germans eavesdropping from across the square grew suspicious of the movement noises and started shelling the house relentlessly.[253] The light tank crews from D Company, 756th, tried setting out on their tank reclamation project but were halted and politely told to stay out of town. The infantry feared the engine noises would only draw more unwelcome German mortar and artillery and complicate their already prickly consolidation efforts.[254] Later, the II Corps asked both commanders of the 133rd and the 168th if they desired air strikes on the nearby hills to aid the efforts. Both commanders flatly refused the offer.[255] At this point, no one wanted any more complications—particularly anything involving airplanes with their reputation for inaccuracy.

At 2045, an unsubstantiated rumor circulated among the Allied ranks warning of a German counterattack successfully breaking across the Rapido further south. The story sent Cannon Company, TD, and mortar crews positioned throughout the valley scrambling for their side arms and extra ammo.[256] The alert persisted for quite some time until the "breakthrough" turned out to be two lost German soldiers who had stumbled into a minefield and blown themselves up.[257] Nevertheless, this silly false alarm highlighted the hair-trigger anxiety levels of the men supporting the line.

At 2200, three Germans soldiers were seen wandering behind 133rd lines, giving the Americans another scare. Two were shot, and the other was captured. The lone survivor said he came from III Battalion, 132nd Grenadier Regiment (44th Infantry Division).[258] About an hour later, two more Germans in town approached 133rd positions with their hands high in the air. One stepped on a mine and was blown to pieces. His surviving comrade reported they had both been assigned to a nearby mortar until an American tank destroyed their bunker.[259]

A German lieutenant captured in the highlands by the 135th Regiment complained about how the German Army in Italy had been experiencing ever greater shortages—particularly with fuel, munitions, and quality soldiers. He also expressed admiration at the effectiveness of Allied artillery and aviation operations, but was especially awed by the seemingly endless stream of Allied munitions, fuel, and reserves pouring into the area. The Allies had "at least three times as many vehicles as the Wehrmacht," the German officer marveled.[260]

The Allies could, indeed, boast a distinct advantage in equipment and materials, but the battle for Cassino also bled them of quality men. Equipment was worthless without experienced operators. After two weeks of combat, each of the three battalions to all three infantry regiments of the 34th Division suffered from heavy personnel losses—some by as much as fifty percent. At full strength an infantry battalion fought with approximately 900 men (five companies of 180 each). The 1st Battalion, 133rd, rolls had fallen to only 506 men, the 100th Battalion fell to 540, and the 3rd Battalion reported a somewhat healthier 659 figure.[261] The three battalions (1st, 2nd, 3rd) of the 135th Regiment, battling along the massif, reported depleted numbers of 655, 592, and 581, respectively. 168th Regiment rolls reported only 442 actives in the 1st, 731 in the 2nd, and 699 in the 3rd Battalions. These numbers are worse than they appear when one considers combat attrition did not fall equally among a battalion's five companies. The three rifle companies almost always suffered higher combat losses because of the dangerous close-quartered nature of their work. Generally, the HQ and heavy weapons companies of a battalion lost fewer men. In reality, many "Red Bull" rifle companies battled on with less than fifty percent authorized troop strength levels. For example, rifle companies A, B, and C of the 1st Battalion, 133rd, reported personnel levels at only eighty-nine, forty-three, and eighty-eight respectively. A, B, and C Companies of the 100th Battalion, 133rd, recorded unit strength at 100, eighty-five, and eighty-six, and the 3rd Battalion of the133rd's I, K, and L Companies were operating with only 108, 122, and 120 men. Without a doubt, A Company of the 168th was the worst off. This battered company was down to only forty enlisted men with no officers left to lead them—and yet these men remained on the line at only twenty-two percent of their table of organization strength.[262] These were enormous burdens for any infantryman to bear.

The 756th Tank Battalion arrived at San Michele on 21 January with a full complement of thirty-eight officers and 642 enlisted men.[263] By 8 February, rolls fell to thirty-two officers and only 574 enlisted men.[264] In eighteen days of battle, the battalion lost seventy-eight men: eighteen were killed, fifteen taken prisoner, twelve seriously wounded and unlikely to return, with thirty-two others either wounded in action or injured badly enough to require hospitalization.[265] Most were tank crewmen. Roughly 360 men in the battalion filled this role, so this loss represented a twenty percent attrition rate. The attached 760th tank company lost another dozen men—fifteen percent of their crewmen.[266] Tank commanders, drivers, and gunners were not easily replaced while in combat and there was no opportunity to properly train new ones.

During WWII, the U.S. War Department instituted a troop "replacement system" based upon a faulty "interchangeable parts" concept. The idea was patterned upon the success of the factory assembly line and the role "standardized parts" played in an age of rapid industrialization. If a brake pad wore out on a truck, or a spring failed in a rifle, an interchangeable spare part restored the unit's function. The War Department believed replacement soldiers should be plugged into fighting units much the same way. Thus, spare solders were "stockpiled" at Replacement Depots

("Repple-Depples") like jeep tires. The concept looked good on paper but proved an abject failure in practice. Combat units are more akin to living, breathing organisms, than to cold, impassive machines. To fulfill their functions, men assigned new roles in unfamiliar surroundings need encouragement, trust, and friendship—all of which required time, training, and mentorship to develop. To meld a collection of strangers into an effective fighting unit, an esprit de corps had to first be built and nurtured away from the battlefield. When thrown into a combat setting, new troops did not simply "plug" into existing units without degrading the morale of everyone involved. The U.S. Army replacement system was a terrible disservice to both the combat veteran fighting in the field and the inexperienced soldier tossed in an unfamiliar foxhole and expected to replace someone else's dead buddy. The better method was to pull an entire unit away from the front line and replace it with a fresh unit every few weeks. Under this type of rotational system, replacements could be introduced into new units and properly integrated away from the crushing pressures of combat. The British preferred this approach and it worked well.[267]

The captured German lieutenant may have marveled at the Allies' seemingly endless stream of vehicles, but tanks—particularly M4s—were in short supply. As of 8 February, the 756th Tank Battalion operated with only twenty-eight medium tanks, twelve light tanks, and thirteen attached mediums from the 760th. Fully stocked, the battalion should have had fifty-three M4s, seventeen M5 lights, plus the seventeen additional M4s from the 760th. Eighteen days of battle claimed a staggering *sixty* tanks—destroyed, captured, disabled or damaged severely enough to require extensive repairs.[268] A tank battalion short twenty percent in tankers but fifty percent in tanks meant trained crews were left standing around with nothing to do.

***

The results of Lt Gen Mark Clark's latest grand offensive were mixed, at best. The 34th and 36th Infantry Divisions achieved some success, but fell far short of attaining the Fifth Army's overall aim of breaking into the Liri Valley. During the day, the British to the south and French to the north also added pressure along the Gustav Line, but failed to crack German resolve anywhere. Snow and cold weather now hampered French operations further north, and those units needed time to reorganize.[269] And despite all the German prisoner griping about battlefield losses, scant supplies, and plummeting morale, somehow these deprived defenders maintained an iron grip on Monastery Hill and most of Cassino while showing little sign of surrendering. On the other hand, the 34th and 36th Divisions had, at best, only a few days of energy remaining to expel them. Afterwards, both divisions would need to be pulled from the line before breaking down completely.

New troops from the 2nd New Zealand Division began pouring into the area during the day, and by mid-afternoon the 5th Brigade (NZ) emplaced two full infantry battalions along the eastern bank of the Rapido.[270] The sudden appearance of dishpan-shaped Brodie helmets suggested "failure" to the weary and frustrated Americans, but this was not true. American determination, bravery, and sacrifice had not been lacking in this ruthless contest. The wretched terrain, elaborate fortifications, and veteran combat experience of the Germans were heavy factors. Nevertheless, American troops from top to bottom began convincing themselves that their troubles must have stemmed from some other nefarious cause. Maj Gen Keyes, in his II Corps daily report to Lt Gen Mark Clark, identified the prime suspect: "Front line troops report Abbey being used as German OP."[271]

The rank and file now grumbled openly for the air force to just flatten the place and spare their lives.[272]

German 242nd Assault Gun Battalion

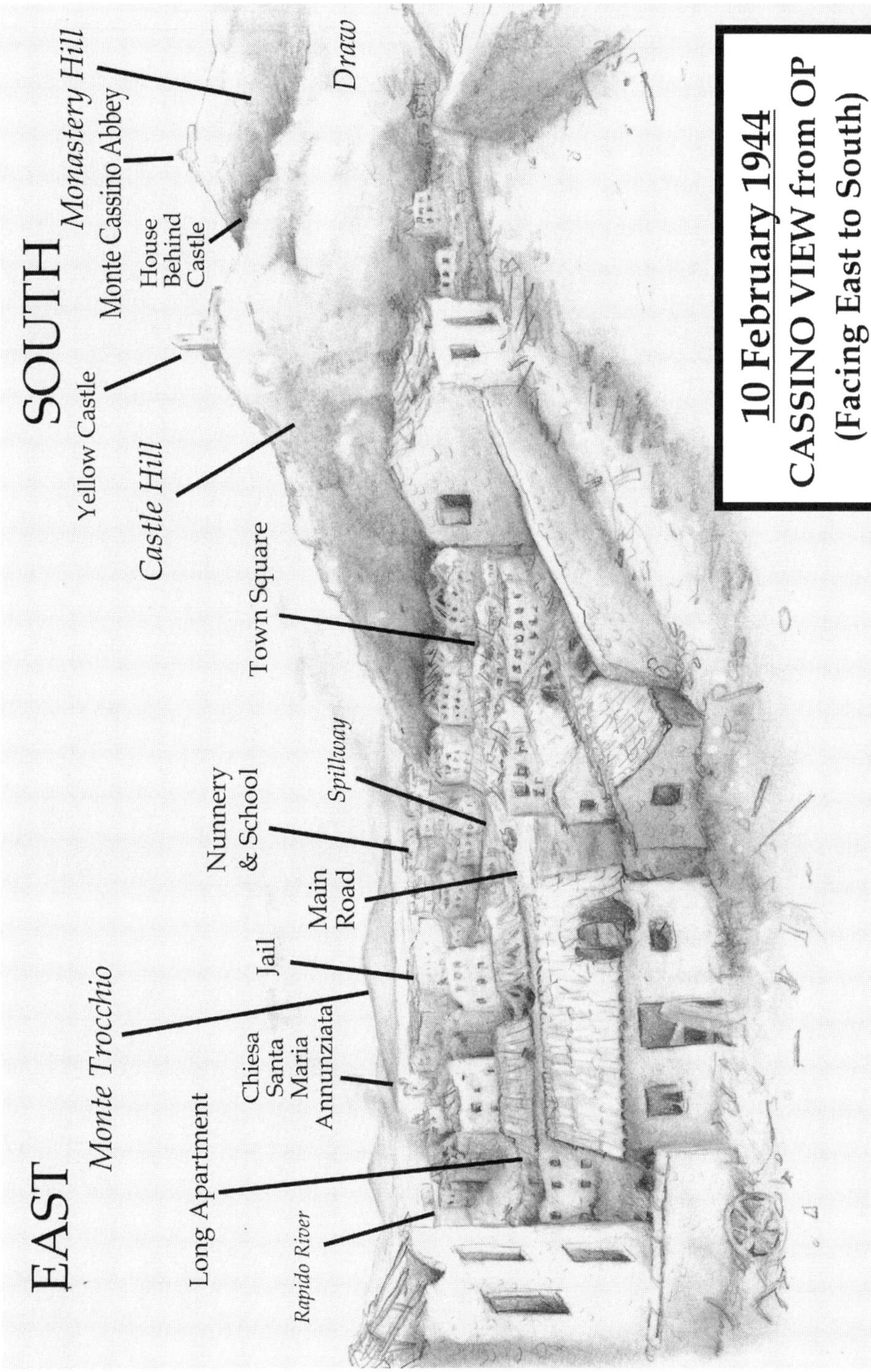

10 February 1944
CASSINO VIEW from OP
(Facing East to South)

CHAPTER FOUR

The Jail: 9 February 1944 to 12 February 1944

After midnight, 9 February, the 756th Tank Battalion dispatched recovery teams into Cassino to retrieve the two immobilized C Company tanks blocking the narrow road across from the jail. Although the crews labored as quietly as possible, the sounds attracted unwelcome German attention. Over the next two hours, the enemy's harassing fire grew so distressing and hazardous that the recovery effort was completely abandoned by 0300 and both tanks were left in place.[1]

The Germans stepped up artillery harassment as well—much of it directed upon American positions in the highlands.[2] At 0100, heavier rounds, whooshing in from Terelle to the north, exploded across 168th and 135th Regiment positions atop the massif. The ordeal lasted a solid hour, before diminishing somewhat, but never ceasing entirely. The 135th complained the shells were exceptionally accurate, and the 168th reported at least thirty-two rounds had burst about their CP.[3] Every so often, a German MG would chatter along in counterpoint.[4] At 0450, some unidentified plane buzzed directly over the 135th Regiment CP and disappeared, unnerving the entire HQ staff.[5] Evidently, the Germans didn't want any Americans to fall asleep.

The 1st Battalion, 133rd, also received a few rounds of artillery after midnight.[6] Several other rounds exploded around 3rd Battalion, 133rd, positions in town,[7] but this relatively light harassment did not compare to the torment falling among the hills nearby. A patrol was dispatched to the northeast corner of town and heard enemy voices near the jail, but when Nebelwerfer rockets started exploding nearby, the five-man team decided to move on. They quietly proceeded westward and listened to MG and rifle fire echoing through the town square. To their rear, off in the direction of the jail, some vehicle motor grumbled to life. At 0200, German mortar fire suddenly burst around them—bringing a discomforting sense to the stealthy intruders they were being watched and followed. The patrol decided, then and there, to end their eavesdropping and return home.[8]

***

The morning arrived with overcast skies, light rain, and poor visibility. The mercury level teased upward to a tepid forty-four degrees, but the damp air delivered a miserable chill.[9] At the quarry, Lt Redle's coffee-fueled tankers awaited orders to move forward. Several days had passed since his crews played a central role in town. On paper, B Company again fielded three platoons, but each was comprised of only three tanks—down from the normal five. Only one officer, Lt Harley, commanded a platoon—the 1st. Both the 2nd and 3rd platoons were commanded by S/Sgt Haspel and Sgt Oliver, respectively. Oliver took over the 3rd Platoon after S/Sgt Johannesen was wounded.[10] Lt Redle's crew included a new gunner, Cpl Frank W. Mielcarski—shuffled over to replace Sgt Wunderlich, who had also been wounded a few days earlier.[11]

Because of the heavy misting, Redle wondered if his tanks would even be called forward at all, but at 0730 the infantry phoned in the request, and Redle dispatched a platoon into the northern edge of town. Sweeting had been right about the jail: the infantry could not maintain any presence there through the night—and now wanted the fortress-like building systematically demolished.[12] The walls were thick and the task daunting, but Redle's tanks began chipping away at the stone and mortar with AP, HE, and new concrete piercing rounds.[13] In dreary damp fog, punctuated by occasional showers, the pounding persisted all morning long.[14] By noon, the cold rain finally yielded to cloudy skies, but the blasting of the jail continued—halting only for a short time when the infantry requested the tanks divert a few rounds into another nearby building.[15]

In the meantime, roughly 200 yards west, other infantrymen focused upon capturing several buildings near the square and the downed bridge. At 1400 hours, Colonel Marshall ordered the 133rd Cannon Company to lay smoke and maintain suppressive HE fire just beyond the buildings at a rate of two rounds per gun per minute—roughly 1,000 per hour.[16] To assist in the effort, Lt Redle dispatched a second tank platoon to town. Along the way, Lt Neal's L Company troops joined forces and the small, armored column passed through I Company positions toward buildings lining the south edge of the square. As Neal's infantry fanned out and assigned targets, the tanks fired slowly and methodically, taking great pains to avoid friendly fire. At one point, the crews concentrated efforts upon one building wall for a full forty-five minutes. Once a hole was finally made large enough, the firing ceased, and Neal's infantry stormed inside and captured an entire floor.[17]

Lt Neal's attack shifted to the east side of the road with the intent of reaching the jail from that direction. The narrow road abutting the spillway and leading past the jail was still clogged with rubble, so Neal reconnoitered ahead on foot to find the best way to clear a pathway for the tanks to follow. After returning, Neal sent a squad back through with instructions to attack the front of the jail. This action would provide a distracting feint so others could clear the road. Neal's remaining men attempted to remove rubble but immediately drew German fire from three nearby houses. Lt Neal now had to devise a plan to capture those positions. Although a frontal assault was never an ideal option, the ruins of Cassino often did not allow an infantry team to flank an objective. This meant a target could only be attacked head on—but only after careful planning and with cunning, timing, and especially teamwork.[18]

After a course of action was devised, and Neal's men dodged and weaved their way toward the houses, two German SP guns hidden deeper in town started firing at them. Redle's tankers, however, found no clear sight lines and could not return fire upon the SP guns. After careful observation, it was determined one gun was masked inside a fortified house several hundred yards south,[19] so the Corps' 8-inch howitzers were called upon to hammer the position. These oversized guns were so accurate that adjustments could be made as tight as ten yards, and the infantry had no qualms about allowing these huge 200-pound shells to explode as close as fifty yards from their positions.[20] Chapmen's men called this practice "sniping with an 8-inch how." A few minutes later, 8-inch shells screamed in from the east and exploded all around the SP gun. The house, however, proved so well fortified that the SP gun never ceased firing.[21] Clearly, only a lucky round had any hope of silencing the irritating thing.[22] Now, in order to shield Neal's men as they worked, Cannon Company was called upon to drop smoke cannisters and lob suppressive HE shells—adjusting placement as the infantry maneuvered.[23] From 1400 to 1840, some 3,000 rounds of all types were dispatched—just in support of this simple operation.[24] In the end, Neal's men consumed the rest of the afternoon clearing three houses lined between the dropped bridge and the jail—and the roadway never did get cleared.

Late in the afternoon, the B Company platoon tasked with pummeling the jail was withdrawn after running out of ammo.[25] In total, Redle's crews dispatched 275 rounds of HE and AP into the jail walls.[26] Some progress was made, but the walls proved fortress thick. The platoon supporting Neal's men was withdrawn as well.[27] Sweeting asked Redle to send another platoon to town to resume firing on the jail. That platoon left the quarry at 1725 and continued with the battering.[28]

At 1655, the 1st Battalion, 133rd, reported success in placing more men upon the steep slope of Hill 193. Despite heavy German MG fire pouring from hidden bunkers spread across the craggy hill, a few American troops even infiltrated the crevices west of the castle.[29] The 100th Battalion spent the afternoon mopping up resistance inside the draw further west.[30]

As dusk succumbed to night, the 3rd Battalion, 133rd, successfully cleared five more houses west of the downed bridge—but still hadn't reached the jail. Two abandoned German halftracks were captured in the process, and were torched to prevent enemy recovery. Engineers appeared in town to begin studying options to repair the downed bridge.[31]

The Germans responded angrily with another night of heavy shelling. At least 100 rounds of medium shells exploded about the barracks just before midnight—mostly arcing in from the west and southwest.[32] One lucky round struck an ammunition pile, setting it afire.[33] Another barrage rolled through the north quarter of town like a giant rototiller—churning across the square, the western draw, and Hill 175—anywhere the Americans seemed to make headway during the day.[34]

As was customary every evening, Sweeting met with Colonel Marshall to coordinate the next day's plans. Afterwards, the energetic lieutenant colonel called together his company commanders to relay the details. Little had changed: the tanks would continue blasting the jail and all other targets designated by the infantry. In the meantime, the 133rd Regiment would consolidate positions.[35] Because the two disabled C Company tanks continued blocking the northern route to jail, the crews were instructed to use alternate firing positions until the wrecks could be removed. B Company was assigned reserve duties at the quarry. C Company, 756th, crews would take their turns in town, while A Company, as usual, lent fire support from across the river. Lt Redle was given an additional responsibility of directing quarry traffic. C Company, 760th, still badly battered after fighting in Cassino a few days earlier, would sit in reserve near Hill 213.[36] The best news of the day was that the 756th suffered no casualties whatsoever—despite all the heavy action.[37]

The day was nearly disastrous, however, for "Red Bull" troops fighting on the massif nearby. At 0500, the 135th Regiment reeled under a surprisingly heavy German counterattack lasting for several hours. Only after great effort and struggle was the intrusion finally repulsed.[38] To regain the upper hand, Fifth Army had arranged for an elaborate aerial assault upon German highland positions. The bombardment was supposed to unfold as five separate waves arriving in sequence during the morning and early afternoon, but poor weather postponed the start until 1000. This delay was the first sign of trouble. The opening attack run was supposed to fly in low from the north heading south—bombing only those areas marked with violet smoke by 34th Division artillery batteries. Instead, the planes appeared from the east heading west and either bombed the wrong places or bombed nothing at all. No violet smoke had fallen ahead of time to show the pilots what to hit. Many bombs fell north of the monastery—exploding among 3rd Battalion, 168th, positions. Worse, the Germans positioned east of the monastery took advantage of the error by launching follow-up Nebelwerfer and mortar rounds upon those same 168th positions—as if their own planes had done the bombing!

An angered 168th command staff phoned the divisional HQ to halt the aerial attacks, but the second wave was already underway. This time the bombs landed behind the monastery and the draw immediately north—striking, at least, some of the areas they were supposed to hit. While departing, however, several planes mistakenly strafed the 168th CP area and ended up wounding an officer. The 168th, again, implored the 34th Division to halt the operation. The request was relayed up to II Corps and then over to the Air Force, to see what could be done. By now, however, the third attack wave was en route.

The winds had dissipated the violet smoke faster than expected, so artillery was asked to drop more. As they did, red smoke started popping up in strange places all over the area. The Germans were craftily dispatching the extra smoke canisters to confuse Allied pilots. The simple ruse worked, and the third wave skipped bombing the massif altogether, opting to strike a more distant German airfield instead. By then, II Corps' request was finally handled and the Air Force cancelled the fourth and fifth waves.[39] Afterwards, the 168th reported the bombings accomplished little and complained bitterly of how one out of every sixteen bombs landed on their own men.[40] They called, instead, for protective artillery barrages for the remainder of the day.[41]

When 3rd Battalion, 133rd, troops in town heard of the debacle, a few swapped a cynical joke that had been circulating among Allied ground forces for some time: "When a British plane comes over, the Germans hit their holes. When a German plane comes over, the British hit their holes. But when an American plane comes over, *everyone* hits their holes!"[42]

The Germans tried capitalizing on the fiasco by launching several counterattacks upon 135th and 168th Regiment positions during the afternoon.[43] The attacks failed. Ultimately, the highlands quietened down again somewhat after darkness,[44] and what had nearly been a disastrous episode returned to an exasperating status quo. Nevertheless, another day had been lost and more men had perished.

The battered 3rd Battalion, 135th, was relieved by the 2nd Battalion, 141st Regiment, near Massa Albaneta, three-quarters of a mile northwest of the abbey.[45] The exchange was slow, arduous, and dangerous because earlier rains had left the ground a sopping, muddy mess. Many trails had eroded and even been washed out completely in places—greatly complicating supply efforts.[46] Mules and mule skinners alike were fatigued after trudging the same, long, perilous route night after night without any meaningful rest.[47] Wounded troops, seeking medical help were screened by skeptical officers posted along the trails. Only those afflicted with the most serious, life-threatening wounds were allowed passage. Others were ordered to return to their posts under the implicit threat of the officers' sidearm.[48]

The mental and physical exhaustion suffered by the common "Red Bull" infantryman fast approached a crisis point. Gnawing fear over the ever-present threat of death darkened many spirits to where some men openly prayed for a swift and painless exit. Fatalistic expressions such as "simply let it happen quickly" or "I will be happy if I don't have to suffer" invaded even the most mundane of conversations.[49]

The unappetizing repetitive food wasn't helping morale either. Many soldiers hadn't enjoyed a hot meal in nearly thirty days.[50] Front-line troops subsisted on bland diets of D-ration "nutrition bars" or pre-packaged K ration boxed meals. These barely palatable "foods" were meant to be eaten only in the short term—perhaps a few days at a time. They provided a man with basic caloric energy and staved off his hunger pangs, but little else. The tankers enjoyed a somewhat more varied diet which included canned C-rations. But three straight weeks of these too had grown monotonous, especially when consuming them at every breakfast, lunch, and dinner.[51] Napoleon once observed: "Une armée marche à son estomac" ("An army marches on its stomach"). A happy soldier is a well-fed soldier. Even the most inspiring general cannot expect a soldier to perform well when his meals are poor.

Napoleon's observation applied not only to food in particular, but logistics in general. A soldier also needed ammunition, and the Fifth Army was running low on artillery shells. In an alarming 9 February message to the II Corps, the Fifth Army reported gun batteries at Cassino had been firing rounds at double the replacement rate for two straight weeks. Analysts projected that the Army's supply chain could not meet current demand until 10 March—another month into the future. As a result, immediate restrictions were placed on the use of 155mm, 105mm artillery rounds and even on M1 rifle cartridges.[52] Consequently, 34th Division artillery batteries expended only 838 rounds of 105mm, 59 rounds of 155mm, and 655 rounds of 3-inch rounds throughout the day.[53] No doubt, the Fifth Army's attempts to organize aerial bombings earlier in the day were due to this embarrassing artillery shortage.

Despite this sour development, Maj Gen Geoffrey Keyes, II Corps commander, dispatched a "rah-rah" letter to the COs of all units under his command. In the message, Keyes urged:

> THE BATTLE FOR CASSINO HAS REACHED ITS DECISIVE STAGE. THE EFFECT ON THE ENEMY AND THE IMPORTANCE HE ATTACHES TO THIS K[E]Y FEATURE ARE EVIDENCED BY THIS STUBBORN RESISTANCE AND HIS REPEATED USE OF RESERVES DRAWN FROM ALL OTHER FRONTS. YOU HAVE ESTABLISHED YOUR SUPERIORITY BY YOUR ACCOMPLISHMENTS WITHOUT RELIEVE OR REST, IN BREAKING HIS LINE AND THROWING BACK HIS DESPERATE COUNTER ATTACKS. TODAY'S AND TOMORROW'S BATTLE IS A FINAL TEST OF COURAGE AND ENDURANCE. VICTORY IS IN SIGHT AND WILL FALL RIGHTFULLY TO THOSE TROOPS AND LEADERS WHO HAVE THE DETERMINED WILL TO WIN.
>
> KEYES.[54]

Keyes insisted his troops would succeed in this final attempt to capture Cassino, despite the misgivings of General Alexander, 15th Army Group commander.[55] The British general privately believed his American subordinate was pushing his men too hard. Alexander would know. He had been commanding corps, armies, and army groups ever since September 1939—through the Fall of France, the evacuation of Dunkerque, the loss of Burma, the victory at 2nd Battle of El Alamein, and during challenging campaigns across Tunisia, Sicily—and now, Italy. Alexander recognized even the world's best soldiers could not keep fighting when utterly exhausted. Nevertheless, he deferred to Keyes' judgment.

***

10 February arrived like every other wretched midnight in Cassino. The dead night air cracked with the blood-curdling screams of Nebelwerfer rockets arching and exploding indiscriminately across the valley. Then, after several terrifying volleys, the racket halted. Mysteriously, at 0130, white flares appeared over the abbey—causing the Americans to wonder what new round of nefarious enemy activities required such steady illumination.[56]

At 0300, the 168th Regiment endured several waves of heavy German mortar and artillery blasts. Many rounds burst about the stone remnants of a medieval fort atop Hill 593.[57] Tellingly, 135th Regiment positions nearby, and 133rd-held sections in Cassino below were left unmolested.[58] Something was brewing in 168th-held territory. Sure enough, at 0400, the Germans launched another forceful counterattack upon 3rd Battalion, 168th, positions around Hill 593. This time, the German wave seemed bound and determined to recapture the hill. Unremitting fire of all types rained in from the south and west. To hold the point, the 3rd Battalion was forced to pull reinforcements from other positions.[59] By dawn's light, the 168th could finally perceive that between 100 to 200 attackers were involved, but by 0730, the Germans finally quit the effort after sustaining heavy losses.[60]

Meanwhile in Cassino, the Germans began casting harassing fire around 0525. The 133rd interpreted the behavior to be only a covering barrage to shift their defensive positions.[61] Shortly afterwards, Sweeting and his support detail arrived at the OP near town to begin another day. As usual, battalion radio and phone links were tested and readied. At 0630, Sweeting phoned Captain Arnold at the quarry and told him to prepare to send the tanks on the infantry's request.[62] A half hour later, just when the infantry was about to resume the push upon the jail, an SP gun hidden deep in Cassino opened fire—rocking the OP with several explosions. Captain Arnold rushed down on foot to find Sweeting and the others unhurt, but the battalion radio links with the assault gun and mortar platoons were completely destroyed.[63] The incident delayed the attack plans, so Sweeting left Arnold with the task of restoring communications and departed for Caira to regroup with Colonel Marshall.[64]

Remarkably, the OP staff restored order swiftly and Captain Arnold had the two battalion radios swapped and operating by 0900.[65] The infantry attempted an advance upon the jail without tanks, but was driven back.[66] Pale, clammy cloud cover hung low over the town, dropping occasional light showers and making the employment of Cannon Company's howitzers impossible.[67] The Germans on Monastery Hill took advantage of the situation by spraying S/A and mortar fire all over the north section of Cassino.[68] By 1000, the sun burned away enough of the dreary haze for Cannon Company to resume fire.[69] The improved visibility also heralded the unwelcome return of the two SP guns hidden deeper in town. The object of their wrath this time was the 100th Battalion OP on Hill 165, and the battering became so severe that the HQ section had to completely flee the position.[70] At noon, the Germans shelled the 3rd Battalion, 133rd, CP at Caira—just as Sweeting arrived to confer with Major Chapman.[71] Neither commander was injured, but the Germans seemed to know precisely where each and every American OP and CP was located.

A new tank/infantry attack on the jail was rescheduled for 1300. Sweeting arrived at the OP near town at 1240 to help coordinate the operation.[72] During the morning, the 3rd Battalion, 133rd, captured several more stone houses utilizing the tried-and-true bazooka blast method.[73] Supplies of hand grenades and TNT blocks, however, were running low.[74] The infantry continued encountering well-fortified positions built inside the homes. These were often constructed from steel-reinforced concrete capable of withstanding even direct 105mm artillery blasts. In some cases, bunkers were resupplied via reinforced tunnels—so artillery had no effect whatsoever.[75] Only tanks firing concrete piercing rounds in close coordination with steely-nerved infantrymen could dislodge the Germans from such places.

Major Chapman's 3rd Battalion learned "shock action" was the key to successfully capturing a position and keeping their own casualties to a minimum. Artillery, mortar, aerial bombardment or supporting tank fire was wasted if not followed immediately with an infantry assault. If a target could be stormed before a stunned enemy could return to their guns, success was all but assured—even a few moments of hesitation allowed the German defenders time to recover and beat back an attack.[76] The most effective way of delivering this devastating, morale-shattering shock was from the barrel of a companion M4 tank.[77]

Under skies still dreary and overcast, a two-tank section from C Company, 756th, trundled from the quarry toward town. The crews halted briefly to dismount and attach tow cables to a tank previously knocked-out near the edge of town. After dragging the charred hulk far enough to gain a clearer passage, the crews returned to their seats and continued.[78] The pair then swung eastward along the back road leading to the jail. Because the two disabled C Company, 756th, tanks still blocked the far end, the new section took up positions behind them and awaited infantry instructions—which came right away. They blasted the jail. They blasted the long nunnery building 200 yards beyond. They blasted nearby houses, creating "shock action" so the infantry could sweep through immediately afterwards. If a house proved too dangerous to approach, the tanks leveled it to the ground. Even if the Germans returned to the ruins afterwards, they were, at least, deprived of overhead protection against mortar and artillery.[79]

After two hours utilizing such close tank support, the infantry secured five more houses,[80] moved closer to the jail, and captured seven prisoners. At one point, Sweeting directed M-10 TD fire into a building north of the jail.[81] By 1500 hours, the jail appeared close to falling.[82] Sweeting alerted his reserve tank crews at the quarry to prepare to storm the town and sweep east of the jail should the infantry breach the walls.[83]

Then the rains hit. Visibility deteriorated rapidly and the townscape washed into featureless blocks of gray. Because the tank crews and supporting artillery could no longer see their targets, the infantry halted, took cover wherever available and shivered beneath steady showers lasting well into the evening.[84] At the same time, weather conditions turned far worse on the nearby massif—where freezing drizzle and blinding snow squalls positively tormented the troops of the 168th and 135th.[85]

The bone-chilling rain foiled the progress of the 100th Battalion as well. The Nisei troops struggled to reduce two tough bunkers near a large house behind the castle. All the while, heavy sniper fire sprayed down on them from the high slope leading up to the abbey. They tried blasting the bunkers with 60mm mortar fire—but without effect. Heavier 4.2-inch mortar support was considered but ruled out due to the proximity of friendly troops. At the 100th's immediate left at the same time, the 1st Battalion attempted to claw up Castle Hill against withering S/A fire pouring down from the ruined castle itself.[86] The rains, however, deprived both battalions of vital smoke cover, and the troops were left clinging against the rocky hillside, soaked to the skin, and unable budge in any direction without drawing fire.[87] They had to remain as such until nightfall, when it was safe to move again.

At 1700, Lt Col Sweeting and Captain Arnold arrived at Major Chapman's 3rd Battalion, 133rd, CP to discuss plans for the following day, but discovered none had yet been prepared or delivered.[88] Sweeting hurried over to Colonel Marshall's CP and the two officers sat down to draft one. The results included strong tank involvement.[89]

At 1900, Sweeting met with all of his company commanders. Lt Perkins was ordered to lead a small force of both C and D Company tanks into town after dark and remove the two disabled tanks near the jail. It was imperative for both to be removed before daylight.[90] After sunrise, Lt Redle's B Company would attack with the infantry. Two tanks would take the road east of the jail where one would assume a spot at the northeast corner and the other would halt about 200 yards southeast of the jail. Redle's remaining tanks would then push from the north. Once the jail fell, tanks would then sweep beyond to the east. One platoon would help secure the large field between the jail and the nunnery, and the other platoon would skirt east of the nunnery to concentrate on the city block nearby.[91] If all went well, the OP would be relocated to Castle Hill by day's end.[92]

The downed bridge near the town square was also discussed. The engineers determined that fill gravel would not be enough to bridge the spillway and a new fifteen-foot bridge had to be constructed instead. Because of German observation, the engineers elected to build the sections away from town, transport the pieces by truck at night, and then use a T2 tank recovery vehicle to position them.[93]

Two 756th men were wounded in action during 10 February: 2nd Lt Andrew D. Orient of A Company, and S/Sgt William Fodor of C Company.[94] The battalion's operational tanks count stood at forty-one, with twenty-eight others still under repairs and twenty-two lost to date. The attached 760th C Company tanks figures were as follows: twelve fit, two under repairs, and eight lost to date.[95] Later that evening, all tanks operating west of the Rapido withdrew to Hill 213 for resupply and maintenance.[96]

Once the meeting concluded, Sweeting sent Captain Arnold to the 3rd Battalion, 133rd, CP to brief Chapman's staff on the new plan.[97] Sweeting also arranged to personally interrogate four German prisoners at his CP in Caira.[98] Although the questioning lasted well over an hour,[99] hardly anything new was gleaned—other than confirmation of an AT gun positioned among a row of block houses west of the nunnery. This location had already been strongly suspected.[100]

At 2200, Major Chapman stopped at the 756th CP in Caira so as to be absolutely clear on the plan.[101] While he met with Sweeting, German artillery pummeled 133rd Regiment positions on Hills 175, 193, and along the entire roadway running from Cassino to the barracks. At one point, phone communications to all three battalions cut out completely on account of severed wires. The 1st and 3rd Battalions tried renewing the attack during the night—particularly targeting buildings at the south side of the square, but intense German mortar and artillery countermeasures made maneuver virtually impossible.[102]

At 2145 a key building west of the square was finally captured and four prisoners were taken. The captives identified themselves as members of the 6th and 7th Companies, 211th Grenadier Regiment (71st Infantry Division).[103] One prisoner reported the 7th Company had been deployed along the spillway, between the downed bridge and the jail, several days earlier. But after enduring intense tank fire, he and his comrades had been forced to flee. They sought refuge at their CP near the nunnery—only to find the location in flames. As a result, the CP staff had been forced to relocate deeper in town. When the American infantry failed to storm the position and the tanks withdrew, however, the Germans returned during the night to those same houses along the spillway.[104] This was one glaring example of how the Americans failed to take full advantage of the tanks' "shock action." Had the infantry stormed immediately and held those houses, the jail's western flank and the square's eastern flank might have fallen to American forces days earlier.

During the mid-afternoon, two other prisoners were pulled from beneath a bridge roughly a hundred yards northeast of the jail.[105] Both were 19-year-olds—one a private and the other a corporal—and yielded a trove of intelligence. They revealed they had been assigned to the position that very morning and gave the exact locations to several MG nests nearby. One light MG was set inside a bunker behind the first house east of the jail, and two others were posted near the jail entrance at the southwest corner. They also reported two SP guns—one equipped with a 75mm and the other with a 105mm gun—lay hidden near the nunnery's church. The young enlistees also confirmed that several other 211th Regiment companies were stationed in town, but the units were running low on men and living off canned rations pre-stocked inside the bunkers. 8 February was the last time any supplies had arrived to them from the rear.[106] They described how American artillery and tank fire had caused countless casualties over the last few days. The 6th Company CP was located inside the jail—but battle attrition had reduced the entire company down to only twenty-two men—ten of whom ran the CP. Another fifteen from the 14th Company were also posted inside the jail. A bunker behind the first house east of the prison also housed nine men—including several prisoners of war. They revealed their battalion CP was located inside a school building much deeper in town and identified Lieutenant Koch as their company commander, Captain Muller as their battalion commander, and Major Knutt as the regimental CO.[107]

This intelligence was extremely useful—if it could be corroborated. Usually, German prisoners were remarkably talkative during interrogations and generally provided trustworthy information.

As brutal as the fighting could be at times, there were still extraordinary incidents of compassion. One night, a team of American litter bearers seeking out the wounded, mistakenly wandered into a German-held part of town. Two German NCOs intercepted them, but instead of harming or taking the men captive, escorted them to their own aid station deeper in town. The Americans were only cautioned to look straight ahead or risk being shot. They arrived to find several wounded American infantrymen lying about the floor. The Germans explained they did not have the proper medicine or supplies to take care of them and even helped load the wounded men upon litters before escorting the Americans back to their lines.[108]

Another time, however, Germans defending a house foolishly shot several American litter bearers clearly operating under Red Cross flags. The men of I Company, 133rd, became so enraged at the sight, they surrounded the building and killed every single German inside, including several who tried surrendering.[109] Under Geneva Convention principles, medics on both sides were unarmed and considered "non-combatants." Shooting one without cause invited summary death. Unfortunately, these same rules were not observed on the European Eastern Front or in the South Pacific.

While German artillery continued falling, Lt Redle met at the quarry near his tank with 1st Lt William F. Bouch. In his capacity as battalion transportation officer, Bouch made rounds each evening sharing the latest aerial photos with every company commander. The two young men were old friends from ROTC training at Creighton, and Redle looked forward to seeing his former classmate each night. The quarry was shielded by high granite on three sides, and generally tucked safely below the trajectory angle of most German artillery. On this particular night, however, a shell burst right on the rocky rim just above Redle's tank, showering both officers with sharp shards of stone. Redle was unhurt, but Bouch's leg was left a mangled mess and the stricken officer had to be evacuated.[110]

Due to ammunition shortage concerns, the 34th Division's artillery activities had been restricted throughout the day. Only seventy-three rounds of 155mm, 172 rounds of 105mm, and 675 rounds of 3-inch artillery were expended over the preceding twenty-four hours.[111] Fortunately, a more detailed review of Allied ammunition stocks had been taken in the meantime. This one overturned the original supply assessment and Fifth Army gun batteries received "all-clear" orders to resume firing their usual ammunition allowances.[112] Sidelined artillerymen, who had been dawdling in sandbagged dens east of the Rapido tossed aside their solitaire cards, rumpled comics and secondhand magazines to return to their familiar camouflaged gun positions.[113] At 2000 hours, Allied batteries erupted again with such ferocity, the entire valley seemed to howl in pain.[114]

German air activity was conspicuously absent. Only two enemy recon aircraft appeared during the course of the day—buzzing briefly over Monte Lungo and Monte Trocchio before disappearing again.[115] The last German air attack occurred 8 February, when three ME-109s divebombed Monte Trocchio, and one of those had been blown from the sky by retributive AA fire.[116]

***

As midnight approached, 1st Battalion, 168th, Regiment troops were relieved by the 141st Regiment in the snow-covered highlands. It was a case, however, of the weak replacing the weaker. Relief for the depleted 1st Battalion, 168th, had been long overdue, but 141st rolls were terribly understaffed as well. Nearly three weeks had passed since the 36th Division's atrocious Rapido crossing beating—and yet many units continued limping along at only fifty percent combat strength.[117] Few replacements could be integrated in the intervening time. This exchange of weary troops attracted a smattering of German artillery fire, but little else. Even the enemy seemed exhausted. By 2300 hours, the sorry swap was complete.[118]

***

At 0430, 11 February, Lt Perkins reported the two disabled C Company, 756th tanks near the jail had been successfully cleared by T2 recovery vehicles.[119] At 0530, the 756th's OP party left Caira for Cassino to prepare ahead of the morning attack.[120] Captain Arnold normally accompanied the OP party, but was delayed an hour while attending to battalion business.[121] As the operations officer (S-3), Arnold enjoyed little sleep. The tall blond Texan worked tirelessly keeping the crews fed, the tanks stocked, and everyone fighting where they were supposed to be fighting. Arnold personally reconnoitered most attack points and supply routes beforehand so he could anticipate and correct any issues.[122] This attention to logistical detail and the humane concern Arnold showed for the tank crews made him a highly respected battalion officer.

Intermittent rain showers continued rolling through the night, keeping everyone everywhere soaking wet and shivering cold.[123] Even hot coffee and the pittance of heat radiating from portable U.S. Army gasoline stoves failed to alleviate the misery.[124] At dawn's first light, faint blue wisps of smoke could be seen rising from the chimneys of the jail and several other houses in town. Evidently, the Germans also needed warmth, so the howitzers of the 133rd Cannon Company pounced on those smoky positions with 75mm HE shells—giving the occupants the extra heat they desired.[125]

As was his early morning custom, Lt Redle set out for town to coordinate plans with the front-line infantry officers.[126] With his tanks assuming the lead this day, Redle was particularly eager about gathering all the details. Generally, the infantry officers pointed out particular walls, buildings or doorways they wanted blasted down so their men could storm inside afterwards. The walk from the quarry to town was the most dangerous part of the journey—as this section of road was under constant surveillance by German observers further south. Very early on, Redle learned the value of hyperawareness, and scanned constantly for any places the Germans might hide mines, MG nests, AT traps or observation posts.[127] Cassino, however, taught him discretion was also essential: one remained hyperalert, but moved without appearing threatening to an enemy observer. As a result, Redle strolled boldly down from the quarry each morning—knowing full well Germans with binoculars were watching his every step. Never once, did he draw fire. All veteran soldiers walked to town showing similar confidence. One day, a new infantry sergeant, fearful of being seen—crept, dodged, and dashed his way down from the quarry. The Germans shot and killed him before he ever reached town.[128] A nervous American made them nervous as well.

Once in town, Redle also never walked directly to an infantry OP or CP. He would, instead, take circuitous routes behind stone walls and around rubble piles to avoid giving away the position.[129] On this day, after completing the perilous journey, Redle tracked down the local infantry officers—only to learn the carefully planned morning attack had been cancelled. The news came as a big surprise and Redle returned to the quarry somewhat perplexed.[130]

Sweeting found Major Chapman at the 3rd Battalion, 133rd, CP and confirmed this last-minute change had been ordered from above.[131] Maj Gen Ryder wanted the 133rd's attack in town postponed until after the 135th and 168th Regiments commenced a new offensive in the highlands later that morning. In the meantime, Chapman's men used the delay to neutralize a few more problem houses while the engineers cleared away more debris—particularly along the east-west roadway abutting the spillway and leading past the jail.[132] Sweeting decided to use the lull to send Redle's tanks into town ahead of the attack. There, his crews would resume pounding the jail and strike another problem building further south.[133] At 0800, Sweeting left for the quarry to communicate this adjustment to Redle's crews.[134]

Meanwhile, a four-man team of mine-sweeping engineers cautiously removed bodies scattered across a minefield near the Rapido.[135] The work was still too dangerous for Graves Registration personnel. Although the weather was always chilly, the temperatures never stayed cold enough to suppress the awful stench of decaying flesh. The nauseating odor was even worse in town. American and German victims had become so intermingled among the collapsed floors, pulverized walls, and blasted debris that none could be recovered until such time as bulldozers could be brought in. As a result, Cassino always reeked of a slaughterhouse sewer.[136] The vomit-inducing stench permeated wet wool clothing and lingered with the pungent body odors of the unwashed living. One could always identify a front-line soldier by his smell alone.

At 1030, 3rd Battalion, 133rd, infantrymen reported more progress assaulting a row of houses near the jail. The 1st and 100th Battalions held steady on Hill 165 and the steep slope below Castle Hill. Two platoons of engineers from A Company, 109th Engineers Battalion wrapped up assigned work filling holes, leveling out sections of roadway, and clearing a wider path along the spillway.[137] As a heavy slew of artillery shells dispatched by 175th Field Artillery Battalion batteries roared, cracked, and boomed across the cloud-shrouded massif,[138] the Americans in Cassino below waited to hear of the progress of their "Red Bull" brethren above.[139]

***

The II Corps' very last attempt to capture Monastery Hill commenced at 1100. Weather conditions were atrocious on account of thick overcast skies, freezing rain mixed with flurries, and persistent biting crosswinds scouring the barren ridges. At times, snow swirled so heavily in pelting squalls that visibility dropped down to only a few feet.[140] Despite these daunting conditions, the haggard, depleted troops of all four American regiments—the 141st, 142nd, 135th, and 168th attacked at once.[141] The 142nd anchoring the far-right flank and holding high ground from Monte Castellone to Point 706—faced off against German-held Colle S'Angelo several hundred yards further west. On the 142nd's left, the 135th pushed toward the ruined Albaneta Farm, also laying to the west. The 1st Battalion, 141st, squeezed between 135th and 168th positions upon the eastern slope of Hill 593, was given the mission of storming over the hilltop to seize German-held hills south of the Albaneta Farm. The 168th on the far-left flank was given the responsibility of taking the abbey.[142] To generate the greatest possible pressure, all four regiments attacked at once—with dim hopes of creating some exploitable breach somewhere in the German line.

As with previous attacks, the Germans showed little reaction at first, but once the Americans crawled out into the open among the rocky crags and crevices, the Germans ratcheted up the S/A and MG fire. Before long, German artillery and mortar also burst heavily all along the American forward line.[143]

Ryder's exact attack instructions to Colonel Marshall were: "When the top of hill falls and they start coming down the side then the 133rd will make an all-out effort to take town."[144] Because of the sagging cloud ceiling, it was impossible to see the hills from the valley, so for the next hour, Marshall's troops were forced to wait for a phone call.[145] By noon, blinding snow made it impossible for the troops fighting on the hills to even see each other.[146] The II Corps, also nervous for news, phoned each of the four regiments involved, but nobody could report anything other than everyone "jumped off on time."[147] Five minutes later, a few more details filtered through and none were promising. The 141st reported "very little if any progress."[148] The 168th was engaged in a "considerable battle from right to left" and the 135th also described moving "very slowly."[149] German defenses showed no signs of cracking anywhere.

By 1330, cracks of frustration, however, began appearing among the American commanders. Colonel Boatner of the 168th complained: "It seems that 593 is the key to the whole situation, we believe Lynch should attack it and just fire on it. As it is, it is holding up the 168th."[150]

Boatner's criticism was misplaced: Lt Col George E. Lynch commanded the 142nd. It was Lt Col Aaron W. Wyatt who was in charge of the 141st.[151] Wyatt's problems had been greatly complicated once the Germans retook Hill 593 the previous night. Wyatt had been told erroneously that this critical hilltop was under American control when he first moved his 1st Battalion troops in the area around the same time.[152] Over the last forty-eight hours, the scrapping over Hill 593 had grown so confusing that nobody really knew who held it at any given moment.[153]

Ryder agreed to pass along Boatner's suggestion to the 36th HQ but admonished his colonel: "Yes but we will not try to run the 36th Division."[154]

Apparently, Boatner's criticism left some sting. Three minutes later, the 141st reported troops progressing toward Hill 593 to help shore up 168th right rear flank.[155] By 1340, the 141st reported troops still on the move, but now it was Boatner's 168th men who had been halted by withering fire and unable to move at all.[156]

***

As the blizzardy highland drama unfolded a mile to the west, all nine of Lt Redle's remaining tanks rolled into town—taking up firing positions across the north edge.[157] One platoon spread out along the road leading to the jail and immediately began blasting into the northwest wall.[158] Another section of tanks covered the repositioning of a third section moving further eastward to fire into buildings south of the jail.[159] A Company, firing from dug-in positions across the river a half-mile away, joined in the pummeling.[160] From their valley vantage point, the A Company crews often observed German vehicles traveling the long switchback road toward the abbey. While monitoring the radio chatter between tank crews, Redle heard S/Sgt Harris of A Company directing his platoon's fire upon a German command car attempting to mount the snaking roadway. Their bracketing had trapped the car between two curves, with no hope of escape. Redle got called away from the radio and never did learn the outcome, but suspected the car didn't survive S/Sgt Harris's firing orders.[161]

The 133rd Infantry kept waiting to hear news of 168th troops spilling down over the hillside, but as of 1400 hours it hadn't happened yet. In the meantime, Redle's tanks blasted into the jail while Nisei troops worked to capture problem bunkers behind the castle. Everybody else in the 133rd fidgeted in a holding pattern.[162]

Around the same time, the Fifth Army staff grew anxious for an update.[163] The 135th had just finished beating back a frenetic German counterattack.[164] The 141st described resistance in their area as "heavy." News from the other two regiments was somewhat more encouraging: the 142nd pressed on between Hills 468 and 569 against "light moderate fire,"[165] while 168th troops "inched forward" toward the monastery.[166] By 1515, 141st troops approached Hill 468 just south of Massa Albaneta.[167] Forty-five minutes later, Companies E and F of the 142nd joined the attack near the hillcrest—despite frantic German shelling of their rear positions between points 444 and 569.[168]

At 1530, Sweeting and Arnold stopped by the 3rd Battalion, 133rd, CP to discuss plan changes.[169] With the day drawing to a close, time had dwindled away to launch any coordinated infantry/tank attack. Throughout the afternoon, though, Redle's crews expended a total of 750 rounds of new concrete piercing ammunition into the thick walls of the jail—some from as close as thirty yards away. The mission was hugely successful—especially so, because no crewmembers had been wounded or killed in the operation.[170] But with ammunition bins nearly barren, Redle's crews withdrew for the evening.[171]

Major Chapman wanted his 3rd Battalion, 133rd, troops to attempt a night attack upon the jail, and felt confident they would triumph.[172] Tanks couldn't support night attacks, so Chapman requested the tank destroyers positioned near the barracks continue blasting the jail's walls until nightfall. Sweeting passed along the major's request with instructions for one round to be fired every three minutes.[173]

***

As dusk descended over the snow swept highlands, visibility remained poor and progress problematic.[174] At 1800, the 135th held a shaky line southeast of the Albaneta Farm with the 1st Battalion on the right and the 2nd Battalion on the left.[175] The 1st Battalion, 168th, reported positions to the left of the 2nd Battalion, 141st, on nearby Hill 593.[176] Both American and German artillery continued exploding in constant cacophony across the frozen massif. During the day, the 34th Division batteries, alone, expended an absurd number of shells: 4,455 rounds of 105mm, 1,345 rounds of 155mm, and 2,000 rounds of 3-inch howitzer.[177] But because of the poor visibility, only five enemy gun flashes could be seen and answered with counterbattery. Twenty-six other locations, however, had been identified via acoustic methods.[178] The artillery batteries did not rest after nightfall. With a new infantry attack forming in town, every big Allied gun barrel remained piping-hot keeping the Germans at bay.

At 1930, Sweeting instructed 1st Lt Robert Kremer, D Company CO, to send two M5s into town and move a disabled German vehicle blocking the roadway north of the jail.[179] A short time later, Sweeting called Colonel Marshall to coordinate tactics for the following morning. Marshall informed him the infantry had no plans involving tanks.[180] Around the same time, Sweeting also learned the 2nd Platoon, A Company, 760th, had been detached from 756th Tank Battalion and reunited with the 760th.[181] With no battle plans and a few less tanks at his disposal, the disappointed battalion commander returned to his CP in Caira for the evening.[182]

At 2030 the 36th Infantry Division reported a German counterattack pouring down from Colle S'Angelo involving heavy mortar and artillery fire. The 3rd Battalion, 142nd, positions bore the brunt of this shocking new assault. Companies I and K heroically held the line, but their combined numbers had dwindled down to only twenty-five defenders.[183] At 2150, the 36th reported their troops had finally taken Hill 468 near the Albaneta Farm.[184] If this report was ever true, the Germans quickly recaptured the position.[185] Hill 593 nearby had also fallen under firm German control.[186] At the same hour, the 168th settled in, established defenses, and dispatched perimeter patrols.[187] The II Corps' day-long attack in the highlands could boast of marginal gains here and there, but had utterly failed to break the German line.

***

Meanwhile, in the north section of Cassino, the 133rd massed before their daring night attack. At 2210, the 1st Battalion shifted positions away from their Castle Hill lines to free troops for the main assault upon the jail—set to commence an hour before dawn. The 100th Battalion ran out of explosives while attempting to capture the two stubborn bunkers behind the Castle, and asked for flamethrowers.[188] These frightening weapons had been tried once earlier in town, but failed to function due to rushed and improper training.[189] Three men from A Company, 109th Engineering Battalion, completed the two hours of necessary practice and reported to the 133rd for duty.[190] In the meantime, the 3rd Battalion, 133rd, dispatched a recon patrol that, somehow, ended up capturing a few more houses.[191]

At midnight, 12 February, an unexpected hush enveloped Cassino. The 3rd and 100th Battalions reported no German activity whatsoever, and the 1st Battalion heard only a few sporadic bursts of artillery fire near them.[192] At 0200, Caira shook under a brief but violent flurry—proving that German batteries had not forgotten about them.[193] All the while, the 1st and 3rd Battalions picked up the pace of their staging. The Germans suspected something was in the works and sprayed generous bursts of MG fire pinging up the darkened streets. [194] The harassing fire grew so persistent that by 0222, the 168th, hearing the racket a full mile away, called to make sure everything was okay.[195] L Company dispatched two separate patrols toward the jail, but the Germans saw them and drove them away.[196]

By 0400, the Germans grew so suspicious over the American nighttime movements that they pounded Caira and the road leading down through the barracks with a flurry of mortar and artillery fire lasting well over an hour.[197] Six parked vehicles in Caira belonging to the 756th Tank Battalion's medical detachment were shredded to bits. Fortunately, no medical personnel had taken refuge in them at the time.[198] By 0525, the mistrustful shelling lessened somewhat—but did not fully subside.

The 136th and 168th suffered under a similar artillery barrage beginning at 0400. Everything from mortar and Nebelwerfer to "heavier stuff" such as 150mm shells burst all around them—mostly shrieking in from positions north of Piedimonte.[199] The men complained of, at least, twenty-seven separate waves of "screaming meemies" exploding all around them. Even by 0530, the intensity hadn't let up at all.[200] "Everyone is calling for counter-battery," the 34th Division G-3 recorded.[201]

Strangely, very little German artillery fell over the north sections of Cassino during the same time span.[202] At 0430, Lt Kremer informed Sweeting that the efforts to remove the disabled German SP gun near the jail were unsuccessful. The T2, attempting to winch the wreck, became stuck and a medium tank had to be called forward to rescue the T2.[203]

At the same time the 100th Battalion reported they were still chipping away at the two problem bunkers. The 1st Battalion had nearly completed repositioning north of the jail—creating a new left flank for the 3rd Battalion.[204] A Company closed at 0430 as C Company filtered in behind them.[205] More patrols were dispatched but could not infiltrate any approach toward the jail without drawing fire.[206]

A full attack jumped off around 0500, but was driven back quickly by mortar and MG fire emanating from the northeast corner of the jail. A second attack was attempted immediately, but was also thwarted by similar resistance. At 0530, the infantry officers pulled the men back and consulted with Colonel Marshall, who in turn, called Sweeting and asked for tank fire at daylight.[207] Redle was then contacted at the quarry and told to ready two of his tanks for the mission.

In the meantime, the 1st Battalion, 133rd, infantry attempted a third attack—this time with C Company flanking around to the east side of the jail.[208] This maneuver split the attention of the jail defenders and allowed A Company to breach the interior in force.[209] The Germans tried regaining control by pounding the jail's northern edge with suppressive artillery and mortar fire, but a crucial American foothold had been established.[210] For the next two hours, a vicious battle raged inside and no one on the outside knew for certain who held the upper hand.[211]

Just prior to dawn, three green flares whizzed high into the western sky. Nebelwerfer screeched and exploded across the highlands upon 168th positions. Then, a red flare followed by a white one blazed into view, and a concentration of both 150mm artillery and Nebelwerfer rockets exploded a little more to the southwest.[212] At least the cloud ceiling had lifted high enough to reveal the hills from the valley.

The morning was cool and damp, bringing fair visibility.[213] By 0807 the 3rd Battalion, 133rd, reported capturing several more houses near the jail.[214] At the same time, the 1st Battalion reported a full company had infiltrated the jail's interior, with more men sweeping outside around the eastern end.[215] Colonel Marshall wanted to be absolutely certain this critical building was completely secure before passing any news up the chain of command.

A half hour later, the 1st Battalion called Marshall again: everything was now firmly under American control. Only ten Germans were found still alive inside the jail.[216]

Finally, the battered stone fortress had fallen.[217]

U.S. Medal of Honor

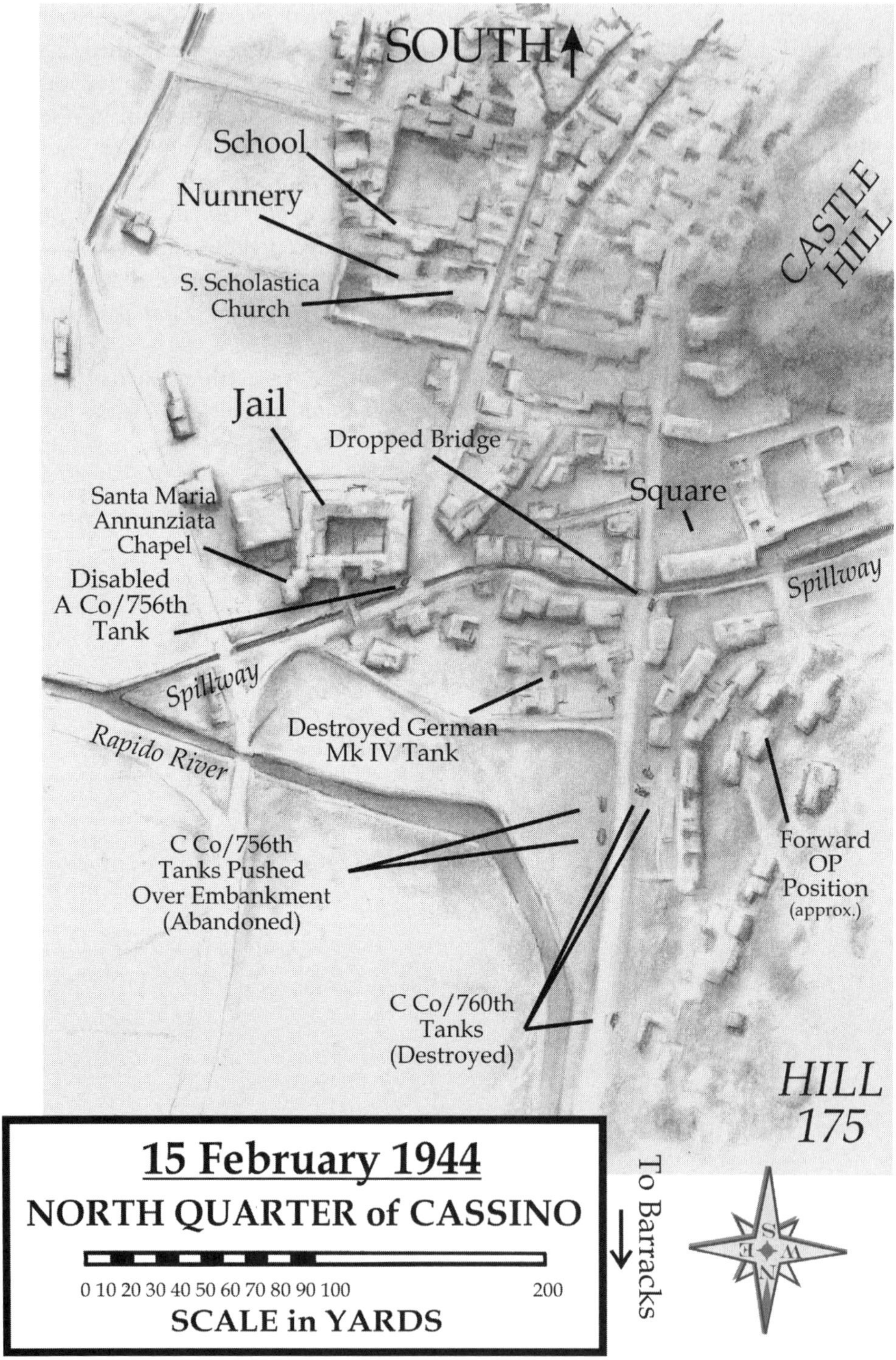
SOUTH
School
Nunnery
S. Scholastica Church
CASTLE HILL
Jail
Dropped Bridge
Santa Maria Annunziata Chapel
Square
Disabled A Co/756th Tank
Spillway
Spillway
Rapido River
Destroyed German Mk IV Tank
C Co/756th Tanks Pushed Over Embankment (Abandoned)
Forward OP Position (approx.)
C Co/760th Tanks (Destroyed)
HILL 175
15 February 1944
NORTH QUARTER of CASSINO
0 10 20 30 40 50 60 70 80 90 100 200
SCALE in YARDS
To Barracks
S
W
E
N

CHAPTER FIVE

Exhaustion: 12 February 1944 to 14 February 1944

At 0835, Lt Col Sweeting arrived at the 133rd Infantry Regiment's Caira CP and learned the good news of the jail's capture.[1] To aid the infantry struggling to expand the battalion's right flank, Sweeting dispatched a section of tanks to town from B Company, 756th's 1st Platoon. Upon arrival, the crews were directed to fire freely into the crumbling buildings along the southern edge of the square—allowing riflemen and BAR men nearby to venture a few yards deeper among rubble piles and collapsed walls.[2] By mid-morning, the efforts led to two more ramshackle houses succumbing to 3rd Battalion squads.[3]

German artillery shells, again, rained down in maelstrom across the highlands and along the battered road leading from Caira into town.[4] The distant shells flashed and burst as rising plumes of smoke and then faded away as delayed thuds echoed across the valley—a dangerous, but strangely intriguing sight to witness from afar. The near ones, however, elicited utter terror: deafening jolts suspending the senses and stunning a victim momentarily inside a whirlwind of splintered stone, pinging metal, choking dust, and nauseating acrid smoke. From 0200 to 0700 an astounding 2,000 German 150mm shells and 210 Nebelwerfer rockets exploded around Caira alone.[5] The barrage reached its highest intensity from 0400 to 0700 hours.[6] By 0820, the bombardment ended on Caira and the road leading to Cassino, but continued falling across the massif.[7] Concerned again over the security of his regiment's right flank, Colonel Marshall inquired on the condition of the 135th and 168th Regiments,[8] and was told communications to both regiments had been out since 0636[9]—probably the result of the phone lines running down to Caira having been severed. Marshall, still troubled, told the 34th Division he would dispatch two of his own officers on foot to contact both regiments and report back.[10]

The 135th Infantry Regiment complained to divisional HQ again about the lack of American counterbattery response: "We were shelled in Caira for 3½ hours this morning. Was anything done this morning?" Divisional artillery explained that their Cub planes could not fly during the night to hunt for German guns, and that their own counterbattery outfit was still recovering after suffering two direct hits.[11]

When questioned again twenty minutes later, divisional artillery replied testily: "We have three OPs looking for enemy guns and they have done some adjusting. We are doing all we can to stop it."[12] Nerves were fraying.

In the meantime, the 3rd and 1st Battalions of the 133rd pressed forward with slow, steady success. The 2nd Chemical Mortar Battalion lobbed their deadly, splintering 4.2-inch rounds deeper into Cassino to help support the advance. This coordinated fire enabled the 3rd Battalion to clear several more houses west of the jail.[13]

At 1032, the 133rd asked for a full company of engineers to come to town, clear mines, and make road repairs for tank passage.[14] Unfortunately, all the 34th Division's assigned members of the 109th Engineers Battalion were given other tasks and unavailable. The 133rd tried contacting the II Corps to beg help from their engineers, but the phone lines were out. At 1105, the 109th Engineers responded, and promised to send any of their available men, but would try to first secure those who had worked in town the previous night—since they already had familiarity with the conditions.[15]

By 1130, both the 1st and 3rd Battalions of the 133rd advanced southward of the jail drawing only S/A fire in the process. Eight more prisoners were captured.[16] Two taken the previous day confirmed the jail had housed the CP to the 6th Company, 211th Grenadier Regiment before its fall.[17] When asked about their food situation, the German prisoners said hot food arrived when American artillery was not too heavy. The food truck stopped at a farmhouse roughly two miles south of town.[18] They also reported their battalion CP had relocated in the nunnery building south of the jail.[19] Two SP guns guarded the CP. They also revealed the white flares signaled "raise artillery fire."[20]

Lt Redle walked down to Cassino, as he did every morning—but in order to locate the infantry officers, he had to meander all the way over to the jail. He found American troops inside delighted to finally enjoy overhead cover again. Scores of discarded German helmets cluttered the hallways and dim cells. Redle had never seen so many lying about in one place. Blood was splattered all over the concrete floors and walls—fresh, slick maroon puddles congealing over older russet stains, with the damp stagnant air of a slaughterhouse. The jail had served as a collecting station for the many casualties suffered under four straight days of intensive tank and artillery fire. Evidently, those casualties were evacuated before the building was overrun. Maimed or dying men no longer needed helmets, so such items were left behind.[21]

At noon, 12 February, Redle ordered a second section of tanks over to the town square to aid the 3rd Battalion.[22] The weather stayed a cool thirty-five degrees, but at least the rain and snow had ceased. The low cloud cover returned, however, bringing poor visibility throughout the area.[23] No aircraft from either side could take to the skies.[24]

The 1st Battalion, 133rd troops crept nearly 200 yards beyond the jail—encountering only sporadic S/A fire and a few odd bursts of artillery here and there.[25]

Apparently, the Germans still reeled over their losses and were uncertain of the location of their own forward line. Nevertheless, the Americans proceeded with extreme caution for fear of a trap. They had been deceived before by such lulls, and there was no way to tell the difference.

The officers Colonel Marshall dispatched to contact the 135th and 168th reported that phone lines to both regiments remained dead, but radio contact with the division had resumed.[26] Marshall was relieved to learn, at least, that both regiments still existed.

At 1240, Maj Gen Ryder phoned Marshall in Caira to discuss the progress of his regiment. Marshall expressed alarm over the communications problems vexing the 135th and 168th above. Because of these worries, he decided to keep the 100th Battalion on Hill 165 to shield the operations of the 1st and 3rd Battalions in town.[27]

Ryder wasn't concerned in the least about the severed phones lines:

"Keep going and shove the 2nd Battalion in around if you have to. Put them on the left if you want. Get buttoned up and shove on through," the old general urged.

The progress of Marshall's troops was one bright spot in the II Corps' 26-hour-old all-out attack. The rest of the area news had been lackluster.

Marshall asked Ryder if any new highland attacks were scheduled for the evening. Ryder replied that his plans were to remain in place, maintain pressure, and patrol toward the abbey. The following evening, however, new orders would be given that he could not yet discuss.[28]

***

By the early afternoon, some severed phone lines were restored, and the 168th provided a more detailed report: the highland situation had remained relatively quiet the past few hours, with no signs of German offensive preparations.[29] The 168th troop positions had been badly battered but still held. Contact patrols with the 135th, 141st, and 142nd reported all three of those regiments also holding steady under relative calm.[30] Conditions were essentially static. The 168th inquired about new orders, and was told to sit tight and await further instructions arriving later in the day. The new orders teased of "relief."[31] Just hearing the word brought hope.

***

At 1330, Sweeting dispatched a section of B Company tanks to the jail in support of the 1st Battalion's advance on the nunnery. Much tank fire was directed into a large school building just beyond the nunnery, which had emerged as a hive of trouble. A bald-headed German appeared on the balcony of a nearby house, to the front of Sgt Hamilton A. Smith's tank. The hatless soldier brazenly raised a rifle and fired an AT grenade squarely at Smith's head. Fortunately, the round missed and exploded off to the rear. Smith, impressed by the man's audacity, dispatched of him nonetheless with a single HE round from his main gun.[32] The infantry operating a short distance away beckoned over S/Sgt Haspel's tank to rescue some buddies trapped on the upper floor of another building. Germans had returned to the lower floor after the Americans had cleared through and moved upstairs. Haspel pulled within thirty yards of the target, fired seven quick rounds of HE into the lower floor, and paused. After a few moments, a smiling infantryman stuck his head out a lower storey window and waved to Haspel. All was well again.[33] A third M4 crew exhausted their entire stock of ammunition firing into the school building further south. After they withdrew, a freshly stocked M4 promptly assumed the vacated position and continued with the steady blasting.[34]

While watching events unfold from the hillside OP near town, Sweeting radioed Sgt Haskell Oliver and told him to prepare to move over to the east side of the jail. From there, his crew could open up a new angle of fire. At the same time, Sweeting alerted the TDs positioned back at the barracks and ordered his battalion mortar platoon to lay covering smoke along the east side of town.[35] As the new smoke dropped and billowed, Sweeting ordered Sgt Oliver to move.

Oliver, a rock-solid, square-jawed[36] rancher from California,[37] took command of Johannesen's tank after the tall blond staff sergeant was seriously wounded in that nighttime artillery attack nine days earlier. Though knocked out during the same incident, the gutsy sergeant recovered and stayed on duty. Oliver and his seasoned crew knew Sweeting was asking them to make a risky move. Once their cover lifted at their new position, they would have little time to identify danger.

Oliver's driver, T/5 Roy L. Anderson, nosed the M4 past the eastern wall as the smoke dissipated. Somewhere deeper inside the town, a large-caliber German AT gun opened fire. A snarling, red-hot round streaked over the heads of American infantrymen crawling across the field between the jail and nunnery—narrowly missing the front corner of Oliver's tank. Anderson instinctively yanked the steering controls into reverse and pulled back behind the protection of the wall. Sweeting's excited voice crackled in over Oliver's radio: he had seen the shot come from the barrel of a German Mark IV lurking at a street junction southwest of the nunnery.

"Should I take care of the infantry's mission first or take care of that tank first?" Oliver asked.

Sweeting's laughter filled their headsets—that same giddy hooting he let fly several days earlier after German MG bullets shredded his overcoat.[38]

Of course, he wanted Sgt Oliver to challenge the Mark IV first!

Because the battalion radio operated on only one open channel, all tank crews listened to the tense drama unfolding. A Mark IV tank was roughly the same size as an M4, but its 75mm main gun was, at least, fifty percent more powerful. It was also better armored and presented a lower silhouette.[39]

Oliver dismounted and peered past the corner of a stone wall. Once he located the menacing German tank through his binoculars, he returned to his crew and had each one dismount in turn to do the same. Afterwards, the five tankers congregated near the hull to discuss their best course of action. Superior teamwork would be necessary to even the odds.

Anderson returned to his driver's position on the left, lowered the seat, and buttoned down the top hatch. As he adjusted his periscope and headset, Pvt George C. Davis slithered down into his seat at the bow gunner's post and checked to make sure the MG belt was properly seated and slackened.[40] Directly behind both men, Oliver and his turret crew also prepared their stations. T/5 Edward J. Sadowski, the burly Pittsburgh steel worker, prepositioned five AP rounds on the turret floor below the loader's seat.[41] He then crouched next to the main gun, swung his left knee across the seat while planting his right foot firmly to the rear. This athletic stance enabled Sadowski's big muscular arms to feed the breech block with almost superhuman efficiency.[42]

The gunner, T/4 Bert L. Bulen, was a small Oklahoman blessed with excellent reflexes and extraordinary vision.[43] As a sport hunter in civilian life, he often astonished his friends by spotting deer in the distance long before anybody else could see them.[44]

Three of these men had trained as a crew since Fort Lewis, and although Sgt Oliver was their new commander, he trained alongside them with other crews.[45] They had become an extremely tight and efficient team—indeed, their very lives depended upon that coordination at this very moment.

Sgt Oliver checked his throat mic and adjusted the commander's seat to a point where his head rose only partway out the hatch, providing him with a wide field of vision. He then asked Anderson to ease the tank forward to the wall's edge and stop. Bulen peered intently through his gun sights while firmly grasping the turret's pistol control grip with his right hand. His muddy left boot hovered just above the fire switch on the floor. Sadowski already had planted an AP round firmly in breech—ready to fly.

Anderson halted the M4 so the crew could draw one more long breath. Oliver asked a final time if they were ready and then gave the order to move forward. Anderson shoved the throttle lever down and threw forward the steering controls. As the tank lurched past the wall, Anderson pulled back the right lever, spinning the frontal plate toward the Mark IV lurking only 200 yards away. At the same time, Bulen swung the turret around and leveled the gunsight's reticle pattern directly on target—firing the first shot before the sights had even settled. The round struck paydirt, and the Mark IV shuddered with a loud bang. As the hot, empty casing ejected from the smoking breech, but before clattering to the floor, Sadowski slammed home another AP round and Bulen fired again. A proficient loader could cycle each nineteen-pound round through the breech every five seconds. Sadowski did it in two. Bulen fired off shells as quickly as the big steeler seated them, and in less than ten seconds, all five AP rounds had been pumped into the smoldering hull of the

Mark IV. Anderson reversed the tank back behind the wall—in case some other unseen SP gun or German tank lurked nearby, intent on vengeance.[46]

Over in the western part of town, the 3rd Battalion continued attacking a long municipal building at the south end of the square and houses in the draw further west. Lt Harley's 1st Platoon supported the effort. Trailing the infantry as closely as possible, Lt Harley worked his tank along a narrow gravel lane leading far up into the rocky draw, shooting whatever targets the infantry called to his attention. Oftentimes, Harley dismounted to lead his driver around tight bends or past hazardous sections of the rugged lane. From time to time the low clouds shrouding the nearby hills lifted slightly, and the young officer could see Germans wearing white camouflaged coverings moving among the rocks and snow near the abbey. The sight was unsettling. At one point, Harley prepared to remount his tank but was astonished to see Lt Redle walking toward him on the lane. Redle was just as surprised to have finally located Harley's tank so far up the draw. Although conditions were extremely dangerous, the B Company commander wanted to be assured Harley's crews weren't lacking supplies and to apprise his South Carolinian platoon leader of other tactical matters. After a brief discussion, Harley dropped down inside his turret and Redle headed back toward town. Moments later, a series of German mortar shells exploded along the lane nearby, sending the infantry scurrying for cover. Another cluster of rounds burst on the opposite side of the tank—this time closer. Harley realized he was being bracketed and ordered his driver to zigzag out of the draw as quickly as possible.[47]

Later that afternoon, Harley's tank returned to the town square to link up with the second tank from his section, commanded by Sgt Hamilton Smith. At the time, Smith had been assisting an infantry team clearing out a block of buildings. The pair became so engrossed in the effort that, at 1600, when Sweeting radioed for them to withdraw for the day, Harley asked to keep fighting until exhausted of all ammunition. At the time, Harley's tank had squeezed inside a narrow alleyway—helping the infantry battle for yet another building. The Germans inside answered with harassing small arms fire and had already taken several unsuccessful rifle grenade shots at Harley's head. Sweeting, impressed by the Citadel graduate's dedication, agreed to the request.[48]

About an hour later, both Harley and Smith tanks exited the square to return to the quarry. Harley's tank slowed near a segment of road the engineers had filled earlier, but the loose gravel gave out and Harley's tank bogged. While the driver struggled to regain traction, three loud grenade bangs jarred the hull in quick succession. The temporarily deafened crew remained calm as Harley's eyes darted back and forth in search of the culprit. A fourth rifle grenade followed—this one penetrated the hull and caused the interior to spark, smoke and hiss. [49] Luckily, no one was hit, but Harley ordered everyone to dismount and hurried them across a ditch to the safety of a nearby house.[50] Sgt Smith's M4, now trapped behind Harley's disabled tank, withdrew west in search of cover.[51]

The incident left Harley hopping mad. He raced all the way to the quarry and requested another tank so he could return to rescue his crew and the other tank. After nightfall, Harley did ride back into town and personally supervised the evacuation of his crew, the rescue of Smith's tank, and the recovery of his own damaged tank.[52] Although Harley's tank didn't catch fire, the grenade damage was irreparable and the wreck was ultimately surrendered to Ordnance.[53] Captain Arnold witnessed the entire incident from the hillside OP and was so impressed by Harley's bravery and dedication, he recommended him for the Silver Star.[54]

The tank section operating east of the jail also withdrew to the quarry for the evening, but Sweeting directed Redle to leave one tank near the jail until the infantry could reposition a 57mm AT gun in the area.[55] By 2130, the AT gun was relocated, and the last B Company tank withdrew for the night.[56]

Sweeting walked to the 133rd CP in Caira for his usual evening meeting with Colonel Marshall.[57] The infantry plans for the following morning were for the 1st and 3rd Battalion to continue pressing deeper into town. As usual, the tanks would provide close fire support. The 100th Battalion, however, was being withdrawn to a reserve position on Hill 175 that very evening.[58]

Sweeting, too, was greatly angered over the destruction of Harley's tank. He didn't, however, blame the Germans for the incident. In his view, the lives of both Harley and Smith crews were jeopardized unnecessarily because their tanks had bogged on a road supposedly "repaired" by the engineers. That same day, Cpl Behymer's tank was also struck by a rifle grenade. No one was wounded in that incident either, and the damaged tank withdrew under its own power.[59] Nevertheless, Sweeting blamed poor road conditions for both incidents. Many other streets remained impassable because of uncleared rubble and unfilled shell craters.[60] After days of politely requesting engineer assistance, the critical bridge near the town square was still down and several active Teller mines remained buried in the roadway—presenting unnecessary deadly hazards for his crews. Such easily corrected issues prevented Sweeting's tank crews from supporting infantry operations more effectively.[61] This time, Sweeting complained directly to Brigadier General (Brig Gen) Frederic B. Butler, the 34th Division's Assistant Commanding General. Butler listened sympathetically and tactfully explained how Colonel Robert E. Coffee's 109th Engineers were also exhausted after being stretched thin for so long. He told Sweeting, however, to send a direct request on his personal authority to Coffee and ask for a company of engineers on a priority basis. If this could not be done, Sweeting was authorized to secure another company from the 235th Engineering Battalion.[62]

The 133rd captured eleven more Germans during the day—all from the 211th Grenadier Regiment and all in the vicinity of the jail. Eight were from the 7th Company, two from the 1st Company and the remaining one was from the 2nd.[63] Each man complained of dreadful attrition and spoke of German companies operating with only thirty, forty or forty-five survivors. American artillery had been responsible for these terrible losses, they said. Earlier in the day, American artillery vaporized one MG crew positioned at the southeast corner of the school, and another barrage placed on the Hotel Continental killed some thirty men from 7 Company in a mere matter of minutes. The prisoners told of another artillery round landing squarely on top of an SP gun positioned south from the jail—blowing it completely apart.[64] To avoid a similar fate, two remaining SP guns withdrew for cover further south during the night of 11 February.[65] One prisoner, a German sergeant, witnessed Oliver's crew destroy the Mark IV earlier, and politely requested to see the "automatic 75 that you are using on us."[66]

***

The American infantry holding the hills near the monastery could advance no further.[67] The surviving troops had become utterly exhausted, and no more clerks, drivers, or anti-tank crews could be called in as replacements. Fortunately, the Germans were no better off—but that didn't mean they wouldn't try to take advantage of the situation. Just before dawn, the Germans unleashed another powerful artillery barrage across all highland positions held by the 34th and 36th Divisions. As thick curtains of shells howled and burst, German troops poured down from Colle S'Angelo in one last desperate attempt to wrest Monte Castellone away from the 142nd Regiment. The Americans responded with determined—often frantic—machine gun, rifle, and mortar fire. The battle raged for four solid hours. At times, combat was so brutal and personal that hand grenades were the preferred weapons used by both sides.[68] By 1100, the counterattack finally petered out and the retreating German survivors left several hundred of their dead littered upon the barren slopes.[69]

The counterattack brought no change to the battle lines.[70] The Germans maintained a firm hold on Colle S'Angelo to the west, the monastery in the east, and the Albaneta Farm and series of ridges in between—effectively blocking entry to the Liri Valley. The old fort ruins atop Hill 593 also remained under German control, although this fact was not apparent to the weary Americans nearby. Because of severed phone lines, fickle radios, and the daunting challenges with sending runners, American commanders in Caira mistakenly believed Hill 593 was still theirs. The 141st Regiment was supposed to occupy the hill, but could never move in close enough to complete the task.

Three weeks had passed since the 36th "Texas" Infantry Division was badly mauled attempting to cross the Rapido, but the unit never received an opportunity to properly reconstitute. The 141st Regiment sent to occupy Hill 593 represented a mere ghost of a regiment. Survivors of the 141st's 1st and 3rd Battalions now totaled only twenty officers and 150 men—a patchwork remnant barely comprising a company. According to the U.S. Army Table of Organization, two full strength battalions fielded seventy officers and over 1,600 men.[71] The 142nd Regiment's personnel numbers also dropped dreadfully low and what little remained of the unit was all but wiped out in the ill-fated attack on the Albaneta Farm. In truth, the 36th Division had been eroded down to only twenty-five percent combat effectiveness. Three weeks of fighting had eliminated seventy-five percent of the division.[72] The 34th "Red Bull" Division was hardly better off. The 168th Regiment had been reduced to 793 effective combat troops spread across three battalions—basically representing only thirty-three percent table strength. The 135th Regiment reported an average of only thirty men per company. In twenty straight days of combat (24 January to 12 February), the 34th Infantry Division lost a staggering 2,341 men: 318 confirmed killed, 1,641 wounded, and another 392 missing—either captured or dead.[73] Most casualties were riflemen, BAR men, or machine gunners from the rifle companies. This was a dreadful price to ask any infantry division to pay.

Allied planners believed the introduction of two fresh British divisions into the area would finally break the Gustav Line.[74] The 4th Indian Division and the 2nd New Zealand Division were summoned from the British Eighth Army with this intention. At 1805 the II Corps signaled a desire to move one or two battalions from the 4th Indian Division to Hill 593 that very night.[75] Ten minutes after the message circulated, Maj Gen Ryder followed with this cautionary dispatch to his field commanders:

"Everyone up there is to be alerted for anything. They are near the breaking point. If anything happens either Colonel Neely, Gen Butler or myself will be alerted at once."[76]

The general did not want any complacency taking root while relief arrived.

The 168th phoned to report a quiet evening. Three patrols had been dispatched and were still out gathering intelligence.[77] The 135th also reported no activity in their area.[78] The 142nd Battalion sent guides to Caira to help the first Indian troops navigate up into the highlands, but as of 2125, nobody had yet returned.[79] In reality, the movement of new troops to Caira wasn't happening.[80] The Indian troops tried arriving aboard their unit's standard four-wheeled trucks, but encountered roads so rutted and muddy that they had to borrow 270 six-wheeled trucks from American units just to reach San Michele.[81] By 2334, word spread that the 4th Indians wouldn't relieve the 141st during the night, after all.[82] The news was disappointing, to say the least.

***

No word had yet been received on relief for the 756th Tank Battalion. For the time being, the crews were expected to continue fighting and maintaining pressure in town alongside the troops of the 133rd. Sweeting moved an A Company, 756th, platoon from across the river and put their crews and those of C Company, 756th, on alert for the following day.[83] The other tank crews, as usual, positioned near Hill 213 or in the quarry area and turned in for some rest. Quiet rumors circulated around Coleman camp stoves of the monastery being bombed soon.[84]

Early in the murky morning hours of 13 February, an engineer team labored removing teller mines and filling crater holes in the roads of town. Sweeting's complaints to Brig Gen Butler finally yielded results. At the same time, the 100th Battalion was pulled back to Hill 175 to take a reserve position.[85] The first two hours after midnight were extremely quiet, and all three regiments of the 34th Division enjoyed some degree of respite.[86] At 0200, however, the silence abruptly ended with the familiar cacophonous call of German artillery and mortar fire. The tempest lasted roughly forty-five minutes—mostly directed toward 168th positions. One shell wiped out the message center and destroyed the regimental radio. Then the dark skies fell silent again.[87] Then, a short time later, the 135th received their turn of harassing MG fire and artillery fire. This unwelcome attention, although not as heavy, lasted through daybreak.[88]

At 0550, German artillery exploded along the road near the Hill 213 assembly area—sending everyone diving for cover. The assault lasted a solid ten or fifteen minutes before shifting southward upon the barracks.[89] Ten minutes later, the concentrations shifted south, yet again—this time to pummel the quarry and road entrance into Cassino.[90] The Germans, however, saved the strongest concentrations for the north end of town itself—rocking 133rd Regiment positions for a full hour.[91] The sunrise attack was intended to catch Americans out and moving about—the hour they were most likely to do so.

At 0650, the 135th and 168th positions received another shellacking—this time from mortar and Nebelwerfer rockets.[92] The 34th Division Artillery dispatched a Cub plane from Monte Trocchio in search of German gun flashes.[93] The air remained cold but the skies cleared to a crystal blue with few clouds—perfect weather for gun spotting.[94] At first, the Americans on the massif feared the beginnings of another counterattack but saw none of the usual troop movements that accompanied prior attacks.[95] Perhaps the Germans were simply repositioning their own hilltop defenses.

The dawn barrage delayed American plans in town by about a half hour. Captain Arnold and the 756th OP party departed for Cassino at 0630 as a platoon of A Company tanks assembled at the quarry.[96] C Company, 756th, waited on alert.[97] At the same time, Sweeting met in Caira briefly with Colonel Marshall before departing for the quarry as well.[98]

The 1st and 3rd Battalions of the 133rd resumed the push into town using their customary cover of smoke and suppressive Cannon Company fire. This time, the engineers stayed through the morning to continue clearing debris and filling road craters.[99] By 0845, the 3rd Battalion reported advancing 100 yards further south on the west side of town, while the 1st Battalion progressed "four or five buildings down on the east side." German resistance hit back stronger than expected.[100] Evidently, the defenders had replenished some of their positions during the evening.

At 0900, the Germans launched a counterattack toward a key road junction southeast of the jail. The ferocity of the attack caught the Americans off guard and forced them to pull back before the incursion could be halted. Sweeting met with Major Chapman, immediately, to formulate plans to regain the lost ground. The two elected to send in the tanks—even though the engineers hadn't completed the necessary road work.[101]

Around 0930, the A Company, 756th, tank platoon made the dismal and sluggish trek down into Cassino—a first time for all four crews.[102] The tankers were utterly shocked at the degree of devastation and death before their eyes. The town's approach looked like a tank graveyard. Six abandoned M4s lay scattered—penetrated and burned by enemy fire. Some were turned over onto their sides. Others sat scorched with broken tracks and guns a kilter. All had been knocked out within 100 yards of the entrance. The narrow ribbon of roadway through was barely passable—bordered by crumbling stone walls on the right and a debris filled riverbed to the left. The rotting dead and parts of the dead were strewn about everywhere—most of whom had once been America's finest. As the platoon split into sections and probed deeper into town, the drivers did their best to avoid crushing the decaying remains, but found the task impossible and just plowed through.[103] The stench was retching.

One section halted near the downed bridge, providing welcome fire support for those infantrymen battling in the town square. The crags and caves lining Castle Hill along with a row of shell blasted buildings lining the south end of the square continued to be the primary focus.[104] Despite days of blasting countless HE rounds into those positions, German resistance remained tenacious. The second section moved westward to the jail—stopping along the spillway to a place where they could place fire into the nunnery.[105] Under blue skies and slightly hazy conditions at ground level and with the solid direction of the infantry,[106] the tank gunners fired and fired and fired without ever running out of targets.

***

Meanwhile, a high stakes drama with international ramifications unfolded all morning long at the 34th Division HQ on Monte Trocchio. At 0630, someone at the HQ thought he saw mortar flashes emanating from the monastery and called the 133rd to confirm. The 133rd responded that they had no OP directly monitoring the abbey and couldn't verify the sighting.[107] At 0810, an operations officer with one of the recently arriving New Zealander units monitored the phone chatter and suggested Maj Gen Ryder agree to an aerial bombing of the abbey. Ryder summarily rejected the notion as too perilous, citing the proximity of his own troops. Alarmed, too, by potential political fallout from the proposal, Ryder promptly contacted Keyes. At 0840, Ryder returned to state more emphatically to the New Zealanders:

"Make it clear with the Air Corps Officer that I will not accept that bombing. I am in command of this sector and will not be responsible nor will I permit any other bombing than what I put out myself."

Ryder's orders were passed on to the Air Liaison officer.[108] At 1050, Air Service Command (ASC) phoned with a short and disturbing message: "Mission on Abbey Called off."[109] Evidently, the New Zealanders presumptuously scheduled bombing runs that very morning—and then tried to nudge Ryder into taking responsibility for the final decision.

The 2nd New Zealand and 4th Indian Divisions were organized under one provisional New Zealand Corps and placed under the command of Lt Gen Sir Bernard C. Freyberg. The 55-year-old Freyberg was a genuine national hero with a distinguished and unassailable war record. He had been wounded in combat nine separate times during his career and received Great Britain's highest military honor: the Victoria Cross.[110] Freyberg was born in England but grew up in New Zealand. During WWI, he participated in the disastrous Dardanelles Campaign and witnessed firsthand the appalling, senseless sacrifice of thousands of New Zealand's best troops in a beachhead meat-grinder known as Gallipoli. The dreadful experience instilled Freyberg with a zeal to succeed while paying the lowest possible cost in lives to his own troops—a goal that naturally made him very popular with his men.[111] He was a tall, confident man blessed with both an imposing physique and a charming, gregarious personality.[112] Freyberg's opinions carried great weight with his peers, and he was never bashful about making them known.

Once the New Zealander general arrived in the area, he sought to secure any and all advantages ahead of the commitment of his own troops into battle.[113] He quickly became convinced that the abbey's capture was the key ingredient to winning the campaign. As early as 9 February, Freyberg began lobbying for a limited air strike to "soften up" the German defenders he suspected were inside. This bombardment was to be followed immediately by Allied infantrymen sweeping over the position.[114] At first, Freyberg's plan garnered little interest from his immediate superiors. Lt Gen Mark Clark, the man to whom Freyberg immediately reported, dismissed all talk of an abbey bombing as a non-starter—both a grievous political and military mistake. Clark remained unconvinced that the Germans were using the abbey militarily—but argued they certainly would if it were destroyed. In such case, he contended, the defenders would be just as difficult to expel from the ruins as those currently defending Cassino.[115] Clark viewed Freyberg as a bit of a prima donna,[116] but in deference to the man's impeccable military stature, referred his opinions (along with Clark's own objections) up to British General Sir Harold Alexander of the 15th Army Group.[117] Alexander was also skeptical—but felt enormous pressure from Prime Minister Winston Churchill to break the Italian stalemate.[118] Alexander wouldn't dismiss Freyberg's ideas completely, and so aspects of it floated further up the command chain into the Allied Forces HQ. There, two Americans—Lt Gen Ira C.

Eaker, commanding all Mediterranean Allied Air Forces, and Lt Gen Jacob L. Devers, deputy to Supreme Allied Commander, Mediterranean Theater, British General Sir Henry Maitland Wilson,[119] morphed Freyberg's pitch into a demonstration of the wonders of strategic air bombing. By 13 February, all that was missing was a formal order to carry out their modified plan.

Wilson booted the monumental decision down to Alexander who, in turn, punted it right back into Freyberg's lap—stating if the big New Zealander still considered the bombing a "military necessity" then Alexander would "reluctantly" agree to it.[120] Freyberg, perhaps feeling isolated, tried securing support from his peer commanders—but found few takers. Maj Gen Fred Walker of the 36th Division steadfastly opposed.[121] Maj Gen Geoffrey Keyes of II Corps also opposed—believing Freyberg was falling into a German trap designed to goad the Allies into an abbey bombing for propaganda purposes.[122] Now, Maj Gen Ryder was his latest equal to rebuff the plan. Despite all these firm rejections from the campaign's best-informed commanders, Freyberg's bombing idea would not die and the debate among the generals persisted.

***

In the meantime, the thankless toil of the common infantryman's war persisted with higher levels of frustration and even lower levels of degradation. At 1245, the 133rd Regiment reported more German shelling than normal falling on their positions. Communications had been knocked out—which meant wire layers had to scamper out among rubble for the umpteenth time to risk their lives making splices. The 133rd was running short on men to do the job—or any job. The 100th Battalion now functioned with only 100 men per company. The previous day, fifty Nisei casualties were evacuated due to trench foot—the rotting of skin off the feet because of long-term exposure to moisture and cold. The 100th Battalion CO, Major Casper Clough, was forced into a field hospital after being wounded yet again. His case must have been particularly grave as the stubborn, dedicated young officer refused to leave his men three weeks earlier—even after suffering severe shrapnel wounds to his hand and arm.[123] Many other 34th Division infantrymen also suffered from trench foot in varying degrees and were, perhaps, days away from becoming forever combat ineffective as well.

The 1st Battalion, 133rd, had fallen to an alarmingly low average of only 110 men per company. The 3rd Battalion, 133rd, was slightly stronger at 117 per company. Hampered with these staffing constraints, the best the 133rd could hope for was to push a bit further into town, where they could then consolidate and hold positions until New Zealand replacements arrived.

Through it all, the nasty work of probing and counter-probing persisted for both sides. A team of Germans, carrying a pickaxe and five S-mines, was seen sneaking around the left side of town. After being fired upon, the intruders scurried away. Seven 3rd Battalion men stationed at the perimeter disappeared and were presumed captured. At one point, up to twenty Germans were seen massing deeper in town. Mortar was used to disperse them. Roughly fifty Germans were suspected of opposing the 3rd Battalion's left flank—stubbornly holding an area encompassing the nunnery and school building. Upon sight or sound of any American activity, torrents of S/A and MG fire would spray out from both buildings. To answer them, the 1st Battalion positioned MGs in the jail with overlapping fields of fire.

During the afternoon, Cannon Company was called to lay a heavy concentration upon German positions deeper inside of town. The Germans responded by blasting the K Company CP with surprising savagery. The two SP guns were suspected as the sources—firing ninety-two rounds in all and registering fifty-four hits. German mortar positions on the south slope of Castle Hill joined in the assault, which only invited an American counter response from artillery batteries. At one point, every weapon in town seemed to be blazing with blind vengeance. Alarmed by the escalating racket, Colonel Marshall alerted his "strongest" 100th Battalion company to prepare to shore up 3rd Battalion positions. By 1320, the 133rd reported eleven men wounded. The shelling abated considerably, at least, but the tit-for-tat S/A and MG fire endured.[124]

At 1500, the 1st Battalion finally requested tank support to quell the exasperating and incessant German fire coming from the nunnery. In response, Sweeting dispatched a section of A Company tanks to the west of the jail.[125] The roadway was still choked with rubble, but the lead tank commander found a fairly stable firing platform along the spillway's edge, offering a tight line of fire between two buildings. In order to bring his main gunsights on a German sniping from an upper storey window several hundred yards further south, the commander kept urging his driver to nudge forward. The driver protested each time, but somehow, the front plate would jut out a few more inches over the spillway and hold. Still unable to strike the target, the commander ordered to edge forward one more time. This time, the tank plunged down into the spillway and rolled over on its side. The crew, shaken but otherwise unhurt, was forced to abandon the tank and make their way back to safety on foot.[126]

German artillery seemed to shift focus all afternoon—with each succeeding barrage zeroing in on a different key American position with the passage of time. At 1530, the 3rd Battalion hillside OP near town shuddered under several blasts, leaving a Cannon Company lieutenant wounded in the aftermath.[127] Then, at 1645, the 141st Regiment CP in Caira was obliterated by a one-in-a-million hit. A 150mm shell skipped down an adjoining rooftop and threaded a stone doorway surrounded by sandbags. The resulting explosion vaporized the regimental commander, Lt Col Aaron W. Wyatt, where he stood and left his XO and entire operations staff seriously wounded. Nearly every survivor needed to be evacuated.[128] A few weeks earlier, this sort of tragedy would have been devastating for unit morale, but at this stage of the battle the survivors merely shook off the dust and returned to their duties—pausing only to duck and ride out the next salvo.

The 109th Engineers devised a solution to the downed bridge near the town square. They decided to build a span and transport it to Cassino during the night. In the meantime, fellow engineers recovered nine more decomposing bodies from the minefields east of The Pimple. Others, with steel nerves and nimble fingers, defused dozens of deadly S-mines in the same area.[129]

By mid-afternoon, Sweeting's tankers concluded their fire missions and withdrew to the quarry and Hill 213 for resupply and rest. At 1730, Sweeting returned from the 133rd Regiment CP after meeting with Colonel Marshall. Once Captain Arnold and the OP party arrived from town around 1800,[130] a company commanders' meeting was convened at the 756th Tank Battalion Caira CP.[131] Lt Redle was informed that his tanks would take rotation the following day. With the jail now secured, their next mission would be to pulverize the tower on Castle Hill. The battalion's tank strength had improved considerably. Fifty tanks were now considered operationally fit, with twenty-two others under repairs. A total of twenty-two had been lost to date. C Company, 760th, reported nine operational tanks with four under repairs and four others lost to date.[132] An attempt to recover two disabled tanks would be made in town that evening, and a T2 would also be sent to help the infantry reposition another towed AT 57mm gun.[133] Major Dolvin was given the task of assisting the engineers with the bridge bypass.[134] Only two men in the battalion—a B Company tank driver and a private in HQ—were wounded during the day, but their injuries were light and both remained on duty.[135]

***

The cloak of night brought welcome calm over the highlands—a benefit to Allied transition plans. Relief troops of the 4th Indian Division had only started trickling in during the day. The 141st Regiment near Hill 593 was supposed to be completely relieved the previous night, but nobody ever arrived.[136] The 142nd Regiment on Monte Castellone received only a handful of relief troops around 1000.[137] Even this modest exchange drew heavy German ire. "We have been getting the shit shot out of us," an exasperated 135th officer phoned the 34th Division HQ at 1040.[138] The caller was assured that the 135th was next on the relief list but would have to wait until later that evening. The 141st and 142nd had been given priority.[139] The 168th sent guides to Caira in hopes of contacting their relief counterparts, but were told they would have to wait until the following day.[140] The Indian troops were delayed this time not by trucks, but by mules—there weren't enough of these poor beasts still living to move supplies from San Michele to Caira.[141] The original plans called for the 4th Indian Division to attack this very night. However, the mule shortage forced a postponement until the following evening.[142]

Later in the day, one extremely brave German officer approached a 142nd position waving a white flag. He asked if American officers would agree to a short armistice the following morning lasting from 0800 to 1100 in the areas of Hills 706 and 711. The truce would allow both sides to collect their dead and wounded in peace. The 36th Division granted the request, but secured a Cub plane to monitor the truce and alerted 36th Division artillery batteries to remain on standby in case of a ruse.[143]

For a few hours that evening, a similar calm reigned over Cassino. But at 2140, when B Company, 100th Battalion, slipped over the regimental right flank to shore up 3rd Battalion positions, harassing gunfire sputtered again from the nunnery.[144] The repositioning was completed by 2200, but the Germans ratcheted up their displeasure by lobbing mortar rockets. Peeved by this, the 1st Battalion, 133rd, then directed their own mortars upon the nunnery.[145] Finally, the Germans capped off the quarrel by tossing several rounds of artillery on the jail.[146] Nothing amounted from this exchange, other than the venting of collective frustration.

***

Dawn broke on 14 February with clear magnificent skies and only a hint of haze drifting over the valley.[147] Even so, the infantrymen of the 133rd had no plans to attack. Personnel rolls had dipped too low to do anything other than hold ground and direct tank fire into suspected German positions. At 0630, three tanks of Lt Harley's 1st Platoon, B Company, arrived at the quarry and awaited final movement orders. Sgt Alfred W. Mancini, Jr., commanded one of the tanks, but the other crews had become so exhausted and depleted that Cpl Ed Farley and T/4 Bert Bulen temporarily commanded the other two.[148] By 0700, Captain Arnold arrived at the forward OP to join the 756th's observation crew who had already been waiting a good forty minutes.[149] From blacked out windows and cracked walls, the men peered across the town square to Castle Hill roughly 300 yards away and watched for any trace of movement. At 0745, after conferring with Colonel Marshall, Sweeting ordered Mancini's tanks to assume positions north of the square. For one full hour, the three M4s blasted the castle tower and walls—hurling AP, HE, and concrete piercing shells at the ancient stonework. Eventually a large portion of wall cascaded down the granite slope, leaving behind an impressive cloud of yellow dust—much to Lt Col Sweeting's delight. Sweeting suspected the wall's collapse now blocked several tunnels connecting German hilltop positions.[150] At 0930, four tanks from A Company assumed positions west of the jail and joined in the castle attack. After forty-five straight minutes of firing, the crews described "good success."[151] Throughout the morning, the Germans tried retaliating by peppering the tanks with intermittent mortar and artillery—but failed to register any direct hits or bring a halt to the mission.[152]

At 1130, Sweeting and Dolvin ventured into town to survey the results and compile information for the New Zealand tankers—which were expected to arrive any day now.[153] The two officers found the bridge near the square still out, but the engineers had successfully removed many dangerous AT mines. The narrow road running next to spillway from the square over to the jail was still clogged with considerable debris. The main street running through town was also choked with rubble—but appeared somewhat negotiable for a tank. The roadway east of the jail showed the most promise for passage—the route was clear and provided the best cover from German hilltop gun positions.[154] The two tank officers were encouraged by the tanks' slow demolition of the castle, but the infantry still complained of ongoing harassment emanating from the nunnery. They decided to call forward more tanks to address the problem.

At 1230, S/Sgt James Haspel's 2nd Platoon, B Company, arrived near the jail. Sweeting took command of one tank and directed the others to fan out across the field between the jail and the nunnery. His intent was to draw German fire—particularly from rifle grenadiers—and destroy them.[155] The plan worked. The Germans, perhaps believing a major American attack was underway, responded by firing everything available at Sweeting's tanks—including artillery. One tank halted briefly beneath a shower of sparks after sustaining a direct hit from a rifle grenade. The hull was penetrated, but the tank did not catch fire and the crew fought on calmly.[156] Any nook or cavity suspected of harboring German guns was pounded repeatedly by Sweeting's fuming wave of M4s weaving back and forth across the field. Windows, entries, alcoves, and porticos flashed, ruptured, and collapsed after receiving blast after blast.

In desperation, the Germans unleashed a concentrated artillery barrage upon the slow, advancing armor. Normally, only a direct hit could seriously damage a tank,[157] but one round exploded off the rear of S/Sgt Haspel's tank and locked his engine down to idle speed. The driver tried shifting through the gears but found the tracks barely budged. Sgt Hamilton Smith, commanding a nearby tank, yelled to Haspel to sit tight as he worked on a solution. Smith was a short, skinny fellow with pale blue eyes, but possessed an indomitable spirit. The Washington State native had been a B Company member since June 1941 and became known to all as the one guy who wasn't afraid of anything. During times of celebration, Smith's comrades also marveled at how his small frame could hold "a lot of whiskey."[158] Early on, he was given the nickname "Snuffy" after the ornery hillbilly character "Snuffy Smith," popularized in the newspaper cartoon sections. Though sloppy and somewhat undisciplined by Army standards, Smith's "can do" manner won Sweeting's inimitable admiration. "He does everything!" Sweeting once marveled to Captain Wilkinson, as the two officers observed a training exercise.[159]

Once the artillery barrage lifted temporarily, Smith shot down from his turret clutching a bag of tools. Despite countless German bullets snapping and hissing past his head, he dashed across the churned and muddy sod to gain cover behind Haspel's rear tank deck. With the battle raging all around him, Smith heaved open the engine hatch and adjusted the idle speed to around 800 RPM before closing up and racing back to his own tank. He clambered inside the safety of his turret just as another volley of shells burst across the field. Though Haspel's tank speed was still hobbled down to a snail's pace, Smith's tinkering provided just enough power for the driver to reverse slowly toward the jail.[160] As he did, Sgt Smith's and Cpl David L. Grate's tanks both backed along serving as protection. Progress proved too slow, so the two commanders dismounted during another lull to attach a tow cable to Haspel's tank, then returned to their turrets and continued fighting. A short time later, the fire mission on the nunnery ended and Haspel's tank was towed completely to safety. Sweeting, witnessing the entire incident from his command tank, was so impressed by their selfless teamwork that he recommended both Smith and Grate for the Silver Star.[161] The honor was enormous, as Sweeting had a very stingy reputation for awarding medals.[162]

At 1515, Sweeting ordered Redle to withdraw the 2nd Platoon from town. He then called forward four additional A Company tanks to assume positions east of the jail. There, they resumed fire on the castle and nearby ridgeline. The mission, lasting until dusk, was deemed successful.[163] That evening, the infantry dispatched patrols to the south and west,[164] while Major Dolvin met with the engineers to finalize plans to position the replacement bridge near the square.[165]

At 1645, the OP party departed Cassino and arrived at the battalion CP in Caira in time for the planning meeting for the next day. In attendance was a guest—Colonel Fry from the 88th Infantry Division—sent to the front as an observer.[166] The 88th Division arrived in Naples only two days earlier.[167] Sweeting informed his tank officers that they would continue similar fire missions the next morning. This time, A and C Company were to be ready to roll into Cassino by 0700.[168] Sweeting was still so pleased with B Company's daytime performance, he told Lt Redle his men earned the following day off. Nevertheless, he cautioned Redle to keep his tanks on standby just in case.[169] Redle's crews sorely needed time to regroup. Four B Company men had been struck by German artillery after returning to the cemetery near Hill 213 after a long day of battle.[170] Two of them—Cpl Eugene H. Rule and T/5 Edward Tomaszewski—were evacuated with life threatening injuries. Rule's femur was fractured in several places by shrapnel and Tomaszewski had been peppered badly in the skull, face, neck, and forearm.[171] Cpl Ralph A. Rutzen and Pfc Kevin F. Brennen were also wounded and required hospitalization. Earlier in the day, ironically, Rutzen's tank was hit three separate times by German rifle grenades—without any of the crew getting hurt.[172] Two other battalion tankers, C Company's Cpl Calvin J. O'Leary and A Company's Pvt John J. Deenihan, were also wounded.[173]

The drawdown of American forces in the area greatly affected the ability of Sweeting's tankers to maneuver. At 2215, C Company of the 776th Tank Destroyer Battalion was relieved of its attachment to the 756th Tank Battalion.[174] Sweeting had relied heavily upon the presence of these TDs concealed amongst the barracks ruins for covering fire. Many times, the M-10's big 3-inch guns protected the M4s as they maneuvered in town. With those TDs now gone, the tankers had to remain especially alert for German SP guns—which had been conspicuously absent for two straight days now.

***

The western highlands had been a hushed hell for most of the day. Under the truce spanning from 0800 to 1000, German and American litter bearers combed the frigid rocks and ravines between Monte Castellone and Point 706 in search of their respective dead. The bitter harvest seemed endless. Unshaven haggard officers from both sides stood together watching wearily over the sorry scene. At first, conversations between rivals were detached and brief, but as the awkward moments ticked by and a glorious morning sun rose higher in the east, cold adversaries warmed into human beings again. Crinkled cigarettes were exchanged. Dirty wallets emerged from wet pockets, and creased photos soon circulated among grimy hands testifying of peaceful lives with wives and children back home. Stories swapped, too, of ancestral connections between America and Germany.[175] Though enemies by uniform, these were still family men with much in common.

German attitudes seemed a bit different from those displayed only three weeks earlier—when the 36th Division was trounced during the Allies' first attempt to cross the Rapido. A few days later on 25 January, the Americans requested a truce to collect their wounded and dead along the river banks. Germans emerged from nearby defenses to assist with the humiliating work. The German officers, though reserved, were quite accommodating—even friendly. Those speaking English freely gave advice to their American counterparts on what aspects had been tactically right or wrong in their disastrous attack—much the way an older brother might lecture a sibling bested yet again in a child's game.[176]

This time around, the Germans were far less patronizing. Evidently, their American rivals had earned some begrudging respect. In truth, the Germans were just as distressed, overstretched, and exhausted. They, too, had to hastily reinforce shaky mountain positions by calling forward any warm body available. Cooks, drivers, and administrative personnel were thrown into foxholes until more seasoned combat veterans could be cannibalized from distant units and rushed into the area. Although these temporary replacements were not particularly effective combatants, their efforts proved enough to prevent the fall of Monte Cassino.[177] The toll in German lives had been horrendous.

Early in the two-hour truce, the Germans asked for an extension of time. The request flowed up the command chain and an additional hour was granted.[178] As the 1100 hour neared however, the adversaries departed from the windswept heights to return to their respective lines—leaving many unclaimed dead still sprawled among boulders to freeze, thaw, and rot over the coming days.[179] The war had to go on, after all.

Early that afternoon, Maj Gen Joseph de Goislard de Monsabert stopped by the 36th Division HQ. When briefed about the 200 German corpses collected under the Red Cross flag that very morning, the 3rd Algerian Infantry Division commander's voice bellowed with enthusiasm:

"Congratulations! Magnificent! You have now partly evened your losses at the Rapido!"[180]

The short white-mustachioed French general was only trying to be encouraging.

***

Later that same afternoon, the Germans proposed another truce for the following morning to resume the macabre collection process. This time, however, the request was denied. More and more relief troops were arriving in Caira, and the ragged Americans holding the hills had already suffered from too many delays. The 7th Indian Infantry Brigade (4th Indian Division) also had aspirations to attack after sundown,[181] but these plans were reconsidered after learning Hill 593 was not under Allied control after all. The fog of battle during the prior 24-hours was to blame.[182] The American survivors, thoroughly expended of energy and eager for relief, fooled themselves into assuming someone from their side still held Hill 593.

During the evening, Indian troops commanded by British officers finally started relieving front-line positions held by the 135th and 168th Regiments.[183] The newcomers were shocked at the utter hellscape awaiting them. Hundreds upon hundreds of corpses from both sides littered the entire rocky massif—not just along Monte Castellone and Point 706—but everywhere. Many had been dead for days, if not weeks—scattered across barren rock or slumped over in holes. Some had been blown to bits by artillery—often friendly fire.[184] Mule carcasses rotted along with fallen men.[185] In places, remains were dispersed and jumbled so many times from repeated shell blasting, it was impossible to tell what part belonged to whom.

"It was like a cemetery up there … devoid of all greenery," one British soldier later related. "Thank God their mothers couldn't see the sadness and indignity of it all," lamented another.[186]

Empty shell casing, jagged chunks of spent artillery fragments, supply package litter also lay scattered everywhere among the shattered rocks and splintered stumps that had once been trees.[187] The entire mountain resembled a refuse pile. These were not the conditions one would expect to find any living creature. Nevertheless, determined survivors of the "Red Bull" and "Texas" divisions endured—hunkered down in wretched pockets among frigid crevices and rock piles. Only 400 fighting men, at best, remained of four proud battalions from three regiments holding the forwardmost positions along the massif.[188] This was all that remained of a mighty 3,200-man force that first attacked along the Rapido only four weeks earlier.

After two straight weeks of mountain fighting, the survivors suffered from severe deprivation and exposure. They hungered and thirsted from lack of supplies. They agonized from pneumonia, flu, and constant respiratory hacking. Their dirty unshaved faces quavered with the sluggish blank stares of men denied countless nights of sleep. The lucky ones wrapped themselves at night in wet frozen blankets and curled up on sharp, uneven rock. The unlucky ones shivered half-submerged in foxholes of snow and melting slush.[189] The eternal cold stiffened everyone's limbs to a point where they could scarcely fire their weapons. The scourge of trench foot was ubiquitous. Many could no longer walk and had to be hoisted out of their icy furrows and carried on stretchers all the way to Caira—a journey taking seven to eight hours to complete.[190] Plummeting temperatures and an inch of fresh snow falling throughout the night only slowed and complicated the troop transfer. As a result, Indian troops continued arriving as late as dawn on 15 February.[191]

The predominance of trench foot was appalling and unforgivable. The onset could easily be delayed with a simple change of socks on a daily basis—even inside wet boots. If the feet were kept dry and massaged from time to time to keep the blood flowing, the debilitating condition could be avoided altogether.[192] This was a basic hygiene requirement known by all—yet inexplicably ignored. Instead, men were sent fighting into snow-covered elevations without proper clothing and ample supplies of socks, and became needless casualties as a result. Many were rendered permanently lame and would never return to battle. Napoleon may have pontificated over the importance of food, but even he ended up foolishly losing his Grande Armée to a Russian winter for lack of proper attire.

The Allies threw a stunning amount of artillery into the effort. During the first two weeks of February, 12,000 rounds of 8-inch artillery, 900 rounds of 240mm howitzer, and a staggering 100,000 rounds of 105mm explosives were fired in support of the infantry's advance. An astronomical 200,000 rounds of Allied artillery of all types were dispatched during those same two weeks. Cannon Company of the 135th Regiment was responsible for firing 22,000 of those rounds.[193]

In the end, the combat infantrymen of the 34th Division were driven beyond their human limits. Despite daunting and brutal conditions, they managed to push two full miles across the craggy massif above and behind Cassino—coming within a few hundred yards of capturing the monastery.[194] Whenever the snow, rain, and mist lifted, these proud troops could clearly see Highway 6 snaking through the valley below—a grand prize laying tantalizingly just beyond their grasp. They truly believed if they pushed a little harder, they would spill down into the Liri Valley and shatter the mighty Gustav Line.[195] This driving ambition made their leaders choose extra ammunition over clean socks every time the mule trains loaded up. Their failure was not for lack of heart or effort.

***

The monastery became the universal symbol to this Allied frustration, and its fate now rested on the desk of the Supreme Allied Commander in the Mediterranean, British General Sir Henry Maitland Wilson.[196] Earlier that morning, Lt Gen Ira C. Eaker, an American commanding all Mediterranean Allied Air Forces, boarded a Piper Cub observation plane along with Wilson's deputy commander, Lt Gen Jacob L. Devers, another American, to study the situation firsthand. For ten minutes, the tiny, green canvas-clad plane circled low and slow only a few hundred yards above the monastery, allowing both generals to take copious visual notes. For fear of revealing their positions below, the Germans dared not fire upon the gadfly of an aircraft.[197] The generals confirmed the obvious: gun positions had been constructed within fifty yards of the monastery's towering edifice. Initially, the Germans assured the Roman Catholic Church they would honor a 300-meter neutral zone surrounding the structure, but broke that vow in early January—essentially paring the zone down to the walls themselves. American artillerymen and mortarmen could not strike them for fear of damaging the abbey, and were angered to no end to see the enemy firing from those positions without fear of retribution.[198] The Germans swore before the world that they would never take advantage of the abbey's sacred interior for military purposes—but were perfectly willing to take advantage of that same abbey's high walls to shoot from the shadows.

Eaker and Devers also believed they saw a radio antenna inside the monastery courtyard, along with soldiers milling about in German uniforms, and even a laundry line draped with *feldgrau* woolens.[199] The II Corps commanding general (CG), Maj Gen Keyes, made several similar reconnaissance flights earlier but never saw anything of the kind.[200] The observation—real or imagined—was enough to convince Eaker and Devers that an air strike was necessary, and that they would be saving Allied lives by doing so.[201] This firm conclusion was passed on to General Wilson.

Clark tried one final time via phone to convince General Alexander of the perils and pitfalls of the idea, but failed to move his British superior.[202] Alexander's judgment was, perhaps, tainted by a sketchy civilian source claiming eighty German troops and thirty machine guns were hidden inside the abbey.[203]

Despite the objections of the top four commanding generals directly overseeing Cassino area ground operations for the past four weeks—Ryder, Walker, Keyes, and Clark—Alexander deferred the momentous decision to newcomer Freyberg, and Wilson concurred with Alexander.[204] Freyberg maintained that the abbey's destruction was a "military necessity." Even last-minute pleadings from General Alphonse Juin, French Expeditionary Forces commander, had no effect.[205] The matter was settled.[206]

Around the 1300 hour that afternoon, a battery of American 105mm howitzers fired fifteen shells stuffed with leaflets and timed to burst over the abbey. The white messages fluttered down all over Monastery Hill. Ironically, not a single sheet landed inside the abbey walls. Typed text in both Italian and English alerted all occupants to leave "at once" but the deadline was utterly unrealistic. "The time has come when we must rain our guns on the monastery itself," the message warned.[207] Most fell uselessly among German speakers who could not read them. One brave refugee, at great personal risk, ventured beyond the abbey's walls to retrieve a flyer for the Abbot. The Abbot took the warning seriously but needed the cooperation of the area's German commanders to comply with the evacuation demands. He dispatched his secretary immediately to make arrangements and the Germans agreed to begin evacuation prior to dawn on 16 February.[208] This timetable, of course, was unknown to the Allies.

Weather became the next concern for the flight planners. With so many friendly ground troops stationed about the area, visibility had to be absolutely pristine to carry out such a precise bombing operation. As cruel fate would have it, the very next day's forecast—15 February—called for perfectly clear skies. The days to follow were projected as cloudy with periods of rain.[209] Pressures at Anzio also factored heavily into these plans. The Germans had been building up forces along the beachhead ahead of a counteroffensive expected to commence at any moment. Once the Germans attacked there, Allied bombers would be unavailable for Cassino.[210]

Originally, Lt Gen Freyberg requested only a small swarm of thirty-six fighter-bombers to carry out a very limited bombing mission upon the abbey. The resulting explosions were supposed to leave the defenders shocked and dazed so Freyberg's troops could storm immediately and easily capture the hilltop. Mysteriously, this modest proposal expanded into a huge spectacle involving hundreds of planes dropping nearly 500 tons of explosives—probably the result of Eaker's encouragement.[211] Even Freyberg got swept up in this lust for destruction, and by 14 February was thoroughly convinced the abbey should be completely flattened to its foundations.[212] Forgotten, somehow, was the whole point to the bombing in the first place: empowering Freyberg's men to immediately seize the ruins before the Germans could recover.[213]

Freyberg's relief troops *were not ready.*

U.S. Silver Star medal

CHAPTER SIX

A Monumental Tragedy: 15 February 1944

The first rays of sunlight unveiled a new bridge spanning the spillway at Cassino's north square. The 109th Engineers finally completed the project by prefabricating sections a half-mile to the north during the day and then trucking them to town at night. With the aid of a 756th Tank Battalion T2 recovery vehicle, a "Class 30" bridge was assembled over the fifteen-foot-wide and six-foot-deep ditch in under two hours and completed by 0430.[1] The structure was just wide and strong enough to accommodate an M4. A secondary wooden bridge, four feet wide, was tacked on one edge to allow for troop movement alongside vehicles.[2]

The sun broke over a clear blue horizon as gusty winds whirled through the valley. Visibility was absolutely pristine—the best since the 34th Division's arrival at the front.[3] The meteorologists were remarkably precise with their 15 February forecast.

The laborious troop relief in the highlands reached a point where remnants of the 135th and 168th Regiments could finally drop back to Hill 213 near Caira.[4] The 133rd Regiment, however, was instructed to maintain their Cassino positions until further relief could arrive.[5] With no infantry attack planned in town, any testing of the new bridge would have to wait.

Sweeting's tankers prepared for another routine day of target shooting on Castle Hill. The OP party arrived at 0615 and Sweeting met with Marshall at the 133rd Regiment CP at 0645.[6] In the meantime, one platoon of A Company tanks lingered with idling engines at the quarry.[7] At 0830, the platoon was told to move into town. Three tanks assumed firing positions near the square while two others halted near the jail. All five gun barrels raised westward and Castle Hill rocked again under unremitting fire.[8] As 0930 approached, another tank platoon—this one from C Company—was dispatched to town with the same mission.[9] A War Department photographer assigned to a task force studying weapons and ordnance squeezed inside one of the tank turrets to document the mission.[10]

***

That same morning, word spread quickly among Allied ranks that the abbey would be bombed, starting at 0930 hours. American officers gazed out in reserved expectation from their HQ hideouts atop Monte Trocchio while motion picture camera crews from the Signal Corps and several news organizations prepared to film the event. Dozens of reporters scribbled their impressions while flipping notepads. John Lardner of *Newsweek* labeled the gathering as "the most widely advertised single bombing in history."[11] Most troops stationed in the valley were excused from their duties to witness the event.[12] Some climbed atop stone walls or high into trees to gain better vantage points,[13] while others clenching binoculars shifted their focus expectantly back and forth between the abbey and surrounding skies.[14] Save for the distant sounds of tank fire in Cassino, this growing sense of suspense made for an unusually quiet morning. American artillery batteries, for the most part, sat silently beneath camouflage netting. The Germans, too, suspected something unusual was brewing and halted their cannon as well.[15]

A holiday-like atmosphere of anticipation washed through the Allied rank and file.[16] The average GI had grown resentful of the abbey, and convinced himself the Germans were watching his every move from behind those high fortress walls overlooking the valley—"Jerry staring down our throat," he grumbled constantly.[17] He certainly didn't believe the Germans would keep a political promise. What else could explain the accuracy of German artillery? What else could explain the stalemate? The Germans were cheating, that's how. He was fed up with fighting in mercurial weather that ranged from cold, miserable, and wet to wet, miserable, and cold. He was sick of wearing a uniform always sodden and malodorous, and lugging around several pounds of caked-on mud that never flaked off. He resented the daily frontal assault orders, the mounting casualties, and the waiting for replacements and essentials that never came. Even Armed Forces radio demoralized him with their daily broadcasts. Elsewhere the war seemed to be going glowingly well, whereas his hardships were summarily ignored. The average GI at Cassino wanted to hear good news about himself again.[18]

The great English playwright William Shakespeare observed: "All the world's a stage, and all the men and women merely players."[19] At certain times and places, this ceaseless human drama produces a Greek tragedy—and a moment arrives when the principals, the chorus and the audience all halt to look skyward for a *Deus Ex Machina* moment of deliverance. The gods then appear and alter the outcome in ways often unexpected.

***

The gods first made their entrance at Monte Cassino around 0925 hours in the form of a low ominous hum in the distance. For the next three minutes, the steady droning grew louder, heavier, and angrier. The first specks appeared in the clear eastern sky like a swarm of tiny hornets,[20] but swelled into waves of resolute four-engine B-17 bombers soaring confidently in wingtip formations. Long silvery contrails tracked their gleaming fuselages as they sailed overhead at 15,000 to 18,000 feet, forming one mighty conveyer belt. As the lead planes approached the abbey and opened their payload doors, spontaneous cheers erupted across the valley.[21] From long thin fuselages, bombs fell as strings of dark tumbling pebbles toward the mountaintop. The sunlit walls of the abbey vanished behind sparkling white flashes and violent jets of flame—all billowing into one enormous thick black plume rising a thousand feet high. Dozens upon dozens of tiny gray figures could be seen scrambling away from the abbey's main gate in desperation,[22] but another slew of bombs exploded around them, and the figures disappeared. The cheering grew raucous, but others just stood in stunned silence.[23] Some allowed tears to roll freely down their blank faces—unable to process the event as deliverance or damnation.[24]

The unearthly spectacle appeared hushed and weirdly beautiful at first, but after a few seconds elapsed, a long banging thunder rolled through the valley and the ground trembled as if the mountain itself was about to collapse.[25] Seemingly endless ribbons of bombs exploded all across the hilltop, one after another—adding deadly grist to a burgeoning, hellish column of black smoke and gray dust. The abbey was nowhere to be seen.

In the span of only a few minutes, 142 Flying Fortresses dropped 287 tons of 500-pound general-purpose bombs and 66.5 tons of 100-pound incendiaries.[26] Once expended, the long ribbon of empty planes veered southward, leaving the sky veiled with a thin layer of engine haze and the mountaintop burning in shrouded silence. A hush of expectancy gripped the audience as brisk easterly winds pushed back the thick curtain of dust and smoke. After a few moments, the abbey could be seen again—shockingly intact and showing little damage. Even the pale blue domed roof of the main basilica remained.[27]

At 0940, a second wave of bombers comprised of forty-seven B-25 Mitchells and forty B-26 Marauders buzzed over, dropping a punishing 140-ton payload of 1,000-pound bombs.[28] The abbey vanished under another slew of explosions, as did a small building nearby rumored to conceal an elevator shaft.[29] A new pillar of dark smoke engulfed the mountaintop.[30] When the heavy veil lifted this time, the basilica was gone and the courtyard buildings had collapsed in smoldering rubble.[31] Small fires licked from several broken windows along the façade, but the monastery's thick outer walls still stood in stubborn defiance.[32]

At 1010, a third wave of medium bombers hurtled in low through the valley, blanketing their payloads across Castle Hill, before climbing sharply, and pummeling the abbey. Heavier fires raged from more windows—and a water tower which withstood the first two waves, tottered over into rubble.[33] Hoots and cheers of approval rose again throughout the valley.[34]

At 1030 hours, II Corps artillery batteries fired an impressive time-on-target barrage combining 266 rounds of 240mm, 8-inch, 4.5-inch, and 155mm shells.[35] All rounds arrived at once to create a monstrous bang rocking the entire valley. Every available Fifth Army artillery battery then joined the attack—firing at will and painting the abbey and surroundings in a ghastly kaleidoscope of flash and plume.[36] This relentless pummeling, halting only when Allied planes appeared, lasted for hours. At 1040, a fourth wave of bombers swept through, dropping scores of incendiaries all over Monastery Hill.[37] By now the vapor trails from the countless radial engines combined with the rising smoke and dust fed by innumerable detonations hung so heavy that the blue sky had turned completely gray.[38]

For the next hour-and-a-half, the aerial attack paused while the artillery carried on, but at 1305 the planes returned. This time a swarm of eighteen medium bombers rumbled past with six others bringing up the rear. Their aluminum bellies split open and more explosives tumbled earthward—scoring direct hits along the monastery's thick stone edifice. Moments later, twenty-four more medium bombers flew through and repeated the scene. When the attack ended, a large section of the abbey's eastern wall finally collapsed in submission. Dozens of fires raged unabated making the ruined interior look like a smoldering volcano.[39] These were the last Allied planes to strike for the day.[40] In all, 256 bombers dropped 453 tons of explosives on an ancient Christian monastery dedicated to serving the Prince of Peace.[41] Fifteen-hundred years of history was destroyed in under four hours.[42]

***

Even as the last bombs struck the abbey, the Germans answered with their own artillery. Retributive shells exploded along the northern road heading out of Cassino. Two jeeps burst into flames and eight men lay either wounded or dead. Fifteen minutes elapsed before an ambulance could reach them.[43]

The fearless war correspondent, Tom Treanor, had departed Cassino for the Anzio beachhead the prior week and missed the entire spectacle.[44] Had he remained, he wouldn't have chosen to mingle among the battery crews, supply personnel, and headquarters staffers spread across the muddy valley nearby, tough as their lives were. He'd want the raw, unvarnished feelings of front-line infantrymen and tankers—and these men were bitter about the bombing. Why did their own High Command wait until fresh troops arrived in the area before acting, they wondered? Were British lives more valuable? The decision seemed like a stab in the back to those still fighting and bleeding amid the ruins of town.[45]

Lt Gen Mark Clark refused to witness the bombing—choosing to instead catch up on paperwork inside his command trailer at Presenzano that morning.[46] In one of those eyebrow-raising ironies of the war, a sixteen-bomb payload intended for the abbey accidentally exploded around Clark's trailer and nearly hit him. Clark was a full seventeen miles away from the target at the time. One might suspect some conspiracy, but another errant payload fell three miles short of Cassino—this batch destroying several parked vehicles behind the rooftop where Lt Gen Eaker stood to observe his "precision bombing" operation in progress.[47] "When an American plane comes over, *everyone* hits their holes."

Once the aerial bombing ceased, several Allied fighter planes escorted a light observation plane above the smoldering monastery. Evidently, the Air Force was eager to evaluate the results and dispatched a photographer to snap pictures.[48] The abbey sustained thirty-five direct hits. The basilica and most buildings around the interior courtyard lay utterly demolished. The exterior walls showed significant damage and a large section on the east had completely collapsed.[49] During the first attack run, some bombs overshot the north wall and skidded into Allied troop positions—killing or wounding forty Indian troops settled in only the night before.[50]

What the observation plane could not record was the utter horror suffered by Italian civilians who sought refuge inside the abbey and were given no time to escape. As many as a thousand people—mostly women, children, and older folk—packed the dark cellars below to pray and wail with the monks and Abbot.[51] The weight of the buildings crumbling above them collapsed portions of the cellars below, crushing the lives out of at least 200—mostly huddled beneath the southeastern wall.[52] Survivors suffered from dreadful injuries—some with severed limbs. Still, others perished after living out their last hours in dark, desolate despair because nobody could reach them to dig them out.[53]

Scores of destitute local men had camped outside the abbey and worked for the Germans in exchange for a little food or cigarettes. Some had been drafted into labor service.[54] These figures were likely the ones the Americans saw scrambling away and mistook as Germans when the first bombs fell. These civilians had no cover whatsoever. Nobody knows how many of them perished in the rain of bombs—or survived and fled only to be down cut down by artillery fire.[55]

Saint Benedict was the founder of the western Christian monastic tradition. His monks lived peaceful, humble, contemplative lives painstakingly preserving great intellectual and artistic treasures of Western Civilization. Because of this devotion, the Roman Catholic Church declared Benedict the patron saint of Europe. After the bombing, Benedict's statue still stood in the courtyard—but his marble head had been blown away.[56]

***

The destruction of the monastery did nothing to ease the burdens placed on Sweeting's tanks in town. That afternoon, the crews continued blasting Castle Hill with the same ferocity they had for many days now. At noon, another section of tanks was brought to the square to aid in the effort.[57] German snipers hidden in the nunnery resumed their mischief as well, and so a section of tanks was shifted at 1330 to silence them. One hour later, the mission was declared a success and the section withdrew.[58] At 1500, another tank section was sent to the square to continue thumping away at suspected German gun positions along the ridge.[59] The targets always exceeded the supply of ammo and so the tanks withdrew empty before sunset. Late in the afternoon, Sweeting met with Colonel Marshall at the 133rd CP to coordinate plans with the infantry for the following day.[60] Tagging along with him was Colonel Fry, who would then spend the night at the 756th CP and witness Sweeting's tanks perform the exact same mission the next morning.[61]

At 1510, more silhouetted figures were seen dashing along the skyline between the abbey and a stone building to the south. Cannon Company of the 168th Regiment blasted them, joined very quickly with heavy concentrations from 34th Division batteries. The figures scattered. At 1515, the 34th Division reported "Jerries are in the Monastery," but provided no source or reason for the belief.[62] Perhaps emerging civilians were misidentified, or perhaps German soldiers were truly starting to filter into the ruins and establish defensive positions. At 1520, even more figures were seen departing the abbey. The artillery struck them again. This time, several fell motionless.[63]

***

The Germans holed around the exterior of the monastery were left severely dazed and disoriented by the bombing, but Freyberg's understrength troops could not take advantage of this temporary shock.[64] By evening, two battalions from the 1st Regiment and one battalion from the 3rd Regiment of the 1st *Fallschirmjäger* Division rushed into positions among the ruins.[65] The main buildings of the monastery may have collapsed, but the thirty-foot thick foundations of the walls remained—providing these elite German paratroopers and machine gun crews with superior protection.[66] While the monks and civilian survivors clawed out and evacuated, the Germans forged a fortress from the rubble—just as Mark Clark predicted and feared.[67]

Germans troops were never stationed in the monastery prior to the Allied bombing.[68] The 78-year-old Abbot, Don Gregario Diamare, attested to this fact many times.[69] For a short time, several German MPs guarded the main gate as a buffer against some 800 hungry, sick, and homeless civilians camped outside.[70] However, as the fighting neared and stray bullets and shell fragments began wounding or killing refugees here and there, the terrified crowd grew unmanageable—eventually bursting through the gate and spilling inside. At that point, the military police left.[71]

The Germans never used the abbey for observation or to stock weapons or materials. It was unnecessary. Nearby buildings, rocky points, and caves provided plenty of other suitable storage places and points from which to monitor the Allies in the valley.[72] General Frido von Senger und Etterlin commanded the five-division strong German XIV Panzer Corps forces opposing Clark's U.S. Fifth Army forces at Cassino. Von Senger was also a practicing Catholic and a lay Benedictine. So respectful was von Senger of the abbey's neutrality that after accepting a dining invitation from Abbot Diamare for Christmas 1943, the German general patently refused to walk near any windows.[73] And the "German radio mast" Eaker spotted while flying 1,200 feet over the abbey was likely the old weather station that had been there for years.[74]

To their everlasting praise, good Germans officers—many practicing lay Catholics—evacuated most of the monastery's transportable treasures to Rome three months earlier for safekeeping. In all, some 70,000 priceless and irreplaceable artworks, scrolls, and manuscripts were preserved for future generations.[75] Their battle to save these works was not only against Allied bombs, but also from the kleptomania of their own National Socialist leaders. Sycophants to Hermann Goering stole fourteen of these works and then shipped them off to the rotund Reichsmarschall, hoping to curry his favor. Goering, of course, kept them.[76]

The Germans also bore enormous blame for this tragedy. After all, they selected this particular area to do battle. Had they truly cared for the monastery's fate, they would have chosen another location to build their "Gustav Line." They also reneged on an earlier promise to maintain a 300-meter neutral zone around the abbey.[77] Inexplicably and inexcusably, General von Senger issued those orders to do so.[78] The Germans then used caves within that zone to store munitions and establish at least one command post, two observation posts, and two machine gun positions.[79] They shifted two SP guns in and out of the zone.[80] They used the abbey's shadow as a military shield. They intended to be provocative and hoped to elicit some undisciplined Allied response. Maj Gen Keyes saw this tactic as no different to when the Germans dangled light armor just beyond Allied gun range in the North African desert—hoping to lure naïve Americans into tank traps. The Germans loved setting traps. This time, they dangled the monastery as bait in an international propaganda snare—into which rushed fools.

***

That night, Freyberg's troops attempted a feeble attack on Hill 593—considered a crucial objective before any major attack on Monastery Hill could launch.[81] Two paltry platoons from one company of the 1st Royal Sussex of 7th Indian Brigade set out and lost half of their men before crossing seventy yards.[82] They encountered a ravine unmarked on their maps, became confused, and failed to find a way through in the darkness. The mission was completely abandoned once the survivors ran low on hand grenades.[83] These men were experienced mountain warfare troops specifically summoned to the highlands for their skills, and thirty-four of them were immediately wasted for nothing.[84]

The Indians were in no position to mount such an attack. Many were still filtering into highland positions. Two entire battalions slogged the trails as temporary porters just to bring up basic supplies for their fighting brethren. The 800 mules dedicated to running supplies from Caira weren't enough. German mortar and S/A fire fell constant as the snowflakes—hampering all movement.[85] As a result, two other Indian battalions sat trapped at San Michele.[86] The Indians were also short on critical ordnance. Forty-eight hours earlier, two transport trucks stocked with grenades and mortar rounds plunged over an embankment during the move to San Michele—depriving the front-line troops of these essential materials.[87] Mountain combat consumed lots of mortar and grenades and sending good men into battle without these necessary weapons and ammunition was unconscionable.

***

The destruction of the abbey gained absolutely no military advantage for the Allies. Despite the crowd-pleasing spectacle, the battle lines remained exactly the same as before. The enemy had not been dislodged and appeared more defiant than ever. This disastrous decision was born of an odd mix of frustration, brashness, and deference. Everywhere else the war progressed well for the Allies—something the American media reported, at times, with gleeful overconfidence.[88] Eisenhower was quoted as saying the war would be over in 1944. *Newsweek* went even further by boldly predicting the war would be over in only four months.[89] As a result, tremendous political pressure was placed upon Generals Wilson, Alexander, and Clark to break the impasse at Cassino. When the ground troops faltered, Lt Gen Eaker rushed onto the scene eager to demonstrate what his "precision" aerial bombing could accomplish. Eaker was not alone in this zealousness. Many in the War Department felt the same—viewing air power with an almost religious veneration.[90] Freyberg maintained that the bombing was a "military necessity," but Lt Gen Clark admitted later: "I was never able to discover on what he based his opinion."[91] Freyberg's troops were not ready to exploit the event. Both he and Eaker knew this and yet the bombing proceeded anyway—simply because the skies were clear.[92] Clark may have been vocal in his opposition, but even he relented after pressing General Alexander: "You give me a direct order and we'll do it." Alexander gave the order and Clark did it.[93] Nobody actually possessed enough conviction to say no.

The bombing was a dreadful political fiasco—one that Hitler's media unreservedly exploited for maximum propaganda benefit.[94] German radio repeatedly condemned the Allied bombing as a "senseless act."[95] Newsreel crews from *Die Deutsche Wochenschau* ("The German Weekly Review") rushed to the ruins to cast Hitler's National Socialists as the righteous defenders of Western Civilization against unprincipled, marauding Anglo-American barbarians. The Allies were put on the defensive—but doubled down, nevertheless, on the fiction that German troops were using the abbey militarily. Worse, they embellished details without providing any supporting shred of evidence. Ahead of the bombing, the pilots were falsely told "heavy guns" had been placed in the monastery.[96] Afterwards, the *New York Times* headline blared "US Blasts Nazis in Mt. Cassino Abbey" with the subtitle: "Historic Abbey Turned By Nazis Into Fortress Before Their Rout." Other American and British newspapers made similar unsupported claims.[97] Most shameful of all, President Franklin Roosevelt flat-out lied during a press conference by asserting: "It was being used by the Germans to shell us. It was a German strongpoint. They had artillery and everything up there in the abbey."[98] None of this was true.

Any Allied "bombing" of Monastery Hill should have been limited to artillery strikes on confirmed German positions near the abbey's exterior walls. Bomber planes were too inaccurate and shouldn't have been employed at all. Any artillery barrage should have followed with an immediate and overwhelming ground assault—but only after enough new troops were in position to do so. The high stone walls would likely have sustained damage, but the innocent civilians and immovable cultural treasures inside would have been spared.

The purposeful destruction of the abbey at Monte Cassino was a moral and political embarrassment, a colossal military blunder, and a monumental tragedy.

Saint Benedict's Cross

CHAPTER SEVEN

Relief: 16 February 1944 to 22 February 1944

M7 "Priest" Assault Gun (1942)

For the haggard tank crews of the 756th Tank Battalion, the abbey's destruction made no difference to their lives whatsoever—except increase speculation on where they might be heading next. Rumors circulated the battalion would take a "boat ride" once the tanks of the New Zealand 19th Armoured Regiment arrived to take their place.[1] With Indian and New Zealand troops still pouring into the area and cramming the roads, that armor relief appeared to be days away.

The attitudes of the tankers over the bombing mirrored those of their infantry brethren: if the Germans occupied the abbey, what took so long to strike them? Others didn't believe the Germans were inside or the bombing was even necessary. Regardless, the abbey's problems lay the next mountain over, and the mess was someone else's concern. The tankers' world revolved around Castle Hill, the nunnery, and the north section of Cassino—burden enough for their guns to chew on.

The German artillery fell with unnerving irregularity and often drew blood. The previous day, T/5 Joe B. Taylor of A Company was struck dead, and Pvt Joseph P. Birtten of C Company fell wounded.[2] With relief finally coming, nobody wanted to be the last unlucky sucker to "buy the farm."[3] In the meantime, all one could do was take cover and ride out each storm of shrapnel with gritted teeth—then pick up the mess afterwards.

The morning of 16 February arrived with bone-chilling temperatures.[4] At 0615, the 756th outpost party set out for their regular OP on Hill 175. Sweeting and Colonel Fry appeared at the quarry at 0720 to coordinate the day's "milk runs" into town.[5] At 0930, a section of tanks parked at the square and blasted German MG positions along the south ridge. At 1130, another section moved near the jail to fire on nunnery targets identified by the infantry.[6] This dangerous work mimicked the routine of a factory job back home. The shift ended in the late afternoon; the tanks withdrew and the OP party returned to the battalion CP at Caira by 1650.[7]

C Company then placed a three-tank platoon at the quarry just in case the 3rd Battalion, 133rd, needed tank support during the night shift.[8]

***

The abbey and adjacent German hilltop positions were again blanketed with bombs that same afternoon. This time approximately a hundred P-40 and P-51 single-engine fighter/bombers spearheaded the effort.[9] Two separate attacks by twin-engine A-26 dive bombers, however, targeted the monastery specifically, leaving the site a "smoldering pile of bricks."[10] One civilian who escaped the abbey bombing the previous day was allowed passage into Allied territory. When questioned by American investigators, the Italian reported as many as 2,500 civilians had taken refuge in the monastery's cellars. He also stated that no Germans were ever among them—nor had they ever placed weapons or observers inside the abbey. He did confirm, however, that one German MG sat about fifty yards from the outer walls and that others had been positioned approximately 200 yards away.[11]

During that same day, the Germans launched their long-anticipated attack on the Anzio beachhead, thirty miles to the west. The enemy offensive, codenamed *Untemehmen Fischfang* (Operation *Catch Fish*), was met by a resolute Allied response. This fluid and dangerous development placed intense pressure on Freyberg to attack the monastery immediately—even though his front-line positions were still understrength and beset with supply problems.[12] Nonetheless, his Indian troops were ordered to seize Hill 593 at midnight. This time, one entire company from the 1st Royal Sussex Regiment stormed the key point and actually took it. A vicious battle raged for two full hours until the beleaguered company ran out of grenades and was forced to retreat—losing seventy men in the ferocious clash.[13] Both attempts to capture Hill 593 cost the Royal Sussex Regiment a total of twelve officers and 162 men over two nights—with nothing to show for these sacrifices.[14] An attack on the abbey itself had not yet even been attempted.

Several days earlier, French General Alphonse Juin lobbied to shift both the Indian and New Zealand division up into the French Expeditionary Forces zone of operations. Rather than continuing the attack on Cassino, Juin proposed driving aggressively northwest to Atina before cutting down into the Liri Valley—thereby bypassing the abbey strongpoint altogether. The plan was rejected because Juin's bypass route crossed mountainous terrain and relied heavily on mule trains for supplies.[15] This was ironic, considering the Indian troops given orders to capture the abbey were severely hampered for the same reasons.

Sensing his last best opportunity slipping away fast, Freyberg decided to use all his available highland forces and attack the abbey directly the following night—even without securing Hill 593 first. Concurrently, New Zealanders in the valley would strike across the Rapido into the southernmost sections of Cassino. Freyberg hoped this combined pressure might crack open a weak point in the German defenses.[16] The plan relied on another big dose of hope.

***

Prior to the break of dawn, 17 February, the 756th OP party reached Cassino to prepare as usual. Visibility was poor, but sunrise arrived rather peacefully for a war zone.[17] At 0610, Lt Redle moved his B Company tanks down from The Pimple area to the quarry in anticipation of making another "milk run." Ten minutes later, however, Lt Col Sweeting informed Redle that the 133rd infantry had no plans for the tanks for the entire day.[18] Colonel Marshall's men hoped a lack of tank activity might cause the Germans to ease up on their mortar and artillery harassment.[19] Nevertheless, Redle's crews remained on stand-by in case conditions changed.

Pressure upon German positions in the north section of Cassino was maintained—but from a distance. At 0830, Sweeting directed the A Company platoon positioned across the Rapido to target a church steeple deeper into town—but the fire rate was restricted to only one tank at a time. The 756th Tank Battalion assault guns and mortars positioned further north fired on additional targets identified by the OP party.[20] A German SP gun hidden roughly 200 yards southwest of the nunnery retaliated by striking at front-line 3rd Battalion troop positions.[21] German artillery joined and set fire to the abandoned A Company tank overturned in the spillway near the jail.[22] This tit-for-tat scuffle lasted until 1600, after which all 756th Tank Battalion gun crews ceased and the OP party departed town for the day.[23]

That same afternoon, fifty-nine more Allied fighter-bombers dropped twenty-three tons of bombs on Monte Cassino,[24] creating new clouds of dust and fanning the flames of several smoldering rubble fires. For a third straight day the abbey was pummeled, and large portions of its outer walls had now collapsed substantially.

***

Evening "rest" at the 756th assembly area, tucked beyond The Pimple, was never restful and sure to include several terrifying artillery barrages. The Germans had registered all the key locations along Hill 213 and made nightly rounds striking targets on their list. By now, Lt Redle had survived so many close calls that he earned a reputation among his peers for living a "charmed life." A gallows joke circulated among the tankers not to be caught next to Redle in battle because he wouldn't be hit, but the guy next to him would. One night, the 756th intelligence (S-2) officer, Captain Robert H. Rydman, dove beneath the nearest tank to ride out one particularly fierce German storm. As the tank buffeted and jerked above him from the deafening concussions, Rydman came to realize someone else lay near him at the other end. "Who's there?" Rydman queried between volleys. A short pause followed. "Redle," the shadowy prone figure answered. A few choice cuss words spilled from Rydman's mouth and both men laughed aloud. Redle was quite aware of the dark joke as well.[25]

Two weeks earlier, Sgt Eugene Wunderlich was the unlucky man hit while standing by Redle—receiving horrific shrapnel wounds to all four limbs. Though promptly evacuated, the 30-year-old sergeant was not expected to survive. Sheer strength of character pulled Wunderlich through and the Prosser, Washington, native became medically stable enough to be transferred to a 36th General Hospital recovery ward in Caserta. His good friend, Sgt Dick Adlard, recovering from wounds suffered in a separate incident, was assigned to the same ward.[26] At one point, Major Dolvin visited both men to offer his personal encouragement.[27] Wunderlich suffered tremendous blood loss from the incident and required periodic blood transfusions. On 17 February, a hospital medic injected Wunderlich with the wrong blood type and killed him accidentally.[28] When word travelled back to B Company, many of Wunderlich's friends were devastated. He had been a popular B Company member since inception in June 1941. Prior to the war, Wunderlich had been offered several college basketball scholarships but elected to remain at home helping his widower father run the family cherry farm. Wunderlich was single and his mother had passed away in 1935.[29]

Contrasting Wunderlich's extreme misfortune was the strange case of S/Sgt Oric Johannesen, another great former high school athlete also wounded during the same artillery incident.[30] Johannesen's muscular back had been pierced by a quarter-sized shrapnel chunk that exited his chest. He was presumed to be in severe mortal danger and quickly evacuated. When the doctors examined his wounds, however, they found no damage at all to his internal organs. Thoroughly perplexed, a 3D body model was consulted to determine how such a large piece of shrapnel could completely miss the heart, lung, liver, arteries, aorta, spleen, etc. They found no conceivable pathway. Thereafter, Johannesen was known as the "miracle man" by the medical staff. Several days later, while still recovering from his torso wounds, the doctors discovered a second piece of shrapnel had passed completely through Johannesen's foot as well. This smaller sliver entered through the top and exited out the sole—yet broke no bone nor severed any tendon.[31] The legend of the "miracle man" only bourgeoned around the hospital.

***

At midnight, four infantry battalions from the 4th Indian Division attacked along a 1,500-yard highland front.[32] The Royal Sussex Regiment, already degraded to only sixty percent effectiveness, attacked on the right toward Hill 593 for the third straight night.[33] Troops of the 9th Gurkha Rifles attacked the middle toward Hill 444 while the 2nd Gurkha Rifles pushed in the direction of the north monastery wall.

The fighting was fierce—featuring heavy MG and mortar fire under the disorienting illumination of German flares bobbing high above. The bloody battle consumed the predawn hours of 18 February. By morning, the Royal Sussex troops suffered 196 more casualties, but still failed to take Hill 593. The 9th Gurkhas attacking in the direction of Hill 444 gained 300 yards before becoming pinned to a hopeless and complete halt. By morning, ninety-four of their troops lay dead or dying. The 2nd Gurkhas pushing upon the abbey wandered into a row of booby-trapped trip wires, and were cut to shreds by withering German MG crossfire. Eleven officers—including the battalion commander—and 138 enlisted men were either killed or seriously wounded in the futile struggle. Any hopes of renewing the attack at dawn were dashed, so the entire offensive was abandoned, and surviving troops withdrew all the way back to their original jump-off points.[34] Again, absolutely nothing was gained.

Allied casualties were atrocious—some 530 men lost among the Indian troops alone—in a nighttime battle lasting only a few hours. German casualties, on the other hand, were light.[35] Three fresh German parachute battalions plus one parachute MG battalion had been rushed in to shore up defensive positions throughout the hills and among the abbey ruins.[36] And despite three straight days of heavy aerial bombardment, German resistance proved surprisingly robust.[37] The Allies falsely assumed that all those spectacular hilltop explosions had blinded German observation and obliterated many of their bunkers nearby. Instead, the Germans emerged from their battered holes, caves, and tunnels as if nothing had ever happened. The realization was demoralizing.[38]

Freyberg pushed for a fourth attack, but British Brigadier General Harry K. Dimoline, commanding the 4th Indian Division, convinced him of the futility of the notion.[39]

Freyberg's broad offensive wasn't a complete failure. During the night, 28th Maori Battalion troops of the New Zealand 2nd Division managed to gain a tenuous bridgehead across the Rapido south of Cassino. After crossing along a railway embankment south of Highway 6, the Maori seized the rail station and adjacent track yards. The feat was unexpectedly good news. In an attempt to get armor across before dawn, engineers worked feverishly in the dark trying to fill huge gaps the Germans had blown in the raised railbed.[40] The race to solidify the bridgehead was now against the sun.

The crews of the 756th Tank Battalion awaited news on both attacks. If the Germans showed any signs of retreat, the tanks might receive swift orders to sweep through town. Although the abbey attack failed, reports of the New Zealander breakthrough to the south sent a bolt of energy through the 756th HQ staff. At 0645, Captain Arnold and the OP party rushed to the ruined north Cassino villa.[41] Under a clear, windy morning,[42] Major Dolvin and Lt Col Sweeting strategized with Colonel Marshall at 0745 at his CP.[43] Marshall's 133rd infantry was woefully understrength—a regiment in name only; and Major Chapman's 3rd Battalion scarcely comprised a company. Only thirty effectives remained of I Company. L Company was down to only forty while K Company fielded seventy. In twenty straight days of combat since the Rapido River crossing, the 3rd Battalion lost a total of fifty-two men killed in action, 174 seriously wounded in action and another twenty-three missing.[44] At this point, the Marshall's men were incapable of spearheading any offensive actions and simply awaited relief. Nevertheless, they could still hold ground, patrol, and lay down suppressing fire and lend assistance any way possible.[45]

The New Zealander engineers came up short in the race to move armor across the railway embankment. The harsh light of dawn revealed everything to German observation, and a counterattack brewed immediately.[46] Within minutes, approximately three platoons of German infantry closed on Maori positions at the rail station behind a hail of bullets. Escorting the Germans troops was an astonishing sight: two captured M4s from Lt Granberry's "lost platoon" with white stars still clearly visible on their hulls. Initially, the appearance of "American" tanks caused hesitation and confusion among the Maori, but once the tanks began firing at them, Allied artillery was called in. The subsequent explosions broke up the German formation and forced the two captured M4s to withdraw.[47]

At 0750, Lt Col Sweeting raced to the British 5th Brigade CP.[48] Even though British Indian forces had not fully arrived in the area, plans were hastily drafted to rush all available troops from the Essex Battalion into northern Cassino should the Maori southern bridgehead hold and expand.[49] The aim was for both forces to link up in the center of town. The support of Sweeting's tanks would be critical. At 0830, Sweeting met with both command staffs for the 5th Brigade and Essex Battalion. A more concrete plan was drafted to attack later in the afternoon—but only if Castle Hill and the abbey fell first.[50] For these positions to fall meant a general German withdrawal was in the works.

In the meantime, Major Chapman's 3rd Battalion, 133rd, probed southward to test German reaction in town. The Germans remained in force and fired back to prove it. At 1000, two A Company tanks were sent to the jail to neutralize German MGs and aid the infantry's delicate advance. At 1020, however, the infantry backed off the pressure and the tank mission was altered to fire on the nunnery and then withdraw.[51] By 1100, the crews completed the task and pulled back.[52] Sweeting contacted Captain Arnold by phone, wanting renewed pressure on German positions in the nunnery and along castle ridge as well.[53] At 1330, four more tanks were dispatched into town. Two took the nunnery mission while the other two blasted away at the ridge.[54]

In the meantime, the abbey was bombed for a fourth straight day.[55] Further south, the struggling Maori holding the Cassino rail station were running short on supplies. Throughout the morning and early afternoon, New Zealand artillery units laid a protective smokescreen over Maori positions, but could not hold off

German troops accompanied by two *Sturmgeschütz* SP guns from inching in.[56] The situation had turned dire.

At 1430, Captain Arnold ordered three tanks from B Company to stage at the quarry.[57] In the meantime, Sweeting held a finalization meeting with the COs of the 5th Indian Brigade, the Essex Battalion with the company commanders for all four tank companies, HQ Company, and his communications officer, Captain Ed Olson in attendance.[58] Having never worked together before, every last coordination detail between the tanks and infantry had to be reviewed and agreed upon—including liaison protocol and the provision of British infantry radios for each company commander's tank.[59] One big caveat remained to the operation: the attack would only launch after the fall of Monastery Hill and Castle Ridge.[60] By 1700, the plan was complete.[61]

As dusk approached, Arnold withdrew the tanks in town and the OP party departed for Caira. The three B Company tanks at the quarry were told to await further instructions and remain in place overnight if necessary.[62]

At the same time, the New Zealand Maori struggling to hold the rail station flirted with disaster. The troops were nearly out of ammunition and could not be reinforced with additional infantry, nor could armor be moved in via the railway embankment. All afternoon, artillery batteries of the 34th and 36th Divisions put up a protective wall of fire to stave off the Germans, but enemy forces had closed in so close now that the risk became too great for causing friendly fire deaths.[63] The two encroaching SP guns, especially, could not be stopped. The toll on the Maori was horrendous. Of the 200 or so troops who originally crossed the Rapido, twenty-two were killed, seventy-eight wounded, and twenty-four went missing. Under covering artillery fire, the few dozen survivors withdrew back across the Rapido atop the damaged railway berm,[64] and the rail station fell back under the firm control of the Germans. With absolutely no evidence showing enemy withdrawal from either the abbey or Castle Hill, the carefully conceived plans for Sweeting's tanks and the Indian troops of the Essex Battalion to sweep down from the north were cancelled.[65]

The "Second Battle of Cassino" spearheaded by Freyberg's "fresh" troops ended in only four days,[66] and battle lines had not moved one iota since the Allied air bombardment of the abbey four days earlier.[67] The only consolation to the situation was the German offensive at Anzio had also stalled. Both sides had fought to a complete draw in Italy, leaving battle planners with much to ponder. As the weather worsened bringing biting winds, freezing rain, and blinding snow, any meaningful offensive became impossible for either side to launch.[68] Nevertheless, Freyberg began drafting plans for Operation *Dickens*—but these would take several days to prepare and did not involve the 756th Tank Battalion.

***

More and more British troops streamed across the Rapido from San Michele. After several nights, the 756th's assembly area nestled along Hill 213 became quite congested. Most of these new soldiers were Indian Sikhs or Gurkhas, but their officers were English. Gurkhas, in particular, had pitched camp near the B Company CP or alongside the tank crews clustered about the cemetery.[69] Though petite in stature—perhaps 5'2" tall and 120 pounds at most—they were extremely disciplined and polite soldiers.[70] As devout Hindus, they rarely associated with anyone other than their officers. Redle's tankers became fascinated watching their new neighbors' habits and customs—trying to square what they saw with what they heard about these strange foreigners. These small, quiet, and unassuming men had ferocious reputations as exceptional nighttime fighters. Gurkhas were legendary for infiltrating German positions undetected and killing the enemy as they slept in their foxholes. Naturally, the Germans were terrified of them.[71]

Upon arrival, the Gurkhas' British officers established a large ordnance dump along the road running up to Caira. Everything from mines, flares, and casks of wine were stockpiled in nice, neat rows. An officers' ration dump—a concept utterly foreign to Americans—was also established near the B Company CP. Both locations had already been well-registered by German artillery observers. Redle tried cautioning the newcomers, but the British major in charge boasted: "You Yanks don't know how to fight. We'll show you how it's done!" When morning arrived, the Germans promptly laid down a precise and orderly artillery barrage—reducing both dumps to hopeless messes.[72]

The cocky British major returned the following night and dallied about the B Company CP awaiting the arrival of a mule train carrying his new shipment of supplies. He informed Redle that he had abandoned the two old dumps and the tankers were free to salvage whatever they wanted. Pfc Clyde Guild rescued a few undamaged boxes of Libby peaches, Nestlé candy bars, canned sardines, and a few other goodies for distribution—knowing the crews would welcome the dietary variety. The major's mule train arrived just after sundown. As the skinners started unpacking, the area was blanketed with another heavy gust of German artillery. After this barrage lifted, only three of the fifty-three mules were still alive. German observers had monitored the major's mule train snaking across the eastern valley before dusk and calculated almost to the minute when it would arrive at Hill 213. The subsequent evening, the British major finally learned his lesson and made certain his mule train arrived well after dark to avoid detection along the way.[73]

German artillerymen seemed to relish showing the British newcomers "how it's done" by sending Indian colonials scurrying for cover every night—killing or wounding some in the process. One night, Sgt Hamilton Smith stood watching the Gurkhas congregate around a roadside water pump near the B Company CP. Each man had stripped down to perform some religious bathing ritual. Just then, the Germans struck hard with artillery. Sgt Smith tried diving beneath his own tank but found the tight space already crammed full of men and had to find cover elsewhere. Once the barrage lifted, fourteen Gurkhas climbed out from under Smith's tank.[74]

On another occasion, a Sikh solder was brought into the B Company CP writhing in pain with a large piece of shrapnel sticking from the bone of his forehead. Lt Redle tried administering a morphine shot, but the man refused the help and became greatly agitated. Later, a sheepish Redle learned that Sikh religious beliefs strictly prohibited the use of painkillers.[75]

During another German artillery attack, the B Company CP communication shed rocked under a series of heavy explosions. When this one ended, Pfc Guild raced over to check on Sgt Daniel Pompey—fearing the worst. As Guild burst through the door, he saw a stunned Gurkha soldier standing stiff against the wall with a hole in his head. With every beat of the doomed man's heart, blood spurted from his gaping wound. The long narrow room was jammed with Gurkha troops—some wounded, others dead. Seated in the far corner behind his regular desk was Sgt Pompey—smoking a pipe and calmly attending to his communication duties.[76] This was the moment Guild realized the war had become too much of a routine for B Company.

***

Throughout the day, German propaganda radio fixated on Monte Cassino. "The abbey Monte Cassino is completely destroyed," the broadcasts blared, "A senseless act of force of the Anglo-American air force has robbed civilized mankind of one its most-valued cultural monuments." Interviews with Abbot Diamare and German General von Senger played repeatedly, assuring the world that the abbey was never used for military purposes and condemning the Allies for failing to provide adequate evacuation notice. Hundreds of innocent civilian refugees were killed, both men testified.[77] Diamare, who had been the monastery's abbot for thirty-five years, wept sincere tears of despair as he recounted the horrors over National Socialist radio.[78] The broadcasts were deeply embarrassing for the Allies. Nevertheless, the U.S. State Department insisted the Germans were lying about respecting the abbey's neutrality.[79] German propagandists hoped the incident would help shore up Italian Fascist support in northern Italy. Partisan activity had been increasing in German-held areas, so printed posters showing the bomb damage and recounting Diamare's testimony of the abbey's neutrality started appearing all over the place.[80]

***

In the predawn hours of 19 February, Captain Arnold and the OP party departed for Cassino to begin another day of tank coordination. At the same time, Lt Col Sweeting met with Colonel Marshall at the 133rd CP—only to discover his infantry had no plans for tank support for the entire day. With relief now rumored to be only two days away,[81] Marshall saw no upside to offensive operations. His men would remain in position, ride out the intermittent mortar and artillery, and respond when appropriate.[82] As a precaution, Sweeting ordered Redle to swap a fresh platoon of tanks at the quarry in case the infantry situation changed. The three remaining tanks from Lt Harley's 1st Platoon took the shift.[83]

Sweeting also learned that C Company of the 760th Tank Battalion would be detached from his command and return across the Rapido at nightfall. The first New Zealander tank units were arriving in the area—meaning the 756th Tank Battalion was perhaps only hours away from being pulled from the line as well. For most tankers, the news was a godsend—but it brought teeth grinding aggravation to Sweeting. Some misplaced guilt over not accomplishing the mission ate away at his conscience. The only tools remaining at his disposal to go after the Germans were his assault guns and mortar crews. The mortars sat hidden across the Rapido to the east and the assault guns were positioned up near Caira. To alleviate his exasperation, Sweeting spent the day at the Hill 175 OP overlooking town, directing 81mm mortar and 105mm howitzer fire wherever he suspected the Germans to be hiding.[84]

The battalion's mortar platoon was comprised of three crews operating off three halftracks.[85] Their 81mm mortars were the same ones used by a "heavy weapons" platoon in an infantry battalion. The weapon was simple, durable, and dependable with a high rate of fire—as many as 800 rounds in a 24-hour period. One big disadvantage, however, was a low muzzle velocity combined with a high trajectory. This allowed shifting winds to wreak havoc with shot precision—a persistent challenge in Cassino. Whenever the winds remained calm, though, the 81mm mortar was extremely accurate.[86]

The six assault gun crews of HQ Company had worked virtually non-stop since their arrival at Cassino.[87] An M7 "Priest" assault gun was fully tracked like an M4 tank, but featured an open top—leaving the crew vulnerable to artillery and airbursts. A 105mm gun belched ample cordite, so the open top was necessary to disperse the fumes. Nevertheless, crews became terribly nauseous during heavy firing sequences and had to often stop and vomit over the side before loading and firing again. To prevent barrel burn-out, crews swabbed the tubes periodically with cold water. S/Sgt Roy Collins, platoon sergeant, allowed only five guns to fire at any given time—always rotating out one gun sequentially for cool down, whether it was needed or not. If a gun showed any signs of seizing up, the crew stopped firing without Collins's "cool down" order. Usually, the problem was rectified quickly with the addition of recoil cylinder oil.[88]

The assault guns fired every day, usually all day long and often at night as well. They were targeted by German artillery bombardments which often lasted several hours at a time, as well as aerial strafing runs—three times in one day on at least one occasion.[89] Firing operations commenced after target coordinates were phoned

North Section of Cassino, 6 February 1944. (National Archives, SC 239682)

One of dozens of German pillboxes buried 1½ miles north of Cassino. (U.S. Army)

A T2 from Service Company, 756th Tank Battalion, removes one of these German pillboxes somewhere north of Cassino. Walls were formed from cast iron, two inches thick. (National Archives, SC 329835)

An M4 crew of C Company, 760th Tank Battalion, waits to be called forward from a defilade position in the drained Rapido riverbed somewhere north of Cassino. (Critical Past)

M4s from the 760th Tank Battalion pass through the captured barracks on a "milk run" to Cassino. View is north. The Pimple (Hill 156) can be seen rising above the ruins on the left. (Citadel Archives and Museum, Charleston, South Carolina)

An abandoned German *Sturmgeschütz* III is examined and recovered from the barracks area by U.S. Army ordnance teams. It was later used for bazooka practice. The steep background hill in the left photo is Hill 215, beyond which lies Cassino. (U.S. Army)

A 756th Tank Battalion M4 sits disabled due to a thrown track two miles north of Cassino. (U.S. Army)

Another M4 victim of Rapido River mud. This track was completely sheared and thrown forward when the driver attempted to reverse out of the situation. (U.S. Army)

The rear idler wheel to this M4 north of Cassino has been clipped by a German AT round, shattering the track and leaving the tank immobilized. (U.S. Army)

A 34th Infantry Division mortar crew operates from the rocky hills north of Cassino. The flooded fields east of the Rapido River can be seen in the distance. (Critical Past)

A 133rd Infantry Regiment MG operator and spotter keep watch on the monastery from Hill 175. (Critical Past)

American infantrymen holding defensive positions east of the Rapido River. (Critical Past)

756th Tank Battalion tanks, an M10 TD, and a medical half-track assemble in the quarry a half-mile north of Cassino. The location, tucked safely under the parabolic reach of enemy mortar and artillery rounds, offered an ideal staging site for all future attacks into the town. (Critical Past)

34th Infantry Division troops heading from Cassino file past an Italian woman and infant near the ruined village of San Vittore. (Critical Past)

A dead German lays sprawled outside the rear entrance of a MG bunker above the quarry. Such positions usually had to be flanked carefully and neutralized by tossing hand grenades. A supporting M4 was much more efficient: one round of AP created an opening. A follow-up HE round through the hole killed the occupants. Consequently, the Germans usually surrendered quickly when an M4 was present. (Critical Past)

Major Dolvin leads a late afternoon attack on Cassino, 3 February 1944. One column of tanks advanced on the narrow road while a second column advanced in the drained Rapido River bed on the left. Smoke was dropped ahead to blind German SP crews hidden in town. (Author created composite of frames taken from Critical Past film footage)

Quarry area, facing north. 756th Tank Battalion M4s depart from the quarry area on a fire mission into the north section of Cassino sometime during the first week of February. Notice the drained Rapido River and the felled trees along the river. The Germans cleared the banks of brush to create MG "killing fields" to the east. (Author created composite of frames taken from Critical Past film footage)

Wide angle view of Cassino taken during an Allied artillery attack on the morning of 6 February 1944. Castle Hill and the town's center bear the brunt. At his point in time, American forces held only the flat ground seen in the lower quarter and the ruined buildings seen in the far right section of this photograph. All other ground remained under firm German control. (National Archives, SC 359292)

The Benedictine monastery as seen from Hill 175. Beleaguered Americans below convinced themselves the Germans were using the neutral site as an observation post. (Critical Past)

Composite taken from Hill 225 showing the extent of flooded fields east of the Rapido River. Only tracked vehicles and six-wheeled trucks could get through further north where the engineers constructed a narrow, raised roadway. (Critical Past)

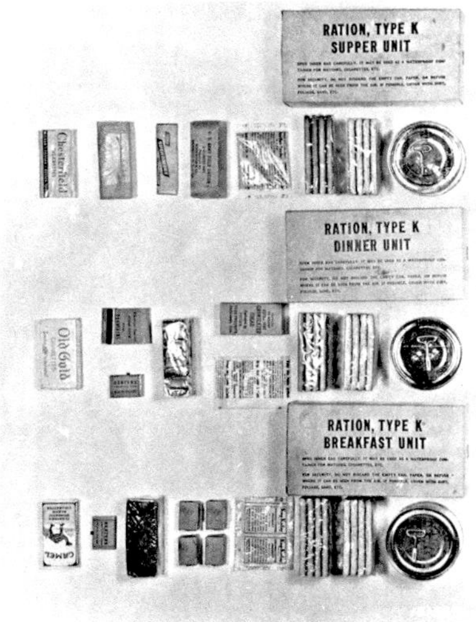

A combat infantryman's sustenance for a day: the three-meal K-ration. Each box was roughly 7" by 4" by 2" in size. (U.S. Army)

A German anti-personnel Schu mine and remnants of a "Screaming Meemie" photographed one mile north of Cassino. (U.S. Army)

Tanks damaged beyond the expertise of 756th mechanics, but otherwise salvageable ended up here—with the 87th Ordnance Company near Presenzano, Italy. (National Archives, SC 312581)

A destroyed C Company, 760th Tank Battalion, M4 sits silently inside the north edge of town showing two AT holes near the bow gunner's position. This was 2nd Lt Leo J. Trahan's tank—knocked out at dusk, 3 February 1944. This photo was taken on 19 May 1944 by Polish forces. Note the advanced destruction of nearby buildings. (S. E., Carpathian Division, 2nd Polish Corps)

Another destroyed C Company, 760th Tank Battalion, M4 near the north entrance of town. This one was hit with AT fire in the final drive, shattering the right drive sprocket and in the lower hull, obliterating the middle boogie wheels and track suspension. This was Sgt Lawrence G. Stander's tank—knocked out on 7 February 1944. Photo taken 19 May 1944. (S. E., Carpathian Division, 2nd Polish Corps)

A third C Company, 760th, M4 knocked out and pointed north near the town's entrance. This photo was also taken in May 1944, after Cassino was finally captured. Nearly five months of bombing left little standing of the jail in the background. (Citadel Archives and Museum, Charleston, South Carolina)

Members of the 242nd Sturmgeschütz Abteilung (Assault Gun Battalion) pose atop one of three M4s captured from Lt James Granberry's "lost platoon" in Cassino during the evening of 2 February 1944. (Archive, St. Barbara, Jüterbog)

One of Lt Granberry's tanks repainted with 242nd markings and put into service of the German army. This was likely Sgt Vaughn's tank as the turret has been removed. Sgt Vaughn's turret was damaged by AT fire before he and his crew were captured. (Archive, St. Barbara, Jüterbog)

The remnants of a German Mark IV tank first knocked out in the north section of Cassino on 6 February 1944. The wreck suffered further damage after countless bombings before this photo was taken three months later. (Polish Institute and Sikorski Museum—London)

Photo taken of the ruined jail area by George Kaye on 18 May 1944 when Cassino finally fell to the Allies. This is likely the A Co. 756th M4 that overturned while firing on the nunnery on 13 February. (Alexander Turnbull Library, Wellington New Zealand)

The commanding views east from Monte Cassino. The Allies suspected the Germans were illegally using the abbey as an observation post. However, countless caves, hollows and outcroppings nearby offer the same panoramic advantages. (U.S. Army)

Numerous aerial flyovers failed to show any clear evidence of German presence inside the abbey compound. Nevertheless, during an overflight on 14 February 1944, Allied Air Forces commander Lt Gen Ira C. Eaker thought he saw a laundry line of gray uniforms strung between buildings. This was enough to convince him that the abbey should be destroyed. (Critical Past)

Messages warning of the abbey's imminent destruction were loaded into artillery shells and fired onto the summit. The monks and civilians inside were given little time to escape: the bombers arrived the next morning. (Critical Past)

Allied bombs destroy the abbey during the morning of 15 February 1944. (Critical Past)

The following three images are combat photos taken in Cassino on the morning of 15 February 1944. They are found in a 27 April 1944 War Department publication called "Report of the New Weapons Board". The photographer is unknown. M4s from A and C Companies, 756th Tank Battalion arrive at the north entrance of Cassino during the morning while the abbey is being bombed. (U.S. Army)

The two overturned C Company, 756th, tanks seen on the left became disabled the week before and were pushed aside to keep the narrow roadway open. (U.S. Army)

The bombed abbey is obscured by dust and smoke as the M4 crews prepare to fire upon nearby Castle Hill on the left. The huge blast holes in the walls of the nearby apartment building were created by tank gunners while supporting infantry operations earlier in the month. (U.S. Army)

15 February 1944, composite view of north Cassino, facing south. Five U.S. Army photos form this remarkable composite of the battle-scarred northern quarter of Cassino. All M4 crews of the 756th Tank Battalion and attached tankers of C Company, 760th, became intimately familiar with this view of the town during the two-and-a-half weeks they fought here. The Germans could not be dislodged from these ruins until May 1944. (Author created composite from U.S. Army "Report of the New Weapons Board" photographs)

Lt Col Sweeting holds two 75mm German AT slugs similar to what knocked out one of his C Company tanks at Cassino, leaving holes in the transmission plate and below the driver's hatch. (U.S. Army)

Captain "Doc" Sarno poses with British Gurkha troops near the 756th's "meat wagon" ambulance after it was destroyed in an artillery attack. (Donald G. Shonka)

Lt Howard Harley, Silver Star recipient for his actions at Cassino. (Ann Harley Skinner)

Sgt Eugene K. Wunderlich (left) and Pfc David J. Orris (right), both mortally wounded at Cassino, 5 February 1944. (David Orris family)

S/Sgt Oric W. Johannesen was seriously wounded at Cassino on 5 February 1944, but became known as the "Miracle Man" by his doctors and returned to B Company in time for Operation *Diadem*. (Oric Johannesen Family)

in to the crews from the forward OP. Next, the guns launched smoke shells to mark the target and awaited adjustment instructions. After a position was properly sighted and confirmed, the guns fired a steady stream of explosive rounds until instructed to halt. At times, battle demands pushed the guns beyond their mechanical limits—an extremely dangerous practice. On a few occasions, the crews kept firing away even with hydraulic bleed valves safeties fully extended. Fortunately, no misfires ever occurred—otherwise the resulting explosion would have likely wiped out an entire gun crew.[90]

One halftrack and several trucks kept the M7s steadily supplied with 105mm howitzer ammunition—driving all the way to San Pietro to obtain new stocks. During the long journey, the drivers were often forced to time German artillery salvos raining down along the main road and speed through. Because all supply runs occurred at night under blackout conditions, every trip was harrowing.[91]

The crews relied on flashlights during nighttime fire missions to adjust the readings on their gun sights. Invariably the batteries ran low on charge and had to be boiled in a number ten can over a Colman single-burner stove to rekindle a few more hours of light. The crews never understood how the same magnificent U.S. Army could keep a steady supply of ammunition flowing but never stocked enough flashlight batteries—despite their many requests.[92] Some Army practices defied logic.

During the afternoon of 19 February, Sweeting directed assault gun fire from the forward OP but grew increasingly disappointed over the outcome. The gun crews were performing well, but German troops could often be seen darting from one position to another only 300 yards away on Castle Hill. Out of pure frustration, Sweeting borrowed an M1 Garand and started sniping at them. After squeezing off a few shots, he stepped back from the window in disgust. Seconds later, the OP villa was inundated with S/A, MG, and mortar fire. Several men dropped from wounds and S/Sgt William Fodor of C Company/756th lay dead from a clean gunshot through his right temple.[93] Fodor had been observing out the same stairwell window from which Sweeting fired and had returned to his post after his commander finished his undisciplined outburst. Not only had Sweeting foolishly given away their OP position, but Fodor had died needlessly as a result of his rash action. Worse, Sweeting savagely berated a young infantry lieutenant afterwards—accusing him of not maintaining a proper look-out and shifting the blame on him for Fodor's death.[94] Captain Arnold, who always maintained a professional persona, was so enraged by what he had witnessed he briefly considered assaulting Sweeting physically—but refrained after regaining control of his senses.[95] Arnold had been Fodor's company commander before assuming the S-3 position, and knew him well from the battalion's earliest days at Fort Lewis. Fodor had always been an upstanding and dependable soldier,[96] and Arnold considered the 25-year-old from Wellsburg, West Virginia, as much of a "friend" as was appropriate between an officer and an enlisted man.[97]

The 756th Tank Battalion had suffered no casualties during the past three days.[98] Now, S/Sgt Fodor became the battalion's last unlucky man to die—and under scandalous circumstances.[99] Battalion medics T/5 Phil Oliva and T/5 Denis Hannan retrieved Fodor's body—but waited until after nightfall to avoid becoming the newest set of battalion casualties.[100]

***

Without question, Lt Col Sweeting was a courageous officer. He led with gusto from the front when the situation demanded it, and never tired of seeking creative solutions to dire tactical challenges. Some men froze in fear when faced with mortal danger. Many others pressed on despite a dry mouth, a heart pounding in the throat, and a loss of bodily functions. Rote training moved their arms and legs. But rare types—like Sweeting—found combat exhilarating and empowering. Sweeting even exhibited a weird giddiness under fire. Ironically, this fearlessness was also Sweeting's worst fault, because he could not control it. Tom Treanor, the intrepid young *Los Angeles Times* reporter, perfectly captured this aspect of Sweeting's personality when he observed:

> He was what his men called battle-happy. When the fighting was on he seemed to be lifted into a sort of exalted state which gave him limitless energy and more or less deprived him of personal fear. He radiated vigor and enthusiasm and had the faculty of communicating a feeling that the battle was an exciting game rather than a terrifying ordeal … Sweeting was the type who could always put things picturesquely. After he'd been in an engagement there was never any difficulty getting a story out of him. It came hot and smoking off his tongue so you got the feel of it.[101]

Real flesh and blood men died in Sweeting's game. They did not wake up again and walk back to camp when the match was over.[102] Somehow this sense of humanity got lost in Sweeting's interactions with others during combat, and his men consequently lost faith he even cared about their survival.

Unlike many West Pointers, Sweeting did not come from a military family. His father and grandfather were common tradesmen. His mother died when he was young, and so a military-minded uncle raised him and had great influence on his character.[103] After reading countless military histories, Sweeting felt drawn to the life of a professional soldier and was admitted to the U.S. Military Academy in 1929. Sweeting believed his next calling was to win great war battles. He once revealed to Lt Redle his belief in reincarnation and that he had been a brilliant commander in the past in the mold of Alexander the Great.[104] Another time, he told his tank driver, Jack Brown, that he saw his future self as a brigadier general with a "dignified" limp due to an old leg wound.[105] A powerful sense of destiny is not an unusual quality to great military leaders—but great military leaders also exhibit great self-discipline in all aspects of their character, as well as respect and appreciation for the men they lead.

Perhaps Sweeting struggled inside with this self-control. Outwardly, he was a nervous and high-strung officer. He had been a heavy smoker and decided to quit the habit, of all times, during the Battle of Monte Cassino—and succeeded in doing so.[106] Better to smoke, however, than betray your OP position in a fit of frustration. Better to wait for infantry support before ordering a platoon of tanks into town—only to promptly lose them. Better to curb a bit of your enthusiasm seeking out a creative solution to a combat challenge in order to factor in the survival of your men. What made Sweeting so exasperating was that he exhibited all the ingredients for greatness, but had not yet figured out how to put them in proper order.

***

At 1500, B Company rotated the platoons on standby at the quarry. Sgt Oliver's 3rd platoon moved in to allow Lt Harley's 1st platoon to withdraw back to Hill 213.[107] By early evening, Sweeting instructed all his company commanders to hold positions, but the assault gun and mortar crews would continue firing on through the night.[108]

Word of Fodor's pointless death spread throughout the battalion and cast a pall over the men's eagerness for impending relief. During the night, the tanks of C Company, 760th, withdrew across the Rapido.[109] The Germans, sensing a transfer in the works, shelled the staging areas surrounding 756th HQ near San Michele without mercy.[110]

On the morning of 20 February, the OP party departed Caira and arrived in town at 0645.[111] No tank activity was planned, but the battalion's assault guns and mortars would continue firing throughout the day. At 1000, the telephone rang at the 756th HQ with a message that C Company, 760th, had been formally detached from the 756th.[112] At 1430, officers from the New Zealand 4th Armoured Brigade met with Sweeting at the 756th CP in Caira to prepare an orderly transfer of duties.[113] The M4 tank crews of the 19th Armoured Regiment, 4th Armoured Brigade, would make the actual exchange. Sweeting briefed the British officers on the tactical situation and furnished them with sketches the battalion had been using as maps.[114] The men agreed that the New Zealand tanks should arrive the following evening. After which, the 756th Tank Battalion would withdraw across the Rapido.[115] American positions would be relieved one tank at a time—but only after a New Zealander tank first took its place. B Company would depart first, followed by C Company and then, finally, A Company.[116] The 756th's assault gun platoon and mortar platoon were instructed to fire all remaining ammunition ahead of the move.[117] The assault guns would do so the following morning and then wait a few hours before moving back across the Rapido.[118]

After nightfall, all battalion vehicles apart from the M4 mediums and T2 retrievers were instructed to move to San Pietro. Ammunition dumps near San Michele were ordered to be packed and moved eastward as well.[119] By 2130 the battalion's entire marching orders for the journey from San Michele to the San Pietro were finalized.[120] Word spread quickly from the battalion's forward positions at Caira, Hill 213, and the quarry out to HQ units at San Michele before finally reaching the rear service units at San Pietro. Afterwards, everyone found sleep difficult from all the excitement.[121] Many were surprised to be moving at all because Cassino had not yet fallen.[122]

Well before sunrise on 21 February, 756th Assistant S-3 Captain Oscar S. Long scurried between HQs coordinating road march plans with the 34th Infantry Division. Due to massive road congestion, movement from San Pietro to a final destination at Alife—36 miles away—required special clearances.[123] At 0845, Sweeting conferred with Colonel Marshall at the 133rd CP one final time. Both commanders looked haggard and drained, but throughout the entire ghastly four-week ordeal, the colonel unwaveringly maintained his trademark handlebar moustache. He did so by meticulously scraping and melting the wax from discarded K-ration cartons.[124] An orderly transition was now their main concern.[125] By 1130, the liaison officer with the New Zealand 19th Armoured Regiment, 4th Armoured Brigade, informed Sweeting that seventeen tanks from his unit would relieve the 756th at midnight.[126]

All morning and afternoon, American artillery batteries blasted German positions to shield relief operations. Every now and then, German batteries retaliated. They seemed to possess an uncanny sense, too, about which units were most vulnerable and showered the 756th HQ area at San Michele with special attention. The sporadic bursts unnerved the weary men packing vehicles, hoping simply to survive the next few hours. Every shriek of an incoming round made them cuss, dash, and dive behind sandbags, beneath foxhole covers and into the tanks themselves. Nobody was ever hit, but one round exploded behind a parked HQ tank—blowing the air cleaner completely away from the rear deck.[127]

At 1430, Sweeting issued final instructions to his remaining company commanders. Fifty minutes later, the Germans heavily shelled Caira, striking a disabled battalion M7 assault gun and setting it on fire.[128] Fortunately, the crew had taken cover some distance away beforehand. For two hours, the steel hulk burned—providing a convenient beacon for further German artillery attacks as dusk set in.[129] After nightfall, the five remaining M7s pulled from Caira and headed toward the Rapido. Sgt Roy Collins looked around one last time at the cold hellish landscape. Several fires raged around them—casting the ruined houses, shops, and tiny courtyards with a sinister orange glow that flickered with every shifting wind. Through one blast hole in the upper storey of a nearby house, he saw a mule carcass rotting in a bedroom. The poor beast had been tossed skyward before crashing through the roof. In the broken branches of an apple tree, the ruptured body of a dead soldier dangled in an ignoble twist—after landing there following some other prior blast.[130]

Collins and the assault gun crews fretted throughout their slow journey eastward, but eventually arrived at San Michele safely.[131]

At 0100, 22 February, the liaison officer with the 19th Armoured Regiment, reported his B Squadron had crossed the Rapido and was ready to relieve the 756th Tank Battalion.[132] Ten minutes later, Sweeting radioed the coded withdrawal order everyone wanted to hear: "The Stars and Stripes have come." B Company moved first, departing the quarry as New Zealand B Squadron's M4A2 Shermans assumed their places. Lt Redle's tanks snaked back to Hill 213, then cut right at the road junction north of the cemetery before heading toward the Rapido.[133] C Company was next, then A Company followed, with the battalion medical detachment bringing up the rear. The retreat was orderly and uneventful, and the last vehicle closed just before dawn at the battalion's pre-designated "intermediate point" in a field off Highway 6 near Monte Trocchio.[134] The crews needed a few hours of rest and the tanks required reservicing before they could proceed to their final destination at Alife—thirty-six more miles to the southeast.

At the same time, the remnants of Colonel Marshall's battered and beleaguered 133rd Regiment finally received their relief in the form of bright, clean Brodie-helmeted troops representing the 6th New Zealand Infantry Brigade. Marshall's men had been fighting far too long below the fifty percent mark of authorized strength and looked like tattered hobos. Their orders were to walk first to an assembly area near San Michele and join their fellow 34th Division survivors before boarding trucks headed to Alife for much-needed recuperation and reorganization.[135] During the march back, one "Red Bull" infantry officer leading fifteen filthy, shabby, and unshaven soldiers passed the B Company tank maintenance crew parked near San Michele. "This does not look like 180 men, does it?" the fatalistic officer muttered to T/5 John J. Roth while trudging by. At that instant, Roth thanked God he was in the maintenance crew and not a tanker on the front.[136]

***

"The battle was best described as a little Stalingrad," a 3rd Battalion, 133rd, officer summarized later.[137] When the 756th Tank Battalion first arrived at Cassino, Allied planes blanketed German positions with leaflets offering a choice between "Stalingrad or Tunis."[138] The flyer was meant to elicit surrender. The chief lesson of Stalingrad, however, was that a highly motivated army on the defensive could annihilate an attacking army—even if forced to fight among city ruins with their backs to a river. The Germans chose Stalingrad—but in the role of the Russians.

A key feature to Lt Gen Freyberg's Operation *Dickens* demanded battlefield conditions even closer to those of Stalingrad. Rather than renewing the attack through the mountains, Freyberg decided the best way to capture the abbey was through the town below. To do so, troops in Cassino had to be withdrawn while the remaining buildings were blitzed into oblivion under another dubious aerial bombardment gambit. The north entrance of town, the square, the OP on Hill 175, the new bridge over the spillway, the jail, every crumbling shop, home, apartment, courtyard, alley, room, and wall that the 756th Tank Battalion and 133rd Infantry Regiment blasted, breached, cleared, and secured through desperation, deprivation, toil, and death over the course of three agonizing weeks would be abandoned again to the Germans.

All in hopes of winning it back again after the bombers thundered away.

New Zealand cap badge

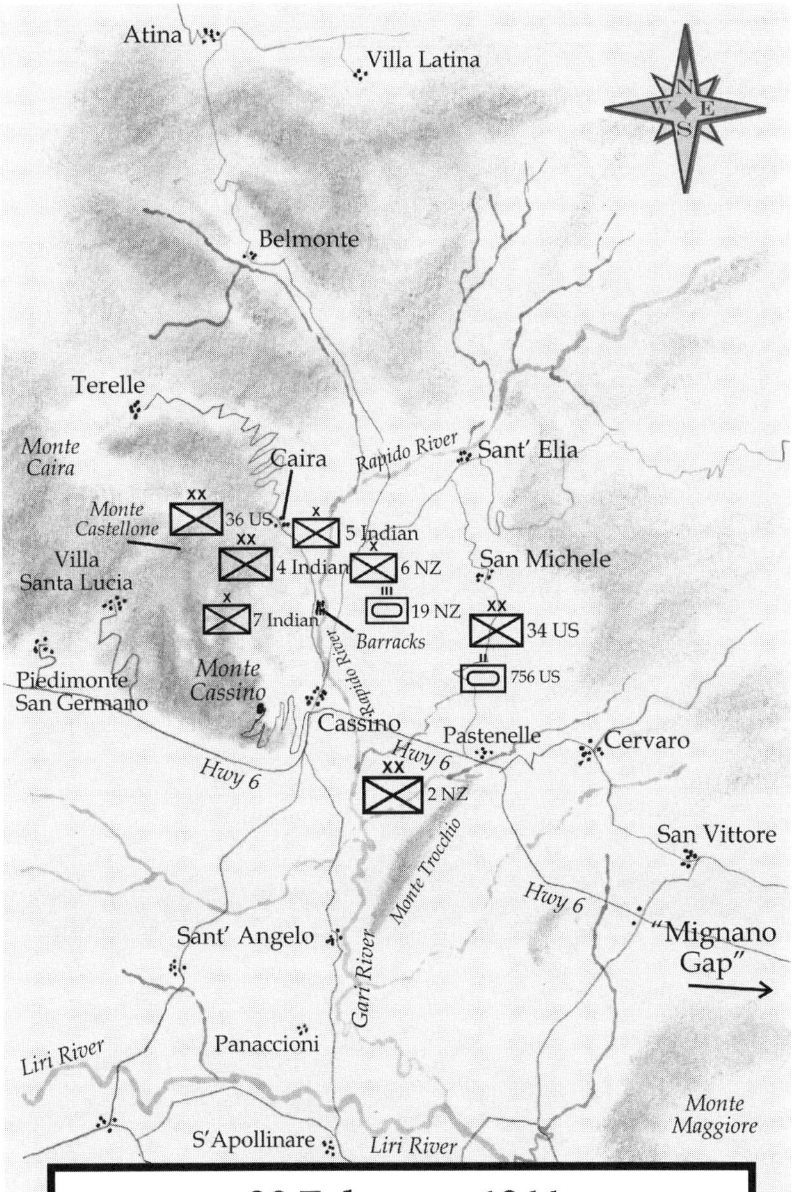

20 February 1944

RELIEF of US 34th INFANTRY DIVISION CASSINO REGION

0 1/2 1 2 3 4

SCALE in MILES

CHAPTER EIGHT

Retrospection: 22 February 1944 to 23 February 1944

The 756th Tank Battalion left Cassino the same way they came: in the dead of night under the dazzling chaotic flashes and thunderous serenading of artillery. At 2230, 22 February, with Captain Arnold leading, the C Company tanks exited the muddy field below Monte Trocchio—then lined up and plodded toward Highway 6 at walking speed. A medical half-track shuffled into place with the small column. Fifteen minutes later, A Company, the Assault Gun Platoon, and a second medical halftrack repeated the process before rumbling off in the darkness as well. Lt Redle waited a predetermined fifteen minutes more before staging his tank crews into the last column segment. The medical ambulance and the maintenance section brought up the rear. After Redle's column reached Highway 6, speed increased to a brisk eight miles an hour and vehicles maintained fifty-yard spacing intervals. Blackout lighting and strict radio silence was maintained.[1]

The nighttime travel weather was clear—no rain or mist for once—but the roads were in an atrocious condition. The heavy beating from the ever-present flow of men and machines coming and going made for a rugged and jarring ride,[2] and because of the influx of fresh British troops packing the opposite lane, the tank drivers' eyes strained to stay extra vigilant. Twenty-four hours earlier, D Company and most of battalion HQ caravanned to Alife to scout out bivouac grounds,[3] arriving just prior to dawn.[4] Along the way, reconnaissance guides were dropped off at key locations to make certain the rest of the battalion did not miss the turns. These guides were then picked up by maintenance section vehicles closing out the column.[5]

After traveling roughly two hours and covering fifteen miles of territory, the tankers cleared the Mignano Gap and passed south of Clark's HQ at Presenzano. Blackout orders were lifted, and all headlights flared on with blinding glory. After forty days of moving without any nighttime light at all, the drivers could finally see clearly again.[6]

Just before reaching this point, however, a tank retriever near the rear of the column—the B Company T2 driven by Pfc Thomas M. Barber and commanded by T/4 Roy R. Kosanke—fell woefully behind. Barber lost sight of the slatted taillights he was supposed to follow and sped up to find them. Kosanke, watching from the turret hatch, feared Barber had left the road. Due to the deafening engine whine and clanging racket of tools and equipment shaking about the interior, Kosanke ducked inside to yell a warning over to Barber. At that instant, he felt the T2 floating airborne and his mind screamed: "Oh Lord, I hope this isn't a canyon!" The nose dropped and a violent jolt followed. The 34-ton vehicle came to rest completely upside down—showering all six horrified occupants with wrenches, bolts, and heavy equipment. For several moments, the dazed men groped about inside pitch darkness amid the dripping of gasoline and battery acid but became too disoriented to find the exit. Up was down and down was up. Luckily, Technical Sergeant (T/Sgt) Morris B. Thompson, trailing in another vehicle, witnessed the T2's taillight slats disappear ahead of him. Barber had missed a critical detour and plummeted over a blown bridge—crashing twenty feet below. Had Kosanke not ducked down inside the turret hatch when he did, he would have surely been crushed to death. Thompson bounded down the steep ravine and grasped the handle to the side hatch, but found it locked from within. "Where is the door?" a bewildered voice inside queried when told to release the handle. The hatch was finally opened, and the crew escaped. Medics examined each man and found places for them to ride in other vehicles. Miraculously, only Pfc Barber—grimacing from a cracked collarbone—was the only injury.[7]

Because of strict radio silence orders, Lt Redle was not informed of the T2 accident until after B Company arrived at Alife. Those six hours of quiet travel gave the young company commander plenty of time to ponder life and take stock of events over the past few weeks.

Redle had survived so many close calls with death he was genuinely shocked to be alive.[8] He had escaped near misses from artillery, mortar, bullets, and high velocity SP rounds howling inches past his ear. Every day for two straight weeks, he had walked in and out of Cassino under the watchful eyes of German observers and yet—never suffered so much as a scratch. This was an astounding realization. Redle concluded the only way he had beaten such astronomical odds was through God's intervention. He knew his family was praying for him—as were 1,500 nuns at his sister's order, the Leavenworth Sisters of Charity, and this knowledge brought Redle immeasurable spiritual comfort.[9]

The coming respite from the front lines would finally allow him to answer his growing stack of mail. Betty, his fiancée, needed reassurances that he was safe. His best friend, Fazendin, wounded four months earlier by a mine near the Volturno river, needed the same. Faz still faced a long recuperation wrapped in a full body cast somewhere back in the States—and relied on nurses to write his letters.[10]

Redle pondered Captain Wilkinson's fate. Those who had witnessed the unfortunate events of 27 January were reasonably convinced Wilkinson and the surviving members of his and Lt Henry's tanks had been captured. But nobody really knew for certain. Redle still found it difficult to accept Wilkie was gone. He had great admiration for his former captain and patterned much of his own leadership style upon the tall Texan's impeccable examples. From time to time, Redle wondered if he was meeting expectations in this new role. Feedback from his peers and the men under his command indicated he was.[11]

Redle was extremely proud of his men. B Company's first days in battle had been brutal—beyond anything anyone could have imagined during training. The unforgiving mud, the early, devastating losses of key leadership, the frequent communication glitches with the infantry, the narrow attack lanes, the claustrophobic maneuvering spots—all represented seemingly insurmountable challenges at times. But through it all, his men endured, adapted, and overcame. Lt Col Sweeting deserved much of the credit. The numerous months prior of exhausting physical fitness exercises, head-numbing gunnery exercises, and rote crew training drills had prepared the tankers well for the rigors of combat. Redle was also thankful for Lt Howard Harley—the only other officer remaining in his company. He was proud to see Harley's bravery recognized by Sweeting and Captain Arnold and that the South Carolinian would be awarded the Silver Star. However, Redle was most proud of his sergeants. Without them, the company simply would not have functioned. Three platoon sergeants, in particular—Johannesen, Haspel, and Oliver—had been outstanding. Because of the early loss of lieutenants, both Haspel and Oliver were forced to lead their respective platoons through most of the battle. Sgt Oliver, especially, had performed exceptionally well. Redle thought Oliver and his entire crew should have received some formal recognition for going head-to-head against that German tank hidden near the nunnery. The incident had become legendary among the battalion rank and file. Sweeting witnessed the encounter firsthand—so why the battalion commander refused to decorate them afterwards was a complete mystery.[12] Sweeting already had a stingy reputation for awarding medals, but Redle considered this particular slight downright unfair—and wondered if some latent jealousy might be involved.[13] 1st Sgt Jack Hogan, too, had been indispensable—keeping the company properly supplied while running and handling all the lieutenant's administrative work so Redle could concentrate strictly on combat. During the upcoming reorganization, Redle would recommend awards and promotions for many of these men.

B Company suffered twenty-two casualties during the battle of Cassino: five men killed, nine wounded, seven captured, and one man injured and evacuated.[14] Out of a company of roughly 100 men, this represented a loss of one in five—certainly not as dire as the infantry's losses, but a tanker was not as easy to replace as a rifleman. A tank platoon leader, commander, gunner, or driver required time and far more extensive technical training to become proficient at their jobs. This was why the battalion needed to withdraw to Alife to reorganize and retrain.

The battalion's survivors were forever changed. All the pre-combat swagger about "killing Krauts" and "getting the job done quickly and going home" ended. Nobody talked that way anymore. Some came through the ordeal with profound religious experiences. During one particularly harrowing German artillery barrage, a B Company tank became hung up near the entrance of town. Crewmember Pvt Cletus J. Offerman saw a woman in a blue dress and white collar step out into the middle of the street amid the bursting of shells. Her appearance was not only foolish, but impossible, as all civilians had long since evacuated town. He then recognized the mysterious woman as his own mother—the very instant the figure disappeared. This was also impossible since his mother had passed away several years earlier. Offerman turned to Pvt Nicholas P. Motto, the driver, and asked if he also saw someone standing in the road. Motto, nodding in disbelief, confirmed seeing a woman in a blue dress. At that moment, the tank mysteriously slipped into reverse and backed out of danger.[15] Other men experienced similar unexplainable events they were reluctant to disclose for fear of ridicule or from concerns they might be losing their grip with reality.

Five B Company tanks were total losses. Two had been destroyed in battle, and three others sunk so deep in mud they had to be abandoned.[16] In all, the 756th Tank Battalion left behind twenty-eight tanks—most unsalvageable. HQ Company lost one during the second attack on the town when Major Dolvin took the lead. D Company lost three others. A Company lost a total of six—most had been hit and burned after the second Rapido crossing of 29 January; and C Company lost eight—three of which had been captured by the Germans. In addition, C Company, 760th, lost five tanks while attached to the 756th—four were wrecks still scattered about the entrance of town.[17] The tracked survivors plodding the long journey back to Alife required extensive servicing due to the heavy wear and tear of battle. Regular maintenance was necessarily neglected to allow the crews rest and recovery during those brief times away from combat.[18] The mud and moisture had worked into everything—acting as a harsh abrasive. Gears, pins, and joints had become contaminated with soil and required a complete cleaning and relubrication. All bogie wheel grease seals also needed replacement.[19] Sticks, stones, rocks, and rubble had lodged up inside the suspension works—fatiguing and cracking the volute springs, track guides, drive sprockets, bogie wheels, and idler wheels.[20] Insufficiently tensioned tracks permitted the accretion of even more debris—chunking out rubber tread blocks and even causing, at times, the entire track to disintegrate.[21] Rubber track blocks were rated to last 800 miles, but the rough roads and rubble-strewn Italian battlefields ground them flat after less than 300 miles of travel. Steel tracks proved more durable, but the crews' sore rumps preferred the rubber over steel "almost universally."[22] Steel track also caused more damage to the bogie wheels—leading to premature replacement.[23] The rough conditions had also degraded transmissions, clutches, and steering bands. None of these repairs could be performed easily upon a battlefield, and it was plainly impossible to clean treads and suspension systems while fighting.[24]

At Cassino, the tanks and their crews had been forced to fight in ways unintended. An M4 medium tank was designed to storm across open fields through rolling countryside—crossing the occasional obstacle—a fence, a rock wall, a ditch, a stream—using speed to flank the enemy. An M4 was not built to ply atop rubble piles for days on end or squeeze down narrow streets with fully depressed main guns firing point blank rounds into basement windows. The crews had not even been trained to fight in cities at all. The concept was completely alien to the two-and-a-half years of armor doctrine pressed inside their heads. The crews had been drilled on the importance of attacking while spread out *en masse*—much like a football team dashing down a gridiron during a kickoff. Enemy tanks were to be avoided in favor of striking an enemy's weakest point. Using speed and shock, the tanks would theoretically penetrate deep inside an enemy formation sowing confusion and despair.[25] Clearly, much Fort Knox "armor doctrine" had been tossed out the window during the Battle of Cassino. In theory, tank destroyers were supposed to destroy German tanks, but the M-10's vulnerable open turret often prevented crews from moving in close enough to do the job under actual battlefield conditions. Thus, confrontations between M4 mediums and German tanks became unavoidable.

Many times, too, the tanks could not maneuver with the benefit of fire support from other tanks. Crews were often forced to operate outside the protection of their battalion, company or even their platoon—attacking not with speed and shock in support of one another, but as one or two lumbering pillboxes shadowing the infantry. In probably the most glaring oversight of all, the infantry and tankers hadn't trained together ahead of time. Nevertheless, the two disciplines were thrust together and expected to hash out any doctrinal differences and somehow succeed under the do-or-die pressures of battle.

Sweeting addressed many of these concerns in his formal Cassino after-action report: "Separate tank battalions should be attached to units whom they are going to support in battle, during training periods prior to action. The value of such attachment is inestimable," he emphasized. Sweeting also recognized that too much tank training had been devoted to battalion, company, and platoon level tactics and not enough to the crews and sections: "All the action emphasized the importance of well-trained crews and sections. Tank commanders must be trained to make decisions quickly. Commanders are frequently knocked out or their radios stop functioning. Individual tankers (knowing the situation and the mission) must then <u>look</u> around and <u>move</u> around to complete the mission." Sweeting also cautioned against the over-reliance of aerial photography in decision-making without having corroborating ground reconnaissance, and called for at least four back-pack sized radios for battalion use. "The present SCR 509 is not suitably portable," he concluded.[26]

Sweeting also noted how the Germans were often caught off guard during late afternoon attacks—particularly after a position was hammered earlier in the day.[27] He believed this weakness wasn't exploited to the fullest. Lt Redle drew other lessons from Cassino—believing the 34th Infantry Division had not been adequately resupplied with men and material after their long, tough slog up the Mignano Gap. These same depleted infantry units were expected to carry the fight beyond the Rapido but lacked the full punch to do so. As a result, Redle believed American losses were unnecessarily high and led to a stalemate.[28] A properly rested and more aggressive infantry moving when Wilkinson's four tanks first breached the Rapido, meant both Hill 213 and the barracks would have likely fallen by nightfall, 27 January. The Germans had been completely stunned by the appearance of Wilkinson's tanks. But the infantry's hesitation allowed the enemy time to adjust—and thus several of Captain Lewis's tanks were knocked out two days later. The infantry was simply too tired to keep up, Redle concluded.[29] When Redle's tank column first attacked Cassino on the afternoon of 2 February, his progress was repeatedly delayed by "mopping-up" operations. The 3rd Battalion, 133rd, was alarmingly understrength at the time.[30] Too few troops had been committed to the attack—slowing down momentum. Redle was convinced that had his infantry support been properly rested and operating at full strength, the Germans would have been routed out of northern Cassino that same afternoon. A German prisoner later confirmed as much.

The offensive failed primarily because the troops were too exhausted—not just at Cassino but along the entire Gustav Line. British X Corps forces to the south and Juin's French forces to the north had also fatigued after months of fighting.[31] Poor weather and the cunning of the German defenders were also factors, but the Allies simply ran out of human energy.[32]

Generals Alexander, Clark, and Keyes were also too predictable and rigid in executing their battle plans and did not emphasize deception to throw the Germans off-guard. All Allied orders and actions telegraphed a singular intention of establishing a local bridgehead across the Rapido with the goal of directing armored units into the Liri Valley to link up with the Anzio forces.[33] As a result, the Germans properly deduced the Allies would focus on capturing Cassino and Monastery Hill and shored up their defenses accordingly.[34]

Even if the 36th Infantry Division had formed a successful bridgehead near Sant'Angelo on 22 January, there's no guarantee the victory would have resulted in columns of armor racing up the Liri Valley.[35] All the battle experiences thus far in Italy had been to the contrary. Somehow, the Germans always seemed to regroup behind another formidable set of defenses without ever retreating very far.

If the 36th Division had instead attacked further north where the Rapido was more fordable, they might have been successful. German defenses in the Caira area were not as strong on 20 January, and Maj Gen Walker's troops might have taken Monte Castellone right away. This would have opened up the tantalizing possibility of spilling troops downhill through nearby Villa Santa Lucia and Piedimonte three miles to the southwest. Highway 6 might have been cut a full five miles west of Cassino,[36] and the Gustav Line could have been pierced without ever capturing Monte Cassino.[37]

By the time the 34th Division crossed the Rapido a week later, the Germans in the sector had strengthened their positions. Even so, the surprise capture of Caira on 31 January, and then Monte Castellone the next morning, created a similar opportunity that was completely squandered. Juin was eager to send his forces over much higher elevations further north to reach the Liri Valley. Why not shift some of his mountain fighters down to Monte Castellone where the highland route was much shorter? A broad front master plan had already been set in motion and the Allied Command was reluctant to alter it—even when plum flanking opportunities fell right into their laps.[38]

The Allied commanders also failed to grasp the strategic value of Hill 593 behind the abbey. The Germans recognized the Hill's importance and, consequently, fought tooth and nail to hold it. Had the Allies concentrated on capturing this point, rather than Monastery Hill, and then focused next on breaking through German defenses at the Albaneta Farm and nearby points, they wouldn't have needed to take the abbey at all.[39] The distance from Hill 593 to the abbey in the southeast was roughly three-quarters of a mile. The distance from Hill 593 to Highway 6 to the southwest was exactly one mile. The attack had been directed the wrong way.

***

Captain Fred L. Schmidt, the 756th Tank Battalion's supply officer, recorded a total of 125 casualties at Cassino.[40] Thirty men were killed, sixteen taken prisoner, and fifty-one wounded and evacuated—fifteen cases were so severe the men were unlikely to ever return to action. Six others were injured in accidents and another twenty-four lightly wounded in action.[41]

Up until ten weeks earlier, the members of the 756th Tank Battalion had trained for over two-and-a-half years as a light tank outfit. In just one month, they transformed into a medium tank outfit. That upgrade required the restructuring of every company and every tank crew. Normally, a medium tank battalion needed a year or more of proper training before entering combat. Eleven days after the 756th's reorganization, the battalion was sent into battle. No other tank unit had been asked to make such a sacrifice.[42]

***

In the cool predawn of 23 February, Redle's tank column plodded through rolling Italian countryside along Highway 623. They crossed back over the Volturno River and rumbled past Alife.[43] About a mile northwest of town, a battalion member flagged them from the road and directed them into an apple orchard.[44] The last company vehicle parked under the cover of a tree just before 0600 and the crack of dawn.[45] The forty-one-mile road journey ended and each man found any comfortable spot available to steal a few hours of sleep.[46] The morning was gloriously beautiful. The sunrise revealed clear weather and a pastoral provincial setting worthy of a postcard.[47] The members of D Company and battalion HQ had already set up much of the facilities during the previous day—and as the sun rose ever higher, a familiar cadence of camp life returned.[48] At a nearby quartermaster facility, the "rugged looking" tankers finally enjoyed hot showers and haircuts, and received a fresh clean set of clothes.[49] After six weeks of using their helmets as wash basins, these simple tasks felt positively luxurious.[50] The kitchen was also fully operational, and the gentle breezes drifting through the orchard carried the mouthwatering aromas of warm cooked food. The men ate heartily.[51]

That evening, numerous card and dice games got underway among the enlisted men, bringing back friendly banter and bouts of raucous laughter after a six-week hiatus. Redle was fascinated by how life could return so quickly to normal. Pfc Bernard J. Shue, a 27-year-old Ohioan,[52] played the part of the company mascot. Shue was short—perhaps 5'2" at most—and undereducated. He lacked the aptitude for most company work other than kitchen jobs or "go for" errand duties—but was a kind, gentle, and trusting soul.[53] Many of his company mates found a soft spot in their hearts for him—except, perhaps, when it came to money. Shue got roped into a cut-throat card game and was losing quickly. T/5 Anthony L. Notoroberto, the New Yorker maintenance clerk with a murky history in the numbers racket, decided to intervene. Up until now, Notoroberto refrained from playing card or dice games because he didn't want to take advantage of his friends, but the injustice he witnessed compelled him to step in as Shue's "manager." That evening, the rural Ohioan walked away with a big smile on his face and $200 in winnings.[54]

Many lessons in war were learned away from the battlefield.

The surviving members of B Company struggled privately with their experiences at Cassino. They had witnessed the toughest fighting of the war. Many suffered from survivors' guilt, with full knowledge their personal perils were nowhere close to over. They were, after all, reorganizing only to fight all over again. As in the past, they trained not knowing where they were going or what they would be asked to do next.

The Gustav Line had not been broken. Germany had not capitulated. This was a long war, and the worst was yet to come.

U.S. Purple Heart medal

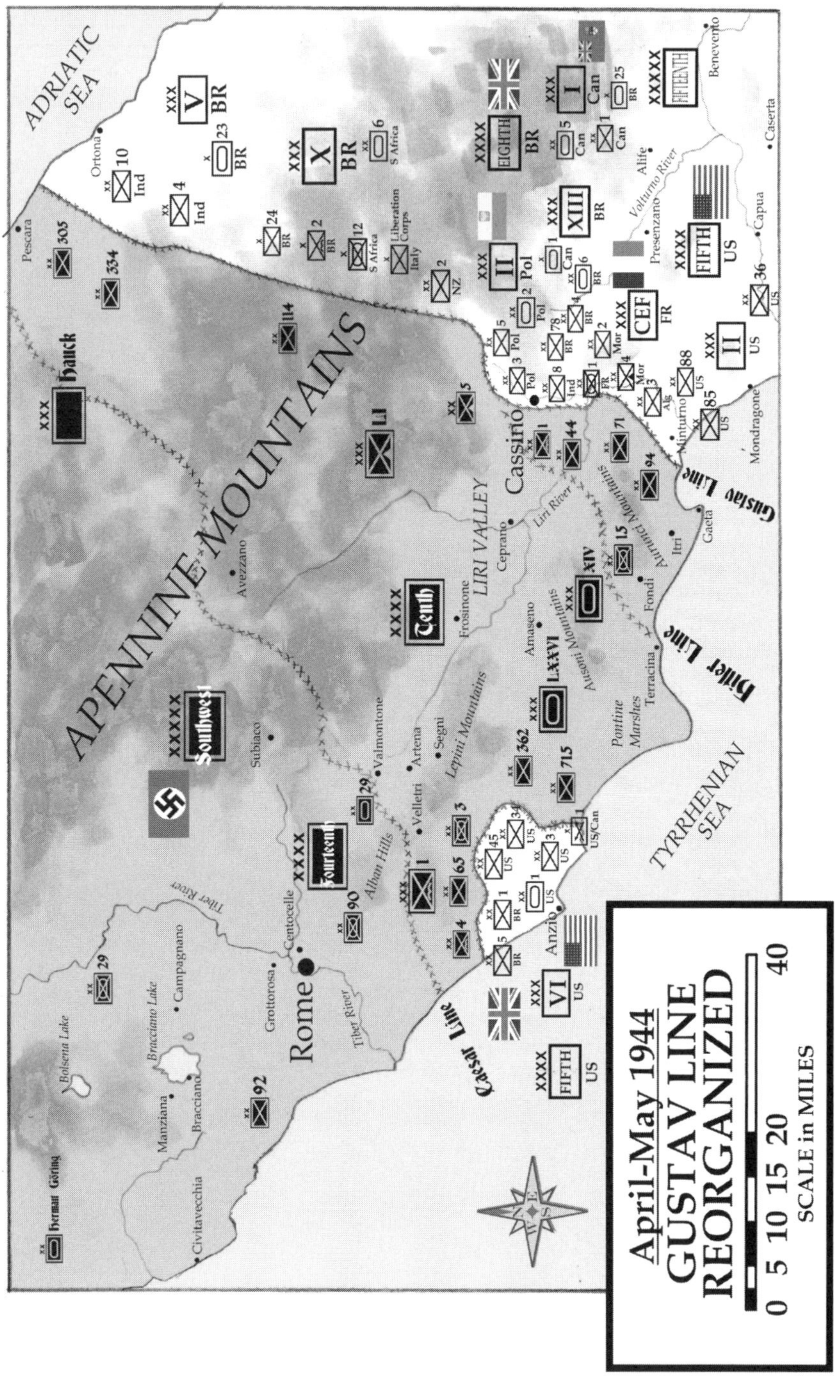
April-May 1944
GUSTAV LINE
REORGANIZED
0 5 10 15 20 40
SCALE in MILES
ADRIATIC SEA
TYRRHENIAN SEA
APENNINE MOUNTAINS
LIRI VALLEY
Gustav Line
Hitler Line
Caesar Line
Cassino
Rome
Anzio
Pescara
Ortona
Avezzano
Subiaco
Frosinone
Cepràno
Valmontone
Velletri
Artena
Segni
Lepini Mountains
Alban Hills
Amaseno
Ausoni Mountains
Aurunci Mountains
Pontine Marshes
Terracina
Fondi
Itri
Gaeta
Minturno
Mondragone
Capua
Caserta
Benevento
Alife
Presenzano
Volturno River
Liri River
Tiber River
Grottorosa
Centocelle
Campagnano
Bracciano Lake
Bracciano
Manziana
Bolsena Lake
Civitavecchia
Tenth
Fourteenth
Southwest
Hauck
EIGHTH BR
FIFTH US
FIFTEENTH
CEF FR
Hermann Göring

CHAPTER NINE

Regroup: 24 February 1944 to 5 April 1944

The brutal combat experiences at Cassino revealed the battalion's natural leaders and Lt Col Sweeting wasted no time reshuffling officer assignments.[1] 1st Lt Ralph L. Hanson was given command of A Company. D Company 2nd Lts Herman J. Kaufmann and William M. Hammer joined Hanson as his platoon leaders.[2] Dispatched to the Personnel Center were 1st Lt Walter L. Greene and 2nd Lt Chestmir F. Brokl.[3] Neither officer was flawed—they just didn't meet Sweeting's high standards.

1st Lt Charles P. Waldron moved from HQ Company to assume command of C Company.[4] 1st Lt Orlando A. Richardson transferred from Service Company to C Company as platoon leader. 2nd Lt Gordon E. Perkins shifted from C to A Company and 2nd Lt Maurice Levenborn was sent packing to the Personnel Center.[5] D Company received two new platoon leaders, both from HQ Company: 2nd Lt Hugo E. Staake and 1st Lt Willis A. Trafton, Jr. 1st Lt Osgood Tower was relieved as battalion liaison officer and promoted to HQ Company commander, and 1st Lt Frank E. Piotrowski was given charge of the Assault Gun Platoon.[6]

B Company welcomed 2nd Lt William H. Newman from D Company as a new platoon leader.[7] Even with the arrival of the tall, handsome 22-year-old, Redle's Company still remained two officers short.[8] Those vacancies would have to wait to be filled in the coming days.

During the mid-afternoon on 24 February, Sweeting convened all thirty-two battalion officers together for a lengthy meeting. The new officer assignments were announced, and a general action plan for the next few days was discussed: the cleaning of clothing and equipment, personal inspections, management of salvage and shortage requisition requests, and the scheduling of vehicle and weapons inspections with Ordnance. Much of the time, however, was spent reviewing, examining, and critiquing past operations—"lessons learned" as the Army called the process. Before the assembly was dismissed, Sweeting encouraged his officers to recommend all qualified enlisted men for awards or promotions and to do so as quickly as possible. He felt it was vital to recognize the natural leaders among the ranks before tank training ramped up again in earnest.[9]

That same evening, a U.S. Army truck halted near camp. Down bounded an unexpected returnee: Captain French Lewis—mostly recovered from his battle wounds and discharged from the hospital earlier that day. Technically, Lewis was AWOL. His orders directed him to the 2nd Replacement Depot. Lewis did report briefly to the vast tent city sprawled across an old racetrack in Naples, but took one look around and hitched a ride on the first truck he could find heading to Alife. "No way in hell" he was going to stay there, Lewis declared upon reporting to Sweeting. The 756th Tank Battalion was home, and Sweeting was just as pleased to put the old battalion veteran back in charge of A Company. Lt Hanson was relieved of his short command and made A Company XO.[10] Lewis's orders, of course, were amended to preserve his clean record. The Army generally looked the other way if a man went "AWOL" to return to combat—particularly when his home unit welcomed his return. The practice was not uncommon among other medically mended officers or enlisted men and underscored the low confidence many placed in the Army's "replacement" system.

A Company's battle-scarred captain may have returned, but with each passing day hopes dimmed of B Company ever seeing Captain Wilkinson again. Although the men had no way of knowing this, at that very moment, "Wilkie" had escaped his German captors and was running free through the Roman countryside. Still, the odds were abysmally low he would ever safely reach Allied lines. B Company was now 1st Lt David Redle's outfit, and his men were slowly acquiring and reflecting his leadership example and personality traits: shrewdness, loyalty, and dependability.

Under Sweeting's mandate, Redle summarily promoted Sgts Hamilton Smith and Haskell Oliver each to S/Sgt.[11] Smith was made 2nd Platoon sergeant while Oliver was made permanent platoon sergeant for the 3rd Platoon. S/Sgt James Haspel returned to 1st Platoon sergeant. All three NCOs displayed brilliant competence and steeled calm at Cassino. Oliver's steady-handed driver, T/5 Roy Anderson, was promoted to sergeant and given command of his own tank.[12] Cpls Harold M. Behymer, Robert D. Danner, Henry E. Gohde, and David L. Grate, Jr., also received sergeant stripes and tank commands. Cpl Frank W. Mielcarksi, who assumed the commander/gunner role in Redle's tank, previously held by the late Sgt Wunderlich, was also promoted to sergeant.[13] Six others received corporal stripes, two T/5s moved up to T/4, five received T/5 stripes, and eleven privates were bumped up to privates first class.[14] Thirty-two men in all—roughly one-third of B Company—received promotions and new responsibilities—all earned as the result of proven reliability under fire. Six weeks of the war's worst combat had transformed B Company from one of the U.S. Army's newest medium tank outfits into one of its most experienced.

Some of the company's wounded began trickling back to B Company to report for duty—medically cleared but forever scarred.[15] Mechanic T/5 Tom Barber returned to work in the maintenance section with a cast on his arm to keep his broken collarbone in place.[16] Army doctors considered one good arm suitable enough to handle a grease can and wrench. Pvt Merle E. Brooks, company radio bearer, returned as well, fortunate that German shrapnel had completely missed severing his spinal cord.[17] Others caught up in the blasts of mines and artillery, such as Sgt Roland Buys, faced long, painful recoveries and would never return to the company.

***

During the remaining days of February, camp life resumed with a familiar tempo: hot meals, shoe-shining orders, bayonet drills, the reservicing of equipment, weapons, and tanks during the day and rest after sundown.[18] Movies and traveling entertainment shows provided visual and auditory delights and local "vino" was always available to dull off-duty anxieties.[19] During downtime hours, the officers drew sensible measures of goodwill out of a 1-ton trailer crammed with gin and cognac "liberated" from a German cache discovered in a Cassino cellar.[20] A few lucky tankers even landed relaxation passes for a few days at an Army rest center in Caserta.[21] These men were the envy of all.

Leisure time spawned rumors and gossip swirled like "wildfire" of the battalion destined for England.[22] During the afternoon of 27 February, however, the hottest chatter centered around Lt Col Sweeting. At 1030 hours, Maj Gen Ryder made a surprise appearance at the 756th HQ. There, the tall lanky general met with Sweeting for nearly an hour before departing to attend other matters.[23] Even before the exhaust of the general's jeep could dissipate among the nearby apple trees, new rumors spread of how Ryder wanted Sweeting for the 34th Infantry Division.[24]

As the 756th prepared to embark on ten days of carefully planned training, the cold Italian rains returned with vengeance.[25] On 29 February, a drawn-out tank and tool inspection was held under an incessant downpour—leaving everyone soaked, shivering, and miserable.[26] The first day of March brought more non-stop rain, and everyone cussed and moaned when told no one could eat until all shoes showed a spotless sheen—a near impossibility under the circumstances. Mercifully, a battalion-wide gun inspection was called off and even routine tank work halted on account of the poor weather.[27]

More pelting rains ushered in an already soggy 2 March,[28] but the real flood washing across camp was news of Lt Col Sweeting's departure. Official orders arrived sending him immediately to Ryder's 34th Infantry Division to assume duties as the new 135th Infantry Regiment commander.[29] Sweeting's promotion, though a hot rumor for several days, still came as a shock—as he had served as battalion commander since the summer of 1942 at Fort Lewis, Washington. Through thick and thin, Sweeting had been the driving force of the unit.[30] After many months of training, drilling, molding, shaping, reorganizing, and finally leading the unit into battle, suddenly their high-energy CO was gone.

Sweeting left behind a mixed legacy—particularly among his officers. He excelled at preparing his men for battle—even going so far as to groom them for his own demise: "All my staff officers and company commanders are trained to be battalion commanders," he frequently stated as a point of pride.[31] And for whatever tactical contingency Sweeting's sharp ingenious mind could conceive, he drilled the battalion crews over and over again—instilling them with a lasting conviction that they could handle any problem thrown their way. This confidence served them well at Cassino, and undoubtedly saved lives. On the other hand, his impetuous, hyperactive disposition had cost lives unnecessarily in the heat of battle and eroded the delicate faith of his officers. Many former admirers grumbled privately of coming to "hate his guts."[32] Sweeting's departure came at the right time for everyone. Ryder landed a new regimental commander with the proven creativity and initiative he so coveted. Sweeting earned a fresh start and a golden opportunity for a full colonel rank—one grade below that brigadier general star he envisioned, and the 756th Tank Battalion gained Major Dolvin as the capable yet humane CO they needed.[33]

Dolvin, too, had been a vital battalion fixture since the earliest Fort Lewis days—serving in the XO position for the past eighteen months. The 28-year-old Georgian shared the same rigorous West Point background as Sweeting and demonstrated similar tactical proficiency and bravery under fire. What set him apart, however, was his small-town humility and a sincere compassion for the troops he commanded. Dolvin always went out of his way to visit any stricken 756er recuperating in the hospital—making sure every wounded warrior knew he was appreciated and not forgotten.[34] As a consequence, everyone in the battalion was excited about having Dolvin as their new commander.[35]

***

The rains continued through 3 March, complicating tank cleaning and maintenance chores as well as practice at the small arms firing range.[36] 1st Lt Redle and 2nd Lt William M. Hammer received three-day passes and left for Sorrento, Italy, to relax in style at the Excelsior Grand Albergo Vittoria Hotel on the Bay of Naples.[37] They returned on 6 March to find the camp still soaking under intermittent showers. The battalion had begun preparations to move fifty miles southeast to Benevento, but the order was postponed on account of the weather.[38]

The next day, 7 March, 1st Lt William R. "Bob" Engfer transferred in from HQ Company to serve as Redle's right hand man. After waiting seven weeks, B Company finally landed their long-overdue XO replacement. The 26-year-old Engfer, originally commissioned in cavalry, brought with him a wealth of experience—serving various assignments in battalion HQ going back as far as July 1943.[39]

On 9 March, tents were struck from beneath the rows of the old apple orchard and all tanks loaded up. The entire battalion formed a column and started rolling forward at 1300—passing first through Alife, then later Benevento before arriving at the small mountain town of Montemiletto: seventy-eight miles of sluggish travel in cloudy weather over roads which were fair at best.[40] B Company's journey took nearly ten hours to complete—having departed at 1400 and arriving just before midnight.[41] Although battalion reconnaissance scouted out the location ahead of the move, the ground proved too soft and wet for the tanks to even depart from the narrow roadway.[42] Because the rustic stone village sat on a hill with an elevation 2,000 feet above sea level, the dank air carried an almost alpine chill.[43]

The next morning, battalion HQ settled into a large municipal building while Service Company established along the village square.[44] The four tank companies spread out among the outskirts in bivouac locations preselected by the reconnaissance team. Under steady sheets of cold driving rain, patchwork patterns of olive drab tents emerged atop the soggy fields and along the mucky slopes.[45]

B Company's bivouac area was a disaster. The HQ was crammed inside a tiny, two-room house near the road, but the tanks had to be parked further down a steep slope. In order to move each one back up onto the road, a winch was employed—requiring an hour-and-a-half of time to complete the transfer of all seventeen tanks.[46] Major Dolvin arrived to conduct a surprise inspection of personal weapons. B Company passed with few deficiencies. A Company, however, assigned to a cluster of four or five homes a short distance away, flunked the inspection. The new battalion commander, obviously setting the disciplinary tone for his command, found many weapons poorly maintained, caked with grime, and even assigned to the wrong individuals. As Dolvin sauntered from weapon to weapon and man to man—describing every deficiency in precise technical detail while chastising the operator—his voice never rose and his trademark grin never left his face.

"He had a unique way of chewing out men while smiling, that made a man want to crawl in a hole because you felt you let him down personally. You did not feel resentment at all, but a strange gratitude." Lewis recounted later, "It was a wonderful trait."

Two days later, Dolvin repeated the inspection. This time, Lewis's men passed with flying colors.[47]

***

B Company's housecleaning had less to do with weapons and more to do with lingering personnel matters and concerns over the atrocious bivouac location. On the morning of 11 March, 2nd Lt William G. Leger was finally released from his limited obligations with the company and sent to the II Corps HQ.[48] Unfortunately, Leger proved unsalvageable for any role in the 756th.[49] His surly presence only rekindled bad memories of that first river crossing attempt on 27 January. It was best for all concerned for him to earn a fresh start elsewhere. With Leger's departure, B Company's active officers dropped to four: Redle, Engfer, Newman, and Harley. At least one more platoon leader was still needed. The rolls for the enlisted, however, swelled to a robust 110 men after the arrival of thirteen newcomers trucked in from the 2nd Replacement Depot on 12 March.[50]

Redle instructed 1st Sgt Hogan to locate a better bivouac site. With the help of Italian-speaking Pfc Joe Cutrone, the two searched the countryside while the remainder of B Company departed for the firing range.[51] The two discovered a yellow two-storey stucco house on flat country just north of Montemiletto. A caretaker living on the property told them the place was a summer home for a woman who lived in a village apartment during the winter. The owner was located and informed of B Company's plans to use the property. She opened the house and Redle's men helped her consolidate her fine china, flatware, and other valuables into one room equipped with a door lock. The rest of the house became B Company's new home.[52]

The CP moved into one of the rooms. Within moments, all corners were crammed with equipment and material belonging to 1st Sgt Hogan, Company Clerk Cpl Grainger J. Butler, Communications Sgt Pompey, jeep driver Pfc Clyde Guild, and a few others like Pvt Merle Brooks and T/4 Carl Mras—who handled all the radio repairs.[53]

S/Sgt Gene Shirley and his supply helper, Pfc Gerald C. Chotin, set up shop in an adjoining room, which quickly became piled full of uniforms and accessories.[54] After nearly three years in the company, Chotin still spoke with such a thick Cajun accent that few could understand him. However, the men learned not to tease him, otherwise he grew rather irate. Strangely, fellow Louisianan Sgt Graffagnini lost much of his accent after only six months.[55]

Another supply helper was Johnny Fatima, the stowaway boy who had been tagging along with the outfit since Morocco.[56] Fatima had become something of a little brother and company mascot. He wasn't supposed to be there, but Sweeting and Dolvin were either unaware of his presence or chose to look the other way.

One of the most popular guys in the company was mail clerk T/5 Irving Shapiro. Every tanker was always pleased to receive mail, but "Shappy" always made the delivery routine even more enjoyable. The Brooklynite's good-humored, upbeat nature served as a daily morale booster for the crews—absorbing barbs and dishing back quips with a thick New York accent that only enhanced the comedic aspects of every verbal exchange. Beneath his entertaining veneer, however, was a concerned and serious man—fiercely loyal to his friends. Because of his Jewish ancestry, Shapiro confided his private fears of German capture.[57]

B Company's yellow country house also featured a huge covered porch along the south side roughly twenty by thirty feet in area—providing a perfect location for field kitchen.[58] Mess Sergeant S/Sgt Raymond W. Colley and his kitchen staff of T/4 Oscar T. Crenshaw, T/5 Guy M. Sheffield, Pfc Earl C. Kilgore, Pfc John K. Wessels, and Pfc Bernard J. Shue went to work immediately unpacking equipment and setting up the stoves.[59] In only a matter of hours, the grateful tank crews lined up for satisfyingly hot home-cooked meals again. The company's popular fresh food program, first instituted during their earlier bivouac days, also resumed. Every day, voluntary money collections were gathered. Colley's crew then boarded the kitchen truck and drove to Naples to procure the raw ingredients. The cooks broke the process down to a science: the money collected was first used to buy liquor, which was, in turn, traded for sacks of flour, sugar, and other foodstuffs being offloaded from supply ships at the docks. Part of these raw staples were taken to the civilian market and bartered away for fresh vegetables and meats.[60] This unauthorized procurement was called "scrounging" and proved quite successful in providing a robust and varied diet for the crews. Each of the battalion's company kitchens engaged in "scrounging" as well—and the officers conveniently looked the other way.[61]

Work on the tanks resumed on 12 March, but field training was called off on account of heavy rain and snow.[62] The men, however, spent the day enjoying three hot meals—all excellent—and dinner was a festive affair, complete with communal songs.[63] Guard duty, as usual, followed later in the evening.[64]

***

On the morning of 13 March, the company commanders convened at the battalion HQ building in Montemiletto, anticipating that the formal orders had finally arrived giving Major Dolvin permanent command.[65] Instead, a distinguished 38-year-old lieutenant colonel walked into the room. He was a confident and fit officer of average build with thick dark hair and a trim moustache below a long Grecian nose.[66] "I am Lieutenant Colonel Glenn F. Rogers, your new battalion commander," he announced directly. Everyone in the room stood flabbergasted.[67] Rogers had arrived fresh from the States, by way of the 9th Armored Division training at Fort Riley, Kansas.[68] He was originally from Morrison, Tennessee, and graduated from the USMA in 1931 with a commission in Cavalry.[69] His service record included a stint as a West Point professor, but he was completely new to combat.[70] Sensing he had big command shoes to fill after Sweeting's tenure and recognizing he was also replacing a familiar and popular Dolvin, Rogers's overall message to his officers was to "relax" and continue with battalion business as usual.[71]

Major Dolvin, the consummate professional, resumed his role as battalion XO—disappointed, nonetheless, about being passed over for command of the battalion he loved. The other officers of the battalion also struggled to understand why the Army failed to promote such a deserving and obvious choice for the position.[72]

***

The weather cleared somewhat but remained stubbornly cold with periodic bouts of flurries. When the clouds lifted, Monte Vesuvius could be seen thirty miles to the southwest—spewing dark ash steadily into hazy skies.[73] The views were extraordinary from the B Company country house—particularly from a relaxing rooftop patio built above the porch and furnished with a set of table and chairs.[74] On one occasion, the men experienced a strange brown snowstorm—the flakes had been tainted with volcanic ash.[75]

As Lt Col Rogers instructed, a normal daily camp life routine continued—combining field training and firing exercises along with classroom work and inspections.[76] At night, the tankers passed the slow hours playing poker, drinking local sparkling wine or pulling guard duty. Others accepted dinner invitations with local families.[77] B Company lost Lt Harley to illness on 13 March—leaving Redle with only three officers again.[78] On 15 March, the men awoke to find eight inches of snow blanketing their tents and surrounding countryside. They stood for reveille as the flurries swirled heavily, but a short time later, the strange blizzard subsided completely and blue skies emerged to reveal a pristine white wonderland.[79] After only two days, the snow had completely melted and the crews were giving their tanks a fresh coat of paint in warm, pleasant weather.[80] One never knew from one day to the next what type of weather might roll through the Italian boot. One day could be temperate and pleasant, followed by another that was cold and rainy or windy and snowy.[81]

On 17 March, the 756th Tank Battalion received official orders to detach from the 34th Division one week hence, but remain with the II Corps—ending rampant rumors about an impending move and settling a few side bets.[82] Both the 34th and 36th Infantry Divisions were camped about the surrounding countryside, but the 34th was in the process of moving out—stoking the recent spike in speculation among the tankers.[83] Evidently, the higher-ups had new plans for the battalion—and thus a fresh round of rumors commenced.

After nearly a week as CO, Lt Col Rogers won the confidence of his officers. He proved to be good-natured and even-tempered with a prankster's eye and "penchant for puns." He had no patience, however, for insincerity and expected straight honesty from his men.[84] In other words, he was mature. At thirty-eight years of age, some of his officers thought he might be a little too mature for the position, and a quiet rumor circulated of Rogers having a brother in the War Department who had pulled strings to land him the combat command.[85] Factual or not, the rumor seemed to explain his surprising arrival. On the other hand, the officers recognized the awkward command situation Rogers had taken and appreciated the remarkable professional restraint displayed by their new CO.[86] To his credit, Rogers made no radical changes to the organization or personnel assignments in the battalion, and genuinely seemed to believe he had nothing to prove by doing so.[87] Again, this was a mark of a steady, established, and confident officer.

Even so, Rogers noted some slippage in discipline and challenged his company commanders to rein in their men—particularly the after-hours behavior. "When I told you to relax, I didn't mean become unglued," Rogers quipped, but with a fixed gaze that bespoke severity.[88]

Captain Lewis stepped out one evening to inspect the A Company guard. He circulated among the tanks and discovered sentries properly posted but a camp oddly quiet with many of the tankers gone. He ventured out to the bivouac perimeter and saw the telltale glow from several cigarettes floating near a shack across the road. Inside, two female camp followers were "entertaining" several of the men. Rather than alert the men to his presence and embarrass them, Lewis retreated to his CP and sent 1st Sgt John Berkouski out with a jeep and driver to break up the party. The two women were then driven to the next town over and dropped off.[89] Afterwards, Berkouski kept a much closer watch on the crews after the sun went down.

1st Lieutenant Redle suffered from a toothache that had become unbearable. Hoping to catch the 34th Division dentist before he shipped out, Redle made a trip over to nearby Benevento. The dentist, a major, had already packed and sent away most of his equipment but still retained a pair of forceps. He filled a water glass halfway with Old Grandad bourbon and told Redle to drink up. Once Redle's speech started to slur he yanked out the offending tooth, dispensed some pain medication, and sent the half-sloshed company commander back to his jeep and driver.

Redle returned to the B Company CP to find a big celebration in progress. In a large knotty pine room on the second floor, many NCOs and a few officers had gathered to toast 1st Sgt Jack Hogan upon word of his battlefield commission to 2nd lieutenant. Officially, the promotion wasn't effective for another week, but that didn't stop the spiked grapefruit juice from flowing late into the night.[90]

In the early morning hours, an unexpected knock was heard at the door. The celebrants opened the latch to find T/4 Joe K. Wright standing with Aldo, the son of the home owner and a medical student in Naples. Earlier that evening, Hogan had secretly posted Wright to guard the kitchen. Foodstuffs had been disappearing steadily and Hogan suspected some of the tank crews were pilfering company supplies for personal use. In reality, Aldo and his friends were the culprits—stealing coffee and butter in particular and then selling these items on the black market in Avellino for profit.

Hogan held Aldo under guard all night. In the morning, Aldo's mother visited the house—fearful about Aldo's failure to return to her apartment in town. When Redle told the woman of the charges against her son, she cried and pleaded for leniency. She explained how Aldo had been adopted, had also been in trouble before, and couldn't afford another black mark on his record. The exchange was particularly awkward because Redle had been the honored dinner guest at the family's apartment only the previous evening. Finally, the company commander agreed not to prosecute so long as she kept Aldo away from the house while B Company occupied the premises.[91] Two days later, the woman returned with her husband. She claimed she needed some sewing material. Redle let her retrieve the items but suspected the couple had ulterior motives. Her husband was a civil engineer, a known Fascist, and had been on Mussolini's payroll in the past. When Redle informed Lt Col Rogers of the incident, the new battalion CO instructed him to maintain a detailed log of all the owners' household property until the company departed.

On 24 March, the 756th Tank Battalion was formally detached from the 34th Infantry Division and attached to the II Corps HQ.[92] Maj Gen Ryder and his battle-hardened "Red Bull" troops were already at sea, bound for Anzio. Steaming with them was Lt Col Sweeting.

The next day, 1st Sgt Hogan received his formal enlisted discharge papers and new commission as a 2nd lieutenant, effective midnight, 26 March.[93] Because of his familiarity with the other enlisted men, Army regulations barred him from remaining in B Company, and so he transferred over to A Company to join Captain Lewis.[94]

Assuming the central role as B Company's new "Top Kick" was staff sergeant, and soon-to-be 1st Sergeant, Alvin Nusz of HQ Company.[95] Supply Sergeant Gene Shirley lobbied for the job and was sorely disappointed over being passed over.[96] A 1st sergeant's responsibilities were enormous. Aside from serving as chief disciplinarian, he was also expected to secure the company's rations, ammunition, supplies, and replacement materials, while tracking every change in personnel or duty status—plus any and all equipment repairs.[97] A supply sergeant's duties were somewhat similar, but Nusz offered the more varied resumé. He had originally served as a tank crewman—proving himself a smart, dependable soldier and quickly becoming a tank commander. Not long after the Salerno landings, when the battalion was still a light tank outfit, Nusz's tank descended along a narrow mountain road. The rocky slopes were saturated from heavy rain and slickened mud coated the road in sections. Nusz rode high out of the turret watching ahead. The tank spun through a hairpin turn when Nusz saw an old Italian man with a mule pulling a wagon suddenly appear at the fore. With no time to slow down and no room to pass, Nusz ordered his driver to turn into the slope. The tank clawed the bank and rolled over. The Italian man, mule, and wagon were fine, but Nusz lay pinned backwards against the ground—half-way out the commander's hatch. If not for the gun mount, his torso would have been snapped in two. He recovered with three damaged vertebrae, but the residual effects prevented his return to the tanks.[98] He shifted to desk work in battalion HQ and proved equally as smart and dependable handling those duties.

Nevertheless, the differences between Hogan and Nusz were striking. Hogan boasted nearly twenty years in the Army, whereas Nusz had served less than three. Hogan was always the rugged, tough, and worldly "man's man," whereas Nusz was thin, quiet, laid-back, and devoutly religious, displaying more of the persona of a gentle angel.[99] Perhaps that's precisely what B Company needed in the trying days ahead: the steady guidance of an angel.

Hogan wasn't the only NCO in the battalion to receive a battlefield commission. Former Battalion Master Sergeant (M/Sgt) John D. Hanson and S/Sgt James L. "Red" Harris of A Company had also recently been promoted to 2nd lieutenant.[100] Hanson reported to A Company earlier and Harris shifted to over B Company as a new platoon leader.[101] Redle knew Harris well. He was an original Fort Lewis inductee with A Company and proved to be an outstanding platoon sergeant at Cassino. The addition of 2nd Lt Harris certainly helped lessen the sting of losing Hogan.[102]

Three days later, on 30 March, another platoon leader appeared at the B Company CP: 2nd Lt Robert M. Gorman, fresh from Personnel Center #9.[103] Redle did not know him at all, so he sat the 26-year-old officer down for an informal chit-chat—mostly to get a sense of his personality and experience.[104] The situation was always thorny for any new officer coming into a veteran outfit—especially a unit recently returned from combat. To win the confidence of battle-tested crews, a green officer was commonly advised to keep his mouth shut, ears open, learn everything he could absorb—and to certainly refrain from tossing commands around unnecessarily. New officers heeding this advice were generally accepted, in time, by their assigned platoons.[105] Once Redle felt an officer had been properly briefed, he walked him over to his platoon and personally introduced him to the platoon sergeant and tank commanders. After that, the officer was on his own.[106]

Another man reporting for duty on 30 March was a familiar face: Pvt Gene Palumbo, returning after a month-long convalesce in the 11th Field Hospital.[107] The tank loader was left so traumatized by his experiences at Cassino, that 1st Sgt Hogan evacuated him to a hospital a few days after the unit pulled from the line.[108] The doctor's diagnosed his case as "battle fatigue," and planned on reassigning him to a rear echelon unit.[109] Pvt Palumbo, however, insisted on returning to B Company—preferring to courageously overcome his fears and rebuild his shattered nerves among comrades. The doctor finally relented and released the anxious private—but only after drafting a confidential sealed letter the private was instructed to present immediately to Lt Redle.[110] The medical orders inside warned Redle not to return Palumbo to a tank crew, so Redle created a place in the company for him as an extra jeep driver.[111] There were some men for which Redle would never make such an exception, but Pvt Palumbo was different. The fact he wanted to be there spoke volumes of his character. He possessed a "heart of gold" and "would do anything for his friends,"[112] and his gregarious, outgoing, and good-natured personality won him many, many friends. Prior to the war, the 21-year-old from Massachusetts enjoyed life as an entertainer in a professional roller-skating act.[113] Obvious people-lovers like Pvt Palumbo suffered the effects of the war at a profound level. Redle never disclosed to Palumbo the contents of the letter, and the new company jeep driver adapted well to his new role—but still struggled whenever he encountered loud artillery fire.[114]

As March closed and April arrived, B Company underwent a few more changes to personnel and duty status assignments. Two T/5s earned promotions to T/4. Three privates became T/5s, and three others landed Pfc stripes.[115] Several men transferred out sick, as four new ones rotated in from the 2nd Replacement Depot on 27 March.[116] T/4 Rufus P. Marin was reduced to private for a lapse in judgement.[117] Other than an instance earlier in the month where Pvt John W. Jarrett went AWOL for three days,[118] conduct in the company had been remarkably disciplined. Then, on 3 April, Lt Redle had to bust T/4 Luther A. Kinsworthy to private for another blunder.[119] Redle sensed a palpable restlessness setting in and the men were growing weary of their daily routine.[120]

The weather turned drier, warmer, and more pleasant.[121] Baseball gloves popped out of barracks bags and games of catch followed. Some men took road trips to Monte Vesuvius or Pompeii, or walks to nearby villages to pass the boredom—but even the new-found friendships with local families in Montemiletto began to feel stale.[122] There were only so many times the tanks could be cleaned, painted or serviced, and only so many ten-mile hikes the officers could arrange to keep the men constructively distracted.[123] Even the gunnery range had grown routine. Every gunner was now able to routinely hit a man-sized target at 500 yards, and most from 1,000 yards away.[124]

What the tankers needed, and the Army failed to provide, was more combined tank/infantry training. By early 1944, many infantry commanders recognized this deficiency, but the U.S. Army was slow to address it. Colonel W. Shephard of the 3rd Infantry Division scolded one visiting War Department observer: "It is the consensus of the officers that these infantry will not go forward without tanks, and will not stay in a defense without tanks. They just won't do it." His boss, Brig Gen John "Iron Mike" O'Daniel concurred: "Tanks and infantry must be trained together ... The same tank battalion should be attached to an infantry division all the time."[125] Lt Col Sweeting made similar recommendations in his Cassino after-action reports. Inexplicably, the tanks and infantry continued training separately, even though the old policy was a proven loser.

Little had changed on the Italian Front in the past six weeks—aside from the repositioning of units or changes in commanders. The U.S. VI Corps still sat at Anzio—but now under the command of Maj Gen Lucian Truscott. Further south, the British X Corps and U.S. II Corps swapped sectors. The Americans now held the coast, and the Brits suffered their round of misfortunes in trying to capture Monte Cassino. The British Eighth Army moved down into the old CEF (Corps Expeditionaire Français) sector north of Cassino so the French could reposition right of the Americans. In effect, the U.S. Fifth Army south of Anzio consolidated along a tight thirteen miles of front stretching from the Tyrrhenian coast to Liri Valley. The British Eighth Army maintained the rest.

British attempts to capture Cassino failed. On 15 March, Clark, Devers, Alexander, Eaker, and Freyberg gathered at Cervaro to observe Allied bombers pound the town to dust.[126] Over the course of the morning, 514 medium and heavy bombers, 300 fighter-bombers, and 280 fighter planes dropped a total of 1,500 thousand-pound bombs on the condemned occupiers.[127] At noon, the aerial attack halted and 746 artillery pieces from the British X Corps, the U.S. II Corps, and the New Zealand Corps opened fire—blasting 200,000 rounds and another 1,200 tons of explosives into what little remained standing. The hellish barrage lasted all afternoon.[128] Freyberg expected the German defenders to be annihilated, but when his troops and tanks tried to sweep through the ruins, they encountered many defenses just as active as before. Worse, the new rubble piles and fresh bomb craters hindered infantry encroachment and all but halted the tanks.[129] Then the rains came and further complicated operations.[130] More heavy bombings, blistering artillery barrages, and Allied infantry assaults followed over the course of a week—and yet everything attempted failed to dislodge the Germans from either the town below or the abbey above. Finally, on 23 March, General Alexander ordered Freyberg to halt the operation, and the New Zealand and British Indian troops withdrew exhausted.[131]

Alexander ordered a realignment and buildup of Allied area forces and decided to wait for more favorable spring weather before launching a new offensive.[132] In the meantime, some 365,000 Germans in central Italy kept Anzio in check, maintained a firm grip on the Gustav Line, and began preparations on a new "Hitler Line" firewall roughly ten miles to the north.[133]

By the start of April 1944, the reshuffling of Allied Forces was nearly complete.[134] Two new American infantry divisions—the 85th and the 88th—were assigned to the U.S. II Corps and placed on the line by the Tyrrhenian coast near the small towns of Scauri, Tremensuoli, and Minturno.

On 5 April, the 756th Tank Battalion received unexpected orders to join the 85th Infantry Division.[135] The restless tankers were given only four days to pack and travel some seventy-five miles from the mountains to the coast. This time, they were no longer combat newcomers assigned to veterans, but combat veterans assigned to newcomers.

U.S. 85th Infantry Division

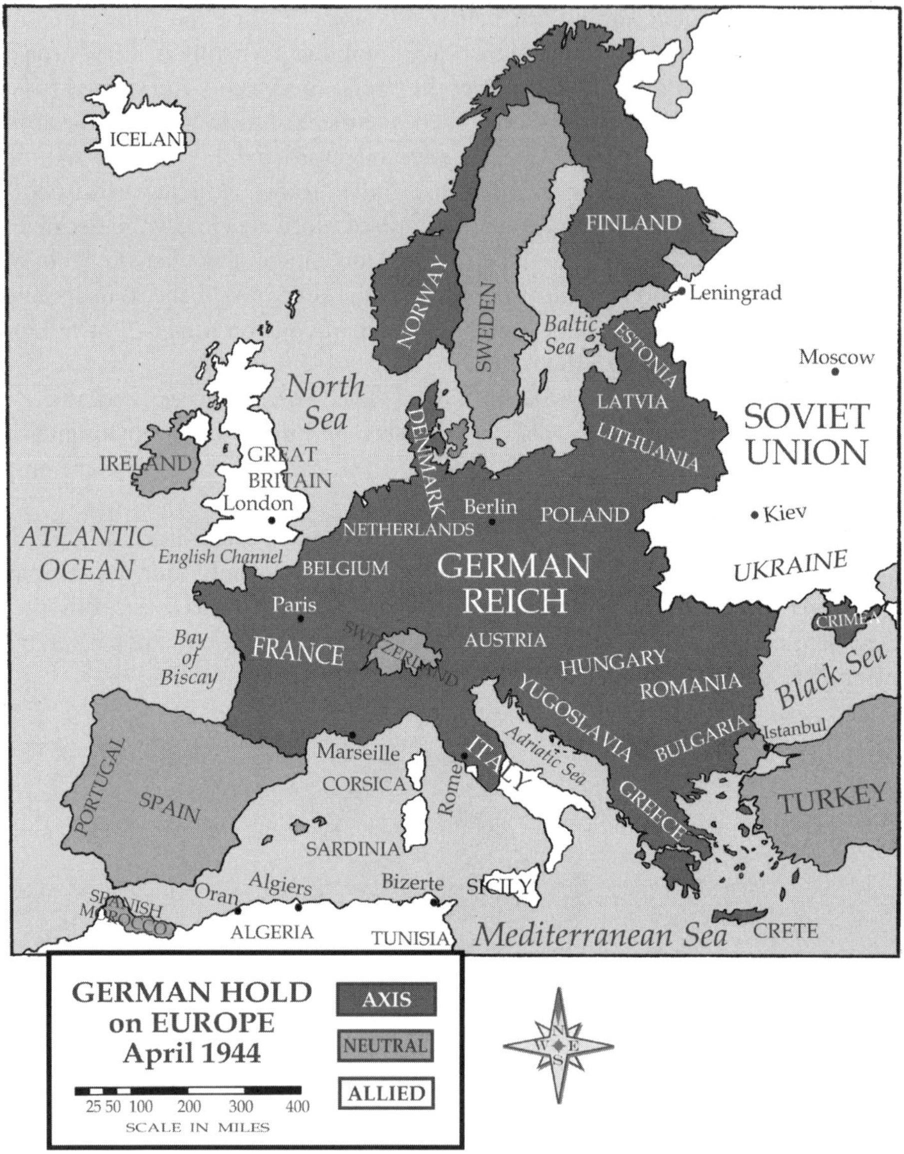
ICELAND
FINLAND
NORWAY
SWEDEN
Leningrad
Baltic Sea
ESTONIA
Moscow
North Sea
LATVIA
DENMARK
LITHUANIA
SOVIET UNION
IRELAND
GREAT BRITAIN
London
Berlin
POLAND
Kiev
NETHERLANDS
ATLANTIC OCEAN
English Channel
BELGIUM
GERMAN REICH
UKRAINE
Paris
CRIMEA
SWITZERLAND
AUSTRIA
Bay of Biscay
FRANCE
HUNGARY
Black Sea
ROMANIA
YUGOSLAVIA
Istanbul
BULGARIA
Marseille
ITALY
Adriatic Sea
PORTUGAL
CORSICA
Rome
SPAIN
GREECE
TURKEY
SARDINIA
Algiers
Bizerte
SICILY
Oran
SPANISH MOROCCO
ALGERIA
TUNISIA
Mediterranean Sea
CRETE
GERMAN HOLD on EUROPE April 1944
AXIS
NEUTRAL
ALLIED
25 50 100 200 300 400
SCALE IN MILES
N
W
E
S

CHAPTER TEN

Custermen: 6 April 1944 to 11 May 1944

GMC 2½ ton 6x6 truck

The 85th Infantry Division had adopted the nickname "Custer Division" in honor of the late Lt Col George S. Custer of Little Big Horn legend. It was strange for an infantry outfit to honor a cavalryman who needlessly lost his life along with the lives of all his troops after blundering into a controversial battle, but the nickname evoked some sense of lineage—which the unit lacked entirely. The division first formed at Camp Custer near Battle Creek, Michigan, in 1917.[1] The outfit shipped overseas in 1918 and promptly split up. Some units remained in England while others formed a training cadre in France. A few other elements saw combat on the Western Front near the end of World War I. At the same time, the 339th Infantry Regiment shipped east to Archangel to fight several skirmishes against Russian Bolsheviks.[2] The division returned home and disbanded in all but name by 1921. After a twenty-one-year hiatus, the "Custer Division" was reactivated 15 May 1942 at Camp Shelby in Mississippi—and despite its historic Michigan origins, the newly formed division trained mostly in Louisiana and California throughout the following year.[3] The unit shipped over to Oran, Algeria, in January 1944 for amphibious training—and then began moving in piecemeal fashion to Naples starting 14 March.[4] By 3 April, the entire division had arrived in Italy but had not yet relocated completely into their assigned sector along the U.S. II Corps front.[5]

Maj Gen John B. Coulter, a cavalry officer with a stocky, medium build and thirty years' experience, commanded the 85th.[6] His tenure began 21 February 1944, when Maj Gen Wade Haislip was tapped to lead the newly activated XV Corps.[7] Coulter instilled an "unimpeachable workmanship" spirit into the training of his green "Custermen"—but over the last six months, his troops were usually divided up and spread out while marching, trucking or shipping somewhere. Now, several days into April 1944, and finally approaching the battlefield, Coulter's men filtered up slowly in stages along forty miles of Italian coastline—toughing through a local transportation shortage.[8] A frenzied supply and logistics staff kept each far-flung element communicating and supplied, and a round red-lettered "CD" shoulder patch tied each man to a mother unit—but this was still a scattered division in search of an identity.

The first 300 Custermen arriving in mid-March promptly trucked to the front as observers.[9] The division's 339th Infantry Regiment soon followed. At the time, the 88th Infantry Division controlled the entire II Corps' five-mile section of the front.[10] The arrival of the 339th allowed the 88th to begin a slow process of shifting northeastward. Ultimately, the 88th Division would move two-and-a-half miles inland to form the Corps' right flank while the newcomer 85th assumed the left flank closest to the coast. Nearly 30,000 troops, totaling the rolls of both divisions, would eventually cram into this narrow five-mile-wide sector. No wonder transportation had become such a challenge.

On 3 April, Maj Gen Coulter established his first forward CP—along with batteries from his 910th and 403rd Field Artillery Battalions—in an olive grove near Monte Massico—roughly four miles south of Cellole and ten miles southeast of the front. The 85th Quartermaster Company, 85th Reconnaissance Troop, 310th Medical Battalion, 310th Engineer Battalion, and 785th Ordnance Company closed five miles south of Coulter's CP at Mondragone on the coast.[11] Because command of the 339th Infantry Regiment shifted temporarily to the 88th until the 85th could arrive in full, Coulter's "division" initially had no infantry.[12] His other two regiments—the 337th and 338th—were still hours or days away from joining him. The 337th, scheduled to arrive late the following day, had just completed additional mountain training some eighteen miles southeast near Sant'Angelo (by Capua), while the 338th continued practicing village attacks and stream crossings at Qualiano even further to the rear—just north of Naples.[13] The 338th's schedule did not have them wrapping up their training schedule until mid-April.[14]

The 88th arrived at the line only a few weeks ahead of the 85th but had already suffered alarming casualty figures: ninety-nine men killed, 252 wounded, and another thirty-six missing. These mounting losses resulted, not because of attacks or counterattacks, but simply from aggressive front-line reconnaissance patrolling and tit-for-tat artillery dueling.[15]

The 88th and 85th Infantry Divisions shared similar histories. The 88th was first activated for World War I, deactivated in 1921, and then reactivated in July 1942 at Camp Gruber, Oklahoma.[16] The unit arrived in Italy in February 1944 by way of North Africa—setting up camp initially at Piedimonte d'Alife before settling along the front.[17] The modern 88th was created with Selective Service draftees uniquely filling out all enlisted ranks.[18] War Department officials were curious as to how a unit comprised mostly of conscripts might perform in combat compared to Regular Army or National Guard divisions blended with draftees and volunteers.[19] The 88th Division members wore a solid blue quatrefoil shoulder patch formed of two intersecting number eights. On casual glance, the shape looked like a four-leaf clover. The design predated the War Department's 1942 personnel plans for the division, but fittingly captured the philosophy behind those ideas.

***

When orders to join the 85th Division arrived, B Company packed swiftly, taking extra measures to leave their country house in immaculate condition. Redle prided his company as being a "first class soldiering outfit." Nothing was taken, nothing was damaged, and the entire premises was left spotless. All items and actions were meticulously documented, and the lengthy logs subsequently turned over to Lt Col Rogers.[20] Because of massive congestion in the area, the 756th orders were to march in two segments. B Company and part of HQ would depart first, by traditional motor convoy. The remainder of the battalion would follow roughly twelve hours later, but with the assistance of a tank transportation trucking outfit.

At daybreak, 7 April, B Company rolled out of Montemiletto, with many of the townspeople interrupting their daily chores to emerge from doors and wave good wishes as the tanks passed.[21] The journey was long, slow, and dusty under clear weather but atop roads in only fair condition. The column snaked west through a congested Avellino, skirted past Naples as Vesuvius belched heavy black smoke skyward before swinging more northwesterly toward the blue coast. The terrain levelled into fertile fields and humble farms while the air warmed noticeably.[22] By noon, Redle's column approached the Volturno River—shrouded in thick chemical smoke concealing a makeshift bridge from German observation planes. Reliving their first Volturno crossing six months earlier, each tank commander dismounted to prudently guide his driver over the twin wheel tracks spanning the river. Upon reaching the opposite bank, the convoy resumed as normal—arriving upon flat fields roughly two-and-a-half miles east of Mondragone around 1330.[23] The entire seventy-five-mile journey took only six hours—a respectable thirteen MPH pace threading along narrow roads universally clogged with trucks running ammo and supplies.[24] Not a single vehicle flagged or broke down. The tank drivers had long mastered road marches in all conditions.

Upon arrival, B Company was officially attached to the 85th Infantry Division.[25] Also joining the division was the 5th Mule Pack Group (Italian), and a carrier pigeon outfit—the 6681st Signal Company.[26] The timing of attachments was somewhat disconcerting—as if armor were an operational afterthought tiered among mules and birds. A tanker could never be sure of his status in a new infantry unit coming fresh from the States. Aside from some fleeting armor exposure while maneuvering in the California desert, the Custermen had received only scant training involving tanks.[27]

B Company's new bivouac area was a living canvas of vibrant pastoral beauty. Recent rain had transfigured the flat fertile landscape with lavish vegetation, showcasing every possible hue of green. Spring dallied in the air as sweet gentle fragrances drifting from nearby orchards festooned of white, pink, and red blossoms.[28] To the west lay Mondragone, a fair-sized seaside beach town of typical Italian beige stone and orange tile architecture. Although most buildings showed damage from previous bombings, it still seemed like a peaceful place. The neighboring Tyrrhenian Sea sparkled like an immense crystal blue gemstone under the high sun—Neptune's bountiful gift of marine sustenance for generations of fisherman dating back thousands of years.[29] Again, Italy was too beautiful of a land to fight a modern war.

Two miles to the north arose a six-mile-long mountain chain somewhat out of place with the flat surroundings. Two 437 and 542-meter peaks named Monte Crestagallo and Monte Pecoraro anchored the east and west ends, with the massive 811-meter Monte Massico holding the center. The feature formed a natural protective wall across a vast river plain ten miles southeast of the Gustav Line—behind which the Allies could amass forces more securely. Many artillery and rear echelon units had already established camps around the area, with more arriving by the hour.[30] In fact, thirteen men from a nearby 105th AA Battalion unit were attached to B Company on a temporary basis so the men could receive rations.[31]

Amid the distant rumble of artillery and periodic droning of heavy Allied bombers passing overhead, Redle's tankers started unpacking and digging in.[32] The tanks were parked under the cover of trees bordering the fields. Only a few farmhouses dotted the area.[33] The only shortcoming to the bivouac choice was the somewhat marshy conditions—an obvious breeding ground for mosquitos and source for malaria.[34]

The remainder of the battalion pulled in later that evening and the following day—most of the tanks offloaded in Mondragone from flatbed trailers pulled by tractor trucks.[35] Earlier, the CO of the trucking company discovered his transporters could not turn around in Montemiletto, so the battalion had to drive their tanks ten miles west to Avelino before loading. After overcoming this initial SNAFU,[36] the remainder of the journey proved uneventful.[37] With the battalion reunited, the familiar sights and smells of camp also returned: freshly dug slit trenches moist with rich dark soil, tarps, and shelter halves attached to tanks in lean-to fashion and flapping in the gentle breezes, the occasional acrid bite of smoldering tobacco, and the omnipresent aroma of fresh coffee brewing atop tiny Coleman stoves.

Sunday 9 April was Easter Sunday. As a devout Catholic, Lt Redle looked forward to attending a Mass scheduled in the battalion area at 1400 hours. However, at 1300, Lt Col Rogers sent for Redle to accompany him on a reconnaissance trip to the front.[38] While enroute by jeep,[39] Rogers explained the infantry wanted a tank force stationed nearby in case of German attack, and B Company was chosen for the mission. Redle's tankers were to begin moving that night.[40]

After skirting around Monte Crestagallo near the coast and driving some eight miles across paper-flat farmland—always with slow moving troops and trucks as fellow travelers—the tank officers arrived at a bridge spanning a seventy-five-yard-wide section of the Garigliano River. German artillery enjoyed harassing the location intermittently. As a consequence, the area was kept permanently blanketed with chemical smoke. Redle and Rogers crossed the bridge and proceeded through the swirling gray mists, which soon broke to reveal the Aurunci mountains looming high across the horizon. Atop foothills at the fore, lay the broken ruins of Minturno and Tufo. To the left, but further in the distance, lay another shattered hilltop village: Tremensuoli. Still much further left, lay the coastal town of Scauri with short conical Monte Scauri as a companion.

Transfer of this two-mile wide slice of the front from the 88th Division to the 85th had kicked into high gear, and troops of every rank and station from both divisions bustled about the area—in vehicles or on foot—carrying, carting or towing every weapon assigned to an infantry outfit.[41] Coulter's Custermen had until 0800 hours, 10 April, to assume control of their territory. Elements of 338th Infantry Regiment arrived the day before, joining the 339th Regiment already holding the line.[42] The 329th Field Artillery Battalion and elements of the 310th Medical Battalion and 85th Reconnaissance Troop had also assumed front-line positions. The Recon troopers primarily patrolled the coast between Mondragone and the Garigliano River, watching for any sign of enemy amphibious infiltration behind the division's position. All these movements, of course, were coordinated with Maj Gen John E. Sloan's 88th Division HQ staff.[43]

The Germans chose this terrain as the battlefield, and naturally retained the advantage as defenders. They held the imposing Aurunci mountain chain five miles in the distance—standing like a stout gray fortress anchored by 1,000 to 1,500-meter-high parapets in the form of Monte Maio on the right and Monte Petrella and Monte Sant'Angelo on the left. The Germans had conceded Minturno and Tremensuoli several months earlier to the British, but still held Scauri at the coast.[44] Their defensives ran west from Scauri along the narrow "Capo d'Acqua" creek weaving between a series of rolling hills beyond Tremensuoli, ranging in height from fifty to a hundred meters. German minefields, barbed wire barricades and gun positions continued northeastward through a grassy valley and the ruined foothill villages of Solacciano and Santa Maria Infante, before continuing into 88th Division territory.[45] Patrols had long determined troops of the German 94th Infantry Division (reinforced) held the territory opposite the U.S. II Corps.[46]

After staring at each other for two months across a static half-mile no-man's-land, both sides had become well established. Critical positions were reinforced with sandbags, timbers, and steel rails. The Germans used the Aurunci mountains as OPs and often subjected any Allied movement they detected with swiftly dispatched concentrations of artillery—usually targeting Minturno, Tufo or the bridge crossing the Garigliano.[47] One favorite focal point was tiny Tremensuoli. The ruined hilltop village position bulged a few hundred yards into their defenses, and this mild salient must have irritated German officers studying the never-moving demarcation lines on their daily maps—and so the narrow roadway leading up to the town came to be known as "Purple Heart Alley" to those Americans tasked with maintaining the unenviable position. If some neglectful GI was seen passing—even fleetingly—inside some broken window frame, German shells would certainly fall within the next twenty seconds.[48]

Tremensuoli was hit particularly hard by German artillery a few days earlier—6 April—exploding during one violent spell at a rate of twenty rounds per minute for fifteen minutes. Allied casualties proved light, but the Germans knew troop repositioning was underway and felt obliged to demonstrate their displeasure.[49] Maj Gen Coulter, fearful that this crafty old enemy might take further advantage of the situation and raid his inexperienced troops during mid-transfer, called upon Lt Col Rogers for tank protection.

Rogers and Redle parked their jeep and set out on foot toward the front—taking great pains to remain in defilade as they approached, periodically rechecking directions and conditions with local troops.[50] They identified the most likely approach for any German incursion as a gentle grassy valley stretching roughly 1,000 yards between the 104-meter high Tremensuoli and 156-meter high Monte Natale further north.[51] Approximately 500 yards northeast of Tremensuoli, they found an abandoned two-storey house tucked behind a wooded hill. The location was perfect: near the middle of the valley—yet affording protection from artillery and concealment for tanks. The house had long since been emptied of occupants and possessions. The second floor had served as some family's living quarters and the ground floor, their livestock barn. Only manure and fleas now remained.[52]

The two officers made their way back to Minturno and learned of another Easter Mass being celebrated in a stone quarry a mile away. They arrived in time for the opening greeting, but a German artillery barrage interrupted the proceedings midway through. The crowd dispersed and regathered once the shelling ended. Fortunately, no one was hit during the melee, the Mass concluded, and Rogers and Redle returned to Mondragone without further incident.[53]

That evening, Redle's tankers moved up to the front. The 85th Division artillery fired a long, heavy barrage to cover the engine noise of the tanks moving into position.[54] Once arrived at the tiny hillside house northeast of Tremensuoli, each tank dispersed about the area, parked beside a tree, and cut their engine. The barrage ceased and the crews made fast work preparing fortifications. Camouflaged netting was first stretched over each tank. Next, sandbags were stuffed with dirt and stacked two high. Then, each tank was momentarily restarted and parked atop the sandbags to form a protected space underneath. Afterwards, the crews evacuated more dirt from below to create a larger living space.[55] The hard, physical work lasted well into the night.

At 0800, 10 April, the 85th Division was formally committed to action for the first time in its history. The left sector of the U.S. II Corps zone had become "Custerman" territory. Even so, not until 14 April did Coulter's troops assume full control of the line. The 339th Regiment, returned to 85th Division control and with three battalions positioned abreast, held the far left flank—5,500 yards of territory opposite Scauri, including the vital Highway 7, running along the sea southwest of Tremensuoli.[56] The 337th Regiment arrived in the area on 5 April to relieve the 351st Infantry Regiment (88th Division),[57] and assumed the remaining 4,000 yards of the division's right flank—from Tremensuoli to the Ausente River.[58] The bulk of the 338th Regiment, however, still training at Qualiano, didn't arrive in the Monte Massico area until 15 April.[59]

Over those same five days, Redle's tankers continued preparing their positions, with a second position added two miles east of Minturno serving as a CP and service area.[60] On two of those nights, the tanks took rotations back to Mondragone for servicing and crew rest—but always returned to the wooded hill before dawn's light.[61] 2nd Lt Howard Harley returned to duty after illness on 13 April.[62] Since Harley had been recommended for promotion, he assisted 1st Lt Engfer with XO duties in the meantime.[63] A new officer, 2nd Lt Bert D. Gilden, joined two days later.[64] The dark bushy haired Gilden was from Bridgeport, Connecticut, and had worked in the publicity department for Warner Brothers Pictures in New York City prior to the war.[65] With all three platoon officer positions already filled, the 29-year-old platoon leader represented a spare—and assumed HQ duties in the meantime.

2nd Lt James "Red" Harris commanded the 1st Platoon. The 27-year-old Harris grew up in Hillsboro, Texas, and was a well-known and popular 756th member. His recently earned a battlefield commission came after long stellar service in A Company. 2nd Lt William Newman had charge of the 2nd Platoon. Newman was a Knoxville, Tennessee, native with a twin brother in the Air Corps.[66] The 22-year-old had already proved his battle mettle at Cassino by calmly commanding a lone M5 light tank on a dangerous test run of engineer Captain Walker Sorrell's Rapido "Skyway" tank route on 29 January 1944.[67] The new officer who arrived two weeks earlier, 2nd Lt Robert Gorman, was given command of the 3rd Platoon.[68] Upon arriving at the front, Lt Redle assigned Newman's 2nd Platoon to the 339th Regiment, and Harris's and Gorman's 1st and 3rd Platoons with the 337th Regiment.[69] The mission was simple: prepare to counter any enemy attack or incursion until relieved at some point in the future.[70]

The 339th had already earned nearly four weeks of experience anchoring the seaside section of the front and grew accustomed to the hazards of nighttime patrolling and sporadic artillery barrages. The rookie troops of the 337th took over positions vacated by the more experienced 351st Infantry Regiment (88th Division) and did their best acclimating to front-line life—which, surprisingly, wasn't so severe. Accommodations were already move-in ready. Foxhole positions had been dug deeply—often tucked behind large rocks or building walls. Such places were then sandbagged and barricaded against mortar and artillery fire.[71] A CP and a kitchen were set up in the battle scarred Minturno city hall. Men on the line were fed at least one hot meal a day, while those in reserve received three.[72] A constellation of OPs was established running from south to north and given code names. "Ferdinand" was a graveyard OP along the Minturno–Santa Maria Infante Road. An old farmhouse sitting 300 yards west of the main line of resistance (MLR), was called "Snuffy's."

Another OP a short distance from "Snuffy's" was dubbed "Mother's Place." Movement between OPs generally occurred after dark and each place served as a staging point or waystation for dispatching and managing nighttime patrols.[73]

Both sides maintained active defenses and circulated regular patrols to maintain security, develop intelligence, or snag prisoners. The Allies had long established a tradition for aggressive patrolling. The British and American infantrymen preceding the 85th Division fanned out each and every evening, no matter how unpleasant the weather conditions—rain, sleet, snow, or ice—scouring over the treacherous rural terrain in search of any new bit of information. With luck, they would sometimes return with a prisoner or two. Maj Gen Coulter, and his G-2, Lt Col Thomas R. McDonald, continued this dangerous, but vital practice.[74]

A patrol leader—usually a lieutenant—planned his mission by sneaking to an observation post by day to study the terrain firsthand and sketch out a course of action. He would next meet with his battalion S-2 to study local maps and any recent aerial photos. Potential dangers and all expected enemy locations were also considered and discussed.[75] The Germans, of course, didn't surrender their secrets easily and countered the incursions by either dispatching patrols of their own or launching nighttime flares to illuminate the intrusion of slinking Americans. At times, the exposed Americans became ensnared in horrific firefights. On one quiet night, a patrol led by 1st Lt Edward R. Halloran, XO to A Company, 337th, was detected near Santa Maria Infante and found themselves embroiled in heated crossfire. Halloran ordered his overmatched men to withdraw while he returned fire from the point position. That was the last they saw of him; the New Yorker had been shot in the head and chest but still kept fighting. Halloran's men returned to their lines safely—but without ever knowing if their selfless XO had been killed or captured.[76]

The German MP-40 machine pistol, with its loud, obnoxious burping sound, struck icy terror into the hearts of Americans. Patrols silently reconnoitering the moonlit lanes and dark field paths beyond Tremensuoli dreaded its rude, unwelcome interruption on a cold silent night.[77] One barrel burst from this so-called "burp gun" was as jarring as a motorcycle without a muffler, and German patrols seemed to relish spraying them as indiscriminately as garden hoses—spitting lead out at a rate of 550 rounds per minute.[78]

Despite the ever-present danger of discovery—leading to certain capture or annihilation—this aggressive patrolling policy produced a clearer and clearer sense of German fortifications and troop strength with each passing night. Over time, the Americans learned that forward enemy positions were not yet fully manned but could be populated quickly if threatened. Minefields and wire barriers blanketed the forward slopes of the closest hills and served as the Germans' first line of defense. These obstacles were intended to slow an attack and funnel survivors toward crestline kill zones where lethal machine guns had been positioned with wide fields of fire and interlocking coverage.[79] Bunkers built into the rear slope of each hill supported the MG crews at the top. On more distant hills, camouflaged self-propelled guns and mortar positions supported the long MG chain holding the forward line. Heavier artillery batteries were located still further to the rear at Spigno, Castellonorato, Maranola, and Formia. Some Nebelwerfer launchers had also been seen on the rear slope of nearby Monte Scauri. Finally, 170mm howitzers and concrete-hardened 5-inch coastal artillery guns entrenched as far away as Gaeta, nine miles to the southwest, were capable of striking Allied positions as far east as Monte Massico. Every day, plodding Piper Cub spotter planes and darting P-38s snapped photos of German emplacements. These were quickly studied by eagle-eyed analysts with magnifying loupes, who meticulously compared every image against previous ones. Then, more infantry patrols were sent out into the night to investigate any suspicious changes identified by photo intelligence.[80] This process was repeated every twenty-four hours.

From prisoner interviews, the Americans identified their area opposition as the German 94th Infantry Division. The unit possessed a long combat record—taking part first in the French Campaign of 1940 before suffering near annihilation at Stalingrad two years later. After reconstituting in July 1943, the 94th was assigned to Italy and had been fighting since October 1943. The Allies considered the 94th a first-class combat outfit. The 274th, 275th, and 276th Grenadier Regiments comprised the bulk of the division's strength and occupied those daunting bunkers opposite Coulter's green troops.[81]

The daytime weather improved tremendously. The days grew longer and warmer under skies light blue and generally free of rain. The vexing mud had become a memory. In fact, a powdery white dust now drifted freely and settled upon the roads and parked vehicles. From time to time an eerie dense evening fog rolled in from the sea or a soft gentle morning mist blanketed the nearby hills and valleys, but always burned away rapidly under the bright rising Italian sun. Patches of receding snow could still be seen clinging to the tallest peaks of the Aurunci mountains to the distant northwest, but the long volatile Italian winter had clearly ended. The flourishing greenery, burgeoning foliage, and blossoming orchards surrounding Minturno now attested to a well-established spring.[82] This proliferation of dense vegetation formed welcome cover for the signal men running wire, the engineers probing minefields, and the ordnance and quartermaster crews busily establishing a vast network of supply and ammo dumps all over the II Corps sector.[83]

The biggest threat to safety was German artillery—which fell intermittently across the area. Over time, the newer and more skittish American troops stopped diving for cover with every barrage and learned how to "sense" the size and trajectory of incoming rounds by sound alone.[84] Only the close ones warranted a mad scramble. The II Corps policy was to answer every German shell with five Allied shells, and the Corps batteries grew so proficient at striking targets, the Germans stopped moving completely during the day. Only at night, when Allied spotter planes could no longer see them, could the Germans replenish supplies or reposition their troops.[85]

***

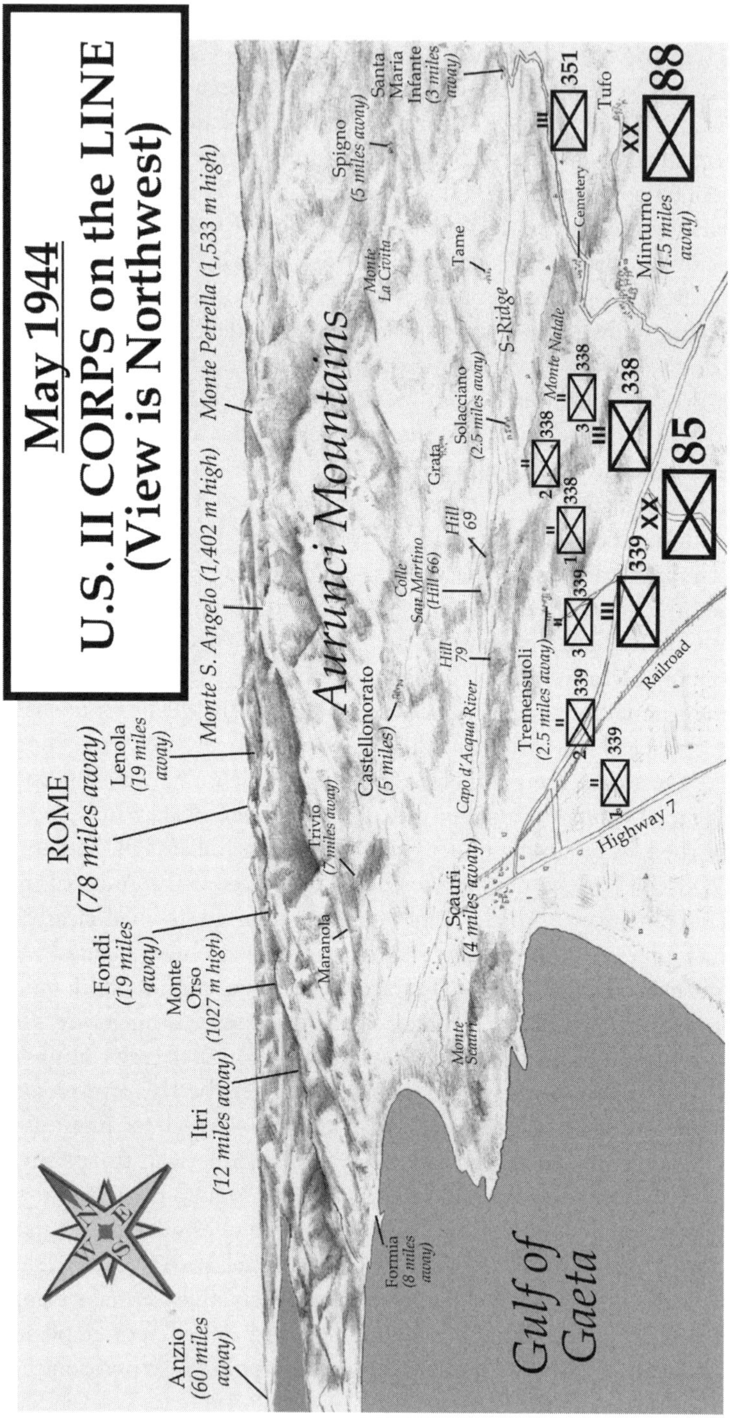
May 1944
U.S. II CORPS on the LINE
(View is Northwest)
ROME
(78 miles away)
Lenola
(19 miles away)
Fondi
(19 miles away)
Monte Orso
(1027 m high)
Itri
(12 miles away)
Anzio
(60 miles away)
Monte S. Angelo (1,402 m high)
Monte Petrella (1,533 m high)
Aurunci Mountains
Trivio
(7 miles away)
Maranola
Castellonorato
(5 miles)
Formia
(8 miles away)
Monte Scauri
Scauri
(4 miles away)
Capo d'Acqua River
Hill 79
Colle San Martino
(Hill 66)
Hill 69
Grata
Solacciano
(2.5 miles away)
S-Ridge
Tame
Monte La Civita
Spigno
(5 miles away)
Santa Maria Infante
(3 miles away)
Monte Natale
Cemetery
Minturno
(1.5 miles away)
Tufo
Tremensuoli
(2.5 miles away)
Railroad
Highway 7
Gulf of Gaeta
339
339
339
339
338
338
338
338
351
85
88
XX
XX
W N E S

From 15 to 30 April, a *sitzkrieg* of sorts reigned along the II Corps line. Aside from the nightly patrols and sporadic bouts of harassing artillery fire, the 85th Division's daily reports invariably led with this mundane summary line: "Sector Quiet."[86] Stockpiles of supplies amassed steadily to the rear, and all units organic to the division took rotations on the front line for the experience and to gain familiarity with the terrain.[87] The 338th, fresh from stream crossing rehearsals held 19–20 April, arrived on the line on 21 April in relief of the 339th. In turn, the 339th dropped back to Monte Massico for additional training.[88]

The Germans never attacked Tremensuoli. Nevertheless, Redle's tankers remained on standby near the MLR for the rest of the month—riding out bouts of light shelling here and there without suffering any casualties.[89] At one point, Redle's crews participated in a massive time-on-target (TOT) exercise with Corps artillery. An air observation plane detected a large concentration of German troops—estimated at a division in size. For a full three minutes, all Allied guns in the area fired according to a predetermined sequencing schedule. Although each gun fired at slightly different times during a volley, the timing allowed for all shells to land at the same instant. The compounding effect proved devastating, and word circulated later among the Allied gun crews of how "German medics were busy on into that night."[90]

On several occasions, Lt Redle escorted his platoon leaders out to key infantry observation posts so they, too, could become familiar with the terrain, artillery protocol, and the other infantry units holding the line. One time they ventured northeast into the CEF sector to visit an OP belonging to a French 90mm artillery battery. They happened to arrive as the OP crew discussed intercepting a certain German motorcycle messenger who passed through like clockwork every day on a road running parallel with the front line. With a stopwatch, the crew practiced several dry fires on a short segment of roadway where the motorcyclist appeared before crossing a small bridge. Once the location was registered, a French sergeant told Redle to be sure to return at the same time the following day. Redle and his platoon leaders returned as instructed and watched the messenger emerge and motor along obliviously. The French crew timed his progress, and then fired a single 90mm round. A few seconds later, both motorcycle and rider disappeared in a heavy flash on the bridge. "Recreational indulgences are *serious* on the front," Redle deadpanned later.[91]

During the third week of April, a series of medals were awarded to roughly a dozen 756th tankers. Bronze Stars went to B Company members T/Sgt Morris B. Thompson, Sgt Haskell O. Oliver, and 2nd Lt (then 1st Sgt) Jack Hogan for heroism at Cassino.[92] Three B Company tankers also received Silver Stars for a higher standard of "gallantry in action" during the same engagement. They were: 2nd Lt Howard M. Harley, Sgt David L. Grate, and Sgt Hamilton A. Smith. Grate and Smith were awarded for towing Sgt Haspel's tank while under fire at Cassino. Harley was recognized for recovering his knocked-out tank and rescuing Smith's crew while under fire.[93] Probably the most deserving Silver Star went to Captain Lewis of A Company for his Rapido River crossing heroics on 29 January—this despite suffering grievous foot wounds.[94]

Many other tankers should have received recognition but didn't. The most glaring oversight involved Sgt Oliver's crew. None received any official honor for confronting and knocking out one very dangerous German Mark IV lurking near the Cassino nunnery two months earlier. And despite Sweeting's promise to Wilkinson at the first Rapido river crossing on 27 January, no posthumous award ever went to 2nd Lt Wayne B. Henry for his daring initiative. Captain Wilkinson, too, was worthy of Silver Star consideration for courageous leadership that same afternoon, but his subsequent capture—through no fault of his own—probably spoiled his chances in Sweeting's eyes. Lt Redle, too, was passed over for consideration—despite several instances of qualifying meritorious action. He felt no regrets, however. When word came through of how the U.S. Army rejected a huge claim filed by the untrustworthy owners of the Montemiletto country house, this news was award enough.[95]

At the same time, the rest of the 756th Tank Battalion continued training near Mondragone. Quiet days were spent servicing tanks, enduring inspections, and taking ten-mile hikes into the nearby mountains.[96] The men enjoyed hot showers and warm caressing breezes sweeping in from the ocean almost daily, but were also required to line up for another round of arm-numbing Typhus shots.[97] There were more tank driving exercises and weapons demonstrations—including a new "snake" device built to destroy minefields.[98] There were also the obligatory U.S. Army lectures meant to be heard by all the troops. In one "less-than-enlightening" seminar, the speaker droned *ad infinitum* on how the nearby swamps were "full of mosquitos and, consequently, malaria."[99] The Army had long perfected methods of boring a soldier into wanting to return to combat.

Lt Col Rogers met with the 85th Division Operations staff almost daily—developing and amending numerous plans for attacks and counterattacks.[100] When not crouched over some table map, the tank battalion commander hiked around the Minturno countryside with Major Dolvin and Captain Arnold—reconnoitering ideal firing positions for the assault gun platoon, mortar platoon, and the remaining tank companies. Oftentimes, their efforts were restricted by local troops out of security concerns.[101]

However, something changed. Although the division's mission continued as the usual "active defense of the left and center sectors of the II Corps by patrolling and artillery fire," the teeming congestion of Allied troops, supplies, vehicles, and ordnance signaled an attack was imminent.[102] On 26 April, the 776th Tank Destroyer Battalion was attached to the 85th Division, and the outfit massed near the Garigliano River by the coast—a sure sign of preparations in the final stages.[103] Two days later, six tank destroyers were sent to the front in direct support of the 338th

Infantry.[104] Mine probing operations by engineering teams intensified—adding grist to an atmosphere of churning tension.[105] German observers reacted with uncharacteristic jitteriness—shifting their nuisance artillery barrages away from 85th Division troop positions to more harried strikes upon the supply routes at the rear. In response, smoke output was increased along the Garigliano to shield the Minturno Bridge, and tank, TD, and engineer bridging units were instructed to move only at night.[106]

Even the 756th tankers rehearsing thirteen miles to the southeast at Mondragone sensed a shift in the status quo. For three straight nights the crews watched from their little camps nestled alongside camouflaged tanks as tracers crisscrossed the skies further south near Naples. The activity didn't seem particularly unusual until the fourth night, 24 April, when all manner of Allied anti-aircraft fire flashed and flickered over Naples with a dazzling frenzy. The awesome display lasted well over an hour and reminded the crews of the futile German air raids they witnessed at Bizerte the summer before.[107] Unlike Bizerte, however, these German intruders successfully bombed one of two key Volturno River bridges at Capua.[108]

The rains returned on 26 April, and a few tankers received four-day passes for rest camp relaxation at Caserta.[109] The sense around the bivouac was these passes would be the last ones issued for a while.

The next day was also cloudy and rainy—and an unwelcome chill filled the air.[110] The crews prepared for a vehicle inspection. Some tanks employed at Cassino still retained rusting barbed wire spooled tightly around their drive sprockets. These thorny remnants could only be cut away after completely removing the tracks.[111] When the inspection took place on 29 April, the harping issue wasn't barbed wire on the exteriors—but dirt in the interiors. One tank revealed a full 1/8 inch of dust caked along the bottom of the engine compartment—another vestige of Cassino.[112]

Redle's B Company tankers had just finished their second week serving as front-line sentinels, and Lt Col Rogers ordered their relief for the following evening. Two platoons from C Company and one platoon from A Company were given the task. At 0530, 30 April, while reconnoitering the area ahead of the transfer, Captain Charles P. Waldron and S/Sgt James M. Riley of C Company became caught in a salvo of German artillery. Once the brief flurry lifted, Waldron lay wounded, but Riley was killed outright.[113] Waldron represented the third C Company, 756th, CO in the past six months cut down by enemy shell fragments at a crucial time. The company appeared to be hexed with a leadership curse. The best ones never seemed to last long enough for actual battle. Nevertheless, the tank transfer took place as planned after nightfall, and B Company returned to Mondragone.[114] The A Company platoon was attached to the 338th Regiment and the two C Company platoons were attached to the 337th.[115] 30 April fell on a Sunday, and many troops attended Catholic Mass or protestant services with congregations noticeably quiet and introspective. The men knew they would be attacking again soon, and the Germans had used the last three months to prepare for them.[116]

***

The war in Europe was still young and far from over. Although the Russian Army had battled to within the old eastern Polish border, and the Americans, British, and French had captured southern Italy, the rest of the continent remained either firmly German or neutral. Everywhere German forces were challenged, they fought with tenacity, ingenuity, and expertise. Rumors of an Allied cross channel attack from England remained rumors, and the only ground war taking place in Western Europe was in central Italy—either along the Gustav Line or at the Anzio beachhead.

The Germans committed twenty-two divisions to the Italian Campaign under the able leadership of Field Marshal Kesselring. The Allies matched this with roughly the same number.[117] Because of poor weather, the slow slog up the Italian boot had turned into a stalemate, and for several months neither side could do much except prepare for drier days ahead. The Germans used the lull to improve minefields, wire obstacles, and concrete pillbox defenses while the Allies amassed fresh troops, supplies, and ordnance while reconfiguring their forces.

Allied 15th Army Group commander, British General Sir Harold Alexander estimated that he needed a three-to-one infantry advantage over the Germans along the Gustav Line before any attack was feasible. By 1 May, that goal was achieved. The U.S. Fifth Army, at a combined strength of over 350,000 troops, amassed along twelve miles of coastal plain stretching from the Tyrrhenian Sea. Anchoring the Fifth's right flank was French Maj Gen Alphonse Juin's CEF—swelled now to four divisions: the 1st Motorized Infantry, 2nd Moroccan Infantry, 3rd Algerian Infantry, and 4th Moroccan Mountain Divisions. The left flank was held by Maj Gen Geoffrey Keyes's U.S. II Corps—with the 85th Infantry Division holding the coast and the 88th Infantry Division positioned inland to the right. The U.S. 36th Infantry Division sat in reserve—awaiting rapid deployment to either the Gustav Line or Anzio, depending on battlefield circumstances.[118] To the right of the U.S. Fifth Army, holding the remainder of the Gustav Line which included the Liri Valley, Cassino, and extended northeast all the way to the Adriatic Sea, was the British Eighth Army—now a multinational force of 265,000 troops encompassing the British V, X, and XIII Corps, the Canadian 1st Corps, the 2nd New Zealand Division, and the 2nd Polish Corps.[119] Alexander had extended the British Eighth Army's responsibilities further southwest to allow for a greater concentration of Lt Gen Clark's forces near the coast.

Clark's Fifth Army also included five divisions at Anzio under the command of Maj Gen Lucian Truscott's U.S. VI Corps. These were the U.S. 3rd, 34th, and 45th and British 1st and 5th Infantry Divisions. The First Special Service Force

(Canadian-American), a brigade sized force, was also assigned to Anzio. Orders for the VI Corps, however, were to monitor progress of the Allied attack on the Gustav Line before attempting a breakout.

Alexander's ambitious attack on the Gustav Line, codenamed Operation *Diadem* would involve over 500,000 troops—the largest Allied offensive to date. The operation required precise coordination on a massive scale. Although the date and time remained indefinite, the plan called upon all Allied forces amassed on the line to strike at once at the earliest opportunity. Only the British V Corps, holding the extreme right flank of the line from a point northeast of Cassino all the way to the Adriatic was ordered to exert pressure while maintaining their line. Everyone else was expected to strike westward and seize ground. Hopefully, this combined pressure of U.S. Fifth Army and British Eighth Army forces attacking at once would crack open an enemy position somewhere along the Liri Valley and blow the Cassino gates open for the long-anticipated drive on Rome.[120]

Diadem placed great expectations upon Lt Gen Mark Clark's U.S. Fifth Army. His forces would attack with two corps abreast, the U.S. II Corps on the left and the CEF on the right, with the ultimate goal of cutting the Itri–Pico Road beyond the Aurunci mountains and eleven miles to the west—a critical German route supplying Gustav Line defenses.[121]

The Fifth Army sector was opposed by the German XIV Panzer Corps consisting of the 94th Infantry Division, 15th Panzer Grenadier Division, 44th Infantry Division, 5th Mountain Division, and elements of Hermann Goering Panzer Division.[122] The Liri Valley featured flat terrain but the land nearer to the coast was rugged and nearly impassable. Roads everywhere were poor: the only good thoroughfares in the area were Highway 7 snaking along the coast and Highway 6 threading up the Liri Valley.[123]

The II Corps sector was most challenging. In order to reach the Aurunci mountains, the 88th and 85th Divisions had to first conquer foothills carved with steep ravines and deep draws bordered by swift moving creeks and streams. Such terrain gave the Germans plenty of places to hide and the enemy enjoyed several months of digging in, laying minefields, installing "armored crab" type pillboxes, and devising shooting lanes and tank traps of every type.[124] The first phase of the attack called for the 85th Division to attack Scauri, the foothills west of Tremensuoli, and the ruined town of Solacciano, with the objective of capturing the tiny town of Castellonorato three miles to the west. Castellonorato anchored a critical pass running between Monte Penitro, Monte Campese, and the sharply rising Aurunci mountains. The capture of the town would also open a coastal alleyway to Trivio, Formia, and Itri further west. At the same time, the 88th Division would attack the crestline village of Santa Maria Infante and an adjacent hill feature called "S-ridge," while French troops attacked down from the north—hopefully, clearing German mountain forces from the side.[125]

The details, of course, on how to achieve these objectives rested with the staff officers at the divisional, regimental, and battalion levels. For the next ten days, lamps and candles burned through the night in camouflaged tents and battle ravaged farmhouses along the Garigliano as those plans were discussed, revised, and finalized.

Redle's B Company spent the first week of May resting and training at Mondragone under blue skies and a radiant sun. Mornings were filled with calisthenics and close order drilling along with the spirited serenading of songbirds and intermittent droning of high-altitude Allied bombers.[126] Tank obstacle course training followed—oftentimes, after sundown.[127] The daily routine waivered little, and with each repetition, the men sensed the gnawing approach of H-hour.[128]

Another Cassino survivor returned to the company—after requiring two months to recover from a severe case of trench foot. Tank driver T/4 Randolph H. Perdue's medical problems began when his tank swamped in the middle of the Rapido river during the first crossing attempt on 27 January. After shivering in waist deep water for nearly twelve hours, Perdue and crew were finally able to safely leave their stricken tank at nightfall. When Perdue removed his boots in the company assembly area, however, his feet promptly swelled up to the point where walking became impossible. He was evacuated and eventually regained functional circulation and sensation, but was told he would never fully recover and could not return to tanks. Fearful he might still end up in an infantry unit, he convinced his doctor to return him to B Company. Redle really had no open positions but made room for the Indianan nevertheless by assigning him as company "troubleshooter"—meaning he just helped where needed. Most of the time, Perdue worked in supply with S/Sgt Shirley. Other times, he assisted the kitchen staff or served as a fill-in jeep or truck driver.[129]

S/Sgt Oric W. Johannesen, the "miracle man" who fully recovered after suffering shrapnel wounds at Cassino that should have been fatal, also rejoined the company on 5 May.[130] Upon returning, Johannesen was given the platoon sergeant position in the 1st Platoon.[131]

S/Sgt Nusz received his formal promotion to company 1st sergeant, and 2nd Lt Howard M. Harley received his expected promotion to 1st lieutenant.[132] Nusz, of course, would remain with the company, but Harley's advancement meant he would likely transfer to another.

Eleven B Company enlisted men returned to duty after relaxing for several days at the Fifth Army Rest Center.[133] Since these were the last of the missing B Company men, their arrival was a sure sign a move to the front was imminent.

Lt Redle had one last matter demanding his immediate attention. Company Mess Sergeant S/Sgt Colley had allowed the allure of personal gain to taint his food-swapping activities with local Italians. Although his infractions were not particularly egregious, they were still inappropriate and shocking nonetheless. Redle had no choice but to remove the wiry Montanan from his plum position and reduce him to the grade of private. Colley was given a tank crewman assignment and cautioned to remain on his best behavior.[134] As a result, Alabaman T/4 Oscar Crenshaw was promoted from cook to become the new B Company mess sergeant.[135]

Orders came down that same morning of 8 May for the tanks of HQ Company and the 1st and 2nd Platoons of B Company to move out from Mondragone after midnight.[136] The 3rd Platoon, maintenance tank, and the maintenance, kitchen, and supply sections would follow later.[137] Nevertheless, all tents were struck and the tanks' rear decks were stacked with tarps, camouflage netting, camp items, crated C-rations, and other supplies.[138] Stoves, ovens, pots, and pans were also carefully packed away aboard the company's kitchen truck. There was no telling how much time would pass before Class B or Class A rations could be served again—weeks, perhaps, months from now. Cooks and cooks' helpers resumed their dual roles moving supplies, rations, gas, and ammunition—a backbreaking responsibility demanding long days and many all-nighters as experienced earlier at Cassino.[139]

Redle's tanks lurched forward at 0030, 9 May, departing the bivouac in a long noisy line. D Company's light tanks and the remaining medium tanks of A and C Companies would follow in the next day or two. Only Service Company would remain in Mondragone indefinitely to continue functioning safely out of range of German artillery.[140] A bright moon hung high in a clear starry sky throughout the entire eighteen-mile journey. Dry conditions swept the inevitable road dust into the eyes of the crews, but other than that, the ride proved uneventful. The HQ tanks stopped at a location three-quarters of a mile east of Minturno at 0300, amidst the thundering of Allied artillery. B Company halted at the 756th's intermediate CP location along Highway 7, roughly a mile west of the Garigliano.[141] The tanks' gas tanks were topped off, bedrolls unpacked, and the crews finally turned in for a short rest at 0540.[142]

On 9 May, the 85th Division forward CP was moved into Minturno, and attack preparations were finalized based upon the classic triangle attack formation. The 339th Regiment reassumed the left coastal flank, with two battalions abreast and one in reserve while the 338th held the inland right with the same configuration. The 337th prepared to move to a reserve location southeast of Tremensuoli between both positions—ready to rush to either flank and exploit any breakthrough. Artillery batteries from the 910th and 329th (105mm), the 403rd (155mm), and the 602nd (75mm) Field Artillery Battalions fired periodically at targets of opportunity from camouflaged gun positions approximately one mile east of Minturno. Deadly 4.2-inch mortars from the 2nd Chemical Mortar Battalion also waited at the ready.[143]

Lt Col Rogers believed the hilly terrain still allowed the employment of four supporting medium tank platoons—two for each regiment.[144] He assigned Lt Redle's B Company to the 339th Regiment on the division's left flank—but concentrated on the right side of the regiment's sector near Tremensuoli. C Company, now led by Captain Donald F. Gourley, would support the 338th on the division's right—through rippled fields saddled between Tremensuoli and Monte Natale.[145] Captain Lewis's A

Company was concealed beneath an orchard along the flat coastal plain southeast of Tremensuoli—serving as a foil should the Germans counterattack from Scauri.[146] The light tanks of D Company would wait in battalion reserve, ready to either reinforce the attack, if necessary, or transport supplies to the advancing medium tank companies during battle. The battalion's assault gun and mortar positions had been established east of Tremensuoli. Their firepower would be attached to the 85th Division artillery at the onset of the attack, but available on call for Lt Col Rogers, if needed. The Recon Platoon would assist the infantry engineers and maintain close radio contact with Rogers—alerting him to any potential tank obstacles and locating feasible tank routes as the attack progressed.[147] Rogers's forward CP had been established about a mile south of Minturno along Highway 7,[148] with the HQ tank section positioned protectively down the road to the west.[149] Communication wire had been strung and supply dumps were established.[150] All that remained were the finishing moves ahead of the attack itself.

Rogers recognized the greatest obstacle threatening the progress of his tank crews was the Capo d'Acqua creek bed running parallel to the front lines roughly a half-mile to the west. The creek was only four feet deep at most, but fifteen feet wide with high banks in many places.[151] The meandering channel was reportedly fordable near Solacciano further north, but this assessment was made from a distance by watching supply-bearing Germans sloshing through the section. These same Germans weren't driving 32-ton tanks over the same spot. During the preceding weeks, Rogers made certain every officer and platoon sergeant in his battalion took turns accompanying the nightly infantry patrols surveying the area. His men returned with worrisome reports of rugged terrain, high terraced slopes, and numerous drainage ditches cutting through the lower rolling fields—all of which complicated any potential tank approach to the Capo d'Acqua itself. The flat plain nearest the coast offered the most favorable topography for tank operations, but funneled into a natural bottleneck at Scauri—where the Germans had excavated a formidable anti-tank ditch, sewn numerous mines, and positioned hidden AT guns.[152] An attack thorough Scauri had been discounted earlier as too costly by division planners. The grounds west of Tremensuoli, though hilly, offered a better option for infantry operations, but Lt Col Rogers could not know if his tanks would get through until actually attempting a crossing. As a consequence, the new battalion commander emphasized the importance of aggressive reconnaissance as the attack progressed. That night, all B Company platoon leaders and section leaders set out on foot investigating possible routes across the Capo d'Acqua.[153] Due to the distance and dangers, they dared not venture too far.

A bloated morning sun rose above flat, gray Monte Massico fifteen miles to the east bringing warm air and good visibility—the twelfth straight day of such beautiful weather.[154] As usual, German artillery shells whined sporadically over the ruins of Tremensuoli—exploding as random clusters around Minturno or along the

Garigliano.[155] On any given day, an average of 150 to 250 enemy rounds fell about the area in similar harassing patterns—but without ever doing much damage.[156] Still, 10 May seemed anything but routine. The uptick in preparatory activity signaled to the regular GIs on the ground that the "lid was going to blow" soon.[157] The prior evening, troops of the 3rd Battalion, 337th, marched to a forward assembly area outside of Tremensuoli, then dispersed and waited—attached now to the 339th at the line as reinforcements.[158] The 1st and 2nd Battalions of the 337th, too, had marched during the night and dispersed in reserve locations roughly a mile more to the southeast, nearer the coast.[159] The 776th Tank Destroyer Battalion had also started moving TDs into forward echelon positions,[160] and that afternoon, General Alexander and Lt Gen Clark stopped by the II Corps CP—another sure sign something major was afoot.[161]

Once evening descended, Lt Redle received orders to move B Company into their final attack positions. Under a moonlit, starry sky with artillery thundering nearby and machine guns clashing further off in the distance, Redle's tank column skirted Minturno heading toward Tremensuoli. The young lieutenant noted with wide-eyed curiosity the presence of enormous 240mm howitzers batteries and another battery consisting of two long 8-inch and 10-inch artillery guns in nearby fields. These Allied guns, usually positioned much further to the rear, now sat easily within range of German 81mm mortars.[162] The emplacement of such powerful weapons so near the MLR convinced him the attack order was imminent and planners expected much ground to be seized by the infantry in the early stages. By 2300, Redle's 1st and 2nd Platoons assumed attack positions 1,500 yards northeast of Tremensuoli. Two tank platoons from C Company rumbled to a stop nearby along the Minturno–Santa Maria Infante Road.[163] A new round of recon patrols ventured deeper down the valley toward the Capo d'Acqua in search of promising tank trails and firing positions.[164]

Dawn, 11 May 1944, arrived warm and cloudy with fair visibility,[165] but cleared to perfection once the sun broke over the horizon.[166] Aside from the infrequent bursting of incoming enemy shells, the morning progressed like every other previous Mediterranean spring day.[167] Fields of bright scarlet poppies bobbed with the gentle caresses of faint sea breezes drifting in from the Gulf of Gaeta. The fresh calming fragrances of flowering Mimosa trees teased of peacetime romantic dalliances. The aged boughs of gnarled orange and lemon trees sagged from the weight of a perpetual bounty of sweet treats—too tempting for any foreign guest to ignore. The Americans ate their fill, but never seemed to unburden the fruit-laden branches.[168] Olive groves and vineyards checkering the countryside began shedding delicate blooms in favor of verdant bounty.[169] Smoke pots obscuring the Minturno Bridge continued, as always, puffing thick clouds of white acrid smoke out across the fertile river plain.[170] No German prisoners had been nabbed during the patrols the previous night and Allied artillery batteries continued belching their barrel fire regularly—as they had for many days now.[171] At times the sounds of the enemy digging and stake driving were heard along the Capo d'Acqua,[172] and, at one point, a spate of German S/A and mortar fire raked through Tremensuoli.[173]

Outwardly, the day may have seemed routine, but the mounting tension among the troops was palpable. All were aware of the impending major Allied offensive and knew an attack order could come at any minute. Truck convoys now ran both day and night. Huge caches of ammunition, fuel, food, and equipment had been deposited under camouflage netting about the area. Tanks, TDs, and artillery guns—also camouflaged—seemingly appeared overnight.[174] Fresh infantrymen had been marched up to the MLR and packed in living conditions far more crowded than even basic training days. Many were now stuffed together inside sandbagged dugouts, or in the numerous scalloped hollows and shallow caves carved into hillsides throughout the area. Other anxious GIs were crammed inside Italian farmhouses with fifteen to twenty-five men sleeping to a room. This was neither customary nor preferred military practice. One random German shell could take out an entire platoon.[175] Many men, sensing time was very short, resorted to last minute letter writing to assuage their nerves and those of families back home.[176] Although most were new to combat, every man knew death would come to someone. Every man chose to believe that "someone" was someone else.

Daylight faded and flickering stars appeared in an indigo sky.[177] Then official verbal orders swept through the waiting ranks: the long-anticipated and new grand Allied offensive against the German Gustav Line would commence at 2300 hours that very night.[178]

***

The 85th Division codenamed their offensive responsibilities under the Operation *Diadem* umbrella as Plan *Scurry*.[179] The plan developed after Maj Gen Keyes, II Corps commander, issued orders on 1 May for both the 85th and 88th Divisions to develop a three-phase plan whereby both units would attack at once in coordination. Since the 88th was considered the more experienced division of the two, the main effort was entrusted to them.[180] Thus, their sector along the Corps' right flank was widened slightly to include the crucial crestline road leading from Minturno north to Santa Maria Infante.[181] The 85th maintained responsibility for the left flank running from the valley north of Tremensuoli down to the coastline.[182] The 88th was to attack Santa Maria Infante, then take a series of hills to the north before swinging westward and seizing Monte Civita and Spigno.[183] At the same time the 85th would drive westward to seize and hold Castellonorato and Monte Scauri with the mission of protecting the Corps' left flank.[184]

The 85th's "Plan *Scurry*" portion of the Corps' orders pertained to only Phase I and developed out of a basic framework established in Maj Gen Coulter's Field Order

#4 issued on 3 May. Those orders directed his commanders to flesh out details for a main attack emanating from division's center at Tremensuoli with the aim of seizing the double peaked sixty-six- and sixty-nine-meter-high San Martino Hill roughly a half-mile west and a 131-meter-high hill dubbed "S-ridge" a half-mile northwest near Solacciano. Under *Scurry* the coastal town of Scauri was to be bypassed and contained in the meantime.[185]

The 339th Regiment would now spearhead the effort with three battalions abreast. The 1st Battalion on the left was given the defensive mission of containing Scauri. The 2nd Battalion, however, would attack aggressively from the center with the mission of capturing Hill 79, 1,200 yards due west of Tremensouli, while the 3rd Battalion on the right pushed beyond the Capo d'Acqua to seize San Martino Hill. The 1st Battalion, 337th, was attached as regimental reserve.[186] At the same time, the 338th Regiment would strike out on the division's right flank from Monte Natale to take the south section of S-ridge.[187] The 88th Division was responsible for securing the north section of the hill.

Use of screening smoke was restricted only to emergencies both night and day—except around the Minturno Bridge.[188] Both the 338th and 339th Regiment received twelve flamethrowers apiece.[189] Infantrymen were instructed to fix bayonets to their rifles.[190] Divisional artillery batteries, tank destroyer crews, and mortar crews prepared to fire on call.[191] Artillery operations, however, were told to continue with no marked increase or decrease in hourly expenditures right up to H-hour—in hopes of maintaining an element of surprise.[192]

The Allies believed they held that advantage. Two German prisoners taken from nearby S-ridge several days prior had been asked specifically if they received any reports of an imminent Allied offensive. Both men knew of no warnings nor of any special measures taken during the past few weeks to repulse one. The prisoners' responses seemed truthful and consistent with those of others. The Germans certainly expected some new Allied offensive—just not on this particular evening. They misinterpreted ongoing heavy motor movement occurring in the British Eighth Army sector as evidence the Allies were still making preparations.[193]

Nevertheless, the Germans waiting further west remained a formidable force. Prisoners reported receiving regular rations and maintaining good morale. After five years of war, some older veterans had become disillusioned, but the younger troops remained "true believers in the Fuehrer" and could be "expected to offer stiff resistance." Despite the steady Allied artillery bombardment day in and day out, the German captives reported casualties as light—with only five men wounded in the past three weeks as a direct result of shell bursts.[194] The Germans seemed quite confident in both their defensive fortifications and their combat prowess. Those opposite the U.S. II Corps sector of the Gustav Line also knew they faced inexperienced American troops from the 85th and 88th Divisions.[195] The enemy, too, took prisoners and employed competent intelligence officers.

A solid month of aggressive patrolling in and around Tremensuoli yielded the II Corps and 85th Division G-2 officers a remarkably clear sense of German unit disposition. They had long established the German 94th Infantry Division opposed them and further determined the 274th Grenadier Battalion anchored the Scauri coastline sector, with the 267th Grenadier Battalion holding San Martino up through S-ridge and the 94th Fusilier Battalion occupying Santa Maria Infante. Many individual company positions were also identified.[196] This knowledge gave the officers of the new American division confidence in their attack plans.

The latest weather forecast helped bolster that confidence. Absolutely no rain was expected for the next forty-eight hours. Skies would remain clear with only scattered mid-level clouds forming at night. Winds should stay light at ten to twelve MPH with good visibility at ten to fifteen miles.[197] These presented near-perfect conditions for artillery operations.

Between 2100 and 2200 hours, the forward CPs for the 339th and 338th Regiments were established in Tremensuoli and a half-mile to the northwest, respectively.[198] Lt Redle's 1st and 2nd Platoons waited patiently nearby for H-hour to arrive. Further to the north, two of Captain Gourley's C Company platoons awaited the same. The tanks were expected to closely follow the infantry once they plunged ahead. If all four platoons progressed without delay, the two remaining platoons from B and C Companies were expected to follow.[199] A platoon of engineers from the 310th Engineer Battalion had been assigned to assist the tanks in reaching the Capo d'Acqua.[200] Recent infantry recon reports raised concerns. Areas along the creek proved boggier than expected. At one spot near Solacciano an average-sized man's boot sunk into mud four to five inches deep.[201]

As the final minutes ticked down to the 2300 H-hour, slight fog appeared in the low valleys. The night remained quiet with little out of the ordinary occurring.[202] American infantrymen quietly crept up into their jump off positions and waited in silence. Redle's tankers tugged their steel helmets over the top of their football style helmets and settled into their crew positions. Several tankers preferred wearing their steel pots backwards to better accommodate radio headsets.[203] Redle always twisted his steel helmet slightly to one side over his small head to keep it in place. His forehead lieutenant bar may have appeared comically off kilter, but his men could always identify their company commander from a distance … from either his cock-eyed helmet or his oversized flapping pants. While at Cassino, even Lt Col Sweeting was known to call Redle "baggy pants" over radio bands so as not to give away his identity to the Germans.[204]

The final five minutes hung like an eternity. Not only were the troops, tankers, and artillerymen of the U.S. 85th Division counting down the seconds while mumbling prayers and fidgeting mindlessly—but 500,000 other Allied soldiers amassed along the Gustav Line did the same. Though surrounded by many, each soldier waited alone in silent desperation—contemplating his fate as the moment of truth drew near.[205]

On this night, no guiding moon hung above them. A high mist rolling across the upper atmosphere caused the few remaining stars to waver and fade before disappearing altogether.[206] As if the heavens refused to witness the earthly hell about to unfold below.

German vehicle symbol

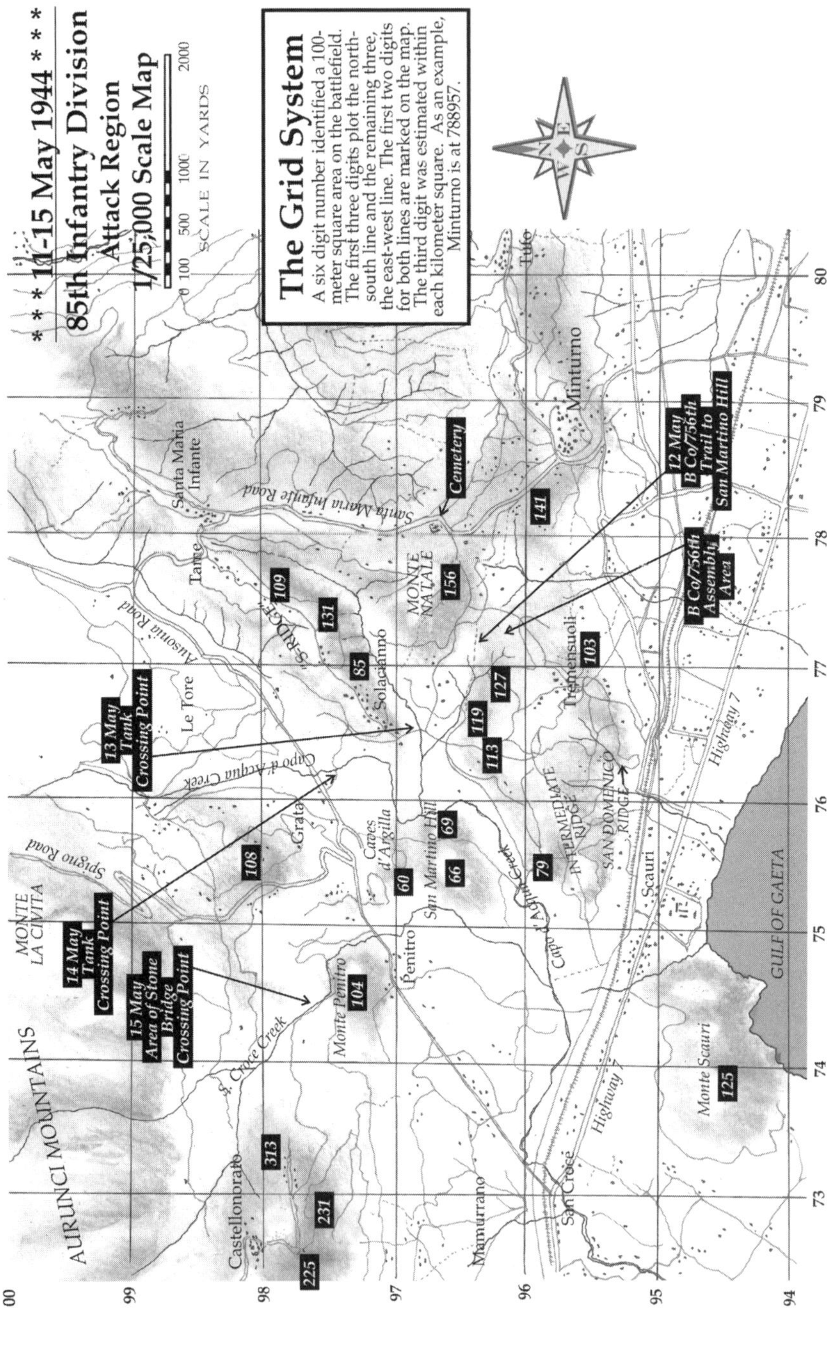
* * * 11-15 May 1944 * * *
85th Infantry Division
Attack Region
1/25,000 Scale Map
0 100 500 1000 2000
SCALE IN YARDS
The Grid System
A six digit number identified a 100-meter square area on the battlefield. The first three digits plot the north-south line and the remaining three, the east-west line. The first two digits for both lines are marked on the map. The third digit was estimated within each kilometer square. As an example, Minturno is at 788957.
N E S W
AURUNCI MOUNTAINS
MONTE LA CIVITA
14 May Tank Crossing Point
15 May Area of Stone Bridge Crossing Point
13 May Tank Crossing Point
12 May B Co/756th Trail to San Martino Hill
B Co/756th Assembly Area
Cemetery
Spigno Road
Ausonia Road
Santa Maria Infante Road
Capo d'Acqua Creek
S. Croce Creek
Santa Maria Infante
Tame
Le Tore
S-RIDGE
Solacianno
MONTE NATALE
Grata
Caves d'Argilla
San Martino Hill
Penitro
Monte Penitro
Castellonorato
Maranola
San Croce
Monte Scauri
Scauri
Tremensuoli
INTERMEDIATE RIDGE
SAN DOMENICO RIDGE
Minturno
Tufo
Highway 7
GULF OF GAETA
225
231
313
104
108
60
66
69
79
113
119
127
85
131
109
156
103
141
125
73
74
75
76
77
78
79
80
00
99
98
97
96
95
94

CHAPTER ELEVEN

Cracking the Gustav Line: 11 May 1944 to 13 May 1944

At precisely 2300 hours, 11 May 1944, a tranquil Italian night erupted in one colossal wall of fire. Allied artillery gun batteries of every caliber—1,660 barrels in all, flashed and belched unbroken fury from beneath thrashing blankets of camouflaged netting positioned along twenty-five miles of front. From Cassino to the Tyrrhenian Sea, American 240mms, Long Toms, 105s, 75mms, and British six-pound and twenty-five-pound cannon rifles ejected high explosives westward as quickly as their crews could feed their ravenous breeches.[1]

For the next half hour, tens of thousands of Allied shells pummeled German positions. The roar was deafening, and the front lines flickered under the steady bursts as if some unsteady twilight tried taking hold.[2] The hellish spectacle reminded British Eighth Army veterans of earlier epic cannon duels at El Alamein, but Allied radio declared this the greatest artillery concentration of the war thus far.[3]

As the ruthless pounding persisted, nervous scouts, pathfinders, and platoon leaders probed forward amidst long dancing shadows seeking the best ways through to meet the enemy. Their skulking brethren soon followed—in waves or streams, depending on the terrain—to take new attack positions along the very edges of the firestorm.[4] Then, at precisely 2330, the barrage abruptly ceased, and the battlefield fell dark again.[5] With wide eyes straining, ears ringing, and hearts beating in throats parched with dread, Allied infantrymen from twenty-five mighty divisions dared breach the Gustav Line. Americans, Brits, French, and Canadians stormed up hillsides, over fields, and across river bridges in a weighted gamble to accomplish what couldn't be done during the past five months: break the excruciating stalemate in central Italy. Only the Polish troops were delayed, under the carefully crafted Allied timetable, from making their final assault on the ruins of Monte Cassino.[6] Their attack would commence ninety minutes later.[7]

The responsibilities placed upon B Company, 756th Tank Battalion, were restricted to a mere 1,000 yards of that twenty-five-mile front, but the challenge was daunting nonetheless. The bowled terrain between Tremensuoli and Monte Natale leading a mile down to the Capo d'Acqua undulated with irregular hillocks and fields. Ditches converged to form crisscrossing gullies and shattered homes, stone terraces, and gnarled olive orchards lined the hillsides. The only way through was a coarse and narrow farm lane. Lt Redle's tanks waited in the protection of the saddled draw between Tremensuoli and Natale for a signal from their assigned infantry—the 3rd Battalion, 339th Regiment—to move forward. The call could come at any minute.[8]

In the meantime, the 3rd Battalion, 339th, under the command of Major Richard S. Smith, spilled down from Tremensuoli with L Company in the lead.[9] Machine guns sputtered staccato bursts of red-traced fire while mortar and cannon company rounds erupted as dazzling flashes beyond the Capo d'Acqua.[10] Lt Redle departed on foot from his tanks with a 756th HQ reconnaissance section and a 310th Combat Engineer Battalion lieutenant and his three-man team, trailing the infantry wave. Their mission was to find the best route for the tanks to reach the river. Anywhere Redle pointed out an impediment, the engineers were supposed to arrange for the necessary repairs.[11]

Hitherto, the German reaction had been muted.[12] The Allied barrage had, indeed, caught them off-guard. However, once the final shells fell and Americans began spilling down from Tremensuoli and Monte Natale, the response was swift and vicious. From well-concealed bunkers beyond the Capo d'Acqua, machine guns spewed back sweeping torrents of death laced with tracers beaded green. Mortar, Nebelwerfer, and artillery fire carefully timed to burst over the open ground upon which the Custermen ventured, quickly found warm flesh.[13] An entire L Company squad passing through Tremensuoli was obliterated in just one flurry of shells. A short time later, a second L Company squad disappeared inside another fiery concentration registered upon the engineer marked trail leading to Hill 113.[14]

In the nearby valley to the north, Redle's team had covered approximately 200 yards when they, too, were hit by a heavy salvo of German mortar and artillery. After hugging the ground and riding out the short barrage, Redle called out into the night for the others. The battalion recon men answered immediately, but the four engineers lay in petrified silence. Finally, after Redle's louder second call, they answered.[15] With everyone accounted for, Redle's team returned to their feet and skulked forward.

Allied artillery crews answered with aggressive counterbattery. Then the German heavy coastal guns at Gaeta opened fire upon the Garigliano further to the rear—still intent on striking the main bridge and severing the U.S. II Corps supply lines.[16] The entire countryside, again, flickered and howled under a hellish array of fuming flashes and blasts.[17] To the 85th's right, troops of the 88th Division moved tentatively north from Minturno toward Santa Maria Infante—drawing a similar murderous reaction from German defenders. Two battalions of 85th's 338th Regiment, under the command of Colonel Alfred A. Safay, advanced toward Solacciano and S-ridge to the northwest, suffering the same.[18]

On the 85th's left, all three battalions of Colonel Brookner W. Brady's 339th Regiment were committed to the attack westward, but Smith's 3rd Battalion had the furthest to go.[19] The 3rd Battalion's objective was the twin peaks "69" and "66" of San Martino Hill just beyond the Capo d'Acqua creek—situated nearly a mile to the west. Despite the hail of bullets and shells and the nightmare of negotiating past S-mine laden fields and rowed concertina wire, L Company managed to reach the Capo d'Acqua shortly after midnight. The swift-moving creek was only fifteen feet wide and three or four feet deep, but the banks on both sides sat six feet high, mimicking a castle moat.[20] The prefabricated solution came in the form of two wood planks eighteen feet long and twenty-four inches wide to serve as footbridges. However, when the bridge-bearing squads stepped forward, the teams and their improvised bridges were smashed and scattered by a crisscrossing barrage of German MG and mortar fire raining down from Hill 79 300 yards to their left, and Hill 69 immediately to their fore.[21] Platoon leaders dropped over dead or wounded in the sudden flurry. Platoon sergeants assumed command for mere moments before they, too, were felled in the ongoing maelstrom of snapping bullets and spinning shrapnel.[22]

The survivors scrambled down into the creek and splashed over to the opposite bank.[23] Weapons, ammo, and radios were shed in the mad dash to survive and get across.[24] K Company, I Company and finally M Company followed, suffering similar losses—but through sheer determination managed to establish a tenuous bridgehead.[25] Along the opposite bank, remnants of platoons quickly organized—in some cases led by a sole surviving NCO—and pressed on.[26] K Company and an L Company platoon moved to the left toward Hill 66 while the rest of the battalion advanced upon Hill 69.[27] Surviving mortar and MG crews of M Company, provided covering fire from the rear.[28]

From the Capo d'Acqua, San Martino did not appear so formidable. The two gentle swells merging as one hill sat only 400 yards wide at the foundation and rose, perhaps, only 120 feet above surrounding fields.[29] To reach it, however, attackers had to cross through even more minefields. Thankfully, these were not as thickly sewn as those along the eastern bank.[30] Both hills were covered in thick grass and denuded of trees—except for four small ones growing at the southern base of Hill 69.[31] Aerial photographs of San Martino indicated the Germans had constructed at least two pillboxes along the forward slope of Hill 66 and maintained outposts on Hill 69. A reinforced company was suspected of holding the reverse side.[32] During the massive Allied artillery barrage proceeding the ground attack, Hill 69 received a dedicated five-minute salvo followed by a full ten-minute concentration on Hill 66, courtesy of the 131st Field Artillery Battalion. An additional 1,200 rounds of splintering 4.2-inch shells were arced onto Hill 66 by the 2nd Chemical Mortar Battalion for good measure.[33]

By 0030, 12 May, Smith's battalion crossed the narrow minefield—losing several more men before reaching the gentle slopes.[34] MG and S/A fire emanated from both hills at a steady and determined rate but failed to slow the advancing Americans—now enraged over the loss of their brethren and resolved to take both objectives. With the high cloud cover breaking and a waning gibbous moon now rising in the east, the forward slope to Hill 69 fell quickly to I Company and a heavy MG section of M Company.[35] The defenders had either perished in the preparatory shelling or vacated their holes at the last minute.[36] The hillcrest fell briefly at 0100, but the Germans counterattacked and captured an entire 3rd Platoon, I Company, squad and a light MG crew before withdrawing again. Shortly afterwards, the 2nd Platoon of I Company retook the height and dug-in along the rear slope.[37]

At the same time, the 3rd Platoon, L Company, bypassed Hill 69 and tried storming up Hill 66. But instead of two pillboxes, they found six, and a vicious, intimate battle followed whereby several pillboxes were eventually knocked out—but only after enormous sacrifice.[38] K Company tried scaling the slope of Hill 66 further south, but were driven back by withering small arms fire emanating from two other pillboxes supported by mortar fire popping from beyond the rear slope. The company commander ordered his 1st and 3rd Platoons to provide a firebase to permit his 2nd Platoon to maneuver on the right, but with a company depleted down to only ninety men, the plan was a crapshoot at best. By this time, the enemy had recognized their loss of Hill 69 and blasted it with heavy concentrations of mortar and artillery fire.[39]

During the same hour, Lt Redle and his recon team ventured 300 yards closer to the creek before drawing another spate of sweeping MG and thick mortar fire. Once this short tempest ceased, Redle again hollered for a headcount and, again, the battalion recon men answered immediately. After calling out several more times for the others and receiving only silence, however, the company commander realized the inexperienced engineers "did not like their initial taste of fire" and had taken off for the rear.[40] Redle and his recon team continued forward, managing to inch within 400 yards of the Capo d'Acqua by 0200. For a third time, the team drew S/A and mortar fire—but this time, the harassment never waned, and the team remained pinned and unable to creep forward any further.[41]

The 3rd Battalion, 339th, battle to take the remainder of San Martino Hill raged on through the night. More hidden pillboxes were discovered on Hill 66, and a depleted K Company attacked each one in turn—but achieved only limited success. German batteries in Castellonorato and Monte Scauri struck back with another deluge of shells.[42] By 0300, part of Hill 66 had succumbed to American control, but the enemy shelling continued unabated.[43] Major Smith called each company for an effective strength report. The numbers were shocking: only twenty-seven riflemen remained in I Company. K Company had only twenty-nine and L Company was down to a mere seventeen. Less than four hours earlier, each company had set out from Tremensuoli with 187 men.[44] The 1938 University of Nebraska graduate Smith grimaced at the disheartening news, and ordered the survivors to dig in, hold their current positions and prepare to repulse any counterattacks sure to come.[45] Next,

Colonel Brady picked up his field phone and ordered K Company from his reserve battalion, the 3rd Battalion, 337th Regiment, to Hill 66 to help reinvigorate the attack.[46]

K Company, 337th, set out promptly from Tremensuoli, but by the time the company crossed the Capo d'Acqua to arrive at Hill 69 before dawn—land mines, and unrelenting artillery and mortar fire had battered their ranks down to only four officers and thirty-five enlisted men. Lacking the necessary numbers to attack Hill 66, the survivors were instead ordered to shore up American positions consolidated on Hill 69.[47]

Around the same time, several hundred yards further to the northwest, Lt Redle and his recon men decided to withdraw before being caught in open daylight.[48] Although his team was unable to creep close enough to the Capo d'Acqua to find a suitable tank crossing location, the plucky lieutenant located two problem ditches and boggy areas along the route in need of prompt attention. After returning to Minturno, Redle passed his observations and recommendations along to the engineers.[49]

As dawn arrived at 0500, the Germans dispatched a fifteen-minute concentration of artillery on Hill 69. As soon as the last shells exploded, a wave of counter-attackers—perhaps a company in size—poured over the crest of Hill 66. Flat trajectory tank fire, likely dispatched from Monte Scauri, supported the advance. L Company immediately called the battalion for mortar and artillery support—which promptly tore into the approaching wave of *feldgrau* wool. After five minutes of fury, the German attack faltered, and the scattered survivors retreated. Unfortunately, one American round fell short, killing the L Company commander and destroying the only radio link between Hill 69 and the rest of the world.[50]

A short time later, the Germans attempted a second counterattack on Hill 66, this one comprised of roughly 200 grenadiers advancing from the south along the Capo d'Acqua with the support of a solitary tank. Divisional artillery batteries were called again for help—and scored a lucky hit atop the creeping tank, thereby dispersing the infantry.[51]

The situation turned dire. Both Major Smith and 339th Regimental commander Colonel Brady realized San Martino Hill was not merely an outpost line as they had assumed prior to the attack, but *the* German MLR.[52] At 0700, Smith contacted Colonel Brady to request reinforcements, but to secure them Brady had to ring up Maj Gen Coulter. The call was not pleasant, but Coulter released the entire 1st Battalion, 337th Regiment to Colonel Brady's care.[53]

Reports were just as frustrating along the rest of the 85th Division's front as well. On the Corps' far left the advance by Lt Col Charles C. Isley's 1st Battalion, 339th, stalled shy of their San Domenico Ridge objective—the southernmost edge of the plateau extending west of Tremensuoli and overlooking Scauri. German mines and MG fire had stymied the effort from the start.[54] The 2nd Battalion, 339th, under the command of Lt Col Charles F. Mudgett, attacked Hill 79, south of San

Martino, but found the heights unexpectedly infested with fifteen bunkers and two full companies from the 274th Grenadier Regiment. As of dawn, fighting remained fierce with neither side prevailing.[55]

To the 339th Regiment's right, two battalions of the 338th attacked Solacciano and the southern half of S-ridge. Resistance encountered was only moderate at first, but stiffened into an insurmountable wall as the night wore on.[56] Of particular impediment were an array of interlocking German MG nests positioned among the stone cottages, vineyards, terraces, and olive groves forming seamless "kill zones" across the hillside's draws and mined wheat fields. Major Vernon A. Ostendorf's 1st Battalion troops became ensnared in this crushing crossfire and failed to reach their intended objectives atop Hills 109 and 131.[57] On the 1st Battalion's left, Lt Col William Mikkelson's 3rd Battalion fared no better. Despite calling in numerous salvos of supporting artillery and attempting several aggressive ground assaults descending, at times, into close-quartered melees fought with only bayonets and hand grenades, the ridgeline ruins of Solacciano remained firmly German.[58] The arrival of dawn found both battalions pinned, heavily debilitated, and unable to inch forward.[59]

The sole Custermen objective met during the night had been the capture of Hill 69 on San Martino, but the cost in lives was atrocious. Upon first light, nearly 400 3rd Battalion, 339th members lay dead or wounded—scattered along a 1,200-yard trail leading from Tremensuoli, down past Hill 131, across the Capo d'Acqua and upon the slopes of San Martino Hill itself.[60] The disconcerting cries and pleadings of the wounded were heard as a cheery morning sun ascended. Evacuation, however, was virtually impossible.[61] The Germans kept a steady rain of deadly mortar and artillery shells falling upon the Hill 69 survivors as ten-minute concentrations every thirty minutes.

Colonel Brady, a 1926 USMA graduate and 1932 U.S. Olympics pentathlete, was determined to hold the division's only clear achievement from the previous evening. The stocky, vigorous Los Angelean[62] kept remnants of his 3rd Battalion, 339th, protected behind a steady shield of artillery and mortar fire until, at 1000, 1st Battalion, 337th troops began advancing through a thick new cover of smoke. The fresh men started out along the same serpentine route the 3rd Battalion, 339th, had followed the night before, and elicited the same German response: heavy artillery, mortar, and MG fire.[63] Four hours later, a battered 1st Battalion, 337th, finally passed through K Company, 339th, positions near Hill 69. Under the midday sun, the gentle grassy slopes of Hill 66 appeared far more formidable. Although the hill was small in size, the MG pillboxes burrowed into its sides could not be destroyed by Allied artillery alone. Even direct hits showed no effect. In desperation, the 337th Battalion S-3 asked for flamethrowers, but none were available.[64] To take the hill, the infantry officers on the ground realized they needed special help: tanks.[65]

1st Lt Redle received the summons around 1330.[66] Lt Col Rogers, returning from the 339th CP in Tremensuoli, told Redle an infantry assault upon Hill 66 was scheduled for 1400. Tank support was deemed "critical" and a crossing of the Capo d'Acqua was to be attempted "at all costs." Rogers added that these orders came straight from Maj Gen Coulter.[67] 1st Lt Howard Harley, stationed at the 339th CP would serve as the tank/infantry liaison for Redle and his crews during the mission.[68]

Redle's crews were already loaded and prepared to fight. At 1345, the 2nd Platoon lurched first out from B Company's intermediate CP in the wooded draw between Monte Natale and Hill 127 to form a column—the least preferred formation, but necessary given the formidable terrain restrictions.[69] Lt Harris's 1st Platoon followed with Lt Redle's tank shuffled in at the fourth tank position.[70] Lt Gorman's 3rd Platoon and the maintenance tank remained in the draw CP as reserve.[71]

The eleven-tank column snaked down the narrow farm path Redle had reconnoitered the night before. Regrettably, the engineers had done nothing to improve the problem areas he had identified. As a result, the drivers often crept at a snail's pace to successfully negotiate over the numerous ruts, shell holes, and washouts along the way. After traveling several hundred yards down the saddled ground tracing the base of "intermediate ridge" west of Tremensuoli, Redle's column obtained a vantage point overlooking the flat grassy fields bordering the Capo d'Acqua. The company commander ordered Lt Newman's platoon to halt and pull over to the side to cover the advance of remaining tanks.[72] Lt Harris's platoon rumbled through with S/Sgt Oric Johannesen assuming the lead position and Lts Harris and Redle holding the third and fourth spots. As the 1st Platoon neared the valley floor, the dirt trail tilted precariously, and Johannesen—fearing his tank might overturn—ordered his driver to drop down to more level ground on the right. The soil proved marshy, and the blond staff sergeant's tank swiftly bogged in viscid muck. Lt Harris crept to the fore and guided the others past the hazard to flat ground near the base of Hill 119 on the left. All five remaining tanks arrived without tipping over. Redle now maintained a close gap at the number three position, watching for any signs of trouble ahead.[73]

San Martino lay 600 yards ahead on the right beyond the hill's edge—swathed in the wafting smoke of heavy battle. Bleak strains of sustained MG bursts and popping rifles testified of unspeakable carnage. Every so often, a violent chain of American artillery shells burst into the side of Hill 66, kicking up thick sheets of soil and sod. Harley's welcome voice crackled in over the radio—providing precise locations on the smokey hill where the infantry encountered the heaviest resistance. While Harris's platoon commenced firing, Redle called for Newman's platoon to move down and join them. During the descent, however, a German AT gun opened fire from the direction of Solacciano, also enveloped in the chaos of battle, some 600 yards to the right. To evade the lethal snarling rounds, Newman ordered his column to find temporary protection in a draw on the left between Hill 119 and 131. While taking cover, Newman's tank clipped the edge of a field ditch and tilted over onto its side. Now out of action, Newman ordered S/Sgt Smith to assume the lead, and the four remaining 2nd Platoon tanks arrived at Redle's position without further drama.[74]

American tank and artillery fire halted momentarily as 1st Battalion, 337th, infantry attempted to move up the slope of Hill 66. German reaction was swift. Enemy artillery poured in from Monte Scauri, Formia, and Castellonorato, and defenders representing the 2nd Battalion, 267th Grenadier Regiment, sprayed scorn from their remaining pillboxes. The American ground attack faltered, and the retreating troops sought refuge back down along the hill base.[75]

Redle's force, now doubled to nine tanks, resumed blasting into Hill 66 with greater ferocity—using the tried-and-true method of piercing pillbox positions with AP followed by HE threaded through the openings. Great care was taken to avoid hitting "doughs"—tanker parlance for American "doughboy" infantrymen who might be huddled nearby. Potential targets were always checked and rechecked with Harley first.[76] Four batteries of divisional artillery contributed a combined sixteen guns to the pummeling. After a few moments, all firing was halted and the brave infantrymen of 1st Battalion, 337th, stormed up the slope.[77] The Germans responded promptly with another violent artillery barrage of their own, driving the Americans back down the hill.[78]

Next, Redle ordered his tanks to move out from along the hillside onto the flat fields bordering the Capo d'Acqua. Following Lt Harley's radio instructions, the crews resumed firing into the Hill 66 bunkers. These new firing angles allowed the crews to also place fire on Hill 79 further to the south. The renewed effort drew German ire swift and accurate. As a new series of enemy artillery shells burst around the repositioned tanks, Redle ordered all drivers to maneuver while firing and instructed the four tanks of Harris's 1st Platoon, in particular, to venture out further in search of a ford across the creek.[79] To conceal the advance, Redle radioed Harley to arrange a smoke drop through his infantry contacts. The request was answered promptly, but the puffing rounds bounded well short of the creek and all over Redle's firing position. Harley called for a second volley to shift further west, but these appeals went unanswered.[80] Evidently, the mortar crews had been overwhelmed with other requests.

As the misplaced smoke dissipated, Redle saw Sgt Graffagnini's tank plodding 200 yards ahead out in the open near the creek. A German artillery round exploded a few dozen yards off one side, followed by a second falling several dozen yards to the other. Recognizing immediately that Graffagnini's tank was being bracketed under the box system,[81] Redle flipped open his company radio band and directed the tall, quiet, and unflappable sergeant to move fifty yards to his right to dodge the next round. He then instructed Graffagnini to search nearby for a promising ford seen on Allied aerial photos. Graffagnini's M4 lumbered along the section of the fast-flowing creek—but found no ford. All the while, the German artillery gun tried to bracket his slow-moving tank, but Redle kept directing his sergeant to points outside the box—forcing the German artillery observer to recalculate from scratch. After observing the trajectory and blast size of several rounds, Redle determined the heavier-caliber fire was likely coming from a German coastal gun—positioned southwest either on Monte Scauri, two miles away, or in Gaeta, nine miles away. It also dawned on him that no AT guns were present, indicating the defenders had considered the deep creek and narrow field as impassable for tanks. The Germans made a similar mistake during the first Rapido river crossing at Cassino on 27 January, but adjusted and moved in SP guns the very next day. Realizing this moment probably represented their best opportunity to cross the creek, Redle urged Graffagnini to keep searching.[82]

Lt Harris, also attempted to reach the Capo d'Acqua by crossing boggy grassland but became mired and threw a track.[83] Though trapped, the crew maintained steady fire into Hills 66 and 79, and the red-headed lieutenant clambered down from the turret to reconnoiter on foot. Stepping past mines and dodging the snap of small arms fire, Harris reached the fifteen-foot-wide channel, but also found no obvious way to cross the four-foot-deep waters and six-foot-high banks. He returned to his crew, radioed Redle with his findings, and concentrated on hitting German targets.[84] A short distance away, Sgt Behymer's tank also threw a track and became another reluctant armored pillbox.[85]

Graffagnini turned the opposite way and continued the search. The determined German coastal gun continued tracking him, but Redle's timely directions kept Graffagnini from being bracketed. By this time, Harris's crew had expended all HE and most AP rounds into San Martino. Using code terms, Harris reported the situation to Redle via radio, but said he intended to retain the remaining AP "just in case." Harris had also been watching the Germans adjust fire on Graffagnini and told Redle he believed he had pinpointed the location of their artillery observer. Redle gave Harris approval to fire a phosphorous round at the spot to test his theory. Sure enough, the artillery stopped—but once the smoke dissipated it started up again. Harris launched another round and the artillery stopped a second time. Harris repeated the process until all five of his phosphorous rounds had been expended.[86]

Harris's actions allowed Graffagnini to complete the quest without further harassment. Unfortunately, no crossing point was ever found. The site circled on the aerial photos had once supported a bridge, but the structure was now gone. Redle immediately radioed Rogers with this disappointing news. Surprisingly, Rogers replied that he was satisfied with the crews' efforts and ordered Redle's tanks to expend all remaining ammunition and return for resupply.[87] The new battalion commander's calm and measured response to bad news was markedly different to that of their previous CO.

All nine of Redle's tanks continued firing their remaining ammunition into the concrete bunkers and steel turrets embedded in the sides of both Hill 66 and Hill 79.[88] At a range of only 600 yards or less, fire placement proved excellent, and the infantry soon signaled their confidence that the German opposition had eroded enough to attempt a new ground attack.[89] At 1630, the firing halted, and Redle's tankers watched with satisfaction as American "doughs" swarmed up the side of Hill 66 against noticeably lighter resistance.[90]

With all 75mm ammunition expended, Redle ordered his crews to withdraw—beginning with Graffagnini, the furthest away. Because of a hopelessly shattered track, Behymer's crew abandoned their M4 and hitched a ride with another crew. Lt Harris believed he could push the track back in place on his tank and asked Redle for assistance. By lining up the drive sprockets to both tanks and employing one well-timed nudge, the track did, indeed, snap back and both tanks reversed toward the hillside. By this time, retributive German artillery again rained heavily all over the area—halting infantry operations on Hill 66 and threatening Redle's retreating tanks. This latest symphony of bursting shrapnel was joined by the coastal gun—this time targeting Redle's tank. One howling heavy-caliber round glanced off the final drive housing on the bow, jolting the crew and leaving a gleaming 1.5-inch gouge in the armor.[91] As his driver took evasive action,[92] Redle radioed Lt Harley to arrange for another smoke screen. Moments later, 81mm white phosphorous blossomed all around the retreating tanks. One round, however, fell directly on the back deck of Redle's tank—forcing the CO to temporarily duck inside his turret to escape the searing heat.[93] Phosphorus sizzled at 5,000 degrees and was virtually impossible to smother once ignited—an obvious concern when the waxy stuff splattered atop an engine compartment holding up to 160 gallons of fuel. Fortunately, fast-burning phosphorous also flamed out after a minute or two. Thankfully, the tank didn't catch fire and Redle resumed the orderly withdrawal of his company.[94]

Although only eight of the eleven tanks from Redle's armored force returned to the B Company intermediate CP near Monte Natale, all crew members arrived safely.[95] Not a single man had been lost or even wounded. All three damaged tanks belonging to Lt Newman, S/Sgt Johannesen, and Sgt Behymer were considered recoverable, but the maintenance section would need to wait until after dark to retrieve them.[96] Although the Capo d'Acqua was not crossed, the mission was considered to be a qualified success. Over 700 rounds of HE and AP had been dispatched into German bunker positions—providing the American infantry with a fighting chance to capture the rest of San Martino Hill. The battle wasn't over, but C Company, 337th, troops now seemed to have gained the upper hand.

***

That same morning and afternoon, the 338th resumed the battle for nearby Solacciano and S-ridge. An attack at 0800 hours failed, but a second one at 1300 gained a toehold inside two ruined stone houses on the village's southwestern edge. This allowed for S/A fire placement upon German positions on the reverse slope of S-ridge—breeding confusion and hesitation among a beehive of enemy mortar and MG crews operating there.[97] Up until this point, German MG fire emanating from

S-ridge had plagued not only the 338th, but the troops of the 88th's 351st Regiment trying to close in on Santa Maria Infante 1,200 yards further to the north.[98] The victory was small, but not enough to crack German resolve. Twelve enemy tanks were spotted in Tame, a tiny hamlet nestled on the north edge of S-ridge west of Santa Maria Infante. The 351st tried bringing up tanks and TDs from Minturno to challenge them, but the roadway was heavily mined and proved impassable.[99]

C Company, 756th, tanks supported the 338th throughout the day, but their track movement had been confined to poor maneuvering ground just west of Monte Natale. Most fire was targeted upon Solacciano. At 0930, Captain Gourley's tanks tried edging closer to support the morning attack, but a deep ditch southeast of the village prevented further advance. Engineers could not be called forward because of heavy artillery and S/A fire. At 1005, the 1st Platoon of C Company, at the request of the neighboring 351st Regiment (88th Division), attempted to move up the Santa Maria Road toward Tame, but found the road already blocked with several 760th Tank Battalion tanks either disabled by mines or knocked out from German AT fire.[100]

At 1900 hours, Lt Col Rogers ordered Lt Redle to lead a restocked B Company up to C Company positions to render assistance. The battalion commander pointed at a point on a map partway up the ridgeline road leading to Santa Maria Infante. During the journey, Redle's column passed two medium tanks knocked out by another large caliber gun. One, an M4, had a huge hole in the turret. The other, an M4A1, had been blown open in the driver position.[101] Neither tank appeared recoverable. Redle located Gourley, but with darkness rapidly descending both companies returned to their respective assembly areas without firing a shot.[102]

Rogers spent the late evening hours shuttling back and forth between infantry battalion HQs and his tank company CPs—catching up on events, planning new attacks and briefing crews ahead of their next missions. At 2100, he stopped into the 339th Regiment CP at Tremensuoli to meet with Colonel Brady. The remaining troops of the 1st Battalion, 337th, and 3rd Battalion, 339th, still held firm positions on the slopes of San Martino Hill. And at that hour, C Company, 337th, closed in upon the crestline against German resistance, now seemingly weakened and beaten.[103] Brady's other two regiments, however, remained deadlocked. At the coastline on the far left, the 1st Battalion, again, failed to take San Domenico Ridge—despite calling forth heavy supporting TD fire from the 776th Tank Destroyer Battalion. The Germans also counterattacked them several times. Each attempt had been thrown back, but a steady rain of artillery falling by way of Monte Scauri and heavy MG fire emanating from many obstinate pillboxes arrayed along San Domenico Ridge forced Lt Col Isley's men to halt and dig in east of Scauri.[104]

Lt Col Mudgett's 2nd Battalion, 339th, faced the regiment's fiercest and bloodiest opposition on nearby Hill 79. After paying a great cost in lives, G Company captured part of the hill and, for a time, held the crest. A German counterattack forced the

Americans off the summit and captured much of F Company holding high ground further east.[105] However, despite prolonged, intense, and vicious pressure from the enemy, G Company maintained hold of their side of the hill throughout.[106] Brady spoke of capturing the rest of Hill 79, and Rogers committed a tank platoon from A Company to the effort. However, during their discussions, reports poured in over the phone lines of yet another German attack in progress on Hill 79 and tank support plans were shelved.[107]

Dawn arrived on 13 May and the Custermen held firm. Despite several German counterattacks throughout the night, the crest of Hill 66 remained 1st Battalion, 337th, territory and nearby Hill 69 endured as a temporary dirt home to 200 or so effectives left from of the 3rd Battalion, 339th Regiment.[108] The morning was spent digging and consolidating positions.[109] Further south, the 2nd Battalion, 339th, struggled to keep a tenuous eastside stake on Hill 79 and the 1st Battalion, 339th, had still not taken San Domenico Ridge. None of these places were tank territory.

Rogers's focus shifted north to the 338th's efforts on Solacciano and S-ridge. Several hours earlier, at 0230, he was ordered by divisional HQ to assist in a morning attack by Colonel Safay's troops on Hill 131. At 0430, Rogers dispatched C Company forward early to reconnoiter a crossing over the ditch running between Monte Natale and S-ridge, but the crews found no way across.[110] The attack commenced in the morning. With Captain Gourley's tanks lending fire support from the valley, two platoons from I Company, 338th, rapidly stormed Hill 131 and captured forty Germans. A counterattack, however, just as quickly forced Safay's men back down into the ravines.[111]

Further west, the 2nd Battalion, 338th, after two failed attempts, finally snuck across the Capo d'Acqua to attack Hill 60 and Caves d'Argilla (clay quarries) 400 yards north of San Martino Hill. The Germans counterattacked almost immediately, but the Americans held their positions.[112]

In the meantime, German artillery and mortar fire fell fiercely around Gourley's ten M4s firing while spread out along the drainage ditch east of Solacciano. The melee prevented engineers from approaching the winding tank obstacle to search for potential crossing sites. At 1000, Rogers risked one of his own reconnaissance teams in the effort, but they, too, were driven back by a storm of bullets. At 1100, Maj Gen Coulter summoned Rogers to his divisional CP in Minturno. The commanding general voiced his impatience over the infantry's failure to hold Hill 131 and wanted to know why the tanks had been delayed. Get them across "at any cost" the general howled.[113]

Rogers returned to Monte Natale and ordered Gourley's crews to select the most promising sites and attempt a crossing—even if they doubted success. For the next two hours, Gourley's M4s paced up and down along the fifteen-foot-wide ditch—testing the crumbling muddy banks at multiple locations. Despite the personal dangers, Gourley and the tank commanders often dropped down from their turrets to reconnoiter further on foot or guide their drivers while testing approaches. The results were mixed. By 1600, eight tanks had either bogged or overturned in the effort, and another was knocked out by German AT fire. Three tanks, however, successfully crossed and advanced upon Solacciano—firing triumphantly into enemy strong points among the shattered homes and stone foundations. Fourteen Germans promptly surrendered, but upon finding no American infantry operating nearby, two bow gunners were forced to dismount and escort the prisoners back to Monte Natale themselves.[114]

At the same time, Rogers ordered Lt Redle to send two platoons and attempt a crossing as well. Lt Harris's 1st Platoon and Lt Newman's 2nd Platoon emerged a few minutes later from behind the southwestern base of Monte Natale—immediately drawing German artillery. Undaunted, the nine M4 mediums spread out in search of another way across. Newman led his four tanks in one direction but found the most promising locations already blocked with knocked out or bogged C Company tanks. The further he probed along the ditch, the heavier the MG and rifle fire raked and pinged across his turret—forcing the handsome lieutenant to keep his head low between the protection of his open hatch plates. With no promising crossing point in sight and fearing he may have inadvertently crossed into enemy territory, Newman radioed Redle—who was intently monitoring communications back at the B Company intermediate CP—and asked for clarification on the whereabouts of the battlelines. Redle had no idea, and suggested Newman turn back and search in the opposite direction. At this point, enemy artillery fell with such intensity that the hulls of Newman's tanks were pelted repeatedly with sod, mud, and stone. Lt Col Rogers arranged for a drop of screening smoke by the Assault Gun Platoon, but disbursement was limited for fear of obscuring the fields of fire to the American infantry and the three C Company tanks operating further north.[115]

At last, S/Sgt Smith signaled that he had located a possible crossing location. His driver squared the tank before the fifteen-foot-wide spot and eased forward tenderly, but the soft bank collapsed. The bow pitched down promptly, burying the main gun barrel in the mucky creek bed. Though lodged at a forty-five-degree angle, the driver tried reversing the treads and shimmying the tank free—but to no avail.[116]

Newman radioed Redle for advice. Redle told him to retrieve Smith's crew and keep searching. Newman plodded ahead further and discovered Sgt David Grate's 1st Platoon tank had been knocked out by artillery. The 24-year-old Ohio[117] sergeant was bleeding from a cheek wound, but both he and his crew were otherwise unharmed.[118] Their immobilized tank, however, sat helplessly out in the open—vulnerable to further shelling. Newman called for Grate's crew to load aboard his tank, but as each man dismounted and ran toward safety, a German rifleman hidden nearby took pot shots at them. Lt Harris, watching nearby, fired phosphorus smoke on two occasions to help shield the transfer, but the German kept shooting—fortunately missing every time. In the end, fifteen men somehow crammed inside or atop Newman's tank.[119]

With dusk descending, Newman decided to return northward and drop off the two rescued crews by Smith's bogged tank—where they could find concealment and better protection until nightfall. After discharging both crews, Newman decided to attempt a crossing at a dubious location further south. Neither he, Harris, or any of the remaining B Company crews found any other spot more promising. The soft bank crumbled just as it had for Smith's driver, and Newman's tank ended up in the same predicament: nose down, rear deck up, and main gun planted firmly into creek muck.[120]

At this point, Lt Redle appeared with a T2 retriever and attempted to remove two bogged C Company tanks at a flat approach near the road south of Solacciano.[121] At 1938, work was interrupted temporarily when thirty-six exhausted German prisoners appeared along the western bank in need of an escort back to Minturno. Two B Company bow gunners brandishing Tommy guns dismounted to carry out the task.[122]

Redle managed to remove one tank, but with night descending rapidly and the three C Company tanks already across but low on ammunition, Lt Col Rogers decided to abandon the effort and regroup before the arrival of morning. After consulting with 338th CO Colonel Safay, Rogers ordered the three C Company tanks to remain in position and assist the infantry for as long as their ammunition held out. He then arranged for ammunition stocks to be deposited near the ditch to help keep the crews firing.[123]

After nightfall, Rogers ordered B Company to return to their CP assembly area out of ambush concerns.[124] In the meantime, Redle's retrieval efforts freed three more tanks. The rest were left for maintenance to recover.[125] Both S/Sgt Smith and Lt Newman's crews abandoned their upturned wrecks to the night and set out on foot for the B Company CP with radio crystals in hand. This was Newman's second tank lost in as many days—the first one still lay unrecovered on its side near Hill 119 only 300 yards away.[126] By 2030, the remnants of the 1st and 2nd Platoons began arriving at the B Company CP for rest and resupply.[127]

At 2045, Rogers consulted with Colonel Safay and ordered the withdrawal of C Company as well. The three tanks attempting to return over the ditch also bogged and had to be abandoned to the expertise of maintenance crews as well. By 2230, all operational C Company tanks returned to their assembly area near Minturno.[128]

At 2235, Rogers received orders to support the 338th Infantry on a new attack at first light. This time, an engineer company and an armored bulldozer were attached to the 756th to assist the tanks along the way. At 2245, Rogers ordered the engineers to construct a crossing over the problem ditch during the night.[129] In the meantime, the B and C Company maintenance crews using three T2 retrievers worked feverishly nearby recovering as many bogged tanks as possible before dawn, 14 May, arrived.[130]

Although the 338th—under the supporting fire from three C Company tanks—succeeded in capturing Solacciano and taking several dozen prisoners throughout the day, Hill 131 remained stubbornly German. A half-company sized American force had temporarily seized the point in the morning, but were soon driven off. By evening, only sixteen riflemen from that original force remained.[131] The 2nd Battalion, 338th, fared better on a flanking mission 700 yards to the west. There, the troops pressed closer upon Hill 60 and Caves d'Argilla despite enduring several counterattacks. The position represented the 85th Division's furthest incursion west and threatened, not only German positions to the rear of S-ridge, but a crucial supply road leading down from Spigno to the coast.[132]

Earlier that morning (13 May), a force of some fifty Germans had also counter-attacked San Martino Hill—yelling and firing machine pistols while storming up the rear slope. The C Company, 337th, defenders, now displaying veteran instincts, patiently allowed the wave to approach within fifty yards of their positions before giving the order to fire. After a few moments of sheer carnage, all fifty German attackers lay dead. The Germans tried a similar mad charge later in the day, but suffered the same fate. After one final futile attempt that evening, the Germans finally quit trying entirely and control of San Martino Hill was never challenged again.[133]

A mile to the northeast, however, the 88th Division failed again to take Santa Maria Infante. The battered hilltop town had become the lynchpin to flushing the Germans from the II Corps' sector.[134] Both morning and afternoon attacks by Colonel Arthur S. Champeny's 351st Regiment had been turned back violently.[135] Elsewhere, however, the 88th made steady progress. On the division's far right flank, the 350th Regiment had taken the heights overlooking Castelforte—allowing the French to attack the key valley town dubbed as "little Cassino" by Allied planners because of similarly bottlenecked terrain.[136]

The modest gains on the flanks did not placate Fifth Army Commanding General Mark Clark. He was particularly disappointed with the 88th Infantry Division's inability to seize Santa Maria Infante and had expected the crestline town to have fallen twenty-four hours earlier.[137] Further to the north, Juin's French Forces succeeded in smashing through the Gustav Line and capturing 940-meter high Monte Maio in dramatic fashion—giving the Allies high ground control overlooking the Liri Valley and threatening both the coastal and Cassino flanks of the XIV Panzer Corps defenses.[138] The British, too, had established two Rapido crossing points and a small bridgehead near Cassino—and although an attack by Polish forces upon the monastery ruins had failed, Clark sensed German resolve along the entire Gustav Line was about to collapse.[139] The tall lanky general was particularly displeased by what he perceived as a lack of aggressiveness in the II Corps' sector.[140] His criticism was, perhaps, unfair.

Juin's seasoned troops could boast of many months of combat experience, whereas both the 88th and 85th Divisions were mostly comprised of conscripts new to the front.

The II Corps commander Maj Gen Keyes, nevertheless, believed battlefield conditions in his sector were about to break dramatically in his favor.[141] Earlier that day (13 May), he called together Sloan and Coulter to evaluate and strategize. Both division commanders also agreed a breakthrough was imminent, resting their optimism upon the steady gains made by their forces on the flanks and the enemy's flagging ability to counter that pressure. Perhaps more importantly, both divisions had stocked up on replacement troops ahead of the 11 May attack and had already replenished their casualty rolls with fresh troops. The Germans could not overcome such personnel losses as quickly.[142] The meeting adjourned with no sense of panic and only minor adjustments to the Corps' battle plan. Divisional boundaries were shifted slightly southward—giving the 88th Division more responsibility for S-ridge while pressing the main effort upon Santa Maria Infante.[143] Hill 131 remained an 85th Division challenge, but the capture of Solacciano to the south and an incursion toward Caves d'Argilla further west made any ongoing defense of the point problematic for the Germans.

Clark arrived at Keyes's CP shortly after the conference and received a fresh assessment of the II Corps' situation. After listening, he left the meeting brimming with Keyes's optimism—even writing in his diary: "We should have Spigno tonight."[144]

The 351st Regiment continued an aggressive attack on Santa Maria Infante well into the night and early morning hours of 14 May—forcing the Germans to finally buckle and withdraw the bulk of their forces. By dawn, all that remained in town were rearguard units and pockets of scattered resistance.[145] As expected, the concession sparked a cascade effect along the entire front in the II Corps sector. Sloan's men pressed quickly on Monte Bracchi, a mile further to the northwest—the final obstacle before sweeping down upon Spigno in the west.[146]

In the 85th Division sector, the Germans also abandoned Hill 79 during the night—allowing the 2nd Battalion, 339th, to finally take the hillcrest and reach those wounded and trapped on nearby Intermediate Ridge.[147] San Domenico Ridge remained a stubborn pocket of resistance, however, and still had not been subdued by 1st Battalion, 339th, troops.[148]

This sudden shift in fortunes caused Maj Gen Coulter to quickly rebalance the day's objectives for his regiments. San Domenico Ridge in the south and Hill 131 to the north had both lost tactical importance. The division's new goal was to cut the Spigno road and push upon Castellonorato further west. In the early morning hours of 14 May, he ordered the 338th to provide a fire base from Solacciano and Hill 60 as the 2nd and 3rd Battalions, 337th, moved across the Spigno road and attacked Hill 108 on the opposite side. The 88th Division's 349th Infantry Regiment was temporarily attached to Coulter's division with the mission of advancing and protecting the north flank of the 337th's attack.[149]

Colonel Oliver W. Hughes, the short, fatherly figure commanding the 337th since January,[150] decided a combined tank/infantry approach was best. The 2nd Battalion and two platoons of tanks would strike Hill 108, with the 3rd Battalion following closely in reserve. Once Hill 108 fell, the infantry and Rogers's tanks would continue probing westward together before making the final attack on Castellonorato.[151] In the predawn hours, Hughes and Rogers hashed out the tank support details. A few hours earlier, at 0200, the engineers reported a crossing had been established over the problem ditch south of Solacciano. Rocks and debris were dumped at the location to allow the tanks to cross over the obstacle.[152] This, however, solved only half the challenge. A way also had to be found across the deeper and wider Capo d'Acqua. One section 300 yards west of Solacciano appeared fordable, and the two officers banked on the skills of the engineers to get the tanks across. The attack was set for the afternoon.

To prepare the way, the reverse slope of Solacciano had to first be swept. At 0430, the 1st Platoon of C Company supported infantry clean-up operations by firing from the southwest slope of Monte Natale.[153] At 0600, Rogers ordered Lt Redle to move B Company across the ditch and attack with troops clearing the far side of S-ridge. Five tanks crossed before the bypass gave out. The armored bulldozer assigned to B Company repaired the damage and the rest of Redle's M4s crossed by 0900.[154]

Redle led the tank column beyond the southwest edge of Solacciano, but had to halt after traveling 100 yards because of a wounded American lying by the sunken road. Redle dismounted and discovered the man—an infantry captain—was delirious after suffering several bullet wounds. Redle assured the officer that help would arrive, climbed back into his tank, and contacted 756th S-3 and recently promoted Major Edwin Arnold. Arnold rushed forward in a jeep to comfort the wounded young man until medics could arrive.[155]

Redle's column lurched forward with the 3rd Platoon taking the lead. Redle's tank and an armored bulldozer followed with the 1st and 2nd Platoons bringing up the rear.[156] Around the time the 3rd Platoon reached flat fields 300 yards northwest of Solacciano and prepared to place fire on Hill 131, the infantry reported the ridgeline clear and requested a change in mission.[157] Some enemy guns had started sputtering from Hill 108 some 1,000 yards to the west and the infantry asked the tanks to respond. Rogers okayed the request, and Redle's tanks went to work firing on any pillboxes, dugouts, trenches, and stone homes they could observe on the distant hillside.[158] A small cluster of homes and caves near the base, identified on local maps as "La Grata," received a lion's share of the gunners' attention.[159]

To gain more favorable firing angles, Redle ordered his tanks to mount the hillside to their rear and fan out. Because the slope was latticed with stone terraces, the drivers took great care to avoid flipping as they mounted each wall. But with the passing of each tank, the ancient walls crumbled down to form a road of sorts. The new high ground achieved allowed the gunners to place direct fire on the main road running from the north. Every so often, escaping German vehicles sped down from Spigno toward the coast, and Redle's gunners picked them off as they emerged. Cars, trucks, towed artillery pieces, and even a *panzerjäger* became easy victims. One German armored car tried escaping down into a sunken side road—only to explode in flames before disappearing.[160] Clearly, the Germans were conceding the area and desperate to regroup and reestablish defenses near Castellonorato.[161]

This free-for-all targeting continued for another hour.[162] At one point, Redle observed Germans scurrying into the network of quarry caves roughly 800 yards off to their left.[163] Next, he saw a flare rocketing over the position followed by a series German artillery shells blossoming across the thick grassland to the fore. Redle knew of an American infantry combat patrol operating in the area and presumed the Germans had detected their presence. Without liaison, however, he couldn't be certain if American "doughs" were near there or not. He directed the tank gunners to fire only AP into the holes and observed carefully. Finally, he directed his own gunner, Sgt Mielcarski to dispatch one round of HE into the position. A split second later, the whirling shell dipped into a cavern—completely blasting out the interior. Redle learned later, a "good number" of Germans died in that explosion.[164]

At this point, ammunition in both the 3rd and 1st Platoons was running low and Redle received instructions from Lt Col Rogers to withdraw to their assembly area, resupply, and await further instructions. By 1100, all B Company tanks returned and Redle realized the Germans hadn't fired so much as a single shot at his crews throughout the entire mission.[165]

U.S. 339th Infantry Regiment

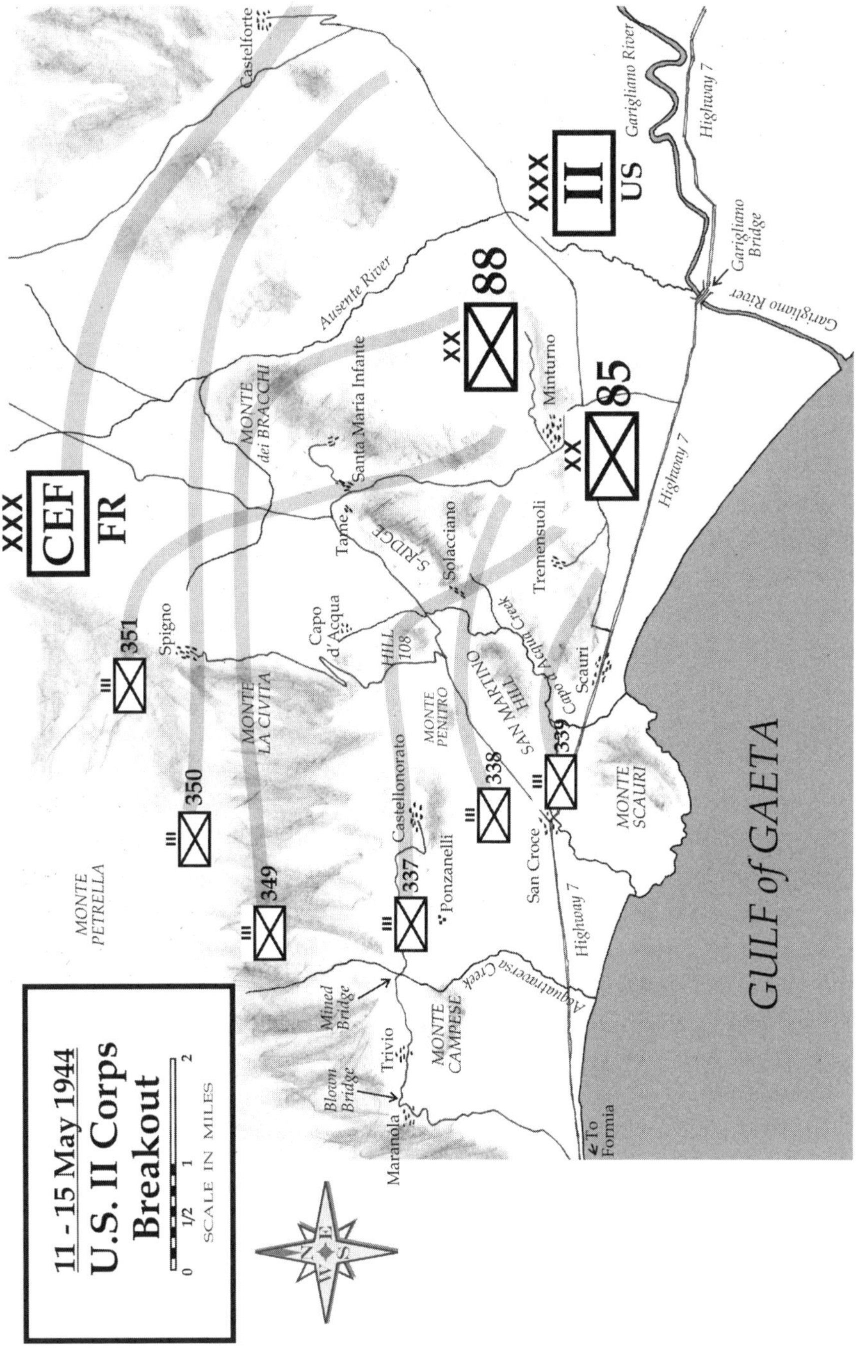
11 - 15 May 1944
U.S. II Corps
Breakout
0 1/2 1 2
SCALE IN MILES
N E S W
XXX CEF FR
XXX II US
XX 88
XX 85
III 351
III 350
III 349
III 337
III 338
III 339
Castelforte
Ausente River
Garigliano River
Garigliano Bridge
Highway 7
MONTE dei BRACCHI
Santa Maria Infante
Minturno
Tame
S-RIDGE
Solacciano
Tremensuoli
Capo d'Acqua
HILL 108
SAN MARTINO HILL
Capo d'Acqua Creek
Scauri
Spigno
MONTE LA CIVITA
MONTE PENITRO
Castellonorato
Ponzanelli
MONTE PETRELLA
MONTE SCAURI
San Croce
Acquatraversa Creek
Mined Bridge
Trivio
MONTE CAMPESE
Blown Bridge
Maranola
To Formia
GULF of GAETA

CHAPTER TWELVE

Castellonorato: 14 May 1944 to 15 May 1944

Details ahead of the afternoon attack rapidly crystalized. At 1000, Rogers received word from the 85th Division G-3 that his entire 756th Tank Battalion was now attached to Colonel Hughes's 337th Regiment. This allowed the battalion commander to shift nearly all his resources into the effort. Two platoons from Captain Lewis's A Company were called over from static anti-tank defensive assignments along the coast and near Tremensuoli. The Tremensuoli positions, in turn, were replaced by a platoon of D Company light tanks. At 1030, Rogers contacted Colonel Hughes for further planning. The two agreed that if the tanks were held up at the Capo d'Acqua, the infantry would still proceed forward. The tanks would then provide fire support from the east bank until a later crossing could be accomplished. The 1500 attack time remained unchanged.[1]

At 1120, Rogers alerted Captain Lewis that his two A Company platoons would lead the attack and ordered him to move into the assault position west of Solacciano immediately. In the meantime, Lewis's 3rd Platoon continued anti-tank duties southeast of Scauri.[2] Lt Redle also received instructions for B Company to support A Company by fire and then follow Lewis's tanks over the Capo d'Acqua once the engineers established a crossing.[3]

At 1245, Rogers sent three tanks from C Company, the armored bulldozer, and a detachment of engineers out to the Capo d'Acqua due west of Solacciano.[4] The infantry massing in the area reported a fordable stream section at this location.[5] To provide the engineers cover as they worked, Rogers ordered a platoon of D Company M5s to transport the mortar platoon to positions in Solacciano. There, the four crews remained on call to lay screening smoke as needed.[6]

By 1330, the engineers commenced work on the crossing but reported swift waters three feet deep flowing between banks eight to ten feet high—not at all "fordable" as the infantry scouts assumed.[7] The team then found themselves under fire. By 1410, the AT and HE fire poured in from Castellonorato so heavily, Rogers ordered the assault guns positioned near Minturno to lay screening smoke along the creek.[8] He also ordered Captain Lewis to move his ten tanks closer to the banks and fire into Hill 108 in response. The counterfire and thick white blanket failed to halt the harassment. By 1500—jump off time—the engineers temporarily drew back the bulldozers and crews out of concern for their safety.[9]

The troops of the 2nd and 3rd Battalions, 337th, waded through the cool stream and poured over the west bank without delay. They met surprisingly little opposition while navigating across 500 yards of flat terrain, featuring thick grassy fields and rows of unkempt brush. Those attacking further to the north didn't have to ford the Capo d'Acqua until first reaching the main road leading north to Ausonia and San Giorgio, as the creek swung sharply northwest once beyond Solacciano. The capture of the two-lane asphalt road was, in and of itself, a major accomplishment—effectively cutting off any remaining Germans forces further north from escape.[10] The objective, Hill 108 and the tiny hamlet of La Grata, still lay 800 yards to the west.[11]

As Hughes's infantrymen closed in on their target, Lewis's gunners fired into pillbox positions in the hillside—effectively suppressing MG fire as the Americans encroached within their range. All the while, the A Company tank captain bustled about on foot—trying to assist the bulldozer crews, now returned to the creek bed, in their work.[12]

At 1630, the engineers gave up on trying to fashion a ford and, instead, requested materials to lay down a bridge. Knowing this might take hours, Rogers directed Captain Lewis and the engineer team to reconnoiter further north for other possible locations.[13] They found a promising spot where the banks dropped down to only four or five feet above water level. The creek bed appeared solid, and the water flowed at only three feet deep. 2nd Lt William M. Hammer, 1st Platoon leader, volunteered to go first. His driver crept slowly over the bank until a good third of his 32-ton tank jutted out over the waters. Suddenly the bank gave way, and the driver gunned the engine at full speed. The front end plummeted with a huge splash, but the desperate spinning treads gripped the bottom. The chassis bounced, leveled out, and then shot up the opposite bank—causing the far wall to collapse into a convenient dirt ramp.[14]

The other tanks of Hammer's platoon followed, pivoted to the right, then fanned out, and advanced. Captain Lewis traversed next, followed by 2nd Lt Roland V. Hunter's 2nd Platoon. All ten tanks crossed the creek without much struggle, but the trail was left a muddy mess and in need of repair. No American infantry were in sight. One hundred yards beyond the creek, the small, armored force encountered a square two-storey farmhouse surrounded by a five-foot high stone wall. A few shots cracked from the position, so the tanks answered with roughly a dozen rounds of HE directed through windows and about the courtyard's corners. As they rolled past, twenty Germans poured out with their hands up. Several wore bloody bandages. Two small squeeze-bore 28/20mm AT guns also lay in ruins next to the walls.[15]

Lewis's iron wave crossed the road and closed in on La Grata and Hill 108—still 600 and 1,000 yards away respectively. American infantry could now be seen passing through the tiny hamlet and edging up the northeastern slope.

In the meantime, Lt Col Rogers surveyed the crossing point and ordered B Company to move down and join A Company to the west. While Redle led his tanks down from Monte Natale, Rogers ordered the engineers to bulldoze smoother ramps on both banks.[16] During the downhill journey, a seized track block on Sgt Louis J. Jarvis's tank caught fire, and Lt Newman ordered the crew to return to the assembly area for repairs.[17] When the remainder of Redle's column arrived by the creek around 1745, they found their CO standing up to his hips in the swiftly moving waters, watching intently as each tank passed through.[18]

At the same time, Lewis's ten tanks reached La Grata just as the infantry neared the hillcrest. German MG fire from the opposite side promptly drove them back.[19] Sporadic artillery fire from the south and southwest also began bursting about the tanks,[20] so Lewis directed his crews to take a position slightly northwest where they could observe both Hill 108 and the switchback road leading down from Spigno. Lt Hammer reported seeing a German 76.2mm SP gun lurking nearby. Strangely, the gray beast wasn't moving, and the barrel was pointed away from them.[21] Lewis told him to fire on it. On a hunch, the lieutenant ordered his driver to drive around to the rear where he tossed several hand grenades down the hatches. The deadly machine had been abandoned, and Hammer's instincts saved at least one precious 75mm round for later use.[22]

Lewis contacted an infantry officer to determine how his tanks could be put to the best use. The officer described the heavy MG fire at the crest and wondered if the tanks could climb the hillside.[23] The 500 yards or so to the crestline was not too severe—perhaps a ten-degree incline at most. The terrain was grassy and smooth with few trees. Lewis radioed his crews to fan out and climb up the slope. As they bowled over the top with infantry closely trailing, German artillery fell heavier, and the irksome 5-inch coastal gun at Gaeta began firing at them—still intent on claiming a tank victim. The tilting action caused two of Lewis's tanks to throw tracks, but the other eight advanced unchecked—knocking out several MG nests and two more AT guns dug into the southern side of the hill.[24] The Germans surrendered in droves—emerging from holes and covered trenches waving white flags. Others posted further down the hill emerged and fled toward Castellonorato.[25] Over eighty prisoners were processed—marched back over the hill and toward Solacciano.[26] Most were engineers from the 194th Engineer Battalion fighting as infantry.[27] Not only was the south face of Hill 108 captured, but a key segment road leading down from Spigno winding along the base. The short battle served as an excellent example of what could be accomplished when tankers and infantrymen worked closely together.

2nd Platoon leader Lt Roland Hunter, however, slumped to his side wounded. While blasting a MG crew into oblivion, either a bullet or shell fragment pierced his arm—shattering the bone and severing an artery. He lost a great deal of blood before his crew applied a tourniquet and evacuated him back to the Capo d'Acqua crossing. From there, Lt Col Rogers took him by jeep to an aid station.[28]

The capture of Hill 108 cleared the way for Colonel Hughes's regiment to next strike Castellonorato, only a mile to the west. However, the sun had since dropped behind the Aurunci mountains, and a mellow orange twilight took hold. To keep his troops fresh, Hughes refrained from moving the 3rd Battalion across the Capo d'Acqua and postponed attack plans until morning.[29] Patrols from the 2nd Battalion, however, were dispatched immediately from Hill 108—seeking the best approaches to scale the magnificent rocky 310-meter-high hill.[30] The task would not be easy. Like Monte Cassino, the ancient stone castle and compact attendant village clinging along the crest had been reduced to ruins after months of shelling.[31] This was an infantryman's challenge. The tanks simply could not follow.

At 1858, Colonel Hughes phoned in one more request to Lt Col Rogers. His infantry, still clearing pockets of resistance north of La Grata, sorely needed fire support. Rogers ordered Captain Lewis to commit a platoon to the task. Because of harassing enemy fire emanating from the Caves d'Argilla area 1,000 yards to the southwest, Lewis ordered his remaining tanks to maneuver and cover the movement. The 338th had allegedly captured the "Argilla" series of clay quarry caves the previous day, and the tankers were cautioned not to fire on it. Evidently, that report was erroneous.[32] By this time, Redle's B Company tanks had arrived at La Grata, so Rogers ordered Redle's crews to keep watch on the southern flank so all of Lewis's tanks could operate further north.[33] Once Lewis's tank accomplished the mopping-up mission, they returned to La Grata in near darkness.

The two tank company commanders met briefly to discuss defensive arrangements.[34] At night, tanks were extremely vulnerable to ambush, and only one infantry company had been positioned nearby. They summoned the infantry captain and found he greatly feared a German counterattack but lacked the confidence he had the necessary numbers to prevail.[35] At 2045, Lewis radioed Rogers. Using coded language, the seasoned tank officer described their concerns.[36] Rogers told Lewis to hold steady and organize defenses with the available infantry. He promised to send men and supplies as soon as possible. After signing off, Rogers next contacted Hughes and requested more troops be sent to shore up the position.[37]

The three officers convened again and decided to arrange forces in a large square along the hill base with one squad of infantry and several tanks placed at each corner. A Company took the right flank and B Company handled the left.[38] A heavy weapons section originally assigned to the infantry company somehow got lost during the taking of Hill 108, and the outfit lacked adequate MG protection. To compensate, Lewis stripped two .30-caliber MGs and all grenades from his two disabled tanks near the hillcrest and lent these weapons to the infantry.[39] The .30-caliber bow guns from four operational tanks were also removed and distributed—providing the "doughs" with six more MG positions and the infantry captain seemed better convinced his men could repulse a counterattack—assumed by all as inevitable.[40]

The left flank lay completely open.[41] Lt Redle's eyes strained to discern any movement among the 700 yards of rolling fields and mottled thickets laying between his tanks and the Capo d'Acqua. His focus gravitated to the caves, especially, low to his 11 o'clock—as they were the mostly likely origination point for trouble. At night, the task was nearly impossible, but German artillery fire fell intermittently and the brief flashes provided him with area "snapshots" from which he could make mental comparisons.[42]

Midnight, 15 May, passed, then 0100 and 0200 hours, but nothing happened. Nobody dared sleep, except for the occasional catnap.[43] The fresh infantry company arrived from Solacciano, as Colonel Hughes had promised, doubling the position's troop strength, and halving the anxiety.[44] Still, no German counterattack materialized.[45]

At 0309, a column of D Company M5 light tanks laden with gasoline cans and ammo cannisters lumbered into La Grata after crossing the Capo d'Acqua. The supply column had been delayed several hours because the ford area needed engineer improvement, but the teams couldn't work because of harassment by German patrols. Counter patrols were organized to enable repairs to continue.[46]

As the M5s arrived, led by A Company XO 1st Lt Ralph Hanson, another barrage of German artillery burst about the area—at times falling close enough to the tankers unloading and scrambling about that several men "blacked out" temporarily from the concussive effects. Nevertheless, Lewis's crews succeeded in gassing up, stowing the new ammo, and storing rations aboard their tanks without sustaining any casualties. Once settled, the crews took turns trying to catch up on sleep.[47]

Just prior to dawn, 15 May, A Company moved with the infantry along the eastern base of Hill 108 while Redle's tanks scaled to the crestline and assumed defilade positions among the foundations of a shattered house.[48] With the first glimmers of daylight, the Germans finally chose to counterattack—beginning with an opening artillery barrage that left one A Company tanker wounded, Pvt Maynard W. Vader—and another dead: Cpl Edwin R. Rittenbach.[49] The ground attack, however, was weak and easily repulsed.[50]

From atop Hill 108, Redle's instructions were to fire on any targets of opportunity—especially to the north and west of San Martino Hill.[51] Redle's crews enjoyed a 180-degree eagle eye view of the battlefield below. To their 9 o'clock lay green San Martino Hill, roughly 1,500 yards away. The reddish Caves d'Argilla clay pits lay a bit closer at 1,200 yards down at their 10 o'clock. To their 11 o'clock, the rocky outline of Monte Scauri anchored the bay roughly 5,000 yards in the distance. To its right sat the hazy gray hump of Gaeta some eight miles further off in the distant blue. Dead ahead at 1,200 yards rose the conical 104-meter-high Monte Penitro and 2,500 yards away at 1 o'clock stood the more severely steeped Castellonorato. These last two points were the 337th Regiment's next objectives.

Redle's gunners were ordered to fire upon any German artillery and mortar positions or moving vehicles—especially those observed within a band of 2,000 to 3,000 yards. Anything closer required extreme caution because American troops could be advancing into the area. At one point during the morning, Redle's tankers could observe American infantrymen attacking toward German troops retreating into the Argilla caves. As done the prior day, the Germans fired red flares overhead and German artillery followed—driving the Americans back. At this point, Redle felt confident his crews could render assistance without causing American casualties. He called for his crews to load concrete piercing ammo—the same shells used so effectively several months earlier upon the jail and Castle Hill in Cassino.[52] These rounds penetrated like an AP slug but carried a small HE filler charge that burst after entry. A quick series of shots sliced into the clay like hot knives through butter—burying the occupants or leaving them too dazed to fight. The infantry promptly stormed the position and captured the survivors.[53] Afterwards, groups of Germans were seen retreating across the fields west of San Martino. Twelve rounds of 75mm HE cut down many of them and brought out the German medics waving Red Cross flags.[54]

In the meantime, the infantrymen of the 3rd Battalion, 337th, massed to the rear of Hill 108, preparing to pass through 2nd Battalion positions and push the fight on to Castellonorato.[55]

At noon, Maj Gen Coulter met his Assistant Division Commander, Brig Gen Lee S. Gerow, his Chief of Staff, Colonel William T. Fitts, Jr., and the entire division staff at the Minturno CP.[56] The haggard team hovered over creased maps and shuffled through smudged messages—jubilant over the news of the last twenty-four-hours. The Gustav Line was clearly shattered, initiating "Phase Two" to the division's offensive plans.[57] San Domenico Ridge fell to the 339th. Hill 108 belonged to the 337th, and Caves d'Argilla had finally succumbed to the 2nd Battalion, 338th.[58] Two miles to the north, the 88th Division swept westward from Santa Maria Infante to seize Monte La Civita and Spigno.[59] Further beyond, French Forces advanced upon the mountain towns of Ausonia and Castelnuevo and overran San Giorgio in the Liri Valley.

The U.S. Fifth Army captured over 2,200 prisoners in four days of fighting—while severely crippling the German 94th Infantry Division and ostensibly wiping the 71st Infantry Division from existence. Thousands of German dead littered the hills and fields from Scauri to the Liri Valley, along with the burned out, twisted hulks of hundreds of their trucks, armored vehicles, SP guns, and artillery pieces.[60] The carnage spread across miles of otherwise picturesque pastoral, mountainous country that had once been the Gustav Line. Virtually every Italian shop, house, and cottage trapped within the zone suffered blast damage of some sort—often reduced to nothing but stone foundations. The two newest American infantry divisions comprising the U.S. II Corps paid dearly for their part in breaking the German line. Sloan's 88th

Division suffered 2,000 casualties in the first three days of the offensive.[61] Coulter's 85th lost 1,100 men in the first forty-eight hours alone.[62]

During the morning of 15 May, Lt Gen Clark sent a personal congratulatory message to both Sloan and Coulter, commending both for conducting themselves in a "glorious manner" and capably training their new divisions for the rigors of combat.[63] Clark's sentiments were sincere, of course, but he also cautioned of further challenges ahead and voiced his expectations of continued success. The Fifth Army commander's sights had already shifted nine miles west beyond the Aurunci mountains to the critical Itri–Pico road. This was rugged territory where the Germans intended to reestablish a new wall of defenses along a new "Hitler Line."[64] Clark intended to pursue them relentlessly and break up the enemy's maddening pattern of finding yet another mountain pass from behind which to fight—as Maj Gen Walker of the 36th Infantry Division described with such resigned exasperation several months earlier.

During the same hour Clark dispatched his written praises to Sloan and Coulter, he verbally directed Maj Gen Keyes, II Corps commander, to dispatch the 88th with all haste across the Aurunci mountains from Spigno to Itri. Concurrently, the 85th was ordered to aggressively pursue remnants of the German 94th Infantry Division along the coastline. To accomplish this, he emphasized, Castellonorato had to be taken without delay.[65] Clark also primed Keyes of his intentions to ship the 85th Division and the II Corps Headquarters to Anzio. Effective at 1200, 16 May, both organizations were to be prepared to move to Naples' port on only seventy-two hours' notice. Later in the day, Clark's orders were put in writing as Fifth Army Operations Instructions No. 18.[66]

Castellonorato represented the lone Gustav Line stronghold remaining in the U.S. II Corps sector. At the top of the steep jagged hill, near the castle and attendant town also lay the ruins of an ancient fortress.[67] Possessing wide panoramic views of the Garigliano plain and the Gulf of Gaeta, Castellonorato had always held historical strategic significance.

At 1300 hours, Lt Col Rogers received word his tanks would support the 337th infantry's attack upon Castellonorato, commencing at 1500 hours.[68] The infantry officers suggested replicating the successful capture of Hill 108 with the tanks and troops storming the crest together. Castellonorato was too steep however, and Rogers explained his tanks could only roll up to the base—after which they could only lend fire support from below at a distance. Rogers directed B Company to accompany the assault wave, and then swing south and west of the hill while the infantry clambered up the slopes. A Company would overwatch B Company's advance and remain prepared to follow the attack if necessary. Rogers also ordered the D Company light tanks to trail B Company and prepare to move to either flank depending upon the severity of the German resistance. C Company waited in reserve near Solacciano.[69]

The 3rd Battalion, 337th, would lead the attack from Hill 108, followed by the 2nd Battalion, 337th.[70] Castellonorato lay roughly 2,500 yards (1.4 miles) away across challenging tank country—rough and rural terrain dotted with olive groves and stone cottages, yet offering plenty of opportunity for defilade. A small dry stream bed listed on maps as "S. Croce" bisected the attack route at 500 yards and represented a potential obstacle.

Another likely impediment lay 700 yards on the left, a small 104-meter-high hill called "Monte Penitro," and a known hive for German MG and mortar positions. I Company, 337th, was given the responsibility of silencing those positions once the attack commenced. L Company would bypass the hill to the right and press on toward Castellonorato.[71]

As Hughes's infantry organized ahead of the attack, Castellonorato was pummeled severely by American artillery fire and the occasional swarm of Allied dive bombers—keeping the crest surrounded with a thick halo of dust.[72] For a time, Redle moved his tanks back to the top of Hill 108 to help "soften" up the target.[73] At 1400, Lt Redle received a call to meet Lt Col Rogers at the bottom of Hill 108 with B Company tanks aligned in column. He halted fire and withdrew his tanks to the base. There, the battalion commander handed Redle a local map, discussed a few last-minute changes and wished good luck to the crews.[74] At 1450, Redle met briefly with the infantry CO to confirm the orders and review the progression of events.[75] Afterwards, the tankers and infantry waited expectantly as the final moments ticked down—watching the sparkling blasts of artillery and aerial bombs falling upon the distant hill, while wondering if the Germans would stubbornly fight to keep those heights or retreat and save their strength for another day.[76]

At 1500 sharp, I Company ventured out from brushwood along the bottom of Hill 108 toward Monte Penitro. German artillery and mortar fire greeted their appearance immediately but failed to slow the advance. Moving abreast, the 1st and 3rd Platoons bounded over the narrow creek bed and advanced up the gentle grassy slope—drawing sporadic S/A fire. Several pillboxes were flanked and swiftly vanquished with little resistance. By 1510, the entire near slope was theirs and dozens of prisoners streamed downhill with their hands high. I Company cleared the ridgeline next, firing upon Germans troops seen retreating into a small thicket on the opposite slope.[77] After taking fifteen minutes to consolidate, the two attacking platoons pursued the retreating Germans but ended up pinned against the hillside from unexpectedly heavy S/A fire. The trapped Americans hunkered down and waited for the bursting of German mortar which inevitably followed in such situations.[78] The 1st Platoon leader, Lt Harry Campbell, encouraged his men to hold steady and promised to bring help—then dashed back over the hilltop.[79]

Around this time, five of Redle's tanks reached the small dry creek bed near Monte Penitro and successfully crossed. Campbell saw the column and rushed down and explained his predicament to the lead tank crew. Twenty minutes after promising his men aid, Lt Campbell triumphantly returned atop the first of five tanks emerging from behind the west side of the hill. His men rallied and pressed forward. Upon seeing the small, armored force, the Germans fled from the small woods toward Castellonorato—dodging tank blasts as they scurried. With the capture of Monte Penitro, I Company of the 337th was credited with killing forty-four Germans and capturing 111 others. In the process, however, sixteen I Company men were killed and another sixteen wounded. One of those killed was I Company Commander, Captain Robert H. White.[80]

On the right flank further to the west, Redle and his remaining tanks slogged across uneven terrain—firing upon Castellonorato targets while maneuvering around stone wall terraces, through pitched olive groves and over field ditches. At first, they attempted to flank further to the right but found no clear way through.[81] While backtracking, a flight of six Allied fighter bombers screamed through the valley to the rear, dropping a slew of white phosphorous bombs. Within minutes, the entire area behind Hill 108 disappeared behind a thick curtain of smoke. Redle wondered for a time if the Air Force had missed their target, but as the smoke dissipated, he could see troops from the 88th Division moving up into the Aurunci mountains.[82]

Redle's tankers arrived at San Croce creek but found no obvious way to cross—except for an old flat stone bridge without abutments or side rails, barely wide enough to accommodate a tank.[83] Certain the crumbling structure would collapse under the weight of a tank, Redle encouraged his crews to keep firing from positions along the northern bank while he sought out a better option. The southeastern edge of Castellonorato Hill lay only 400 feet away and the rising slope offered plenty of targets with a clear, unobstructed field of fire. At the same time, around 1630, Lt Col Rogers directed one platoon of D Company light tanks to search further along the dry creek for other crossing sites.[84]

An infantry officer approached Lt Newman asking for assistance. His men were pinned down along the southern slope of Castellonorato and needed tank support. Redle decided to risk crossing the bridge and one gallant crew volunteered to go first. To shield the attempt, Rogers ordered the battalion mortar crews to drop smoke further west.[85] Cement dust wisped, and the weathered stone arch creaked under the passing pressure of thirty-two tons, but the ancient span held—not only for the first tank but all thirteen of Redle's company.[86] Once across, Redle ordered Lt Harris's 1st Platoon to fan out to the right as Lt Newman's 2nd Platoon rolled forward. Lt Gorman's 3rd Platoon was then dispatched wide to the left to assume an overwatch position. The company commander's radio had been faltering the entire afternoon—fading in and out at inopportune times and slowing progress. Finally, the set stopped working altogether, and Redle resorted to using dismounted bow gunners to run messages between tanks.[87]

Heavy German bullet and mortar fire poured down from the bolder strewn heights, and machine guns chattered from the flats along nearby ditches.[88] The ground offered flatter maneuverability areas with fewer terraces and plenty of trees for cover. For the first time that day, Redle could deploy his tanks in a line and bring all firepower to bear on any targets pointed out by the infantry. The line rolled forward around 1700, silencing local opposition and yielding a quick haul of prisoners.[89] Coordination with the infantry, however, was spotty as they had virtually no experience with tanks,[90] but a system emerged whereby the tankers simply observed where the infantry fired and joined in the effort. The results proved excellent. On average, two rounds of HE fired into a German position brought out the white flags.[91] Evidently, the Germans had not placed AT guns in the immediate area to challenge Redle's crews.

Using covering fire from the other tanks, Lt Newman's 2nd Platoon advanced toward the southeastern base of the hill where the requesting infantry officer's men still lay pinned. During the journey, however, Sgt Jarvis's fussy tank threw a track and Sgt James H. Gilkerson exhausted his ammo—leaving only Newman and Sgt Mancini to continue. The infantry officer led them through a small pass on the Scauri side of the hill. They drew some AT fire but accomplished the mission. In time, the rest of B Company joined them along the southeastern hill approach and watched with satisfaction as infantrymen clambered up the rugged slope toward the ruined village at the peak.[92] The terrain was far too rough for the tanks to follow but every now and then, their coaxial MGs or 75mm cannon were called upon to assist the "doughs" closing in upon the crestline while dusk settled over the battlefield.[93]

As B Company operated along the base of Castellonorato Hill, Lt Col Rogers ordered the D Company crews to add reinforcing fire while protecting the battalion's left flank. The movement of the M5 lights drew hostile fire from several houses near the Caves d'Argilla—a surprising development as the area was supposed to have been cleared of enemy two days earlier.[94] M4 mediums from A and C Companies responded by blasting the stone homes and forcing the survivors to surrender. Afterwards, both companies advanced toward Castellonorato by crossing the same stone bridge Redle's crews used earlier.[95]

That same afternoon and early evening, the 338th Regiment advanced from Solacciano and the Caves d'Argilla down the Ausonia road toward San Croce and Highway 7 near the coast—taking the tiny hamlet of Penitro along the way.[96] At the same time, the 339th pressed toward Monte Scauri.[97] These advances threatened to sever German lines and provoked a spirited counterattack—causing the Americans to stop shy of their objectives.[98]

Further to the north, however, the 88th Division moved from La Civita into the Aurunci mountains virtually unimpeded, capturing several key ridges while flanking right of Castellonorato.[99]

At 1800, Redle's crews were heavily engaged firing from the valley floor in support of 2nd Battalion, 337th, troops moving from Point 234 along the crestline. There, the men encountered communication wire running between several OPs, but no

Germans. As they pressed on toward town, however, the fighting flared again—sporadic and waning, but deadly nonetheless. In the meantime, D Company, holding B Company's rear flank, was engaged in rounding up snipers and processing prisoners sent down from the slopes by the advancing infantry.[100] By 1900, Castellonorato fell, and Hughes's men poured down the rear slope, mopping up stragglers while capturing several abandoned SP guns and artillery pieces.[101] The Germans chose to tactically concede the hill and withdraw from the area. Hughes's men welcomed this decision with a "grim exuberance."[102]

Around this same time, Maj Gen Coulter contacted Lt Col Rogers through the divisional liaison officer assigned to the 337th Regiment. The general wanted a reconnaissance of the tiny crossroads town of San Croce and ordered Rogers to send light tanks there to "take a quick look back of Monte Scauri and return with any information gained." The assignment was dubious but the order was direct. San Croce lay nearly three-quarter-of-a-mile south in an area the Germans savagely defended only a few hours earlier. The sun had already set, and out of a necessity for speed, no infantry would accompany the force. Rogers ordered two D Company platoons forward in the dwindling twilight, but counselled the crews to zigzag while progressing. He also ordered one A Company platoon to protect the mission's left flank by moving cross country through a nearby orchard. As the tanks prepared to depart, the liaison officer relayed Coulter's additional instructions for Rogers not to lose any tanks. Coulter's orders seemed contradictory, but Rogers interpreted the general's intention was to avoid any heavy engagements.

D Company travelled no further than 200 yards when a small 28-20mm AT gun hidden further down the road claimed a victim. The stricken tank smoked, and the four-man crew bailed out for the protection of the nearest ditch. Then a second M5 shuddered under a heavy clang—sending four more men scrambling for their lives. The other tanks maneuvered for cover and attempted to locate the source of fire, but in the fading light the task proved impossible. By 1945, Rogers ordered the remaining M5 tanks to give up the effort and withdraw to La Grata for the night.[103]

With Castellonorato relatively secure, 337th scouts ventured westward in search of the German MLR. With dusk falling heavily, Redle's tanks remained on standby at the bottom of the hill, lending occasional fire to the mopping-up operations. A Company sat a few hundred yards east, monitoring the San Croce crossroads. At 2000, several rounds of German AT fire howled past the tankers' heads in both areas of operation. Then, the big German 5-inch coastal gun unleashed unexpected hell. The first round punched through the turret of Sgt Clyde F. Cogdill's tank of the 3rd Platoon, B Company—blowing open the chest of Pfc Verner L. Kreitlow and killing him instantly.[104] The interior flared of molten steel, blood, and bits of flesh, and in the aftermath, gunner Cpl Raymond T. Brown hunched over in agony from multiple wounds while Sgt Cogdill stood behind him dumbfounded: his lower jaw was completely gone.[105]

Redle, parked in his tank a short distance away, saw and heard the sickening jolt and scanned south immediately for the culprit. A second round howled by—blowing the pioneer tools and personal items from the rear deck of Lt Gorman's tank. Judging from the flat trajectory, Redle deduced the source was not Gaeta eight miles away, but Monte Scauri only one mile to the south. He first ordered his driver and then radioed Lt Gorman and the other tanks to move closer to the hillside for cover.[106] While advancing, two more HE rounds exploded against the side of Gorman's tank, causing the radial engine to cough and sputter. Gorman's crew was unharmed and his tank reached safety, but the tall, thin upstate New Yorker was left emotionally dazed.[107]

Fortunately, Cogdill's tank failed to catch fire, and driver T/4 Joe K. Wright maintained the presence of mind to also move the damaged hulk to safety.[108] Sgt Roy L. Anderson and several other tankers rushed over to help extricate Cogdill and Brown from the damaged turret. Brown was a peppered mess, but Cogdill's wounds were downright shocking. With his lower jaw completely missing, and the sergeant's tongue hung freely down to the chest of his blood-soaked coveralls.[109] First aid and crude compresses were administered to both men, and Redle sent for infantry medics—who were exasperatingly slow in responding.[110] Eventually, help arrived and both men were evaluated, stabilized, and evacuated. Brown went to the 85th Division Clearing Station, but Cogdill was dispatched straight to the 11th Field Hospital.[111]

Alarmed by the loss of three tanks in fifteen minutes and seeing "no useful purpose would be served by their remaining exposed to anti-tank fire" as darkness descended, Lt Col Rogers ordered A and B Companies to pull back to La Grata for the evening. Smoke cover laid by the battalion's assault guns helped shield the M4s and they backtracked.[112] Lt Gorman's tank was temporarily abandoned due to its faulty engine. T/4 Wright grimly drove his damaged tank back to the assembly area with the mangled body of his friend, Kreitlow, still crumpled behind him in the loader position.[113]

Word of the late-day tank losses and especially Cogdill's horrific wounds spread rapidly throughout battalion ranks.[114] The muscular 34-year-old was well-known and admired by many—having first been inducted in March 1941 and serving as a fixture in the outfit ever since inception.[115] Over time, the unmarried, rugged Nebraskan built a rock-solid reputation as a courageous and dependable tanker.[116] A soldier suffering such wounds never returned and often didn't survive. Cogdill's sudden departure felt like a stiff kick to the gut to his comrades.

The infantry's scouting push took them a full 2,000 yards west of Castellonorato in the direction of Trivio and Maranola—two small towns nestled upon the saddle between 355-meter-high Monte Campese to the south and main Aurunci chain to the north.[117] The Germans seemingly retreated into this narrow 500-yard-wide corridor. The probing halted temporarily while more aggressive pursuit plans were drawn.[118]

At 2200, a swarm of German planes screamed low through the night, dropping flares over the 756th Tank Battalion's assembly area. For many long anxious moments, the tankers waited for bombs to fall or artillery blasts to follow—but nothing happened.[119]

A half hour later, Lt Col Rogers received orders to report to the 337th CP near Monte Natale. There, he learned from Colonel Hughes that Maj Gen Coulter wanted the light tanks to, again, engage in dubious reconnaissance. This time the M5s were to proceed "at once from Castellonorato along the Trivio road to gain and maintain contact with the enemy" and "report all information gained"—on the "assumption" the Germans were withdrawing. Rogers stood momentarily incredulous. So much was flawed about the order it took a few seconds to unpack a response. Finally, Rogers politely explained to Hughes how his tanks couldn't climb Castellonorato in the day, so they certainly couldn't do so at night, and that his gunners' sights were useless in the dark, leaving the tanks defenseless and completely vulnerable to ambush.[120] In short, his crews were technically incapable of carrying out the mission. Rogers wasn't refusing orders, of course. This would be unprofessional, and clear grounds for court martial. He was, however, asking the general for clarification. Rogers's hoped just raising these concerns might change the general's mind, but by simply requesting clarification, he gained something valuable: time.

At this late hour, Coulter was preoccupied and couldn't immediately return Rogers's call. The entire 85th Division sector bustled with activity. G-2, G-3, S-2, S-3 reports, field messages, and recon summaries flooded the divisional staff tables in Minturno, and preparations were underway to renew the offensive at dawn. The 349th Regiment of the 88th Division had just been attached temporarily to the 85th as part of those plans. During the day, the 349th successfully attacked from La Civita over the rocky ridges north of Castellonorato—maintaining remarkable pace on a right flank parallel to the 337th's drive. The Germans misjudged the terrain as too rugged for infantry operations and failed to prepare adequate defenses.[121] By midnight, both the 2nd and 3rd Battalions of the 337th advanced a full 400 yards west of Castellonorato to establish a firm new forward line.[122] These late-night developments delayed Coulter from answering Rogers's earlier call.

Finally, at 0130, 16 May, the general called the 337th CP to speak to the tank battalion commander. Rogers tried explaining his crews' constraints, but the general was unmoved and unconvinced—even threatening to relieve the lieutenant colonel of his command if he did not carry out the orders in full.[123] The call ended abruptly with that understanding.[124]

When Rogers returned to La Grata and relayed the orders to his staff, the tank officers clearly sensed his angst. Although Coulter had masterfully prepared his division for infantry operations, the cavalry-commissioned general seemed to lack a basic understanding of tank capabilities or limitations. During the weeks of planning prior to Plan *Scurry*, the general often expressed skepticism over their use. Now, after four days of combat, his armor expectations had swung 180-degrees into the realm of the unrealistic.[125] A few hours earlier, those same impractical demands led to needless tank losses and casualties. Rogers's men understood the terrible dilemma their battalion commander had been put in, but as he explained preceding events and outlined how the recon mission would unfold, a subtle subtext emerged to reveal his true motivations.

Rogers would protect them.

U.S. 338th Infantry Regiment

CHAPTER THIRTEEN

Bursting Through: 16 May 1944 to 21 May 1944

Before Lt Col Rogers left the 337th CP near Monte Natale, he alerted both the battalion reconnaissance section and D Company by radio to prepare for action. Then Rogers stalled for time. He remained with Colonel Hughes studying maps, aerial photos, and messages while sorting details from the most recent phone and radio reports. Not until 0330, did the battalion commander return to La Grata to brief his staff and those directly involved in the mission. The tanks would not be sent blindly into the night without topside sentries. The recon section was instructed to ride the rear decks of the M5s and serve as protective "infantry"—a new role for them. Rogers opened a map and directed the column to take one particular winding road up the eastern side of Castellonorato Hill. Once there, the recon section would dismount and walk alongside the tanks as they climbed cautiously. The column was told to remain in radio contact with Rogers the entire time. Finally, at 0400, D Company departed.

Once the M5s arrived, however, they discovered the route—which the 85th Division HQ had misidentified as a road—was merely a furrowed cart trail, much too narrow for light tanks.[1] With dawn only moments away, the mission effectively ended before it could even begin. In the intervening hours, Hughes's infantry had consolidated safely west of Castellonorato—negating the need for the recon anyway. Rogers had masterfully complied with orders without needlessly jeopardizing his crews. His tacit, nuanced solution to the dilemma did not escape the notice of his appreciative officers.[2]

***

During the predawn hours of 16 May, infantry patrols dispatched throughout the 85th Division sector returned with reports of enemy withdrawal all along the line.[3] Coulter pressed his men harder—ordering a dawn attack to keep the Germans off guard. If Highway 7 could be secured, Formia would certainly fall next—opening a direct avenue to Itri and Terracina.[4] The 338th was tasked with cutting Highway 7 at San Croce and assuming the division's left flank, seaward drive toward Formia. The 339th would follow behind, clearing out Scauri and Monte Scauri. At the same time, the 337th would continue pushing west overland from Castellonorato on the right flank.

At 0615, Lt Col Rogers received orders to contact Colonel Hughes and coordinate tank/infantry operations. The 337th's attack toward Trivio was set for 0800. Because of difficult terrain north of Castellonorato, armor could not immediately join. Rogers recommended his tanks approach along the south side of the hill before swinging north to join the infantry attack in progress. He also requested an engineer platoon and bulldozer to aid in the advance. Hughes readily agreed to everything.[5]

At 0730, Rogers contacted his company commanders to relay the plan: B Company would take the lead, followed by A and C Companies. D Company had been recalled from their unsuccessful recon mission and instructed to anchor the rear.[6] All four tank companies were short several tanks due to mechanical attrition. C Company was down to ten tanks while B Company operated with only eight.[7] The column progressed from La Grata without incident until arriving at a dry stream bed southwest of Castellonorato by 1000 hours. A small wooden bridge, rated for only four tons, offered the only obvious way across. One of Redle's crews tested the structure. The timbers creaked and compressed down a good three inches under the 32-ton weight of a passing tank, but miraculously held. The rest of B Company and part of A Company followed—taking up firing positions along the far bank to cover the passage of the rest of the battalion. Bursting German mortar shells greeted the tankers' arrival, but eventually subsided upon realizing the harassment had no effect. The bridge, however, now showed signs of catastrophic failure, so the engineers were called forward to bulldoze a bypass. By 1200, all vehicles had successfully crossed, and the advance resumed.[8]

In the meantime, Hughes's infantrymen had halted 400 yards short of Acquatraversa creek—a mountain spillway running down from the Auruncis, bisecting the battlefield before tracing along the eastern edge of Monte Campese.[9] Sporadic German MG and mortar fire forced a pause until tank support could arrive. To the south, the 338th succeeded in taking San Croce but slowed their westward drive along Highway 7 under the steady bursting of German mortar rounds falling from nearby Monte Campese and coastal artillery shells dispatched from distant Gaeta across the bay.[10]

Rogers contacted Hughes and learned a renewed infantry attack would commence at 1500 hours. The new offensive would be coordinated with the 338th pressing along Highway 7 near the coast.[11] Redle's tankers resumed the lead—arriving among infantry positions around the tiny hamlet of Ponzanelli lying 500 yards due east of Monte Campese.[12] Captain Lewis's A Company assumed positions on the left, with C Company halting behind both—prepared to assist wherever needed. D Company assumed protective defilade positions along the battalion's right flank while the HQ mortar platoon dispersed along the streambed to the rear—ready to lay down smoke on call. The assault guns positioned back at La Grata prepared to do the same. In the meantime, infantry officers pointed out to the tank crews any enemy position seen on the slopes of Monte Campese or in Trivio, 1,000 yards away on the right.

The attack launched on schedule. The 3rd Battalion, 337th, on the left and supported by Lewis's tanks, pressed toward Monte Campese under a steady rain of German mortar and MG fire. Redle's tanks, following the 2nd Battalion, 337th, toward Trivio on the right, encountered the same. The terrain was rough—an irregular patchwork of fields and terraces bordered by crumbling stone walls and haphazard ditches—making maneuver extremely difficult.[13] Lt Newman saw a German emerge from a hole near the foundation of a house roughly 100 yards ahead. The *feldgrau* figure grabbed a ladder and draped a big white flag in a tree before returning to his burrow. Newman's crew withheld fire upon seeing the signal. A short time later the same *landser* emerged again to gather up some personal belongings. He then pulled down the sheet and started skulking away. Enraged by the ruse, Newman's bow gunner cut down the scammer with a quick burst of .30-caliber MG fire. The foolish man died clutching his only hope for survival.[14]

Somewhere on the left side of the slope of Monte Campese, a German AT gun began firing—slowing the advance of both A and B Companies.[15] But after two hours, the infantry, reached the Aquatraversa under vanquishing fire provided by the 756th tankers.[16] Lt Harris accidently broke his hand—an easy thing for a tank commander to do during combat inside a rotating turret amidst jolting breeches and thumping hatches. The injury was serious enough to warrant immediate evacuation.[17] His departure left B Company with only two officers on the battlefield: Redle and Newman. Lt Gorman, still shaken over the prior day's events, sat emotionally incapacitated at La Grata.[18] 1st Lt Harley had since transferred over to C Company,[19] and XO Lt Engfer was overseeing tank recovery efforts near Solacciano. A spare platoon leader, 2nd Lt Bert Gilden, could not be brought over from HQ and properly integrated until later. Making matters worse, Redle's radio transmitter had failed yet again, leaving Newman as the only officer who could communicate with the crews.[20] Despite these handicaps, Redle's tanks joined the infantry along Acquatraversa—only to find no way across.[21]

By late afternoon, the infantry started digging in along the deep mountain creek—taking a breather and a K-ration break before resuming the effort.[22] Colonel Hughes was in the process of bringing more troops into the area. His 1st Battalion, released from a four-day attachment to the 339th, pulled back off San Martino Hill to Tremensuoli where the troops received hot meals, fresh supplies, and awaited transport trucks.[23] These extra troops, however, were not expected to arrive ahead of the next attack set for 1800 hours.[24]

An hour into the new offensive, Hughes contacted Rogers and asked him to shift some tanks north to the main road connecting Castellonorato with Trivio. A small bridge on that route spanned the Aquatraversa—offering a vehicular way across.[25]

Rogers directed Redle to the position, but AT fire coming from three directions quickly halted the advance. In response, Rogers ordered Captain Gourley to swing his C Company tanks around B Company positions and take the lead.[26] The AT fire persisted—snarling in from Monte Campese to the southwest, the Acquatraversa bridge location to the northwest, and a ridgeline due north. The fire coming from the north was the most surprising, as this was high ground supposedly cleared earlier by 349th Regiment infantrymen.[27] At 1830, Rogers ordered B Company to pull back east and then move north in support of Gourley's tanks. D Company was alerted to provide right flank protection.[28]

At 1933, Captain Gourley reported arriving in view of the bridge. The AT fire had halted, but small arms fire pinged constantly off his company's tank hulls and no friendly troops could be seen anywhere. Gourley also said the bridge appeared to be mined, as evidenced by a telltale ridge of dirt piled neatly across the middle.[29]

Redle's tanks and supporting infantry arrived roughly 300 yards north of Ponzanelli—drawing fire from four nearby German MGs. Redle's gunners flooded the area with coaxial .30-caliber MG fire of their own and the German guns fell forever silent.[30] After searching awhile, Redle finally found Gourley's tanks in what appeared to be a large agricultural nursery, six to eight city blocks in size, filled with trees and shrubs—still awaiting infantry that never arrived.[31] With dusk settling rapidly and no clear idea where the MLR had shifted, the two company commanders contacted Rogers by radio for further guidance. Lt Kremer, in charge of D Company, also radioed similar concerns at 2015. His M5s were being pelted by small arms bullets but the crews withheld fire until verifying the location of friendly troops. Rogers contacted Hughes and the 337th CO informed him some Germans had infiltrated their lines. With darkness approaching and no way of knowing who was firing from where, the tanks withdrew back to La Grata.[32] Along the way, Lt Newman picked up Lt Moultrie Patton of D Company, whose tank had been knocked out by AT fire mere moments before.[33]

Hughes's 2nd and 3rd Battalions kept fighting until 2100, when division orders arrived calling for a halt until 0450 in the morning.[34] Neither battalion pushed very far beyond the Acquatraversa and both the Monte Campese and Trivio objectives remained German strongholds.[35] At 2100, however, the 1st Battalion, 337th, finally de-trucked near Castellonorato, and Hughes received a timely infusion of fresh men.[36]

At 0215, 17 May, Rogers received divisional confirmation of the 337th Regiment's attack upon Trivio set for 0450. The timetable was determined as part of II Corps-wide offensive designed to place maximum pressure on the retreating Germans.[37] Delay requests were not accepted. Because of difficulties in moving gasoline and ammunition over the congested roads near Santa Maria Infante, however, Rogers notified Hughes of his doubts the tanks would be ready in time, but gave his personal assurances the crews would arrive as soon as possible.[38]

The gas and ammunition arrived at La Grata around 0530, and the crews loaded up and moved out roughly an hour-and-a-half later. A Company led, followed by D, B, and C Companies.[39] Enroute, however, the order was reshuffled to A, B, C, then D Company.[40] The tanks arrived at the Acquatraversa, crossed the small bridge (since de-mined), and headed toward Trivio. The infantry's morning gains were impressive. Monte Campese had been stormed by 3rd Battalion, 337th, infantrymen after an hour-long artillery shellacking.[41] Trivio, too, had fallen. Captain Lewis's A Company tanks snaked through the empty ruined village unmolested at 0900 but were halted by a blown bridge roughly a half-mile west of town, just shy of Maranola. The 2nd Battalion, 337th, was fighting in town as evidenced by the sights and sounds of nearby gunfire. Rogers called forth the engineers and notified Colonel Hughes of the new delay. The crews waited—wearily studying Formia and Gaeta sprawled below in the distance. Every so often German artillery shells burst all around them. One unlucky A Company driver was stuck by shrapnel and required evacuation.[42] By 1100, a bypass was completed but Hughes told Rogers to wait in place until further orders.[43] Maranola had just fallen.[44] The reports pouring in were so good, the colonel didn't even need tanks at the moment. In fact, with so much ground taken, Hughes was busily moving his CP to Trivio just to keep pace.[45]

Along the coast, the news was even better. With Monte Campese neutralized, the 338th, attacking along Highway 7, stormed across the Acquatraversa and advanced a full two miles to the outskirts of Formia.[46] The 339th Regiment, too, overran an abandoned Scauri and subdued a lightly defended Monte Scauri. With both objectives taken, the entire regiment was ordered to move up behind Hughes's men at Trivio during the afternoon of 17 May.[47]

The battle shifted up into the bald craggy ridges and draws west of Maranola.[48] This was, in no way, tank country. After consulting with Hughes, at 1415 Rogers issued orders for A Company to remain in a support position near Maranola, but for the rest of the battalion to withdraw to a new bivouac location a half-mile southwest of Castellonorato.[49] There, on flat fertile fields, the remainder of the day was spent cleaning and oiling all guns and equipment.[50] And, for the first time in six days, the crews found rest.

***

By evening, 17 May, 338th troops pushed deeply into Formia—finding the town booby-trapped, heavily mined, and protected with scattered pockets of resistance. Total occupation of the town, however, was delayed until morning on account of heavy coastal gun fire howling in from Gaeta.[51]

The quick fall of Formia and seizure of high ground west of Maranola convinced Lt Gen Mark Clark to cancel his contingency plans for moving the 85th Division to Anzio. The division's original projected drive through Itri to Terracina would continue.[52] Progress along the entire Fifth Army front had been stellar the past forty-eight hours. The 88th Division and French Forces pushed so quickly up into the Auruncis the Germans never had an opportunity to regroup behind their prearranged "Dora Line." The Germans, too, suffered from a sudden intelligence disadvantage. Thousands of their troops had been captured, whereas very few Allied prisoners had fallen into their hands. Without vital interrogation information, the German commanders operated in a fog over the composition and strength of the forces pressing hard upon their rearguard units.[53]

The French progress was especially impressive. Juin's forces had crossed the Auruncis from the Ausonia corridor to reach the outskirts of Esperia, bordering the Liri Valley. By the morning of 18 May, Algerian colonial troops swarmed down from the mountains and through Esperia. Pico, the CEF's next objective, nine miles to the west, now fell within artillery range.[54]

The 756th Tank Battalion saw no action during 18 May, and the Custermen ventured beyond Formia to take Monte Conca late that evening. Capture of this critical coastal hill completely sealed off those Germans still retreating from Gaeta and secured the only route inland to Itri.[55] The event certainly marked a milestone—but not one nearly as monumental as had occurred twenty miles to the north: Monte Cassino had finally fallen. That same morning, Polish forces swept through the ruins of the pulverized monastery and triumphantly raised their national colors.[56] The grueling five-month siege was finally over—leaving 20,000 German and 55,000 Allied soldiers dead or wounded.[57] Thirty of those Allied dead were 756th tankers.

All four tank companies of the 756th used the day to reorganize and perform more complex maintenance work.[58] The tracks on some tanks had to be pulled to replace bullet-damaged idler and boogie wheels.[59] The respite gave the crews time to take inventory of their surroundings. The scene was not pleasant. American and German dead littered the nearby hills, attracting flies and maggots. The hot Italian sun had already baked and bloated their bodies to a scorched black or gangrenous yellow. The foul odor made the troops retch. Italian citizens began emerging from their cellar holes and mountain hideouts—filing past the busy tankers while lugging ragged belongings on their backs with worried stares on their faces. The lucky ones found homes with missing roofs. The unlucky ones found only piles of stone.[60]

At 0730 the next morning, 19 May, Lt Col Rogers received orders to move one tank company to Formia to help support infantry operations. Rogers gave Captain Gourley's C Company the assignment. At 0900, Gourley's column reached the Castellonorato–Trivio Road but were halted by troops passing through on priority orders. Rogers contacted Division HQ for a resolution. A half hour later, orders coming straight from Maj Gen Coulter directed C Company to return to the battalion area and await further instructions.[61]

At 1147, Rogers heard from Maj Gen Coulter again. This time the battalion commander was instructed to meet with the CO of the 1st Armored Group (formally called the 1st Tank Group) for new orders. Rogers left promptly for Scauri, where the group colonel was supposed to be touring, only to be directed on to Formia. After a fruitless search wasting several hours, Rogers contacted the G-3, II Corps at 1400, and learned new orders had been cut for the battalion to report to the CO of the 2nd Armored Group—twenty miles away in the French sector. Rather than engage in another fruitless jeep chase, Rogers raised the 2nd Armored Group by phone. At 1500, confirmation arrived: the 756th Tank Battalion was ordered to immediately travel north of Ausonia, locate and occupy an assembly area near San Giorgio, and await a new assignment.[62]

Rogers obtained traffic clearance to begin moving at 1700 in cloudy, rainy weather. Travel was smooth—over blacktop mostly, but from time to time the long column slowed, then halted due to some delay ahead. While idling among the ruins of one small town, Redle was struck by the plight of destitute civilians milling about and picking through the rubble. One Italian man bitterly cussed the Germans for stealing all his cellar hams. A young woman paced the road near a cemetery cradling an eight-month-old infant in her arms. The baby had been dead for several days.[63] By 2100 hours, surrounded by the irregular thudding of French artillery batteries firing into the sunset, the battalion set up camp in a lush green field one-and-a-quarter miles northeast of San Giorgio, and attachment to the 85th Infantry Division officially ended.[64]

The next morning, 20 May, the crews awaited word on their next assignment—rumored to arrive later in the day. At 1130, the 2nd Armored Group ordered one company to move south of Ausonia and await further instructions. Puzzled, Rogers sent his Battalion S-3, Major Edwin Arnold, to the 2nd Armored Group HQ for clarification. Arnold returned a short time later, explaining one company was needed for an armored task force. The remainder of the battalion would receive a separate assignment later. Rogers gave B Company the job and at noon, Redle's tankers drove out of San Giorgio for Ausonia ten miles to the south—back down the same road they came in on the night before.[65] With such confusing and contradictory orders flying about, few wondered why the roads were so congested.

B Company arrived at their bivouac location around 1830, but were instructed to remain in column. The setting was odd. The uniforms, weapons, equipment, and vehicles were all American, but the language used was French. Closer scrutiny revealed many wearing "Adrian"-style backboned helmets,[66] and French tricolor or Moroccan red star themed markings and flags adorning the vehicles, equipment, and shirtsleeves—which only added to the quirkiness.

A friendly French major approached Redle, speaking excellent English, and identified himself as his liaison. He welcomed Redle to the 4th Moroccan Mountain Division (4th DMM) and informed him B Company was hereby assigned to *Groupe*

Blindé ("Armored Group") of the division. *Groupe Blindé* was commanded by a Major Dodelier and was comprised of tank destroyers (American M-10 models), halftracks, and other armored vehicles, but lacked organic M4 medium tanks.[67] The French major then informed Redle *Groupe Blindé* would be departing shortly … through Formia.[68] The news filtering down the column was met with chuckles, groans, and disbelieving shakes of the head. After journeying in haste some fifty miles in less than twenty-four hours, the B Company crews found themselves passing through the very place they started from. Combat made more sense.

***

Meanwhile at San Giorgio, the remainder of the 756th Tank Battalion endured their own day of confusion. At 1400, Rogers was told to report for orders at the CP for the French First Motorized Infantry Division (1st DMI). He arrived and was told to appear again at 1900. Rogers returned as instructed—only to be told the 756th had been detached from the 1st DMI and attached to the Third Algerian Infantry Division (3rd DIA). Rogers rushed over to the 3rd DIA HQ and learned the 756th was to move out promptly for Sant' Oliva, ten miles to the west, and report to Colonel Bonjour. He raced back to the battalion assembly area by 2105, alerted the companies, and dispatched Major Arnold with reconnaissance teams and billeting parties ahead of the move.[69]

The battalion tanks and trucks rolled out in the dark atop a meandering mountain route through Esperia, which was every bit as congested as it was perilous. Along one hairpin turn, the Germans had blown a culvert. French engineers filled the hole with sandbags. The edge gave out under the passing weight of Captain Lewis's lead tank, causing it to roll over completely on its turret. If not for the presence of several large boulders, the tank would have continued tumbling down into a steep valley below. The crew was left battered and bruised—but otherwise unhurt—amidst the jostling of loose ammunition and hand grenades and managed to slither out of one unblocked hatch reeking of gasoline and oil. Captain Lewis took charge of a 2nd Platoon tank to keep his company moving. No one venturing within a few yards of Lewis or his crew dared light a cigarette for a while.[70]

At 0300, the 756th Tank Battalion (less B Company) arrived at a bivouac location on the slope of Hill 640 near Sant' Oliva. The crews were instructed to take a short rest and prepare to attack Pico first thing in the morning.[71]

Whether handling the unholy stresses and demands of combat or negotiating through the exasperating, contradictory, and Byzantine demands of Army protocol away from combat, Lt Col Rogers's placid demeanor never changed. He was a consummate professional and had since earned the deep trust of his officers and enlisted men alike. What the battalion may have lost in the creative drive and brashness of Lt Col Sweeting, they gained in the confidence, maturity, and perspective of Rogers. The enlisted men, especially, respected their new battalion commander for his practicality and modesty. Standard operating procedure during an artillery attack demanded the crews immediately halt the tanks, fuel up, and dig slit trenches. During one such attack, the crews—already exhausted—asked to forego the slit trenches and take cover beneath the tanks instead. Rogers agreed to bending the rules. Sweeting would have never done so.[72] On another occasion, T/4 Ralph Donley was driving for the lieutenant colonel while under fire. During the course of operations, the turret rotated completely to the rear and Rogers ordered Donley to "back up" via intercom. Donley followed instructions, only to hear Rogers immediately ordering him to "halt" and "back up" again. After repeating this a third time, Donley realized Rogers had become confused by the turret position.

"… but Colonel, I am backing up," Donley replied.

"Oh yes, you're right, Sergeant!" Rogers acknowledged before correcting his instructions.

Sweeting would have never humbly admitted such a mistake, Donley thought at the time.[73] Small personal gestures like these were huge gestures to the enlisted men as a whole—and became the comforting grist of conversation among the average Joes huddled around Coleman stoves gulping their morning coffee. It assured them their commander saw them as fellow human beings.

***

While the 756th moved to Sant' Oliva, B Company plodded south with the *Groupe Blindé* column from Ausonia, past familiar La Grata, Hill 108, and Castellonorato. They snaked along Highway 7 through battle damaged Formia on the coast, then turned west into the setting sun. Their Custermen associates had since cleared Gaeta and advanced three miles inland just beyond Itri. The column followed their trail—threading the scenic mountain gap leading to the battle-scarred but still picturesque town before turning north along the Itri–Pico road. After rolling about a mile, *Groupe Blindé* arrived near the tiny hamlet of Sant' Elmo around 2230 and dispersed among fields, orchards, and olive groves along the eastern side of the road.[74] The French liaison promptly appeared to reestablish contact with Redle and apprise him of future plans. Redle introduced the mannerly major to B Company's communication sergeant and fluent French speaker, Sgt Daniel Pompey. Citing prudence, Redle suggested Pompey be stationed with a short-wave radio at the French CP to avoid any misunderstandings. The major nodded politely and replied he didn't believe the extra step was necessary—but agreed to Redle's request nevertheless.

Before departing, the major turned to Redle and closed: "Bed your men down. We won't need you until later tomorrow."[75]

His syntax sounded peculiar to the American ear. For a moment, Redle wasn't sure if his friendly French liaison was referring to men or horses.

Fighting with the French was going to be *une affaire intéressante.*

U.S. 337th Infantry Regiment

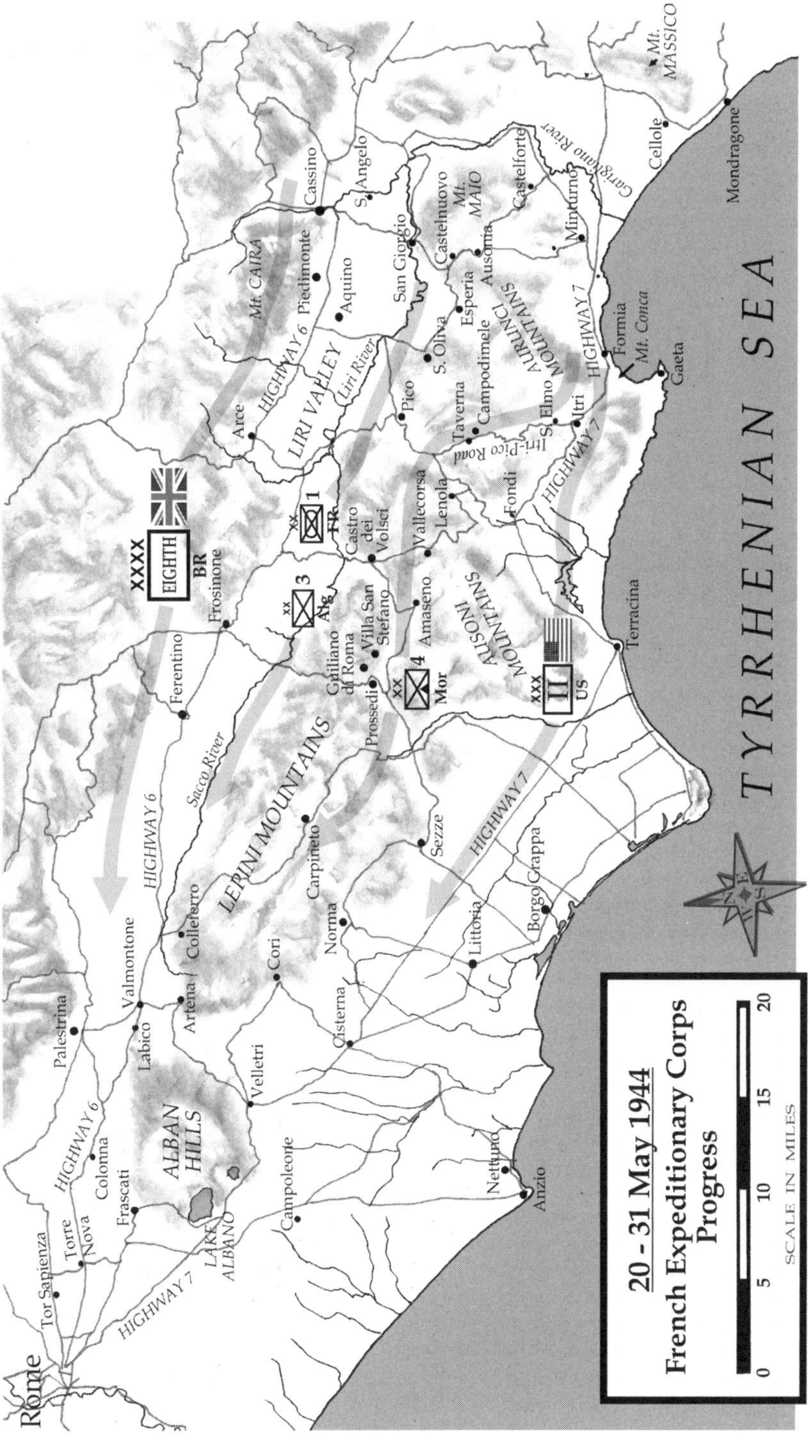
20 - 31 May 1944
French Expeditionary Corps
Progress
0 5 10 15 20
SCALE IN MILES
TYRRHENIAN SEA
Rome
Tor Sapienza
Torre Nova
Frascati
Colonna
HIGHWAY 6
HIGHWAY 7
LAKE ALBANO
ALBAN HILLS
Palestrina
Labico
Valmontone
Artena
Colleferro
Velletri
Campoleone
Nettuno
Anzio
Cisterna
Cori
Norma
Littoria
Borgo Grappa
Carpineto
LEPINI MOUNTAINS
Sezze
Sacco River
Ferentino
Frosinone
XXXX
EIGHTH
BR
Prossedi
Giuliano di Roma
Villa San Stefano
Amaseno
4 Mor
3 Alg
1 FR
XX
XXX
II
US
Castro dei Volsci
Vallecorsa
Lenola
AUSONI MOUNTAINS
Terracina
Fondi
Itri-Pico Road
Arce
LIRI VALLEY
Liri River
Pico
Taverna
Campodimele
S. Elmo
Itri
S. Oliva
Esperia
AURUNCI MOUNTAINS
Formia
Mt. Conca
Gaeta
Aquino
Piedimonte
Mt. CAIRA
Cassino
S. Angelo
San Giorgio
Castelnuovo
Mt. MAIO
Ausonia
Castelforte
Minturno
Garigliano River
Cellole
Mondragone
Mt. MASSICO

CHAPTER FOURTEEN

Living the War with the French: 21 May 1944 to 31 May 1944

The mighty *feldgrau* dam had finally burst. From the high Apennines down to the Tyrrhenian coast, hundreds of thousands of Allied troops stormed across the Gustav Line by foot, tire, and track.[1] To prevent the Germans from regrouping and establishing yet another defensive bulwark, all Allied units were urged to maintain a close and vigorous pursuit. The British Eighth Army, attacking on the Allies' right flank, was responsible for clearing the Liri Valley and bordering heights to the northeast. The U.S. Fifth Army, on the left flank, was tasked with charging up the rugged Ausoni and Lepini mountain chains while slogging through the swampy lowlands running from Terracina to Cisterna. The goal was to link up with Anzio forces, then steamroll with the British Eighth Army into Rome.

The Fifth Army's section of front spanned roughly twenty miles. Keyes's U.S II Corps continued pursuit on the coastal left, while Juin's CEF Forces pressed through the mountainous right. Lt Redle's small seventeen-tank company was placed squarely in the middle—foreigners assigned to *Groupe Blindé* of the French 4th Moroccan Mountain Division in an unfamiliar role supporting skirmishing armored mountain recon troops.[2] War was as strange as it was brutal.

Groupe Blindé was the only armored component of larger, regimental-sized French *Groupe Cherrière* formed to sweep the peaks and valleys of German resistance. This task force, commanded by Colonel Paul Cherrière, was comprised of four battalions of light mountain infantry: two from the 6th Moroccan Tirailleurs Regiment (6th RTM),[3] and two battalions of Goumier troops from the 1st Tabor Group.[4] A battalion from the 69th Mountain Artillery Regiment and a company of engineers from the 82nd Engineers Battalion rounded out the force.[5]

The Operation *Diadem* breakout had restored French confidence. That swagger, perhaps, had never really disappeared, but it certainly hadn't been allowed to shine either—until Lt Gen Mark Clark put the CEF on his Army's right flank, at the center of the entire operation. Clark had no other choice. His best and most experienced divisions—the 1st Armored and 3rd, 34th, and 45th Infantry Divisions had been shifted to shore-up Anzio. The 36th was still rebuilding and the 85th and 88th were completely green outfits. The CEF was his only option, and the French seized the opportunity and excelled. Italy may not have been their beloved *Patrie*, but the CEF fought as aggressively as if it were. The British fought to avenge Dunkirk. The French fought to avenge all of 1940.

At the early morning hour of 0500, 21 May, the B Company CP radio in the Sant' Elmo camp crackled with a familiar voice. Sgt Pompey, serving as liaison in the *Groupe Blindé* CP further up the road, exclaimed loudly how the French wanted tanks "right now!" Strangely, no Germans were attacking, and no other emergency existed. Redle asked for further explanation, but Pompey had been given nothing more. The company commander drew a deep breath and told Pompey to relay the message that B Company would report once the men had eaten and properly prepared their tanks. For the next hour or so, Redle pondered diplomatic ways of informing his French associates how Americans weren't accustomed to jumping at blind orders and a more considerate method of communication would need to be employed.[6]

B Company joined the gathering column. An advance guard was organized comprised of one platoon of medium tanks, one platoon of light tanks, one platoon of M-10 tank destroyers and other various armored half-tracks and recon vehicles. Redle assigned the 3rd Platoon to the task.[7] Lt Gorman was still not settled enough to resume command, so S/Sgt Oric Johannesen was placed in temporary command—swapping his #4 tank and crew in place of tank #14.[8] The day's objective was Lenola—a small valley town approximately ten miles to the northwest. To get there, *Groupe Blindé* had to advance along Highway 82—a long, narrow, and twisting valley road with high mountains on either side. Redle had been assured the flanking high ground along the way would be cleared concurrently by Goumier infantrymen. The "Goums" were fierce, swarthy Moroccan tribesmen valued for their fighting skills—especially with knives. They dressed in flowing robes of striped earthen colors and head turbans—wearing helmets only when under fire.[9] They were led by a mix of tribal chieftains and French officers—which often did not result in good discipline or communication.[10]

The French first directed S/Sgt Johannesen's platoon to a draw to the west—roughly a quarter-mile away from Sant' Elmo.[11] This side mission, commencing at 0730, was to provide direct fire support to the Goums operating along the crestline while guarding against any German counterattack. After an hour, Johannesen's tanks returned to the roadway at the head of the column. Redle questioned this placement but was told this was how the French preferred to proceed.[12]

By 0830, the *Groupe Blindé* column cleared Sant' Elmo.[13] After traveling roughly two miles, the long line of vehicles snaked through a series of switchback roads before passing through the small farming hamlet of San Nicola. The entire journey essentially traced along a sparsely populated canyon floor flanked by inhospitable barren rocky hills with patches of scrub trees and parched grasses clinging to fissures. And although travel thus far had been relatively uneventful, Redle kept wondering if the Goumiers had really cleared the gray 700-meter heights to either side and from which bend a dreaded German AT gun would make an inevitable appearance. The terrain wreaked havoc with FM radio communications.[14] At times, Redle had no idea what was happening—even a few hundred yards ahead of him.

After negotiating through another two miles of switchback turns, *Groupe Blindé* began drawing S/A and MG fire. Roughly a mile ahead lay the valley town of Taverna and adjacent hilltop village of Campodimele. Much of the resistance originated from the right, along the slopes just below the crestline village. S/Sgt Johannesen's tanks spread out as wide as the narrow road would allow and dispatched counterfire.[15] After a while, the German response slackened, and then dwindled down to nothing. In the meantime, Lt Redle walked up to observe the action. An Italian woman was seen slowly sauntering the narrow ribbon of roadway leading up to Campodimele—carrying a heavy crate atop her head. Redle told Johannesen's crews to watch the woman closely to see if she hesitated or reacted in any way which would suggest Germans were still lingering in the area. The woman reached town as if she hadn't a care in the world.[16] Redle considered this strong evidence the Germans had drawn back.

By early afternoon, the advance guard leading *Groupe Blindé* proceeded along the valley floor toward Taverna, which also fell without much fight. However, Johannesen's crews had expended most of their ammunition, so Redle ordered their withdrawal and for the 1st Platoon to take the lead. With 2nd Lt Harris out with a broken hand, 2nd Lt Bert Gilden now had command. One tank developed mechanical trouble, so only Gilden's remaining four could proceed. Soon after 1300, the 1st Platoon arrived in Taverna.[17] Two M4s were dispatched immediately north of town to overwatch a French engineering crew repairing a blown section of roadway. The rest of the force—four M-10 tank destroyers, five M3A1 half-tracks, five M5 light tanks, five jeeps, a small detachment of engineers, plus Gilden's two remaining M4s—waited in Taverna. During the pause, Lt Gilden wandered the town streets seeking out the French officer in charge to gain a better understanding of his orders. One French 1st lieutenant, claiming to be in charge, provided him with one set of orders. Another 1st lieutenant, commanding the TD platoon, told Gilden something entirely different. Both officers spoke only French. Gilden understood the language to some degree, but sought out an English-speaking officer to clarify the contradictions. He found one, only to be told the French major commanding all of *Groupe Blindé* was also in charge of the advance guard. The cosmopolitan New Englander never did get a straight answer.

The half-dozen or so French officers waiting in Taverna met to discuss proceeding. Lt Gilden listened intently, hoping to glean any useful information. The officers seemed confused. Some discussed placing the light tanks ahead of the M-10s in the marching order. Others disagreed. No one seemed to have any definitive idea of the whereabouts of their supporting Moroccan infantry battalion—but presumed they had taken the ridgeline on the left north of town. Another French armored task force was supposed to be moving down from the north to rendezvous with them in the valley beyond Taverna. Whether that force was arriving or not, no one knew for sure. Gilden learned, at least, that their next objective was a crossroads lying 1,200 yards north of town. To attack it, however, the French decided to proceed without first establishing contact with the Goumiers—presumably on the left—and without employing preliminary foot reconnaissance. They hoped the sheer weight of their thundering armor would be enough to drive off any Germans defending the intersection. The 29-year-old American was unimpressed with the plan, but in no position to offer alternatives.

The line of departure was established 400 yards north of town. An artillery barrage arranged for 1500 commenced as scheduled—and the crossroads 800 yards ahead shuddered under the short, violent blitz. Once the bombardment lifted, Lt Gilden finally received specific orders: lead the column on point until his tanks met AT resistance, then withdraw and wait for further instructions. Gilden was incredulous. His orders were lawful and direct, but completely contrary to U.S. Army armor doctrine—which stressed the importance of attacking along defilade approaches with room to maneuver and supporting fire. Gilden's only recourse was to advise the other three tank commanders to move cautiously down the road in a series of bounds. Each road curve represented a bound limit, and passage through every bend would be protected by a supporting tank with a wide field of fire.

The advance guard column left the line of departure at 1600. For the next 600 yards, Gilden's platoon probed judiciously ahead using this bound method. As they approached a final curve, Gilden's #1 tank successfully gained an overwatch position while Sgt Graffagnini's tank #2 nosed slowly around the road bend. The rude searing snarl of an AT round whooshed past the tall, thin sergeant's head. Graffagnini strained to find the source. The gun sat somewhere at the crossroads—but the thick trees and rugged terrain limited his field of vision. A second round slammed into the turret but failed to penetrate—lodging instead into spalled gleaming steel as if frozen in time.[18] The suspended slug was a 75mm round from a PaK 40 towed AT gun.[19] The crew sat stunned momentarily by the concussive clang and then continued scanning ahead for telltale movement. If they could spot the gun, one dispatched HE round of counterfire would kill the crew and abruptly end the threat. Gilden's crew, a short distance away, also searched in desperation. A third round completely missed Graffagnini's tank, and Gilden, realizing they were pressing their luck, radioed the sergeant to withdraw. The AT gun was simply too well hidden.

Next, German artillery exploded all along the column route north of town. Clearly, the advance guard had been under observation the entire time. The barrage was not heavy but irritating enough to halt operations and force the French officers to revisit their options. The sloped terrain did not allow for the tanks to properly disperse, and the road bend only permitted passage of a single vehicle at a time. One knocked-out tank would certainly bottleneck the rest. Out of sheer futility, an M-10 tank destroyer fired three ineffectual rounds of HE down into the valley and in the general direction of the crossroads, after which the advance column was ordered to draw back to Taverna at 1800.[20] Nothing was accomplished, and Graffagnini's crew was lucky to have escaped unharmed. Later that evening, *Groupe Blindé* finally made contact with the Goumiers on the left, and the fierce Moroccans easily overwhelmed the crossroads defenses under cover of darkness—taking thirty prisoners.[21]

Gilden's 1st Platoon was pulled back from Taverna to the B Company assembly area south of town for resupply and rest. Both the 2nd and 3rd Platoons were already there.[22] During the day, only one B Company tanker was wounded and evacuated—20-year-old tank driver T/5 Edward D. Durham, pierced by artillery shell fragments to the thigh.[23]

Gilden met with Redle to review the day's events. Redle was impressed with the new platoon leader's tactical understanding and coolness under fire. Both officers agreed the M4s were too slow and awkward to serve as point vehicles—especially on such restrictive terrain. Any advantage in firepower had been negated. The M-10 TDs were also not positioned properly to support the movement of the medium tanks.[24] Neither American was impressed by French armor coordination with supporting infantry.[25] These were basic concepts drilled in the U.S. Army field manuals. Redle concluded a "difference in system of operating" existed between the two armies and he faced a prickly command challenge bridging those discrepancies. Liaison was already problematic due to the language barrier, and the English-speaking French major of whom Redle saw only occasionally was not enough interaction to smooth out these tactical differences.[26]

The young company commander was also accustomed to working within a battalion structure. This was the first time his company had been "farmed out" exclusively to another unit.[27] All three of his platoons were spread out, complicating proper control of his company.[28] He realized he could not be everywhere at once and would need to rely increasingly upon the skill and judgment of his platoon leaders and platoon sergeants. His meeting with Lt Gilden assured him that the 1st Platoon was in good hands, and Lt Newman was already a proven combat leader guiding the 2nd Platoon. Leadership of the 3rd Platoon however, remained an open question—with Lt Gorman still suffering from nervous trauma due to the tragic events at Castellonorato the prior week.

***

The next morning at 0800, 22 May, Redle dispatched Lt Newman's 2nd Platoon to Taverna for a turn spearheading the advance guard. One tank was out for repairs so Newman proceeded with only four. During the night, the Goumiers had cleared the valley a full mile-and-a-half north to the critical road junction leading west toward

Lenola. Lt Gilden's 1st Platoon formed a roadblock at the intersection, while Newman and the advance guard turned left through the mountain gap toward Lenola.

The attacking force was commanded by French Lt Renail[29] and given the mission of taking the small town. Newman's four M4s assumed the lead, followed by an assortment of scout cars, and four tank destroyers. The small column passed through the three-mile gap without incident.[30] Five-hundred yards shy of the Fondi–Lenola crossroads, the tanks and vehicles halted while a pre-arranged artillery barrage pummeled the small intersection. With the help of some late joining infantry, the intersection was captured, and Lt Newman's tanks turned toward the picturesque hilltop town—lying approximately 1,000 yards to the north, but obscured by trees, walls, and stone farmhouses lining the crooked hillside roadway. The advance was cautious and slow with Newman setting the pace from the lead tank. The 22-year-old platoon leader closed the distance by ordering his driver forward a few dozen yards, and then halted to gauge enemy reaction before moving again. About half-way to town, Newman pulled alongside a roadside home and was shocked to see eight Germans emerge from the interior with their hands high, but with rifles and MG pistols still dangling from their shoulders. Any one of them could have easily shot the unsuspecting lieutenant through the head. As his gunner, Cpl Raymond S. Getz, kept the coaxial MG trained upon the group, Newman hailed Lt Renail by radio. After several anxious minutes, the French lieutenant appeared on foot. He promptly searched the house, found a ninth man, then disarmed the group and marched them toward the rear. Newman glanced down at his watch. The time was 0930.

From this vantage point, he could see most of Lenola still several hundred yards ahead. Many of the tightly packed homes and shops showed heavy bombing damage from an Allied air attack several months earlier.[31] Through a worn binocular set he observed Germans moving everywhere—many strolling casually about the streets as if it were a normal Monday morning. Newman then scanned the high adjacent hills, hoping to see French infantrymen closing in along the slopes, but none were evident. Lt Renail returned, and the two officers discussed options. Newman wanted to wait for more Goumier troops to appear before proceeding. Renail—believing no AT guns were present and only MGs opposed them—preferred attacking the town immediately. Newman convinced the French officer, at least, to first move up the four TDs to an overwatch position. Nine Moroccan scouts from the recon platoon were also called forth to help protect the tanks. Five scouts took up places upon the back deck of Newman's tank, and the remaining four clambered atop Sgt Jarvis's M4 holding the number two spot. After the coarse leather-skinned North Africans settled in and the four French M-10s grumbled to a halt nearby, Renail ordered Newman's platoon forward.

Newman and Jarvis successfully cleared another prominent road bend when an AT gun erupted from somewhere in town. The third tank, commanded by Sgt David Grate,[32] shuddered from a direct hit and began smoking. Newman and Jarvis did not see the source but continued rolling forward—firing confidently in hopes of shattering the unseen AT gun crew's nerves. Newman turned his head briefly and counted five crewmembers tumbling out of Sgt Grate's tank. Everyone, at least, was accounted for.

Newman arrived at a road junction just short of town. Roughly 175 yards ahead, he saw the ominous gray hull of either a German tank or SP gun parked along the narrow road. He immediately ordered his driver to reverse behind the safety of a nearby wall—causing the Moroccan scouts to jump to the ground seeking cover. For several minutes, he and Jarvis fired into town—believing the original German tank, SP or AT gun lurked somewhere among the densely packed buildings. In the meantime, S/Sgt Hamilton Smith, commanding the fourth tank, tried scraping by Grate's burning M4 to render assistance. A German tank hiding in town appeared briefly and fired upon Smith's vulnerable machine—also setting it on fire. Smith and all his crew barely escaped with their lives. Then, the killer panzer—clearly a Mark IV—vanished like a ghost among the alleyways.[33]

After firing six or seven more retributive rounds, Sgt Jarvis's main gun jammed, and the crew was unable to clear the breech. With a cannon now essentially useless, Newman ordered the sergeant to back up as far as the other two burning tanks and abandon the vehicle. As Jarvis reversed, Newman shadowed along several dozen yards to his front, firing and providing cover for both retreating tanks. The Mark IV sniped at them several times but missed. Just as the two slow-moving tanks neared the bottleneck, however, an AP round shattered the right sprocket and pierced the final drive to Newman's tank—peppering bow gunner Pfc Francis Payne with steel fragments to the hand, leg, and both feet.[34] Newman ordered his tank to be abandoned and helped pull the stricken 26-year-old free of his hatch. Newman glanced down at his watch in disbelief. The hands showed only 1000.[35] The last half hour had dragged by like half a day.[36]

French medics attended to Payne;[37] his wounds were not life-threatening, but serious enough to require evacuation. Three crewmembers from Sgt Grate's tank and two of S/Sgt Smith's crew also suffered light wounds but remained on duty.[38] Newman's entire platoon had been neutralized. Two tanks spewed smoke and flame fueled by bursting ammunition as the other two sat helplessly disabled on the roadway ahead. How no one in the crews had been killed was a miracle.

For the remainder of the morning, the four French TDs fired at three German tanks seen prowling about town. One was finally caught in the open and set afire. For a moment, Newman considered returning to his stricken tank to man his platoon's only remaining operational cannon, but the German tank up the road kept firing at them. The harassing shots sailed harmlessly overhead, indicating to Newman that his trapped tank sat safely in a defilade position, but the young lieutenant saw little reason to risk further lives with little chance of gain.[39] The battle for Lenola now belonged to the French.

That afternoon, Goumier troops from Brig Gen Augustin Guillaume's 1st Moroccan Tabor Group (GTM) poured down over the high hills to the east and south.[40] This was the expected rendezvous force Lt Gilden heard the French officers discussing the previous afternoon. Using sheer numbers, the town was enveloped and swarmed against relatively light opposition—yielding over 250 German prisoners. Most came from the 276th Grenadier Regiment. By 1900, Lenola had fallen.[41]

Lt Newman and his crews walked back from Lenola without their knocked-out tanks, passing through Lt Gilden's roadblock before arriving at Taverna, where B Company had moved the bivouac.[42] The unnecessary loss of Lt Newman's entire platoon angered Redle. This was yet another example of French commanders ordering "hey, you guys just go ahead" while they sat back and watched.[43] Because he was a low-ranking officer caught in a Byzantian chain of command, Redle could not fight this battle alone. He needed the intervention of Lt Col Rogers.

At that moment, the rest of the 756th Tank Battalion had successfully assisted French forces of the 3rd Algerian Division in taking the critical junction town of Pico, five miles to the northeast—thus crushing any German hope of holding their "Hitler Line."[44] As a result, the battalion was detached from the 3rd DIA, attached to the 4th DMM and in the process of reuniting with B Company at Taverna.[45] The journey required a slow backtracking march over that same, long congested route leading south from Ausonia through Formia and north through Itri.[46] Through Major Arnold's masterful management and Major Dolvin's advance party efforts, the battalion closed camp several miles north of Itri by 2300 and established a forward CP in Taverna. Captain Lewis's A Company was then positioned on the outskirts of Campodimele by 0300, 23 May.[47]

Redle learned Lt Col Rogers, too, tangled repeatedly with French officers over the proper use of his armor. Many times, he was never even informed of the mission's objective. At least Rogers had the necessary rank to appeal directly to the *groupe* general, which did bear some results—but only after engaging in a "fruitless visit from one officer to another, each referring the inquirer to someone else." On one occasion, Rogers's attempt to see the commanding general "resulted in being referred to a major, who referred me to another major, who referred me back to the general."[48] This lack of tank/infantry coordination, in particular, stunned Rogers, as the French had previously received American-led training in North Africa.[49] "As a result of uncertainty, our troops became dubious and hesitant, even over perfectly proper orders," Rogers recounted.[50] Majors Dolvin and Arnold and Captain Lewis were also unimpressed by their experiences thus far.[51] Not only did the tank officers have to fight a stubborn German enemy, but educate their amiable French allies on the proper use of medium tanks.

That very evening, a far more alarming deficiency emerged involving the French Goumier troops: undisciplined behavior. The American tankers, however, would only learn hints of the sheer wickedness in the days to follow. After Lenola fell, many

Italian civilians hiding in the nearby hills began returning to their homes—believing they had finally seen deliverance. The Goums separated the women from their men and raped them—repeatedly. Any distraught husband, son or father who intervened was either beaten, killed, or sexually violated as well. Fifty women weren't enough to satisfy demand, so the Goums expanded their depraved frenzy to include children and old men.[52] The town was also ransacked and robbed of any item of value. Nearby Campodimele suffered under similar atrocities,[53] but the men of the 756th camped below in Taverna had no inkling of the crimes occurring on the hilltop only a half-mile away.

After only a few days of action, however, the tankers had witnessed enough to feel discomfort over their association with the Goums. One A Company tank crewmember was nearly shot accidentally by four insensible Goumiers chasing after a cat for a meal. The Moroccans weren't hungry—just bored and seeking out a delicacy.[54] Captain Lewis witnessed Goumier troops building fires at night—even though Germans on adjacent hills could see them. During the day, the Goums openly defecated on the very same mountain trails trod by their brethren.[55] These were not the hallmarks of a disciplined army. Even the Goumiers' formidable reputation was called into question. Sgt Roy Anderson, commanding B Company tank #14, asked a French-Canadian officer about a rumor circulating of a Goum killing twenty Germans. The French officer chortled at the suggestion—claiming Goums "couldn't count" and doubted any of his men were capable of such a feat.[56]

Despite such disciplinary deficiencies, the CEF, nevertheless, managed to crack through both the Gustav and Hitler Lines in under two weeks. Not only was the pathway to Rome blown open, but the Allied forces trapped at Anzio could now break free.[57] In fact, the Operation *Buffalo* Anzio breakout was set to commence at daybreak, 23 May. All other Allied forces—from the U.S. II Corps near the coast, to the CEF in the Lepinis and the British Eighth Army in the Liri Valley—were expected to maintain maximum pressure along the front and keep the Germans on their heels.[58]

Under this mandate, the CEF ordered the Mountain Corps to drive hard from Lenola toward Castro dei Volsci to the northwest.[59] A map showed the distance as only seven-and-a-half miles, but the road distance was more than double, and skirted along the lower western slopes of several 1,100-meter-high mountains. Vallecorsa, another hilltop town sure to be crawling with Germans, marked the midway point. This, again, was not tank country.

It was the 3rd Platoon's turn to join the French advance guard of *Groupe Blindé*. They were the only B Company platoon available anyway. Newman's 2nd Platoon no longer had tanks, and Gilden's 1st Platoon had been assigned roadblock duties north of Taverna until noon, at least.[60] In a cool dawn drizzle, the crews greased their tanks, loaded up on extra ammunition, and departed for Lenola at 0800.[61] Lt Gorman believed his nerves had finally settled enough and agreed to lead. Partway through the journey, however, the young lieutenant became so sick to his stomach, he had to climb down from his turret and walk back. S/Sgt Johannesen took charge a second time.[62]

At 1000, Johannesen's five crews set out from Lenola, again, in single column at the fore of the French advance guard column. The terrain gave them no other option. The thin roadway quickly became a rising ribbon of asphalt hewn precariously from forty-five-degree slopes of majestic mountains—lifting the armored force several hundred feet up above the green Vallecorsa valley floor. They traveled four miles without incident until arriving at a blown bridge at a ravine marked "Vi e Cupa" on their maps.[63] With nowhere to go, the column halted as engineers rushed forward to survey the situation. The French crew in the first TD immediately following Johannesen's platoon used the lull to dismount and hunt for souvenirs. As soon as they departed, German artillery began raining down along the head of the column. With no crew at the controls, the Germans easily adjusted fire and set the unattended TD ablaze—thus trapping the other American tanks. Johannesen's crews enjoyed only 400 yards of roadway within which to maneuver and avoid further bracketing—yet they managed to do so all afternoon under Johannesen's calm leadership.[64] As the engineers hauled stone and gravel to fill the blown section of road, Johannesen's crews fired on a few pesky German snipers hidden on the northwestern hillside, just beyond the ravine. After a few exchanges the sniping ended, and Johannesen and Pvt Merle Brooks set out on foot seeking assurance the Germans had fled the area. They returned with four captured *landsers*. Later, the S/A sniping started back up again, but was abruptly silenced under a new flurry of 75mm HE rounds.[65]

That same morning and afternoon, Lt Col Rogers was overwhelmed with all sorts of activities—from moving C, D, and Service Companies up from Itri and establishing a new constellation of CPs near Lenola, to coordinating a multitude of plans with the French.[66] Nevertheless, the unflappable battalion commander kept close tabs on Johannesen's predicament. Originally, Rogers wanted to dispatch some C Company tanks forward to allow Johannesen and all of B Company a few days to rest and reorganize. The tight terrain and the knocked-out TD, however, would not allow such a transfer. At 1800, Rogers ordered the Assault Gun Platoon to move to Lenola and provide fire support to Johannesen, just in case the busy staff sergeant needed the extra help.[67]

At 2130, with dusk descending, the engineers successfully bypassed the blown bridge at Vi e Cupa and Johannesen's crews proceeded forward—finding the most promising defilade positions along the road and settling in for the evening.[68] A short time later, Lt Redle arrived on foot to check on them. The crews were dog-tired, and fuel was running low.[69] Redle arranged for supplies to be brought in on foot throughout the night. Relief, however, would have to wait until tomorrow.

At the same time, B Company's new CP opened on the outskirts of Lenola and the maintenance section went to work retrieving Newman's tanks.[70] Three were retrieved but tank #9 was completely burned and unsalvageable.[71] Lt Gilden's 1st Platoon rejoined the company in Lenola after performing roadblock duties for nearly thirty-six hours straight. Gilden's crews were dog-tired as well.

The next morning, 24 May, Johannesen's tanks resumed the attack, nosing around a narrow mountain road bend to finally observe Vallecorsa lying two miles due north. Johannesen and a second tank ventured forth a full mile down the road—protecting French engineers as they patched more blown sections of asphalt.[72] The French infantry began closing in upon Vallecorsa from the valley and nearby hills, and Johannesen's crews lent fire support when requested.[73] The Germans responded with heavy stretches of artillery fire. Johannesen had to, again, keep moving to avoid bracketing. Because of flying shrapnel, the engineers gave up repair work until nightfall. Nevertheless, Johannesen stayed to protect the team and did not withdraw his platoon until after 2130. By then, C Company tanks had arrived in relief.[74] When Johannesen's crews finally rejoined B Company outside of Lenola a short time later; they were utterly exhausted from fighting nearly thirty-six hours straight without sleep.

***

B Company spent the next day, 25 May, resting and performing first echelon (front line) maintenance of their tanks while the rest of the battalion carried the fight to the outskirts of Vallecorsa under *Groupe Bondis*.[75] The B Company bivouac was located in empty fields about a half-mile south of Lenola, tucked along the northwest footing of a small hill also dubbed "San Martino."[76] The officers had just received their monthly U.S. Army liquor allotment and Lt Redle and Lt Bob Engfer could finally sit down and converse face-to-face without the stresses of combat or rushed movement orders. Engfer was doing an excellent job as company XO. Keeping the tanks supplied and operational was a round-the-clock responsibility few could manage well. Redle also enjoyed Engfer's company. Like Dave, the lanky Minnesotan possessed an unassuming, down-to-earth personality.[77] In no time, Engfer was singing the popular Armed Forces radio song "Mairzy Doats and Dozy Doats,"[78] while the rest of the company decided the time had come for both officers to take a bath. A few days earlier, the Goums had dragged a bathtub out of a nearby farmhouse and into the open field. Water was warmed and poured into the abandoned tub. Each officer was instructed to "wash up." Redle went first and left the dirty water for Engfer—who followed up signing and laughing. It was a light-hearted break for everyone away from the madness of war, which was never very far away.[79]

In fact, some of the horrors endured by the civilians of Lenola became more evident. A local farmer told of how his modest home had been spared harm from the Germans and Allied shells—only to be ransacked by marauding Moroccans.[80] Redle witnessed a local Italian man complaining to a French captain of a Goum raping his daughter. The captain asked the civilian to identify the rapist. Once he did, the officer promptly pulled out his pistol and shot the accused soldier dead.[81] Other French officers were less concerned—even blasé or dismissive of the unconscionable behavior of their own troops. Captain Lewis learned that some French officers actually enticed their colonial troops into action by promising them all the wine, goats, and women they could find in the area. Another English-speaking French captain explained to him, rather unconvincingly: "You [Americans] have good rations, a post exchange, beer, chocolate, cigarettes, good coffee, and R & R. Look at my troops. We have nothing. We live mostly off the land." Lewis had seen the pyramidal tent brothels set up earlier in the French battalion assembly areas. Moroccan women were trucked in and put between blanket partitions eight cots to a tent while the Goumiers lined up outside, patiently waiting turns with the prostitutes inside.[82] The French officer was not being honest with himself and had shirked his responsibilities as a leader. He treated his troops like animals and consequently they behaved that way. These were still men, perfectly capable of controlling themselves.

While the tankers regrouped south of Lenola, the French major serving as B Company's liaison invited Lt Redle to his CP for lunch. Redle agreed, believing the affair might last only a half hour. While enroute, the Germans opened up with a short, but intense, artillery barrage targeting a road intersection ahead. Redle dismounted from the jeep and instructed driver Pvt Palumbo, to return to Lenola. The barrage lifted, and Redle walked up to the intersection and discovered three French scout cars and one half-track destroyed. All occupants were dead. He left the road to walk cross-country toward the major's CP and turned to witness the German artillery pound the intersection a second time. One extremely brave French motorcyclist slalomed around the blasts—somehow threading through without losing his life. Redle and the motorcyclist reached the CP at the same time. The American lieutenant watched in wonder as the driver dismounted with a large piece of shrapnel lodged in the back of his head. He saluted a French colonel, handed him a message, and waited for the colonel to sign his reply. He then took the message, saluted again, remounted the motorcycle, and drove back through the continuing barrage.[83]

The French CP was situated inside a stone country house surrounded by mature shade trees. Four or five tables had been arranged outdoors complete with white tablecloths, full settings of china, and fine flatware. Redle was seated among the French officers as 6'4" tall Senegalese troops dressed in pristine white jackets and red fez caps served them various courses. This picnic-like atmosphere amidst the surrounding blare of war seemed even more absurd to Redle than the stoic motorcyclist's conduct. The lunch, of course, was delicious and the conversation polite, lively, and light. Still, Redle couldn't get over a gnawing sense of guilt for attending such frivolity when much serious work needed to be done. One French officer perceiving Redle's restlessness remarked: "We expect to make about ten miles today. If it were Americans, you would make thirty miles."[84] His comment reminded Redle of another conversation he had two weeks earlier with a French artillery major stationed near the Gustav Line. That Frenchman had remarked: "The French live the war, the British live the war and the Germans live the war, but you Americans *fight* the war."[85] After two hours, the gala luncheon finally concluded and Redle walked back to his CP outside of Lenola—appreciative of the French hospitality but further behind in his more pressing duties as a fighting U.S. Army tank company commander.[86]

***

The Allied news for 25 May around Italy was all positive. After two days of battle, the 90,000 troops of the U.S. VI Corps crammed at Anzio had finally broken free. The First Special Service Forces cut Highway 7 below Cisterna as the U.S. 1st Armored Division punched through further north—devastating the German 362nd Infantry Division in the process. As a result, the U.S. 3rd Infantry Division rushed in to seize Cisterna itself.[87] That same day, elements of the 85th Infantry Division linked up with Anzio forces near Borgo Grappa—unifying both forces for the first time.[88] The Germans, fearing Allied momentum would ultimately split their defenses, were forced into a full-scale withdrawal from southern Italy.[89] Originally, the main objective of Maj Gen Lucian K. Truscott Jr.'s VI Corps was the capture of Highway 6 at Valmontone—potentially trapping the German Tenth Army.[90] This rapid shift in Allied fortunes, however, caused Lt Gen Mark Clark to recalibrate his plans. A tantalizing opportunity opened for his Fifth Army to be the first Allied troops to march triumphantly into Rome and proved too tempting to pass up, so Clark instead ordered his divisions to concentrate on the Alban Hills and drive upon the Eternal City. This modification was controversial. Although Clark had been given broad leeway by General Alexander to "exploit" battlefield conditions, the decision tested the limits of that mandate. Truscott and many of Clark's divisional commanders were also not pleased with this decision—believing the opportunity of crushing the German Tenth Army was the bigger prize. Clark countered that the destruction of the German Tenth Army was no sure thing, but the capture of Rome was. Clark also harbored secret knowledge he could not share with his subordinates: the imminent landings at Normandy. Italy would soon become a backwater campaign, and the American general was determined to see the men of the U.S. Fifth Army receive the public recognition they deserved.[91]

These decisions by both Allied and German high commands had an almost immediate effect on the mountain fighting in the CEF sector. During the evening of 24 May, the French Goumiers tried storming Vallecorsa but were viscously thrown back several times.[92] By the morning of 25 May, however, the Germans had not only conceded the town—but much of the valley north.[93] The roads, however, were too damaged and terrain too unforgiving for the passage of 32-ton medium tanks.

During the afternoon, Lt Col Rogers dispatched his lighter 15-ton D Company M5 tanks north of town on reconnaissance. By 1500, one platoon ventured to within two miles of Castro dei Volsci—halted only by blown bridges. By then, French engineers had repaired the main road leading up through Vallecorsa well enough for Rogers to send his C Company mediums in support.[94]

By evening, 25 May, Redle's B Company was ready to resume its place in the battalion's combat rotation. Lt Newman's 2nd Platoon had been fully restored to five operational tanks.[95] Lt Gorman was relieved of his place in B Company and sent back to Personnel Center #6 with an uncertain future.[96] His combat nerves had been completely shot. 2nd Lt Harris, out with a broken hand, was transferred to the 103rd Station Hospital and not expected to return for another month.[97] To fill the 3rd Platoon leader vacancy, 2nd Lt Andrew D. Orient transferred in.[98] The 32-year-old Pennsylvanian had served previously in HQ and A Companies of the 756th, but this was his first assignment in B Company.[99] No sooner did Orient arrive when he, Lt Gilden, S/Sgts Johannesen and Oliver, and Sgt Jarvis were dispatched on a foot reconnaissance to review C Company positions two miles north of Vallacorsa.[100]

The adjacent valley to the west, harboring the town of Amaseno, was the French Mountain Corps' next objective.[101] Blown bridges and damaged roads, however, slowed vehicular advance.[102] German tactics had shifted away from hard defensive stands to softer delaying actions. At noon, 26 May, 2nd Lt Hugo E. Staake, commanding the 1st Platoon of D Company, 756th Tank Battalion, led his light tanks all the way in to Amaseno and reported the route clear. French TDs and a recon platoon were supposed to accompany him but failed to appear. Lt Staake proceeded without them. A column of C and D Company tanks, led by Major Dolvin, joined Staake in town after dark.[103]

Contact with the enemy was finally made on the road north of Amaseno, and a dawn attack, 27 May, was planned with French forces supported by C and D Company tanks. The terrain, however, prevented the effective use of armor. Nevertheless, the French infantry easily prevailed over scant resistance. Attack plans to take the towns of Prossedi and Villa San Stefano immediately followed.[104] B Company moved to Vallecorsa by mid-afternoon as battalion reserve.[105] In the late afternoon, the attack commenced. By 1800, C Company was in Prossedi, but the advance upon Villa San Stefano was halted due to another blown bridge and heavy concentrations of German artillery fire.

After nightfall, Lt Col Rogers requested permission from the French to swap out C Company tanks with A Company tanks. The French officer in charge of 4th DMM armor, Major Dodelier, agreed to the plan but told Rogers such relief was unnecessary as no plans existed for the use of armor the following day. Nevertheless, Rogers made the swap—while the rest of the battalion moved up into a dusty Amaseno.[106] The next morning at 0830, 28 May, Lt Col Rogers and Major Arnold walked into the *Groupe Louchet* HQ to find a French staff agitated because "the tanks had not attacked at dawn." Flabbergasted, the two American officers, along with Captain French Lewis of A Company, scrambled to correct the misunderstanding. The French wanted tanks supporting a drive from Prossedi north to Giuliano Di Roma. Lewis promptly called upon one of his platoons to join the mission in progress.[107]

That same afternoon, B Company moved to Amaseno and Gilden's 1st Platoon was assigned roadblock duties along the Amaseno–Vallecorsa road.[108] Newman's 2nd Platoon engaged in a fire support mission on a road junction to the north connecting Prossedi with San Steffano. The French infantry, however, failed to take their objectives and withdrew.[109]

By early evening, 28 May, the Germans in the area were clearly retreating northwest toward Highway 6 and French forces struggled to maintain an aggressive pursuit. Troops could not be moved fast enough. The roads, already poor, were clogged by troops and idling vehicles creeping at a snail's pace. Confusion set in with commanders on the proper location of the MLR, which in turn, caused objectives to shift around by the hour. Word of those changes filtered down to the men fighting in the field. A Company had taken a bridge and road junction north of Prossedi earlier in the afternoon.[110] To gauge German reaction in the nearby town of Giuliano, Lt Hammer led his platoon into the hilltop village and radioed back that the streets were clear. Around the same time, Lt Col Rogers was ordered to commit a tank company to *Groupe Guillaume*, so he dispatched his Battalion S-2, Captain Robert Rydman to *Groupe Guillaume* HQ for guidance on holding Giulano. The baffled French claimed they had no orders to hold the town, so Hammer's platoon was withdrawn. With evening approaching, Rogers inquired with *Groupe Guillaume* about properly supporting A Company holding the road junction north of town. Infantry and AT guns needed to be moved in before nightfall. After some back-and-forth messaging, the French finally told Rogers to withdraw A Company at 1515, which Rogers promptly did. Forty-five minutes later, the French ordered Rogers to retake the junction—but by then German infantrymen had retaken the position and Captain Lewis's tanks had to drive them out again. Worse, enemy tanks were now reportedly seen operating on the back of a hill just to their north. At 1930, the French reversed their plans and ordered A Company to withdraw again—this time for good.[111]

A Company was next ordered to prepare for a move to Carpineto Romano—some fifteen miles to the northwest through mountainous country.[112] Just after midnight, 29 May, B Company was ordered to assume A Company's missions at Prossedi and Villa San Stefano under *Groupe Louchet*. Redle tried complying promptly, but because of congested traffic, couldn't depart Amaseno and cover the five miles of required distance until 0730.[113] Lt Orient's 3rd Platoon was directed into roadblock positions south of Villa San Stefano.[114] The company HQ and maintenance section halted in Prossedi while the 1st and 2nd Platoons moved another mile north—with the mission of retaking the same bridge roadblock position vacated by A Company the prior night.[115]

Lt Gilden's platoon led the mission, supported by French infantry, TDs, and artillery.[116] This time, the French regimental commander in charge—a Colonel Maullet—demonstrated a firm grasp of tank/infantry coordination.[117] He called together Redle, Gilden, the French TD platoon leader, and his infantry leaders ahead of time. A simple and clear plan was sketched out whereby the TDs would cover the movement of the tanks and a company of infantry. An artillery barrage on the objective would precede the attack. Time was set for 0900. Following the conference, the officers made a foot reconnaissance to better understand the terrain and discuss the particulars before returning to the line of departure. As expected, a twenty-minute artillery barrage commenced at 0840. As soon as the last shells exploded, Gilden's five tanks rolled forward across flat ground paralleling the road as Moroccan infantry fanned out and trotted alongside. Gilden's gunners laid down suppressive fire and the infantry easily overwhelmed the position. Two companies of German infantry fled out of fear—abandoning a perfectly intact 7.5cm PAK 41 towed AT gun. Two German Mark IV tanks supposedly bolted as well. At no time were the American tanks and French infantry out of contact with each other, and the operation unfolded as a textbook example of tank/infantry coordination—this, despite the language barrier.[118] The attack succeeded because of attentive leadership, basic planning, and a little observation beforehand.

Lt Newman's 2nd Platoon, too, enjoyed a rather fruitful day. Eight-hundred yards north of Giuliano sat a hilltop cemetery and large church. French infantry closing in upon the position became stymied by several German MGs hidden among the crypts and along the church walls. Newman's crews operating from high ground along the road north of Prossedi, provided fire support. The lowland between Prossedi and Giuliano, had been carved through by nature with numerous creeks, ravines, and gullies, and thus completely impassable, so Newman's crews were restricted to a firing distance ranging between 2,500 and 3,000 yards. To make the most of their ammunition, Newman ordered each crew to fire only twenty-five to thirty rounds total—devoting half to either the cemetery or the church. Only one tank fired at a time, after which Newman studied the destructive results of each shot through his binoculars and ordered an adjustment. Using this method, the German MGs were permanently silenced. A Mark IV tank appeared near the cemetery just before dark. Newman had one of his tanks fire three rounds of AP on it, but at such a great distance the spent slugs failed to penetrate—and only bounced harmlessly off the hull. The crew switched to HE and scored several more direct hits but failed to set fire to the skulking gray tank. Surprisingly the German crew didn't return fire, choosing only to wiggle back and forth on occasion—the way a restless bull might shake off horseflies. After firing twenty rounds, Newman's crew gave up the effort as futile.[119]

After resupplying in Prossedi, Newman's platoon returned to the same positions the next morning, 30 May, to lend fire support. The infantry, however, had advanced beyond a crossroads northwest of Giuliano with the tactical situation well under control. As a result, Newman's crews weren't called upon to fire a single shot throughout the day.[120]

In the meantime, Lt Orient's 3rd Platoon moved out from roadblock positions south of Villa San Stefano to attack Giuliano from the southeast with French Moroccan infantry of the 2nd Battalion, 6th Infantry Regiment.[121] The tanks were delayed somewhat by a roadblock fashioned from felled trees by German engineers. One tank threw a track while circumventing a demolished section of roadway. Orient's remaining four tanks were given the overall objective of taking the cemetery and church 800 yards north of town—the same positions Newman's crews fired upon the day before. When they arrived, however, they discovered the Goum troops had already overwhelmed the position. The German Mark IV tank still sat there—abandoned.[122] Apparently, Newman's long-distance targeting had done more damage than he realized.

The day turned oppressively hot. In the mid-afternoon, Lt Redle drove out to survey Gilden's road block positions a mile north of Prossedi. After visiting each crew and complimenting them for their fine attack the previous morning, Redle departed.[123] Soon after, a French naval officer touring the front stopped by with his driver to chat to the crews.[124] Lulled by a long period of inaction and seeking respite from their sweltering tank interior, Sgt Harold M. Behymer and his crew dismounted to greet the French officer. At that very moment, the Germans struck the position with a flurry of artillery shells.[125] Behymer collapsed with the first burst, splayed open in the back. Fellow crewman Pvt Cletus J. Offerman, standing by him, was blown to the ground, bleeding from the left hand, and splattered with his sergeant's blood and visceral fat.[126] Behymer appeared dead, but the French officer—sprawled and bleeding nearby—groaned with life. Offerman grabbed ahold of the Frenchman, pulled him under the tank as the bursts fell heavier, then gave him a shot of morphine to ease his agony. Once the short, violent attack lifted, Offerman climbed into the tank and radioed for medical help.[127] T/4 Frank C. Manak and T/5 Leak H. Smitherman also lay wounded from the barrage. The 31-year-old Manak had been hit in the jaw and was taken to the 93rd Evacuation Hospital.[128] Smitherman, a 21-year-old North Carolinian, had been hit multiple places in the abdomen. He was evacuated promptly to a French field hospital nearby.[129] Offerman's hand was bandaged, and he remained on duty.[130]

Shockingly, Behymer's disfigured 6'2" 192-pound frame still registered a weak pulse, so the 24-year-old sergeant was rushed away by ambulance along with prayers for a miracle. Sadly, the blue-eyed Akron, Ohio, native passed away before arriving at the 403rd Clearing Station.[131] Behymer was one of Redle's most dependable sergeants. He had been the gunner in the tank trailing Redle the night they tried rescuing Lt Granberry's platoon in Cassino.[132] He was always an enthusiastic soldier and quite proud of the praise he had received from Redle only moments prior to his death.[133] Unfortunately, Behymer's crew let down their guard by leaving the tank and congregating nearby. Almost certainly, the Germans had them under observation and took advantage of the moment. The only shred of value Redle could draw from the tragedy was to remind his crews to remain inside their tanks while manning roadblocks and to always expect the unexpected.[134]

By 1830, all B Company tanks assembled near the CP at a crossroads south of Prossedi.[135] Redle learned Sgt David L. Grate had also been wounded during the day with another nasty shrapnel gash to the cheek. A medic had bandaged the 23-year-old's face so the stubborn young tank commander could remain on duty.[136] This was Grate's fifth wound in only ten days. Earlier, he had been singed with second degree burns while escaping a flaming tank and peppered with shrapnel to the thigh, among other battle injuries—yet he remained steadfast. Redle made absolutely certain the northeastern Ohioan received a Purple Heart.[137]

Other elements of the 756th Tank Battalion had also assembled nearby.[138] Only A Company and a platoon of D Company light tanks was missing—all still engaged in combat further west in the mountains around Carpineto.[139] The campaign to take the Lepinis was drawing to a close, and an air of expectation swirled around camp over the battalion's next assignment.

Morning and afternoon, 31 May, were spent on first echelon maintenance. The kitchen rejoined B Company and the crews received a decent breakfast and lunch.[140] At 1600, Lt Col Rogers pulled into camp and told Lt Redle to climb aboard his jeep.[141] While en route to the French HQ, Rogers explained A Company was about to attack near Carpineto but orders had come through that might change everything. Upon arrival, both officers learned the 756th Tank Battalion had been detached from the CEF and attached to the U.S. II Corps effective immediately.[142] The new assignment required relocation to Cisterna—some twenty-five miles to the southwest. All units not engaged in combat were required to move by 2100 hours that evening.[143] Major Arnold departed with a billeting party at 1800. Part of the advance detail included B Company's 1st Sgt Alvin Nusz. Rogers informed Captain Lewis to proceed with attack plans and expect relief from the 755th Tank Battalion sometime that evening.[144]

Rogers tried arranging for a tank transport, but discovered the trucking outfit could not reach them on account of inadequate bridges in the area.[145] At 1945 the march commenced with B Company leading, followed by C and D Companies and the Assault Gun Platoon. A half hour into the journey, the route was changed on account of snarled traffic along the Cisterna–Cori road. Mortar Platoon crews, acting as guides, were quickly dispatched to direct the column to take an alternate route leading to Norma. All vehicles made the turn off Highway 7. The assembly area was located in flat fields roughly a half-mile east of Highway 7 along the Norma road. The crews were thankful just to be out of the twisting mountains and traveling across flat ground again. B Company arrived at 2200, with the last vehicles of the battalion closing by 2330.[146] The twenty-five-mile journey had been covered in just over two hours.[147] A Company reported delays because the Germans had temporarily blocked their exit from Carpineto, but expected to move the following morning.[148]

Rogers contacted the G-3, II Corps, and learned the 756th would likely be attached to the 1st Armored Division's "Task Force Howze" the following day.[149] Fighting with the French had been a strange adventure. Everyone looked forward to working with Americans again.

French Expeditionary Forces

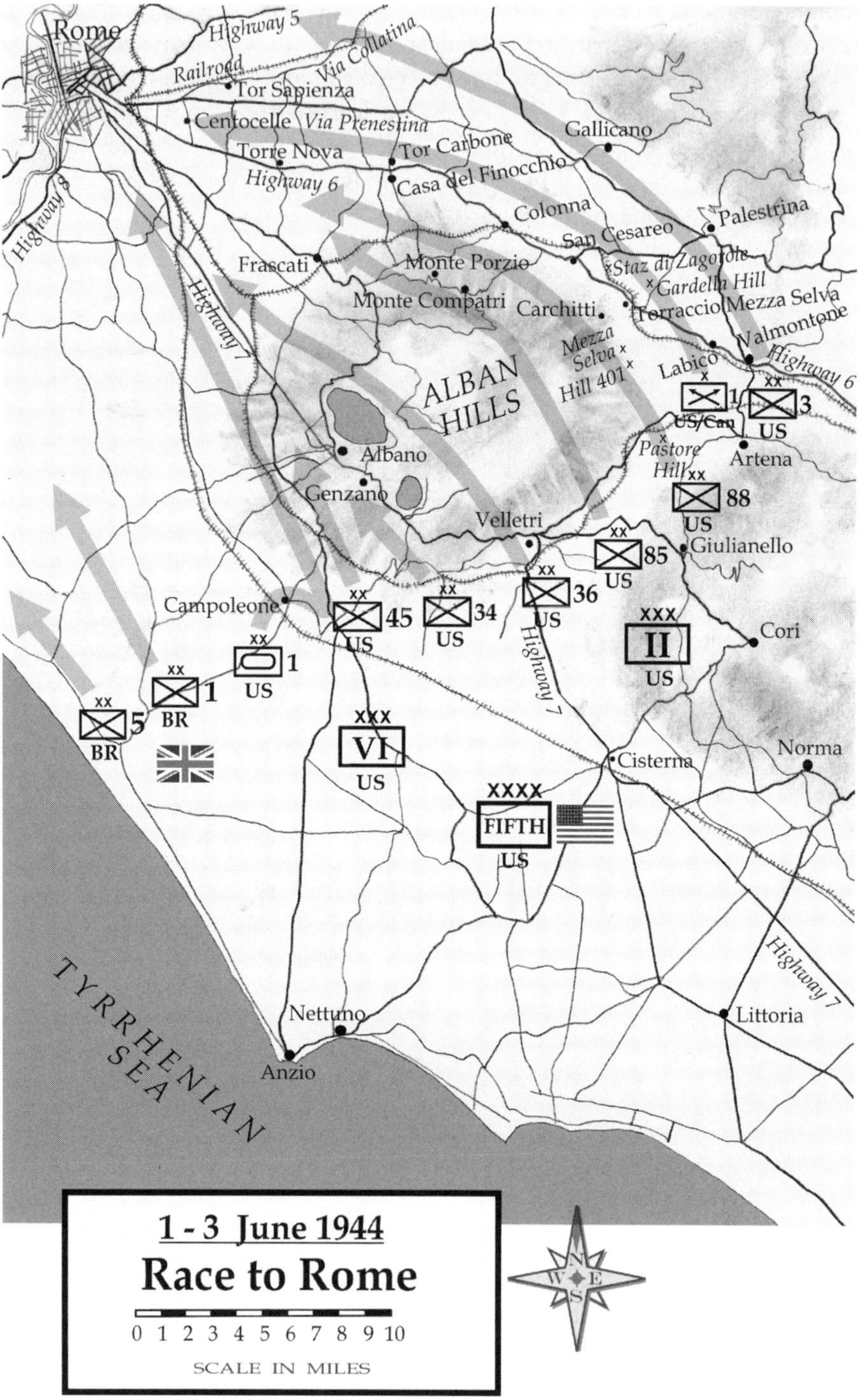

1 - 3 June 1944

Race to Rome

0 1 2 3 4 5 6 7 8 9 10

SCALE IN MILES

CHAPTER FIFTEEN

Race to Rome: 1 June 1944 to 3 June 1944

U.S. ¼-ton 4x4 "jeep" truck

In AD 536, a Byzantine army under the command of Flavius Belisarius marched up the boot of Italy to reconquer Rome from the Ostrogoths. The king fled and the city succumbed unopposed.[1] In the 1400 years since, no other power had conquered Rome from the south. Now, the Eternal City lay only twenty miles to the northwest of Lt Gen Mark Clark's rapidly advancing Fifth Army. History beckoned and victory seemed inevitable.

A massive cresting tidal wave of Allied men, weapons, and vehicles closed in upon Rome along a thirty-mile front. The U.S. VI Corps held the left flank—with the British 5th and 1st Infantry Divisions driving along the coast, and the U.S. 1st Armored, and 45th, 34th, and 36th Infantry Divisions pressing upon the Alban Hills. The U.S. II Corps shifted from the coastline to the right flank—through a fertile farming gap between the Albans and Lepinis toward critical Highway 6. The 85th Infantry Division held the left, the 88th took the middle while the newly added 3rd Infantry Division drove north upon Valmontone. Tanks on loan from the 1st Armored Division organized under Task Force Howze were added to the II Corps to provide armor punch and jacks-of-all-trades First Special Service Force troops helped augment Maj Gen Keyes's offensive options. By 1 June, Clark saw his quickest avenue into Rome lay with Keyes's divisions skirting north of the Albans along Highway 6.[2]

Before Keyes's men could swing west into this corridor, however, Valmontone had to fall. This crossroads town and the adjacent high ground overlooking Highway 6 was the original objective of Operation *Buffalo*—and still crucial to Allied designs for crushing the German Tenth Army. Maj Gen John "Iron Mike" O'Daniel's 3rd Infantry Division was given the honor. Juin's CEF, still mopping up in the Lepinis, was ordered to cut Highway 6 near Colleferro and then move northwest to Palestrina, providing right flank cover to II Corps operations. The British Eighth Army, facing tough German resistance, still lagged in the Liri Valley.[3]

As this grand stage was set for a final drive into Rome, American colonels and generals regressed to their days of cut-throat "intermurder" gridiron games while cadets at West Point. Competition turned fierce among them over who would ultimately claim that "first in Rome" grand prize—and the 756th Tank Battalion became the football.

At 0930, 1 June, the 756th was formally attached to Task Force Howze, operating with O'Daniel's 3rd Infantry Division.[4] This ad hoc armored force was commanded by Colonel Hamilton H. Howze—a colleague of Lt Col Rogers dating back to their USMA days. "Ham" Howze graduated in 1930, one year ahead of Rogers.[5] Both were cavalry men.[6] Rogers promptly established liaison with the 3rd Division HQ in anticipation of working with his old friend.[7] A Company, however, was still delayed in the Lepinis at Carpineto, and had yet to rejoin the battalion—complicating those plans. Then, as Howze's tankers and the 3rd Division became deeply drawn into combat operations along the Artena–Valmontone road,[8] the attachment was shunted temporarily to the side.

In the meantime, the men of the 756th prepared for combat and acclimated to their new surroundings.[9] The devastation in and around Cisterna was total. Four months of non-stop fighting had completely leveled the town. The dead still lay where they had fallen, attracting swarms of flies. Destroyed vehicles and ordnance of every type littered the bomb-cratered landscape. Several knocked out Tiger tanks sitting silently in the distance attracted the interest of the tankers—who could not resist the impulse to walk over and inspect the monstrous machines more closely.[10]

At 1515, Rogers received a message from the II Corps HQ reporting a change in plans. The 88th Infantry Division had now claimed the 756th away from Howze. Rogers reported immediately to the 88th Division HQ and was told to move the battalion to a new assembly area north of Giulinello around midnight and to "be prepared to enter combat on short notice."[11] Fortunately, Captain Lewis's A Company had finally left Carpineto and was expected to rejoin the battalion within the next few hours. By 1900, Lewis's tankers rolled into camp and the battalion was whole again.[12]

During the afternoon, B Company received a new officer from Personnel Center #6: 1st Lt Robert L. Gilman.[13] The 24-year-old New Hampshire native arrived as a spare platoon leader. Redle had offered Johannesen a battlefield commission, but the tall, blond staff sergeant politely declined.[14]

Sad news circulated around camp over the death of T/5 Leak Smitherman. The 22-year-old member of Sgt Behymer's crew survived two days in a French hospital near Amaseno before succumbing to his abdominal wounds. Numerous blood transfusions weren't enough to save the young unmarried North Carolinian.[15] Smitherman had served in the Army for nearly a year and a half.[16]

After nightfall, Redle took his three platoon leaders on a reconnaissance trip to nearby Cori—roughly seven miles to the north. They found the battle-scarred mountain town abandoned, save for a few American troops. Nighttime flak bursting along the coast was a common occurrence, and the four officers had grown accustomed to the intermittent flashing and rumbling the way a city dweller ignores the din of a bustling street.[17] The growing whine of approaching airplane engines, however, sent the group scrambling for cover. Two German ME-109s screamed through, dropping a slew of butterfly bombs.[18] Fortunately, no one was killed or injured.[19]

At 2300, the 88th Division G-3 ordered Rogers to move to the new assembly area and prepare for action.[20] Under a waxing gibbous moon, the battalion set out within the hour from their temporary camp three miles southeast of Cisterna, and dispersed among wheat fields two miles north of Giulianello around 0300, 2 June.[21] Along the way, a solitary German plane strafed the jeep carrying T/5 Guild, Sgt Pompey, and S/Sgt Johannesen—fortunately missing both vehicle and occupants.[22]

At 0330, Maj Gen John E. Sloan, commanding the 88th, ordered Rogers to immediately contact the 351st Infantry Regiment and support their attack at daylight.[23] Rogers sent a liaison officer, but the regiment's CP had since moved to an unknown location. By 0415 the 351st's new CP location was discovered and Rogers took a team of officers and platoon sergeants—one from each company—along with him for further instructions. Lt Orient and S/Sgt Oliver represented B Company.[24] The team arrived at 0500 and discovered one infantry battalion already attacking Mezza Selva Hill—roughly a half-mile southeast of Carchitti and two miles south of Highway 6. Regimental commander, Colonel Arthur S. Champeny, wanted tanks moved up quickly in support of the attack, but didn't know the exact location of his men. Rogers dispatched a liaison officer to find them and report back by 0630.[25]

At that same hour, the "Rock of the Marne" 3rd Division cut Highway 6 at Valmontone allowing the Marnemen to storm the town.[26] A German pullback during the night had created a sector-wide vacuum the U.S. II Corps scrambled to fill.[27] The general orders hadn't changed: the 3rd Division's responsibility was to secure Valmontone and push five miles north to Palestrina. The 88th, striking from the Corps' middle was to cut Highway 6 near San Cesareo, then turn west toward Rome. The 85th protected the Corps' Albano flank on the left.[28] What remained fluid and confusing, however, were combat operations at the regimental level and below. Orders simply could not keep up with events on the battlefield—especially in the morning.[29]

Champeny's 351st had just relieved 338th Infantry Regiment (85th Division) positions roughly two-and-three-quarter miles due west of Artena at 0200 that very morning. After a hasty reconnaissance, the 3rd Battalion, 351st, began attacking northwest from Pastore Hill at 0400, with the 2nd Battalion echeloned slightly to the rear on the left.[30] Champeny's men expected difficult resistance as they were being thrown against enemy positions defended by tough, highly motivated members of the Hermann Goering Division. Surprisingly, the attack began well. German MGs and snipers were quickly silenced by a combination of solid artillery support and good infantry work. Confusion set in, though, when the 3rd Battalion Commander, Major Charles P. Furr, was told Hill 401—situated roughly a mile northwest of Pastore Hill—had been cleared and occupied. Furr, his S-3, and operations sergeant moved up to the position and encountered fifteen Germans instead. A brief firefight ensued. The Germans were driven off, but Furr's S-3 and operations sergeant were both left wounded in the encounter.[31] This was not an environment to send in tanks without a clear idea of where they were going.

By 0700, Lt Col Rogers gained a clear enough grasp of infantry positions to order the battalion to move four miles northwest to Mezza Selva. B Company led, followed by the assault guns, then C, A, and D Companies.[32] Because of time constraints, many platoon leaders were not properly briefed and had no idea of where they were heading.[33] After marching approximately 500 yards north up the narrow asphalt road, the column was supposed to turn northwest and roll cross-country to Pastore Hill. Orient's 3rd Platoon, leading the column, and Gilden's 1st Platoon, immediately following, made the proper turn. Newman's 2nd Platoon, however, missed it and continued moving northeast toward Artena. The low morning sun and dusty conditions contributed to his confusion.[34] Newman wasn't the only officer making the mistake. All of Captain Gourley's C Company also missed the turn.[35] The lost tankers realized their error only after drawing AT fire and seeing no supporting American infantry whatsoever. A few quick radio calls to battalion HQ clarified the situation, the tankers backtracked to safety but spent the rest of the morning seeking out their comrades.[36]

Redle's orders were to contact the 351st Infantry and "give them whatever support we could." He was only provided a general idea of where to find them.[37] With C Company temporarily lost, Captain Lewis's A Company orders were amended to keep contact with Redle and support his crews wherever necessary.[38] After advancing perhaps a mile beyond Pastore Hill without finding the infantry, Redle halted the column for fear of ambush. He called forward Lt Gilden and the two set off on foot through rolling country in search of the front lines. After probing ahead cautiously for forty-five minutes and covering some 400 yards, they finally located a 351st CP operating in some caves located in a shady coppice. Redle offered the service of his tanks to the officer in charge, and the two quickly agreed upon a method of attack. The infantry would ride on the back decks from one hilltop objective to the next, then dismount to storm the crest while the tanks maneuvered in leaps and bounds dispatching supporting fire.[39] Newman's tanks joined the operation just as it commenced.[40]

This simple approach proved successful throughout the morning and early afternoon. The terrain allowed for textbook tank operation: open and rolling with fields, thickets, and farmhouses offering plenty of defilade options with ample room for maneuver. This was also one of the rare times B Company moved and fired as a complete unit according to their training. Two platoons set up a fire base, while one tank platoon and supporting infantry stormed an objective a few hundred yards away. As soon as one hilltop was taken, the tanks sped on to the next—and platoons took turns "leap-frogging" in the attack role.[41]

German counterfire evaporated with the approach of the American M4s.[42] Many *feldgrau* uniforms fled. Others remained silent and tried concealing themselves in dugouts and holes. If they chose not to surrender, the infantry soon coaxed them out with hand grenades.[43] All manner of abandoned German equipment was also captured.[44]

By 1100, Redle's tanks overwhelmed Mezza Selva Hill.[45] The supporting infantry identified several homes in a nearby hamlet as targets. Firing had just commenced when, in the doorway of one stone house, appeared an American waving a white flag. The guns halted as infantrymen stepped forward to investigate. Out of the house appeared two more Americans and nine German soldiers holding their hands high. The three Americans, captured earlier, were thankful to be repatriated. After flanking these houses, the tanks drew AT fire from two directions, so Redle ordered his tanks to take temporary cover in a wooded area ahead.[46]

The capture of Mezza Selva allowed Colonel Champeny to move his 2nd Battalion to the left of his 3rd Battalion. Up to this point, the high ground to the southwest—foothills of the Albans falling inside the 85th Division's sector—restricted his regiment to employing only one attacking battalion. Now, the 351st's zone of operation widened and force could be multiplied. Captain Lewis's A Company tanks could also be employed more effectively. The 3rd Battalion cleared the town of Carchitti and the 2nd Battalion continued pushing north-northwest toward San Cesareo.[47]

With the fall of Carchitti, the 3rd Battalion and Redle's tanks swung north toward Highway 6.[48] Using the same tank/infantry fire and maneuver methods, one-and-a-half miles of ground was quickly captured, and by 1630 the critical highway was cut near Torraccio Mezza Selva.[49] Resistance proved shockingly light.[50] The roadway was explored and Lt Col Rogers ordered Redle to establish a roadblock in a wooded area approximately 1,000 yards to the west.[51] Lt Orient's 3rd Platoon was assigned the task, and the crews settled into position with guns pointed east toward Labico.[52] Redle's other platoons maneuvered into overwatch positions nearby.

Every now and then, German vehicles appeared on the highway and were either knocked out by infantry bazooka teams or by Redle's tankers.[53] At one point, Redle saw thick black smoke rising near the 2nd Platoon area and feared one of his tanks had been hit. None were. S/Sgt Hamilton Smith had just knocked out a massive German 170mm self-propelled artillery gun attempting an escape.[54]

The infantry fanned out among the wheat fields and red poppies in rolling hills north of the highway.[55] The 350th Infantry Regiment, operating right of the 351st, pressed north to take Gardella Hill.[56] In the meantime, the 2nd Battalion, 351st, attacked San Cesareo two miles to the west. By late afternoon, a three-mile section of Highway 6 had fallen under 88th Division control and the 351st Regimental CP moved to an old factory building near Stazione di Zagorole north of the highway and prepared the next phase of attack. The roadway was strewn with all manner of destroyed or abandoned German vehicles and artillery pieces. German aircraft periodically strafed the men as they moved, and somewhere in the distance an irksome 20mm gun kept firing at them.[57]

With the sun setting in the west and the infantry fanned out approximately 600 yards away, Redle caught sight of a small German convoy moving along a more distant hill. One of the vehicles was a large half-track crammed with thirty or forty soldiers.[58] Redle called out the range to his gunner, Sgt Frank Mielcarski, and watched through his binoculars while American infantry began firing into the small column. As the black helmets piled off to engage, Mielcarski fired. A split second later, the entire vehicle disappeared in a blinding flash and enormous explosion. Any soldier still aboard was instantly vaporized and those nearby were reduced to flying limbs scattered across a hundred yards of field. Absolutely nothing remained of the twelve-ton half-track, and a five-foot-deep crater scarred the roadway. Redle concluded a German pioneer (engineer) outfit must have been on board—overladen with as much weight in explosives as men.[59] A second half-track, not nearly as combustible, was also knocked out and the survivors surrendered. A 75mm crew abandoned their truck and towed gun outright and ran away.[60]

After sundown, the 756th Tank Battalion became the football again in a battle among commanders competing to be the first in Rome. At 2100, Rogers learned his battalion had been detached from the 88th and assigned to the II Corps. A short time later, this new assignment was amended to Task Force Howze. Colonel Howze's tanks had just been detached from the 3rd Infantry Division and reverted to II Corps HQ control. Howze was told to submit alternate attack plans for the following day.[61] Before midnight, however, the attachment shifted back to the II Corps before returning to the 88th all over again.[62] Rogers's liaison officers and teams were driven frantic trying to keep pace and, at one point, had no clue to which headquarters they were supposed to report.[63] After midnight, the assignment was firmly established as Task Force Howze, and Rogers met his tall square-jawed friend to discuss two separate plans for attacking Rome: one involved an advance slightly to the south of Highway 6 and the other attacked along roads further north. Rogers returned to his own CP at 0200, 3 June, for an hour or two of sleep while awaiting a II Corps decision on which plan would be adopted.[64]

At 0600, Rogers received a call from the battalion liaison officer with Task Force Howze reporting the 756th had been reassigned to the 88th Infantry Division all over again. Furthermore, the tanks were supposed to have attacked with the 350th and 351st Infantry Regiments nearly two hours earlier—at 0430. The situation was beyond exasperating, but Rogers remained his usual calm. He dispatched liaisons out to locate the 351st and 350th Regimental CPs and told A and B Companies to prepare for action. C and D were placed on reserve call.[65] Lewis and Redle already had their tanks ready to roll by 0540—believing they would be attacking with Task Force Howze. A cavalry trooper trotted up to Captain Lewis's tank and pointed to a jeep parked off on a trail nearby.

"There's someone over there that wants you!" he barked gruffly.

Lewis trotted over to the jeep to find 88th Division Assistant Commanding General Brig Gen Paul W. Kendall waving a walking stick, already screaming his head off. The captain's frozen salute was completely ignored.

"Why in the hell aren't you up there? Shit! You were supposed to be up there at 0300 this morning! What the fuck are you doing back here? You goddamn tankers are never where you should be!"

"Sir," Lewis calmly replied, "Sir, our last orders were to be ready to move at 0600 and we are ready."

"Captain, you better be goddam sure you are right. Where in the hell is your battalion?"

"Back up this trail about a half-mile, sir."

"Then get your battalion commander the hell down here, and Captain, you damn well better be right!"

Lewis returned to his tank and dispatched a jeep to retrieve Lt Col Rogers. Five minutes later, Rogers arrived and also received an earful of expletives from the irate general. After allowing Kendall to vent, Rogers coolly explained the change in attachment orders—which didn't please the general but at least calmed him considerably.[66] Once their conversation concluded, Kendall waved for Lewis to walk over.

"Captain, it's a damn good thing you were right," he closed.

Then his jeep wheeled around and disappeared in a cloud of trail dust.[67]

***

The II Corps opted for the plan where Task Force Howze attacked on the right flank of Highway 6 while the 88th Division advanced on the left. Colonel Hamilton H. Howze normally commanded the 13th Armored Regiment of the 1st Armored Division. On 26 May, the week prior, Howze was put in charge of a spearheading attack force designed to deliver a heavy punch. Over 100 tanks from two tank battalions—one medium and the other light—of his 13th Armored Regiment formed the core.[68] Augmenting this fire power were tank destroyers from B Company, 701st Tank Battalion, armored cars from the 81st Reconnaissance Squadron, and artillery from the 24th Field Artillery Regiment—a British 105mm outfit.[69] Howze's attached infantry changed from time to time. On this day, troops from the 88th's 1st Battalion, 349th Infantry Regiment, and 3rd Division combat-seasoned veterans of the 1st Battalion, 7th Infantry Regiment, clustered atop the warm, dusty tank decks.[70]

Howze's tanks rolled in from Labico with a bright warm morning sun rising behind them. The small town situated along Highway 6, two miles west of Valmontone, fell the day prior, but Howze felt his crews had been overly cautious—perhaps because several tank commanders had been shot in the head by German snipers hiding in the nearby hills. Three tanks had also been knocked out—victims of skilled German gunners of the Hermann Goering Division. The tall, rugged Texan resolved his crews would be more aggressive henceforth.[71]

As Howze's force staged near La Torre, Lt Col Rogers ordered Captain Lewis's A Company to join the 350th Infantry Regiment on the right flank of the 88th Division's attack. By 0800, the 350th had already moved two miles west of San Cesareo—somewhere between Colonna and Monte Compatri. Redle was ordered to take B Company to a Highway 6 road junction roughly 300 yards past San Cesareo in support of Lewis's tanks.[72] Because the 756th would be operating adjacent to Howze's tanks, with both forces maneuvering and firing inside a corridor only a mile or two in width, the chance for friendly fire errors were high. To avoid any tragic misidentifications, Rogers met with Colonel Howze at 0930 in the middle of Highway 6. After comparing orders, pouring over maps, and discussing options, the two decided to coordinate the attack closely together. Howze's 3rd Battalion, 13th Armored Regiment, M4 tanks transporting 1st Battalion, 7th Infantry Regiment, infantrymen would attack on the 88th's right flank south of Highway 6, pressing toward Colonna.[73]

At 1000, both Captain Lewis and Lt Redle reported their companies were in position. At the same time, C and D Companies of the 756th moved in along Highway 6 to assume closer reserve positions.[74] The attack commenced at once and the 350th Infantry Regiment achieved immediate success skirting the north edge of Monte Campatri toward Monte Porzio—both hilltop towns were separated by roughly a mile of distance. The terrain was fairly open. Field terraces presented Lewis's tankers with some mobility challenges, but the drivers maintained a steady pace with the advancing infantry while the gunners blasted German rear guard positions in houses, hamlets, and road intersections along the way.[75]

Howze's tanks crossed somewhat tougher terrain featuring vineyards, olive groves, taller terraces, and higher hills.[76] Nevertheless, by noon, both forces achieved their primary objectives. The advance halted at a road junction west of Monte Porzio amidst sporadic sniper and AT fire. During the drive, the 7th Infantry Regiment, in particular, captured dozens upon dozens of German prisoners.[77]

Near the base of Monte Porzio, Rogers met briefly with Brig Gen Kendall and informed him of his intentions to return the 756th three miles north to continue the westward advance along Highway 6. Kendall approved of the plan.[78]

Rogers's tankers linked back up with Howze's task force, attacking west of Colonna. At the same time, German AT guns west of the railroad station were challenging Howze's advancing column. After a coordinated tank/infantry assault, the Germans guns fell back.[79]

At 1400, as Rogers and Howze met again to align operations, a Cub spotter plane buzzed by at treetop level carrying Maj Gen Keyes, commander of the II Corps. The tiny plane banked then turned back toward Allied territory—releasing a single fluttering message before disappearing. The paper was retrieved and brought to the colonel:

"Howze—get these tanks moving!" Keyes had scribbled.[80]

Howze gazed over at Rogers and asked the 756th commander if he wanted to formally join his task force. Rogers looked back at his old USMA friend with a conspiratorial smirk. After a quick call to the G-3, II Corps, the attachment was made official and immediate.[81] Moments later, Lt Col Rogers's buoyant voice crackled in over the 756th Battalion radio band:

"To hell with the 88th Division, we are with Howze's task force."

Word of Kendall's early morning tirade had circulated quickly among battalion members, and the tankers were equally pleased to hear of the change.[82]

Howze instructed Rogers to strike out along the southern side of Highway 6 while Lt Col Bogardus "Bugs" S. Cairns's 3rd Battalion, 13th Armored Regiment, spearheaded the main effort along the highway's northern side. Troops of the 1st Battalion, 7th Infantry, jumped aboard Rogers's tanks while 1st Battalion, 349th, infantrymen climbed atop Cairns's mediums. The two long columns of tanks and infantrymen set out from Colonna for the crossroads towns of Casa del Finocchio and Tor Carbone, three miles to the west-northwest.[83] The 756th encountered more rugged ground, but Cairns's 3rd Battalion had to contend with German AT guns.[84] Combat was sporadic for both columns, but the German rear guard teams were generally overmatched and either surrendered after only a few minutes of battle or withdrew to fight again later. Intent on keeping the retreating Germans off balance, Howze pushed his tankers into taking risks they normally wouldn't dare attempt—even going to the extreme, at one point, of ordering a platoon to barrel up the road at full speed until fired upon. The tactic resulted in the fiery loss of the lead tank and crew—causing Howze great anguish, but did allow his column to advance a full 3,000 yards in less than thirty minutes.[85]

In the meantime, Rogers's tanks and infantry rounded up an additional 200 prisoners on their parallel drive along the south.[86] Redle's B Company crews claimed a hand in processing twenty of them.[87] The terrain grew more challenging once Highway 6 swung northeast to skirt around the base of a broad hill.[88] The attack halted momentarily as Rogers and Howze met again on Highway 6 to adjust their plans. They decided to shift the 756th behind Cairns's column near Tor Carbone before assuming a parallel advance to the north.[89] Captain Lewis was radioed to bring A Company forward and report for new orders. Lewis found both officers at an intersection pondering a roadmap laid across the hood of a jeep.

"Lewis, if you can get over there in a hurry, you might get some gravy," Howze gushed while pointing to another intersection on his map several more kilometers west.[90]

After prudently comparing maps, Lewis climbed aboard his tank and sped off with all of A Company and a trailing platoon of M5 lights from D Company. They reached their objective a few minutes later: a "Y" crossing on Highway 6 where the left road led to Rome and the right road veered off to the north. The only German stragglers the tankers encountered along the way were riding aboard a slow lumbering truck, which was promptly captured, and the hapless prisoners processed by D Company crews. Lewis established roadblocks on all three roads and waited—like hungry funnel spiders deep in the brush. A short time later, a German sidecar motorcycle carrying a captain buzzed into their snare and was captured. Every so often, another unsuspecting truck or vehicle tried passing through, only to be challenged, stopped, and impounded, and the occupants, processed and taken out of the war. One of the captured trucks carried five large marmite pots of hot stew, which Lewis's crews set aside for their own consumption later.[91] Howze did promise "gravy."

While C Company and the remainder of D Company moved up behind Lewis's position to set up additional roadblocks along the curved highway, B Company parked in column toward the rear. Somehow, a German car slipped through the D Company section and sped toward Redle's tanks. Upon seeing the long row of American M4s teeming with infantrymen, however, the driver stopped his vehicle, leapt out, and promptly dropped to his knees in the middle of road, hands tightly clasped as if in prayer. Infantrymen rushed up to search his pockets and take him into custody. The portly, rosy-cheeked German had been so fearful of being blown off the road, he didn't bother to turn off the engine. Upon inspection, the odd-looking vehicle was identified as an amphibious Volkswagen *Schwimmwagen*—the first the tankers had ever seen. The infantry took possession of the small jeep-like car and turned it over to Ordnance.[92]

At the same time, a mile to the west, the rest of Task Force Howze pressed beyond Casa del Finocchio against heftier delaying AT fire. Cairns's M4 crews overcame the resistance through standard fire and maneuver, but Highway 6 now passed over a series of gentle rolling hills covered with trees, homes, and terraces, offering a slew of new places for an enemy to hide. The Germans employed AT guns at each hillcrest that had to be located and destroyed or driven back—at the cost of several more of Cairns's tanks and crews. Nevertheless, the armored advance outpaced the walking infantry, and many pockets of resistance were sidestepped in favor of maintaining overall speed. At times, Howze's CP trailing behind Cairns's long column, came under attack with S/A and MG fire from those circumvented Germans. The lagging infantry worked to clear out such places. At one point, the bypassed harassment poured in so thick, Howze and Rogers were forced to take cover in a roadside ditch until their supporting infantry arrived. Amidst the snap of bullets and pinging of shrapnel, Rogers, a devotee of great literature, quipped: "You know, I wonder what would Walter Mitty do in a case like this?"[93]

Another time, Howze's jeep driver, armed only with a pistol, disappeared into a clump of scrub trees by the side of the road to answer the call of nature. He emerged a few minutes later with twenty German soldiers—all walking in a row with their hands up. Apparently, the sounds of Howze's tanks rumbling nearby convinced them to surrender to the startled corporal.[94]

The 88th Infantry had also pressed in closer upon Howze's left flank—complicating operations and raising tempers. At one point, a brigadier general pulled rank and took one of Howze's attached infantry companies to clear out a pocket of resistance in his territory. The theft left Howze somewhat exposed on his flank, but the colonel figured the Germans were too disorganized to attack him—which turned out to be true.[95] What Howze lost in infantry, however, was gained later when a wandering tank destroyer company ended up joining his column. The TD outfit, enthused to finally find a home, somehow got lost earlier and had been overlooked in the II Corps' mad dash for Rome.[96]

Three times, Allied planes strafed Howze's column—even though the colonel was "meticulous" about regularly reporting his progress and position to the II Corps HQ. Howze's CP was assaulted directly on one of those runs—by five P-40 Warhawks attacking from one direction and then banking around to strike from another. This incident occurred despite the presence of numerous yellow smoke canisters Howze's men had tossed on the road identifying themselves as friendly troops to the pilots.[97]

Late in the afternoon, the Germans ambushed Cairns's lead column from a cluster of factory buildings halfway between Tor Carbone and Torre Nova.[98] Several M4s were knocked out in a matter of minutes. Cairns pulled back to allow for the infantry to mass and for artillery support to be organized. When a large, coordinated attack was finally launched, however, the Americans found the factory completely vacated. Cairns's tanks pressed on toward Torre Nova, only to be hit again with AT fire from the next hillcrest.[99] Nevertheless, the Americans could now see Saint Peter's Dome, less than ten miles ahead, rising from the heart of Rome.[100] The ultimate objective was, at least, in sight.

While Howze's main force, spearheaded by 3rd Battalion, 13th Armored Regiment, tanks pressed west, Rogers's 756th Tank Battalion shifted north and then west to protect the right flank. Lt Redle's B Company spearheaded the effort out of Tor Carbone.[101] Lt Newman's 2nd Platoon took point with Lt Gilden's 1st Platoon trailing. Newman's platoon had already shrunk down to only three operational tanks—as S/Sgt Smith's developed mechanical problems after striking a shell crater the prior day, and Sgt Gilkerson's tank had completely sheared a drive shaft.[102] Lt Orient's 3rd Platoon remained back on Highway 6 near Colonna on roadblock duty. B Company's specific orders were to move to a road junction 2,000 yards north and 1,000 yards west of Highway 6 on the Via Prenestina and set up a road block in an attempt to capture a German artillery unit seen escaping.[103] The attack called for speed, so the attending infantry from A Company, 7th Infantry Regiment, piled atop the sun-warmed tank decks.[104] Anticipating German AT guns would challenge their incursion at some point, Redle ordered the tanks to advance up the narrow northern road in 300-yard intervals.[105]

Upon reaching Via Prenestina, Newman's tanks turned west toward Rome. The road cut slightly into a hill while curving gently to the right. As Newman's tank emerged from the hill's edge to observe a bridge approximately 200 yards ahead, German artillery and MG fire greeted their appearance—causing the column to halt and seek cover.[106] At the same time, an AT gun fired at one of Gilden's tanks and missed, but wounded several riflemen huddled on the deck.[107] The infantry dispersed into the nearby fields and set to work driving off the Germans—who were evidently trying to maintain a roadblock of their own. In the process, one especially aggravating MG in a house 500 yards beyond the bridge was silenced by Newman's tanks.[108] Eventually, the Germans were driven off, but at the cost of one dead and thirteen American wounded.[109] Redle regretted that his small force hadn't been assigned a recon component, otherwise he would have pressed the attack more aggressively westward. His orders, however, were to consolidate in place for the evening.[110]

As the B Company roadblock was firmly established, A and C Company tanks ferrying B and C Company, 7th Regiment, infantrymen formed roadblocks another 2,000 yards to the northwest along the Via Collatina. Resistance there proved non-existent.[111] The previously seen column of horse-drawn German artillery was observed moving in the distance and the tanks opened fire—causing great carnage.[112]

Around dusk, Lt Col Rogers contacted Colonel Howze and reported the north flank had been secured against light resistance.[113] Howze was particularly pleased to hear of the destruction inflicted upon the fleeing German artillery column—again, calling the spoils "gravy."[114] And the "gravy" kept coming. Almost as soon as A Company's roadblocks were established, German vehicles continued driving in from the east—sometimes alone, other times in groups.[115] All seemed unaware their escape routes through Rome had been severed. They were stopped, confiscated, and the occupants were taken prisoner. At one point, an entire convoy of some thirty vehicles and 130 soldiers was captured—including a lieutenant colonel. Another time, two mobile 88mm guns were confiscated.[116] A sedan carrying a German quartermaster general and his dog also wandered into the trap, but the general seemed more concerned about the fate of his dog and sedan than becoming a prisoner.[117] Not a single American died in the operation, although four Germans were killed.[118] "We had gotten even for Cassino!" Captain Lewis boasted later.[119]

At 2200, C Company tanks passed through A Company positions to form a new roadblock on the Via Collatina, 1,200 yards further west.[120] A beautiful orange sunset didn't seem to stem the steady stream of frantic German traffic flowing in from the east. An entire field hospital—including all the doctors, nurses, and patients—was intercepted on the Via Collatina and taken prisoner. In the B Company area, an ordnance battalion was also captured—along with several screened-in buses jammed full of lathes, drills, and other specialized machine tools. The 3rd Platoon tank driver and B Company armorer, T/4 Joe K. Wright, happily poured through all the equipment, pulling out anything useful for gun repairs.[121] A small supply convoy also pulled up and surrendered a short distance away. The investigating infantry returned with three prisoners and a big barrel of pickles.[122]

In the diminished twilight, three ME-109s suddenly appeared at 500 feet and flew directly toward B Company's roadblock. For several anxious seconds, the Americans watched the angry growling planes approaching. The haul of captured German vehicles in the fields sitting nearby must have fooled the pilots over who was on the ground. To everyone's astonishment, the three ME-109s wagged their wings in acknowledgement while thundering by. The grateful Americans waved back.[123]

Lt Col Cairns's tanks, parked under cover near Torre Nova 4,000 yards to the southwest, weren't as fortunate. The German pilots knew American tanks were hiding along Highway 6 and harassed the main thoroughfare without mercy. Several Task Force Howze vehicles were hit and caught fire—further marking the locations for future attacks.[124] B Company XO Lt Engfer and 1st Sgt Nusz had also been strafed while moving B Company's HQ and maintenance sections through Colonna. Fortunately, neither man was harmed.[125]

Miraculously, nobody in the entire 756th Tank Battalion had been killed or wounded during the long day of heavy action.[126] Luck certainly played a role, but the unit had long since become battle-hardened and all the crews professionals. The only B Company "casualty" for the day was Sgt Graffagnini, who came down ill and was sent to the 16th Evacuation Hospital.[127] The battalion also lost Major Dolvin—not to injury or illness, but to promotion. The 191st Tank Battalion had been badly decimated in the Anzio Breakout commencing on 23 May. The battalion commander, XO, and most of the officers had been wounded or killed on the first day—leaving the outfit essentially leaderless.[128] Dolvin certainly earned a battalion command, but rebuilding this once-proud tank battalion back from their dirt-low morale would require all his command and organizational skills—and immediately.[129] Few 756ers were given the opportunity to wish their long-serving battalion XO a proper farewell before the popular officer with his trademark slow Georgia drawl quickly packed and departed.

***

After nightfall, Task Force Howze halted their advance outside of Torre Nova. Cairns's battalion, normally fielding over fifty tanks, had been reduced to only eighteen serviceable M4s.[130] A long-range flat-trajectory duel with German forces continued for some time, but the results proved ineffectual. Eventually, both sides abandoned the tit-for-tat prodding and retired for the evening.[131] Howze also retired to his crossroads CP in a stout brick house to take stock of the day's events and catch some sleep. An air observer informed the colonel that, earlier in the day, some forty German tanks were seen pulling back from his advance. Howze admitted had he heard this detail at the time, it would have "scared me silly."[132]

Around midnight, elite troops from the First Special Service Forces (FSSF) filtered up into Howze's positions—first, in dribs and drabs, and then as a veritable flood. The arrival of this brigade-sized outfit not only doubled the number of Allied troops in Task Force Howze's sector, but altered the entire character of the attack. Next, Brig Gen Robert T. Frederick, the FSSF's dashing, slender 37-year-old commander sauntered into Howze's CP sporting a confident smile beneath his Clark Gable moustache. His neck was wrapped in a bandage covering recent battle wounds.[133] His tough, weather-beaten hands held the II Corps orders instructing both forces to merge for the final assault on Rome—set to commence at 0400, 4 June, with Frederick serving as overall commander. Normally, an ambitious young colonel might feel slighted about the change. Howze was delighted. Taking the streets of Rome was an infantryman's job, and Frederick's men were the best infantrymen in the Allied Forces.[134] Howze knew the time had come for his tanks to shift into a support role.

As Frederick's three regiments spread out in the dead of night and formed a line west of Cairn's and Rogers's two resting tank battalions, the two officers met in Howze's cramped little brick roadside house to plan history.[135]

U.S. 13th Armored Regiment

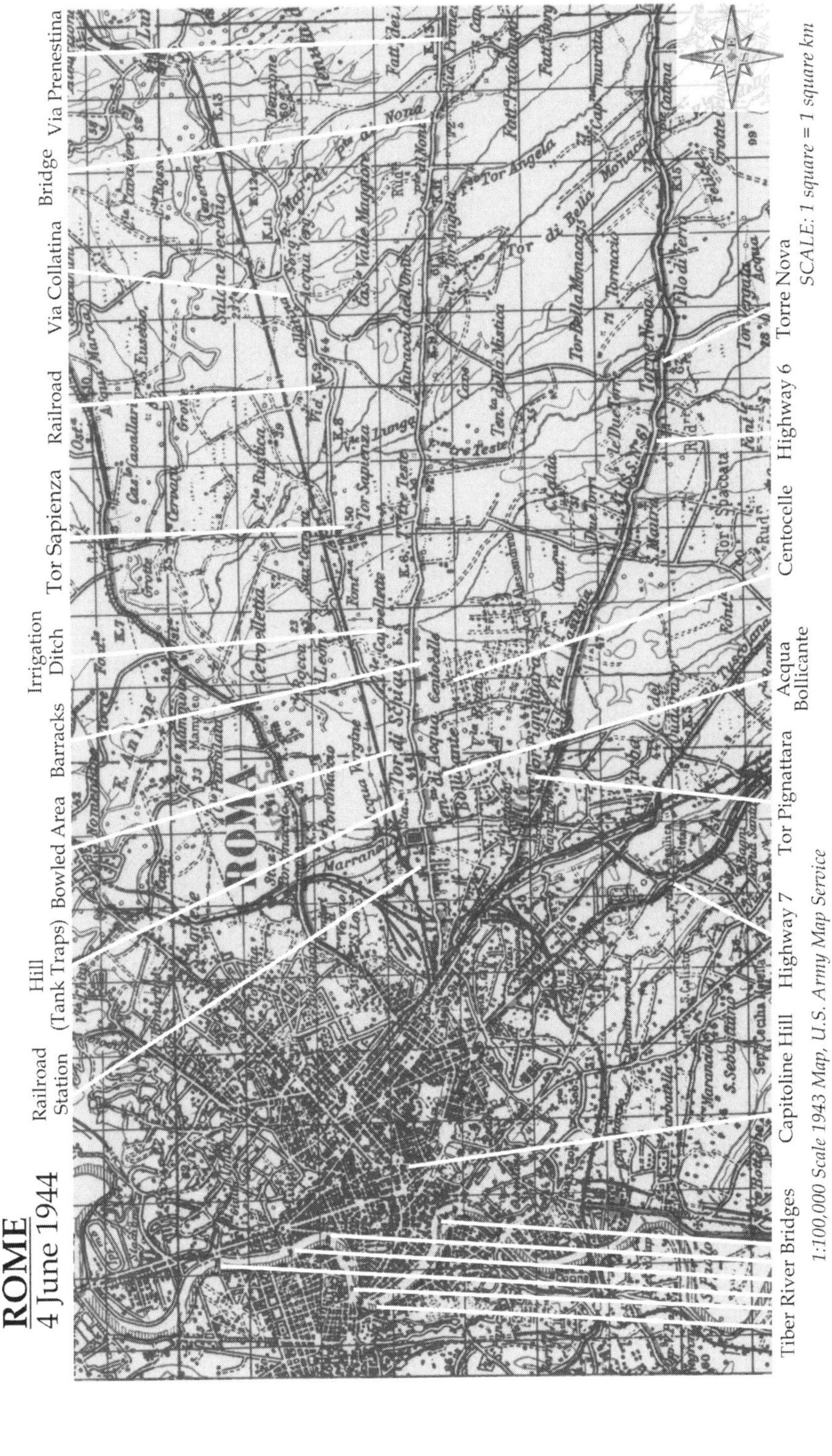

ROME
4 June 1944

1:100,000 Scale 1943 Map, U.S. Army Map Service

CHAPTER SIXTEEN

Liberators: 4 June 1944 to 5 June 1944

The First Special Service Force was activated in Helena, Montana, on 20 July 1942, as a specialized airborne winter-fighting outfit under the command of (then) Lt Col Robert T. Frederick. Single male volunteers in tip-top physical condition from ages twenty-one to thirty-five were recruited from all over the Pacific Northwest and Canada to fill out the rolls—generally pulled from self-reliant demanding outdoors occupations such as ranching, prospecting, trapping, hunting, and lumberjacking. Only the very best candidates were accepted.[1] Originally, the outfit was supposed be dropped in German-occupied Norway as a saboteur force, but the idea was shelved after no one could figure out a way of bringing them back.[2] Training continued regardless and "Forcemen" became proficient in all aspects of warfare ranging from winter, amphibious, mountain, airborne, and infantry operations to hand-to-hand encounters. Each member also became adept at firing every small arm and arming any explosive found in the U.S. arsenal.[3] Forcemen even designed and manufactured a special stiletto-style knife with a "skull-crusher" pommel handle for their exclusive use.[4] Their arm patch was an upright red spearhead embroidered inside with a white stitched "USA" and "Canada" forming a "T." The U.S. Army viewed them as multifaceted "shock troops" ready to be sent into any situation anywhere.[5]

Like its individual members, the FSSF was structured as a lean, independent combat outfit.[6] Every level utilized fewer personnel than equivalent infantry units. The three regiments contained only 600 men each. A regiment comprised only two battalions of three companies each, and a company comprised only three platoons of two sections each. A section had between nine to twelve men. Service units, of course, rounded out the rolls, but even with those numbers added in, the entire FSSF consisted of only 2,608 men at full strength.[7]

Frederick, now a full colonel, built the FSSF from the ground up. Not only did the 1928 USMA graduate[8] with movie-star looks possess a razor-sharp intellect, but a calm and charismatic demeanor—no matter how dire the situation seemed. His unflappable attitude proved infectious, and his Forcemen came to believe there was no challenge they couldn't meet. Frederick also treated his men like sons, so consequently, they came to love him as a father.[9]

The FSSF first combat operation occurred in June 1943, when the outfit was sent to expel Japanese troops off the island of Kiska in the Alaskan Aleutians. The Japanese chose to withdraw a few days before the FSSF arrived, so combat was light.[10] In November of the same year, the FSSF was sent to join the U.S. Fifth Army in southern Italy.[11] Their first real combat came in early December 1943, when they were tasked with dislodging German defenders off Monte La Difensa in the Mignano Gap. The 3rd Infantry Division tried, but failed. The FSSF succeeded by scaling 200-foot-high cliffs considered impassable by the Germans. The U.S. II Corps hoped the 960-meter heights might succumb in three days—Frederick's Forcemen captured the crest in only two hours. Several more tough mountains fell to the FSSF in the weeks that followed, before the unit was pulled and rushed to shore up Anzio.[12]

Maintaining a reputation for versatility, the FSSF shifted from rugged mountaineers to terrifying nighttime commandos. Raids at Anzio were designed as brief, violent affairs, deep behind enemy lines. Participants blackened their faces to avoid detection. Whenever an FSSF team struck, it destroyed everything at the target—and left behind paper stickers with the unit's arrowhead insignia intended to demoralize those discovering the aftermath. The tactic worked and the Germans nicknamed the intruders "Black Devils" out of fears they could never hear the FSSF teams coming.[13]

At the time of the Anzio breakout on 23 May 1944, the FSSF had attritted down to about 1,500 men. Frederick, who always chose to lead from the front, had already been wounded several times—yet always returned quickly to lead again. The Black Devils took Artena, and then pressed on through Valmontone—suffering a forty percent casualty rate in the process. By the time Frederick's men joined with Howze's forces late 3 June, the FSSF was operating with only 1,000 effectives.[14] Nevertheless, the Black Devils still fought like a force three times their size—which is why they were now commanded by a brigadier general rather than a colonel.

Lt Gen Clark specifically called upon Frederick's FSSF and Howze's task force to secure eight critical bridges over the Tiber.[15] Although Rome had been declared an "open city" by the retreating Germans the previous day, Clark wasn't taking any chances.[16] The Germans still utilized rearguard tactics while vacating the city. Sabotage of those bridges would greatly inhibit his Army's ability to pursue the fleeing enemy once Rome fell.

Competition among Allied forces to be the first to breach the city limits remained cutthroat. Elements of the U.S. VI Corps' 1st Armored, 36th, and 34th Divisions closed in rapidly from the southeast, but the II Corps' FSSF and 85th and 88th Divisions, pressing from the east, held the advantage.[17]

***

Before daybreak, Redle's tank crews arose, ate breakfast, and topped off their tanks with ammo and fuel. Lt Orient's 3rd Platoon had moved up from Colonna during the night—making B Company whole again.[18] The company formed an expectant column with the rest of the 756th, drove three miles west to Tor Sapienza, then cut the engines, and patiently waited. A cheery sun ascended beyond hazy Apennine mountains further east. Boisterous American soldiers dressed in unkempt uniforms riding two and three to a motorcycle, or crammed atop jeeps like circus clowns, sped through toward Rome. Open bottles of wine passed eagerly between them. Redle noticed their red spearhead patches but didn't recognize the unit.

"What a bunch of undisciplined soldiers. I certainly wouldn't want to work with them," the company commander remarked to his gunner, Sgt Frank Mielcarkski.[19] The 26-year-old Chicagoan only shook his head in disbelief.[20]

A short time later, around 0630, Lt Col Rogers drove up in his jeep and told Redle to jump in. As they pulled away, Rogers explained he was gathering each of his company commanders together for a meeting in Tor Sapienza with the officers from their latest attachment: the 3rd Regiment, First Special Service Forces.[21] Redle wasn't familiar with the outfit, so Rogers pointed to the troops who had moved up among them that morning. Now Redle shook his head in disbelief.[22]

At that same moment, two-and-a-half miles to the southwest, two companies from the 1st Regiment, FSSF, riding eight armored cars from A Company, 81st Armored Reconnaissance Battalion, and tanks from Lt Col Cairns's 3rd Battalion, 13th Armored Regiment, tested the Via Casilina (Highway 6) entrance into Rome.[23] The morning was eerily quiet. Warning leaflets, signed by Allied 15th Army Group Commander, General Sir Harold Alexander, had been dropped on Rome at daybreak promising liberation and advising citizens to avoid the fight but "do everything possible to protect public services, transportation facilities and communications … and go on with your regular work." "Your job is to save the city," Alexander urged, "ours is to destroy the enemy." [24] The fluttering notices cleared the streets of traffic.

Earlier, Brig Gen Frederick arranged for one of his company commanders, Captain Mark Radcliff, to probe ahead with an ad hoc team of eighty-one pathfinders packed aboard eighteen jeeps. Radcliff's team's job was to paste direction signs along the route for the following troops. Two photographers, a motion picture cameraman and a journalist, hitched rides. Radcliff's unit passed the "Roma" sign at 0620 and breached the city limits, only to be driven back promptly by S/A fire.[25] Frederick's armor column arrived a short time later and tried pressing past the white and blue Roma sign. German AT fire knocked out the two lead tanks, and heavy S/A fire halted the infantry.[26] Frederick, riding in a half-track near the front, ordered his men and tanks to pull back while recon teams bounded forth among the buildings. The first teams returned with reports of seeing at least four enemy SP guns, five tanks, and approximately 350 infantrymen.[27]

By then, six jeeps and two armored cars had pulled up behind Frederick's stalled column. Lt Gen Mark Clark and Maj Gen Geoffrey Keyes bounded out from their seats and asked the FSSF commander for an update. Frederick explained the reasons for the delay and outlined his plans to outflank the resistance to the north.[28] Clark approved, but emphasized the need to secure the Tiber bridges as quickly as possible.[29] As a gift, Fredrick had one of his men retrieve the nearby "Roma" sign for the Fifth Army commanding general.[30] Hoping to hurry the process, Keyes ordered Cairns to immediately take a platoon of tanks into the city and attempt to overrun the roadblock—even though the remaining recon teams had not yet reported back.[31]

At 0715 Cairns led his five tanks directly into the city. After traveling 100 yards and rounding a road bend, two AT guns opened fire, knocking out Cairns's lead tank and the second in his column. As flames engulfed both tanks, Cairns's surviving crew members and the three remaining tanks returned to the starting point. Cairns asked Keyes for permission to resume their earlier flanking timetable. Keyes agreed.[32] Clark departed, and Frederick asked the II Corps commander the reasons behind the rush.

"France is going to be invaded from England," Keyes replied. "We've got to get this in the newspapers before then."[33]

That same hour, in the lobby of a small hotel in Tor Sapienza, Rogers's company commanders met with Lt Col Edwin A. Walker and his 3rd Regiment, FSSF, staff.[34] Major Arnold and a liaison team were dispatched promptly to Walker's CP, and a basic mode of operation was discussed and agreed upon.[35] To assure close tank/infantry coordination, a rudimentary communication system employing hand signals and message runners was also established. Brig Gen Frederick soon arrived and introduced himself. He described the ferocity of the enemy rearguard actions encountered earlier on Highway 6 and his strategy for the remainder of the day. Frederick would continue leading the column involving his 1st Regiment and Cairns's tanks on a flanking operation through the suburbs of Centocelle and Acqua Bollicante—just south of the Via Prenestina. Colonel Howze would eventually lead the remainder of forces (2nd and 3rd Regiments, 756th Tank Battalion, and 1st Battalion, 7th Infantry Regiment) in support. To allow room for Frederick's task force to maneuver, Howze's attack would not commence until mid-afternoon.[36] The charismatic young general departed almost as quickly as he arrived, and the tankers returned to their column and waited. At 0800, B and C Companies were ordered to move out of the column and take up positions around Tor Sapienza to ward off any possible German counterattack.[37]

The morning sky was a clear and beautiful blue. Around 0900, the tankers of A and D Companies—still in column but moved into defilade positions near the road—noticed a swarm of P-40 American fighters approaching high over the horizon. Standard Operating Instructions (SOI) required the crews to toss out yellow smoke grenades, marking the location as "friendly" to the pilots. No sooner had the tankers done so, when the planes veered sharply in their direction and lined up their wing-mounted .30-caliber machine guns. Seconds later, the shocked tankers and infantry were pummeled with trails of sweeping bullets—ducking heads and sending men scrambling. "My God! I've seen everything now!" Captain Lewis exclaimed as the stunned tank crews tossed out more grenades until the entire column was billowing in yellow smoke. The effort proved pointless. The planes simply circled back around and strafed them a second time before finally departing. The aftermath revealed at least fifteen tankers wounded—four seriously—and two shredded jeeps. An untold number of American infantrymen, plus a few German prisoners, also lay wounded or dead. Captain Lewis, livid and bleeding heavily from his ear from bullet splatter, radioed battalion HQ and threatened to open fire on the American planes with .50-caliber MGs if they returned. Rogers, in turn, radioed Colonel Howze, who immediately informed the II Corps of the incident and provided the location of Rogers's tanks to prevent any recurrence.[38]

At 1000, B Company's orders were amended to form roadblocks in and around Tor Sapienza.[39] Redle's crews promptly complied, and the wait resumed.

At 1100, two British Spitfires started a new strafing run on A and D Company positions—but ceased and wiggled their wings upon seeing the yellow smoke. Two vehicles were slightly damaged in the initial bullet fire. Rogers radioed Colonel Howze a second time—this time arguing more vehemently for II Corps intervention. "Our men were dangerously close to using the anti-aircraft machine guns against the last strafing attack," Rogers declared. As luck would have it, both Keyes and Clark were visiting Howze's HQ at that very moment and the colonel promised to inform both commanding generals of the incident. Afterwards, the careless aerial attacks completely ceased.[40]

In the meantime, Frederick's forces struck northwest from Tor Pignattara—making steady headway against German opposition hidden among the homes and angled streets of Acqua Bollicante.[41] Cairn's G Company tanks acted as the chief flanking force and successfully surprised and destroyed nine armored vehicles—causing the survivors to flee deeper into the city.[42] Behind them, units from the 88th Infantry Division—including tanks from the 752nd Tank Battalion—tangled with pockets of German resistance still lingering in the eastern suburbs.[43]

Further to the south, lead elements of the U.S. VI Corps also reached the outskirts of Rome. The 1st Armored and 36th Infantry Divisions exchanged—not only wrathful bullets and bursting shells with German rearguard units—but barbed words with one another over control of Highway 7. Finally, Maj Gen Truscott had to step in and order Maj Gen Fred Walker's "Texas Division" to vacate Highway 7 so the tanks could pass.[44]

By late morning, Colonel Howze grew weary of sitting on his hands while listening to the radio and phone traffic. During Keyes and Clark's visit to his CP, the cavalry officer proposed opening a new avenue of attack into Rome by sending his forces across the Aniene River further north. The suggestion was instantly dismissed for falling outside the II Corps sector. On two other occasions, Howze asked Frederick for permission to attack along the railroad line paralleling Via Prenestina several hundred yards to the north—allowing clearance for both of their task forces to operate. Frederick demurred both times. Finally, Howze cleverly convinced one of Frederick's own staff officers to make the same suggestion. This time, the FSSF general assented and Howze went to work organizing his attack.[45]

Around noon, Howze convened all his commanders at Tor Sapienza for another planning meeting. In attendance were: Lt Col J. F. R. Akehurst, commanding the 2nd Regiment; Lt Col Edwin A. Walker, commanding the 3rd Regiment; Lt Col Frank M. Izenour, commanding the 1st Battalion, 7th Infantry Regiment; and Lt Col Rogers of the 756th Tank Battalion. Various other artillery and liaison officers also contributed to the discussion. The compressed time schedule did not allow for complicated plans. In brief, Akehurst's 2nd Regiment would lead the attack astride the railroad line heading west into Rome.[46] Rogers's entire battalion would provide the necessary tank support with two medium tank companies coordinating closely with both of Akehurst's FSSF battalions. Redle's B Company would support the 1st Battalion moving south of the tracks while Captain Gourley's C Company would support the 2nd Battalion Forcemen moving along the north side.[47] A and D Companies would follow Gourley's tanks in reserve. Basic operating rules were established: Special Forces troops would precede the tanks in all densely packed areas to avoid ambush. The tanks and ground forces would also remain in close contact at all times—even during delays, and the earlier agreed-upon system of hand signals and runners would be employed. It was noted that because the railbed was raised on a high mound of gravel, little, if any fire support could be provided to either side. Because of this, the more exposed right flank would attack slightly ahead of the left—allowing for Rogers to move his reserve tanks into support positions, if necessary. Time of attack was set for 1500.[48]

For the next two hours, Rogers raced around by jeep making certain all his pieces were set. A platoon from D Company was dispatched 2,000 yards north with a team of Forcemen to guard a key Aniene River bridge and watch for German encroachment. The battalion's Assault Gun Platoon moved into fire support positions and an artillery observer was ordered to remain at Rogers's side for the remainder of the day. Finally, Rogers directed his XO, Major Arnold, to establish an observation post with an unobstructed view of the railroad route inside a high tower in Tor Sapienza.[49]

At 1450, B Company moved into jump-off positions in a wooded area near bowled terrain 1,200 yards west of Tor Sapienza.[50] Lt Orient's 3rd Platoon assumed the point position, followed by Newman's 2nd Platoon tanks. Gilden's 1st Platoon crews found overwatch positions and settled in. Four tank destroyers from the 701st also moved into support positions.[51] Gourley's C Company followed twenty minutes later—pulling up on the right flank just north of the railroad embankment.[52] All the while, Akehurst's Forcemen filtered up through the nearby fields and trees.

The attack was postponed a half hour to allow for Walker's trailing 3rd Regiment to make some final adjustments, but when it finally commenced at 1530, the tanks and troops moved like "clockwork."[53] The first obstacle was an irrigation ditch, which was traversed without too much difficulty.[54] The tanks and infantry progressed across more open fields toward a barracks complex, seamlessly coordinating efforts and neutralizing enemy resistance as if they had trained together for months. Each infantry platoon worked exclusively with one section of Redle's tanks. Whenever German MG or S/A fire was encountered, the infantry whistled forward an M4 and the problem vanished with the flashes of a few rounds of HE.[55] Redle was impressed with how the smaller teams of Forcemen moved with such cool, professional efficiency and quickly regretted his earlier prejudicial remark to Mielcarski.[56] No operational detail had been left to chance. Every Forceman even carried an instruction sheet written in Italian for soliciting local help in securing the Tiber bridges. The barracks fell quickly, bringing in the first haul of German prisoners. The 88th Division, operating further south among the homes of Centocelle, had been stymied by opposition coming from those same barracks all day long.[57]

Next, the infantry set out across green wheatfields toward a small hill 1,000 yards to the west. After crossing nearly 200 yards of open ground, an abrupt firestorm of German MG, S/A, and mortar fire pinned the Forcemen down in the tall grass. At least three men were hit—one killed instantly from a gunshot wound to the chest, another lay twitching in violent death throws, his brains spilling out upon a rock.[58] Redle and his platoon leaders tried searching for the sources through their field glasses, but they proved impossible to pinpoint. Redle ordered Orient's tanks to move out into the fields to gain a better vantage point.[59] The move drew immediate German AT fire.[60] Orient's tanks halted momentarily while the Forcemen regrouped and started inching forward again—making certain to always remain in close contact as agreed earlier.[61] Redle watched with sheer admiration as these "exceptional" Special Service troops timed every bound forward to coincide with the German MG crews changing out their belts. Then he noticed something very peculiar: some crazy Signal Corpsman was standing upright in the same field taking motion pictures of everything.[62]

Redle had little time to ponder the odd sight. An infantry runner climbed upon the side of his tank and pointed to a farm silo off to the right. German MG fire had been spraying intermittently from the top. Mielcarski promptly zeroed in the main gun and blew off the entire roof. The messenger left with a huge grin on his face. A short time later, however, he returned. This time, MG fire was spewing out from along the silo's base, so Mielcarski knocked down the entire structure.[63]

Orient's tanks ventured further out into the fields to maintain pace with the infantry's advance. Suddenly, Cpl Lloyd R. Stout's #13 tank shuddered under a sickening metallic thud. Stout's driver, T/4 Joe K. Wright was killed instantly from wounds to the abdomen and head.[64] The loader, 32-year-old Pvt Paul N. Cardullo, lost his leg from the knee down.[65] Fortunately, the tank was slow to catch fire. Stout, though wounded in the buttocks and hip,[66] helped the four surviving crewmembers to the ground, where they took refuge near their smoldering tank and applied a torniquet to Cardullo's shredded stump. When a German bullet shattered Pvt Hulin Long's tibia, however, the survivors scattered—leaving Cardullo alone.[67]

As S/Sgt Oliver moved his #14 tank within forty yards of Stout's survivors, creating a screen, the AT gun fired again—shattering a track and leaving him immobilized.[68] Rather than abandon the tank, Oliver and crew searched steadfastly for the source. As they did, several more AT shots battered the hull. One round glanced off the turret behind the radio, putting a small hole in the armor.[69] The others failed to penetrate. On the last shot, Oliver's gunner, T/4 Bert L Bulen, finally saw a telltale gun flash in a distant haystack. He immediately fired on the location and watched the straw erupt into a huge ball of orange flames, revealing a shattered German Mark IV tank beneath. Several other "haystacks" stood suspiciously along the road nearby. Oliver clicked on the battalion band and radioed all nearby armor crews to target them. Thirty seconds later, three more German Mark IVs were set aflame by combined M4 and TD fire.[70]

Oliver's crew continued providing fire support from their immobilized tank until exhausting all ammunition—knocking out three more German MG guns in the process. At one point, the 26-year-old Californian rancher dismounted and braved his way through a hail of bullets to cradle Cardullo and pull him closer to the safety of his own tank.[71] As the battle abated, Oliver dismounted, again, to check for more survivors in or around Stout's smoldering tank.[72] Cardullo, perhaps delirious from shock, asked Oliver to retrieve a bottle of wine from the turret. Oliver checked, but the bottle had shattered.[73] He also noticed T/4 Wright was clearly dead.

One Forceman, moving through the fields ahead, spotted another hidden AT gun—this one with an exposed crew—and sniped the gunner. The rest of the crew scattered, and the Forceman beckoned Redle's tanks forward.[74] However, at this point the only 3rd Platoon tank still in operation was Lt. Orient's M4. A third tank developed engine trouble and the fourth was beset with a seized main gun.[75] Redle ordered Lt Newman's 2nd Platoon forward and arranged for Gilden's 1st Platoon and the four tank destroyers to shift into new support positions.[76] While the tanks reconfigured, the advancing infantry halted near a seven-foot-high cyclone fence topped with three-strands of barbed wire. An infantry runner was dispatched back to Redle for assistance. Redle immediately ordered Orient forward to crush the obstacle. As the 33-year-old lieutenant neared the fence, however, a red ball of fire roared just past the front of the hull—narrowly missing T/4 Jesse B. Rickerson's driver's position. Orient backed up promptly, then radioed Redle for advice. Redle suggested to try advancing again—but not as far while being prepared to reverse. Everyone else was radioed to observe. Orient edged forward and again drew another near miss. This new AT fire clearly emanated from the 88th Division's sector to the south. Howze was alerted, and the careless friendly fire promptly halted. A few moments later, a Special Forces rifleman gave the "all clear" signal with three quick gun shots. This time, Orient advanced unmolested.[77]

With the fence now trampled, an entire platoon of Forcemen advanced up the small hill, with Orient's tank and Newman's 2nd Platoon closely following.[78] German resistance in the area had completely collapsed and prisoners emerged to be marched to the rear.[79] Along the hillcrest, the Germans had dug a series of cone-like holes to serve as anti-tank obstacles. Although the Rome city limits only lay perhaps 100 yards away, Redle's tanks could go no further. The mission, however, was to deliver the FSSF troops to city limits but not actually go in.[80] That accomplished, Redle's crews halted and awaited a new set of orders. C Company and A Companies operating along the north side of the tracks, reported arriving at a similar position, with lead elements halting about 1,000 yards short of the main railyards. Opposition in their area had been relatively light.[81]

Redle dismounted to take inventory of his surroundings. While inspecting the trap holes, he came upon a red-headed German 1st lieutenant sitting in the grass. His leg had been shot off above the knee. Redle offered his counterpart a shot of morphine but the officer, speaking perfect English, refused the offer—saying he had already received a dose from an American infantryman. He explained he was responsible for all the defenses in the area and handed Redle a onionskin map overlay:

"Lieutenant, you made a superb attack. Perhaps you would like to have this."

The map showed the positions for four tanks, one AT gun, fourteen machine-guns, and 111 riflemen.[82] After engaging in a little more conversation, Redle learned the wounded man was from Berlin, but then left the defeated German to contemplate his new future as a prisoner while Redle carried on with the business of war.[83]

After studying the tank obstacles, Redle determined to move beyond them—just in case new orders arrived sending them forward. On the hill base to the left, he noticed a number of parked M4s waiting along the nearby Via Prenestina.[84] He approached and saw deck markings for the 752nd Tank Battalion, then located the battalion commander and asked for permission to move his B Company tanks along the road to clear past the hill obstacles. The battalion commander refused—saying his tanks were preparing to advance once a Mark IV tank spotted up ahead was destroyed. From this new vantage point, however, Redle saw a way through for his tanks without using the road or leaving their sector. Redle's tanks advanced beyond the obstacles, and for a fleeting moment, the company commander considered breaching the city limits just for the accolades. The wayward thought was banished almost as soon as it crossed his mind. Redle was, above all, a man of his word.[85]

***

Rome had already been breached by Frederick's men and Cairns's tankers, but at a much higher cost. Frederick's flanking operation succeeded, but his 1st Regiment commander, Colonel Alfred C. Marshall Jr., had been shot dead through the forehead on the city streets while seeking out a missing company.[86] The German Tigers and

SP guns continued to plague Cairn's tank crews in an urban game of cat-and-mouse, and G Company nearly caught eight of them escaping along the Via Prenestina around 1700. Unfortunately, the M4s had perched atop a bank fifty yards away from the thoroughfare and couldn't depress their guns low enough to hit the fleers—nor could the Germans elevate their guns high enough to strike back at their adversaries. Shouts of tanker frustration and dismay were heard all over the battalion's dedicated FM radio band. No doubt, the German panzer radio bands carried the same. Two Mark IVs and a Tiger, however, were hit and set ablaze before disappearing west among the six-storey apartments and factory buildings.[87]

A short time later, the 2nd and 3rd Regiments, FSSF, linked up with the 1st Regiment at G Company's knoll top position.[88] The Forcemen split up into teams and ventured deeper into the city, toward the critical Tiber River bridges three miles away.[89] Here and there, they encountered scattered pockets of resistance, involving the exchange of gunshots—but these were short-lived, futile engagements. With most Germans gone, Romans began pouring out of shuttered apartments in droves, showering their grimy liberators with affection and offers of assistance.[90] As the result of civilian aid, Frederick's Special Force troops reached the bridges before nightfall and started the process of securing each one.[91] As promised, the Germans didn't drop them into the Tiber. Many Americans expressed astonishment the Germans had kept their word.[92]

Frederick called upon Rogers to provide two tank companies to serve as overnight bridge security. On a hilltop overlooking Rome with a tired bloated orange sun slowly sinking behind Saint Peter's Basilica three miles to the west, Rogers asked Captains Lewis and Gourley for a volunteer to take the job. D Company was already committed.[93] Either A or C Company could go. Recognizing both the historical significance and the rewarding opportunity of mingling with the overjoyed locals, both Lewis and Gourley jumped at the assignment. Rogers pulled out a coin to determine a winner. Gourley won the flip, and his C Company crews got to go enjoy the festivities.[94]

With evening falling, more Allied units filtered into the Eternal City: the U.S. 1st Armored, 3rd, 34th, 36th, 85th, and 88th Infantry Divisions—discovered an Italian city refreshingly intact for once and a populace overjoyed to see them. Conditions remained hazardous nevertheless.[95] German Resistance still flared in the northern and western quarters from scattered, uncoordinated units trying to evade capture—and in the dark unfamiliar streets, Allied units sometimes mistook each other for the enemy. Elements of the 351st Infantry Regiment, attempting to capture a Tiber River bridge, mistook FSSF troops already stationed there as Germans. A firefight ensued. Brig Gen Frederick, who happened to be inspecting the position at the time, was grazed in the knee and elbow in the crossfire. One American was killed, and several others were also wounded in the SNAFU.[96] Allied friendly fire incidents, such as these, dulled the luster to an otherwise triumphant day.

At 2230, Redle's three B Company platoons withdrew east to Tor Sapienza for the evening and reunited with the company's HQ and maintenance sections—repositioned from Colonna only five hours earlier.[97] Lt Orient's 3rd Platoon, especially, needed the respite to reorganize. Cpl Stout, Pvt Cardullo, and Pvt Long were all sent to the 95th Evacuation Hospital.[98] Stout, hopefully, would return in a few weeks. Cardullo, now missing a leg, would be heading home. Long's gunshot to the leg could go either way.[99] Another tanker, Pfc Ford T. Draeger, bandaged up as the result of minor neck burns, remained on duty.[100]

The death of T/4 Joe K. Wright, especially, dampened moods around the bivouac. Wright had been with B Company since inception, 1 June 1941.[101] He was not only a skilled tank driver, but a gifted and enthusiastic machinist and gun repairman. The 27-year-old Oregonian and Bronze Star recipient was not married but left behind a sister and widower father.[102]

As soon as Redle's tank pulled into the bivouac, Lt Col Rogers and the popular battalion surgeon,[103] Captain "Doc" Sarno, walked over to greet him as he dismounted. Rogers extended a firm handshake and congratulated the B Company commander on his promotion while Sarno proudly pinned a set of silver captain bars to Redle's collar.[104] His official date of rank was listed as 31 May 1944, but Redle had been serving as B Company commander for over four months now.[105] The delay had been, more or less, an oversight. The battalion was simply too preoccupied in fighting a war in the meantime, and because those challenges continued, the ceremony was very brief indeed. There would be no further parties, steak dinners or friendly shoving matches to celebrate Redle's accomplishment.

2nd Lt William H. Newman also received a well-earned promotion. The new 1st Lt Newman, though only twenty two years old, had consistently proven himself a courageous and competent officer. Never once did the young Tennessean waiver in the execution of his duties.[106]

***

Throughout the night of 4 June and early morning hours of 5 June, 756th C and D Company tanks stood guard on the approaches of five different Tiber River bridges. At 0800, Colonel Howze relieved the crews, and the entire battalion assembled near Tor Sapienza at 1030. One hour later, the battalion was officially detached from the FSSF and reattached to the 88th Infantry Division. Lt Col Rogers sent the requisite liaison team to the 88th HQ by early afternoon, but at 1410 word travelled back that the 756th would not see action until 6 June—so the tankers used the extra time to clean equipment or wash, shave, and rest.[107]

The U.S. Fifth Army consolidated its hard-fought gains in and around Rome—savoring the day as local liberators and Allied media darlings. Lt Gen Mark Clark entered the city at 0730 via Highway 6 riding in a jeep with his loyal Chief-of-Staff,

Maj Gen Alfred M. Gruenther—getting lost for a time in the maze of streets before a friendly priest pointed them in the direction of City Hall on Capitoline Hill, their destination.[108] Other jeeps carrying Maj Gen Keyes, Maj Gen Truscott, and hordes of doting newspaper correspondents also arrived on Capitoline Hill—gliding past the famous Colosseum and throngs of exuberant Romans jamming the roadside along the way.[109] These magnificent scenes, captured by both film and pen, became instant, timeless highlights in a war characterized by endless scenes of vast material destruction and human suffering.

Clark's U.S. Fifth Army was actually a 369,356-member multinational army with 231,306 Americans, 42,908 British, and 95,142 French serving under the tall, lanky American's command.[110] And from the landings at Salerno in September 1943 to the liberation of Rome on 4 June 1944, this same multinational army suffered more than 124,000 casualties—with 35,014 occurring in just the last three months alone.[111] Some criticized Clark for catering to the media—mistaking his publicity appearances as shameless self-promotion, but the commanding general only saw himself as representing all those men fighting beneath him:

"We intended to see that the people back home knew that it was the Fifth Army that did the job and know the price that had been paid for it," he wrote later in his memoirs.[112]

His motivations were really that simple.

Clark was not a perfect battlefield commander. He made mistakes that cost lives, but he learned and moved ahead. He gave his Fifth Army Rome because Rome made them feel appreciated, and appreciated warriors are more motivated warriors. Clark, through all his faults, understood this very basic human need. A long war still lay ahead.

The British may have instead preferred that Clark push his Fifth Army through Valmontone on the fair chance—but no hard guarantee—of trapping the German Tenth Army. Those orders, however, were not explicit and did allow the American general to exercise his best judgment. Clark chose Rome because the city had always been the Allies' stated goal.[113] Clark chose Rome before the enemy could even consider turning the city's beautiful streets and historical monuments into another Cassino. Clark chose Rome because his Fifth Army paid a very heavy price getting there and earned the honor. Clark chose Rome because a war-weary American public also thirsted for a morale boost. The 15th Army Group commander General Sir Harold Alexander, to his credit, allowed the U.S. Fifth Army this moment of glory and never publicly questioned his subordinate general's decision until after the war.[114]

***

The 756th Tank Battalion's life among liberated Romans lasted a mere twenty-four hours. At 2300, 5 June, the 88th Division directed the battalion to move five miles north of Rome and report to the 91st Cavalry Reconnaissance Squadron.[115] The column passed through a nighttime city looking more like a garrison town. Signal corpsmen shuttled about, stringing communications lines along the streets, so the tankers tied down their radio antennas to avoid striking the crisscrossing labyrinth of telephone and electrical wires. One A Company tank antenna snapped free nonetheless and struck a live streetcar wire—frying out the radio in a brilliant shower of sparks.[116] B Company jeep driver, T/5 Clyde Guild, chose this night to ride atop a tank deck—a rare event. One low hanging phone line clipped him along the helmet lip, launching both the pot and liner skyward and nearly yanking the startled 19-year-old over the edge. He regained his balance and suffered a nasty neck scrape, but had the strap been fully clasped below his chin, Guild would have been decapitated.[117] At 0500, 6 June, the column halted at a road junction on Highway 3 near Grottarossa. Under the high umbrella branches of majestic Italian stone pine trees, the crews formed a new bivouac near the ancient Tiber.[118]

No sooner was Rome liberated when a debate raged over which Allied unit arrived first. The 88th claimed one of their Reconnaissance Troop patrols crossed the city limits at Highway 6 coordinates 799647 around 0715 hours.[119] Lt Col Bogardus Cairns's diary entry shows his 3rd Battalion, 13th Armored Regiment, tanks breached town the same time.[120] Captain Mark Radcliff, leading a FSSF recon effort that morning believed his team crossed at least an hour earlier.[121] The Fifth Army, probably pressed with more important matters, seemed to recognize all claims and the dispute was never settled to anyone's satisfaction.

At the same time, another ambitious officer also seeking his place in the history books was Lt Col Harry W. Sweeting. The former 756th Tank Battalion commander wanted his current unit—the 135th Infantry Regiment—to be the first into the city. After taking his jeep out on an ill-advised reconnaissance jaunt toward the Tiber River, however, both driver and regimental commander lost their bearings and became prisoners of war.[122]

First Special Service Forces

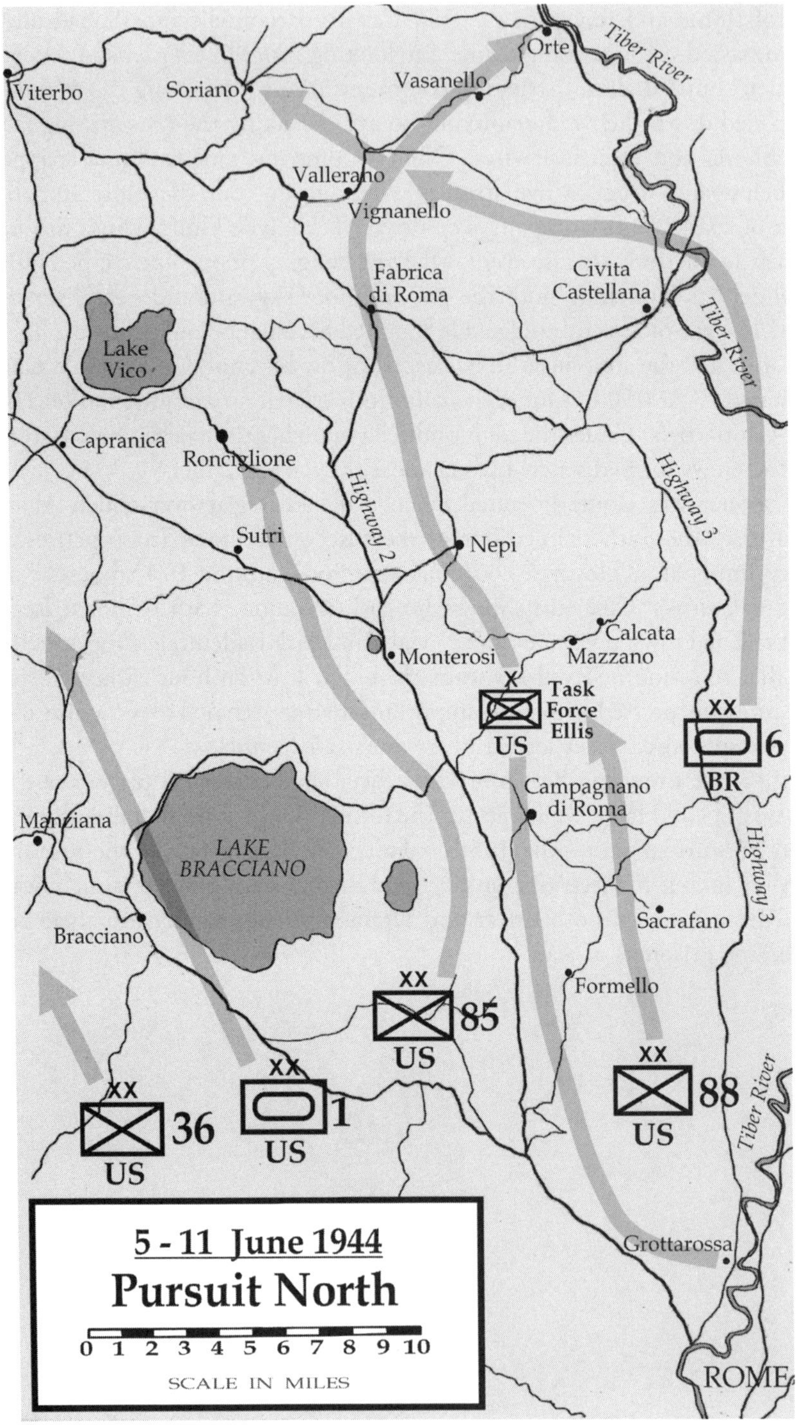
Orte
Tiber River
Viterbo
Soriano
Vasanello
Vallerano
Vignanello
Fabrica di Roma
Civita Castellana
Lake Vico
Capranica
Ronciglione
Highway 2
Highway 3
Sutri
Nepi
Calcata
Monterosi
Mazzano
Task Force Ellis
US
XX
6
BR
Campagnano di Roma
Manziana
LAKE BRACCIANO
Sacrafano
Bracciano
Formello
85
88
36
1
Grottarossa
ROME
5 - 11 June 1944
Pursuit North
0 1 2 3 4 5 6 7 8 9 10
SCALE IN MILES

CHAPTER SEVENTEEN

Chase North: 6 June 1944 to 10 June 1944

At 0730, 6 June, Lt Col Rogers, 756th Tank Battalion HQ staff and company commanders arrived at an old quarry site just east of the Tiber River banks near the tiny hilltop town of Grottarossa.[1] This was the time and place they were supposed to meet Lt Col Charles A. Ellis, 91st Cavalry Reconnaissance Squadron and "Task Force Ellis" commander. Ellis, however, was running late with other meetings and hadn't yet arrived.[2] At 0800, the 756th was put on thirty-minute movement alert, nonetheless.[3] Finally, at 0930, a small column of half-tracks and jeeps carrying Ellis and his CP team pulled in hurriedly.[4] The morning's agenda had already fallen behind schedule, but for good reason. The slender 52-year-old cavalry colonel bounded down upon the ochre soil to make a few short opening remarks.[5] He then tugged a paper from a crowded breast pocket and read aloud a late-breaking dispatch announcing a successful Allied invasion in Normandy, France. The news drew a hearty round of cheers, but Captain Redle figured the British had to be ecstatic.[6] The "Tommies" had been fighting this European war three years longer than their American cousins.

Word of a cross-channel invasion, itself, came as no surprise. A buildup of troops and materials in England—expanding openly over many months—was no military secret, and the establishment of a second front in France had always been the Allies' public position. Rather, the news brought welcome relief to hundreds of thousands of Allied troops still slogging up the Italian boot. No longer were they alone in shouldering the Western European war flank. On the other hand, this new northern France campaign was sure to steal much of the limelight away from their future efforts. Lt Gen Mark Clark's frenetic push to take Rome suddenly made sense, but the U.S. Fifth Army's bask in glory lasted for only one day.[7] Any later, and the liberation of Rome would have been relegated to a "Page 2" event.

Ellis, a cavalry veteran of World War I and experienced Secret Service agent prior to the Second,[8] wasted no time explaining his action plan. The Brooklynite had been commanding bold reconnaissance operations in the 91st Cavalry since Operation *Torch*.[9] In short, with the Germans still retreating north, the job of Task

Force Ellis was to aggressively pursue, overwhelm and destroy all lesser-sized enemy rearguard operations encountered and, hopefully, take a substantial bite out of their hindquarters.[10] The assigned sector fell between Highway 2 on the left and Highway 3 on the right—fertile, rolling country populated with small towns and farms.[11] At the same time, the U.S. 85th Infantry Division would operate in the sector on the left, while the 6th South African Armoured Division moved in the right sector.[12]

Task Force Ellis was first formed a week earlier by Maj Gen Keyes to compete with Task Force Howze in the dash for Rome.[13] While Howze pressed along Highway 6, Ellis pushed ahead of 88th Division positions further to the south toward Highway 7. Both forces were comprised similarly of recon troops bolstered with tanks, tank destroyers, and motorized infantry, and given dedicated artillery support. A few of Howze's men may have breached the city limits ahead of Ellis, but Ellis's men claimed they were the "first unit of combat strength" to enter Rome a few hours later, at 1312 hours.[14]

The firepower at Ellis's disposal was now even greater than his Rome task force. The normal personnel strength of a cavalry "squadron" was roughly equivalent to a tank battalion—but organized as six "troops" instead of six companies. As a fully "mechanized" outfit, all recon troopers traveled and maneuvered aboard jeeps, M-8 "Greyhound" scout cars, half-tracks, M5 light tanks or trucks. Nobody walked. Committed in support of Lt Col Ellis's 91st Cavalry Reconnaissance Squadron were two TD companies from the 804th Tank Destroyer Battalion, the 3rd Battalion of the 351st Infantry Regiment (motorized aboard trucks), one company from the 313th Engineer Combat Battalion, and the entire 756th Tank Battalion. A battery of 105mm howitzers from the 913th Field Artillery Battalion were also attached.[15] Task Force Ellis had expanded from a squadron to a regiment-sized armored reconnaissance force—unleashed, not only to seek out the enemy, but to wreak havoc once found.

Ellis explained the Fifth Army's objectives were broad but flexible—so the officers should always expect last-minute changes. Aggressive pursuit of the Germans was a given. The seaport of Civitavecchia, forty miles northwest of Rome, and an airfield complex at Viterbo, laying more to the north, were Clark's intermediate goals. The port would remove the necessity of maintaining many miles of supply lines, ammo dumps, and circumvent sluggish ground troop transport up through central Italy. The airfields would bring southern Germany within Allied bomber range.[16] The overall objective for Task Force Ellis was to achieve a phase line a few miles east of Viterbo—running from the towns of Orte to Soriano.[17] Both towns lay nearly forty miles due north of Rome's city center.

Task Force Ellis's immediate objective was to take the towns of Mazzano and Calcata—lying a more modest twenty miles to the north. The task force would attack as two columns—sometimes adjacent, sometimes in tandem.[18] Each column would be led by a recon troop, followed by one medium tank company, and one

TD Company—a much more effective arrangement than the French approach. One company of infantry would ride the tank and TD decks. The remainder of the force would follow in reserve. Rogers assigned Captain Lewis's A Company to "Red Column" on the left. Captain Gourley's C Company went to "Blue Column" on the right, while Redle's B Company and Kremer's D Company trailed in reserve.[19] Time of attack was set for 1530.[20]

The attack commenced on time with both columns moving northwesterly for several miles, passing scores of wrecked or deserted enemy vehicles and abandoned gas dumps burning alongside the road.[21] Although not a single German could be seen, citizens of every Italian village and hamlet along the way emerged from modest stone country homes and shops to cheer the Americans as they raced through.[22]

Finally, at 1700 hours, as Red Column neared Formello, artillery concentrations began to burst about the entrance of the town—barring entry. The propellant charges, however, clearly exploded to the rear—indicating friendly fire. Lt Col Rogers, riding near the column's head, radioed both Ellis's mobile CP further to the rear and the 88th Division HQ near Rome for help. Neither knew who was responsible. Finally, after an investigation which took nearly an hour, the 117th Cavalry Reconnaissance Squadron—moving ahead of the 85th Division further west—admitted to directing the salvos. Some other Allied unit had mistaken Ellis's column for retreating Germans and tried blocking them with fire.[23]

Upon reaching Formello, Blue Column turned northeast toward Sacrafano, but found the town clear of Germans.[24] Red Column proceeded northwest toward Campagnano di Roma. After covering nearly four miles, the lead scout cars drew S/A and AT fire coming by way of Highway 2 further east.[25] Artillery support was called in while Captain Lewis's A Company tanks bolted forward, spread out over the valley floor, and returned fire. The German AT gunners, shielding the rear of an escaping column, showed no signs of backing down. A tit-for-tat duel persisted well past sunset with neither side gaining the upper hand. Lewis's gunners ended up firing at faint muzzle flashes in the darkness.[26] Finally, at 2130, the German guns stopped firing altogether. Apparently, the retreating column had slipped out of range.

Shortly after, Lt Col Rogers directed A Company to consolidate and establish nighttime security with their infantry, a messenger arrived carrying written 88th Division orders to "continue without pause." Rogers tried contacting Lt Col Ellis for confirmation, but the task force commander's CP was out of radio range. As the senior officer present, Rogers ordered Red Column to resume the advance. The tanks and TDs, however, were extremely vulnerable to nighttime ambush, so the infantry was ordered to dismount and walk alongside while the armor moved in measured bounds.[27]

Next, Rogers radioed Captain Redle, trailing about a mile to the rear, and directed him to halt his tanks and get a good night's rest. B Company would take the lead the next morning.[28] Redle's tanks crossed a field three miles north of Formello and pulled beneath the cover of a tree line.[29] Looking back, the crews noticed their treads had churned up dozens of white potatoes growing in the soft soil. The kitchen crew harvested a portion and served up a rare treat of French-fried potatoes as a late-night snack. Afterwards, the crews turned in with full bellies.[30]

In the meantime, Red Column continued moving northwesterly through the dark, but did not meet any resistance until 0230, 7 June.[31] Here, at a Y junction meeting Highway 2, two-and-a-half miles beyond Campagano di Roma, the leading recon troop drew enemy fire—small arms crackle followed swiftly with the vicious green snarls of AT rounds cutting through the night.[32] Lewis's tanks lurched forward a second time, dispatching blazing red AT fire in response; Lt Hammer's M4 assuming the lead. The spectacle quickly took on an appearance of a wild Fourth of July celebration—complete with streams of flaring tracers, strobed flashing of bursting shells, and sparkling spray of ricocheting bullets. The exchange was not particularly effective, but several German vehicles were eventually set afire along the highway. Lt Hammer's tank managed to creep within 100 yards of Highway 2, but sustained an AT hit to the drive sprocket, shattering the track and leaving the tank immobilized. Fortunately, Hammer's crew was unharmed. Many trapped Germans chose to surrender to attendant American infantrymen, maneuvering in along the flanks, but an even larger number escaped.[33] By 0430 the nighttime skirmish dwindled. Reports of a column of German tanks retreating over a ridge 2,500 yards to the north, however, caused an upsurge in fire. One Mark IV was hit and set ablaze before the remaining panzers disappeared altogether and the gunfire exchange completely ceased. In the end, over forty German vehicles had been destroyed and an estimated 200 enemy killed.[34] Out of vulnerability concerns for his flanks, Rogers ordered a halt in movement and for the establishment of roadblocks.[35]

At dawn, Blue Column had pulled up behind Red Column positions. Rogers ordered Gourley's C Company to pass through A Company's line and continue the pursuit north. Captain Lewis's crews were physically exhausted and nearly out of fuel and ammunition. Rogers told them to sleep the rest of the morning—their first meaningful rest in three days.[36] Redle's refreshed B Company crews and fully stocked M4s arrived at 0630, 7 June, followed by Captain Kremer's D Company lights. Another small task force was formed after a brief reorganization—this one designed to probe five miles northeast through Mazzano and to Calcata—another mile-and-half beyond. A recon platoon comprised of scout cars, halftracks, and five light tanks took the lead, with Redle's 1st, 2nd, and 3rd Platoons following.[37] Infantry piled atop the tank decks.[38] Not a single hint of resistance was encountered the entire way, and by 1100, Mazzano was secured.[39] Plans to proceed further to Calcata were cancelled on account of poor terrain and Redle's task force was ordered to hold in place for the remainder of the day.[40] For once, Redle's company finally drew the lucky long straw.

At 1800 hours, the 756th liaison alerted Rogers of new attack plans in the works and advised the battalion commander to "get in on the plans before the plans became orders."[41] Rogers arrived a short time later at Lt Col Ellis's CP, two miles south of Campagnano. Major Arnold also appeared at Rogers's request. Ellis wanted the advance to the final Orte–Soriano objective line to proceed as two columns. Rogers was fine with the idea, but asked for halts at night to allow the reservicing and refueling of tanks and rest for the crews. Tanks, Rogers explained, were basically blind at night. The battalion commander also wanted to know the disposition of Allied forces on their flanks. Other than the general sector assignments, Ellis had not been given specific up-to-date information. Progress of the 85th Division on the left flank was especially murky. Rogers expressed concerns over the long supply lines. The Orte–Soriano phase line lay a full forty miles from Rome. Supply dumps and infantry protection teams needed to be established along the entire route. Ellis agreed to all of Rogers's recommendations and promised formal orders would be sent later.[42]

Rogers and Arnold left for Mazzano afterwards. At 0100, 8 June, word arrived that the new orders had been delayed until morning. At 0615, Ellis finally pulled into Rogers's Mazzano CP 1,500 yards west of town. Maps were distributed to all company commanders and a general attack plan was outlined. "Left" and "Right" columns were established with senior infantry commanders placed in charge of each column. Gourley's C Company M4s were assigned to the Left Column and Redle's B Company was placed in the Right Column. A and D Companies followed in reserve.[43]

At 0900, all columns moved out in tandem along Highway 2, passing scores of German vehicles, guns, and dead troops—still smoldering after losing their encounter with Captain Lewis's gunners the prior day. They skirted by Monterosi, then departed Highway 2 for secondary roads passing through sunny green rolling farmland. Only the occasional bursting of shells in the hills ahead or the rising smoke and lingering dust from a distant bridge demolition signaled any German presence.[44] Finally, after covering nearly fourteen miles, C Company met stiff resistance between Fabrica di Roma and Vallerano.[45] Two recon light tanks and one C Company M4 were promptly knocked out by close range AT and *Panzerfaust* fire, and the infantry ran forward to form a hasty defense.[46]

B Company followed the same route in the "Right Column." During the journey, Lt Orient's M4 developed engine trouble and had to drop out of column. Lt Gilden temporarily took charge of both the 1st and 3rd Platoons.[47] As Right Column neared the outskirts of Fabrica, some AT gun fired several rounds at them. Like hound dogs catching whiff of a rabbit's scent, the armored recon platoon bolted on toward town.[48] The infantry dismounted from Gilden's tanks to organize a skirmish line, but the tank lieutenant had to caution the troops to move further back to give his crews proper maneuvering space. Fortunately, the AT fire was inaccurate and Gilden's crews answered with a few rounds of HE "security" fire after assuming covered positions. At the same time, Captain Redle ordered Lt Newman and S/Sgt Smith, following behind in the 2nd Platoon, to dismount and reconnoiter along a nearby ridgeline. By that point, the recon platoon returned, and ordered a cease fire. The town had already been taken. Nobody ever determined who was behind the AT gunfire.[49]

Afterwards, Lt Gilden passed his observations on infantry preparedness along to Major Charles P. Furr, commander of the 3rd Battalion, 351st Infantry Regiment—specifically proposing the rapid formation of skirmish lines away from the tanks when first encountering resistance. Gilden also suggested the infantry conceal themselves with foliage while riding the tank decks. Gilden's tankers had worked with Furr's men on 2 June during the drive on Rome, so the two officers had some established familiarity. The young major, always seeking improvement, readily instituted Gilden's suggestions. At the same time, the tank commanders were cautioned to supervise the placement of infantrymen atop their tanks, and to keep the front areas clear of riders to allow the gunners wide fields of fire.[50]

By early evening, the infantry probing ahead of the Left Column reportedly breached Vallerano. Orders came through at the same time from Brig Gen Kendall, 88th Division Assistant Commanding General, for all elements of Task Force Ellis to clear the roads in the vicinity of Vallerano and Fabrica to allow passage of the 6th South African Armoured Division.[51] The sector lines had been redrawn and the British unit was shifting west as a consequence.[52] When it was learned, however, that the infantry had not entered Vallerano, but were still held up by S/A fire 1,000 yards short of town, supporting C Company tanks were granted a temporary exemption from the order.[53]

Captain Redle's B Company passed through Fabrica around dusk and halted roughly two miles south of Vallerano.[54] No further advances were planned for the evening.[55] Then, under cover of darkness, the few Germans holding Vallerano, retreated northward like gray ghosts—and another Italian village joined the growing list of the liberated.[56]

The next morning, at 0825, 9 June, Lt Col Rogers received new orders to proceed northeast to the final objective: the Orte–Soriano Line.[57] He directed B Company to assemble on the Fabrica–Vignanello road and prepare to lead Right Column. Major Arnold was dispatched by jeep to coordinate with the rest of the task force, but soon discovered orders had not yet arrived for the other units. Finally, at 1025, Left Column started moving. Upon clearing Vallerano, however, the column halted west of Vignanello due to a clog of parked tanks belonging to the 6th South African Armoured Division. Major Arnold, again, was sent scrambling around for a solution.[58]

In the meantime, the Right Column advanced northeast beyond Vignenello to Vasanello; infantry, as usual, riding atop the tanks and TDs while a recon platoon of scout cars and halftracks led the charge. The entire six-mile journey through neatly rowed orchards and gently rolling farmland felt more like a summer "joyride" through eastern Iowa than a deadly hunt for a dangerous enemy. Not a single German appeared to spoil the mood. At Vasanello, the column halted briefly for Lt Newman's 2nd Platoon to assume a turn at the fore, knocking Gilden's 1st Platoon to the second spot, ahead of Captain Redle's command tank and Lt Orient's crews.[59]

The "joyride" continued for another four miles, but the terrain grew more wooded, hilly and jagged. Their objective was Orte, a walled medieval town sitting atop a hill overlooking a Tiber River bend and a nearby bridge spanning the fifty-yard-wide waterway. At 1500, upon descending a narrow hillside road and nearing a crossroads 800 yards west of town, the leading recon troops finally drew sniper fire and slowed to a halt. The crackling fusillade grew thick enough to call forth Newman's tanks.[60] Then, German artillery bursts joined the angry chorus, with the heavier gunfire arching in from across the river.[61]

Newman arrived, and a quick coordination plan was drawn to advance recon teams, tanks, and infantry around to the Tiber bridge on the northeast side of town. The officers agreed to barrel through the resistance in column. Once they started rolling, however, the lead recon car drew a flurry of AT fire and spun around for safety. The advance halted momentarily as Newman, watching from the lead tank, studied the hilltop town 600 yards off to the right. He could see a few civilians walking about, but no Germans. He radioed Redle for advice. The captain suggested that the next time the AT gun fired to "make a run for it" while the crew reloaded. At the same time, Redle ordered Lt Gilden's 1st Platoon to maneuver into position and lay screening smoke beyond the crossroads. Newman timed the run, but also encountered AT fire too frequent for a single gun. After surviving two glancing rounds—one tearing away the driver's periscope assembly, Newman backed out of the field of fire and the advance halted for a third time. No sooner had he stopped when the artillery shells started bursting again—this time walking up from the road junction in sequence toward his position. Newman radioed Redle for permission to back up further, which was immediately granted. While retreating, however, a shell struck a nearby tree—showering the hull with shrapnel. Newman received a nasty nick in the back, but, fortunately, the wound wasn't serious.[62]

Redle recognized Right Column had run into another infamous German AT "Bowling Alley" whereby several AT guns were brought to bear on a single spot. As usual, the enemy selected a bottleneck location where the terrain allowed for the passage of only one vehicle at a time. The German artillery continued falling. The pattern seemed haphazard and inaccurate,[63] but when one round struck a communications scout car 100 yards ahead of Redle,[64] the captain decided to call for support from the 756th Assault Gun Platoon. Unfortunately, all FM radios were out of range. Finally, a message was successfully placed through an infantry SCR-193 AM band. Right Column waited, but nothing happened.[65]

The Americans delayed until nightfall before approaching the road junction and passed through without incident. Afterwards, the recon platoon and infantry stormed up into town—finding the narrow streets completely free of Germans. Redle's tanks followed, taking up supporting firing positions along the hill base. By midnight, the small town was declared clear.[66] However, when a recon scout car tried approaching the Tiber bridge, the main span shuddered with a bright flash and deafening bang before dropping into the river.[67] The Germans registered the final word.

To guard against counterattack, Redle positioned four tanks at a roadblock west of the road junction. A section of tanks was sent up into town while the rest remained spread out along the base below.[68] German artillery fell intermittently through the night, but dissipated completely by morning.[69] Many townspeople, emerging at dawn, hadn't realized that Americans troops had moved in during the night. Upon discovery, a large, joyous celebration was quickly arranged—complete with wine, pasta, and chicken held beneath a gently fluttering Stars & Stripes raised in honor above the town square.[70]

At noon, 10 June, orders came through for Task Force Ellis to officially dissolve and for British units to move into the area as relief. As a consequence, the 756th Tank Battalion was promptly released from the 88th Division and attached to the 1st Armored Group.[71] The tankers were instructed to backtrack, carrying infantry, to an assembly area two-and-a-half miles northwest of Campagnano.[72] The 6th South African Armoured Division still maintained road priority; and the A and C Company tanks, halted with the Left Column in Soriano, faced more congestion through which to navigate.[73]

B Company tanks arrived first at the bivouac around 1400. The kitchen, HQ, and maintenance sections arrived at 2030—making the company whole again, and the more mundane administrative demands of command resumed for Captain Redle.[74] Sgt Graffagnini returned from illness.[75] Long-time B Company tank driver, T/4 John H. Senior, drew a lucky transfer to return home on rotation.[76] The popular and humorous B Company cook,[77] T/5 Guy H. Sheffield, went AWOL the previous day, and Redle had to demote him to private.[78]

That same evening, Major Arnold arrived at the 1st Armored Group CP in Rome. At first, the 756th XO was instructed to assemble the battalion south of Rome, but at 2100, the tall, blond major contacted Rogers in Campagnano to report their eight-hour attachment to the 1st Armored Group had promptly ended. The 756th Tank Battalion had been placed, instead, under Fifth Army control—in reserve.[79] The change was very odd.

"What the hell is going on? Who ever heard of a fighting tank battalion being in Army reserve? Something special must be coming up!" Captain Lewis pondered.[80]

Redle let others ruminate over the significance. Task Force Ellis had just finished chasing the Germans for four exhausting days across forty-five miles and hadn't really

Captain Edwin Olson (holding helmet) and Major Welborn Dolvin (seated behind the jeep steering wheel) take a meal break during unit reorganization after the battle of Cassino. The man in the background is unidentified. (Edwin B. Olson)

B Company mail clerk T/5 Irving Shapiro holds a kitten as 1st Sgt Jack Hogan stands to his left. The man on Shapiro's right is unidentified. (Paul Ranspach family)

T/4 Roy Kosanke (left) and Sgt Hamilton A. Smith (right) pose in Class A uniforms while at Fort Ord, 1942. (U.S. Army Armor and Cavalry Collection)

2nd Lt James L. Harris is presented the Bronze Star for his actions at Cassino by Lt Col Glenn F. Rogers in April 1944. (Doyle Cody collection)

Tankers of the 756th pose for a group photo while training near Montemiletto. These are probably members of D Company. Notice the loose coverall work uniforms. Many have blank armor insignia sewn on the left chest, while others do not. Armor patches with an embroidered "756" did not appear until later in the war. Until then, some tankers inked or handstitched "756" in the yellow area out of a sense of unit pride. (Paul Ranspach family)

Happy children of Montemiletto gather around two 756th tankers outside a building on the town square used to temporarily accommodate the Battalion HQ and medical staff. More than likely, the youngsters are hoping for candy. More than likely, the tankers have some they will give. (Paul Ranspach family)

View from Minturno of Scauri (right foreground), Monte Scauri (Middle) and Gaeta (left background). (Citadel Archives and Museum, Charleston, South Carolina)

Easter Mass is held by Father Kennedy near Minturno on 9 May 1944. This was likely the Mass Redle and Rogers attended, although they cannot be identified in this photo. (Citadel Archives and Museum, Charleston, South Carolina)

349th Regiment infantrymen walk past the cemetery north of Minturno on 14 May 1944. This hilly terrain was poor for tank operations. (National Archives, SC 377803)

12 May 1944. A 756th Tank Battalion M4 passes a British M4 knocked out earlier in the year near the cemetery north of Minturno. View is west. Notice the billowing road dust—a pervasive problem in springtime Italy. (National Archives, SC 190187)

A mortar squad from M Company, 351st Infantry Regiment, walks the same route on 12 May 1944. They are heading north to Santa Maria Infante. (National Archives, SC 364689)

Aerial photo of a rebuilt Minturno with Santa Maria Infante to the north. Image was taken April 1946, nearly two years after Operation *Diadem*. Markings are by the author. (National Archives, SC 320985)

Civilians wash clothing in the Capo d'Acqua creek prior to the war. Because of its high banks, this fifteen-foot-wide waterway became an effective tank obstacle for German defenders a few years later. (National Archives, RG 407, Box 12738)

The eastern slope of San Martino "Hill 66" shows numerous German pillboxes and dugouts. A few trees line the Capo d'Acqua in the foreground while the barren peaks of the 1,402-meter-high Monte S'Angelo (left) and 1,533-meter-high Monte Petrella (right) rise five miles away in the distance. (National Archives, RG 407, Box 12738)

U.S. dive bombers strike Monte Scauri on 16 May 1944. To the left is Scauri and the Gulf of Gaeta. To the right, part of Tremensuoli can be seen atop the hill. (National Archives, SC 377799)

Close-up of a typical German MG bunker. This particular one on San Domenico Ridge was captured by the 339th Infantry Regiment at great cost. (National Archives, RG 407, Box 12738)

4.2-inch mortar crew from D Company, 2nd Chemical Mortar Battalion, operating near Tremensuoli. (Citadel Archives and Museum, Charleston, South Carolina)

88th Division HQ jeep passes a 756th M4 with a thrown track on the Minturno–Santa Maria Infante road. The M4 is likely from C Company and may have hit a Teller mine. This was rough country for tank operation. (Citadel Archives and Museum, Charleston, South Carolina)

16 May 1944. The ruins of Castellonorato. (National Archives, SC 191199)

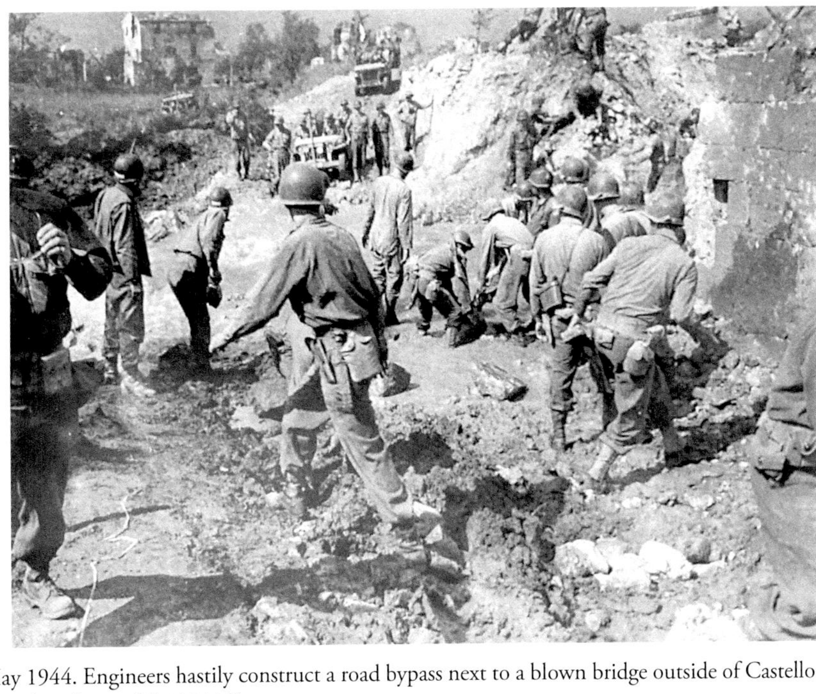

16 May 1944. Engineers hastily construct a road bypass next to a blown bridge outside of Castellonorato. (National Archives, SC 191198)

16 May 1944. An operational German Marder III 75mm SP gun, captured near Castellonorato, is driven to Ordnance. (National Archives, SC 364689)

A destroyed 5-inch coastal gun captured at Gaeta. The Germans turned these guns inland toward Minturno during the Allied breakout of 11–15 May 1944. One was responsible for killing one B Company tanker and seriously wounding two others.

18 May 1944. U.S. II Corps infantrymen, heading toward Itri, follow narrow mountain footpaths near Monte S' Angelo. Tanks simply could not traverse this terrain. (National Archives, SC 191381)

Goumier troops and pack mules walk past a French-crewed American M8 self-propelled 75mm howitzer in the Aurunci mountains. (U.S. Army)

A Moroccan Goumier, wearing a mix of tribal clothing and modern weaponry, sharpens his bayonet in Sicily. "Goums" were fierce fighters but not properly disciplined by their French officers. (U.S. Army)

On a rare day of rest, Lt Redle takes a bath in a tub outside Lenola on 25 May 1944. (David D. Redle)

Pfc Vernor L. Kreitlow, killed in action, 15 May 1944. (Verner Leslie Kreitlow family)

T/5 Leak H. Smitherman, died of wounds, 1 June 1944. (Smitherman family)

A destroyed German Tiger tank is examined by U.S. troops near Cori, Italy, on 1 June 1944. (Citadel Archives and Museum, Charleston, South Carolina)

2 June 1944. U.S. 3rd Infantry Division troops move guardedly through the ruins of Valmontone. The Allies' capture of this key town severed Highway 6 as an avenue of retreat for German forces withdrawing towards Rome. (National Archives, SC 190574)

An M4 from H Co, 13th Armored Regiment, carrying mounted FSSF troops rolls past the "Roma" sign on Highway 6 on the morning of 4 June 1944. A short time later, this very sign was taken down and given to Lt Gen Clark as a war trophy. (National Archives, SC 190655)

On the morning of 4 June 1944, Lt Gen Mark Clark (three stars) studies a map of Rome with mustached FSSF commander Brig Gen Robert T. Frederick as II Corps commander Maj Gen Geoffrey Keyes (two stars) looks on. Notice the knife hanging on Frederick's hip with the "skull crushing" pommel. All Forcemen carried this special knife. (Citadel Archives and Museum, Charleston, South Carolina)

4 June 1944. Brig Gen Frederick (center) sits at his informal CP on a hillside only sixty yards from the city limits of Rome. He is likely awaiting reports from recon teams sent in earlier. Notice his bandaged neck. Frederick had been wounded several days earlier but refused hospitalization. (National Archives, SC 377812)

4 June 1944. An M4 from Task Force Howze burns near the Centocelle train station on Highway 6 outside the Rome city limits. (National Archives, SC 377811)

Late afternoon, 4 June 1944. FSSF and 351st Regiment troops move up the Via Prenestina near the main rail yards. M4 in foreground is likely from the 3rd Battalion, 13th Armored Regiment. Destroyed Tiger tank can be seen further ahead. (Citadel Archives and Museum, Charleston, South Carolina)

4 June 1944. The 191st Tank Battalion (supporting the 34th Inf Div) waits on Highway 6 for the signal to enter Rome. Major Dolvin had just assumed command of this unit two days prior. At this point, the German hold on the city was broken, and an orderly Allied entrance became the chief challenge. (Citadel Archives and Museum Charleston, South Carolina)

Another column of American armor, including an open-topped M-10 tank destroyer, enters Rome on 4 June 1944. By now, the mood among Fifth Army troops had grown confident and expectant. Photo was taken along the Via Casilina (Highway 6). (U.S. Army)

Captain Mark Radcliff and his FSSF recon team are mobbed by jubilant Romans as German forces flee from the city. (Citadel Archives and Museum, Charleston, South Carolina)

4 June 1944. Lt Gen Mark Clark tours Rome in triumph. His controversial decision to take the city ahead of a chance to annihilate the German Tenth Army, nevertheless boosted the morale and public profile of his battered U.S. Fifth Army. (U.S. Army)

8 June 1944. Lt Gen Clark departs the Vatican after meeting with Pope Pius XII. At Clark's side is his Chief of Staff, Maj Gen Alfred M. Gruenther. Monsignor Walter Carrol is seated in front next to driver Sgt Joseph Adayeh. (National Archives, SC 191256)

18 June 1944. U.S. Army divisional commanders gather at the Fifth Army HQ. Left to right: Brig Gen Robert T. Frederick (FSSF), Maj Gen John B. Coulter (85th Inf Div), Maj Gen Ernest B. Harmon (1st Armored Div), Maj Gen John W. O'Daniel (3rd Inf Div), Maj Gen William W. Eagles (45th Inf Div) and Maj Gen John W. Sloan (88th Inf Div). The 756th Tank Battalion fought under every one of these commanders while in Italy. (National Archives, SC 220363)

Captain French G. Lewis, CO of A Company, and Captain Edwin B. Olson, 756th Tank Battalion Communications officer display a captured German flag somewhere in Italy. (French G. Lewis)

756th Tank Battalion CO, Lt Col Glenn F. Rogers; Captain Edwin B. Olson and Battalion S-2, Captain Robert H. Rydman, take a break from staff duties to pose for a photo. After Cassino, Rogers was brought in to replace a promoted Lt Col Sweeting. Although not as tactically creative as Sweeting, Rogers's competence, maturity, and concern for the well-being of his men gained the quick admiration and loyalty of the battalion. (French G. Lewis)

B Company Supply Sergeant Gene Shirley with "Piccolo Stronza," the unmannerly company mascot. (Paul Ranspach family)

Lt Col Glenn F. Rogers and Major Edwin "Cotton" Arnold attending Allied planning meetings in either Rome or Naples during the summer of 1944. (Glenn F. Rogers)

Sgt Roy L. Anderson (left) and S/Sgt Haskell O. Oliver (right) of the 3rd Platoon. Oliver received the Silver Star for his heroic actions on 4 June 1944. (Family of Roy Leonard Anderson)

Sgt Roy L. Anderson (left) and T/4 Bert L. Bulen, gunner for S/Sgt Oliver. Bulen was blessed with extraordinary eyesight—which helped make him one of the best gunners in the battalion. (Family of Roy Leonard Anderson)

caught up with them. No doubt, the 756th Tank Battalion would be sent to fight them again somewhere else.

The 26-year-old captain unrolled his thick Klondike bag beneath the undercarriage of his #17 command tank and crawled inside. At that moment, Redle just wanted sleep.

U.S. 88th Infantry Division

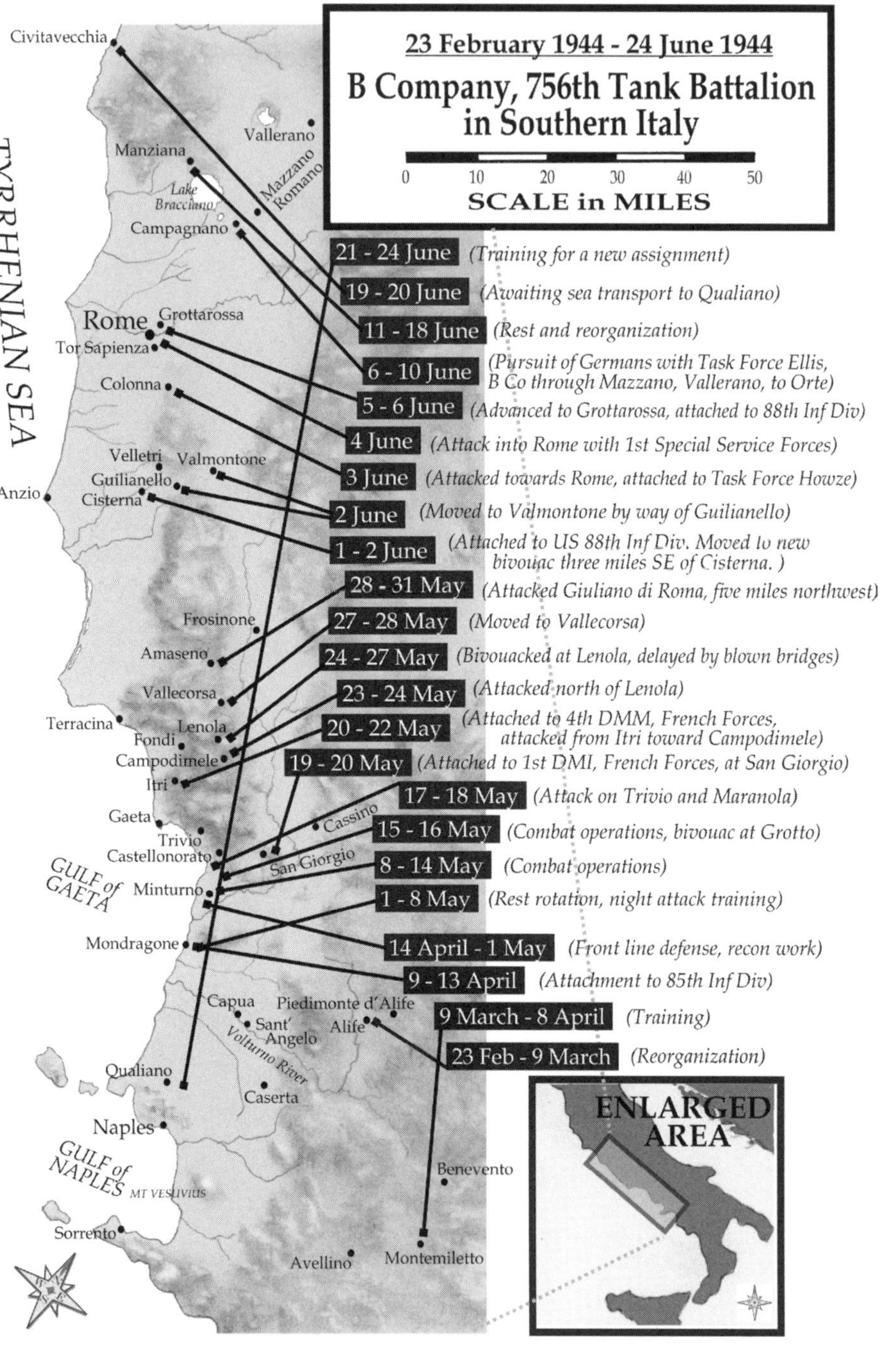
23 February 1944 - 24 June 1944
B Company, 756th Tank Battalion in Southern Italy
0 10 20 30 40 50
SCALE in MILES
21 - 24 June (Training for a new assignment)
19 - 20 June (Awaiting sea transport to Qualiano)
11 - 18 June (Rest and reorganization)
6 - 10 June (Pursuit of Germans with Task Force Ellis, B Co through Mazzano, Vallerano, to Orte)
5 - 6 June (Advanced to Grottarossa, attached to 88th Inf Div)
4 June (Attack into Rome with 1st Special Service Forces)
3 June (Attacked towards Rome, attached to Task Force Howze)
2 June (Moved to Valmontone by way of Guilianello)
1 - 2 June (Attached to US 88th Inf Div. Moved to new bivouac three miles SE of Cisterna.)
28 - 31 May (Attacked Giuliano di Roma, five miles northwest)
27 - 28 May (Moved to Vallecorsa)
24 - 27 May (Bivouacked at Lenola, delayed by blown bridges)
23 - 24 May (Attacked north of Lenola)
20 - 22 May (Attached to 4th DMM, French Forces, attacked from Itri toward Campodimele)
19 - 20 May (Attached to 1st DMI, French Forces, at San Giorgio)
17 - 18 May (Attack on Trivio and Maranola)
15 - 16 May (Combat operations, bivouac at Grotto)
8 - 14 May (Combat operations)
1 - 8 May (Rest rotation, night attack training)
14 April - 1 May (Front line defense, recon work)
9 - 13 April (Attachment to 85th Inf Div)
9 March - 8 April (Training)
23 Feb - 9 March (Reorganization)
TYRRHENIAN SEA
Civitavecchia
Vallerano
Manziana
Mazzano Romano
Lake Bracciano
Campagnano
Rome
Grottarossa
Tor Sapienza
Colonna
Velletri
Valmontone
Guilianello
Cisterna
Anzio
Frosinone
Amaseno
Vallecorsa
Terracina
Lenola
Fondi
Campodimele
Itri
Gaeta
Cassino
Trivio
Castellonorato
San Giorgio
GULF of GAETA
Minturno
Mondragone
Capua
Piedimonte d'Alife
Sant' Angelo
Alife
Volturno River
Qualiano
Caserta
Naples
GULF of NAPLES
MT VESUVIUS
Benevento
Sorrento
Avellino
Montemiletto
ENLARGED AREA

CHAPTER EIGHTEEN

Summer Respite: 11 June 1944 to 24 June 1944

1st Sgt Alvin Nusz grabbed the corners of Captain Redle's Klondike bag and mischievously pulled his CO out into blinding morning sunshine. The battalion had just been ordered—not back into battle—but on a two-week rest stint along the shores of Lake Bracciano, several miles to the west.[1] A few hours later at 1030, 11 June, the battalion pulled south onto Highway 2, then turned westward, tracing along the southern shore of the five-mile-wide lake, before arriving in the resort town of Bracciano on the western edge. A gentle drizzle dampened the first leg of the twenty-one-mile journey, but soon acquiesced to warm sun and blue skies.[2] A South African tank outfit, already lining the streets, squeezed tightly against the storefronts to allow the passage of their American counterparts—creating barely two-feet of clearance. During the slow-moving process, Redle had concerns German planes might appear, but none ever did.[3]

The companies dispersed beneath tall stately oaks growing in the area.[4] A Company remained near Bracciano, but B Company established a bivouac one mile southwest of Manziana, three miles further west of the lake.[5] Technically, the 756th's new orders attached them to the 1st Armored Division for "training," but no actual training occurred.[6] The first few days were spent cleaning and repairing.[7] Clothes needed to be washed of fleas,[8] and most of the tanks sustained track damage—requiring replacement.[9] Since 11 May, the battalion marched and fought nearly every day—logging an average of 600 road miles per combat vehicle.[10] Every tank, jeep, truck, and half-track needed new engine oil and a thorough regreasing of all moving parts.[11]

The men, too, needed to refresh. The month-long campaign to take Rome resulted in the deaths of eighteen enlisted and the wounding of another eight officers and seventy-six enlisted men.[12] Although these losses were not nearly as severe as those sustained at Cassino, the crews still needed time to rest, regroup, and integrate a new batch of replacements sure to arrive. The cool swimming waters of Lake Bracciano brought welcome respite when each day's work was done.[13] Time was also set aside daily for the men to simply "relax."[14]

Several B Company tankers received promotions. Cpl Ralph A. Rutzen became a sergeant; Cpl Luther A. Kinsworthy, a T/4; T/5 Francis A. Fischer, a T/4; and T/5 Clyde W. Guild, Pfc William J. McInrue, and Pvt Raymond W. Colley were all appointed as corporals. Three others became T/5s, while six privates were upgraded to privates first class. At the same time, twelve new privates joined the company as replacements.[15] The spare officer, 1st Lt Robert L. Gilman, moved to C Company.[16]

Redle received an official complaint about the behavior of one of his tank commanders, Sgt Roy L. Anderson. Apparently, the Illinoian angered Maj Gen Truscott—of all people—on a mountain road a few weeks earlier. Redle's men recognized their captain had two walks: the normal one and the "you're in trouble one" where he approached with both arms clasped tightly behind his back. Anderson saw the latter. Redle described the general's complaint and demanded an explanation.

Anderson recounted the incident: his tank was rolling down a narrow mountain road with the driver "riding the hell out of the left brake" in order to avoid going off the hill. The whole way, Anderson watched gravel and stones shift from beneath the right tread and tumble down a slope at least 500 feet to the bottom. Coming up the other way, Anderson saw a jeep with two stars on the front. Both vehicles halted and Truscott shouted, "Get that damn thing over!" Anderson took a moment to glance down the forbidding slope and then welcomed the general to send his own driver over to try "because if he pulls the tank over, it will roll down that hill until next month." The general did not appreciate the sergeant's offer but did back down from his demands. As a solution, all five of Anderson's crew helped Truscott's driver turn the jeep around so both vehicles could return to the bottom of the mountain. "You're going to hear about this," Truscott warned upon departing. "I hope I'm still living to hear about it," Anderson shot back.

Anderson forgot about the incident entirely until Redle approached him with that walk. After Anderson finished, the captain gave the tall sergeant a reassuring pat on the back: "I'm still behind you," Redle smiled.[17]

Redle and Nusz were required to produce an after-action report of all the company's activities from 10 January through 11 June 1944. The two sat down, pouring over a handwritten daily record maintained by 1st Sgts Hogan and Nusz over the five-month time span, and drafted a condensed typewritten report. A bottle of sweet vermouth, split between the two of them over several nights, helped brighten the tedium. Each of the three platoon leaders were also required to record their experiences and observations.[18]

At some point over the last four months, Supply Sgt Gene Shirley and cook Guy Sheffield had purchased a Brazilian screw-tail monkey from an Englishman serving in the British Eighth Army. Though male, the animal was already inaptly named "Piccolo Stronza"—meaning "Little Bitch" in Italian—improperly constructed with confused word gender endings.[19] The high-strung creature displayed a host of flawed behaviors—including crazed shell shock at the sound of gunfire—yet still became an entertaining, treasured company mascot of sorts. Shirley dressed Piccolo in a tiny U.S. Army uniform and tried encouraging good behavior from the excitable little creature. Captain Redle even "promoted" Piccolo on occasion. The monkey eventually rose to the rank of staff sergeant, but lost every stripe after urinating all over company supplies.[20] Another time, the unprovoked primate bit T/4 Randolph Perdue on the wrist—drawing blood and leaving a scar.[21] Worse, Piccolo often exhibited a grossly inappropriate public masturbation habit.[22] "He is not the type of monkey one would have around the drawing room as his habits are not above reproach," one 756th officer reported in a letter home to his wife—without going into detail.[23] Even so, Piccolo's poor antics never got him booted from the company entirely.

While bivouacked at Bracciano, the 756th tankers were issued passes to visit Rome in shifts. Some received day-only visits, while others scored R & R (Rest and Relaxation) lasting up to three days.[24] Nearly everyone in the battalion earned a turn, and the men actually enjoyed donning their dress uniforms, peaked caps, and ties for a change.[25] Beautiful women seemed to stroll everywhere and a horse and buggy tour around town only cost a dollar.[26] Popular destinations included the Colosseum, the old Roman Forum, and Saint Peter's and Saint Paul's Basilicas.[27] The Vatican, of course, hit the top of the tourist list for any Catholics in the battalion. Pvt Cletus Offerman earned a three-day pass but was short on cash. Captain Redle loaned his fellow Catholic the necessary funds, and Offerman enjoyed once-in-a-lifetime experiences participating in a parade review before General Eisenhower and receiving a personal blessing from Pope Pius XII, which he later said passed through his body like an "electric shock."[28] Captain Redle also toured Rome and received the Pope's blessing—but his came as part of a much larger audience of over 5,000 GIs.[29]

Captain Lewis enjoyed three full days of R & R in Rome—his first pass or leave of any kind since departing Fort Lewis two years earlier. While enjoying a smooth, refreshing beer in the bar of the Excelsior Hotel, Lewis struck up a lively conversation with two captains and a 1st lieutenant from the 135th Infantry Regiment. When the three officers discovered Lewis was from the 756th Tank Battalion, however, their mood soured considerably. Sweeting was the reason.

"Why the hell didn't you keep him?" one complained.

"I ought to whip your ass for sending him to us!" exclaimed another.

"Why are you raising hell with me?" Lewis countered, "Your general had him transferred to your division and gave him your regiment."

The three officers were particularly upset over Sweeting needlessly getting several officers killed with "his screwy ideas." Lewis could only listen and nod in sympathy.

Later, Lewis learned Sweeting and his jeep driver had been captured ten days earlier, during the drive on Rome.[30] This news surprised him, although it shouldn't have. At some point, the colonel's luck was bound to run out.[31]

On 15 June, the 756th was detached from both the Fifth Army and the 1st Armored Division.[32] The next morning, the unit was attached to Allied Forces

Headquarters and the 3rd Infantry Division.[33] Captain Oscar Long, assuming the role of battalion S-3 after Dolvin's departure and Arnold's elevation to XO, became a major.[34] Rumors swirled of the battalion heading to Naples for amphibious training.[35]

For the next three days, the tankers relaxed and worked near Lake Bracciano and listened as gossip grew.[36] Finally, official confirmation came on Sunday 18 June: the battalion was ordered to pack up and move out to the port of Civitavecchia by 0800 the following morning.[37] Many men grumbled over being short-changed several days of a promised "two weeks" of rest.[38] Several—including three privates from B Company—foolishly went AWOL in futile protest.[39]

The order was amended to an earlier 0430 departure time. The crews were awakened at 0300, a column formed, and the twenty-seven-mile road march to the coast was completed by 0630.[40] The town, itself, had been devastated from previous Allied aerial attacks—so the column waited on the outskirts until space became available near the loading docks.[41] At 2000, the 756th Tank Battalion was beckoned forward and packed aboard several waiting LSTs. B Company loaded up entirely inside LST-174.[42] The men unpacked their bedrolls and slept inside the dimly lit hold alongside their tanks while the LSTs pulled away from the docks after dusk.[43]

The men woke the next morning, 20 June, to find their LSTs, not at sea, but anchored off Civitavecchia.[44] The delay, measured by warm briny breezes and the gently rocking motion of the waves, was not at all unpleasant, and the Navy food was delicious as usual. The men had nearly forgotten how enjoyable life was without dust.[45]

At 1800, the anchors were hoisted and the small convoy left harbor headed southeast.[46] The shore of the mainland was still visible as darkness descended and the crews turned in for another night of sleep alongside their tanks.[47] At 1600, 21 June, the convoy pulled into Pozzuoli harbor, west of Naples.[48] The enormous doors on each LST's prow parted and the tanks drove out onto concrete quays among towering stacks of cargo, long rows of olive drab vehicles, and bustling servicemen. Another battalion column promptly formed, followed by an eight-mile road march north to Qualiano. At 1945, the tanks halted among apple and plum trees one-mile north of town. The men fashioned tents from shelter halves and set to work constructing a new camp.[49] This small patch of Italian farmland would become their home for the foreseeable future.

The Fifth Army Invasion Training Center had moved from Oran to Naples. This newly christened "Invasion Training Center" was administered directly by Allied Forces HQ under British General Sir Henry Maitland Wilson—the highest command in the Mediterranean Theater. Clearly, amphibious operations hadn't ended with the Normandy landings. This recent attachment to Allied Forces HQ and relocation to Qualiano meant something truly major was in the works—as Captain Lewis had suspected two weeks earlier. At least the 756th Tank Battalion would face this new challenge while joined with their old friends of the 3rd Infantry Division.[50]

On 23 June, sad news filtered through the B Company bivouac of the passing of Pvt Paul Cardullo on 11 June—a company member for over a year. The 32-year-old loader lost his foot during the battle for Rome, and then his life a week later due to medical complications.[51] The upstate New Yorker was unmarried, but left behind a mother, father, and a Catholic priest brother.[52]

Cardullo's unexpected death was not only a stark reminder of the brutal battles already fought, but of even tougher ones still ahead. The men speculated over how long hostilities might last. They knew they were winning, but few battle-hardened veterans voiced any optimism for a swift end. Many concluded the war in Europe wouldn't wrap up until 1946, and the Pacific war would continue raging another two years beyond that. A rather reserved catch phrase "Golden Gate in '48" made the rounds.[53] 1948 was another four years into the future. In effect, they had accepted war as life.

On 24 June 1944, B Company's official roster listed one captain, two 1st lieutenants, one 2nd lieutenant, and 112 enlisted men.[54] Who among them would still be around in six months, let alone four years?

The tankers camped in Qualiano had survived six months fighting seemingly impossible missions—in places tanks were never designed to go: muddy rivers, rubbled cities, and tight mountain trails—lasting weeks on end. These were not Sweeting's "screwy ideas" sending them off to fight in these outrageous situations, but the United States Army. The entire war was screwy.

Now that screwy war demanded these tankers should train as submariners.

Allied Forces headquarters

The Main Gate at Monte Cassino, April 1944

APPENDIX ONE

Glossary, Phonetic Alphabet, and Military Clock

Term	Description
A-trains	The part of an army unit that is engaged in the combat area
Airburst	Artillery or mortar round intended to explode overhead
AP	Armor piercing
Assembly Area	Area for final adjustments before battle, usually a mile or two from the front
AT gun	Anti-tank gun (towed or self-propelled)
AWOL	Absent without leave
B-trains	The part of an army unit supporting an army unit in combat but located away from combat
BAR	Browning Automatic Rifle
Bivouac	A temporary encampment without shelter
Bn	Battalion
Burp Gun	American nickname for German submachine gun
Caliber	The internal diameter of gun bore (expressed in inches or millimeters)
Cav	Cavalry
CEF	Corps Expeditionaire Français
CG	Commanding general
CO	Commanding officer
Co	Company
CP	Command post
Defilade	Arranging forces by using natural obstacles to avoid enemy fire
Div	Division

Doughboy	Slang term used by tankers to describe an infantryman
DOW	Died of wounds
Echelon	The formation and maneuvering of troops in step-like fashion
EM	Enlisted man or men
Feldgrau	Greenish-gray color of German WWII uniforms
First Echelon Maintenance	Regular vehicle maintenance carried out by the operator or the crew
G-2	Intelligence officer/section, division or Army level
G-3	Operations officer/section, division or Army level
GHQ	General headquarters
GO	General orders
GSW	Gunshot wound
H-hour	Start time of an operation
HE	High explosive
Heer	German Army
Howitzer	Artillery cannon that dispatches rounds on parabolic trajectories
HQ	Headquarters
Inf	Infantry
KIA	Killed in action
Landser	Common German infantryman or riflemen
LST	Landing ship, tank
LWA	Lightly wounded in action
MG	Machine gun
MIA	Missing in action
mm	Millimeter (25.4 mm equals 1 inch)
Mortar	Muzzle loading, low velocity artillery with a short range
MP	Military police
MPH	Miles per hour
NCO	Non-commissioned officer
NZ	New Zealand
OCS	Officer candidate school
OD	Olive drab
Panzer	German word for tank or armor

Panzerfaust	"Tank fist" (German handheld AT rocket)
Pillbox	Small concrete structure housing an MG or AT gun
PW	Prisoner of war
R & R	Rest and relaxation
RCT	Regimental combat team
Regt	Regiment
ROTC	Reserve Officers' Training Corps
RPM	Revolutions per minute
S-1	Personnel officer/section, battalion or regimental level
S-2	Intelligence officer/section, battalion or regimental level
S-3	Operations officer/section, battalion or regimental level
S-4	Logistics officer/section, battalion or regimental level
S/A	Small arms (refers to hand held rifles, pistols, machine pistols)
SFW	Shell fragment wound
Shot	Tanker slang for armor piercing (AP) round
SNAFU	An acronym for "Situation Normal All F*cked Up"—an error
SP	Self-propelled (refers to a motorized AT gun—usually with caterpillar tracks)
Sv	Service
SWA	Severely wounded in action
T/O	Table of organization
T/O&E	Table of organization and equipment
TD	Tank destroyer
Tk	Tank
TOT	Time on target, coordinated artillery fire timed to deliver all rounds on a target at once
USMA	United States Military Academy at West Point, New York
WIA	Wounded in action
WP	White phosphorus—used for marking or blinding a target
XO	Executive officer

WWII U.S. Army Phonetic Alphabet			
ABLE	HOW	OBOE	VICTOR
BAKER	ITEM	PETER	WILLIAM
CHARLIE	JIG	QUEEN	X-RAY
DOG	KING	ROGER	YOKE
EASY	LOVE	SUGAR	ZEBRA
FOX	MIKE	TARE	
GEORGE	NAN	UNCLE	

MILITARY CLOCK

APPENDIX TWO

756th Tank Battalion Casualties Day-By-Day at Cassino 1944

Source: 756th Tank Battalion Morning Reports from 10 January to 1 April 1944 for Companies Headquarters (HQ), A, B, C, D, and Service (Sv). (Medical Detachment is not represented.)

Key: KIA: Killed in Action; DOW: Died of Wounds; PW: Prisoner of War; SWA: Seriously Wounded in Action and evacuated; WIA: Wounded in Action and evacuated; IIA: Injured in Action and evacuated; LWA: Lightly wounded in action and remained on duty. ***Names in bold*** *represent combat deaths.*

14 Jan DOW: **T/4 Gus T. Markos** [C] (*died 17 Jan*)
WIA: Cpl Baldemar S. Pantoja [C], Pfc James F. Feeney [C]
LWA: T/5 Lewis Paxton [C]

25 Jan KIA: **Cpl Dean R. Clow** [HQ]

26 Jan SWA: S/Sgt Bernard H. Gaugler [C]
WIA: Pvt Merle E. Brooks [B]

27 Jan KIA: **2nd Lt Wayne B. Henry** [B], **Cpl Paul P. Tirpak** [B], **Pvt John F. Bacha** [B], **Pvt Engvald S. Hindrum** [Sv]
DOW: **Pfc Isaac J. Boose** [C] (*died 28 Jan*)
PW: Capt Charles M. Wilkinson [B], S/Sgt Carl T. Crawford [B], Sgt Leland P. Campbell [B], Cpl Charles H. Coleman [B], T/4 Edward A. Avettant [B], T/5 Louis A. Laliberty [B], Pfc Hubert S. Shew [B]
WIA: 2nd Lt Roland V. Hunter [A]
IIA: T/4 John S. Nichols [A], Pvt Virgil V. Kriz [A]
LWA: T/5 Earl V. Giesige [Sv], Pfc James A. McNamara [C]

28 Jan KIA: **Pfc Norval N. Clayton** [HQ]
SWA: Pvt John Rodriguqez [HQ]
WIA: Cpl Norman S. Lindow [HQ], T/5 Otis E. Hyles [HQ], Pfc James B. Patty [HQ], Pvt Alex P. Reed [HQ]
LWA: Pvt Joseph Czerkas [A], Pvt Albert C. Schmall [C]

29 Jan	KIA: **Sgt Raymond V. Galbraith** [A], Cpl **Joseph J. Olbyk** [A], **T/4 Herman J. Bayless** [A], **Cpl William F. McGill** [A], **Pfc Clyde M. Long** [C], **Pvt Harvey J. Arrington, Jr.** [C], **Pvt Edward J. Dudzinski** [A], **Pvt Alfred R. Shanahan** [A] DOW: **T/5 Rudolph A. Sharbutt** [C] (*died later the same day*) SWA: S/Sgt Thomas P. Ames [A], T/4 Leroy Doolittle [A], Cpl Nazario Martinez [A], Pvt Vincent P. Ciccerelli [A], T/5 Sam A. Liberto [D] WIA: Capt French G. Lewis [A], 1st Lt Robert L. Gilman [A], 1st Lt David Loeb [C], Sgt Herman C. Kirtley [C], Cpl Frank H. Linderman [A], T/4 Earl Hollon [A], T/5 Lewis Paxton [C], T/5 William B. Toler [C], Pfc Edgar P. Ayers [C], Pfc Frank J. Casper [A], Pfc Ignacio F. Jimenez [A], Pfc Richard F. Makynen [A], Pvt Bernard L. Cohen [C], Pvt Donald G. Isakson [C]
30 Jan	KIA: **Pfc Louis E. Cottonware** [D] LWA: Sgt Robert J. Holloway [D]
31 Jan	KIA: **Pvt Albert T. Gober** [A], **Pvt Darrell D. Shryer** [A] SWA: Sgt Howard A. Harrison [A], Cpl Edwin R. Rittenbach [A], Cpl Mike Sudvary, Jr. [A] IIA: Sgt Ithel R. Adlard [HQ] LWA: Sgt Norman C. Fuller [A], Cpl Chester A. Duvinski, [A], Pfc Stanley J. Kotarski [D]
1 Feb	WIA: 1st Lt Ralph Hanson [HQ] LWA: 2nd Lt John J. Czakowkski [B], Pvt Lee P. Barnes [D]
2 Feb	WIA: 2nd Lt Howard F. Michael [C], Pfc Walter E. Burg [C] LWA: Sgt James M. Riley [C], Pfc Rocco Peluso [C]
3 Feb	KIA: **Pfc Wilbur M. Lewis** [C], **Pvt William S. Keoke** [C] DOW: **Sgt Edwin Holmquist** [C] (*died 6 Feb*), **T/5 Lee Roy Jones** [C] (*date unknown*) PW: 2nd Lt James W. Granberry [C], Sgt James Vaughn [C], Cpl George C. Dugger [C], T/4 Erwin E. Tompkins [C], T/4 James W. Nichols [C], T/5 Jeff D. Goddard [C], Pfc Lowell M. McMurtrey [C], Pvt Charles F. Foley [C], Pvt Eric L. Biegler [C] WIA: 1st Lt William R. Engfer [HQ], Cpl Edward J. Clark [HQ] LWA: Maj Welborn G. Dolvin [HQ], S/Sgt Charles N. Goodloe [D], T/4 Howard J. Bowers [Sv]
4 Feb	IIA: T/4 Cullen B. Ward [Sv], Pfc Victor W. Scholz [HQ]
5 Feb	KIA: **Pfc David J. Orris** [B] (*died later the same day*) DOW: **Sgt Eugene K. Wunderlich** [B] (*died 17 Feb*) SWA: Sgt Roland L. Buys [B], T/4 Malcolm L. Smith [HQ] WIA: S/Sgt Oric W. Johannesen [B]

6 Feb	LWA: T/5 William E. Stiles [D]
7 Feb	LWA: Pvt Thomas E. Mawhiney [Sv]
8 Feb	KIA: **S/Sgt Dennis W. Grigsby** [C], **Pvt Ralph Morrison** [C] LWA: S/Sgt Willam Fodor [C], Sgt Millard J. Parrish [C], T/4 Albert C. Voegele [C], T/4 William F. Holton [C]
10 Feb	WIA: 1st Lt William F. Bouch [Sv], 2nd Lt Andrew D. Orient [A]
13 Feb	LWA: T/4 Arend Strand [B], Pvt Louis P. DiRocco [HQ]
14 Feb	SWA: Cpl Calvin J. O'Leary [C], Cpl Eugene H. Rule [B], T/5 Edward Tomaszewksi [B] WIA: Cpl Ralph A. Rutzen [B], Pfc Kevin F. Brennan [B], Pvt John J. Deenihan [A]
16 Feb	KIA: **T/5 Joe B. Taylor** [A] WIA: Pvt Joseph P. Birttnen [C]
19 Feb	KIA: **S/Sgt Willam Fodor** [C] WIA; Cpl Richard E. Wills [C], Cpl Chester D. Preddy [C]
21 Feb	IIA: Pvt George C. Davis [B]

Analysis: The 756th Tank Battalion arrived at the front on 11 January and departed 22 February 1944—a span of forty-three days. During that time, this 750-man unit suffered 125 combat casualties—a sixteen percent rate. This number does not seem high until one considers that most were highly specialized and trained medium tank crewmembers. The 756th Tank Battalion had three medium tank companies and one light tank company—with about 100 men in each company. In reality, the 756th Tank Battalion lost a full company of tankers during that short period. Thirty were killed, sixteen captured, fifty-one were wounded and evacuated (fifteen with life-threatening wounds), and another six were injured and required hospitalization. Twenty-four others were wounded but did not require time away from duty.

A closer look at the types of casualties (those greater than LWA) reveals a shockingly high loss of leadership: all three medium tank company commanders were casualties (one captured, two wounded and evacuated), nine lieutenants were lost (one killed, one captured, seven wounded and evacuated), six staff sergeants and nine sergeants were also lost—these were the battalion's "doer" platoon leaders and tank commanders. The gunners and tank drivers (corporals, T/4s, and T/5s) also suffered greatly: with losses of seventeen, nine, and ten respectively. A great deal of training was required to become a proficient tank driver or gunner. These men were not easily replaced. This is why the battalion had to be pulled from the line in mid-February for reorganization.

APPENDIX THREE

34th Infantry Division Effective Strength Table, 9 February 1944

SECRET SECRET

HEADQUARTERS, 34TH INFANTRY DIVISION
UNITED STATES ARMY

9 February 1944

EFFECTIVE STRENGTH TABLE BY UNIT
As of 2400 hrs., 8 February 1944

	133rd Infantry			135th Infantry			168th Infantry		
	Off	WO	EM	Off	WO	EM	Off	WO	EM
Hq & Hq Co.	18	2	117	13	1	131	18	1	131
Service Company	10	3	130	11	3	148	12	2	111
Cannon Company	8		122	6		130	6		113
A.T. Company	7		155	7		143	5		114
Medical Det.	12		92	7		105	10		100
TOTAL	55	5	616	44	4	657	51	3	569
Hq & Hq Co. 1st. Bn.	9		116	8		119	10		126
Company A	4		85	6		95	0		40
Company B	6		37	4		160	5		50
Company C	4		84	3		101	1		60
Company D	6		155	5		154	4		146
TOTAL 1st. Bn.	29		477	26		629	20		422
Hq & Hq Co. 2nd. Bn.				11		119	8		119
Company E				2		100	5		147
Company F				5		85	5		136
Company G				5		114	5		141
Company H				5		146	6		159
TOTAL 2nd. Bn.				28		564	29		702
Hq & Hq Co. 3rd. Bn.	11		116	8		122	10		128
Company I	4		104	2		78	4		151
Company K	5		117	3		101	4		125
Company L	6		114	4		127	6		116
Company M	5		177	3		133	5		151
TOTAL 3rd. Bn.	31		628	20		561	29		671
100th Inf. Bn. (Sep)									
Hq & Hq Co.	15	1	139						
Company A	5		95						
Company B	4		81						
Company C	6		80						
Company D	4		110						
TOTAL	34	1	505						
TOTAL REGIMENT	149	6	2226	118	4	2411	129	3	2364

H. L. S.

APPENDIX FOUR

Allied Forces Chain of Command, Cassino, Italy, January 1944

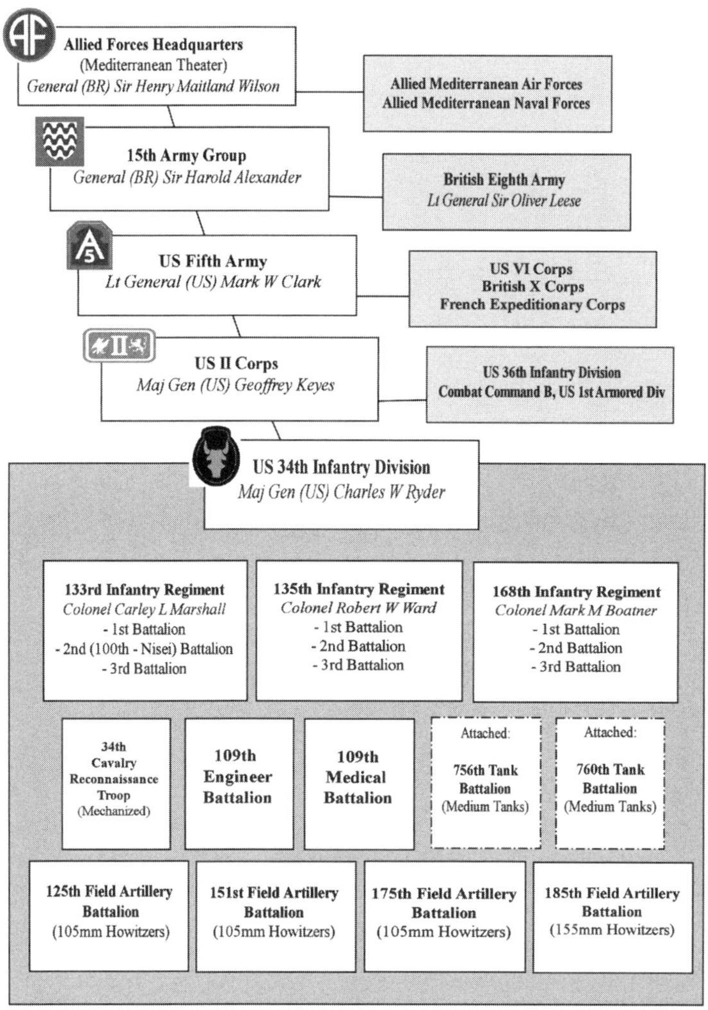

APPENDIX FIVE

Order of Battle, II New Zealand Corps, February 1944

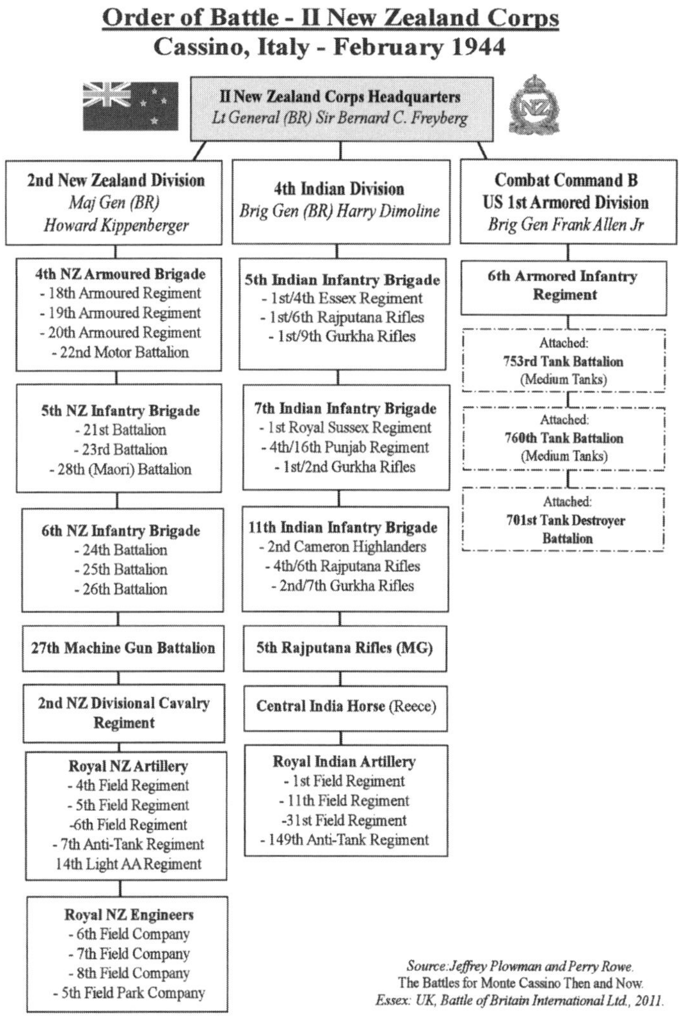

APPENDIX SIX

10 February 1944 S-3 Operations Overlay, 168th Infantry Regiment

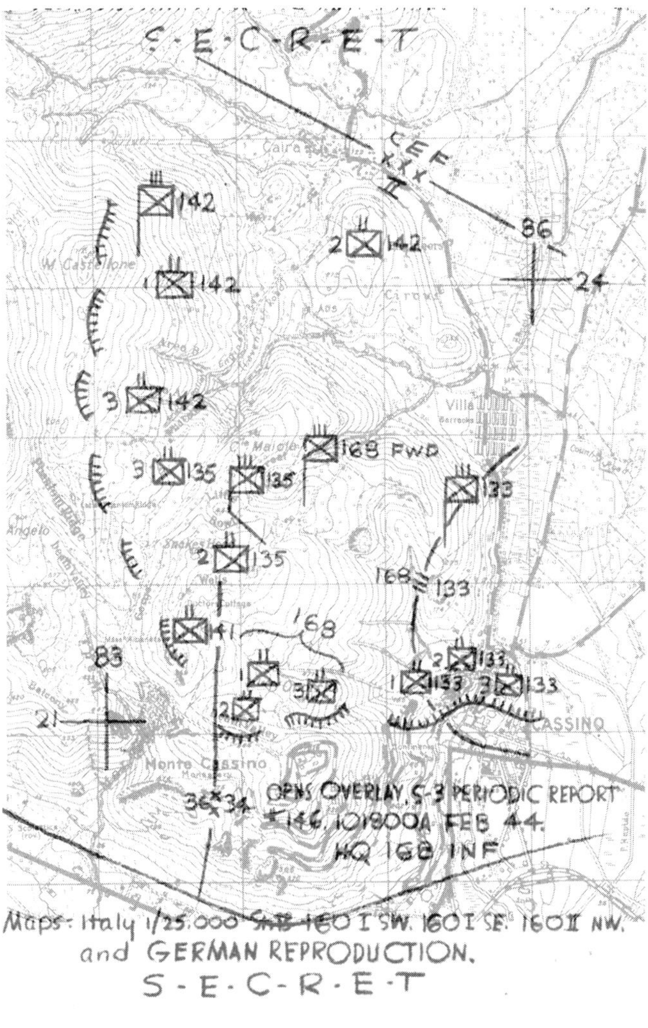

APPENDIX SEVEN

13 February 1944 Disposition of Battalions Overlay, HQ 133rd Infantry Regiment

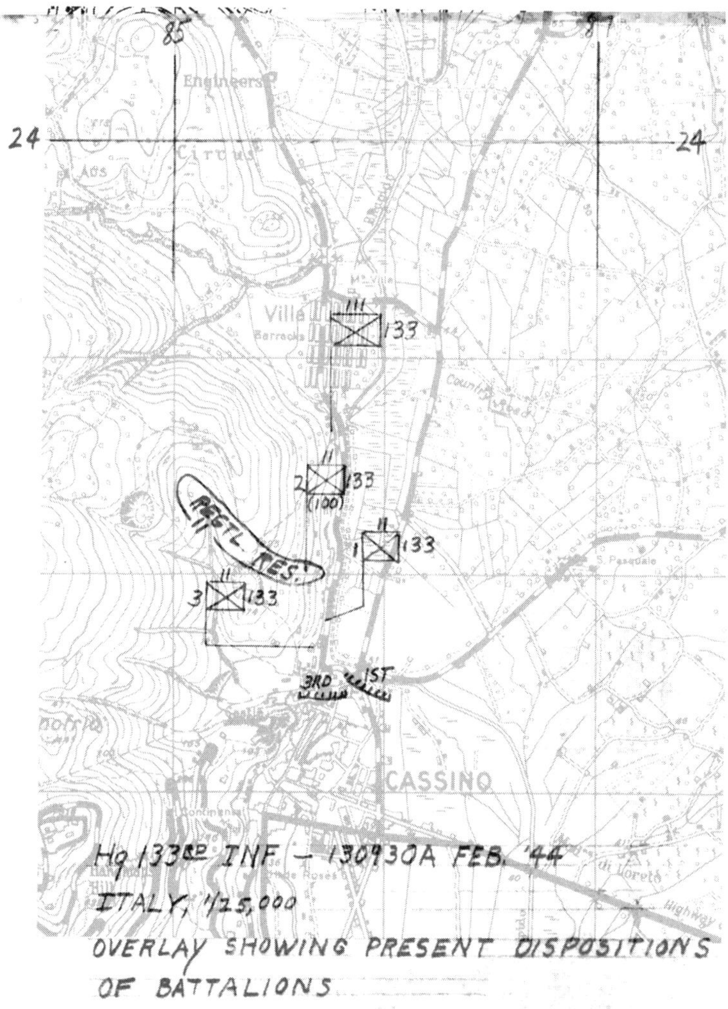

APPENDIX EIGHT

756th Unit Journal Map of North Cassino

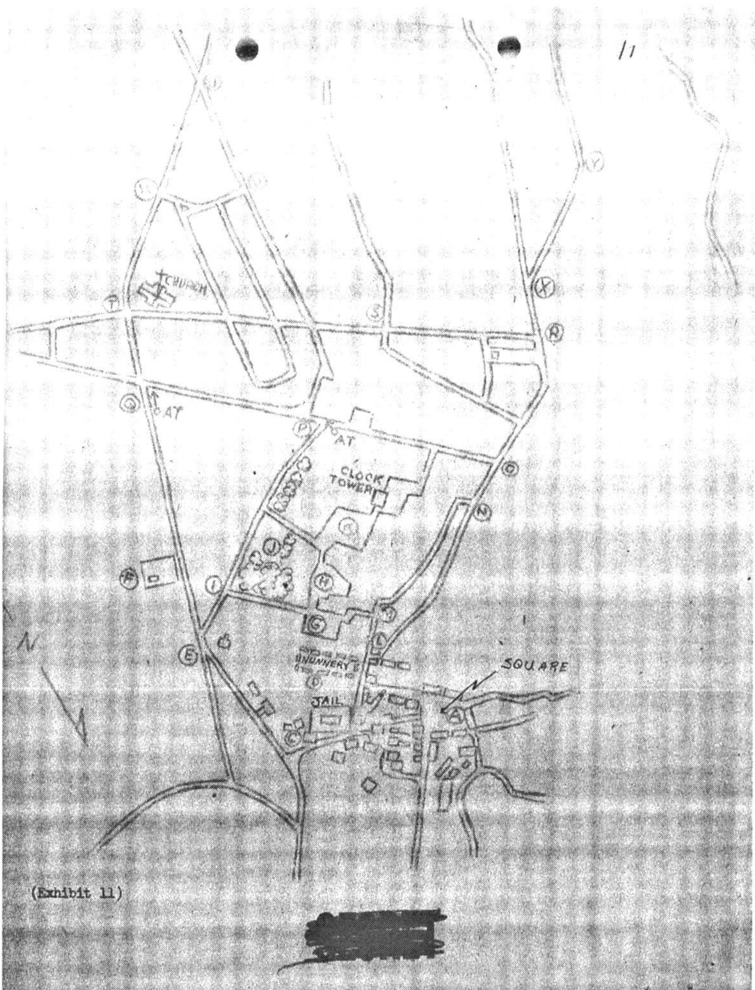

APPENDIX NINE

Cassino 756th Tank Losses Listing

No.	Tank U.S.A. [illegible] No.		History
			"D" Company (Light Tanks)
1.	W-3043972	......	Hit idler blown off, engine pan knocked off.
2.	W-3043979	......	Has been hit.
3.	W-3044461	......	Hit mine, front suspension system gone and dr[illegible] sprocket bent. Track off - salvageable.
			Hq. Company
12.	-3022758	......	Hit and burned.
			"A" Company
3	W-3066202	......	Needs new wiring and new or rebuilt engine. Bogged down, has been under water.
7.	W-3032543	......	Hit and completely burned out.
8.	W-3065930	......	Hit and completely burned out.
10.	W-3022729	......	Hit and completely burned out.
21.	W-3022560	......	Broken track - in good shape and repairable. (Radio has been removed, inition wires cut, hatch locked.)
22.	W-3058786	......	Turned over in ditch, burned.
			"B" Company
4	W-3065879	......	Bogged down, has been under water, Needs new wiring and new or rebuilt engine.
5.	W-3036580	......	" " " " " " "
6.	W-3010829	......	" " " " " " " "
9.	W-3010899	......	Hit and burned out.
11.	W-3066500	......	
			"C" Company
1.	W-3066033	......	Bogged down, has been under water. Needs new wiring and new or rebuilt engine.
2.	W-3015872	......	" " " " " " "
13.	W-3066453	......	In Rapido dry river bed. Not penetrated or burned. Suspension partially gone. Right sid[illegible]
16.	W-3065658	......	On side over 5 ft. wall. Burned out.
19.	W-3053832	......	" " " " " " " "
20.	W-3015444	......	On side, salvageable.
-	W-3065888	......	Missing
-	W-3053637	......	Missing.
			760th Tank Bn. **"C" Company**
14	760th)		
15	760th)		
17	760th)	......	Hit and burned.
18	760th)		
23	760th)		

\-\-\-\-\-\-\-\-\-\-\-

NOTE: Light tanks in blue letter[illegible]

APPENDIX TEN

B Company, 756th Tank Battalion, Roster for 11 May 1944

Source: B Company/756th Tank Battalion Morning Reports from July 1943 through 11 May 1944

1st Lt David D. Redle
1st Lt William R. Engfer
1st Lt Howard M. Harley, Jr.
2nd Lt Bert D. Gilden
2nd Lt Robert M. Gorman
2nd Lt James L. Harris
2nd Lt William H. Newman

1st Sgt Alvin Nusz
T/Sgt Morris B. Thompson
S/Sgt James E. Haspel
S/Sgt Oric W. Johannesen
S/Sgt Haskell O. Oliver
S/Sgt Gene B. Shirley
S/Sgt Hamilton A. Smith
Sgt Roy L. Anderson
Sgt Harold M. Beymer
Sgt Clyde F. Cogdill
Sgt Robert. B. Danner
Sgt James H. Gilkerson
Sgt Henry E. Gohde
Sgt Charles J. Graffagnini
Sgt David L. Grate, Jr.
Sgt Louis J. Jarvis
Sgt Alfred W. Mancini, Jr.
Sgt Frank W. Mielcarski
Sgt Daniel Pompey
T/4 Bertie L. Bulen
T/4 Roy C. Burdette
T/4 Oscar T. Crenshaw
T/4 Earl W. Cunningham
T.4 Roy R. Kosanke
T/4 Frank C. Manak
T/4 Carl A. Mras
T/4 Randolph H. Perdue
T/4 Jesse B. Rickerson, Jr.
T/4 John J. Roth
T/4 Henry J. Sanislow
T/4 Werner G. Sprattler
T/4 Joe K. Wright
Cpl Raymond T. Brown
Cpl Joseph Cutrone
Cpl Melville E. Corson
Cpl Ed Farley
Cpl Leonard D. Froneberger, Jr.
Cpl Raymond S. Getz
Cpl Butler J. Granger
Cpl Alexander L. Huffman
Cpl Marvin E. King
Cpl Luther A. Kinsworthy
Cpl Lotka U. Kupriance
Cpl Donald E. LaDue

Cpl George W. Minnick, Jr.
Cpl Lloyd R. Stout
Cpl Steve Vargo
T/5 Thomas M. Barber
T/5 Merle E. Brooks
T/5 John Dufalla
T/5 Edward D. Durham
T/5 Donald W. Fischer
T/5 Francis A. Fischer
T/5 Clyde W. Guild
T/5 Albert A. Jaksys
T/5 Rufus P. Marin
T/5 Anthony L. Notoroberto
T/5 Elbert Rainwater
T/5 Paul A. Saale
T/5 Edward J. Sadowski
T/5 John H. Senior
T/5 Irving Shapiro
T/5 Guy H. Sheffield
T/5 Leak H. Smitherman
T/5 Bernard C. Wammes
T/5 Frank M. Ware
Pfc William R. Boyer
Pfc Gerald C. Chotin
Pfc George C. Davis
Pfc Ford T. Draeger
Pfc Robert F. Gilbert
Pfc Earl C. Kilgore
Pfc Harold H. Matthies
Pfc William J. McInrue
Pfc Delmar P. McIntyre
Pfc Nichols P. Motto
Pfc Francis Payne
Pfc Reynold Peters
Pfc Raymond R. Reid
Pfc Frank M. Schafer
Pfc Bernard J. Shue
Pfc John K. Wessels
Pvt Filimon Aragon
Pvt William H. Buisset
Pvt Harding Burcham
Pvt Paul N. Cardullo
Pvt John S. Carter
Pvt Raymond W. Colley
Pvt Valentine Crowe
Pvt Thomas F. Devlin
Pvt Dual F. Dishner
Pvt Robert L. Duncan
Pvt Frank Freeman, Jr.
Pvt Anton E. Fricke
Pvt Ruben F. Fries
Pvt Michael Gautieri
Pvt Glenn R. Gordon
Pvt John W. Jarrett
Pvt Verner L. Kreitlow
Pvt Hulin Long
Pvt Reuben B. Mapes
Pvt James W. Martin
Pvt Oscar W. McEntire
Pvt Merrill L. Moor
Pvt Cletus J. Offerman
Pvt Gene Palumbo
Pvt Philip Rodriquez
Pvt Edward C. Shea
Pvt Walter F. Smith
Pvt Emil A. Tikkanen
Pvt Olaf I. Ulvestad
Pvt George D. Wallace
Pvt Merton E. Weatherwax

APPENDIX ELEVEN

Lt Col Rogers's Castellonorato Map, 15–19 May 1944

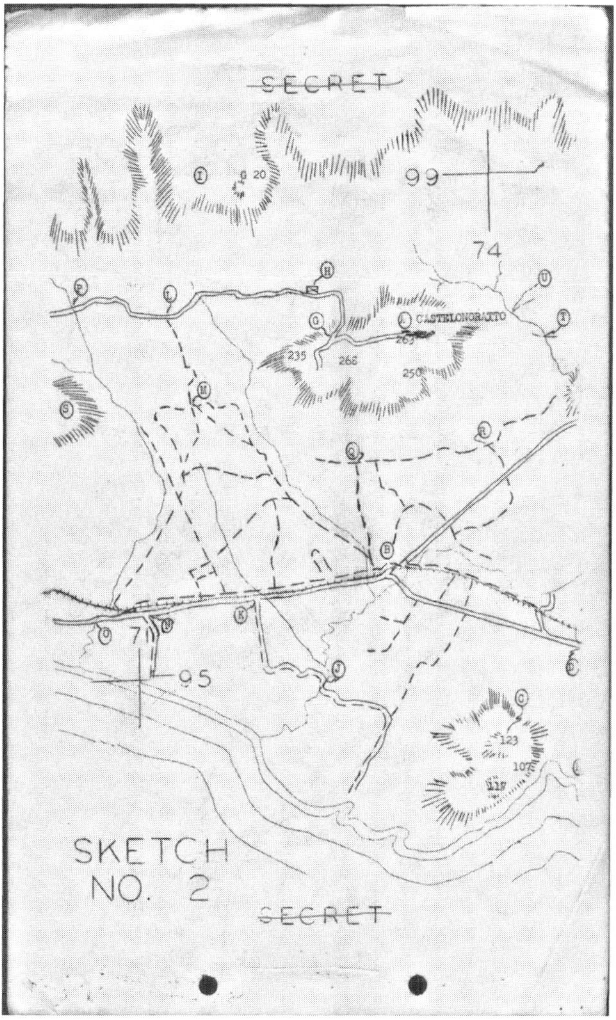

APPENDIX TWELVE

Lt Col Rogers's Rome Map, 3–4 June 1944

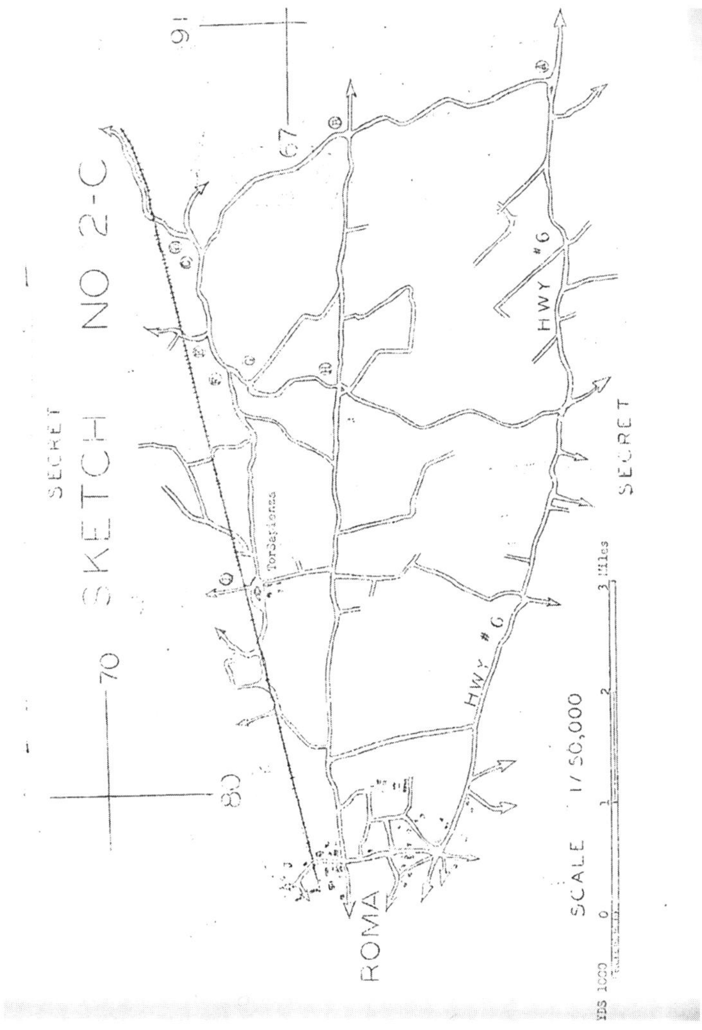

Special Acknowledgments

In addition to Melinda Woofter, Russell Danby-Jones, A. Harding Ganz, Tim Stoy, Ron Lowther, David A. Redle, Bernard "Bud" Fink, Victor "Tory" Failmezger, Susan Strange, Sydney Soderberg, Dave Kerr, and Jeffrey Plowman for contributions already described in the "Special Acknowledgements" section of Part One of this series, I would like to add special thanks to the following people for their particular contributions to Part Two:

Jacqueline Davis, Director of the Fort Sam Houston Museum, for providing me with biographical details and reference photos of Lt Col Charles A. Ellis.

Reid DeMass, student researcher at The Citadel in Charleston, South Carolina, for spending many hours scanning rare photos from General Mark Clark's WWII photo albums.

Bob Holt, 752nd Tank Battalion historian, for help with chapter work and photos related to the march on Rome.

Loïc Jankowiak, for reviewing my chapter work involving the FSSF, alerting me to several errors, and helping me develop additional details.

Bob Jones, 337th Infantry Regiment historian and webmaster to www.337thinfantry.net. Bob provided me with many invaluable photographs and little-known historical details for the chapters covering the 85th Infantry Division.

Stefan Karpiniec, for sharing personal photos of the two 760th Tank Battalion tanks knocked out in Cassino in early February 1944. The photos, taken 19 May 1944, came from his father, 2nd Lt Zdzislaw Karpiniec of the Carpathian Division, Polish 2nd Corps, but the photographer was an unknown comrade with the initials of S.E.

Wolfgang Loof, curator for the *Sturmartillerie* collection under the *Garnisongeschichte Jüterbog St. Barbara* (www.hl-barbara.de), an historical society in Jüterbog, Germany, dedicated to preserving nearly 130 years of local military history. The *Sturmartillerie* service branch began in the Jüterbog area during the 1930s. Wolfgang provided me with photographs and critical background details on the 242nd *Sturmgeschütz-Abteilung* (Assault Gun Battalion).

Glenn F. "Jeff" Rogers, Jr., retired U.S. Army Lt Col, USMA Class of 1966, and son of Lt Col Glenn F. Rogers, for reviewing and correcting my draft—especially for proper military nomenclature and accuracy.

Bibliography

Published Books

Ankrum, Homer R. *Dogfaces Who Smiled Through Tears*. Lake Mills, Iowa: Graphic Publishing Company, 1988.

Ashcraft, Howard D. *As You Were: Cannon Company, 34th Infantry Division, 168th Infantry Regiment, World War II.* Richmond, Virginia: Ashcraft Enterprises, 1990.

Atkinson, Rick. *The Day of Battle: The War in Sicily and Italy, 1943–1944*. New York, New York: Henry Holt and Company, LLC., 2007.

Barry, Steven Thomas. *Battalion Commanders at War: US Army Tactical Leadership in the Mediterranean Theater, 1942–1943.* Lawrence, Kansas: University Press of Kansas, 2013.

Bishop, Chris, and Chris McNab, eds. *Campaigns of World War II Day by Day*. Hauppauge, New York: Barron's Educational Series, Inc., 2003.

Blumenson, Martin. *Mark Clark: The Last of the Great World War II Commanders*. New York, New York: Cogdon & Weed, Inc., 1984.

Blumenson, Martin. *Salerno to Cassino.* Washington, D.C.: Center of Military History, U.S. Army, 1993.

Böhmler, Rudolf. *Monte Cassino: A German View*. Maximilian Verlag GmbH & Co, 1956. Reprint, South Yorkshire, UK: Pen & Sword Military, 2015.

Bond, Harold L. *Return to Cassino: A Memoir of the Fight for Rome.* Garden City, New York: Doubleday & Company, Inc. 1964.

Bull, Stephen and Gordon L. Rottman, *Infantry Tactics of the Second World War.* Oxford, UK: Osprey Publishing Ltd., 2008.

Caddick-Adams, Peter. *Monte Cassino: Ten Armies in Hell.* New York, New York: Oxford University Press, 2012.

Clark, Mark W. *Calculated Risk.* New York, New York: Harper and Brothers Publishing, 1950.

Delaney, John P. *The Blue Devils in Italy: A History of the 88th Infantry Division in World War II.* Nashville, Tennessee: The Battery Press, Inc., 1988.

Duus, Masayo Umezawa. *Unlikely Liberators, The Men of the 100th and 442nd*. English Translation. Honolulu, Hawaii: University of Hawaii Press, 2006.

Eisenhower, Dwight D. *Crusade in Europe*. Garden City, New York: Doubleday & Company, Inc., 1948; Dolphin edition, 1961.

Fazendin, Roger. *The 756th Tank Battalion in the Battle of Monte Cassino, 1944*. Cave Creek, Arizona: Stories Unlimited, 1991. Reprint. Lincoln, Nebraska: iUniverse Inc., 1991.

Fisher, Jr., Ernest F. *U.S. Army in World War II, The Mediterranean Theater of Operations: Cassino to the Alps*. Washington, D.C.; Center of Military History, U.S. Army, 1993.

Froeschle, Helmuth O. *Our Story of the 760th Tank Battalion, WWII*. Reprint. Victoria, Canada: Trafford Publishing, 2007.

Ford, Ken. *Cassino 1944: Breaking the Gustav Line*. Oxford, UK: Osprey Publishing Ltd., 2004.

4eme Division Marocaine Officers, *Avec la 4eme Division de Montagne, 4eme Division Marocaine.* Mulhouse-Dornach, Switzerland: Braun & Cie, 14 Octobre 1945.

Gaujac, Paul. *Le Corps Expéditionnaire Français en Italie.* Paris, France: Histoire & Collections, 2003.

Gooderson, Ian. *Battles in Focus: Cassino.* London, UK: Brassey's, 2003.

Graham, Dominick. *Cassino: Battle Book No. 16.* New York, New York: Ballantine Books, Inc., 1970.

Green, Michael. *M4 Sherman: Combat and Development History of the Sherman Tank and All Sherman Variants.* Osceola, Wisconsin: Motorbooks International Publishers & Wholesalers., 1993.

Green, Michael and Gladys Green. *Weapons of Patton's Armies.* Osceola, Wisconsin: MBI Publishing, 2000.

Hapgood, David, and David Richardson. *Monte Cassino.* Garden City, New York: Double Day & Company, Inc, 1984.

Hart, Steven and Russell Hart. *German Tanks of World War II.* London, UK: Brown Packaging Books Ltd., 1998.

Hougen, Lt. Col. John H. *The Story of the Famous 34th Infantry Division.* Reprint. Nashville, Tennessee: The Battery Press, 1979.

Howe, George F. *Old Ironsides: The Battle History of the 1st Armored Division.* Washington, D.C.: Combat Forces Press, 1957; Reprint, Nashville, Tennessee: The Battery Press, 1979.

Howze, Hamilton H., *A Cavalryman's Story: Memoirs of a Twentieth Century General.* Washington, D.C.: Smithsonian Institute Press, 1996.

Huff, S/Sgt. Richard A., ed. *The Fighting 36th: A Pictorial History of the Texas Division in Combat.* Austin, Texas: 36th Division Association, 1945.

Jentz, Tom and Hilary Doyle. *Sturmgeschütz III and IV 1942–45.* Oxford, UK: Osprey Publishing, 2001.

Laurie, Clayton D. *The U.S. Army Campaigns of World War II: Rome-Arno* (CMH Pub 72-20). U.S. Army Center of Military History, 1994.

Mikolashek, John B. *General Mark Clark: Commander of America's Fifth Army and Liberator of Rome.* Havertown, Pennsylvania: Casemate Publishers, 2013.

Parker, Matthew. *Monte Cassino: The Hardest-Fought Battle of World War II.* New York, New York: Doubleday, 2004.

Pimlott, John. *The Historical Atlas of World War II.* New York, New York: Henry Holt and Company, Inc., 1995.

Plowman, Jeffrey, and Perry Rowe. *The Battles for Monte Cassino Then and Now.* Essex, UK: Battle of Britain International Ltd., 2011.

Rottman, Gordon L. *World War II Infantry Fire Support Tactics*, Oxford, UK: Osprey Publishing, 2016.

Schultz, Paul L. *The 85th Infantry Division in World War II.* Washington, D.C.: Infantry Journal Press, 1949.

Smith, E.D., *The Battles for Monte Cassino.* New York, New York: Charles Scribner & Sons, 1975.

Springer, Joseph A. *The Black Devil Brigade: The True Story of the First Special Service Force.* Pacifica, California: Pacifica Military History, 2001.

Stanton, Shelby L. *Order of Battle U.S. Army, World War II.* Novato, California: Presidio Press, 1984.

Taggart, Donald G. *The History of the Third Infantry Division in World War II.* Reprint, Nashville, Tennessee: The Battery Press, 1987.

Treanor, Tom. *One Damn Thing After Another.* Garden City, New York: Doubleday, Doran & Company, Inc., 1944.

United States Army. *752nd Tank Bn.* 1945. (PDF version downloaded from Bangor Public Library), World War Regimental Histories. Book 60. http://digicom.bpl.lib.me.us/ww_reg_his/60, accessed 20 April 2021).

Wallace, Robert. *The Italian Campaign.* Morristown, New Jersey: Time-Life Books, Inc., 1978.

Werner, Bret. *First Special Service Force 1942-44.* Oxford, UK: Osprey Publishing Ltd., 2006.

White, Nathan W. *From Fedala to Berchtesgaden: A History of the Seventh United States Infantry in WWII.* Providence, RI: Bickford Engraving & Electrotype Co., 1947.
Youngdahl, Herbert M. *The Other Side of War.* San Francisco, California: Robert D. Reed Publishers, 2000.
Yeide, Harry. *The Infantry's Armor: The US Army's Separate Tank Battalions in World War II.* Mechanicsburg, Pennsylvania: Stackpole Books, 2010.
Zaloga, Steven J. *Anzio 1944: The Beleaguered Beachhead.* Oxford, UK: Osprey Publishing, 2005.

Unpublished or Self-Published Books and Dissertations

Esposito, Cheryl. *The 756th Tank Battalion in the European Theatre.* Privately printed, 1999.
King, Maj Glenn L. "From Salerno to Rome: General Mark W. Clark and the Challenge of Coalition Warfare." Thesis, Master of Military Art and Science, Military History, US Army Command and General Staff College, Fort Leavenworth, Kansas, 2007.
Kosanke, Roy. "756th Tank Battalion Reunion Book." 756th Tank Battalion Association, late 1980s. Photo-scanned.
Mudd, Lee. "History of the 756th Tank Battalion and the Development of the Tank-Infantry Team in World War II." Thesis, Johns Hopkins University, 2000.
Sterner, C. Douglas. *Go For Broke: A Tribute to the Nisei Warriors of WWII.* Legal Help for Veterans, PLLC, 2018. (Downloaded from https://homeofheroes.com/wp-content/uploads/2021/06/Go-for-Broke-final.pdf, accessed 23 June 2021.

War Department Field Manuals, Training Manuals, Regulations, and Organizational Tables

Unless specified otherwise, all items listed below were published by the US Government Printing Office in Washington, D.C., at time of release.

Army Regulations AR 850–150, Authorized Abbreviations and Symbols—13 November 1943 and 18 September 1944, with supplements.
Employment of Tanks with Infantry FM 17–36, War Department, 13 March 1944. Reprint. West Chester, Ohio: The Nafiziger Collection, Inc., 2000.
Table of Organization No 7–14, War Department, Washington, D.C., 26 February 1944, Infantry Cannon Company.
Table of Organization No. 17–25, War Department, Washington, D.C., 15 September 1943, Medium Tank Battalion.
Table of Organization No. 18–27, War Department, Washington, D.C., 15 March 1944, Tank Destroyer Gun Company, Tank Destroyer Battalion, Self-Propelled.
Technical Manual TM 12–427, Military Occupational Classifications of Enlisted Personnel—July 12, 1944.

Fort Benning Monographs

Obtained and downloaded as PDF files at: https://www.benning.army.mil/Library/Donovanpapers/wwii/index.html, accessed 20 April 2021.

Captain Wyndham Bammer. "Operations of Company K, 339th Infantry (85th Infantry Division) in the Attack of Hills 66 and 69, Near Tremensuoli, Italy, 11–12 May 1944 (Personal Experience of a Weapon Platoon Leader)." Advanced Infantry Officers Course 1948–1949.

Captain John M. Davies, III. "The Operations of Company I, 3rd Battalion, 337th Infantry (85th Infantry Division) at Castellonorato, Italy 11–15 May 1944, During the Breaching of the Gustav Line. (Rome-Arno Campaign) (Personal Experience of a Platoon Leader)." The Infantry School, Fort Benning, Georgia, Advanced Infantry Officers Course 1947–1948.

1st Lt Belfrad H. Gray, Jr. "The Crossing of the Rapido River and Occupation of Positions Above Cassino, Italy, by Company 'I', 168th Infantry (34th Infantry Division) 27 January–15 February 1944 (Rome-Arno Campaign) Personal Experience of a Squad Leader." The Infantry School, Fort Benning, Georgia, Advanced Infantry Officers Course 1947–1948.

Captain James A. Luttrell. "The Operations of the 168th Infantry (34th Infantry Division) in the Rapido River Crossing, 28 January–10 February, 1944. (Rome-Arno Campaign) (Personal Experience of a Cannon Company Commander)." The Infantry School, Fort Benning, Georgia, Advanced Infantry Officers Course 1948–1949.

Primary Source Official Documents, Reports, and Lists

National Archives and Records Administration (College Park, MD). Many original US Army Records, including WWII enlistment records and casualty lists are housed at this facility. A tiny amount of material has been digitized and is available for download online at: https://www.archives.gov/, accessed 20 April 2021.

34th Infantry Division, (Army Records Group 407, Boxes 8172 & 8173) for dates: 23 January to 13 February 1944 includes the following materials:
Communications to the Fifth Army HQ, French CEF HQ, & II Corps HQ
II Corps G-3 Reports, Counterbattery Reports
34th Infantry Division G-3 Journal, G-3 Reports, G-2 Reports, Field Orders, & Messages
34th Infantry Division Artillery S-3 Reports
1st Tank Group S-3 Reports
105th AA AW Battalion S-3 Reports
109th Engineering Battalion S-3 Reports
133rd Infantry Regiment S-3 Reports, Patrol Reports
135th Infantry Regiment S-3 Reports
168th Infantry Regiment S-3 Reports
756th Tank Battalion S-3 Reports
776th Tank Destroyer Battalion S-3 Reports

337th Infantry Regiment, (Army Records Group 407, Box 10720):
Operations Reports, May 1944

85th Infantry Division, (Army Records Group 407, Boxes 10662, 10669, 10675, 10680, & 10690)
Field Orders, May 1944 (Box 10690)
G-2 Reports, 10–20 May 1944 (Box 10669)
G-3 Daily Reports, 1–11 May 1944 (Box 10675)
Report of Operations, April–May 1944 (Box 10675)
Report of Operations, May 1944 (Box 10675)
Operation Reports by Maj Gen Coulter, May 1944 (Box 10662)

G-3 Journal File, 16–30 May 1944 (Box 10680)
85th Inf Div Photograph Album (Box 12738)

88th Infantry Division, (Army Records Group 407, Box 10855)
G-3 Reports, 1–10 June 1944

U.S. II Corps, (Army Records Group 407, Box 2669)
II Corps "G-3 Journal File," 30 April–31 May 1944

756th Tank Battalion, (Army Records Group 407, Boxes 16769–16772): 1943 Unit History, 1944 Unit History, Commander's Narratives, Unit Journal, Rosters, Field Orders & "Yellow" Orders.

Records of World War II Prisoners of War, 1942–1947, documenting the period 12/7/1941–11/19/1946 at National Archives website: https://aad.archives.gov/aad/series-list.jsp?cat=WR26, accessed 20 April 2021.

World War II Army Enlistment Records, documenting the period ca. 1938–1946, at National Archives website: https://aad.archives.gov/aad/series-list.jsp?cat=WR26, accessed 20 April 2021.

National Personnel Records Center (St Louis, MO): Microfilm images of the "Morning Reports" to each US Army company are kept at the NPRC. These are daily records of the location and basic activities of the company as well as any changes of duty status to all personnel assigned to the company. https://www.archives.gov/st-louis, accessed 20 April 2021.

756th Tank Battalion: B Company: June 1941–Feb 1946 (May & June 1943 missing from NPRC),
A, C, D, HQ, & Service Companies & Medical Detachment: 1941–1944 (select dates)
133rd Infantry Regiment HQ Co: January 1944 (select dates)
168th Infantry Regiment, HQ Co, 2nd Bn HQ, 3rd Bn HQ, E, F, G, H, I, K and L Cos: January 1944 (select dates)
760th Tank Battalion, Co C: Feb 1944 (complete month)

Dwight D. Eisenhower Library (Abilene, Kansas): U.S. Army: Unit Records, 1917–50, 756th Tank Battalion, Box 146.
B Company 756th Tank Battalion, Unit Journal, January–September 1944.

U.S. Army Human Resources Command (Fort Knox, KY): The US Army HRC keeps the original "Graves Registration" Individual Deceased Personnel Files (IDPF) for all those US Army members killed in action in World War II. www.hrc.army.mil, accessed 20 April 2021.
IDPF Files for the following: John F. Bacha, Harold M. Behymer, William Fodor, Wayne B. Henry, Verner L. Kreitlow, Ralph E. Obermire, Andrew D. Orient, David J. Orris, Paul T. Tirpak, Leak H. Smitherman, Kinnon R. White, Eugene K. Wunderlich, Joe K. Wright.

American Battlefield Monuments Commission: American WWII overseas graves listing with the "American Battlefield Monuments Commission" at: http://www.abmc.gov/, accessed 20 April 2021.

U.S. Government Records at Ancestry.com:
Obtained through website subscription at: http://www.ancestry.com, accessed 20 April 2021.
Social Security Death Index.

United States Army WWII Draft Cards 1940–1947.
United States Census for 1920, 1930, and 1940.
U.S. Select Military Registers, 1862–1985.
U.S., WWII, Hospital Admission cards 1942–1945.

United States Military Library, digital collections:
Cadet class yearbooks accessed from: https://usma.libguides.com/welcome, accessed 20 April 2021.
Broom, Thad A., ed., *Howitzer* West Point, NY: United States Corps of Cadets, 1930.
Jones, Wilber S., ed. *Howitzer*. West Point, NY: United States Corps of Cadets, 1931.

US Army Registry of Officers:
Books downloaded in PDF form from: https://archive.org/, accessed 20 April 2021.
United States Army. ***Official US Army Register.*** Washington, D.C.: War Department, The Adjutant General's Office, United States Government Printing Office. 1941, 1943, 1944, 1945, and 1946

Combined Arms Research Library (CARL): CARL is part of the US Army's Combined Research Center. The purpose of CARL is to serve as an online resource to the General Staff College but a vast amount of historical documents and declassified material has been digitized and is available to the general public for online research and download. CARL is an extraordinary resource for WWII historians. http://usacac.army.mil/organizations/cace/carl, accessed 20 April 2021.

Allied Forces. *Report by the Supreme Allied Commander Mediterranean to the Combined Chiefs of the Staff on the Italian Campaign, 8 January 1944 to 10 May 1944*. Washington, D.C.: US Government Printing Office, 1944.
The Armor School. *Maintenance of Armor in World War II.* Research Report, Officers Advanced Course, Fort Knox, Kentucky, 1949–1950.
85th Infantry Division: Minturno to the Apennines, produced by HQ of the 85th Inf Div, Infantry Division, Information-Education Section, 1944.
History of the Second Chemical Mortar Battalion, Ernest Muller, Salzburg, Austria, 1945.
91st Cavalry Reconnaissance Squadron Operations Reports, 1 November 1943 to 20 February 1945 (Colonel T. Q. Donaldson Summary, dated 28 February 1945).
91st Cavalry Reconnaissance Squadron After Action Reports, May 1944 through May 1945.
Peek, Clifford H., ed. *Five Years, Five Countries, Five Campaigns: An Account of the One-Hundred-Forty-First Infantry in World War II.* Munich, Germany: F Bruckmann KG, 1945.
751st Tank Battalion "Reports of Action of the 751st Tank Battalion," 1943–45.
760th Tank Battalion "Operations in Italy, January 1944," "Operations in Italy, February 1944," & "Operation in Italy, May 1944," After Action Reports.
34th Infantry Division, Lessons Learned in Combat, November 7–8 1942–September 1944. Italy, September 1944.
Walker, Maj Gen Fred L., "Comments on the Rapido River Crossing, January 1944," Library USA CGSC Ft Leavenworth KS, 1960.
United States Army. *A Military Encyclopedia Based on Operations in the Italian Campaigns 1943–1945.* G-3 Section, Headquarters 15th Army Group, 1945.
United States Army, *Fifth Army History, Part IV, Cassino and Anzio, 16 January 1944–13 March 1944.* Florence, Italy: L'Impronta Press, 1944.
United States Army, *Fifth Army History, Part V, The Drive to Rome, 1 April–4 June 1944.* Milan, Italy: Pizzi and Pizio, 1945.

United States Army. *Report of the New Weapons Board.* Washington, D.C.: Army Service Forces. 27 April 1944.

Primary Source Letters, Diaries, Memoirs, Photos, and Miscellaneous

Bernhard, George. "Life in the Service," undated (10 pages) Transcribed diary entries. George Bernhard was a tank crewman in A Co/756th Tank Battalion. (Copies included in French Lewis's personal documents.)

Donley, Ralph. "Recollections," (5 pages). Written for the author and dated 8 March 2005.

Haspel, James E. Interview by Pamela G Patrick on 18 September 1984, (6 pages). (Photocopies provided to the author by Haspel's family.)

Lewis, French. Personal papers, notes, news articles, memoirs, letters, military orders, and letters pertaining to the 756th Tank Battalion, (~2,100 pages). (Photocopies provided to the author by Grieg Lewis, son.)

Offerman, Dick. (Son of Cletus J. Offerman, B Company/756th Tank Battalion). "My Dad was a Tanker." Biography, letters and photos, December 2005, (65 pages). (PDF version provided to the author.)

Olson, Edwin B. War Recollections, Early 2000s (12 pages). (Photocopies provided to author by Edwin B. Olson.)

Ranspach, Paul. Wartime diary dated from 15 September 1943 to 23 October 1945 and photos, (76 pages). Ranspach was a member of both B and D Companies, 756th Tank Battalion. (Photocopies provided to the author by the Ranspach family through the 756th Tank Battalion Association.)

Redle, David D. "B Company, 756th Tank Battalion Added Recollections" memoirs. (14 pages), (1999). (Photocopies provided to the author by David D. Redle.)

Redle, David D. "B Company History" memoirs. (38 handwritten pages), 2004. (Presented to the author at interview 13 March 2004.)

Redle, David D. Interview by Ron Lowther, 11–12 August 2012 in Akron, Ohio, audio tapes provided to the author.

Richter, Arthur F. "Arthur F Richter's Experience in WWII" memoirs. (26 pages), 2007. (Photocopies provided to the author by Arthur F. Richter.)

Primary Source Interviews and Correspondence

756th Tank Battalion Veterans:

Includes letters, e-mails, phone conversations, personal interviews, photos and documents shared with the author.

B Company Veterans:

Roy Anderson, Clyde Guild, Alfred Mancini, Gene Palumbo, Randolph Perdue, David D. Redle, Arthur Richter, Henry Sanislow, Charles M. Wilkinson

Other 756th Tank Battalion Veterans:

Jack Brown (HQ Co), Roy Collins (HQ Co), Jack Deenihan (A Co), Ralph Donley (HQ Co), Edwin B. Olson (C & HQ Co), French G. Lewis (A, B & HQ Cos), Alfred Westle (D & Sv Cos)

756th Veterans' Families and Friends:

Ed Brennan (son to Kevin F. Brennan of B Co), Dave Deputy (Grandson of Frank Deputy, A Co), Earl L Hanson (nephew to Ralph L. Hanson, A Co), Family to James Haspel (B Co), Greig Lewis (son to French Lewis of A, B & HQ Cos), Dick Offerman (son of Cletus Offerman of B Co), Martha Ours, (daughter of Anthony F. Melfi of B Co), Family to Haskell O. Oliver (B Co), Family to Paul Ranspach (B & D Co), Family of Glenn F. Rogers, Alfreda Sadowski (wife to Ed Sadowski of B Co), Bob Shonka, son to Donald G. Shonka (A Co), Michael Thompson (son to Morris B. Thompson of B Co), Family of Charles M. Wilkinson (B Co), Family of Eugene K. Wunderlich (B Co)

Motion Pictures and Photographs

Stock footage available at: www.criticalpast.com, accessed 20 April 2021:
"Battle of Monte Cassino, Italy, US Troops on Mountainside ..."
"Battle of Monte Cassino, Italy. Views of town and Abbey, as US troops prepare ..."
"Scenes from the Battle of Monte Cassino, Italy, during World War II."
"Soldiers of 2nd New Zealand division at the Battle of Monte Cassino ..."
"United States 5th Army Soldiers shell the town of Cassino, Italy during World War II."
"US Army units shell the town of Monte Cassino, Italy, during World War Two."

Internet Articles

1st Bn/337th Infantry Regiment National Archives records ("History of Operations, April 1944" & "337th Operation Report, May 1944") downloaded from: https://www.337thinfantry.net/unit.php, accessed 9 May 2021.

"125th Field Artillery History" at: http://www.vets-hall.org/125th-field-artillery-history, accessed 9 May 2021.

133rd Inf Regt Commander's Narrative for January 1944 by Col Marshall, transcribed and posted by the 34th Infantry Division Association at: http://www.34ida.org/history/133_narr_history.html, accessed 20 April 2021.

351st Infantry Regiment Operations Report for June 1944, transcribed at https://www.351inf.com/opsreports/June-1944, accessed 9 May 2021.

776th Tank Destroyer Battalion January and February 1944 Unit Journals, Operation Reports and Unit History (PDF form) obtained at: http://tankdestroyer.net/units/battalions700s/274-776th-tank-destroyer-battalion, accessed 9 May 2021.

Charles A. Ellis memorial at www.findagrave.com/memorial/63098731/charle-a-ellis, accessed 9 May 2021.

Headquarters 351st Inf Regt., *History of 351st Inf Reg in World War II.* 1945, booklet downloaded from https://www.351inf.com/collections, accessed 9 May 2021).

"Iowa Medal of Honor Heros" "Second Lieutenant Paul F. Riordan" at http://www.iowahistory.org/museaum/exhibits/medla-of-honor/riordan_p_wwii/, accessed 17 May 2015.

Jones, Jr., Robert W. "Race to Rome" (From Veritas, Vol. 2, No. 2, 2006) at https://arsof-history.org/articles/v2n2_race_to_rome_page_1.html, accessed 9 May 2021.

Medal of Honor citation under "Paul F. Riordan" at https://homeofheroes.com/medal-of-honor-citation/world-war-ii-medal-of-honor-recipients/, accessed 29 March 2015.

"Rome-Arno 1944" CMH Publication 72-20, at https://history.army.mil/html/books/072/72-20/index.html, accessed 7 May 2022.

"Unit Journal of Cannon Company, 133rd Infantry, January–March 1944" transcribed at: http://www.34infdiv.org/history/133cannon/4401.html, accessed 18 May 2015.

Endnotes

Chapter 1

1 34th Inf Div G-3 Report, 180001 to 180002 February 1944, (National Archives, Army Records Group 407, Boxes 8172 and 8173).
2 34th Inf Div G-3 Journal, 2 February 1944 (0607 entry), (National Archives, Army Records Group 407, Boxes 8172 and 8173).
3 34th Inf Div G-2 Report, 120001 to 120002 February 1944, (National Archives, Army Records Group 407, Boxes 8172 and 8173).
4 34th G-3 Journal, 2 February 1944 (0720 entry). Sniper position given as 852227.
5 135th Inf Regt S-3 Report, 180001 to 180002 February 1944, (National Archives, Army Records Group 407, Boxes 8172 and 8173).
6 Maj Kermit R. Hansen was the officer's name according to: Hal Boyle, "Nazis' Cassino Defense System Crumbling." *Oakland Tribune* (Oakland, California), 1 February 1944, 3; Maj Hansen was with the 141st Inf Regt/36th Inf Div according to: S/Sgt. Richard A. Huff, ed, *The Fighting 36th: A Pictorial History of the Texas Division in Combat,* (Austin, Texas: 36th Division Association) 1945, listed on page 41 of the roster section.
7 756th Tank Battalion Commander's Narrative for January and February 1944, 25, (National Archives, Army Records Group 407, Boxes 16769–16772): 59th Field Artillery Battalion is the unit reported as supporting this effort.
8 133rd Inf Regt S-3 Report, 180029 to 180030 January, 1944, (National Archives, Army Records Group 407, Boxes 8172 and 8173); 760th Tank Battalion "Operations in Italy, February 1944" (Combined Arms Research Library downloaded from http://usacac.army.mil/organizations/cace/carl).
9 II Corps G-3 Report, 1 February 1944, (National Archives, Army Records Group 407, Box 2669).
10 34th G-3 Journal, 1 February 1944 (1845 entry).
11 Ibid., (2135 entry).
12 34th Inf Div Operational Instructions dated 2 February 1944; Locations for each: Colle S' Angelo (825224), Hill 706 (829231), Massa Albaneta (835217), and S and SE slopes of Hill 516 (844209) (Monte Cassino).
13 34th G-3 Journal, 1 February 1944 (0845 entry), gives the ultimate objective for the 133rd as a line from 850205 (halfway up the hill to the abbey) to 862198 (Cassino rail station area).
14 34th G-2 Report, 120031 January to 120001 February 1944.
15 756th Tank Battalion S-3 Report, 180001 to 180002 February 1944, (National Archives, Army Records Group 407, Boxes 8172 and 8173); 756th Commander's Narrative for January and February 1944, 24–25.
16 756th Unit Journal, 2 February 1944 (0730 entry), (National Archives, Army Records Group 407, Boxes 16769–16772).
17 Homer R. Ankrum, *Dogfaces Who Smiled Through Tears.* (Lake Mills, Iowa: Graphic Publishing Company, 1988), 399–400.
18 34th G-3 Journal, 2 February 1944 (0745 entry).
19 Roger Fazendin, *The 756th Tank Battalion in the Battle of Monte Cassino, 1944,* (Cave Creek, Arizona: Stories Unlimited, 1991; Reprint. Lincoln, Nebraska: iUniverse Inc., 1991), 89: Redle recollection, (Reprint version cited throughout this book, unless otherwise noted). Birthdate was 9 March 1921 according to Fraizer's gravestone shown at www.findagrave.com.

20 "High Mark in Courage is Reached," *Des Moines Tribune* (Des Moines, Iowa), 16 November 1943, 1; "Rockwell Praised for Ridge Attack," *Council Bluffs Nonpareil* (Council Bluffs, Iowa), 17 November 1943, 5.
21 Tom Treanor, *One Damn Thing After Another* (Garden City, New York: Doubleday, Doran & Company, Inc.), 1944, 260. Treanor and other reporters list Fraizer as from Jamestown, New York, but his enlistment record and 1940 Census (www.ancestry.com) lists nearby Ellicott Township as his hometown and his draft registration card (United States Army WWII Draft Cards 1940-1947, at www.ancestry.com) lists Falconer, specifically.
22 David D. Redle letter, 10 January 2009.
23 Redle letter to Gene Palumbo, 25 November 1986. The record does not say where the C Company tanks entered the riverbed, but the likely location was where the river and road were closest just south of the barracks.
24 Treanor, *One Damn Thing*, 260–61; Treanor, Tom. "First Block of Houses in Cassino Was Taken by 38 Yanks and 5 Tanks," *The Gazette* (Cedar Rapids, Iowa), 10 February 1944, 11.
25 Fazendin, *756th at Cassino*, 89–90: Redle recollection.
26 34th G-3 Journal, 2 February 1944 (0755 entry).
27 756th Unit Journal 2 February 1944 (0730 entry). This MG may have been at location 853227, according to 34th G-2 Report, 120001 to 120002 February 1944; 34th G-3 Journal, 2 February 1944 (0755 entry).
28 34th G-3 Journal, 2 February 1944 (0955 entry mislabeled as "0855"). Position of lead elements reported at 857226.
29 B Company/756th Tank Battalion Unit Journal, 2 February 1944, (Dwight D. Eisenhower Library, Abilene, Kansas: U.S. Army: Unit Records, 1917–50, 756th Tank Battalion, Box 146).
30 34th G-3 Journal, 2 February 1944 (0828 entry).
31 David D. Redle interview by Ron Lowther, 11–12 August 2012 in Akron, Ohio, (audio tapes provided to the author).
32 B Co/756th Morning Report, 23 April 1944, (National Archives, National Personnel Records Center, St Louis, Missouri), "Record of Events" for 2 February; 756th S-3 Report, 180001 to 180002 February 1944.
33 Redle interview by Lowther, 11–12 August 2012.
34 756th Commander's Narrative for January and February 1944, 24–25, 756th Unit Journal, 2 February 1944 (0935 entry); Fazendin, *756th at Cassino*, 89–90: Redle recollection. Lt Trafton was in charge of the mortar platoon. These were 81mm mortars mounted on the backs of M3 half-tracks.
35 Fazendin, *756th at Cassino*, 89–90: Redle recollection.
36 Redle letter, 25 January 2004.
37 756th Unit Journal, 2 February 1944 (0935 entry).
38 Fazendin, *756th at Cassino*, 90: Redle recollection.
39 Ankrum, *Dogfaces Who Smiled Through Tears*, 400–01.
40 Fazendin, *756th at Cassino*, 90: Redle recollection.
41 Redle letter, 25 January 2004.
42 Fazendin, *756th at Cassino*, 90, Redle describes this mysterious round only as a "concrete piercing fused shell." It was probably some form of an M61 HE/APT-C (armor piercing round with a small high explosive filler).
43 Redle interview by Lowther, 11–12 August 2012.
44 34th G-2 Report, 120027 to 120028 January 1944: This description comes from a captured German.
45 Fazendin, *756th at Cassino*, 90: Redle recollection; Redle interview by Lowther, 11–12 August 2012.
46 Fazendin, *756th at Cassino*, 90-91: Redle recollection; 756th Unit Journal, 2 February 1944 (1009 entry): The time was 1009 and the location in road was at 858218.
47 Fazendin, *756th at Cassino*, 91: Redle recollection.
48 Redle interview by Lowther, 11–12 August 2012.
49 Ankrum, *Dogfaces Who Smiled Through Tears*, 409; Higgins was from Wyoming, Pennsylvania, according to Treanor, *One Damn Thing*, 261, and Hovey, Graham. "Yanks Digging In On Outskirts of Cassino," *The San Francisco Examiner* (San Francisco, California), 5 February 1944, 5.
50 Ankrum, *Dogfaces Who Smiled Through Tears*, 408–09.
51 "Yanks' Pranks In Italy Offer Comedy Relief," *The Times* (Munster, Indiana), 15 March 1944, 26. The source of this story was Sgt Bud Van Steenbergen of Shelden, Iowa. Lt John Kiely from Marshalltown, Iowa, was the Heavy Weapons Platoon CO involved.

52 34th G-3 Journal, 2 February 1944, (1050 and 1109 entries).

53 34th G-3 Report, 180001 to 180002 February 1944; Ankrum, *Dogfaces Who Smiled Through Tears*, 400-01: According to Ankrum the L Co CO was Lt Dennis Neal, and the K Co CO was Lt Horatio Long; 34th G-3 Journal, 2 February 1944 (0745 entry): K Co's role was to remain in support of the other two companies throughout the day.

54 Ankrum, *Dogfaces Who Smiled Through Tears*, 409–10. Ankrum's book is a rich resource for details, but he is often off with names or times when compared to the G-3 and S-3 Journals and Reports. Ankrum writes that Sweeting was the one who talked to Neal, but Sweeting was not there nor could he have been there at that time. The tank officer could have only been Redle. Ankrum also says a tank was abandoned after grenades were thrown on the back deck. The author cannot corroborate this incident anywhere else, so it was left out of the narrative. Ankrum could be relaying an embellished "infantryman's version" of the German pillbox attack on Redle's passing tank.

55 "'Have a Good Toehold' on Cassino, Yank Shows Reporter," *Democrat and Chronicle* (Rochester, New York), 5 February 1944, 2: Fraizer account.

56 Ankrum, *Dogfaces Who Smiled Through Tears*, 409–10.

57 Redle interview by Lowther, 11–12 August 2012.

58 Redle letter to Palumbo, 25 November 1986: This location appears to be at 858222. Jeffrey Plowman and Perry Rowe, *The Battles for Monte Cassino Then and Now* (Essex, UK: Battle of Britain International Ltd., 2011), 90; Redle did not recall Michaels by name but did recall he was a "replacement lieutenant" in C Company.

59 34th G-3 Journal, 2 February 1944 (1040 entry).

60 Ibid., 1 February 1944 (0845 entry) and 2 February 1944 (1050 and 1109 entries): These sites were at 858222 and 585228. One is the location of the dropped footbridge that blocked the C company tank platoon.

61 34th G-3 Journal, 2 February 1944 (1055 entry).

62 756th Unit Journal, 2 February 1944 (1100 entry).

63 B Co/756th Unit Journal, 2 February 1944; Redle letter, 30 January 2008. Redle said he remained deaf in that ear for several hours and believes that had the German gun crew bore sighted his approaching tank, he would have been killed.

64 756th Unit Journal, 2 February 1944 (1100 entry): Redle's position was 857220. Gun position was recorded at 857217.

65 Ibid.

66 Ibid., (1120 entry).

67 34th G-2 Report, 120001 to 120002 February 1944.

68 34th G-3 Journal, 2 February 1944 (1225 entry).

69 Ibid., (1140 entry).

70 Fazendin, *756th at Cassino*, 91.

71 A few weeks later, Sgt Riley was listed as the 2nd Platoon sergeant (S/Sgt) commanding #9 tank, according to a C Co/756th manning chart found in French Lewis personal papers.

72 Plowman, *Battles for Cassino*, 92.

73 756th Unit Journal, 2 February 1944 (1205 entry).

74 Ibid.

75 Ibid., (1225 entry): This was probably Riley's incident; Redle letter, 30 January 2008; 756th Unit History, 1944, GO #31 II Corps dated 27 April 1944: Riley was awarded the Silver Star for this. According to 756th Unit History for 1944, GO #31 II Corps dated 27 April 1944, B Company driver, T/5 Norwood H. Meisinger, of Minneapolis, Minnesota, also received the Bronze Star "for meritorious service in combat on 2 February 1944 in Italy." It is unclear if this recognition was because of this particular incident or, later, when Redle took two tanks into town at dusk. Meisinger was a driver to one of the two other B Co tanks.

76 Redle letter to Palumbo, 25 November 1986; Lt John F. Harmon became 2nd Platoon leader later according to C Co/756th manning chart in Lewis personal papers; Fazendin, *756th at Cassino*, 91–92: Redle recollection.

77 Fazendin, *756th at Cassino*, 92: Redle recollection; 756th S-3 Report, 180001 to 180002 February 1944; Plowman, *Battles for Cassino*, 90: The German ATs were likely Metzger's assault guns. A round from Gefreiter Teppe's SP gun hit Riley's hatch cover; Redle interview by Lowther, 11–12 August 2012.

78 Plowman, *Battles for Cassino*, 92; British Pathe newsreel/photos from 3 February 1944 accessed at www.criticalpast.com; it is presumed that this tank threw a track, but it could have been due to another mechanical problem. B Co/756th Morning Report, 23 April 1944, "Record of Events" for 2 February reports two tanks were hit and damaged. Perhaps this refers to Redle's tank receiving the gouge earlier and Riley's hatch cover being hit. No other damage is officially recorded, although Ankrum claims grenades set the back of a tank on fire.
79 C Co/756th Morning Report, 3 February 1944.
80 34th G-2 Report, 120001 to 120002 February 1944.
81 Infantry reported as moving just south of the 220 grid line at this time, according to the 34th G-3 Journal, 2 February 1944 (1450 entry).
82 34th G-3 Journal, 2 February 1944 (1330 entry).
83 133rd Infantry Battalion Cannon Company Unit Journal, January–March 1944," transcribed at: http://www.34infdiv.org/history/133cannon/4401.html, 2 February, and 27 March 1944.
84 34th G-3 Journal, 2 February 1944 (1510 entry): 3rd Bn reported along 857218 to 853218 grid line at this time, the quarry is at line 220.
85 Ibid., (1530 entry).
86 Treanor, *One Damn Thing*, 260–61.
87 Fazendin, *756th at Cassino*, 92: Redle recollection.
88 34th G-3 Report, 120001 to 120002 February 1944.
89 34th G-3 Journal, 2 February 1944 (1910, 1915, and 1941 entries).
90 34th G-3 Report, 180001 to 180002 February 1944.
91 34th G-3 Journal, 2 February 1944 (1910, 1915, and 1941 entries).
92 Ibid., (1915 entry).
93 Ibid., (1330 entry).
94 Ibid., (1345 cntry).
95 Ibid., (1350 entry).
96 34th G-3 Report, 180001 to 180002 February 1944.
97 34th G-3 Journal, 2 February 1944 (1250 and 1300 entries).
98 Ibid., (2052 and 2110 entries). Implied in the entries.
99 Ibid., (1706 entry): Location given is at 856221 which seems to show a house on the 1944 1/25,000 scale map. This particular group said they were from the 5th Company of the 211th Grenadier-Regiment.
100 756th Unit Journal, 2 February 1944 (1630 entry); Redle's location reported as 858222. The Unit Journal reports Arnold contacted Redle at this time (probably via radio or message), but Redle only remembers Sweeting giving the orders.
101 Redle letter to Palumbo, 25 November 1986; Redle interview by Lowther, 11–12 August 2012.
102 Redle letter to Palumbo, 25 November 1986.
103 Redle mistakenly recalled Granberry was from A Co, but he was from C Co.
104 756th Unit Journal, 2 February 1944 (1725 entry); Fazendin, *756th in Cassino*, 92.
105 756th Unit Journal, 2 February 1944 (1715 entry).
106 Ibid., (1740 entry); B Co/756th Morning Report, 23 April 1944, "Record of Events" for 2 February.
107 756th Unit Journal, 2 February 1944 (1755 entry).
108 Ibid., (1745 entry).
109 Ankrum, *Dogfaces Who Smiled Through Tears*, 409; Treanor, *One Damn Thing*, 262–63. There is some conflict in the surviving record over Fraizer's condition. Ankrum claims Fraizer was wounded in the foot earlier in the day and did not return. Treanor, however, does not mention Fraizer getting wounded at all, and reports he was still in command that evening. Redle also recalls Fraizer was in command at this point. The author assumes all accounts are essentially factual and concludes Treanor and Redle may not have known Fraizer was wounded earlier and Ankrum might not have known Fraizer returned to command.
110 34th G-3 Journal, 2 February 1944 (1815 entry); 34th G-3 Report, 180001 to 180002 February 1944.
111 34th G-3 Journal, 2 February 1944 (1755 entry).
112 Ibid., (1815 entry).
113 Ibid., (1800 entry).
114 Ibid., (1820 entry).
115 756th Unit Journal, 2 February 1944 (1820 entry).

116 Treanor, *One Damn Thing*, 261.
117 Fazendin, *756th at Cassino*, 92: Redle recollection; 756th S-3 Report, 180001 to 180002 February 1944.
118 756th Unit Journal, 2 February 1944, (1840 entry).
119 Fazendin, *756th at Cassino*, 92–93: Redle recollection.
120 756th Unit Journal, 2 February 1944 (1900 entry); B Co/756th Unit Journal, 2 February 1944.
121 Fazendin, *756th at Cassino*, 92: Redle recollection.
122 Ibid., 93, Redle specifically recalls the German AT rounds traced red flames, not the usual green.
123 Ibid., 93–94; Redle interview by Lowther, 11–12 August 2012.
124 Ankrum, *Dogfaces Who Smiled Through Tears*, 409–10; 34th G-3 Journal, 2 February 1944 (1941 entry); 34th G-3 Journal, 2 February 1944 (1941 entry); B Co/756th Morning Report, 23 April 1944, "Record of Events" for 2 February; Plowman, *Battles for Cassino*, 90.
125 756th Unit Journal 2 February 1944 (1910 entry): Redle advanced as far as 857219, and was told to withdraw to 857227; Plowman, *Battles for Cassino*, 90; Fazendin, *756th at Cassino*, 92–94: Redle recollection; Redle letter to Palumbo, 25 November 1986.
126 Treanor, *One Damn Thing*, 261.
127 Ranspach diary, 3 February 1944.
128 Redle interview by Lowther, 11–12 August 2012.
129 Redle interview, 11 September 2009.
130 Redle letter to Palumbo, 25 November 1986.
131 Donald G. Taggart, *The History of the Third Infantry Division in World War II* (Reprint, Nashville, Tennessee: The Battery Press, 1987), 571; Fazendin, *756th at Cassino*, 93; Peter Caddick-Adams, *Monte Cassino: Ten Armies in Hell* (New York, New York: Oxford University Press, 2012), 117.
132 34th G-3 Journal, 2 February 1944 (2015 entry).
133 Fazendin, *756th at Cassino*, 104–105.
134 Plowman, *Battles for Cassino*, 90; Peter Caddick-Adams, *Monte Cassino: Ten Armies*, 117. Wolfgang Loof (curator with Garnisongeschichte Jüterbog St. Barbara, a German artillery historical society in Germany) email, 8 June 2021: First name confirmed as Edwin.
135 756th Unit Journal, 2 February 1944 (1930 entry); 34th G-3 Journal, 2 February 1944 (2145 entry): Location of square is 858214.
136 Fazendin, *756th in Cassino*, 95–98.
137 Implied by the record, although some—but not all—crew members may have been captured either from this tank or the fourth tank knocked out in Granberry's column (see footnote 141).
138 Treanor, *One Damn Thing*, 262.
139 Fazendin, *756th at Cassino*, 95-96: Eric Biegler recollection. Biegler was the loader in Sgt Vaughn's tank and describes the German flash grenade that burned Lt Granberry's face as "phosphorous," but according to Gordon L. Rottman, *World War II Infantry Fire Support Tactics*, (Oxford, UK: Osprey Publishing, 2016), 23, the Germans did not have the capability of producing phosphorous smoke—but instead used hexachloroethane-zinc.
140 Fazendin, *756th in Cassino*, 98.
141 The true number of Granberry's men taken prisoner ranges from as low as ten to a high as thirteen—so members of another tank crew could have also been captured. The C Co/756th Morning Reports lists thirteen total MIAs (twelve on 3 February 1944 and one more listed retroactively on 13 February 1944). Ten names on this list are also listed in the NARA WWII Prisoner of War database: 2nd Lt James W. Granberry [C], Sgt Edwin Holmquist [C], Sgt James Vaughn [C], Cpl George C. Dugger [C], T/4 Erwin E. Tompkins [C], T/4 James W. Nichols [C], T/5 Jeff D. Goddard [C], Pfc Lowell M. McMurtrey [C], Pvt Charles F. Foley [C], and Pvt Eric L. Biegler [C]. Sgt Holmquist died of wounds in captivity several days later. Three others: T/5 Lee Roy Jones [C], Pfc Wilbur M. Lewis [C], and Pvt William S. Keoke [C], had duty statuses changed later from MIA to DOW (Jones) and KIA (Lewis and Keoke). It is not recorded if any or all of these three men died while in captivity.
142 Fazendin, *756th in Cassino*, 96; Plowman, *Battles for Cassino*, 90; Plowman identifies *Oberleutnant* Metzger and his platoon crews as the Germans who took Granberry's tankers prisoner and captured their M4s. Wolfgang Loof (emails to the author, 29 April, 3 May, and 16 June 2021) identifies Wachtmeister (Platoon Sergeant) Herbert Berneis, in particular, as directly responsible for capturing Lt Granberry's tanks. Berneis was later awarded the German Cross in Gold for this action. Berneis survived the war. The 242nd Cassino After Action

Report records Metzger's crews were pleased to discover the captured American tanks laden with coffee, tea, chocolate, cookies, and other delicacies that "exceeded our expectations."

143 Treanor, *One Damn Thing*, 261: Treanor mistakenly believed four tanks were trapped ahead when a fifth was knocked out. At the time, Granberry's platoon only had four tanks, so three tanks were trapped, not four. Plowman, *Battles for Cassino*, 90: Plowman reports the Germans deemed the M4 "perched over the ditch" as unrecoverable and thus destroyed it with explosives. There could be some confusion over the location of this "ditch." The author assumes the "ditch" refers to the spillway and bridge near the town square. Clearly, the third tank in Granberry's four tank platoon became hopelessly hung up on this bridge (either attacking or retreating) and the crew abandoned the tank—leaving Granberry and Vaughn trapped in the town square. The 756th records, however, show no destroyed tank at this small bridge, nor is a destroyed tank mentioned in the unit journals at this position when the engineers repair the bridge in the days that followed. The author believes the Germans eventually recovered the M4 at the bridge (capturing a total of three M4s) but destroyed the fourth tank in Granberry's column. The fourth tank had been knocked out and abandoned closer to the entrance of town near the Rapido. This was the tank Redle found abandoned by the crew, and blocking the entrance of town when his tank section attempted to rescue Granberry that same evening. Eventually, this fourth tank was bulldozed aside by US forces and overturned into the riverbed.

144 756th Unit Journal, 2 February 1944 (1925, 1930, and 1940 entries).

145 Ibid., (1945 entry).

146 34th G-2 Report, 120004 to 120006 February 1944.

147 Captain James A Luttrell, "The Operations of the 168th Infantry (34th Infantry Division) in the Rapido River Crossing, 28 January–10 February, 1944. (Rome–Arno Campaign) (Personal Experience of a Cannon Company Commander)." The Infantry School, Fort Benning Georgia, Advanced Infantry Officers Course 1948–1949, 16.

148 Plowman, *Battles for Cassino*, 90; Redle letter, 30 January 2008; Ankrum, *Dogfaces Who Smiled Through Tears*, 400–401.

149 34th G-3 Journal, 2 February 1944 (2025 and 2150 entries): Location of Hill 324 is listed as 851227.

150 Ibid., (2234 entry).

151 Ibid., (1510 entry).

152 34th G-3 Report, 180001 to 180002 February 1944.

153 34th G-3 Journal, 2 February 1944 (2052 and 2110 entries).

154 Ibid., (1915 entry).

155 Ibid., (2200 entry); 34th Inf DivG-3 Report, 180031 January to 180001 February 1944, accompanying map dated 2 February 1944 1800hrs shows positions as follows: 3rd Bn/133rd with L Co on right, I Co on left, and K Co following closely behind. C Co/133rd was due east with B Co to the SE and A Co behind.

156 133rd S-3 Report, 180002 to 180003 February 1944.

157 34th G-3 Journal, 2 February 1944 (2320 entry).

158 Ibid., (2005 and 2320 entries).

159 Ibid., (2200 entry).

160 Ibid., (2340 entry).

161 Ibid., (1330 entry): These four routes were: "Rd W of river, river itself, Road N of river and Portella rd. They will converge on Cassino."

162 Ibid., (2005 entry).

163 Ibid., (2320 and 2340 entries).

164 Ibid., (2045 and 2050 entries).

165 Ibid., (2200 entry).

166 756th Unit Journal 2 February 1944 (2400 entry); 34th G-3 Journal, 3 February 1944 (0940 entry).

167 756th Unit Journal, 2 February 1944 (2145 and 2330 entries): According to 2 February 1944 S-3 map, the 133rd CP was located approximately at 886230, putting Col Marshall's command operations in a house approximately 1.5 miles due east of the barracks.

168 Lee McCardell, "McCardell Under Fire With Yanks In Final Attacks On Cassino Forts," *The Baltimore Sun* (Baltimore, Maryland), 6 February 1944, 1; Lee McCardell, "Two Infantry Battles For Cassino Described," *The Baltimore Sun* (Baltimore, Maryland), 7 February 1944, 1.

169 Figuratively, of course. But Treanor reports Sweeting became "obsessed" with destroying those guns.

Chapter 2

1 34th G-3 Journal, 3 February 1944 (0225 entry).
2 Ibid., (0030 and 0055 entries).
3 Ibid., (0405 entry).
4 Ibid., (0125 entry).
5 Ibid., (0259 entry).
6 Ibid., (0408 and 0535 entries): Position was 852224.
7 Ibid., (0050 entry): This was probably not referring to a Rapido bridge, but to another one over a tributary stream.
8 756th Commander's Narrative for January and February 1944, 25.
9 756th Unit Journal, 3 February 1944 (0600 and 0655 entries).
10 Ibid., (0700 entry).
11 34th G-3 Journal, 3 February 1944 (0615 and 0725 entries): The location given is 857216, but the spillway is actually located closer to 857215; Fazendin, *756th at Cassino*, 95-96: Eric Biegler is the source for the "swastika flag" reference, although he does not say at what point in time the flag was placed on the tank. The author believes the flag was placed earlier, so German artillery observers would know not to target it.
12 Ibid., (0615 entry).
13 Ankrum, *Dogfaces Who Smiled Through Tears*, 402: The German tank was disabled by Lt Richard Lohren's men of C Co. Lohren credits one man named "Cox" in particular for shooting out the "prisms" so the crew was blinded. Lohren also reports Cox killed all the men who tried to escape. Some of this seems to be confirmed by 34th G-3 Journal, 3 February 1944 (0725 entry), with "they think the knocked out an AT gun."
14 756th Unit Journal, 3 February 1944 (0740 entry): The location is 859216.
15 34th G-3 Journal, 3 February 1944 (0755 entry).
16 756th Unit Journal, 3 February 1944 (0800 and 0820 entries); 34th G-3 Journal, 3 February 1944 (0940 entry): This is a direct quote from Sweeting.
17 Fazendin, *756th at Cassino*, 94: Redle recollection.
18 756th Unit Journal, 3 February 1944 (0905 entry).
19 133rd S-3 Reports, 180002 to 180003 February 1944, and 180003 to 180004 February 1944; Ankrum, *Dogfaces Who Smiled Through Tears*, 402.
20 34th G-3 Journal, 3 February 1944 (0900 entry).
21 Ibid., (1010 entry).
22 Ibid., (1100 entry).
23 Ibid., (1110 entry).
24 Ibid., (0725 entry).
25 Ankrum, *Dogfaces Who Smiled Through Tears*, 403; "Rockwell Praised for Ridge Attack," *Council Bluffs Nonpareil* (Council Bluffs, Iowa), 17 November 1943, 5; "Villiscan Receives Christmas Present from Gen. Clark," *Council Bluffs Nonpareil* (Council Bluffs, Iowa), 1 August 1944, 3: Neal was from Villisca, Iowa, and received a battlefield commission after the Battle of Fondouk Pass in April 1943. He was promoted to 1st lieutenant, personally, by Lt Gen Mark Clark on Christmas Day, 1943.
26 Ankrum, *Dogfaces Who Smiled Through Tears*, 403.
27 Ibid., 403–05; "Former Nebraskan makes 'one man raid' on enemy in Cassino fighting," *Lincoln Journal Star* (Lincoln, Nebraska), 28 July 1944, 8. This involved close quarters fighting over rugged terrain using hand grenades, athletic maneuvering and point-blank shooting. One of Neal's men, 37-year-old Pfc Leo J. "Pop" Powers was awarded the Medal of Honor for singlehandedly taking out three MGs positions and is also credited with capturing seventeen Germans during this assault.
28 133rd Cannon Co Unit Journal, 3 February 1944.
29 Ankrum, *Dogfaces Who Smiled Through Tears*, 404; 34th G-3 Journal, 3 February 1944 (0830 entry): Reports that C Co/135th was "strung along S slope of Hill 324." Perhaps K Co/133rd contacted these men; "Sea Breeze Youth Aids Cassino Drive," *Democrat and Chronicle* (Rochester, New York), 3 February 1944, 2; Ankrum says Long was a captain, but the 3 February 1944 news article lists him as a lieutenant.
30 Lee McCardell, "Battle for Cassino Viewed by McCardell," *The Evening Sun* (Baltimore, Maryland), 10 February 1944, 4.

31 Lee McCardell, "McCardell Tells of First Battle," *The Evening Sun* (Baltimore, Maryland), 7 February 1944, 1.; The Italian-speaking sergeant was Sgt Bert Guizzetti from Des Moines, IA. Pvt Nelson Brewer of Newport News, VA assisted.
32 Plowman, *Battles for Cassino*, 91; 34th G-3 Report, 1800 3 February to 1800 4 February 1944; 34th G-3 Journal, 3 February 1944 (0940 entry).
33 34th G-3 Journal, 3 February 1944 (0705, 0720, and 0740 entries); Plowman, *Battles for Cassino*, 91.
34 34th G-3 Journal, 3 February 1944 (0830 entry).
35 Ibid., (1510 entry).
36 756th Unit Journal, 3 February 1944 (0905 entry).
37 34th G-3 Journal, 3 February 1944 (0940 and 1330 entries).
38 756th Unit Journal, 3 February 1944 (1230 entry): Location given is 857227. The 1944 1/25,000 scale map shows several houses on the hillside of Hill 225 and one was the likely location for the 3rd Bn CP.
39 34th G-2 Report, 021200 to 031200 3 February 1944; 1st Tank Group S-3 Report, 180002 to 180003 February 1944; 34th G-3 Report, 180002 to 180003 February 1944.
40 34th G-3 Journal, 3 February 1944 (0940 entry).
41 756th Unit Journal, 3 February 1944 (1230 entry): Quarry location is 858223.
42 34th G-3 Journal, 3 February 1944 (1320 entry): Incident happened at 1255.
43 105th AA AW Bn Periodic Report, 28 January 1944 to 4 February 1944: No hits on German aircraft were observed either.
44 34th G-3 Journal, 3 February 1944 (1225 entry).
45 Ibid., (1330 entry).
46 Ibid., 1944 (1330 entry).
47 Ibid., (1330 entry).
48 Treanor, *One Damn Thing*, 260.
49 Martin Blumenson, *Salerno to Cassino* (Washington, D.C.: Center of Military History, U.S. Army, 1993), 378–79; Plowman, *Battles for Cassino*, 91.
50 756th Unit Journal, 3 February 1944 (1500, 1555, 1630, and 1640 entries).
51 Treanor, *One Damn Thing*, 262.
52 Ibid., 262–63; 133rd S-3 Report, 180002 to 180003 February 1944; McCardell, Lee. "McCardell Tells of First Battle," *The Evening Sun* (Baltimore, Maryland), 7 February 1944, 1.
53 Fazendin, *756th at Cassino*, 98–99: Redle and Oric Johannesen recollections.
54 Redle interview by Lowther, 11–12 August 2012.
55 Redle letter to Palumbo, 25 November 1986; Helmuth O. Froeschle, *Our Story of the 760th Tank Battalion, WWII*, (Reprint. Victoria, Canada: Trafford Publishing), 2007, 86–87; 760th Tank Battalion "Operations in Italy, February 1944."
56 Redle letter to Palumbo, 25 November 1986.
57 Redle letter, 4 April 2010: In this letter, Redle writes that Johannesen was not pleased with this assignment as he had to put his life on the line "a second time" (perhaps referring to the incident earlier at the barracks). Redle noted that as company commander, his crews were often issued direct orders by Sweeting, Dolvin or Arnold on tank deployment matters without his input or advice.
58 756th Unit Journal, 3 February 1944 (1500, 1555, 1630, and 1640 entries): Location is 858218. This is the same location where Redle reported an "anti-tank ditch."
59 34th G-3 Journal, 3 February 1944 (1620 entry): Position of the house is 854240. North face of Pimple is 855238. The only way these positions could have been hit with flat trajectory shells was from the north.
60 34th G-3 Journal, 3 February 1944 (1622 entry).
61 756th Unit Journal, 3 February 1944 (1645 entry): Location is 858217.
62 34th G-3 Journal, 3 February 1944 (1627 entry).
63 Tom Jentz and Hilary Doyle, *Sturmgeschütz III and IV 1942–45* (Osprey Publishing: Oxford, UK, 2001), 17.
64 Fazendin, *756th at Cassino*, 99: Redle recollection.
65 Oric Johannesen enlistment record at World War II Army Enlistment Records, documenting the period ca. 1938– 1946, at National Archives website: https://aad.archives.gov/aad/series-list.jsp?cat=WR26, accessed 20 April 2021.

66 756th Unit Journal, 3 February 1944 (1710 entry); Redle interview by Lowther, 11–12 August 2012; David A. Redle (son) email, 14 May 2014: In retrospect, Redle amended the Fazendin account of the driver's death as erroneous, and believed the driver lost a leg, but survived. The author could not identify who this driver was. The record shows several possible candidates; Fazendin, *756th at Cassino*, 99; McCardell, Lee. "McCardell Tells of First Battle," *The Evening Sun* (Baltimore, Maryland), 7 February 1944, 1: McCardell witnessed this event from the nearby hillside while tagging along with the troops clearing out ruined homes.

67 Redle letter, 4 April 2010.

68 Redle interview by Lowther, 11–12 August 2012; Fazendin, *756th at Cassino*, 99.

69 Plowman, *Battles for Cassino*, 91; Fazendin, *756th at Cassino*, 99–100; Redle letter to Palumbo, 25 November 1986. Johannesen may have already done so on his own initiative.

70 Fazendin, *756th at Cassino*, 100; Redle interview by Lowther, 11–12 August 2012.

71 756th Unit Journal, 3 February 1944 (1710 entry).

72 Treanor, *One Damn Thing*, 263–64: Trahan's platoon was down to four tanks due to the loss of one earlier at Caira; Tom Treanor. "Treanor, First Correspondent in Cassino, Give Eyewitness Story of Battle," *The Los Angeles Times* (Los Angeles, California), 6 February 1944, 1–2.

73 133rd S-3 Report, 180003 to 180004 February 1944; Treanor, *One Damn Thing*, 263–65; Froeschle, *Our Story of the 760th*, 86–87; 760th Tank Battalion "Operations in Italy, February 1944."

74 Treanor, *One Damn Thing*, 263–64.

75 Ibid., 264–65.

76 Plowman, *Battles for Cassino*, 91–93; Blumenson, *Salerno to Cassino*, 378; Lee McCardell, "Snow, Cold Bog Down Fighting in Italy," *The Evening Sun* (Baltimore, Maryland), 14 February 1944, 1.

77 133rd S-3 Report, 180003 to 180004 February 1944.

78 Treanor, *One Damn Thing*, 262–63.

79 34th G-3 Journal, 3 February 1944 (1730 entry); 133rd S-3 Report, 180003 to 180004 February 1944.

80 34th G-3 Journal, 3 February 1944 (1730 entry).

81 Treanor, *One Damn Thing*, 264.

82 M Company was the 3rd Battalion's "heavy weapons" company used to support the other three rifle companies. A heavy weapons company was comprised of two MG platoons, each with four .30-caliber M1917A1 water-cooled heavy MGs, and a platoon of six 81mm mortar tubes, (Rottman, *WWII Infantry Fire Support Tactics*, 28).

83 Tom Treanor, "Treanor, First Correspondent in Cassino, Give Eyewitness Story of Battle," *The Los Angeles* Times (Los Angeles, California), 6 February 1944, 1, 2.

84 Treanor, *One Damn Thing*, 263–64.

85 Tom Treanor, "Treanor, First Correspondent in Cassino, Give Eyewitness Story of Battle," *The Los Angeles Times* (Los Angeles, California), 6 February 1944, 1, 2.

86 756th Unit Journal, 3 February 1944 (1730 and 1740 entries).

87 Ibid., (1740).

88 Ibid., (1730, 1740, and 1752 entries).

89 Treanor, *One Damn Thing*, 262–63: German tracer was described by Treanor as an "incandescent green streak."

90 Tom Treanor, "Treanor, First Correspondent in Cassino, Give Eyewitness Story of Battle," *The Los Angeles Times* (Los Angeles, California), 6 February 1944, 1, 2.

91 Treanor, *One Damn Thing*, 263–64; Froeschle, *Our Story of the 760th*, 86–87 and casualty list on page 102; 760th Tank Battalion "Operations in Italy, February 1944"; 756th Unit Journal, 3 February 1944 (1752 entry); Blumenson, *Salerno to Cassino*, 378–79. The two men killed were: Pfc Ralph E. Obermire (MIA) (Wagner, S.D.) and Pvt Kinnon R. White, Jr (MIA) (Pensacola, Fla), according to the IDPFs for both men. The tank was an M4A1 model with War Department #3058586 and crewed by Obermire, White, Isabella, Tedder, and Trahan. White is listed as the loader and Obermire the bow gunner. Obermire was not recovered until June 1944 and White was not found until December 1944. Both remains were removed from rubble outside the tank. The author theorizes that British forces removed the remains during subsequent combat operations and used the tank interior as cover; Tom Treanor, "Treanor, First Correspondent in Cassino, Give Eyewitness Story of Battle," *The Los Angeles Times* (Los Angeles, California), 6 February 1944, 1, 2: Treanor writes that the bow gunner suffered a broken leg, and the rest of the crew escaped, but this was clearly erroneous.

92 C Co/760th Morning Report, 6 February 1944.

93 Ibid. 2nd Lt Leo J. Trahan was from New Orleans and Cpl John P. Isabella was from Schenectady, New York. A third man, Pvt Carl W. Tedder from Pine Mt Valley, Georgia is also listed as LWA the same day and was part of this crew. According to NARA hospitalization records, Tedder was wounded in the buttocks, hip, and hand by shell fragments.

94 Speculative on Dolvin's behavior. He had no radio at this point.

95 756th Unit Journal, 3 February 1944 (1753 and1830 entries); Froeschle, *Our Story of the 760th*, 86–87; 760th Tank Battalion "Operations in Italy, February 1944"; 34th G-3 Journal, 3 February 1944 (1752 and 1810 entries).

96 Tom Treanor, "Treanor, First Correspondent in Cassino, Give Eyewitness Story of Battle," *The Los Angeles Times* (Los Angeles, California), 6 February 1944, 1, 2; Treanor, *One Damn Thing*, 262–64.

97 Treanor, *One Damn Thing*, 264–65.

98 Froeschle, *Our Story of the 760th*, 86–87; 760th Tank Battalion "Operations in Italy, February 1944."

99 Treanor, *One Damn Thing*, 265. Speculative on Dolvin's actions, but he wouldn't have left town unless he was satisfied with the positioning of the remaining armor.

100 34th G-3 Journal, 3 February 1944 (1810 entry).

101 Tom Treanor, "Treanor, First Correspondent in Cassino, Give Eyewitness Story of Battle," *The Los Angeles Times* (Los Angeles, California), 6 February 1944, 1, 2.

102 Speculative that Dolvin stopped and used the field phone at Fraizer's CP. He had no radio, and yet he called in at 1630. This would have been twenty minutes after he departed town. Treanor saw Dolvin too, so it is reasonable to believe Dolvin phoned from Fraizer's CP; 756th Unit Journal, 3 February 1944 (2145 entry). Dolvin reported three operational tanks. This means either he was not aware of the one tank abandoned in the shell hole or he may have known of the two men from Sgt Upchurch's crew reclaiming the tank afterwards and manning the main gun.

103 Treanor, *One Damn Thing*, 264; 756th Unit Journal, 3 February 1944 (1900 entry).

104 34th G-3 Journal, 3 February 1944 (1830 entry).

105 Treanor, *One Damn Thing*, 262–65.

106 Tom Treanor, "Treanor, First Correspondent in Cassino, Give Eyewitness Story of Battle," *The Los Angeles Times* (Los Angeles, California), 6 February 1944, 1, 2: Van Steenbergen was from Sheldon, Iowa.

107 133rd S-3 Report, 180003 to 180004 February 1944.

108 133rd S-3 Report, 180003 to 180004 February 1944; 34th G-3 Journal, 3 February 1944 (1730 entry); Treanor, *One Damn Thing*, 264–65.

109 34th G-3 Journal, 3 February 1944 (1715 entry): Just east of 1st Bn at 875213.

110 34th G-3 Journal, 3 February 1944 (1725 entry): Companies A and B were attached to the 34th Inf Div during this time according to *History of the Second Chemical Mortar Battalion*, (Ernest Muller, Salzburg, Austria, 1946), 24. This unit utilized 4.2-inch mortars greatly feared by the Germans.

111 34th G-3 Journal, 3 February 1944 (1610 entry); 109th Engineers Bn S-3 Report, 180002 to 180003 February 1944: Eight flame throwers were delivered to 133rd by these engineers.

112 Ibid., (1355 entry).

113 Froeschle, *Our Story of the 760th*, 105–6; Pvt Frank J. Costanza of Bronx, New York, and Pfc Lawrence J. Chapman of Bettendorf, Iowa. Remaining in Upchurch's tank were Cpl Edward R. Lizenby of Winchester, Illinois, and Pfc David W. Callahan of Auburn, New York, according to Tom Treanor, "Treanor, First Correspondent in Cassino, Give Eyewitness Story of Battle," *The Los Angeles Times* (Los Angeles, California), 6 February 1944, 1, 2.

114 Treanor, *One Damn Thing*, 265. Treanor was the first Allied war correspondent in Cassino. Lee McCardell, a competing reporter, wrote that an "intense rivalry" took place among war correspondents for the honor, but McCardell freely admitted that he had no desire to earn the distinction … choosing instead to wait until after the city was taken. (Lee McCardell, "Stubborn Yank Infantry Drive is Making History At Cassino," *The Evening Sun* (Baltimore, Maryland), 5 February 1944, 1.)

115 34th G-3 Journal, 3 February 1944 (2115 entry): B Co at 860216, just NE of jail.

116 Ibid., (2250 entry).

117 Redle letter to Palumbo, 25 November 1986; 34th G-3 Journal, 4 February 1944 (0611 entry).

118 34th Division Artillery G-3 Report, 180002 to 180003 February 1944: Period of time from noon 2 February to noon 3 February. Totals were as follows: 7,753 (105mm howitzer), 1,004 (155mm howitzer), and 972 (3" rounds).

119 34th G-3 Journal, 3 February 1944 (2115 and 2250 entries); 34th G-3 Report 180003 to 180004 February 1944.
120 Ibid.: At first these guns are reported as 57mms but later this is changed to 37mm guns.
121 It is unclear from the record exactly when the Germans recovered this tank, but it had to be sometime after 0610 (3 February) when American infantry patrols last observed the tank still stuck on the bridge. It is also unclear exactly when this bridge was dropped, but it happened sometime before 2100, 5 February, when the 34th G-3 Journal starts reporting bridge work in the north part of town by engineers.
122 Ankrum, *Dogfaces Who Smiled Through Tears*, 410, 3rd Bn surgeon was Capt Mizock of Chicago, Illinois.
123 34th G-3 Journal, 3 February 1944 (2250, 2320, and 2345 entries): Tanks were sent to test bridges on Highway 6 at 860209, and 867207 (across the Rapido to SE of town).
124 756th Unit Journal, 3 February 1944 (2045 entry).
125 34th G-3 Journal, 4 February 1944 (0110 and 0340 entries).
126 Ibid., (0100 entry).
127 756th Morning Report casualties listed for 3 February were: Pfc Wilbur M. Lewis [C], and Pvt William S. Keoke [C], (KIA); Sgt Edwin Holmquist [C], (DOW on 6 February); T/5 Lee Roy Jones [C], (DOW, date not given); 1st Lt William R. Engfer [HQ], and Cpl Edward J. Clark [HQ], (WIA, but it's not reported to what extent these men were wounded; Maj Welborn G. Dolvin [HQ], S/Sgt Charles N. Goodloe [D], and T/4 Howard J. Bowers [Sv], (LWA).
128 T/4 rank is listed as Bower's postwar rank and may not have been his rank at this time.
129 Fazendin, *756th at Cassino*, 53–54, Cullen Ward Account; Service Co/756th Morning Report, 4 February 1944: Ward listed as IIA on this date, so this was likely the night it happened.
130 34th G-3 Journal, 4 February 1944 (0050 entry).
131 34th G-3 Report, 180003 to 180004 February 1944: Objective given was 854214.
132 34th G-3 Journal, 4 February 1944 (0212, 0311, 0340, and 0611 entries): 1st Bn position reported as 858216 (just N and NE of jail).
133 Ibid., (0115 entry).
134 34th G-3 Journal, 4 February 1944 (0135, 0317, and 0355 entries).
135 34th G-3 Report, 180003 to 180004 February 1944; Graham Hovey, "Yanks Digging In On Outskirts of Cassino," *The San Francisco Examiner* (San Francisco, California), 5 February 1944, 5.
136 34th G-3 Journal, 4 February 1944 (0611, 0620, and 0624 entries).
137 756th Unit Journal, 4 February 1944 (0800 entry).
138 Froeschle, *Our Story of the 760th*, 105–6.
139 756th S-3 Report, 180003 to 180004 February 1944; 760th Tank Battalion "Operations in Italy, February 1944."
140 760th Tank Battalion "Operations in Italy, February 1944", 11.
141 "Dale F. Pride," (Obituary) *The Springfield News-Leader* (Springfield, Missouri), 17 October 2003, 14.
142 34th G-3 Journal, 4 February 1944 (0840 entry).
143 Ibid., (0840 and 0845 entries).
144 133rd Cannon Co Unit Journal, 4 February 1944.
145 B Co/756th Unit Journal, 4 February 1944; B Co/756th Morning Report, 4 February 1944.
146 II Corps G-3 Report, 120003 to 120004 February 1944: Location of infantry/tanks was 858216, which put them left of the main road in the block of homes between the river and the spillway.
147 Plowman, *Battles for Cassino*, 92.
148 "34th Infantry Division, Lessons Learned in Combat, November 7–8 1942–September 1944." Italy, September 1944. Testimony of Maj Warren C. Chapman, 133rd Inf Regt, 5; Ankrum, *Dogfaces Who Smiled Through Tears*, 412.
149 34th Inf Div "Lessons Learned in Combat," Chapman account, 7–8.
150 Blumenson, *Salerno to Cassino*, 379.
151 Plowman, *Battles for Cassino*, 94: This spillway is called the Torrent San Silvestro.
152 133rd Cannon Co Unit Journal, 4 February 1944.
153 34th G-3 Journal, 4 February 1944 (1030 entry).
154 S-3 Report, 180003 to 180004 February 1944.
155 756th Commander's Narrative for January and February 1944, 29.

156 133rd S-3 Report, 180003 to 180004 February 1944; 34th G-3 Journal, 4 February 1944 (1140 and 1230 entries): Streambed position at 866213. One enemy tank and infantry reported at 858216—which is right next to the jail.

157 II Corps G-3 Report, 120004 to 120004 5 February 1944; 133rd Cannon Co Unit Journal, 4 February 1944.

158 Redle interview, 19 February 2002; 756th Unit History, 1944; GO #31 II Corps dated 27 April 1944: Harris was awarded the Bronze Star citation for "For heroic achievement in action from 4 February 1944 to 19 February 1944" for this incident and other critical fire support he directed; Fazendin, *756th at Cassino*, 128.

159 34th G-3 Journal, 4 February 1944 (1030 and 1817 entries); 133rd S-3 Report, 180003 to 180004 4 February 1944: Relief unit positions listed at 854227 (1st Bn/133rd less A Co), 855219 (A Co/133rd), and 873214 (100th Bn/133rd).

160 756th S-3 Report, 180003 to 180004 February 1944; 1st Tank Group S-3 Report, 180003 to 180004 February 1944; 776th TD Bn S-3 Report, 180003 to 180004 February 1944.

161 133rd S-3 Report, 180003 to 180004 February 1944.

162 34th G-3 Journal, 4 February 1944 (1916 and 1935 entries).

163 Ankrum, *Dogfaces Who Smiled Through Tears*, 410.

164 34th G-3 Journal, 4 February 1944 (1835 entry).

165 Redle letter to Palumbo, 25 November 1986; Henry Sanislow interview, 15 September 2006.

166 James E. Haspel interview by Pamela G. Patrick, 18 September 1984.

167 756th S-3 Report, 180003 to 180004 February 1944: Tanks were positioned at 855238.

168 756th Unit Journal, 4 February 1944 (0940 entry).

169 Ibid., (1200 entry).

170 776th TD Bn S-3 Report, 180002 to 180003 February 1944.

171 756th Unit Journal, 4 February 1944 (1600, 1700, 2100, and 2300 entries): Location of hill is 856223; Treanor, *One Damn Thing*, 258.

172 Ranspach diary, 5 February 1944.

173 Treanor, *One Damn Thing*, 258–59: Date is approximate.

174 34th G-2 Report, 021200 to 031200 February 1944: Two of these prisoners were Indians from the 10th British Army in Libya who were captured and forced to serve as orderlies in the German Army; 34th G-2 Report, 021200 to 031200 February 1944: Location captured is 858214.

175 Stephen Hart and Russell Hart. *German Tanks of World War II* (London UK: Brown Packaging Books Ltd., 1998), 62–65. An M4's M3 75mm main gun fired at only 2030 feet per second.

176 34th G-2 Report, 021200 to 031200 February 1944: Interrogation report # 189; Riedmaier's claim of destroying four M4s is confirmed by the unofficial unit history of the 242 Assault Gun Battalion with this entry: "*Während der Kämpfe um Cassino geriet Wachtmeister Riedmaier nach vorbildlich erfolgreichem Einsatz und Abschuß von vier Sherman-Panzern in Gefangenschaft.*" This translates roughly as: "During the battles for Cassino, Wachtmeister Riedmaier was taken prisoner after exemplary successful use and shooting down of four Sherman tanks." (Loof email and attachments, 8 June 2021).

177 34th G-3 Journal, 4 February 1944 (1330 entry).

178 Luttrell, "Operations of the 168th Infantry … Rapido River Crossing", 17.

179 I and L Cos/168th Morning Reports for 27–31 January 1944 period: Only one man is listed as died of wounds (DOW) during this period. He had been evacuated and was recorded as such two days later by the hospital.

180 Haspel interview by Pamela G. Patrick, 18 September 1984, Individual Deceased Personnel File (IDPF) for Pvt John F. Bacha (B Co/756th) includes references to three other men from the 168th Inf Regt who turned up missing and their remains were never recovered: S/Sgt Paul R. Nelson and Pfc John K. Sayro for A Co and Pvt Valdemero Mattos Jr of I Co. These men were likely killed by artillery or mines and their bodies were subsequently lost in the days and weeks that followed—probably as the result of subsequent blasts of artillery.

181 Edwin B. Olson letter, 30 May 2001.

182 B Co/756th Morning Report, 6 February 1944; IDPF for Paul T. Tirpak: "Report of Burial" completed 9 February 1944 shows he was first buried near Cervaro. Dog tags were not imprinted (probably destroyed). He was identified by his wallet, paybook, and personal effects. Finger prints were also taken. His file contains no evidence of first being buried by the Germans.

183 Arthur Richter interview at 756th Tank Bn reunion in Omaha, Nebraska, 16 September 2004.
184 IDPF for Wayne B. Henry (German records contained within): Henry's US burial report was filed on 8 February 1944; B Co/756th Morning Report, 12 February 1944.
185 Redle letter, 4 April 2010.
186 Ranspach diary, 5 February 1944.
187 34th G-3 Journal, 4 February 1944 (1845 entry).
188 Ibid., (2222 entry).
189 Ibid.
190 Blumenson, *Salerno to Cassino*, 381; 34th G-2 Report, 120003 to 120004 February 1944.
191 Blumenson, *Salerno to Cassino*, 381; Incoming message #16 to 34th G-3 received at 1008 by radio from CEF G-3 on 5 February 1944.
192 34th G-3 Journal, 03 February 1944 (1730 entry); Ken Ford, *Cassino 1944: Breaking the Gustav Line* (Oxford, UK: Osprey Publishing Ltd., 2004), 45 and 49.
193 34th G-3 Journal, 03 February 1944 (1730 and 1930 entries): Positions recorded at 840230 and 829268; 34th G-3 Report 180002 to 180003 February 1944.
194 Born 1888, United States Army. *Official US Army Register* (Washington, D.C.: War Department, The Adjutant General's Office, United States Government Printing Office, 1945), 515.
195 United States Army, *Fifth Army History, Part IV, Cassino and Anzio, 16 January 1944–13 March 1944*, (Florence, Italy: L'Impronta Press, 1945), 93.
196 Blumenson, *Salerno to Cassino*, 378; Lt Col John H. Hougen, *The Story of the Famous 34th Infantry Division* (1949; reprint, Nashville, TN: The Battery Press, 1979), "The Second Phase of Cassino" (unnumbered pages).
197 34th G-3 Journal, 5 February 1944 (0445 entry).
198 Ibid., (0005 entry).
199 756th Unit Journal, 4 February 1944 (1600, 1700, 2100, and 2300 entries); Location of hill is 856223. Treanor, *One Damn Thing*, 258.
200 756th Unit Journal, 5 February 1944 (0200 entry): Position of the gun placement was 858223.
201 756th Unit History, 1944: March list.
202 756th Commander's Narrative for January and February 1944, 29.
203 34th G-2 Report, 120003 to 120004 February 1944; II Corps G-3 Report, 120004 to 120005 February 1944.
204 34th G-3 Journal, 5 February 1944 (0550 and 0635 entries); 133rd S-3 Report 180004 February to 180005 February 1944.
205 34th G-3 Journal, 5 February 1944 (0635 entry).
206 Ibid.
207 133rd S-3 Report 180004 February to 180005 February 1944: Castle Hill, alternately called "Hill 193" was situated at 854214.
208 34th G-3 Journal, 5 February 1944 (0700 and 0725 entries).
209 Ibid., (0730 and 0810 entries).
210 Ibid., (0945 entry): The position given was 854217, which is not technically Castle Hill, but the western wall of the draw.
211 Ibid.
212 135th S-3 Report, 180004 to 180005 February 1944; 133rd Cannon Co Unit Journal, 5 February 1944.
213 34th Inf Div G-3 Journal, 5 February 1944 (0730 entry): Positions were reported on Hills 593 and 563 and location 835214. One Co was also reported at 841214 and two other companies at 847215.
214 Ibid., (1055 entry): Location of tanks was 852213. It turns out later these were *Sturmgeschütz* IIIs; II Corps G-3 Report, 120005 to 120006 February 1944. A "Cub" was a single engine, two-seater prop plane constructed of wood and canvas. Although they flew low and relatively slow, the enemy was often reluctant to fire on them for fear of giving away positions. Their biggest threat was German fighter aircraft.
215 B Co/756th Morning Report, 23 April 1944, "Record of Events" for 5 February.
216 34th G-2 Report, 120005 to 120006 February 1944; 34th G-3 Journal, 5 February 1944 (1328 entry).
217 34th G-3 Journal, 5 February 1944 (1405 entry): Position was 844207. This location is only about 100 yards due south of the abbey.
218 34th G-2 Report, 120005 to 120006 February 1944: Position of enemy tanks was near 854214.

219 756th Unit Journal, 5 February 1944 (0900 entry): The 59th Field Artillery Bn was attached to the 756th until 2200, 7 February 1944, according to the 756th Unit Journal, 7 February 1944 (2200 entry). This attachment is a testament to Gen Ryder's confidence in Sweeting's abilities.
220 756th Unit Journal, 5 February 1944 (1300 entry).
221 Treanor, *One Damn Thing*, 268–70.
222 Fazendin, *756th in Cassino*, 105–06: Redle recollection. Redle does not state exactly when this happened, but it occurred near the quarry. Because the Germans still held nearby ridges, this was likely the time.
223 34th G-3 Journal, 5 February 1944 (1837 entry); II Corps G-3 Report, 120005 to 120006 February 1944: AA claims to have shot down two of the planes; II Corps G-3 Report, 120006 to 1200007 February 1944: 133rd Cannon Co Unit Journal, 5 February 1944; 34th G-2 Report, 120005 to 120006 February 1944; 34th G-3 Journal, 5 February 1944 (1408 entry).
224 756th Unit Journal, 5 February 1944 (1600 entry).
225 Ibid., (1700 and 1830 entries).
226 Ibid., (1630 entry).
227 34th G-2 Report, 120005 to 120006 February 1944; 133rd Cannon Co Unit Journal, 5 February 1944.
228 Redle letter, 3 January 2001.
229 133rd Cannon Co Unit Journal, 5 February 1944.
230 34th G-3 Journal, 5 February 1944 (1515 and 1615 entries).
231 Ibid., (1515 entry).
232 Plowman, *Battles for Cassino*, 96.
233 Lee McCardell, "Snow, Cold Bog Down Fighting in Italy," *The Evening Sun* (Baltimore, Maryland), 14 February 1944, 1.
234 Treanor, *One Damn Thing*, 255.
235 34th Inf Div "Lessons Learned in Combat," Chapman account, 7.
236 Plowman, *Battles for Cassino*, 96.
237 34th Inf Div "Lessons Learned in Combat," Chapman account, 7.
238 Ibid., 5; Ian Gooderson, *Battles in Focus: Cassino 1944* (London, UK: Brassey's, 2003), 72–73.
239 34th Inf Div "Lessons Learned in Combat," Chapman account, 7.
240 Michael and Gladys Green, *Weapons of Patton's Armies* (Osceola, Wisconsin: MBI Publishing, 2000), 36–39.
241 Blumenson, *Salerno to Cassino*, 381–82.
242 Caddick-Adams, *Monte Cassino: Ten Armies*, 119; Robert Wallace, *The Italian Campaign* (Morristown, New Jersey: Time-Life Books, Inc., 1978), 137.
243 Plowman, *Battles for Cassino*, 96.
244 34th Inf Div "Lessons Learned in Combat," Chapman account, 7.
245 Ibid., 8.
246 34th G-3 Journal, 5 February 1944 (2100 entry).
247 Ibid., 7 February 1944 (2115 entry).
248 Ibid., 5 February 1944 (1715 entry).
249 Ibid., (2100 entry).
250 133rd S-3 Report, 180005 to 180006 February 1944; 34th G-3 Journal, 5 February 1944 (2120 and 2130 entries); II Corps G-3 Report, 120005 to 120006 February 1944: This report claims the 1st Bn/133rd actually captured Castle Hill before a German counterattack drove them off; Plowman, *Battles for Cassino*, 96.
251 34th G-3 Journal, 5 February 1944 (2220 entry).
252 756th Unit Journal, February 1944, message exhibits.
253 756 S-3 Report, 180004 to 180005 February 1944: Reports 1800 hours, 5 February 1944, tank positions as follows: One platoon of tanks of Co C/760 Tk Bn in Cassino, Co B less one platoon plus one platoon C Co/756 at 855238. Co C/760 Tk Bn less one platoon plus one platoon Co A at 855238.
254 Redle letter, 7 January 2007.
255 Redle interview by Lowther, 11–12 August 2012; Redle letter, 6 July 2001.
256 Redle letter 6 July 2001; IDPF for David J. Orris; US World War II Hospital Admission Card Files, 1942–1954 (www.ancestry.com): Orris was evacuated and given blood transfusions, but died a few hours later.
257 Redle letter, 7 January 2007; Johannesen obituary, *The World* (Coos Bay, Oregon), 31 March 2004, 5.
258 Redle letter, 7 January 2007; "On Furlough" *The Coos Bay Times* (Marshfield, Oregon), 16 September 1944, 3.

259 1930 and 1940 Census; Roland Lindsay Buys draft card, United States Army WWII Draft Cards 1940–1947; B Co/756th Morning Report, 5 February 1944: The details of Buys injuries were not recorded but he was originally listed as "SWA."
260 B Co/756th Unit Journal, 5 February 1944.
261 Redle believes this commander was either Cogdill or Oliver.
262 Redle letter to Palumbo, 25 November 1986; Fazendin, *756th at Cassino*, 94: Redle recollection.
263 34th G-2 Report, 120003 to 120004 February 1944.
264 Ibid.
265 Ibid., 120004 to 120005 February 1944: PW interrogation report #194.
266 Ibid., 120006 to 120007 February 1944: PW interrogation report #199.
267 Ibid., 120003 to 120004 February 1944: PW interrogation report #192.
268 Ibid., 120004 to 120005 February 1944: PW interrogation report #194.
269 Ibid.: AT guns reported at 856218 (north first four-way crossroads in town), 857212, and near church.
270 Ibid.
271 Ibid., 120003 to 120004 February 1944: PW interrogation report #193.
272 Ibid.
273 Ibid., 120004 to 120005 February 1944: This prisoner, taken by the 135th Inf Regt was reported to be the battalion Sergeant-Major of the 132th Inf Regt.
274 US Army, *Fifth Army History: Part IV*, 90.
275 135th S-3 Report, 180004 to 180005 February 1944.
276 B Co/756th Morning Report, 23 April 1944, "Record of Events" for 5 February.
277 B Co/756th Morning Report, 5 February 1944: Czajkowski may have had ongoing issues with his wounded hand.
278 Redle letter, 25 January 2004.
279 Redle interview by Lowther, 11–12 August 2012.
280 Redle letter, 25 January 2004.

Chapter 3

1 Tom Treanor, "Battles Rage Through Night Within Cassino," *The Los Angeles Times* (Los Angeles, California), 9 February 1944, 1.
2 Treanor, *One Damn Thing*, 266.
3 Ibid., 267. At this point, command of the German 2nd Platoon, 242nd Assault Gun Battalion had changed over to *OberLt* Fritz-Werner Pohl. *Oberleutnant* Metzger was seriously wounded on 4 February 1944. (Loop, emails 29 April and 3 May 2021).
4 34th G-3 Journal, 6 February 1944 (0115 entry).
5 Ibid., (0120 entry).
6 Ibid., (0448 entry).
7 Ibid., (0445 entry).
8 Ibid., (0540 entry).
9 Ibid., (0600 entry).
10 760th Tank Battalion "Operations in Italy, February 1944"; Froeschle, *Our Story of the 760th*, 74 (roster) and 87–88; 756th S-3 Report, 180005 to 180006 February 1944.
11 Froeschle, *Our Story of the 760th*, 105: S/Sgt Pinckney D. Upchurch of Galatia, Illinois; Cpl Edward R. Lizenby of Westchester, Illinois; and Pvt David W. Callahan of Auburn, New York, were each awarded the Bronze Star for this action. Upchurch was recognized for leading and holding the position while Lizenby and Callahan (from Upchurch's crew) were recognized for manning the nearby disabled tank lodged in the shell hole.
12 C Co/756th Morning Report, 6 February 1944; According to Froeschle, *Our Story of the 760th*, 89, Sgt Fenner and his crew also left town at this time on the back of a tank commanded by Sgt Harmon. Fenner's crew had abandoned the tank lodged in the shell hole two days prior.
13 760th Tank Battalion "Operations in Italy, February 1944"; Froeschle, *Our Story of the 760th*, 74 (roster), 87–88: Gleissner recollection.

14 34th G-3 Journal, 6 February 1944 (0615 entry).
15 135th S-3 Report, 180005 to 180006 February 1944.
16 34th G-3 Journal, 6 February 1944 (0715 entry).
17 Froeschle, *Our Story of the 760th*, 88: Gleissner recollection. He identifies his crew as follows: "My driver was Gray, his assistant driver was Wurm, the loader was Kump and the gunner was Jaster."
18 Ankrum, *Dogfaces Who Smiled Through Tears*, 409–10.
19 Froeschle, *Our Story of the 760th*, 88.
20 Ankrum, *Dogfaces Who Smiled Through Tears*, 410: Ankrum credits Sgt Van Steenbergen with picking off the Mark IV crew with his rifle as they abandoned the tank; 34th G-3 Journal, 6 February 1944 (0743 entry); 34th G-2 Report, 120005 to 120006 February 1944; 756th Commander's Narrative for January and February 1944, 30; The 756th Unit Journal (6 February 1944) records the time the Mark IV was knocked out as 0900. It appears to have been struck numerous times; 756th S-3 Report, 180005 to 180006 February 1944; 776th TD S-3 Report, 180006 to 180007 February 1944; Several units took some credit for hitting this tank. The 185th Field Artillery Bn also reports one observed direct hit on a German tank. This was likely the same incident. (34th Artillery, S-3 Report, 180006 to 180007 February 1944.)
21 Froeschle, *Our Story of the 760th*, 88.
22 C Co/760th Morning Report, 8 February 1944; Froeschle, *Our Story of the 760th*, 102 (casualty list): 2nd Lt Eugene Gleissner was from Mishawaka, Indiana.
23 34th G-2 Report, 120005 to 120006 February 1944; II Corps G3 Report, 120005 to 120006 February 1944.
24 II Corps G3 Report, 120005 to 120006 February 1944.
25 Ibid.
26 Ibid.
27 34th G-3 Journal, 6 February 1944 (0940 entry); 133rd S-3 Report, 180004 February to 180005 February 1944. Captain James R. McClymont becomes Acting S-3 per 133rd S-3 Report, 180005 to 180006 February 1944.
28 756th Unit Journal, 6 February 1944 (0800 entry); 756th CP located in Caira at 858249, 3rd Bn/133 CP at 857222.
29 Ibid., (0830 entry).
30 Ibid., (0830 and 0900 entries). Location of infantry OP was 857219.
31 34th G-3 Journal, 6 February 1944 (1155 entry).
32 756th Unit Journal, 6 February 1944 (1400, 1600, and 1800 entries).
33 34th G-3 Journal, 6 February 1944 (1020 entry); location 854233; 133rd Cannon Co Unit Journal, 6 February 1944.
34 34th G-3 Journal, 6 February 1944 (1155).
35 34th G-2 Report, 120005 to 120006 February 1944.
36 133rd Cannon Co Unit Journal, 6 February 1944.
37 34th G-2 Report, 120005 to 120006 February 1944: Location 858212.
38 Ibid.: PW interrogation #198 source is S/Sgt Michael Tescak from Hq III Bn of 132nd Inf Regt who claimed he deserted because he saw "no sense for an Austrian fighting a losing battle for the Germans."
39 133rd Cannon Co Unit Journal, 6 February 1944.
40 Ibid.
41 Ibid.
42 34th G-3 Journal, 6 February 1944 (1200 entry).
43 133rd Cannon Co Unit Journal, 6 February 1944: The operation ended at 1945 that evening; 34th G-3 Journal, 6 February 1944 (1610 entry).
44 34th G-3 Journal, 6 February 1944, (1520 and 1557 entries).
45 Hougen, *34th Infantry Division*, "The Second Phase of Cassino."
46 34th G-2 Report, 120005 to 120006 February 1944.
47 34th G-3 Journal, 6 February 1944 (2120 entry).
48 Ibid., (1340 entry).
49 Ibid., (1405 entry).
50 Ibid., (2105 entry).
51 Ibid., (2120 entry).

52 133rd S-3 Report, 180005 to 180006 February 1944.
53 133rd Cannon Co Unit Journal, 6 February 1944.
54 34th G-3 Journal, 6 February 1944 (1610 entry).
55 Redle interview by Lowther, 11–12 August 2012.
56 Froeschle, *Our Story of the 760th*, 104.
57 Ibid., 88: Later, Stoppenhagen joked darkly: "I got my hair parted from a bullet fired from a church steeple."
58 760th Tank Battalion "Operations in Italy, February 1944"; Froeschle, *Our Story of the 760th*, 87 and 104: For this action, T/4 Stoppenhagen was awarded the Silver Star.
59 34th G-3 Journal, 6 February 1944 (1810 entry).
60 Ibid., (1950 entry).
61 109th Engineers Bn S-3 Report, 180006 to 180007 February 1944: A platoon of C Co did the job.
62 756th S-3 Report, 180005 to 180006 February 1944: location 855238.
63 Ibid.
64 B Co/756th Morning Report, 23 April 1944, "Record of Events" for 6–11 February; Fazendin, *756th at Cassino*, 115 and 120.
65 756th S-3 Report, 180005 to 180006 February 1944: A Co tank platoon location at 871228.
66 Froeschle, *Our Story of the 760th*, 88: Gleissner recollection.
67 Ibid., 87–88, from the 760th records these relief tanks were from Lt Pride's 2nd Platoon/A Co and arrived the evening of 7 February. The author believes the correct evening of arrival was 6 February.
68 756th Unit Journal, 6 February 1944 (2100 entry) records "C.O. Co. 'C' 760th Tank Bn dispatches 4 tanks to CASSINO to relieve the 3 in there." The author believes those three tanks were unable to withdraw and remained in position until the following evening—probably because the road conditions didn't allow for it. The four relief tanks were probably used primarily to transport ammunition and supplies.
69 According to the 760th Tank Battalion "Operations in Italy, February 1944," Stoppenhagen's crews were unable to withdraw until Lt Pride's crews relieved them the following evening (7 February). No reason was given.
70 Lee McCardell, "Snow, Cold Bog Down Fighting in Italy," *The Evening Sun* (Baltimore, Maryland), 14 February 1944, 1.
71 E.D. Smith, *The Battles for Monte Cassino* (New York, NY: Charles Scribner & Sons, 1975), 72.
72 Blumenson, *Salerno to Cassino*, 381; 34th G-3 Journal, 7 February 1944 (1523 entry); II Corps G-3 Report, 120007 to 120008 February 1944.
73 Caddick-Adams, *Monte Cassino: Ten Armies*, 120–21.
74 US Army, *Fifth Army History: Part IV*, 93.
75 *Army Register 1941*, 152; *Army Register 1945*, 170.
76 John B. Mikolashek, *General Mark Clark: Commander of America's Fifth Army and Liberator of Rome* (Havertown, Pennsylvania: Casemate Publishers, 2013), 11.
77 Martin Blumenson, *Mark Clark: The Last of the Great World War II Commanders* (New York, New York: Cogdon & Weed, Inc., 1984), 16.
78 Blumenson, *Salerno to Cassino*, 381.
79 Smith, *Battles for Monte Cassino*, 72–73.
80 Ankrum, *Dogfaces Who Smiled Through Tears*, 399.
81 133rd Cannon Co Unit Journal, 7 February 1944.
82 34th G-2 Report, 120006 to 120007 February 1944.
83 133rd S-3 Report, 180006 to 180007 February 1944.
84 34th G-3 Journal, 7 February 1944 (0528 entry).
85 Ibid., (0528 entry).
86 Ibid., (1523 entry).
87 Ibid., (0200 and 0202 entries).
88 133rd S-3 Report, 180006 to 180007 February 1944; 34th G-2 Report, 120006 to 120007 February 1944.
89 776th TD S-3 Report, 180006 to 180007 February 1944; 1st Tank Group S-3 Report, 180006 to 180007 February 1944.
90 34th G-2 Report, 180007 to 180008 February 1944.
91 34th G-3 Journal, 7 February 1944 (0825, 0907, and 1710 entries).

92 Ibid., (1700, 1915, and 2018 entries).
93 Internet article "125th Field Artillery History" at http://www.vets-hall.org/125th-field-artillery-history: This incident alone accounted for half of the battalion's casualties for the entire war.
94 1st Tank Group S-3 Report, 180006 to 180007 February 1944.
95 II Corps Counter Battery Report, No. 86 from 061800 to 071800 February 1944.
96 Ibid.
97 Ibid.
98 135th S-3 Report, 180006 to 180007 February 1944.
99 Hougen, *34th Infantry Division*, "The Second Phase of Cassino"; *Army Register 1945*, 973.
100 34th G-3 Journal, 7 February 1944 (1945 entry).
101 133rd Cannon Co Unit Journal, 7 February 1944.
102 Ibid.
103 Ibid.
104 776th TD S-3 Report, 180006 to 180007 February 1944.
105 756th Unit Journal, 7 February 1944 (2000 entry).
106 760th Tank Battalion "Operations in Italy, February 1944."
107 Froeschle, *Our Story of the 760th*, 87, 102 (casualty list) and 104 (Silver Star Citation): Sgt Lawrence G. Stander was awarded the Silver Star for his attempts to rescue Cail. Stander was from Promontory, Utah; Cpl Earl W. Shipman was from Eau Claire, Wisconsin; and Pvt Maurice A Cail was from Vallejho, California; 760th Tank Battalion "Operations in Italy, February 1944"; 34th G-3 Journal, 7 February 1944 (2320 entry); 756th Unit Journal, 7 February 1944 (2200 entry); 34th G-2 Report, 180007 to 180008 February 1944.
108 756th Unit Journal, 7 February 1944 (0300 entry); 756th Commander's Narrative, January and February 1944, 30–31.
109 Treanor, *One Damn Thing*, 269.
110 756th Commander's Narrative, January and February 1944, 29–30.
111 Ford, *Cassino: Breaking Gustav Line*, 49; Annex No 1 to FO #16, 34th Inf Div, dated 071500 February 1944.
112 Ford, *Cassino: Breaking Gustav Line*, 49.
113 36th Inf Div disposition dated 7 February 1944.
114 34th Inf Div FO #16 (Fragmentary) dated 071000 February 1944; 133rd Cannon Co Unit Journal, 7 February 1944.
115 Ibid., Accompanying map; Ibid.
116 34th Inf Div FO #16 (Fragmentary) dated 071000 February 1944.
117 Ibid.
118 Smith, *Battles for Monte Cassino*, 69; Ford, *Cassino: Breaking Gustav Line*, 49.
119 34th G-3 Journal, 7 February 1944 (2320 entry).
120 Ibid.
121 Treanor, *One Damn Thing*, 267.
122 Ibid., 266, Carter was from Montgomery, Alabama.
123 Ibid., 266; Tom Treanor, "Battles Rage Through Night Within Cassino" *The Los Angeles Times* (Los Angeles, California), 9 February 1944, 1; 34th G-3 Journal, 8 February 1944 (0032 entry).
124 Treanor, *One Damn Thing*, 266.
125 Ibid., 267.
126 Ibid., 266; 34th G-3 Journal, 8 February 1944 (0032 entry); "Treanor Bunks with Iowans Fighting Germans in the Streets of Cassino," *The Gazette* (Cedar Rapids, Iowa), 15 February 1944, 3.
127 34th G-3 Journal, 8 February 1944 (0430 entry).
128 "Battles Rage Through Night Within Cassino" *The Los Angeles Times* (Los Angeles, California), 9 February 1944, 1; Treanor, *One Damn Thing*, 267; 34th G-3 Journal, 8 February 1944 (0430 entry).
129 Plowman, *Battles for Cassino*, 98.
130 Smith, *Battles for Monte Cassino*, 73; Huff, *Fighting 36th*, "Hills above Cassino," (no page numbers).
131 Gooderson, *Cassino 1944*, 71; Blumenson, *Salerno to Cassino*, 379; Ford, *Cassino: Breaking Gustav Line*, 49.
132 Matthew Parker, *Monte Cassino: The Hardest-Fought Battle of World War II* (New York, New York: Doubleday, 2004), 141.
133 Blumenson, *Salerno to Cassino*, 380.

134 Ankrum, *Dogfaces Who Smiled Through Tears*, 418.
135 Ibid., 419: At an E Co/135th position, one man in a three-man BAR team lost his senses and tried climbing out of his foxhole during a particularly heavy artillery attack. His two partners quickly grabbed his legs to pull him back only to discover the top half of the man was gone.
136 34th G-2 Report, 120004 to 120005 February 1944.
137 Blumenson, *Salerno to Cassino*, 379.
138 34th G-2 Report, 120004 to 120005 February 1944.
139 Dominick Graham, *Cassino: Battle Book No. 16*, (New York, NY: Ballantine Books, Inc., 1970), 62–63.
140 Ibid., 63.
141 Smith, *Battles for Monte Cassino*, 72.
142 Ankrum, *Dogfaces Who Smiled Through Tears*, 398.
143 Luttrell, "Operations of the 168th Infantry … Rapido River Crossing", 21.
144 1st Lt Belfrad H. Gray, Jr., "The Crossing of the Rapido River and Occupation of Positions Above Cassino, Italy, by Company 'I', 168th Infantry (34th Infantry Division) 27 January–15 February 1944 (Rome-Arno Campaign) Personal Experience of a Squad Leader", The Infantry School, Fort Benning, Georgia, Advanced Infantry Officers Course 1947–48, 18.
145 David Hapgood and David Richardson, *Monte Cassino* (Garden City, New York: Double Day & Company, Inc, 1984), 84.
146 Hougen, *34th Infantry Division*, "In Hills Above Cassino", Various photos.
147 Gray, "Crossing of the Rapido, I Co/168th," 18–19.
148 Smith, *Battles for Monte Cassino*, 74.
149 Graham, *Cassino: Battle Book*, 63; Gray, "Crossing of the Rapido, I Co/168th," 18.
150 Graham, *Cassino: Battle Book*, 64.
151 Smith, *Battles for Monte Cassino*, 69; Harold L. Bond, *Return to Cassino: A Memoir of the Fight for Rome* (Garden City, New York: Double Day & Company, Inc., 1964), 70.
152 Graham, *Cassino: Battle Book*, 63.
153 Ankrum, *Dogfaces Who Smiled Through Tears*, 419.
154 Hapgood, *Monte Cassino*, 84.
155 34th G-3 Report, 180007 to 180008 February 1944.
156 135th S-3 Report, 180006 to 180007 February 1944: Location 834207.
157 Location 843208.
158 34th G-3 Report, 180007 to 180008 February 1944; 34th G-3 Journal, 8 February 1944 (0625 entry).
159 Annex No 1 and Annex No 1-B to FO #16, 34th Inf Div dated 071500 February 1944, and attached maps.
160 34th G-3 Journal, 8 February 1944 (various entries).
161 34th G-3 Journal, 8 February 1944 (0448 and 0630 entries); 133rd S-3 Report, 180007 to 180008 February 1944.
162 756th Unit Journal, 8 February 1944 (0600, 0610, and 0635 entries); According to the 34th Artillery, S-3 Report, (180006 to 180007 February 1944), at this time, the location of each of the 133rd Bn CPs were as follows: 1st Bn 133rd CP at 855220 (near Hill 175), 100th Bn 133rd CP 849240 (west side Hill 213), 3rd Bn/133rd at 859228 (SE corner barracks).
163 Treanor, *One Damn Thing*, 267–68.
164 Ibid., 268–69.
165 Ibid.
166 34th G-3 Report, 180007 to 180008 February 1944; 133rd Cannon Co Unit Journal, 8 February 1944.
167 34th G-3 Journal, 8 February 1944 (0530 and 0605 entries).
168 Treanor, *One Damn Thing*, 268–69.
169 Blumenson, *Salerno to Cassino*, 381–82; This unit was the II Corps Artillery (71st Field Artillery Brigade prior to March 12, 1944) according to Shelby L. Stanton. *Order of Battle U.S. Army, World War II* (Novato, California: Presidio Press, 1984), 341 and 351.
170 133rd S-3 Report, 180007 to 180008 February 1944; US Army, *Fifth Army History: Part IV*, 92–93; Treanor, *One Damn Thing*, 268–69; According to Fazendin, *756th at Cassino*, 98, at this time the jail was where Lt Granberry and his captured crews were being held. This testimony comes from Sgt James T. Vaughn who was there. American prisoners were also being held in a nearby building. The jail held but the nearby building

collapsed—killing both the Germans and Americans inside. Afterwards, Granberry and his tank crews were moved out of the jail and away from Cassino; Lee McCardell, "Cassino Battle Shifts To Foot of Monastery," *The Baltimore Sun* (Baltimore, Maryland), 9 February 1944, 1.

171 34th G-3 Journal, 8 February 1944 (0645 entry); Plowman, *Battles for Cassino*, 98.

172 Annex No 1 to FO #16, 34th Inf Div dated 071500 February 1944.

173 Treanor, *One Damn Thing*, 269.

174 133rd S-3 180007 to 180008 February 1944.

175 II Corps G-3 Report, 180007 to 180008 February 1944: The time was around 0645.

176 133rd S-3 Report, 180007 to 180008 February 1944.

177 760th Tank Battalion "Operations in Italy, February 1944"; Froeschle, *Our Story of the 760th*, 87 and 102 (casualty list): It is unclear which crewmembers belonged to which tank. Two were killed and two were wounded from A/Co 760th on 8 February: Cpl Graham M. Hare (Hemp, North Carolina); T/5 Azra J. Buchholtz (MIA) (La Crosse, Wisconsin); Pvt Harold G. Boyer (MIA) (La Grange, Missouri); It is reasonable to believe the two MIAs were from the same tank as it burned. Two members of C Co/760th were also wounded, so it's possible that the second tank in Pride's platoon was a C Co tank. The wounded from C Co/760 on 8 February were: T/5 Raymond K. Janow (Spring City, Tennessee), and Pfc Chester E. Garner of C Co/760. Garner received a bullet wound to the hand (unknown which one) on 8 February, and was hospitalized per Morning Report C Co/760th, 8 February 1944.

178 Ankrum, *Dogfaces Who Smiled Through Tears*, 428.

179 Treanor, *One Damn Thing*, 269.

180 756th Unit Journal, 8 February 1944 (0645 entry); 756th Commander's Narrative for January and February 1944, 31.

181 34th Inf Div "Lessons Learned in Combat," Chapman account, 5.

182 34th G-3 Journal, 8 February 1944 (0712 entry): The round hitting the OP was described here as a "dud" but it was more likely to have been an AP shot.

183 34th G-3 Journal, 8 February 1944 (0730 entry).

184 Treanor, *One Damn Thing*, 269–70: Treanor recalled watching the three tanks knocked out by the SP gun the most terrifying sight of his entire war experience. Interestingly, he described the German SP gun flashes as the color "red" and not green. Sadly, Treanor did not survive the war. He died 18 August 1944 in a jeep accident while covering the combat in northern France.

185 34th Inf Div "Lessons Learned in Combat," Chapman account, 5.

186 Treanor, *One Damn Thing*, 270; 756th Commander's Narrative for January and February 1944, 31–33.

187 Medal of Honor citation under "Paul F. Riordan" at https://homeofheroes.com/medal-of-honor-citation/world-war-ii-medal-of-honor-recipients/; Ankrum, *Dogfaces Who Smiled Through Tears*, 428; Lee McCardell, "Snow, Cold Bog Down Fighting in Italy," *The Evening Sun* (Baltimore, Maryland), 14 February 1944, 1.

188 Internet article "Iowa Medal of Honor Heros" "Second Lieutenant Paul F. Riordan" at http://www.iowahistory.org/museum/exhibits/medla-of-honor/riordan_p_wwii/

189 Ibid.

190 Ibid.

191 34th G-3 Journal, 8 February 1944 (0735 entry).

192 756th Unit Journal, 8 February 1944 (0745 entry).

193 756th Commander's Narrative for January and February 1944, 31.

194 756th Unit Journal, 8 February 1944 (0745 entry): Width is an estimate based upon aerial photos.

195 Ibid., (0845 entry).

196 Froeschle, *Our Story of the 760th*, 87; 760th Tank Battalion "Operations in Italy, February 1944": Pride's battered platoon could not be reconstituted until after 20 February.

197 756th Unit Journal, 8 February 1944 (0845 entry).

198 Ibid., (0700 and 0725 entries); 756th Commander's Narrative for January and February 1944, 30–31.

199 II Corps G-3 Report, 180007 to 180008 February 1944.

200 133rd Cannon Co Unit Journal, 8 February 1944; 133rd S-3 Report, 180007 to 180008 February 1944.

201 133rd S-3 Report, 180007 to 180008 February 1944: Position given was 852213—roughly 100 yards away from the road switchback

202 34th G-3 Journal, 8 February 1944 (0810 entry).
203 Ibid., (0735 entry).
204 34th Inf Div G-2 Report, 180007 to 180008 February 1944; 34th G-3 Journal, 8 February 1944 (1055 entry); 133rd Cannon Co Unit Journal, 8 February 1944; 34th G-3 Journal, 8 February 1944 (0840 entry); 133rd S-3 Report, 180007 to 180008 February 1944; Plowman, *Battles for Cassino*, 96–97: This feat was accomplished by Pvt Masao Awakuni who crept in close and hit it on his second shot; Ankrum, *Dogfaces Who Smiled Through Tears*, 416, Awakuni was awarded the Distinguished Service Cross for this action; Teletype message dated 081500 from II Corps CG to CG Fifth Army and others.
205 133rd S-3 Report, 180007 to 180008 February 1944.
206 Plowman, *Battles for Cassino*, 96.
207 34th G-3 Journal, 8 February 1944 (0845, 0905, and 1044 entries).
208 34th Inf Div "Lessons Learned in Combat," Lt Col Joe L. Bourne, 168th Inf Regt, account, 31.
209 756th Unit Journal, 8 February 1944 (0845 entry): Location of roadway identified as 858216.
210 Ibid., (0950 entry).
211 Ibid., (0845 entry): The name of the C Co platoon leader was not recorded, but circumstantial evidence suggest he may have been 2nd Lt George W. Pope (C Co Morning Reports January–February 1944, Perkins undated post-Granberry manning chart).
212 756th Unit Journal, 8 February 1944 (0845 entry).
213 34th G-2 Report, 180007 to 180008 February 1944; 133rd S-3 Report, 180007 to 180008 February 1944.
214 756th Unit Journal, 8 February 1944 (1320 entry).
215 Ibid., (1400 entry).
216 Ibid., (1430 entry).
217 34th G-3 Journal, 8 February 1944 (1345 entry).
218 756th Commander's Narrative for January and February 1944, 32.
219 34th G-3 Journal, 8 February 1944 (1445 entry); 133rd S-3 Report, 180007 to 180008 February 1944.
220 34th Inf Div "Lessons Learned in Combat," Chapman account, 5.
221 756th Commander's Narrative for January and February 1944, 32: Location of house was 858216. Several houses fit the description.
222 756th Commander's Narrative for January and February 1944, 32.
223 Same location as described early at 858216.
224 According to Morning Reports, 756th Casualties for 8 February 1944 were: KIA: S/Sgt Dennis W. Grigsby [C], Pvt Ralph Morrison [C]. LWA: S/Sgt Willam Fodor [C], Sgt Millard J. Parrish [C]. T/4 Albert C. Voegele [C], T/4 William F. Holton [C]. It is not clear from the record when or where Morrison was killed and Fodor, Parrish, Voegele or Holton were wounded.
225 756th Commander's Narrative for January and February 1944, 32; 756th Unit Journal, 8 February 1944 (1515 entry); 756th S-3 Report, 180007 to 180008 February 1944.
226 756th Unit Journal, 8 February 1944 (1600 entry).
227 This house was at 858216 according to the 756th Commander's Narrative for January and February 1944, 32; 34th G-3 Journal, 8 February 1944 (1520 entry): L Company near "215 line" and K Company at "856215", roughly 200 yards east of L Co.
228 756th Commander's Narrative for January and February 1944, 32.
229 756th Unit Journal, 8 February 1944, 1730; 756th Commander's Narrative for January and February 1944, 32: Assembly area was at 853240.
230 756th Commander's Narrative for January and February 1944, 32–33.
231 34th G-3 Journal, 8 February 1944 (1600, 1604, and 1605 entries).
232 756th Unit Journal, 8 February 1944 (1800 entry).
233 34th G-3 Journal, 8 February 1944 (1520 entry).
234 756th Unit Journal, 8 February 1944 (1800 entry).
235 756th Commander's Narrative for January and February 1944, 32–33.
236 133rd S-3 Report, 180007 to 180008 February 1944.
237 34th G-3 Journal, 8 February 1944 (1345 entry).
238 133rd S-3 Report, 180007 to 180008 February 1944: Coordinates given were: 1st Bn on NW slopes of Hill 193 (854214). 100th Bn in general vicinity of 852213. 3rd Bn in N edges of Cassino, vicinity 858217; II

Corps G-3 Report, 180007 to 180008 February 1944, differed slightly by reporting 1st Bn at base of Hill 193 (853214) and 100th Bn on Hill 165 (852213); 34th G-3 Report, 180007 to 180008 February 1944.
239 34th G-2 Report, 120008 to 120009 February 1944.
240 756th Commander's Narrative for January and February 1944, 33.
241 Plowman, *Battles for Cassino*, 98.
242 34th G-3 Journal, 8 February 1944 (1650 entry).
243 34th G-3 Journal, 8 February 1944 (1345 entry).
244 Plowman, *Battles for Cassino*, 98. These German paratroopers were from the 1st Fallschirmjäger Regiment.
245 34th G-3 Journal, 8 February 1944 (1830, 1900, and 1905 entries).
246 Ibid., (1805 entry); Teletype message dated 081500 from II Corps CG to CG Fifth Army and others.
247 34th G-3 Journal, 8 February 1944 (1345 entry); 34th G-3 Journal, 8 February 1944 (1655, 1700, and 1745 entries); 34th G-3 Journal, 8 February 1944 (1830 entry).
248 756th Commander's Narrative for January and February 1944, 33.
249 Ibid.
250 756th Unit Journal, 9 February 1944 (0300 entry).
251 Ibid., 8 February 1944 (2000 entry).
252 34th G-3 Journal, 8 February 1944 (1755 and 1805 entries): Records plural "AT guns" but only two are presumed from the earlier 4 February records.
253 Herbert M. Youngdahl, *The Other Side of War* (San Francisco, California: Robert D. Reed Publishers, 2000), 44, 53.
254 756th Unit Journal, 8 February 1944 (2400 entry) and 9 February 1944 (0300 entry).
255 34th G-3 Journal, 8 February 1944 (various entries and 2315).
256 133rd Cannon Co Unit Journal, 8 February 1944.
257 Ibid., 9 February 1944.
258 34th G-3 Journal, 8 February 1944 (2200 entry).
259 Ibid., (2318 entry).
260 34th G-2 Report, 120008 to 120009 February 1944.
261 As of 2400, 8 February 1944 according to the 34th HQ, 9 February 1944, "Effective Strength Table by Unit" report. Numbers totaled to include officers. The 133rd number broke down as follows: 1 Bn/133rd: 29 O, 477 EM; Co B reduced to 6 O, 37 EM (A at 4 O and 84 EM; C at 4 O and 84 EM; D at 6 O and 155 EM.) 3rd Bn/133rd at 31 O and 628 EM (I Co at 4 and 104; K at 5 and 117; L at 6 and 114; M at 5 and 177.) 100th Bn/133rd at 35 and 506 (A 5 and 95, B 4 and 82, C 6 and 80, D at 4 and 110.).
262 34th HQ, 9 February 1944, "Effective Strength Table by Unit" report.
263 756th Tank Bn Unit Journal, 21 January 1944.
264 Ibid., 8 February 1944.
265 The 756th Morning Reports from 21 January through 8 February 1944, record that some of those wounded in action returned to duty within this time frame. These figures to not include those lightly wounded who did not miss duty time.
266 Froeschle, *Our Story of the 760th*, 102; seventeen tanks with five crewman each totals eighty-five.
267 Redle phone conversation, 15 September 2000; Dwight D. Eisenhower, *Crusade in Europe* (Garden City, New York: Doubleday and Company, Inc., 1948; Dolphin edition, 1961), 482: Eisenhower expressed regrets for keeping the 34th, 45th, 3rd, and 1st Infantry Divisions fighting on the line so long: "When kept too long in the fight, they (veteran organizations) not only become subject to mental weariness; the most venturesome and aggressive amongst them—the natural leaders—begin to suffer an abnormally high percentage of losses. Consequently the periodical relief of units form the front lines is mandatory to the preservation of efficiently."; King, Maj Glenn L. "From Salerno to Rome: General Mark W. Clark and the Challenge of Coalition Warfare." Thesis, Master of Military Art and Science, Military History, US Army Command and General Staff College, Fort Leavenworth, Kansas, 2007, 80.
268 756th S-3 Report, 180007 to 180008 February 1944: Figures were determined by taking the 7 February numbers (Thirty medium tanks, twelve light tanks available in the 756th, plus the sixteen additional medium tanks from the 760th. Fifty-five total tanks to date were reported lost or under repairs) and adding the five losses for 8 February (two with the 756th, and three with the 760th).
269 II Corps G-3, 120007 to 120008 February 1944; 34th G-2 Report, 120008 to 120009 February 1944.

270 Teletype message dated 081500 from II Corps CG to CG Fifth Army and others.
271 Ibid.
272 Ralph Donley diary, 9 February 1944.

Chapter 4

1 756th Unit Journal, 8 February 1944 (1515 entry) and 9 February 1944 (0300 entry); 756th Commander's Narrative for January and February 1944, 33: Location for both tanks was 858216; Alfred Westle letter to Redle dated 11 August 2000 describes a very similar event. Westle and Roy Kosanke may have been on this detail.
2 34th G-3 Journal, 9 February 1944 (0005 entry).
3 Ibid., (0540 entry); 135th S-3 Report, 180008 to 180009 February 1944.
4 34th G-3 Journal, 9 February 1944 (0055, 0115, 0225, and 0330 entries).
5 Ibid., (0450 entry).
6 Ibid., (0020 entry).
7 Ibid., (0055, 0115, 0225, and 0330 entries).
8 Ibid., (0345 entry).
9 34th Inf Div G-2 Report, 120008 to 120009 February 1944; 1st Tank Group S-3 Report, 180008 to 180009 February 1944.
10 Roy Anderson phone conversation, 28 June 2001.
11 Redle letter, 7 February 2001.
12 756th Commander's Narrative for January and February 1944, 33.
13 756th Unit Journal, 9 February 1944 (0735 entry).
14 776th S-3 Report, 180008 to 180009 February 1944.
15 36th G-3 Report, 16008 to 159909 February 1944; 756th Unit Journal, 9 February 1944 (1130 entry); 133rd Cannon Co Unit Journal, 8 February 1944.
16 133rd Cannon Co Unit Journal, 9 February 1944.
17 756th Unit Journal, 9 February 1944 (1445 and 1515 entries); 756th Commander's Narrative for January and February 1944, 33.
18 34th Inf Div "Lessons Learned in Combat," Chapman account, 6.
19 133rd Cannon Co Unit Journal, 9 February 1944.
20 34th Inf Div "Lessons Learned in Combat," Chapman account, 7.
21 133rd Cannon Co Unit Journal, 9 February 1944.
22 Ankrum, *Dogfaces Who Smiled Through Tears*, 426: Ankrum claims both guns were destroyed by two infantry sergeants by setting fire to spilled Coleman stove fuel. One sergeant is unidentified and the other was a Sgt Drewis. Ankrum reports both were later awarded Silver Stars for their actions. Drewis did receive this medal, but the unit records do not record how these SP guns were destroyed.
23 133rd Cannon Co Unit Journal, 9 February 1944.
24 Ankrum, *Dogfaces Who Smiled Through Tears*, 426–27.
25 756th Unit Journal, 9 February 1944 (1657 entry).
26 Redle interview by Lowther, 11–12 August 2012.
27 Presumed, based upon the record.
28 756th Unit Journal, 9 February 1944 (1725 and 1735 entries).
29 34th G-3 Journal, 9 February 1944 (1655 entry).
30 Ibid., (2250 entry).
31 Ibid., (2049 and 2250 entries); Lee McCardell, "Cassino Fight Rages in Rain," *The Baltimore Sun* (Baltimore, Maryland), 11 February 1944, 1.
32 34th G-3 Journal, 9 February 1944 (2250 entry).
33 Ibid., (0920 entry).
34 Ibid., (2250 entry).
35 756th Commander's Narrative for January and February 1944, 33.
36 756th Unit Journal, 9 February 1944 (2030 entry).

37 756th Commander's Narrative for January and February 1944, 33; 760th Tank Battalion "Operations in Italy, February 1944": Records only one light injury (LIA) for 9 February 1944 (Pvt Kenneth J. Vogel of A Company).
38 34th G-3 Journal, 9 February 1944 (0700 and 0750 entries).
39 Ibid., (0819, 1015, 1017, 1022, 1030, 1032, 1035, 1050, 1220, 1235, and 1900 entries).
40 Ibid., (1700 entry).
41 Ibid., (1900 entry).
42 Youngdahl, *Other Side of War*, 56.
43 34th G-3 Journal, 9 February 1944 (1700 entry); 34th G-2 Report, 120009 to 120010 February 1944.
44 34th G-3 Journal, 9 February 1944 (2045, 2049, and 2342 entries).
45 Location was 832228 according to the II Corps G-3 Report, 120009 to 120010 February 1944; The 3rd Bn/135th was down to twenty officers and 552 (I Co– 2, 77; K Co– 3, 99; L Co– 4, 123) enlisted men according to HQ 34th 10 February 1944 "Effective Strength Table by Unit" report.
46 Peek, Clifford H., ed. *Five Years, Five Countries, Five Campaigns: An Account of the One-Hundred-Forty-First Infantry in World War II* (Munich, Germany: F. Bruckmann KG, 1945), 43.
47 Peek, *Five Years, Five Countries*, 46.
48 Hapgood, *Monte Cassino*, 144.
49 Howard D. Ashcraft, *As You Were: Cannon Company, 34th Infantry Division, 168th Infantry Regiment, World War II* (Richmond, Virginia: Ashcraft Enterprises, 1990), 85.
50 Fazendin, *756th at Cassino*, 137–38: Redle recollection.
51 Froeschle, *Our Story of the 760th*, 84: Froeschle lists their C-Ration diet as follows: Breakfast: tomato juice, dehydrated cereal, canned bacon, hardtack biscuits, canned butter, dehydrated coffee, sugar, and milk. Dinner: dehydrated soup, dehydrated rice, canned roast beef, green peas, hardtack biscuits, canned butter, hard candy, powdered orangeade. Supper: meat and vegetable stew (canned), dehydrated biscuits and fruit spread, evaporated apricots, milk, coffee, sugar.
52 Message from 5th Army to II Corps 9 February 1944, signed by Capt James G. Patterson.
53 34th Artillery S-3 Report, 180008 to 180009 February 1944.
54 756th Unit Journal, February 1944, Exhibit 13.
55 Smith, *Battles for Monte Cassino*, 74.
56 34th G-3 Journal, 10 February 1944 (0130 entry).
57 Plowman, *Battles for Cassino*, 110.
58 34th G-3 Journal, 10 February 1944 (0300 entry).
59 Ibid., (0800 entry).
60 Ibid., (0650 and 0745 entries): Hill 593 is at 835216; 34th G-2 Report, 120009 to 120010 February 1944.
61 34th G-3 Journal, 10 February 1944 (0525 entry).
62 756th Unit Journal, 10 February 1944 (0530 and 0630 entry).
63 Ibid., (0700 entry).
64 Ibid., (0735 entry).
65 Ibid., (0900 entry); 756th Commander's Narrative for January and February 1944, 33.
66 34th G-3 Journal, 10 February 1944 (0830 and 0920 entries); A II Corps teletype message dated 10 February, 0912 hours, claimed that two tanks supported the infantry attack on jail at 0730, but this claim is not supported by the 34th G-3 Journal, the 756th Unit Journal or Sweeting's February report. This is probably what was *supposed* to have happened had the OP not been shelled at 0700.
67 776th S-3 180009 to 180010, February 1944; 91st Recon Sq. S-3 Report, 10 February 1944.
68 Teletype from II Corps CG dated 100912 to all stations.
69 133rd Cannon Co Unit Journal, 10 February 1944.
70 34th G-3 Journal, 10 February 1944 (1005 entry).
71 756th Unit Journal, 10 February 1944 (1200 entry).
72 Ibid., (1215 and 1240 entries).
73 34th G-3 Journal, 10 February 1944 (1125 entry).
74 Ankrum, *Dogfaces Who Smiled Through Tears*, 412.
75 Wallace, *The Italian Campaign*, 137.
76 34th Inf Div "Lessons Learned in Combat," Chapman account, 5.

77 Ibid.: Chapman is quoted in this interview: "There is no fire more devastating and morale shattering than well-directed tank fire."
78 756th Unit Journal, 10 February 1944 (1400 entry); Use of tow cables was the customary method and is presumed to have been utilized here.
79 34th Inf Div "Lessons Learned in Combat," Chapman account, 7.
80 756th S-3 Report, 180009 to 180010 February 1944.
81 756th Unit Journal, 10 February 1944 (1400 entry).
82 756th Commander's Narrative for January and February 1944, 33; 756th Unit Journal, 10 February 1944 (1500 entry).
83 34th G-3 Journal, 10 February 1944 (1406 entry).
84 133rd Cannon Co Unit Journal, 10 February 1944; 756th Unit Journal, 10 February 1944 (1500 entry).
85 34th G-3 Journal, 10 February 1944 (1548 entry); 36th G-3 Report, 160010 to 155910 February 1944.
86 34th G-3 Journal, 10 February 1944 (1406 entry).
87 Masayo Umezawa Duus, *Unlikely Liberators, The Men of the 100th and 442nd* (English Translation. Honolulu, Hawaii: University of Hawaii Press, 2006), 123.
88 756th Unit Journal, 10 February 1944 (1700 and 1720 entries).
89 756th Commander's Narrative for January and February 1944, 33–34.
90 756th Unit Journal, 10 February 1944 (1830 entry).
91 Ibid., (1900 entry).
92 756th Commander's Narrative for January and February 1944, 34.
93 34th Inf Div "Lessons Learned in Combat," Lt Col Robert E. Coffey account, 60–61.
94 756th Morning Reports, 10 February 1944.
95 34th G-3 Report, 180009 to 180010 February 1944.
96 756th S-3 Report, 180009 to 180010 February 1944.
97 756th Unit Journal, 10 February 1944 (2000 entry).
98 Ibid., (1730, 2015, 2050, and 2245 entries); 756th Commander's Narrative for January and February 1944, 34.
99 756th Unit Journal, 10 February 1944 (2200 entry).
100 756th Commander's Narrative for January and February 1944, 34.
101 Ibid., 33–34; 756th Unit Journal, 10 February 1944 (2200 entry).
102 34th G-3 Journal, 10 February 1944 (1845 entry).
103 Ibid., (2145 entry).
104 34th G-2 Report, 120012 to 120013 February 1944, PW interrogation report #205.
105 The position of bridge was 859216.
106 34th G-2 Report, 120012 to 120013 February 1944, PW interrogation report #205: PWs were Pvt Heinz Wahl, age 24, and Pvt Paul Dreisbach, age 21. Both reported two years of service.
107 34th G-2 Report, 120012 to 120013 February 1944, PW interrogation report #206: Pvt Siegfried Lehrmann and Cpl Albin Grywatz.
108 Ankrum, *Dogfaces Who Smiled Through Tears*, 414–15.
109 Ibid., 415: The story's source was Lt. Higgins.
110 Redle interview by Lowther, 11–12 August 2012; Service Co/756th Morning Reports, 10 February 1944. Redle recalls Bouch's wounds were serious enough for him to be sent home.
111 34th Artillery G-3 Report, 180009 to 180010, February 1944.
112 34th G-3 Journal, 10 February 1944 (1930 entry).
113 Lee McCardell, "Cassino's Defense System Described," *The Baltimore Sun* (Baltimore, Maryland), 1 February 1944, 1.
114 34th G-3 Journal, 10 February 1944 (2015 entry).
115 II Corps G-3 Report, 120010 to 120011 February 1944.
116 Ibid., 180007 to 180008 February 1944; 34th G-2 Report, 180007 to 180008 February 1944.
117 36th G-3 Report, 16008 to 159909 February 1944; 34th G-3 Journal, 10 February 1944 (2150 and 2155 entries).
118 34th G-3 Journal, 11 February 1944 (0030, 0046, and 0048 entries).
119 756th Unit Journal, 11 February 1944 (0430 and 1100 entries): It is not recorded if these tanks were recovered for reservicing or simply moved and abandoned. One or both of these tanks could have been rolled over

into the nearby Rapido flood plain. (See photo taken on 10 February 1944 on page 94, Plowman, *Battles for Cassino*.) The author believes at least one of the overturned tanks came from Lt Granberry's ill-fated 2 February platoon.
120 756th Unit Journal, 11 February 1944 (0530 entry).
121 Ibid., (0645 entry).
122 756th Unit History, 1944: Legion of Merit citation for Capt Arnold, dated 3 November 1944.
123 133rd Cannon Co Unit Journal, 11 February 1944.
124 "Snow, Cold Bog Down Fighting in Italy," Lee McCardell, *The Evening Sun* (Baltimore, Maryland), 14 February 1944, 1: Shockingly, only one stove was issued to each platoon.
125 133rd Cannon Co Unit Journal, 11 February 1944; "Battle for Cassino Viewed by McCardell," Lee McCardell, *The Evening Sun* (Baltimore, Maryland), 10 February 1944, 4.
126 Redle interview by Lowther, 11–12 August 2012.
127 Redle letter, 29 April 2003.
128 Fazendin, *756th at Cassino*, 114–115.
129 Ibid.
130 Speculative, based upon the unit journal timelines.
131 756th Unit Journal, 11 February 1944 (0740 entry).
132 756th Commander's Narrative for January and February 1944, 33–34.
133 Ibid.
134 756th Unit Journal, 11 February 1944 (0800 entry).
135 109th Engineers Bn S-3 Report, 180010 to 128011 February 1944.
136 Ankrum, *Dogfaces Who Smiled Through Tears*, 428.
137 109th Engineers Bn S-3 Report, 180010 to 128011 February 1944.
138 34th G-3 Journal, 11 February 1944 (1110 entry).
139 Ibid., (1030 entry).
140 Luttrell, "Operations of the 168th Infantry … Rapido River Crossing", 23.
141 34th G-3 Journal, 11 February 1944 (1115 and 1145 entries).
142 Attack map overlay 34th Inf Div, 11 February 1944 (see book appendices).
143 II Corps G-3 Report, 120011 to 120012 February 1944; 34th G-2 Report, 1200110 to 120011 and 1200110 to 120011 February 1944; 135th S-3 Report, 180010 to 180011 February 1944; 34th G-3 Journal, 11 February 1944 (1030, 1040, and 1045 entries).
144 34th G-3 Journal, 11 February 1944 (1030, 1040, and 1045 entries).
145 Ibid., (1150 entry).
146 34th G-3 Journal, 11 February 1944 (1140 entry); Huff, *Fighting 36th*, "In the Hills Above Cassino."
147 34th G-3 Journal, 11 February 1944 (1200 entry).
148 Ibid., (1205 entry).
149 34th G-3 Journal, 11 February 1944 (1400 entry); 168th S-3 Report, 180010 to 180011 February 1944.
150 34th G-3 Journal, 11 February 1944 (1330 entry).
151 Plowman, *Battles for Cassino*, 98.
152 34th G-3 Report, 180010 to 180012 February 1944.
153 Plowman, *Battles for Cassino*, 98.
154 34th G-3 Journal, 11 February 1944 (1332 entry).
155 Ibid., (1335 entry).
156 Ibid., (1340 entry).
157 Fazendin, *756th at Cassino*, 124.
158 756th Unit Journal, 11 February 1944 (1200 entry).
159 Ibid., (1300 entry).
160 Ibid., (1400 and 1500 entries).
161 Fazendin, *756th at Cassino*, 128.
162 34th G-3 Journal, 11 February 1944 (1358 entry).
163 Ibid., (1402 entry).
164 Ibid., (1400 and 1415 entries).
165 Ibid., (1420 entry): 569 misidentified as "369" in journal.

166 Ibid., (1515 entry).
167 Ibid.
168 Ibid., (1600 entry).
169 756th Unit Journal, 11 February 1944 (1615 entry).
170 B Co/756th Morning Reports.
171 Fazendin, *756th at Cassino*, 124: Speculative on departure time. The unit journal doesn't exactly say when they left, but it must have happened before Sweeting's 1730 meeting.
172 756th Commander's Narrative for January and February 1944, 34.
173 756th Unit Journal, 11 February 1944 (1530 entry).
174 135th S-3 Report, 180010 to 180011 February 1944.
175 Ibid.: Line from 836218 to 837221.
176 Ibid.
177 34th Artillery S-3 Report, 180010 to 180011 February 1944.
178 II Corps Counterbattery Report No. 90, 180010 to 180011 February 1944.
179 756th Unit Journal, 11 February 1944 (2115 entry).
180 756th Commander's Narrative for January and February 1944, 34; 756th Unit Journal, 11 February 1944 (2120 entry).
181 34th G-3 Journal, 11 February 1944 (1830 entry).
182 Speculative, based up on journal times.
183 34th G-3 Journal, 11 February 1944 (2023 entry): Location of the attack was 828230.
184 Ibid., (2148 entry): This appears to be a "fog of battle" report. The II Corps G-3 Report, 120011 to 120012 February 1944 claimed the following: "141st 1 and 2 Bns on Hill 593 (835215) and S slopes 100 yds toward Hill 569 (836214) 2nd Bn at 831225. 142nd 2nd Bn advanced and captured Hill 468 (831217) late 11 February. Several enemy counterattacks repulsed." This did not seem to be the case after the fact.
185 Plowman, *Battles for Cassino*, 98–99.
186 34th G-3 Journal, 11 February 1944 (2148 entry).
187 Ibid., (2225 entry).
188 Ibid., (2210 entry).
189 Ibid., 2330 entry).
190 109th Engineers Bn S-3 Report, 180011 to 180012, January 1944; United States Army, *A Military Encyclopedia Based on Operations in the Italian Campaigns 1943–1945* (G-3 Section, Headquarters, 15th Army Group, 1945), 529: The unit journals and daily reports do not record direct evidence of flamethrower use by the 133rd Inf Regt, but this US Army encyclopedia claims they were used "for street fighting at Cassino."
191 34th G-3 Journal, 11 February 1944 (2330 entry).
192 Ibid., (0012 entry).
193 756th Unit Journal, 12 February 1944 (0200 entry).
194 34th G-3 Journal, 12 February 1944 (0212 entry).
195 Ibid., (0222 entry).
196 Ibid., (0239 entry).
197 Ibid., (0435 entry).
198 Ranspach diary, 12 February 1944.
199 34th G-3 Journal, 12 February 1944 (0410 entry).
200 Ibid., (0600 entry).
201 Ibid., (0530 entry).
202 Ibid., (0415 entry).
203 756th Unit Journal, 12 February 1944 (0430 entry).
204 133rd S-3 Report, 180011 to 180012 February 1944: Location provided for 1st Bn staging is 858215.
205 Location of A Co was 858216.
206 34th G-3 Journal, 12 February 1944 (0415 entry); 756th Unit Journal, 12 February 1944 (0400 entry).
207 756th Unit Journal, 12 February 1944, 0530 entry.
208 133rd S-3 Report, 180011 to 180012 February 1944; C Co position was 859214.
209 34th G-3 Journal, 12 February 1944 (0535 entry).
210 Ibid., (0525 entry).

211 Ibid., (0535 entry).
212 Ibid., (0615 entry).
213 133rd S-3 Report, 180011 to 180012 February 1944.
214 34th G-3 Journal, 12 February 1944 (0807 entry).
215 Ibid., (0810 entry); 756th Commander's Narrative for January and February 1944, 34–35.
216 34th G-2 Report, 1200110 to 120011 February 1944.
217 34th G-3 Journal, 12 February 1944 (0845 entry).

Chapter 5

1 756th Unit Journal, 12 February 1944 (0835 entry).
2 Ibid., (1115 entry): 1st platoon was the likely unit involved because of later events involving Lt. Harley; 756th Commander's Narrative for January and February 1944, 34–35.
3 34th G-3 Journal, 12 February 1944 (0845 entry).
4 Ibid., (0807 entry).
5 Ibid., (1315 entry): The position given was in the vicinity of 845246 (SW Caira).
6 Ibid., (0817 entry).
7 Ibid., (0820 entry).
8 Ibid., (0810 entry).
9 Ibid., (0812 entry).
10 Ibid., (0812 and 0845 entries).
11 Ibid., (0900 entry).
12 Ibid., (0925 entry).
13 133rd S-3 Report, 180011 to 180012 February 1944.
14 34th G-3 Journal, 12 February 1944 (1032 and 1130 entries).
15 Ibid., (1105 entry).
16 Ibid., (1130 entry).
17 34th G-2 Report, 1200110 to 120011 February 1944: The 211th Grenadier Regiment was part of the German 71st Infantry Division.
18 Ibid.: The location was 854192—which shows on the map as a farmhouse south of the railroad.
19 Ibid.: The location was 857214.
20 Ibid.
21 When the 34th Division was relieved later by British and New Zealand units, the jailhouse was retaken by the Germans. Fazendin, *756th in Cassino*, 124; Redle interview by Lowther, 11–12 August 2012.
22 756th Unit Journal, 12 February 1944 (1200 entry).
23 34th G-2 Report, 120012 to 120013 February 1944.
24 II Corps G-3 Report, 120011 to 120012 February 1944.
25 34th G-3 Journal, 12 February 1944 (1240 entry).
26 Ibid., (0950 and 1130 entries).
27 Ibid., (0812 entry); 133rd S-3 Report, 180011 to 180012 February 1944.
28 34th G-3 Journal, 12 February 1944 (1240 and 1245 entries).
29 Ibid., (1205 and 1330 entries).
30 Ibid., (1220 and 1423 entries).
31 Ibid., (1230 entry).
32 Fazendin, *756th at Cassino*, 124: Based upon the circumstances Redle describes, this was the likely day.
33 Haspel interview by Pamela G Patrick on 18 September 1984: This incident may have occurred on another date but seems to fit best here according to the unit journal timeline.
34 756th Unit Journal, 12 February 1944 (1330 entry).
35 Ibid., (1415 entry).
36 Charles M. Wilkinson letters, 20 December 2001 and 31 May 2005.
37 Richter phone conversation, 13 February 2002.
38 Redle interview by Lowther, 11–12 August 2012.

39 The most common gun on a Mark IV was the 75mm Kampfwagenkanone 40, which fired an AP round up to 3,100 feet per second. In comparison, the M4's 75 mm M2 gun fired an AP round around 1,900 feet per second.
40 Redle letter, 5 October 2000.
41 Ibid.
42 Redle interview by Lowther, 11–12 August 2012.
43 Redle letter, 5 October 2000.
44 Fazendin, *756th at Cassino*, 127; Redle interview by Lowther, 11–12 August 2012.
45 Anderson joined B Company a few weeks before the outfit shipped to Casablanca.
46 Redle interview by Lowther, 11–12 August 2012.; Fazendin, *756th at Cassino*, 125–27; Redle letter, 5 October 2000; 756th Unit Journal, 12 February 1944 (1400 entry); 756th Unit Journal, 12 February 1944 (1530 entry). This incident does not fully match any written entries in the unit journals or in Sweeting's after-action reports—and yet the story and details were well known to many 756th veterans. The closest unit journal match seems to be this 12 February 1400 entry: "One tank near jail moves to vic of 'C.' Fire is rec'd by SP located at M. Fire is returned and SP withdraws." (See book "Appendix 8" for map locations.) The author believes a reasonable explanation for the puzzling "SP withdraws" notation may be that the German tank retreated after first firing on Oliver and Sweeting could no longer see it from his OP. Oliver's crew, however, could still see it and destroyed the tank without Sweeting's knowledge. It's also entirely possible that the clerk simply missed this detail and Sweeting forgot to include the incident in his commander's narrative.
47 Fazendin, *756th at Cassino*, 116–118: Howard Harley recollection.
48 Ibid.; 756th Unit History,1944, GO #31 II Corps dated 27 April 1944; 756th Unit Journal, 12 February 1944 (1600 entry).
49 756th Unit Journal, 12 February 1944 (1700 entry).
50 756th Unit History, 1944, GO #31 II Corps dated 27 April 1944; 756th Commander's Narrative for January and February 1944, 34.
51 B Co/756th Morning Report, 23 April 1944, "Record of Events" for 12 February; B Co/756th Unit Journal, 12 February 1944.
52 756th Unit History, 1944, GO #31 II Corps dated 27 April 1944; 756th Commander's Narrative for January and February 1944, 34; Fazendin, *756th at Cassino*, 117: Harley recollection; 756th Unit Journal, 12 February 1944 (1710 entry); 756th Unit Journal, 13 February 1944 (0230 entry): This tank was actually recovered at 0230.
53 B Co/756th Morning Report, April 1944, Record of events for 12 February.
54 Fazendin, *756th at Cassino*, 117: Harley recollection.
55 34th G-3 Journal, 12 February 1944 (1130 entry).
56 756th Commander's Narrative for January and February 1944, 34–35; 756th Unit Journal, 12 February 1944 (2100 entry).
57 756th Unit Journal, 12 February 1944 (1730 entry).
58 34th G-3 Journal, 12 February 1944 (2200 entry).
59 B Co/756th Unit Journal, 13 February 1944. The journal reports this happened on the 13th, but it's more likely it was the 12th as B Company was pulled back for rest on the 13th.
60 Fazendin, *756th at Cassino*, 124–28.
61 756th Unit Journal, 12 February 1944 (1735 entry).
62 34th G-3 Journal, 12 February 1944 (2020 entry).
63 34th G-2 Report, 120012 to 120013 February 1944.
64 This may have actually been the tank that Oliver and his crew destroyed. The PW may not have seen the destruction but witnessed the aftermath and presumed artillery destroyed it.
65 34th G-2 Report, 120012 to 120013 February 1944; PW interrogation report, #205.
66 Redle interview by Lowther, 11–12 August 2012; Redle letter, 5 October 2000; Fazendin, *756th at Cassino*, 127.
67 Ford, *Cassino: Breaking Gustav Line*, 53.
68 Maj Gen Fred L. Walker, "Comments on the Rapido River Crossing, January 1944," (Fort Leavenworth, Kansas: Library USA CGSC, 1960), 19.
69 Walker, "Comments on the Rapido River Crossing," 19.

70 34th G-3 Journal, 12 February 1944 (1630 entry).
71 Parker, *Monte Cassino*, 141.
72 Smith, *Battles for Monte Cassino*, 74; Gooderson, *Cassino 1944*, 74; Blumenson, *Salerno to Cassino*, 383.
73 Plowman, *Battles for Cassino*, 99.
74 Ford, *Cassino: Breaking Gustav Line*, 53.
75 34th G-3 Journal, 12 February 1944 (1805 entry).
76 Ibid., (1815 entry).
77 Ibid., (2125 entry).
78 Ibid., (2155 entry).
79 Ibid., (2116 entry).
80 II Corps G-3 Report, 120011 to 120012 February 1944.
81 Plowman, *Battles for Cassino*, 110.
82 34th G-3 Journal, 12 February 1944 (2335 entry).
83 756th Unit Journal, 12 February 1944 (2130 entry).
84 Ranspach diary, 11 February 1944.
85 756th Unit Journal, 13 February 1944 (0430 entry); 34th G-3 Journal, 13 February 1944 (0700 entry).
86 34th G-3 Journal, 13 February 1944 (0010, 0012, and 0014 entries).
87 Ibid., (0240 and 0405 entries).
88 Ibid., (0400, 0440, and 0535 entry).
89 Ibid., (0550 and 0605 entries).
90 Ibid., (0615 entry).
91 Ibid., (0635 entry).
92 Ibid., (00636 and 0650 entries).
93 Ibid., (0636 and 0700 entries).
94 II Corps G-3 Report, 120012 to 120013 February 1944; 133rd Cannon Co Unit Journal, 13 February 1944.
95 34th G-3 Journal, 13 February 1944 (0650 entry).
96 756th Unit Journal, 13 February 1944 (0630 entry).
97 Ibid., 12 February 1944 (2130 entry).
98 Ibid., 13 February 1944 (0700 entry).
99 34th G-3 Journal, 13 February 1944 (0850 entry).
100 Ibid., (0845 entry).
101 756th Unit Journal, 13 February 1944 (0900 and 0910 entries).
102 It's presumed that four crews made this journey as two sections were later employed. Also, due to attrition, most platoons were operating at this time with only three or four tanks.
103 Fazendin, *756th in Cassino*, 72–73: Jack Deenihan recollection.
104 756th Unit Journal, 13 February 1944 (1000 and 1130 entries).
105 Ibid., (1100 and 1215 entries).
106 133rd Cannon Co Unit Journal, 13 February 1944.
107 34th G-3 Journal, 13 February 1944 (0630 entry).
108 Ibid., (0835, 0840, and 0845 entries).
109 Ibid., (1050 entry).
110 Parker, *Monte Cassino*, 155; Duane Schultz, "Bombing the Abbey" *WWII History* magazine, December 2018, 14.
111 Parker, *Monte Cassino*, 155.
112 Hapgood, *Monte Cassino*, 148–149; Duane Schultz, "Bombing the Abbey" *WWII History* magazine, December 2018, 14.
113 Parker, *Monte Cassino*, 160.
114 Caddick-Adams, *Monte Cassino: Ten Armies*, 137–139; Hapgood, *Monte Cassino*, 152–53; Plowman, *Battles for Cassino*, 108.
115 Gooderson, *Cassino 1944*, 83.
116 Duane Schultz, "Bombing the Abbey" *WWII History* magazine, December 2018, 14.
117 Gooderson, *Cassino 1944*, 81.
118 Duane Schultz, "Bombing the Abbey" *WWII History* magazine, December 2018, 14.
119 Ibid.

120 Plowman, *Battles for Cassino*, 109.
121 Hapgood, *Monte Cassino*, 159.
122 Plowman, *Battles for Cassino*, 108.
123 C. Douglas Sterner, *Go For Broke: A Tribute to the Nisei Warriors of WWII* (Legal Help for Veterans, PLLC, 2018), 16.
124 34th G-3 Journal, 13 February 1944 (1245 entry); 34th G-3 Journal, 13 February 1944 (1320 entry).
125 756th Unit Journal, 13 February 1944 (1500 entry).
126 756th Cassino book, 72–73, Deenihan recollection; 756th Commander's Narrative for January and February 1944, 35.
127 133rd Cannon Co Unit Journal, 13 February 1944; Lt was Lt Raner.
128 Peek, *Five Years, Five Countries*, 47: Lt Col Aaron W. Wyatt was from New York.
129 109th Engineers Bn S-3 Report, 180012 to 180013 February 1944.
130 756th Unit Journal, 13 February 1944 (1530, 1545, 1700, and 1730 entries).
131 Ibid., (1800 entry).
132 34th G-3 Journal, 13 February 1944 (1900 entry).
133 756th Commander's Narrative for January and February 1944, 34–35.
134 Ibid., 35; 756th Unit Journal, 13 February 1944 (1900 and 1930 entries).
135 B Co/756th Unit Journal, 12 February 1944; 756th Morning Reports, 13 February 1944: These men were T/4 Arend Strand [B] and Pvt Louis P DiRocco [HQ]. US World War II Hospital Admission Card Files, 1942–1954: Strand suffered shrapnel wounds to the face and forehead.
136 34th G-3 Journal, 13 February 1944 (0700 entry).
137 Ibid., (1000 entry).
138 Ibid., (1040 entry).
139 Ibid., (1230 entry); 34th Inf Div Operational Instructions dated 13 February 1944.
140 34th G-3 Journal, 13 February 1944 (1000 and 1040 entries).
141 Plowman, *Battles for Cassino*, 110.
142 34th G-3 message No 94 dated 122245A.
143 34th G-3 Journal, 13 February 1944 (1750 and 2230 entries); Walker, "Comments on the Rapido River Crossing," 19.
144 34th G-3 Journal, 13 February 1944 (2140 entry).
145 Ibid., (2225 entry).
146 Ibid., (2345 entry).
147 133rd Cannon Co Unit Journal, 14 February 1944.
148 B Co/756th Unit Journal, 14 February 1944. It is not known why Lt Harley wasn't involved, but a possible reason is he was pulled for liaison work.
149 756th Unit Journal, 14 February 1944 (0630, 0700, and 0720 entries).
150 Ibid., (0745 entry), Fazendin, *756th at Cassino*, 118: Harley recollection; B Co/756th Unit Journal, 14 February 1944.
151 756th Unit Journal, 14 February 1944 (0930 entry); 756th Commander's Narrative for January and February 1944, 35.
152 Presumed, judging from the listing of 756th Tank Bn casualties for the day.
153 756th Unit Journal, 14 February 1944 (1130 entry).
154 756th Commander's Narrative for January and February 1944, 35.
155 756th Unit Journal, 14 February 1944 (1230 entry): "CO moved with this platoon" interpreted by the author as he assumed command of one of the tanks. Knowing Sweeting's personality, this was most likely the case. The 2nd Platoon, B Company is presumed as the 1st Platoon already expended ammo on the castle that morning.
156 Ibid.
157 Steven Thomas Barry, *Battalion Commanders at War: US Army Tactical Leadership in the Mediterranean Theater, 1942–1943* (Lawrence, Kansas: University Press of Kansas, 2013), 110: Citing Alvin D. Coox and L. Van Loan Naisawald "Survey of Allied Tank Casualties in World War II," (Operations Research Office of Johns' Hopkins University, Washington, D.C.), Technical Memorandum, 31 March 1951, 26–28.
158 Randolph Perdue, 13 January 2004 phone conversation.

159 Wilkinson letter, 31 May 2005; Wilkinson letter to Redle, 14 August 1989.
160 Redle letter, 2 May 2002.
161 756th Unit History for 1944, GO #31 II Corps dated 27 April 1944; Both Silver Stars were awarded. Grate was from Geauga Lake, Ohio. Smith was from Kingston, Washington.
162 Redle interview 13 March 2004; Redle letter 2 May 2002.
163 756th Unit Journal, 14 February 1944 (1515 and 1630 entries).
164 Ibid., (1430 entry).
165 756th Unit Journal, 14 February 1944 (1630 and 2000 entries).
166 Ibid., (1715 entry); First name and middle initial not given, but most likely Col James C. Fry, CO of the 350th Inf Regt. John P. Delaney, *The Blue Devils in Italy: A History of the 88th Infantry Division in World War II* (Nashville, Tennessee: The Battery Press, Inc., 1988), xiii, 181, and 298.
167 Delany, *The Blue Devils in Italy*, 38.
168 756th Unit Journal, 14 February 1944 (1645 and 1900 entries).
169 Redle letter, 30 January 2008.
170 B Co/756th Unit Journal, 16 February 1944.
171 US World War II Hospital Admission Card Files, 1942–1954. Neither man returned to unit. Rule was hospitalized until May 1944. Tomaszewski's wounds required plastic surgery and was hospitalized until September 1944.
172 B Co/756th Unit Journal, 16 February 1944; US World War II Hospital Admission Card Files, 1942–1954: Rutzen was wounded in the hand by shell fragments.
173 756th Morning Reports, 14 February 1944; B Co/756th Morning Report, 16 February 1944; B Co/756th Morning Report, 23 April 1944, "Record of Events" for 13–21 February; According to Kevin F. Brennan's separation papers and 11 January 2014 email from his son, Ed, Kevin was a loader in a tank and suffered multiple shrapnel wounds.
174 756th Unit Journal, 14 February 1944 (2215 entry).
175 Parker, *Monte Cassino*, 143–44; Hapgood, *Monte Cassino*, 188.
176 Walker, "Comments on the Rapido River Crossing," 14 and 16.
177 Smith, *Battles for Monte Cassino*, 69.
178 Walker, "Comments on the Rapido River Crossing," 19.
179 Parker, *Monte Cassino*, 143–44; Hapgood, *Monte Cassino*, 188–89.
180 Walker, "Comments on the Rapido River Crossing," 19.
181 Ibid.; 34th G-3 Journal, 13 February 1944 (1740 entry).
182 Plowman, *Battles for Cassino*, 110.
183 Hougen, *34th Infantry Division*, "Fighting Reserves."
184 Bond, *Return to Cassino*, 78, 90.
185 Ankrum, *Dogfaces Who Smiled Through Tears*, 430.
186 Parker, *Monte Cassino*, 171: First quote attributed to Jack Turner, a Royal Sussex Veteran. Second quote attributed to B. Smith, a signaler with the 4th Indian Division.
187 Ankrum, *Dogfaces Who Smiled Through Tears*, 430.
188 Graham, *Cassino: Battle Book*, 70–71.
189 Luttrell, "Operations of the 168th Infantry … Rapido River Crossing," 23.
190 Hougen, *34th Infantry Division*, "Supplies and Medical Aid" and "Fighting Reserves"; Gray, "Crossing of the Rapido, I Co/168th," 22; Wallace, *The Italian Campaign*, 137; Fazendin, *756th at Cassino*, 137–38.
191 Gray, "Crossing of the Rapido, I Co/168th," 19.
192 34th Inf Div "Lessons Learned in Combat," 1st Sgt Gerald J. Gregor testimony, 10; Unites States Army, *Military Encyclopedia of Italian Campaign*, 519–21.
193 Blumenson, *Salerno to Cassino*, 379–80.
194 Wallace, *The Italian Campaign*, 136.
195 Ibid., 137.
196 Implied. Devers, Wilson's deputy, was dispatched the next day on a perilous flight over the abbey to survey the situation firsthand. No formal order from Wilson exists on the bombing of the abbey, but he would have and should have had the final authority to authorize any strike, according to Gooderson, *Cassino 1944*, 82.
197 Blumenson, *Salerno to Cassino*, 408.

198 Plowman, *Battles for Cassino*, 106–108.
199 Ibid., 107–08; Gooderson, *Cassino 1944*, 82.
200 Plowman, *Battles for Cassino*, 108.
201 Gooderson, *Cassino 1944*, 82.
202 Plowman, *Battles for Cassino*, 109; Blumenson, *Salerno to Cassino*, 406–07; To his credit, after the war Mark Clark admitted that the decision to bomb the abbey was a mistake—although he fell short of taking any direct responsibility—insisting, instead, that he opposed it throughout. Parker, *Monte Cassino*, 163; Clark said that had Freyberg been one of his own Corps commanders, he would have dismissed his request.
203 Parker, *Monte Cassino*, 164. These shaky reports included observing "flashes from field glasses" in a window and of a military radio antenna inside the courtyard. In 34th Inf Div G-2 Report, 120008 to 120009 February 1944, a "Civilian Report" passed on by the CIC (Civilian Counter Intelligence Corps) tells of an Italian frequented the abbey several times in the thirty days prior to 7 February 1944. He claimed eighty officers and soldiers and thirty MGs were positioned in the abbey. The CIC was controversial in that the program relied on paid informants.
204 Blumenson, *Salerno to Cassino*, 406–07; Plowman, *Battles for Cassino*, 108–09. Controversy has swirled over this decision ever since. Much of it rests upon two issues: whether the Germans were using the abbey for military purposes and who was ultimately responsible for the decision to drop the bombs. After nearly eighty years, the historical record seems clear on the first question: The Germans were NOT using the abbey for military purposes. The second question is less clear. The Allied chain of command shows any decision to bomb would have been Gen Wilson's to make. However, it is difficult to believe that Gen Wilson, a very competent, thorough, and politically astute commander, would have made such a momentous decision alone in a vacuum. Afterall, the abbey's destruction affected delicate political arrangements involving the Vatican and threatened to raise the ire of millions of Catholics around the world. Wilson's decision *must have been* given prior approval from the highest levels of British and American governments. Although direct evidence of Churchill's or Roosevelt's involvement is scant to non-existent, this author has seen too many historical examples of crafty politicians setting up "fall guys" and employing "plausible deniability" in similar situations. The fact that Wilson did not lose his job and retire in obscurity after this controversial order—but remained in command of the theatre until November 1944, was awarded a prestigious promotion to field marshal, and then enjoyed a distinguished postwar diplomatic career seems to speak volumes.
205 Blumenson, *Salerno to Cassino*, 409.
206 Hougen, *34th Infantry Division*, "The Bombing of the Abbey"; Parker, *Monte Cassino*, 163–64.
207 Hapgood, *Monte Cassino*, 191; Plowman, *Battles for Cassino*, 109.
208 Blumenson, *Salerno to Cassino*, 409; Gooderson, *Cassino 1944*, 84; Smith, *Battles for Monte Cassino*, 88.
209 Graham, *Cassino: Battle Book*, 79.
210 Plowman, *Battles for Cassino*, 112; Smith, *Battles for Monte Cassino*, 88–89; Gooderson, *Cassino 1944*, 83–84.
211 Hapgood, *Monte Cassino*, 200.
212 Blumenson, *Salerno to Cassino*, 409.
213 Ibid., 408.

Chapter 6

1 756th Unit Journal, 15 February 1944 (0430 entry).
2 34th Inf Div "Lessons Learned in Combat," Coffey testimony, 60–61; 756th Commander's Narrative for January and February 1944, 35.
3 133rd Cannon Co Unit Journal, 15 February 1944.
4 34th G-3 Journal, 13 February 1944 (1230 entry); 34th Inf Div Operational Instructions dated 13 February 1944.
5 Hougen, *34th Infantry Division*, "Fighting Reserves."
6 756th Unit Journal, 15 February 1944 (0615 and 0645 entries).
7 Ibid., (0650 entry).
8 Ibid., (0830 entry).
9 Ibid., (0930 entry).

10 United States Army, *Report of the New Weapons Board* (Washington, D.C.: Army Service Forces, 27 April 1944).
11 Hapgood, *Monte Cassino*, 201–02.
12 Duane Schultz, "Bombing the Abbey" *WWII History* magazine, December 2018, 8.
13 Ibid.
14 133rd Cannon Co Unit Journal, 15 February 1944; Duane Schultz, "Bombing the Abbey" *WWII History* magazine, December 2018, 10.
15 Hapgood, *Monte Cassino*, 202.
16 Ibid., 201–02; Duane Schultz, "Bombing the Abbey" *WWII History* magazine, December 2018, 8.
17 Ashcraft, *As You Were*, 82; Hapgood, *Monte Cassino*, 143, 167, and 169; Duane Schultz, "Bombing the Abbey" *WWII History* magazine, December 2018, 8; Tom Treanor, "The Home Front" *The Los Angeles Times* (Los Angeles, California), 1 February 1944, 2.
18 Ashcraft, *As You Were*, 81–82.
19 Spoken by the character Jaques in Shakespeare's play *As You Like It*, Act II, Scene VII, Line 138.
20 Duane Schultz, "Bombing the Abbey" *WWII History* magazine, December 2018, 10.
21 Ashcraft, *As You Were*, 83.
22 Blumenson, *Salerno to Cassino*, 411.
23 Hapgood, *Monte Cassino*, 202–03; Parker, *Monte Cassino*, 165 and 173; Gray, "Crossing of the Rapido, I Co/168th," 19; After the war, Alexander justified the bombing as having a positive effect on the Allied troops who fought there and witnessed its destruction.
24 Haspel interview by Pamela G Patrick on 18 September 1984.
25 Duane Schultz, "Bombing the Abbey" *WWII History* magazine, December 2018, 10.
26 Allied Forces, *Report by the Supreme Allied Commander Mediterranean to the Combined Chiefs of the Staff on the Italian Campaign, 8 January 1944 to 10 May 1944* (Washington, D.C.: US Government Printing Office, 1944), 25; Gooderson, *Cassino 1944*, 84.
27 Hapgood, *Monte Cassino*, 202–03.
28 Allied Forces, *Report by the Supreme Allied Commander Mediterranean*, 25.
29 133rd Cannon Co Unit Journal, 15 February 1944.
30 Gooderson, *Cassino 1944*, 84.
31 Hapgood, *Monte Cassino*, 203.
32 Allied Forces, *Report by the Supreme Allied Commander Mediterranean*, 25.
33 133rd Cannon Co Unit Journal, 15 February 1944.
34 Donley diary, 15 February 1944.
35 Blumenson, *Salerno to Cassino*, 411.
36 Gooderson, *Cassino 1944*, 84.
37 133rd Cannon Co Unit Journal, 15 February 1944.
38 Duane Schultz, "Bombing the Abbey" *WWII History* magazine, December 2018, 10.
39 133rd Cannon Co Unit Journal, 15 February 1944.
40 Duane Schultz, "Bombing the Abbey" *WWII History* magazine, December 2018, 10.
41 Ibid.
42 Ibid.
43 133rd Cannon Co Unit Journal, 15 February 1944.
44 Treanor, *One Damn Thing*, 270–71.
45 Blumenson, *Salerno to Cassino*, 413; Luttrell, "Operations of the 168th Infantry … Rapido River Crossing," 25.
46 Gooderson, *Cassino 1944*, 84.
47 Hapgood, *Monte Cassino*, 203.
48 Ashcraft, *As You Were*, 83–84.
49 Plowman, *Battles for Cassino*, 113 and 115; Hapgood, *Monte Cassino*, 211; Lee McCardell, "Cassino Battle Shifts To Foot of Monastery," *The Baltimore Sun* (Baltimore, Maryland), 9 February 1944, 1: McCardell told of three civilians who "stepped back through our lines" and estimated abbey refugee numbers at "several hundred."
50 Ford, *Cassino: Breaking Gustav Line*, 56; Blumenson, *Salerno to Cassino*, 413.

51 Duane Schultz, "Bombing the Abbey" *WWII History* magazine, December 2018, 10; Hapgood, *Monte Cassino*, 211–12.
52 Plowman, *Battles for Cassino*, 113 and 115; Hapgood, *Monte Cassino*, 211–12: The best local estimate puts the civilian death count at 230. One hundred and forty-eight skulls were recovered from the ruins after the war. Other victims were likely pulverized and never counted or recovered; Ford, *Cassino: Breaking Gustav Line*, 56; Allan Mallinson, "How St Benedict's abbey survived Goths, Saracens and Nazis" *Catholic Herald* magazine, 17 May 2019, 23.
53 Hapgood, *Monte Cassino*, 209–10.
54 Ibid., 73–74.
55 Ibid., 219–220; Blumenson, *Salerno to Cassino*, 411.
56 Green, Col John H., "The Battles for Cassino" *After the Battle Number 13: Cassino Battlefield Tour* magazine, 1985, 8; Hapgood, *Monte Cassino*, 209.
57 756th Unit Journal, 15 February 1944 (1200 entry).
58 Ibid., (1330 and 1430 entries).
59 Ibid., (1500 entry).
60 Ibid., (1600 and 1645 entries).
61 Ibid., (1645 entry).
62 34th G-3 Journal, 5 February 1944 (1515 entry): The source may have been 133rd troops fighting in the north section of town and up the steep hill toward the castle at the time.
63 133rd Cannon Co Unit Journal, 15 February 1944.
64 Ford, *Cassino: Breaking Gustav Line*, 56.
65 Ibid., 56–57; One company of the 1st Royal Sussex Regiment consisting of only three officers and sixty-three men attempted to take the abbey under cover of darkness but were driven back and sustained heavy losses. Chris Bishop and Chris McNab, eds. *Campaigns of World War II Day by Day* (Hauppauge, New York: Barron's Educational Series, Inc., 2003), 132; Plowman, *Battles for Cassino*, 113.
66 Gooderson, *Cassino 1944*, 84.
67 Hougen, *34th Infantry Division*, "The Bombing of the Abbey"; Duane Schultz, "Bombing the Abbey" *WWII History* magazine, December 2018, 14; Gooderson, *Cassino 1944*, 84.
68 Graham, *Cassino: Battle Book*, 79; Hapgood, *Monte Cassino*, 212 and 238; Fazendin, *756th at Cassino*, 123–24: Long after the war, the destruction of the abbey remained controversial even with the veterans of the 756th. Some, like Redle, believed the bombing was unnecessary and counterproductive; others, like Robert Kremer, remained convinced the Germans were using the abbey to direct artillery fire.
69 Duane Schultz, "Bombing the Abbey" *WWII History* magazine, December 2018, 10.
70 Parker, *Monte Cassino*, 162.
71 Hapgood, *Monte Cassino*, 129 and 136.
72 Duane Schultz, "Bombing the Abbey" *WWII History* magazine, December 2018, 10; Hapgood, *Monte Cassino*, 129, 236–42: Hapgood lays out a convincing case.
73 Hapgood, *Monte Cassino*, 89.
74 Ibid., 185–86.
75 Duane Schultz, "Bombing the Abbey" *WWII History* magazine, December 2018, 10.
76 Hapgood, *Monte Cassino*, 60: Fortunately, these works were discovered in a salt mine after the war and repatriated.
77 Plowman, *Battles for Cassino*, 106–07.
78 Hapgood, *Monte Cassino*, 90.
79 Ibid., 101–02 and 239; Caddick-Adams, *Monte Cassino: Ten Armies*, 151.
80 Hapgood, *Monte Cassino*, 239.
81 Gooderson, *Cassino 1944*, 85.
82 Duane Schultz, "Bombing the Abbey" *WWII History* magazine, December 2018, 14.
83 Plowman, *Battles for Cassino*, 118-22; Allied Forces, *Report by the Supreme Allied Commander Mediterranean*, 25.
84 Plowman, *Battles for Cassino*, 122; Gooderson, *Cassino 1944*, 84–85.
85 Allied Forces, *Report by the Supreme Allied Commander Mediterranean*, 25.
86 Plowman, *Battles for Cassino*, 112.

87 Ibid., 110.
88 Hapgood, *Monte Cassino*, 147–48 and 171.
89 Ibid., 95.
90 Ibid., 200.
91 Wolfgang Saxon, "Gen. Mark Clark Dies at 87; Last of the World War II Chiefs, Conqueror of Rome," *The New York Times* (New York, New York), 17 April 1984, 1.
92 Hapgood, *Monte Cassino*, 195; Plowman, *Battles for Cassino*, 113.
93 Hapgood, *Monte Cassino*, 173.
94 Graham, *Cassino: Battle Book*, 79; Plowman, *Battles for Cassino*, 116: The 78-year-old abbot and General von Senger were interviewed on German radio by 18 February—both declaring the abbey was never used by Germans and protesting all aspects of the bombing—including the fact the allied leaflets were dropped late and gave little warning an attack was imminent.
95 Plowman, *Battles for Cassino*, 116.
96 Blumenson, *Salerno to Cassino*, 414-15; Hapgood, *Monte Cassino*, 199.
97 Hapgood, *Monte Cassino*, photo between pages 218 and 219.
98 Ibid., 214; Duane Schultz, "Bombing the Abbey" *WWII History* magazine, December 2018, 10–11.

Chapter 7

1 Ranspach diary, 16 February 1944.
2 756th Morning Reports, 16 February 1944.
3 WWII slang describing a soldier killed in action.
4 133rd Cannon Co Unit Journal, 16 February 1944.
5 756th Unit Journal, 16 February 1944 (0615 and 0720 entries); 756th Commander's Narrative for January and February 1944, 35.
6 756th Unit Journal, 16 February 1944 (0930 and 1130 entries).
7 Ibid., (1650 entry).
8 Ibid., (1815 entry).
9 Blumenson, *Salerno to Cassino*, 417.
10 133rd Cannon Co Unit Journal, 16 February 1944; Donley diary, 16 February 1944.
11 Blumenson, *Salerno to Cassino*, 413: Blumenson does not provide the gender of the civilian.
12 Gooderson, *Cassino 1944*, 84.
13 Ibid., 85; Plowman, *Battles of Cassino*, 118–22.
14 Plowman, *Battles of Cassino*, 122.
15 Ford, Cassino: *Breaking Gustav Line*, 53–54.
16 Gooderson, *Cassino 1944*, 85–86.
17 133rd Cannon Co Unit Journal, 17 February 1944.
18 756th Unit Journal, 17 February 1944 (0600, 0610, and 0620 entries).
19 756th Unit Journal, 16 February 1944. Yellow order dated 16 February and signed by Lt Verus Langham (liaison officer.); 756th Commander's Narrative for January and February 1944, 35.
20 756th Unit Journal, 17 February 1944 (0830 and 1000 entries); 756th Commander's Narrative for January and February 1944, 35: Records "tank guns at quarry" located at 858222 as participating. It's unclear if these were M4s or the HQ assault guns moved temporarily to this position. An A Company tank platoon also fired from 872225 on the east side of the river.
21 756th Unit Journal, February 1944, message dated 17 February 1944 and signed at 1930 by Lt Verus Langham.
22 Ibid.
23 756th Unit Journal, 17 February 1944 (1600 entry).
24 133rd Cannon Co Unit Journal, 17 February 1944; Blumenson, *Salerno to Cassino*, 417; Allied Forces, *Report by the Supreme Allied Commander Mediterranean*, 25.
25 Fazendin, *756th at Cassino*, 115.
26 Redle letter 7 January 2007.
27 Ibid.

28 Wilkinson letter, 31 May 2005; Redle interview by Lowther, 11–12 August 2012.
29 IDPF for Eugene K. Wunderlich; US WWII Hospital Admission cards 1942–1945; Dale Wunderlich (nephew) email, 10 June 2009.
30 Johannesen obituary, *The World* (Coos Bay, Oregon), 31 March 2004, 5: He played basketball, football, track, and softball.
31 Redle letter, 7 January 2007.
32 Gooderson, *Cassino 1944*, 87.
33 Hapgood, *Monte Cassino*, 229.
34 Gooderson, *Cassino 1944*, 87–88; Plowman, *Battles of Cassino*, 124.
35 Ibid.; Hapgood, *Monte Cassino*, 229; Ford, Cassino: *Breaking Gustav Line*, 56–57: One company of the 1st Royal Sussex Regiment consisting of only three officers and sixty-three men attempted to take the abbey under cover of darkness and were driven back—sustaining heavy losses.
36 Gooderson, *Cassino 1944*, 88; Plowman, *Battles of Cassino*, 124; Hapgood, *Monte Cassino*, 229–30; John Pimlott, *The Historical Atlas of World War II* (New York, New York: Henry Holt and Company, Inc., 1995), 142–43.
37 Donley diary, 16 February 1944.
38 Ashcraft, *As You Were*, 84.
39 Hapgood, *Monte Cassino*, 229–30.
40 Plowman, *Battles of Cassino*, 125–26; Gooderson, *Cassino 1944*, 86; Allied Forces, *Report by the Supreme Allied Commander Mediterranean*, 25.
41 756th Unit Journal, 18 February 1944 (0645 and 0745 entries).
42 133rd Cannon Co Unit Journal, 18 February 1944.
43 756th Unit Journal, 18 February 1944 (0645 and 0745 entries).
44 Blumenson *Salerno to Cassino*, 383.
45 133rd Inf Regt Commander Narrative (Col Marshall) for February 1944.
46 Plowman, *Battles of Cassino*, 125–26.
47 Ibid., 130–31.
48 756th Unit Journal, 18 February 1944 (0750 entry): Location not given, but was likely in Caira. A British "Brigade" was similar in size to a US "Regiment."
49 Gooderson, *Cassino 1944*, 86.
50 756th Unit Journal, 18 February 1944 (0830 entry).
51 Ibid., (1020 entry).
52 Ibid., (1100 entry).
53 Ibid., (1110 entry).
54 Ibid., (1330 entry).
55 Allied Forces, *Report by the Supreme Allied Commander Mediterranean*, 25.
56 Plowman, *Battles of Cassino*, 131.
57 756th Unit Journal, 18 February 1944 (1430 entry).
58 Ibid.
59 756th Commander's Narrative for January and February 1944, 35–36.
60 756th Unit Journal, 18 February 1944 (1430 entry).
61 756th Commander's Narrative for January and February 1944, 36.
62 756th Unit Journal, 18 February 1944 (1600 entry).
63 Allied Forces, *Report by the Supreme Allied Commander Mediterranean*, 25.
64 Gooderson, *Cassino 1944*, 88; Plowman, *Battles of Cassino*, 131.
65 756th Commander's Narrative for January and February 1944, 36.
66 Gooderson, *Cassino 1944*, 88–89.
67 Blumenson *Salerno to Cassino*, 417.
68 Ibid., 418; Gooderson, *Cassino 1944*, 89; Bishop, *Campaigns of WWII Day by Day*, 132; This extended into a two-week hiatus. The third major attack on Cassino began 15 March and ended unsuccessfully on 22 March 1944.
69 Fazendin, *756th at Cassino*, 116–18: Redle recollection.
70 Parker, *Monte Cassino*, 152.

71 Ibid.; Fazendin, *756th at Cassino*, 138–39: Redle recollection.
72 Fazendin, *756th at Cassino*, 138–39: Redle recollection.
73 Ibid.
74 Ibid.
75 Ibid.
76 Guild interview, 15 September 2006; Guild phone conversation, 11 February 2004.
77 Blumenson, *Salerno to Cassino*, 407; Plowman, *Battles of Cassino*, 116–17. Ten years after the war, Von Senger, a lay Benedictine, insisted that the abbey was never occupied by German forces prior to the bombardment.
78 Duane Schultz, "Bombing the Abbey" *WWII History* magazine, December 2018, 10.
79 Ibid., 10–11.
80 Ibid., 10; Hapgood, *Monte Cassino*, 224.
81 756th Unit Journal, 19 February 1944 (0530, 0830, and 0900 entries).
82 133rd Inf Regt Commander Narrative (Col Marshall) for February 1944.
83 756th Unit Journal, 19 February 1944 (1500 entry).
84 756th Commander's Narrative for January and February 1944, 36.
85 Table of Organization No. 17–25, War Department, Washington, D.C., 15 September 1943, Medium Tank Battalion; Fazendin, *756th at Cassino*, 83–84: Willis Trafton recollection. Mortar platoon was commanded at this time by Lt Willis Trafton. S/Sgt John Daniels was his platoon sergeant.
86 Green, *Weapons of Patton's Armies*, 65.
87 Fazendin, *756th at Cassino*, 81–82: Ithel "Dick" Adlard recollection. Although the 15 September 1943 US Army Medium Tank Battalion T/O listed only three 105mm guns in the HQ Assault Gun Platoon. The 756th doubled the unit size to six by consolidating the other three 105mm guns assigned to A, B, and C Companies.
88 Ibid., 81: Roy Collins recollection.
89 Ibid., 83: Raymond Norris recollection.
90 Ibid., 82: Adlard recollection.
91 Ibid., 83: Norris recollection.
92 Ibid., 82: Adlard recollection.
93 IDPF for William Fodor.
94 Olson phone conversation, 7 July 2013.
95 Lewis undated letter to Fazendin, Lewis personal papers.
96 Fazendin, *756th at Cassino*, 106, 110, and 119.
97 IDPF for William Fodor; Fazendin, *756th at Cassino*, 106: French Lewis recollection; "Killed—Army," *The Pittsburgh Press* (Pittsburgh, Pennsylvania), 3 May 1944, 2.
98 756th Morning Reports, 17, 18, and 19 February 1944.
99 Ibid., 19 February 1944: Cpl Richard E. Wills, (C Co), and Cpl Chester D. Preddy, (C Co), were wounded 19 February, but it is unknown if they were also in the OP at the time or elsewhere.
100 Fazendin letter to French Lewis, 10 May (1992); Fazendin, *756th at Cassino*, 119–120, Denis Hannan recollection.
101 Treanor, *One Damn Thing*, 258.
102 Ibid.
103 Ibid., 259.
104 Redle interview, 13 March 2004.
105 Jack Brown interview, 16 September 2006.
106 Treanor, *One Damn Thing*, 258.
107 756th Unit Journal, 19 February 1944 (1500 entry).
108 Ibid., (1900 entry).
109 756th Commander's Narrative for January and February 1944, 36.
110 Donley diary, 20 February 1944.
111 756th Unit Journal, 20 February 1944 (0615 and 0645 entries).
112 Ibid., (1000 entry).
113 Misidentified strangely in both the 756th Unit Journal and Sweeting's Commander's Narrative as the "5th NZ Armored Regiment." No such unit existed.

114 756th Commander's Narrative for January and February 1944, 36.
115 756th Unit Journal, 20 February 1944 (1430 entry).
116 756th Commander's Narrative for January and February 1944, 36.
117 756th Unit Journal, 20 February 1944 (1900 entry).
118 756th Commander's Narrative for January and February 1944, 36.
119 756th Unit Journal, 20 February 1944 (2130 entry).
120 756th Commander's Narrative for January and February 1944, 36.
121 Donley diary, 21 February 1944.
122 Ranspach diary, 22 February 1944.
123 756th Unit Journal, 21 February 1944 (0530, 0545, and 0600 entries).
124 "Colonel," *Des Moines Tribune* (Des Moines, Iowa), 3 July 1950, 1; "Remember Col. Carley L. Marshall ..." *The Honolulu Advertiser* (Honolulu, Hawaii), 1 February 1954, 10; "Colonel's Moustache," *Des Moines Tribune* (Des Moines, Iowa), 29 October 1968, 1.
125 756th Unit Journal, 21 February 1944 (0845 entry).
126 Ibid., (1130 entry); 756th Commander's Narrative for January and February 1944, 36.
127 Donley diary, 21 February 1944.
128 756th Commander's Narrative for January and February 1944, 36; 756th Unit Journal, 21 February 1944 (1710 entry).
129 Donley diary, 21 February 1944.
130 Fazendin, *756th at Cassino*, 149: Collins recollection.
131 Donley diary, 21 February 1944.
132 New Zealander tanks were organized as follows: A "regiment" was equivalent to an American battalion. A "squadron" was equivalent to company and a "troop" was equivalent to a platoon; 756th Unit Journal, 21 February 1944 (1430 entry) and 22 February 1944 (0100, 0110, 0200, and 0600 entries).
133 Ibid., 21 February 1944 (1500 entry).
134 Ibid., 22 February 1944 (0100, 0110, 0200, and 0600 entries); IP point referenced in 756th Unit Journal, 21 February 1944 (1500 entry).
135 133rd Inf Regt Commander Narrative (Col Marshall) for February 1944: The 133rd completed the move to Alife by 0020 hours, 23 February 1944; Blumenson *Salerno to Cassino*, 418.
136 Fazendin, *756th at Cassino*, 149: John M. Roth recollection.
137 Ankrum, *Dogfaces Who Smiled Through Tears*, 429: The officer was Capt. Donald Nabity, Adjutant for 3rd Bn/133rd.
138 Parker, *Monte Cassino*, xv.

Chapter 8

1 756th Unit Journal, 22 February 1944 (1530 and 2230 entries).
2 Donley diary, 23 February 1944.
3 756th Unit Journal, 21 February 1944 (2245 entry).
4 Ibid., (0630 entry).
5 Ibid., (1530 and 2230 entries).
6 Fazendin, *756th at Cassino*, 149–52.
7 Ibid.; B Co/756th Morning Report, 24 February, 1944, reports Barber out as "sick." US World War II Hospital Admission Card Files, 1942–1954: reports Barber had a broken bone in the hand and lists nothing about the collarbone.
8 Redle interview by Lowther, 11–12 August 2012.
9 Ibid.
10 Fazendin, *756th at Cassino*, 152–53.
11 Redle letter, 29 April 2003.
12 Fazendin, *756th at Cassino*, 125.
13 Redle letter, 2 May 2002.
14 B Co/756th Morning Report, 21 February 1944: This was Pvt George C Davis. US World War II Hospital Admission Card Files, 1942–1954: Davis had a "crushed between objects" thorax injury requiring sutures.

15 Offerman, Dick (Son of Cletus J. Offerman, B Company/756th Tank Battalion), "My Dad was a Tanker." Biography, letters, and photos, December 2005, 65 pages, copy provided to the author, 18.
16 B Co/756th Morning Report, 21 April 1944 "Record of Events" for 27 January.
17 756th Tank Battalion NARA records: map and listing of Cassino tank losses.
18 The Armor School. *Maintenance of Armor in World War II.* Research Report, Officers Advanced Course, Fort Knox, Kentucky, 1949–1950, 76.
19 Ibid., 70.
20 Ibid., 63.
21 Ibid., 69, French Lewis was a source for this detail.
22 Ibid., 62–63.
23 Ibid., 63.
24 Ibid., 69–70.
25 Barry, *Battalion Commanders at War*, 114.
26 756th Commander's Narrative for January and February 1944, 37–38.
27 Ibid., 37.
28 Fazendin, *756th at Cassino*, xxxiii.
29 Ibid., 1: Redle recollection.
30 Ibid., 1, 93–94: Redle recollection.
31 Ford, *Cassino: Breaking Gustav Line*, 49.
32 Blumenson, *Salerno to Cassino*, 382–83.
33 Walker, "Comments on the Rapido River Crossing," 24.
34 Ford, *Cassino: Breaking Gustav Line*, 45: Von Senger moved his best troops from the 90th Panzer Grenadier Division opposite the British X Corps in the south to shore up Cassino itself.
35 Walker, "Comments on the Rapido River Crossing," 25.
36 Ibid., 4.
37 Ibid., 28.
38 Rudolf Böhmler, *Monte Cassino: A German View* (Maximilian Verlag GmbH & Co, 1956. Reprint, South Yorkshire, UK: Pen & Sword Military, 2015), 204–05: Böhmler, the author of this work, was battalion commander of the 1st Bn /German 3rd Paratrooper Regiment and fought at Cassino. He maintains that Cassino should have been bypassed by the Allies in favor of Juin's plan for taking Atina. He believes Rome could have been reached without ever striking Cassino. Böhmler doesn't seem to have much respect for Freyberg's approach.
39 Hapgood, *Monte Cassino*, 178.
40 Fazendin, *756th at Cassino*, 149: Fred Schmidt is the source.
41 Numbers arrived at through Morning Reports study done by the author (see appendices). These totals are slightly higher than Schmidt's 125 casualty figure reported by Fazendin.
42 Ranspach diary, 30 January 1944.
43 756th Unit Journal, 21 February 1944 (1500 entry).
44 756th Commander's Narrative for January and February 1944, 37: Exact location was 265048.
45 Ibid.; 756th Unit Journal, 23 February 1944 (0600 entry).
46 756th Unit Journal, 23 February 1944 (0600 entry).
47 Ranspach diary, 22 February 1944.
48 756th Unit Journal, 22 February 1944 (0630 entry).
49 Redle recollections in Lewis personal papers; Fazendin, *756th at Cassino*, 154: Redle recollection: Redle recalls this happened "before they left Cassino" but Lewis recalls it happened at arriving at Alife. Considering logistics, the author believes Lewis's memory is probably more accurate on this detail. Ranspach diary, 23 February 1944: Ranspach's description of the men.
50 Lewis draft for Fazendin in Lewis personal papers; Fazendin, *756th at Cassino*, 182: Lewis recollection.
51 Ranspach diary, 23 February 1944.
52 Bernard Shue, enlistment record.
53 Clyde Guild interview, 2007 September 13.
54 Fazendin, *756th at Cassino*, 154–55; Redle recollection; Redle recollections in Lewis personal papers; Shue was from Holmes County, Ohio.

Chapter 9

1 Ranspach diary, 23 February 1944.
2 D Co/756th Morning Reports, 23 February 1944.
3 A Co/756th Morning Reports, 24 February 1944.
4 C Co/756th Morning Reports, 23 February 1944.
5 Ibid., 24 February 1944; Lewis undated letter to Fazendin.
6 D Co and HQ Co/756th Morning Reports, 23 February 1944.
7 D Co/756th Morning Reports, 23 February 1944.
8 Redle letter, 28 June 2009; 1940 Census; "Lt W H Newman Reaches N. Africa", *The Knoxville News-Sentinel* (Knoxville, Tennessee), 20 June 1943, 18.
9 756th Unit Journal, 24 February 1944 (1515 entry).
10 A Co/756th Morning Reports, 24 February 1944; Lewis undated letter to Fazendin.
11 B Co/756th Morning Reports, 1 March 1944.
12 Anderson phone conversation, 28 June 2001; Anderson interview, 27 September 2003.
13 B Co/756th Morning Reports, 1 March 1944.
14 Ibid.: Pvt Melville Corson, Pfc Leonard Froneberger Jr., T/5 Raymond Getz, Pfc Lotka Kupriance, Pfc Donald Ladue, Pfc George W. Minnick Jr (all six appointed to Cpl). Two others promoted from T/5 to T/4. Pfcs Thomas Barber, Clyde Guild and three others appointed T/5. Eleven others were appointed Pfc.
15 Ranspach diary, 24 February to 7 March 1944.
16 B Co/756th Morning Reports, 26 February 1944.
17 B Co/756th Morning Reports, 27 February 1944: Brooks reported to the 106th Clearing Co the following day—possibly as a result of wound complications and returned to duty on 10 March 1944.
18 Donley diary, 28 February 1944.
19 Ranspach diary, 24 February to 7 March 1944.
20 Lewis papers: Fred Schmidt letter, 6 September 1988.
21 Donley diary, 24 February 1944.
22 Ranspach diary, 24 February to 7 March 1944.
23 756th Unit Journal, 27 February 1944 (1030 and 1100 entries).
24 Ranspach diary, 24 February to 7 March 1944; 756th Unit Journal, 28 February 1944.
25 756th Unit Journal, 29 February 1944; 756th Commander's Narrative for January and February 1944, 37.
26 Donley diary, 29 February 1944.
27 Ibid., 1 March 1944.
28 Ranspach diary, 24 February to 7 March 1944.
29 Ankrum, *Dogfaces Who Smiled Through Tears*, 451; Lee Mudd, "History of the 756th Tank Battalion and the Development of the Tank-Infantry Team in World War II." Thesis, Johns Hopkins University, 2000, 38; Fazendin, *756th at Cassino*, 152 and 182: Lewis recollection; Lewis documents: officer lists.
30 Fazendin, *756th at Cassino*, 182: Lewis recollection.
31 Olson phone conversation, 13 July 2007.
32 Ibid.
33 Olson phone conversation, 5 September 2008: Sweeting's proclivity toward pettiness also irritated his officers as time went on. For example, he refused to grade any officer other than himself with the highest physical rating of "superior." He once told Ed Olson, who deserved a superior rating as well: "Olson, I can't give you a superior rating, but I'm inventing one for you of 'excellent plus.'" At the time, "excellent" was the grade immediately below "superior." "This was the way Sweeting was," Olson told the author. It's also interesting to point out that Olson was not one of those officers harboring any resentment toward Sweeting.
34 Redle phone conversation, 15 August 2005; Redle letter to Harry Yeide, 30 January 2008.
35 Lewis draft for Fazendin; Fazendin, *756th at Cassino*, 184: Lewis recollection; Olson phone conversation, 5 September 2008.
36 Donley diary, 3 March 1944.
37 Redle military records.
38 Ranspach diary, 24 February to 7 March 1944; Donley diary, 6 March 1944.

39 HQ Co/756th Morning Reports, July 1943 rations list; B Co/756th Morning Reports, 6–7 March 1944. Engfer actually arrived at B Company at 1700 after being released from the 38th Evac Hosp for some unknown illness.
40 Donley diary, 9 March 1944; Ranspach diary, 8, 9, 10, and 11 March 1944; 756th Unit History, 1944, Change of Station list.
41 B Co/756th Morning Reports, 9 March 1944.
42 Donley diary, 10 March 1944; Fazendin, *756th at Cassino*, 155: Redle recollection.
43 Ranspach diary, 8, 9, 10, 11 March 1944.
44 Ibid.
45 Donley diary, 11 March 1944.
46 Fazendin, *756th at Cassino*, 155: Redle recollection.
47 Lewis draft for Fazendin; Fazendin, *756th at Cassino*, 184–86: Lewis recollection.
48 B Co/756th Morning Reports, 11 March 1944.
49 Fazendin, *756th at Cassino*, 13: Redle recollection.
50 B Co/756th Morning Reports, 12 March 1944.
51 Redle interview, 13 March 2004.
52 Fazendin, *756th at Cassino*, 155: Redle recollection.
53 Redle interview, 19 January 2002; Redle letter, 2 March 2001.
54 Guild phone conversation, 11 February 2004.
55 Redle interview, 13 March 2004.
56 Redle, David D. "B Company, 756th Tank Battalion Added Recollections" memoirs. (14 pages), (1999). (Photocopies provided to the author by David D. Redle.)
57 Mras letter to Redle, 25 November 1997; Redle letter, 2 May 2002; Guild interview, 13 September 2007; Guild phone conversation, 11 February 2004.
58 Fazendin, *756th at Cassino*, 155: Redle recollection.
59 Redle letter, 14 February 2003; Redle interview, 13 March 2004; Guild phone conversation, 11 February 2004.
60 Lewis draft for Fazendin: This was A Company's experience, no doubt replicated by the other kitchen sections.
61 Fazendin, *756th at Cassino*, 184: Lewis recollection.
62 Donley diary, 12–14 March 1944.
63 Ranspach diary, 12 March 1944.
64 Ibid.
65 Ibid., 13 March 1944.
66 Various photos.
67 Fazendin, *756th at Cassino*, 185: Lewis recollection; 756th Unit History, 1944, records Rogers took command on 11 March, but did not physically arrive until 13 March.
68 Fazendin, *756th at Cassino*, 185: Lewis recollection; Lewis draft for Fazendin: Lewis wrote "8th Armored," but probably meant the 9th Armored Division. The 8th Armored Division trained at Fort Knox and Camp Polk, Louisiana, before shipping to England in November 1944. The 9th Armored Division was activated at Fort Riley, Kansas, in June 1942, and moved to California in June 1943, and Camp Polk, Louisiana in October 1943, before shipping to England in September 1944. (Source: Stanton, *Order of Battle U.S. Army*, 59–60.)
69 Jones, Wilber S., ed. *Howitzer* (West Point, NY: United States Corps of Cadets, 1931), 235; Mudd, "History 756th," 38.
70 Redle phone conversation, 15 September 2000.
71 Lewis draft for Fazendin.
72 Lewis personal papers: Olson letter 24 November 1990; Fazendin, *756th at Cassino*, 112 and 185.
73 Fazendin, *756th at Cassino*, 182: Lewis recollection.
74 Ibid., 155: Redle recollection.
75 Ibid., 182: Lewis recollection; Lewis draft for Fazendin: The exact date is not provided, but this event occurred one day during this station.
76 Donley diary, 16 March 1944.
77 Ranspach diary, 13 March 1944.

78 B Co/756th Morning Reports, 13 March 1944: Harley transferred to 109th Clearing Co at 0930 as sick, but his illness was not specified.
79 Donley diary, 15 March 1944; Ranspach diary, 16 March 1944.
80 Donley diary, 17 March 1944.
81 Ibid., 18–26 March 1944.
82 Ranspach diary, 17 March 1944.
83 Ibid., 8, 9, 10, and 11 March 1944. The 34th Inf Div's movement orders arrived 11 March. By 17 March, the division was loaded at the port of Bagnoli and sailing for Anzio—a process completed by 26 March 1944.
84 Wilber S. Jones, ed, *Howitzer* (West Point, NY: United States Corps of Cadets, 1931), 235.
85 Long recollection in Lewis papers.
86 Redle letter to Harry Yeide, 30 January 2008.
87 Lewis draft for Fazendin.
88 Redle interview, 16 September 2005.
89 Fazendin, *756th at Cassino*, 185: Lewis recollection.
90 Redle recollections for Fazendin.
91 Fazendin, *756th at Cassino*, 156: Redle recollection.
92 B Co/756th Morning Reports, 22 March 1944. Lewis 756th HQ attachments document dated 8 May 1945: B Company was formally detached two days earlier.
93 B Co/756th Morning Reports, 25 and 26 March 1944; Ranspach diary, 18–26 March 1944.
94 Redle interview, 19 February 2002.
95 B Co/756th Morning Reports, 27 March 1944; Ranspach diary, 27 March 1944.
96 Perdue phone conversation, 31 January 2004.
97 Richter letter, 12 January 2007; Arthur F. Richter, "Arthur F Richter's Experience in WWII" memoirs, (26 pages), 2007, (Photocopies provided to the author by Arthur F. Richter).
98 Redle letter, 24 June 2002; Randolph Nusz (son of Alvin Nusz) interview, 18 September 2002.
99 Guild interview, 15 September 2006; Guild phone conversation, 11 February 2004.
100 Ranspach diary, 18–26 March 1944.
101 B Co/756th Morning Reports, 27 March 1944. These were the first battlefield commissions in the battalion according to French Lewis's notes for Fazendin book.
102 Fazendin, *756th at Cassino*, 182: Lewis recollection.
103 B Co/756th Morning Reports, 30 March 1944.
104 Gorman draft card, United States Army WWII Draft Cards 1940–1947.
105 Fazendin, *756th at Cassino*, 183: Lewis recollection.
106 Redle interview, 19 January 2002.
107 B Co/756th Morning Reports, 24, 26 February and 27, 30 March 1944.
108 Redle letter, 23 September 2008; Redle letter, 28 June 2009; Redle letter, 28 June 2008.
109 Redle phone conversation, 15 September 2000.
110 Palumbo letter to Redle, 13 November 1986.
111 Redle letter 23 September 2008: Redle believes the doctor was named Major Campbell; Redle letter, 28 June 2008; Redle letter to Palumbo, 25 November 1986; Palumbo interview 16 September 2006; Redle letter 13 February 2001.
112 Redle letter, 13 February 2001.
113 Palumbo letter to Redle, 13 November 1986; Palumbo obituary.
114 Palumbo interview, 16 September 2006; Redle phone conversation, 15 September 2000.
115 B Co/756th Morning Reports, 5 April 1944.
116 Ibid., 27 March 1944.
117 Ibid., 21 March 1944: "SummCM case #9 HQ 756th Tk Bn" cited, but reason not given.
118 Ibid., 2 and 5 March 1944.
119 Ibid., 3 April 1944: Reason not given.
120 Donley diary, 26 March to 4 April 1944.
121 Ranspach diary, 3 April 1944.
122 Donley diary, 7 April 1944.
123 Ibid., 5 April 1944.

124 Anderson phone conversation, 28 June 2001.
125 Harry Yeide, *The Infantry's Armor: The US Army's Separate Tank Battalions in World War II* (Mechanicsburg, Pennsylvania: Stackpole Books, 2010), 80–81.
126 Böhmler, *Monte Cassino: A German View*, 213.
127 Blumenson, *Mark Clark*, 196.
128 Böhmler, *Monte Cassino: A German View*, 212.
129 Ibid., 215.
130 Blumenson, *Mark Clark*, 196.
131 Schultz, Duane, "Bombing the Abbey," *WWII History* magazine, December 2018, 15.
132 Captain Wyndham H. Bammer, "Operations of Company K, 339th Infantry (85th Infantry Division) in the Attack of Hills 66 and 69, Near Tremensuoli, Italy, 11–12 May 1944. (Personal Experience of a Weapon Platoon Leader), Advanced Infantry Officers Course 1948–1949, 5; Blumenson, *Mark Clark*, 197; "Rome-Arno 1944" CMH Publication 72-20, at http://history.army.mil/brochures/romar/72-20.htm, 15; Paul L. Schultz, *The 85th Infantry Division in World War II* (Washington: Infantry Journal Press, 1949), 61.
133 CMH "Rome-Arno," 16.
134 United States Army, *Fifth Army History, Part V, The Drive to Rome, 1 April–4 June 1944* (Milan, Italy: Pizzi and Pizio, 1945), 3.
135 Lewis personal papers: 756th HQ attachments document dated 8 May 1945.

Chapter 10

1 85th Infantry Division: Minturno to the Apennines, produced by HQ of the 85th Inf Div, Infantry Division, Information-Education Section, 1944 (http://usacac.army.mil/organizations/cace/carl), 1.
2 Schultz, *85th Division in WWII*, 2–3.
3 85th Inf Div, *Minturno to the Apennines*, 2–3; Don Jones chapter review notes, email 13 February 2021.
4 85th Inf Div, Report of Operations, April 1944 (NARA Army Records Group 407, Box 10675); 85th Inf Div, *Minturno to the Apennines*, 3; Schultz, *85th Division in WWII*, 45–49.
5 Schultz, *85th Division in WWII*, 57–58.
6 85th Inf Div, *Minturno to the Apennines*, Forward (unnumbered); Schultz, *85th Division in WWII*, 18–19.
7 Jones chapter notes, email 13 February 2021.
8 Schultz, *85th Division in WWII*, 57–58.
9 Ibid.
10 Delaney, *The Blue Devils*, 47.
11 Schultz, *85th Division in WWII*, 57–58; 85th Inf Div, Report of Operations, April 1944: The original division staging area was at Bagnoli, Italy.
12 85th Inf Div, Report of Operations, April 1944.
13 Schultz, *85th Division in WWII*, 58.
14 85th Inf Div, Report of Operations, April 1944.
15 Delany, *Blue Devils*, 46–47 and 53–54, The division arrived 5 March in relief of the British X Corps.
16 Ibid., 7–8.
17 Ibid., 39.
18 Ibid., 46.
19 Ibid., 60.
20 Fazendin, *756th at Cassino*, 156: Redle recollection.
21 Donley diary, 7 April 1944.
22 Redle, "B Company Added Recollections."
23 Donley diary, 9 April 1944; Fazendin, *756th at Cassino*, 156: Redle recollection; B Co/756th Morning Report, 8 April 1944; Redle recollections for Fazendin book.
24 Delany, *Blue Devils*, 57.
25 B Co/756th Morning Report, 8 April 1944.
26 Schultz, *85th Division in WWII*, 57–58; 85th Inf Div, Report of Operations, April 1944.
27 Schultz, *85th Division in WWII*, 33. The only mention of tank involvement was of a stint of desert training. It's unclear from the unit's official history if the 85th Division practiced any extensive tank/infantry tactics at all.

28 Donley diary, 11 April 1944.
29 Donley diary, 19 April 1944.
30 Delany, *Blue Devils*, 57.
31 B Co/756th Morning Report, 9 April 1944: This unit was not relived of attachment until 10 May 1944—one day before the attack.
32 Delany, *Blue Devils*, 57.
33 Fazendin, *756th at Cassino*, 186: Lewis recollection.
34 Donley diary, 9 April 1944.
35 756th Unit History, 1944, Change of Station list.
36 WWII American slang acronym for "Situation Normal All Fucked Up."
37 Fazendin, *756th at Cassino*, 186: Lewis recollection; 756th Unit History 1944, Change of Station list; Lewis draft for Fazendin; 85th Inf Div, Report of Operations, April 1944.
38 Redle recollections and rosters.
39 Obviously, they drove the ten miles. A jeep was the likely transport.
40 Fazendin, *756th at Cassino*, 157: Redle recollection; Redle recollections for Fazendin book: Redle recalls this, but the actual "official" move did not take place until 15 April.
41 Schultz, *85th Division in WWII*, 58.
42 Ibid., 58–59: These units were L Company and one platoon from M Company.
43 Ibid., 58–59; 85th Inf Div, Report of Operations, April 1944.
44 Ernest F. Fisher, Jr., *U.S Army in World War II, The Mediterranean Theater of Operations: Cassino to the Alps* (Washington, D.C.; Center of Military History, U.S. Army, 1993), 45.
45 85th Inf Div, *Minturno to the Apennines*, 6–7.
46 Bammer, "K Co/339th on Hill 66 and 69," 5; Fisher, *Cassino to the Alps*, 46.
47 Schultz, *85th Division in WWII*, 61and 66.
48 Ibid., 61.
49 "Duels: Allied and Axis Heavy Guns Roaring in Cassino Sector" *News-Journal* (Mansfield, Ohio), 6 April 1944, 1, 3.
50 Speculative, given the dangerous conditions.
51 756th "Report of Action Against Enemy" 1–30 April 1944.
52 Fazendin, *756th at Cassino*, 157: Redle recollection; Redle recollections for Fazendin book.
53 Redle, "B Company Added Recollections."
54 Ibid.
55 Fazendin, *756th at Cassino*, 157: Redle recollection; Redle recollections for Fazendin book.
56 85th Inf Div, Report of Operations, April 1944.
57 Ibid.
58 85th Inf Div, *Minturno to the Apennines*, 4.
59 85th Inf Div, Report of Operations, April 1944.
60 During 14 April through 30 April, B Co was situated at 805952 and 776964. 756th 1944 history, Change of Stations list; B Co/756th Morning Report, 14–15 April 1944; 85th Inf Div, Report of Operations, April 1944.
61 Redle recollections for Fazendin book; Fazendin, *756th at Cassino*, 157: Redle recollection. The official record shows the actual attachment to the 337th and 339th took place on 15 April.
62 B Co/756th Morning Report, 13 April 1944.
63 On alternate occasions, Redle told the author that Engfer and Harley were XOs during this time. The issue was not clarified before his passing in 2015. The Morning Reports and B Co Unit Journal record is clear, however: Engfer was the XO and Harley was present but not in charge of any platoon at this time.
64 B Co/756th Morning Report, 15 April 1944.
65 "Bert Gilden, 56, Novelist, Dead" *The Bridgeport Post* (Bridgeport, Connecticut), 5 April 1971, 1, 2; NARA Photo dated 15 August 1944.
66 1940 Census; "James Edmund Newman makes First Lieutenant" *The Knoxville News-Sentinel* (Knoxville, Tennessee), 24 May 1945, 26.
67 Boyle, Hal. "Alabama Engineer Found Way to Get Tanks Across the Rapido" *Nashville Banner* (Nashville, Tennessee), 3 February 1944, 12; "Lt W H Newman Helped Puncture Gustav Line" *The Knoxville Journal* (Knoxville, Tennessee), 14 March 1944, 8.

68 Redle told the author that officers were often assigned to B Company that he never saw until they were needed to replace a battlefield casualty. Perhaps this was the case with Gorman because Redle never mentioned him until he was brought in later.
69 85th Inf Div, Report of Operations, April 1944; 756th "Report of Operations Against Enemy," 1–30 April, 1944.
70 756th "Report of Operations Against Enemy," 1–30 April 1944.
71 85th Inf Div Operation Reports by Maj Gen Coulter, May 1944 (NARA, Army Records Group 407, Box 10662).
72 1st Bn/337th Infantry Regiment National Archives records ("History of Operations, April 1944") downloaded from: https://www.337thinfantry.net/unit.php
73 Ibid.; 85th Inf Div, *Minturno to the Apennines*, 6.
74 Schultz, *85th Division in WWII*, 61–63.
75 Ibid.
76 1st Bn/337th Inf Reg, History of Operations, April 1944; Halloran was killed: "Body of Lt Edward Halloran Comes Home to U.S. Today" *The Tablet* (Brooklyn, New York), 10 December 1949, 8.
77 Redle letter, 24 June 2002.
78 Schultz, *85th Division in WWII*, 65.
79 1st Bn/337th Inf Reg, History of Operations, April 1944.
80 Schultz, *85th Division in WWII*, 65; HQ staff, 85th Inf Div, *Minturno to the Apennines*, 6–7.
81 Schultz, *85th Division in WWII*, 60–63; 1st Bn/337th Inf Reg, History of Operations, April 1944.
82 85th Inf Div, *Minturno to the Apennines*, 8; Schultz, *85th Division in WWII*, 67.
83 Delany, *Blue Devils*, 58.
84 1st Bn/337th Inf Reg, History of Operations, April 1944.
85 Schultz, *85th Division in WWII*, 66–67; 85th Inf Div, *Minturno to the Apennines*, 8.
86 85th Inf Div, Report of Operations, April 1944.
87 Bammer, "K Co/339th on Hill 66 and 69," 6.
88 85th Inf Div, Report of Operations, April 1944.
89 756th "Report of Operations Against Enemy," 1–30 April 1944, 1.
90 Redle recollections for Fazendin book.
91 Fazendin, *756th at Cassino*, 157–58: Redle recollection; Redle recollections for Fazendin book.
92 756th Unit History, 1944, GO #29 34th Inf Div dated 21 April 1944; Other 756th Bronze Star recipients at this time were: T/Sgt Joseph M. Giles of Provo, Utah", Sgt Doyle K. Cody of Whitestown, Indiana, and T/Sgt Clifton Howell, of Los Angeles, Calif.
Ibid.
93 Fazendin, *756th at Cassino*, 116; 756th Unit History, 1944, II Corps HQ General Order #31 dated 27 April 1944. Both incidents are described in Chapter 5 of this book.
94 756th Unit History, 1944, 34th Inf Div General Order #29 dated 12 April 1944.
95 Fazendin, *756th at Cassino*, 156: Redle recollection.
96 Donley diary, 10, 12, 13, and 25 April 1944.
97 Ibid., 19 April 1944; Ranspach diary, 25 April 1944.
98 Donley diary, 18 April 1944. Donley describes what was probably a "Bangalore Torpedo"—not new to warfare but perhaps new in the eyes of the enlisted tankers.
99 Ibid., 17 April 1944.
100 756th "Report of Operations Against Enemy," 1–30 April 1944, 1; 337th Inf Regt Operations Reports, May 1944, (NARA Army Records Group 407, Box 10720).
101 756th "Report of Operations Against Enemy," 1–30 April 1944, 1.
102 85th Inf Div, Report of Operations, April 1944.
103 85th Inf Div, *Minturno to the Apennines*, 8.
104 Schultz, *85th Division in WWII*, 67.
105 Delany, *Blue Devils*, 58.
106 Ibid., 58–59.
107 Donley diary, 20–24 April 1944.
108 Ranspach diary, 25–26 April 1944.

109 Ibid., 26 April to 3 May, 1944.
110 Donley diary, 27 April 1944.
111 Ibid., 28 April 1944.
112 Ibid., 29 April 1944.
113 756th "Report of Operations Against Enemy," 1–30 April 1944, 1.
114 B Co/756th Morning Report, 30 April 1944.
115 756th "Report of Operations Against Enemy," 1–30 April 1944, 1; 756th Unit History, 1944, Change of Station list; 85th Inf Div, G-3 Daily Reports, (NARA, Army Records Group 407, Box 10675), No. 27, 080030 April to 080001 May 1944.
116 Donley diary, 30 April 1944.
117 Bammer, "K Co/339th on Hill 66 and 69," 4.
118 Schultz, *85th Division in WWII*, 70.
119 CMH, "Rome-Arno," 16–17.
120 Schultz, *85th Division in WWII*, 69.
121 Bammer, "K Co/339th on Hill 66 and 69," 6.
122 Ibid., 4.
123 Ibid., 3–4; Schultz, *85th Division in WWII*, 68.
124 US Army, *Fifth Army History, Part V*, 10.
125 Fisher, *Cassino to the Alps*, 45.
126 Donley diary, 2 May 1944.
127 Ibid., 1 May 1944.
128 Ibid., 3–7 May 1944.
129 Perdue phone conversations, 28 December 2001 and 7 January 2004; B Co/756th Morning Reports, 24 February, 8 and 20 March, 4 and 27 April 1944; US World War II Hospital Admission Card Files, 1942–1954.
130 B Co/756th Morning Report, 5 May 1944.
131 Presumably, this assignment was made by seniority and S/Sgt Haspel became a spare platoon sergeant.
132 Ibid., 5 and 8 May 1944. Nusz's promotion officially occurred 8 May. Harley's promotion was dated 27 April but not recorded until 5 May.
133 B Co/756th Morning Report, 8 May 1944.
134 Redle letter, 30 October 2000; Redle interview, 13 March 2004; Wilkinson letter, 19 December 2001; B Co/756th Morning Report, 8 May 1944.
135 Perdue phone conversation, 31 January 2004; Redle interview, 13 March 2004.
136 B Co/756th Morning Report, 9 May 1944.
137 B Company "Journal of Events from 8 May to 27 May."
138 Redle letter, 3 January 2001.
139 Ibid., 14 February 2003.
140 Sv Co/756th Morning Report, 20 May 1944.
141 B Company "Journal of Events from 8 May to 27 May": Position was at 791937.
142 Donley diary, 8 May 1944; HQ Co/756th Morning Report, 10 May 1944.
143 85th Inf Div, Report of Operations, May 1944 (NARA Army Records Group 407, Box 10675): 10 May 1944 map; Schultz, *85th Division in WWII*, 70–72; *History of the Second Chemical Mortar Battalion* (Ernest Muller, Salzburg, Austria, 1945), 24–25, downloaded from http://usacac.army.mil/organizations/cace/carl
144 756th Commander's Narrative for 11 May to 11 June 1944, 1–2.
145 Fazendin, *756th in Cassino*, 161 and 204; Lewis correspondence, letter from Gourley Jr (son) to Lewis, 2 March 1995.
146 756th Commander's Narrative for 11 May to 11 June 1944, 1–2; Fazendin, *756th in Cassino*, 188: Lewis recollection; Lewis draft for Fazendin.
147 756th Commander's Narrative for 11 May to 11 June 1944, 1–2.
148 II Corps, G-3 Journal, 30 April–31 May 1944, (NARA, Army Records Group 407, Box 2669), 11 May 1944 (1650 entry): Position given as 788938.
149 Donley diary, 9 May 1944.
150 HQ Co/756th Morning Report, 10 May 1944.
151 Bammer, "K Co/339th on Hill 66 and 69," 7.

152 756th Commander's Narrative for May 11 to June 11, 1944, 1–2.
153 B Company "Journal of Events from 8 May to 27 May."
154 85th Inf Div, G-3 Daily Reports, No. 36, 080009 May to 080010 May 1944.
155 Donley diary, 10 May 1944.
156 85th Inf Div, Report of Operations, May 1944.
157 Donley diary, 10 May 1944.
158 337th Inf Regt Operations Reports, May 1944.
159 85th Inf Div G-3 Daily Reports, May 1944, (NARA Army Records Group 407, Box 10675); G-3 Periodic Report No. 36, 080009 May to 080010 May 1944: 1st Bn/337th CP reported at 794936, 2nd Bn/337th CP reported at 797934.
160 85th Inf Div, Report of Operations, May 1944.
161 II Corps, G-3 Journal, 10 May 1944 (1445 entry).
162 Fazendin, *756th in Cassino*, 158: Redle recollection.
163 756th Commander's Narrative for 11 May to 11 June 1944, 2–3.
164 B Company "Journal of Events from 8 May to 27 May."
165 85th Inf Div G-3 Daily Reports, No. 37, 080010 May to 080011 May 1944.
166 Delany, *Blue Devils*, 62.
167 85th Inf Div G-2 Reports, May 1944, (NARA Army Records Group 407, Box 10669), 101500 to 111500 May 1944.
168 Donley diary, 10 May 1944.
169 Schultz, *85th Division in WWII*, 67.
170 Delany, *Blue Devils*, 62.
171 Fisher, *Cassino to the Alps*, 42–43; Delany, *Blue Devils*, 59.
172 85th Inf Div G-2 Reports, 101500 to 111500 May 1944: Activity heard at locations 759953, 759959, 762956.
173 Ibid.: Rounds came in from 759953 at 1100.
174 Ranspach Diary, 11 May 1944; II Corps, G-3 Journal, 11 May 1944 (0830 entry); 85th Inf Div, Report of Operations, May 1944.
175 Delany, *Blue Devils*, 59.
176 Ibid.; Schultz, *85th Division in WWII*, 71.
177 Delany, *Blue Devils*, 62.
178 Donley diary, 11 May 1944; Bammer, "K Co/339th on Hill 66 and 69," 6.
179 II Corps, G-3 Journal, 11 May 1944; 85th Inf Div maps.
180 US Army, *Fifth Army History, Part V*, 55.
181 Schultz, *85th Division in WWII*, 70–72; 85th Inf Div, Report of Operations, May 1944.
182 Bammer, "K Co/339th on Hill 66 and 69," 5.
183 85th Inf Div, Field Orders, May 1944, (NARA Army Records Group 407, Box 10690), 1200 11 May 1944 attack plans "Phase II and III."
184 Ibid.; US Army, *Fifth Army History, Part V*, 56.
185 85th Inf Div, Report of Operations, May 1944.
186 Bammer, "K Co/339th on Hill 66 and 69," 6.
187 85th Inf Div, Report of Operations, May 1944; Bammer, "K Co/339th on Hill 66 and 69," 6.
188 II Corps, G-3 Journal, 11 May 1944 (1825 entry).
189 Ibid., 1944 (1445 entry).
190 85th Inf Div, Field Orders, 3 May 1944 attack plans labeled "Phase I."
191 Ibid.; II Corps, G-3 Journal, 11 May 1944 (1604 entry).
192 85th Inf Div, Field Orders, 3 May 1944 attack plans labeled "Phase I."
193 Fisher, *Cassino to the Alps*, 42–43.
194 85th Inf Div G-2 Reports, 091500 to 101500 May 1944, IPW Report "Annex #1 to G-2 Report #31 IPW Report."
195 Ibid.
196 Ibid.: Cpl M. Hilsceer and Cpl A. Endruweit were the PWs (deserters picked up at 798964); G-2 Maps dated 10, 12, 13 May 1944; Bammer, "K Co/339th on Hill 66 and 69," 5 and 7.

197 85th Inf Div G-2 Reports, 101500 to 111500 May 1944.
198 II Corps, G-3 Journal, 11 May 1944 (2200 entry): 339th was positioned at Tremensuoli. 338th was positioned NW by a half-mile at 778964.
199 756th Commander's Narrative for 11 May to 11 June 1944, 1–2.
200 85th Inf Div, Field Orders, 3 May 1944 attack plans labeled "Phase I."
201 85th Inf Div G-2 Reports, 091500 to 101500 May 1944; This boggy area was a field east of Hill 37 (766973), near Solacciano.
202 Fisher, *Cassino to the Alps*, 45–46.
203 Jack Brown interview, 16 September 2006.
204 Redle interview, 15 September 2006.
205 Schultz, *85th Division in WWII*, 73.
206 Ibid.; 85th Inf Div, *Minturno to the Apennines*, 10; Fisher, *Cassino to the Alps*, 45–46.

Chapter 11

1 Schultz, *85th Division in WWII*, 73; Martin Blumenson, *Mark Clark: The Last of the Great World War II Commanders* (New York, New York: Cogdon & Weed, Inc., 1984), 202; CMH "Rome-Arno," 17–18; Fisher, *Cassino to the Alps*, 43: British 8th Army artillery guns numbered 1,060 and US Fifth Army guns numbered 600 for a total of 1,660.
2 85th Inf Div, *Minturno to the Apennines*, 10; Schultz, *85th Division in WWII*, 73–74; Captain John M. Davies, III. "The Operations of Company I, 3rd Battalion, 337th Infantry (85th Infantry Division) at Castellonorato, Italy 11–15 May 1944, During the Breaching of the Gustav Line. (Rome-Arno Campaign) (Personal Experience of a Platoon Leader)." The Infantry School, Fort Benning, Georgia, Advanced Infantry Officers Course 1947–48, 8–9.
3 Delany, *Blue Devils*, 62; Ranspach diary, 12 May 1944.
4 85th Inf Div, *Minturno to the Apennines*, 10; Schultz, *85th Division in WWII*, 73–74.
5 Fazendin, *756th at Cassino*, 158: Redle recollection.
6 Delany, *Blue Devils*, 62; Blumenson, *Mark Clark*, 202; CMH "Rome-Arno," 17–18.
7 Fisher, *Cassino to the Alps*, 43.
8 B Co/756th Unit Journal, "Journal of Events 8 May to 27 May."
9 Bammer, "K Co/339th on Hill 66 and 69," 8; Schultz, *85th Division in WWII*, 81; 85th Inf Div, *Minturno to the Apennines*, 10.
10 Schultz, *85th Division in WWII*, 73–75.
11 Fazendin, *756th at Cassino*, 158: Redle recollection.
12 II Corps, G-3 Journal, 11 May 1944 (2321, 2323, and 2328 entries).
13 Schultz, *85th Division in WWII*, 74; Delany, *Blue Devils*, 62; Bammer, "K Co/339th on Hill 66 and 69," 11–12; 85th Inf Div, *Minturno to the Apennines*, 10.
14 Schultz, *85th Division in WWII*, 81–82.
15 Fazendin, *756th at Cassino*, 158: Redle recollection; B Company Journal: "Company B, 756th Tank Battalion Commanding Officer's Narrative for Period 11 May to 10 June '44."
16 Delany, *Blue Devils*, 62.
17 Donley diary, 12 May 1944; II Corps, G-3 Journal, 11 May 1944 (2346 and 2350 entries) and 12 May 1944 (0005 entry).
18 II Corps, G-3 Journal, 11 May 1944 (2346 entry).
19 Schultz, *85th Division in WWII*, 85.
20 Ibid., 82.
21 Ibid., 74; 85th Inf Div, *Minturno to the Apennines*, 12.
22 Schultz, *85th Division in WWII*, 76, 81–82; Bammer, "K Co/339th on Hill 66 and 69," 8.
23 Schultz, *85th Division in WWII*, 81–82.
24 Bammer, "K Co/339th on Hill 66 and 69," 14.
25 Schultz, *85th Division in WWII*, 82.
26 Bammer, "K Co/339th on Hill 66 and 69," 13.

27 Schultz, *85th Division in WWII*, 82–83.
28 Bammer, "K Co/339th on Hill 66 and 69," 8; Schultz, *85th Division in WWII*, 82–83.
29 US Army, *Fifth Army History: Part V*, 64–65.
30 Schultz, *85th Division in WWII*, 74.
31 Bammer, "K Co/339th on Hill 66 and 69," 7.
32 Ibid., 7, 9–10.
33 Ibid.," 8; US Army, *Fifth Army History: Part V*, 64–65.
34 Schultz, *85th Division in WWII*, 81–82.
35 Ibid., 83; Bammer, "K Co/339th on Hill 66 and 69," 13; II Corps, G-3 Journal, 12 May 1944 (0035, 0045, and 0055 entries); The journal also reports K and L Cos on Hill 69, staging ahead of an attack on Hill 66.
36 Bammer, "K Co/339th on Hill 66 and 69," 12–13.
37 Schultz, *85th Division in WWII*, 82–83; Bammer, "K Co/339th on Hill 66 and 69," 13.
38 Schultz, *85th Division in WWII*, 83.
39 Bammer, "K Co/339th on Hill 66 and 69," 13–14.
40 B Co/756th Unit Journal "Commander's Narrative 11 May to 10 June 1944."
41 Ibid.
42 Schultz, *85th Division in WWII*, 83–85.
43 Ibid.; II Corps, G-3 Journal, 12 May 1944 (0300 and 0330 entries).
44 Schultz, *85th Division in WWII*, 83–85.
45 Bammer, "K Co/339th on Hill 66 and 69," 14; 85th Inf Div, *Minturno to the Apennines*, 14; "Silver Star Award to Lt Col Smith," *The Lincoln Star* (Lincoln, Nebraska), 28 October 1944, 5; Smith was later awarded the Silver Star for his leadership on 12 May 1944.
Ibid., 337th Inf Regt Operation Report, May 1944, downloaded from https://www.337thinfantry.net/index.php, accessed 11 June 2020.
46 Schultz, *85th Division in WWII*, 84–85.
47 Ibid., 337th Inf Regt Operation Report, May 1944, downloaded from https://www.337thinfantry.net/index.php, accessed 11 June 2020.
48 B Co/756th Unit Journal "Commander's Narrative 11 May to 10 June 1944."
49 Ibid.; II Corps, G-3 Journal, 12 May 1944 (0620 entry): Redle's patrol was likely described in this entry: "Col, 310 Engr: A recon patrol (of about 12 men) went fwd to stream bed in rear of Hill 69 where they were taken under heavy flat trajectory fire (shelling) from M SCURI. Trail that far OK for Tanks." It's interesting to note the engineer CO's conclusions regarding the tank trail are more positive then Redle's observations.
50 Bammer, "K Co/339th on Hill 66 and 69," 15–16; Schultz, *85th Division in WWII*, 83.
51 US Army, *Fifth Army History: Part V*, 65; 85th Inf Div, *Minturno to the Apennines*, 15; II Corps, G-3 Journal, 12 May 1944 (0717, 0737, 0740, and 1145 (msg time 0820) entries).
52 Schultz, *85th Division in WWII*, 84–85.
53 Ibid., 85; II Corps, G-3 Journal, 12 May 1944 (0408 entry): The 1st Bn/337 was alerted to move and join 3rd Bn/339th at 0408.
54 Schultz, *85th Division in WWII*, 75–77; US Army, *Fifth Army History: Part V*, 66.
55 US Army, *Fifth Army History: Part V*, 66; Schultz, *85th Division in WWII*, 77; Fisher, *Cassino to the Alps*, 54–56.
56 85th Inf Div, Report of Operations, May 1944.
57 Schultz, *85th Division in WWII*, 74–75.
58 Ibid., 74, 86; US Army, *Fifth Army History: Part V*, 62–64.
59 Schultz, *85th Division in WWII*, 86; 85th Inf Div, *Minturno to the Apennines*, 12–13; Fisher, *Cassino to the Alps*, 55.
60 Bammer, "K Co/339th on Hill 66 and 69," 18.
61 Ibid., 15.
62 Schultz, *85th Division in WWII*, 55–56.
63 Ibid., 85–86; 85th Inf Div, *Minturno to the Apennines*, 14–15.
64 II Corps, G-3 Journal, 12 May 1944 (1210 entry): The 337th S-3 was told all flamethrowers were on the line with the 1st Bn/339th.
65 II Corps, G-3 Journal, 12 May 1944 (1105 entry) (msg timed at 1000): "Tk Comdr to report to CO 339 to arrange to give all Tk Support possible."

66 B Co/756th Unit Journal "Commander's Narrative 11 May to 10 June 1944."
67 Ibid., 2–3; Fazendin, *756th at Cassino*, 158: Redle recollection.
68 Presumed to be Lt Harley's location.
69 B Co/756th Unit Journal "Commander's Narrative 11 May to 10 June 1944"; The time of departure is provided by Rogers, 756th Commander's Narrative for 11 May to 11 June 1944, 2–3.
70 B Co/756th Unit Journal "Commander's Narrative 11 May to 10 June 1944."
71 B Co/756th Unit Journal "Journal of Events 8 May to 27 May."
72 2nd Lt William Newman, "Narrative of Actions of Second Platoon of Company B, 756th Tank Battalion for Period 11 May to 10 June"; B Co/756th Unit Journal "Commander's Narrative 11 May to 10 June 1944."
73 B Co/756th Unit Journal "Commander's Narrative 11 May to 10 June 1944"; Fazendin, *756th at Cassino*, 159: Redle recollection.
74 B Co/756th Unit Journal "Commander's Narrative 11 May to 10 June 1944": Likely location is based upon the maps and circumstances; B Co/756th Unit Journal "Journal of Events 8 May to 27 May."
75 US Army, *Fifth Army History: Part V*, 64–65; 337th Inf Regt Operation Report, May 1944.
76 Exchange presumed according to standard procedure.
77 Bammer, "K Co/339th on Hill 66 and 69," 16–17; US Army, *Fifth Army History: Part V*, 64–65.
78 Bammer, "K Co/339th on Hill 66 and 69," 16–17.
79 B Co/756th Unit Journal "Commander's Narrative 11 May to 10 June 1944"; B Co/756th Unit Journal, "Actions of 2nd Platoon, 11 May to 10 June."
80 B Co/756th Unit Journal "Commander's Narrative 11 May to 10 June 1944."
81 Redle letter, 28 June 2009: Redle described this bracketing system as follows: "The Germans used a box in adjusting artillery fire. I think it was like this: 1) Give coordinates to target. Fire one. 2) Adjust distance by increasing range. If the adjuster thought the round was 200 meters long, he adjusted 400 meters shorter. He then made an adjustment to the left or right in the same manner. After he had determined the box with the target in the middle, he'd divide them in half and fire for effect."
82 B Co/756th Unit Journal "Commander's Narrative 11 May to 10 June 1944"; Fazendin, *756th at Cassino*, 159–61: Redle recollection.
83 Fazendin, *756th at Cassino*, 161: Redle recollection.
84 756th Commander's Narrative for 11 May to 11 June 1944, 3.
85 B Co/756th Unit Journal "Journal of Events 8 May to 27 May."
86 Fazendin, *756th at Cassino*, 161: Redle recollection.
87 Ibid., 159–61: Redle recollection; B Co/756th Unit Journal, "Actions of 2nd Platoon, 11 May to 10 June."
88 756th Commander's Narrative for 11 May to 11 June 1944, 3; Fazendin, *756th at Cassino*, 159–61: Redle recollection; Bammer, "K Co/339th on Hill 66 and 69," 16–17.
89 B Co/756th Unit Journal "Commander's Narrative 11 May to 10 June 1944."
90 756th Commander's Narrative for 11 May to 11 June 1944, 3; Schultz, *85th Division in WWII*, 85–86: For their bravery in taking and holding Hill 66 between 12–16 May 1944, C Co/337th, received the Distinguished Unit Citation by the War Department (General Orders No. 81, dated 14 October 1944).
91 Redle letter, 7 February 2001.
92 The driver's name is unknown. T/4 Arne Strand rotated home a week earlier according to the B Co Morning Reports; II Corps, G-3 Journal, 12 May 1944, 1455 message: "Ex O 756 Tk Bn says En SP guns attacking our Tks Vic HILL 66 and 69."
93 Fazendin, *756th at Cassino*, 161: Redle recollection.
94 Rottman, *WWII Infantry Fire Support Tactics*, 23.
95 B Co/756 Morning Report, 20 May 1944, "Record of Events": Redle's column arrived at the CP around 1700.
96 II Corps, G-3 Journal, 12 May 1944, 1800 msg.
97 Schultz, *85th Division in WWII*, 86; Fisher, *Cassino to the Alps*, 54–55; US Army, *Fifth Army History: Part V*, 62–64.
98 Fisher, *Cassino to the Alps*, 55.
99 US Army, *Fifth Army History: Part V*, 62–64; II Corps, G-3 Journal, 12 May 1944 (1655 entry).
100 756th Commander's Narrative for 11 May to 11 June 1944, 2–3; 760th Tk Bn "Operations in Italy–May 1944, Section II, Attack on Santa Maria": C Co/760th lost eight tanks in this incident—most to mines. Cassino veterans 1st Lt Eugene E. Gleissner and S/Sgt Pickney D. Upchurch were wounded in this action.

101 Fazendin, *756th at Cassino*, 161: Redle recollection: These were likely C Co/760th tanks that struck mines and were subsequently destroyed by the Germans to prevent recovery.
102 Ibid.; 756th Commander's Narrative for 11 May to 11 June 1944, 2–3.
103 US Army, *Fifth Army History: Part V*, 64–65.
104 Bammer, "K Co/339th on Hill 66 and 69," 16–17; Schultz, *85th Division in WWII*, 75–79; 85th Inf Div, *Minturno to the Apennines*, 12–13.
105 US Army, *Fifth Army History: Part V*, 66; Schultz, *85th Division in WWII*, 77–81; II Corps, G-3 Journal, 12 May 1944 (0210 and 0230 entries).
106 Schultz, *85th Division in WWII*, 77–81, 86; Bammer, "K Co/339th on Hill 66 and 69," 16–17; 85th Inf Div, *Minturno to the Apennines*, 13: G Co/339th received the Distinguished Unit Citation (War Department General Orders No. 81, dated 14 October 1944) for this action. The 1st platoon leader of G Company, 1st Lt Robert T. Waugh, was awarded the Medal of Honor for singlehandedly taking out several German pillboxes while taking the Hill. Sadly, the 25-year-old from Augusta, Maine, was killed in action several days later. "Lieutenant Who Broke Gustav Line Single-Handed Honored" *The Berkshire Eagle* (Pittsfield, Massachusetts), 10 October 1944, 2.
107 756th Commander's Narrative for 11 May to 11 June 1944, 2–3.
108 US Army, *Fifth Army History: Part V*, 64–65.
109 85th Inf Div, Report of Operations, May 1944; 85th Inf Div, *Minturno to the Apennines*, 14–15.
110 756th Commander's Narrative for 11 May to 11 June 1944, 3–4.
111 Fisher, *Cassino to the Alps*, 67.
112 US Army, *Fifth Army History: Part V*, 64.
113 756th Commander's Narrative for 11 May to 11 June 1944, 3–4.
114 Ibid.; II Corps, G-3 Journal, 12 May 1944 (1525 entry): Infantry mistakenly reported six tanks had crossed and all bogged down.
115 756th Commander's Narrative for 11 May to 11 June 1944, 3–4.
116 B Co/756th Unit Journal, "Actions of 2nd Platoon, 11 May to 10 June."
117 David L. Grate enlistment record.
118 B Co/756th Morning Report, 15 May 1944.
119 B Co/756th Unit Journal, "Actions of 2nd Platoon, 11 May to 10 June."
120 Ibid.
121 Ibid.
122 756th Commander's Narrative for 11 May to 11 June 1944, 4.
123 Ibid.
124 Ibid.
125 B Co/756th Unit Journal "Commander's Narrative 11 May to 10 June 1944."
126 Ibid.; B Co/756th Unit Journal, "Actions of 2nd Platoon, 11 May to 10 June."
127 B Co/756th Unit Journal "Journal of Events 8 May to 27 May."
128 756th Commander's Narrative for 11 May to 11 June 1944, 4.
129 Ibid.; II Corps, G-3 Journal, 13 May 1944 (0300 entry).
130 Fazendin, *756th at Cassino*, 161: Redle recollection; B Co/756th Unit Journal, "Actions of 2nd Platoon, 11 May to 10 June"; II Corps, G-3 Journal, 13 May 1944 (1900 entry): The location of the stuck tanks was 766967; 14 May 1944 (0200 entry): Three tank retrievers reported operating in area 765970.
131 Fisher, *Cassino to the Alps*, 67.
132 US Army, *Fifth Army History: Part V*, 64; II Corps, G-3 Journal, 13 May 1944 (0320, 0327, 0615, and 0630 entries): Clearly the Caves d'Argilla hadn't yet been captured according to the II Corps G-3 Journal.
133 85th Inf Div, *Minturno to the Apennines*, 15; Schultz, *85th Division in WWII*, 85–86; US Army, *Fifth Army History: Part V*, 64–65; II Corps, G-3 Journal, 13 May 1944 (0600, 0710, and 0720 entries).
134 Delany, *Blue Devils*, 67.
135 Ibid.; US Army, *Fifth Army History: Part V*, 62–64; Fisher, *Cassino to the Alps*, 67; Böhmler, *Monte Cassino: A German View*, 258.
136 Delany, *Blue Devils*, 62–63.
137 Fisher, *Cassino to the Alps*, 65–66.

138 CMH "Rome-Arno," 17–18; Fisher, *Cassino to the Alps*, 56, 62.
139 CMH "Rome-Arno," 17–18.
140 Fisher, *Cassino to the Alps*, 65.
141 Ibid.
142 Ibid.
143 Ibid.
144 Ibid.
145 Schultz, *85th Division in WWII*, 86–87.
146 US Army, *Fifth Army History: Part V*, 67; Fisher, *Cassino to the Alps*, 71.
147 US Army, *Fifth Army History: Part V*, 66.
148 Schultz, *85th Division in WWII*, 77.
149 Fisher, *Cassino to the Alps*, 74; 85th Inf Div, Report of Operations, May 1944.
150 Schultz, *85th Division in WWII*, 48.
151 Fisher, *Cassino to the Alps*, 74–75.
152 756th Commander's Narrative for 11 May to 11 June 1944, 4–7; Fazendin, *756th at Cassino*, 162: Redle recollection: Redle called this form of engineer work "rip-rapping."
153 C Co/756th Morning Reports, 20 May 1944, "Record of Events."
154 Fazendin, *756th at Cassino*, 162: Redle recollection; 756th Commander's Narrative for 11 May to 11 June 1944, 4.
155 Fazendin, *756th at Cassino*, 162: Redle recollection: Redle doesn't specify how Arnold arrived, but a jeep was the most likely method.
156 B Co/756th Unit Journal "Commander's Narrative 11 May to 10 June 1944."
157 Ibid.; 756th Commander's Narrative for 11 May to 11 June 1944, 4.
158 756th Commander's Narrative for 11 May to 11 June 1944, 4–5.
159 B Co/756th Unit Journal "Journal of Events 8 May to 27 May." The hamlet is also listed as "La Grata" and often called "Grotto" in the records.
160 Fazendin, *756th at Cassino*, 162: Redle recollection; B Co/756th Unit Journal "Commander's Narrative 11 May to 10 June 1944."
161 Böhmler, *Monte Cassino: A German View*, 258.
162 Fazendin, *756th at Cassino*, 162: Redle recollection.
163 This may have been the Caves d'Argilla (clay quarries) area.
164 B Co/756th Unit Journal "Commander's Narrative 11 May to 10 June 1944."
165 B Co/756th Unit Journal "Journal of Events 8 May to 27 May"; B Co/756th Morning Report, 20 May 1944; B Co/756th Unit Journal, "Actions of 2nd Platoon, 11 May to 10 June": Newman's 2nd Platoon was down to only three tanks and didn't fire a single shot during this mission—presumably because they brought up the rear and helped provide flank protection; Fazendin, *756th at Cassino*, 162: Redle recollection.

Chapter 12

1 756th Commander's Narrative for 11 May to 11 June 1944, 4–5.
2 Fazendin, *756th at Cassino*, 189: Lewis recollection.
3 756th Commander's Narrative for 11 May to 11 June 1944, 5.
4 C Co/756th Morning Report, 20 May 1944, "Record of Events": The three tanks crossed the ditch east of Solacciano at 1330, but the location is misidentified as the Capo d'Acqua. C Company tanks never crossed the Capo d'Acqua west of Solacciano ahead of A Company.
5 II Corps, G-3 Journal, 13 May 1944 (1930 entry): Gives the location of "stream N of Solacciano" crossing at 766974, but these are the coordinates for Solacciano.
6 756th Commander's Narrative for 11 May to 11 June 1944, 6; HQ Co/756th Morning Report, 20 May 1944, "Record of Events."
7 756th Commander's Narrative for 11 May to 11 June 1944, 5.
8 HQ Co/756th Morning Report, 20 May 1944, "Record of Events."

9 756th Commander's Narrative for 11 May to 11 June 1944, 5; George Bernhard, "Life in the Service," undated (10 pages) (Transcribed diary entries.) George Bernhard was a tank crewman in A Co/756th Tank Battalion. (Copies included in French Lewis's personal documents.)
10 This roadway crossed the Capo d'Acqua. Why it wasn't used by tanks to cross the creek is a mystery. A likely reason is that the Germans blew the bridge at this location. The road leading down from Spigno behind Hill 108 seemed to be more important to them.
11 Fisher, *Cassino to the Alps*, 74–75; US Army, *Fifth Army History: Part V*, 68.
12 Fazendin, *756th at Cassino*, 189: Lewis recollection.
13 756th Commander's Narrative for 11 May to 11 June 1944, 5.
14 Bernhard "Life in the Service"; Fazendin, *756th at Cassino*, 189: Lewis recollection: The 1st Platoon crossed first, then Capt Lewis's tank, followed by the 2nd Platoon.; Fisher, *Cassino to the Alps*, 75; A Co/756th Morning Report, 20 May 1944 "Record of Events": This crossing took place at 1700; 756th Commander's Narrative for 11 May to 11 June 1944, 5.
15 Fazendin, *756th at Cassino*, 190: Lewis, recollection; Bernhard "Life in the Service"; These AT guns weighed about 500 pounds, sat only 2½ feet high and had a 5'8" foot barrel. They fired a 28mm round that was "squeezed" down the barrel to achieve high velocities—leaving the end only 20mm in size and traveling up to 4,500 feet a second. These guns were more than capable of knocking out an M4.
16 756th Commander's Narrative for 11 May to 11 June 1944, 5.
17 B Co/756th Unit Journal, "Actions of 2nd Platoon, 11 May to 10 June."
18 Fazendin, *756th at Cassino*, 163: Redle recollection; B Co/756th Morning Report, 20 May 1944; B Co/756th Unit Journal "Commander's Narrative 11 May to 10 June 1944."
19 Fisher, *Cassino to the Alps*, 75; US Army, *Fifth Army History: Part V*, 68.
20 756th Commander's Narrative for 11 May to 11 June 1944, 5–6.
21 This was likely an open back Marder II or Marder III SP AT gun.
22 Bernhard "Life in the Service."
23 Ibid.
24 Ibid.; Fazendin, *756th at Cassino*, 190: Lewis recollection.
25 Fisher, *Cassino to the Alps*, 75.
26 85th Inf Div, *Minturno to the Apennines*, 15–16; 337th Inf Regt Operation Report, May 1944.
27 US Army, *Fifth Army History: Part V*, 68.
28 Bernhard "Life in the Service"; Bernhard misidentifies Hunter as "Hammer" but then correctly reports Lts Hill and Hammer as "still working with the doughboys" later that day. It is not recorded which arm Hunter was wounded or how he was transported to the creek.
29 Fisher, *Cassino to the Alps*, 75; 85th Inf Div, Report of Operations, May 1944.
30 Davies, "Operations of Co I, 337th Inf Regt, Castellonorato, Italy 11–15 May 1944," 12.
31 US Army, *Fifth Army History: Part V*, 68.
32 756th Commander's Narrative for 11 May to 11 June 1944, 6–7; II Corps, G-3 Journal, 13 May 1944 (1545 entry): "Both F & E Cos in CAVE d'ARGILLA area not consolidated as yet," (and 1716 entry): "E & F Cos taken CAVE d'ARGILLA & have consolidated with 339 at coordination point."
33 756th Commander's Narrative for 11 May to 11 June 1944, 5–6; B Co/756th Unit Journal, "Actions of 2nd Platoon, 11 May to 10 June."
34 Fazendin, *756th at Cassino*, 163: Redle recollection.
35 Ibid., 190–91: Lewis recollection.
36 Radio communications is presumed. Rogers does not record exactly how this exchange took place. It seems doubtful that phone lines had been run yet or a foot messenger was used.
37 756th Commander's Narrative for 11 May to 11 June 1944, 5–6.
38 Ibid., 6; B Co/756th Unit Journal "Journal of Events 8 May to 27 May"; B Co/756th Unit Journal, "Actions of 2nd Platoon, 11 May to 10 June."
39 B Co/756th Unit Journal "Commander's Narrative 11 May to 10 June 1944."
40 Fazendin, *756th at Cassino*, 190–91: Lewis recollection.
41 B Co/756th Unit Journal "Commander's Narrative 11 May to 10 June 1944."
42 Fazendin, *756th at Cassino*, 163 and 191.
43 Bernhard "Life in the Service."

44 B Co/756th Unit Journal "Commander's Narrative 11 May to 10 June 1944."
45 Fazendin, *756th at Cassino*, 163 and 191; Bernhard "Life in the Service."
46 756th Commander's Narrative for 11 May to 11 June 1944, 6.
47 Ibid., 6; Fazendin, *756th at Cassino*, 191: Lewis recollection; Bernhard "Life in the Service."
48 Fazendin, *756th at Cassino*, 163: Redle recollection.
49 Ibid., 191: Lewis recollection; 756th Unit History 1944; Bernhard "Life in the Service."
50 US Army, *Fifth Army History: Part V*, 68.
51 756th Commander's Narrative for 11 May to 11 June 1944, 6.
52 Michael Green, *M4 Sherman: Combat and Development History of the Sherman Tank and All Sherman Variants* (Osceola, Wisconsin: Motorbooks International Publishers and Wholesalers., 1993), 79: These were likely M61 AP-HE rounds that did not see widespread use until later in the war.
53 Fazendin, *756th at Cassino*, 163: Redle recollection: This position was later used by Battalion Maintenance whose members later told Redle the caves were filled with dead Germans. This incident is very similar to the one Redle described the day before and could be one and the same. Redle, however, described the events as taking place from different hills.
54 B Co/756th Unit Journal "Journal of Events 8 May to 27 May."
55 US Army, *Fifth Army History: Part V*, 68; Davies, "Operations of Co I, 337th Inf Regt, Castellonorato, Italy 11–15 May 1944," 12; 337th Inf Regt Operation Report, May 1944.
56 Schultz, *85th Division in WWII*, 87.
57 85th Inf Div, *Minturno to the Apennines*, 17–18.
58 Ibid., 16; 85th Inf Div, Report of Operations, May 1944.
59 Delany, *Blue Devils*, 78–79.
60 US Army, *Fifth Army History: Part V*, 69.
61 Fisher, *Cassino to the Alps*, 73.
62 Schultz, *85th Division in WWII*, 87.
63 Ibid., 87–88.
64 US Army, *Fifth Army History: Part V*, 67.
65 Fisher, *Cassino to the Alps*, 73–74.
66 US Army, *Fifth Army History: Part V*, 69; Schultz, *85th Division in WWII*, 88–89.
67 Fisher, *Cassino to the Alps*, 74.
68 756th Commander's Narrative for 11 May to 11 June 1944, 6–7; Davies, "Operations of Co I, 337th Inf Regt, Castellonorato, Italy 11–15 May 1944," 12.
69 756th Commander's Narrative for 11 May to 11 June 1944, 6–7.
70 Davies, "Operations of Co I, 337th Inf Regt, Castellonorato, Italy 11–15 May 1944," 12.
71 Ibid.
72 US Army, *Fifth Army History: Part V*, 68.
73 B Co/756th Unit Journal "Commander's Narrative 11 May to 10 June 1944."
74 Fazendin, *756th at Cassino*, 163–64: Redle recollection.
75 B Co/756th Unit Journal "Commander's Narrative 11 May to 10 June 1944."
76 US Army, *Fifth Army History: Part V*, 68.
77 Davies, "Operations of Co I, 337th Inf Regt, Castellonorato, Italy 11–15 May 1944," 13.
78 Ibid., 17.
79 Ibid., 13–14; Jones chapter notes, email 13 February 2021.
80 337th Inf Regt Operation Report, May 1944; Davies, "Operations of Co I, 337th Inf Regt, Castellonorato, Italy 11–15 May 1944," 13–14: The author was not able to pin down exactly which B Company platoon participated in this action, but it was likely Lt Gorman's 3rd Platoon since Davies records "five" tanks were involved. Both the 1st and 2nd Platoons were depleted from earlier action. Davies goes on to say the tanks pursued the Germans 500 yards down a cart path before one threw a track.
81 B Co/756th Unit Journal "Commander's Narrative 11 May to 10 June 1944."
82 Ibid.
83 Ibid.
84 756th Commander's Narrative for 11 May to 11 June 1944, 6.
85 HQ Co/756th Morning Report, 20 May 1944, "Record of Events."

86 The number of tanks is an estimate. According to Lt Newman, his 2nd Platoon was short two tanks and Sgt Grate's 1st Platoon tank, hit by artillery on 13 May, was not likely recovered nor replaced by this time.
87 Fazendin, *756th at Cassino*, 164: Redle recollection; 756th Commander's Narrative for 11 May to 11 June 1944, 6; B Co/756th Unit Journal "Commander's Narrative 11 May to 10 June 1944."
88 756th Commander's Narrative for 11 May to 11 June 1944, 6; B Co/756th Unit Journal "Commander's Narrative 11 May to 10 June 1944."
89 Ibid., Fazendin, *756th at Cassino*, 164: Redle recollection.
90 Redle letter to Harry Yeide, 30 January 2008.
91 756th Commander's Narrative for 11 May to 11 June 1944, 6.
92 B Co/756th Morning Report, 20 May 1944, "Record of Events."
93 B Co/756th Unit Journal, "Actions of 2nd Platoon, 11 May to 10 June"; Fazendin, *756th at Cassino*, 164: Redle recollection; The "pass" Newman describes was likely the 150 yards or so of ground between Castellonorato Hill and Monte Penitro. Redle recalls the Germans wore white covered helmets during this battle—holdovers, perhaps, from winter fighting.
94 756th Commander's Narrative for 11 May to 11 June 1944, 6.
95 A Co and C Co/756th Morning Reports, 20 May 1944, "Record of Events"; Bernhard "Life in the Service."
96 US Army, *Fifth Army History: Part V*, 68.
97 85th Inf Div, Report of Operations, May 1944.
98 85th Inf Div, *Minturno to the Apennines*, 17–18; Schultz, *85th Division in WWII*, 89.
99 85th Inf Div, Report of Operations, May 1944.
100 756th Commander's Narrative for 11 May to 11 June 1944, 6.
101 Schultz, *85th Division in WWII*, 89; Davies, "Operations of Co I, 337th Inf Regt, Castellonorato, Italy 11–15 May 1944," 14–15; 756th Commander's Narrative for 11 May to 11 June 1944, 6: Rogers records six 50mm AT guns and two 76mm AT guns captured during the day, but does not say by whom or from where.
102 Schultz, *85th Division in WWII*, 89; 85th Inf Div, *Minturno to the Apennines*, 17–18.
103 756th Commander's Narrative for 11 May to 11 June 1944, 7; Fazendin, *756th at Cassino*, 192: Lewis recollection.
104 IDPF Kreitlow; Kreitlow was an unmarried farmer from Dows, Iowa, born in 1910.
105 Fazendin, *756th at Cassino*, 164: Redle recollection; B Co/756th Unit Journal "Journal of Events 8 May to 27 May"; 756th Commander's Narrative for 11 May to 11 June 1944, 7; Redle letters 12 January 2007, 1 June 2001, and 28 June 2009; Redle measured the hole in Cogdill's tank later and found it was 5" in diameter; US World War II Hospital Admission Card Files, 1942–1954.
106 Fazendin, *756th at Cassino*, 164: Redle recollection.
107 B Co/756th Unit Journal "Journal of Events 8 May to 27 May"; Redle letter 28 June 2009; Gorman draft card, United States Army WWII Draft Cards 1940–1947.
108 Redle later recommended Wright for the Bronze Star for this action. This was awarded 8 June 1944 (85th GO summary complied by Don Jones, historian of 337th Inf Regt, https://www.337thinfantry.net/index.php, accessed 11 June 2020.
109 Anderson phone conversation, 20 June 2009; Perdue phone conversation, 28 December 2001.
110 Redle letter, 12 January 2007.
111 B Co/756th Morning Reports, 18 and 19 May 1944: Brown did not return to B Company, but survived the war. "Raymond T. Brown" Obit, *The Courier-Journal* (Louisville, Kentucky), 7 March 1977, 5; "24 Kentuckians are Wounded," *The Park City Daily News* (Bowling Green, Kentucky), 29 June 1944, 7.
112 756th Commander's Narrative for 11 May to 11 June 1944, 7; A Co, B Co, and Co/756th Morning Reports, 20 May 1944, "Record of Events"; B Co/756th Unit Journal, "Actions of 2nd Platoon, 11 May to 10 June."
113 B Co/756th Unit Journal "Journal of Events 8 May to 27 May."
114 Ranspach diary, 15 May 1944.
115 Clyde Cogdill enlistment record; "Eight Nebraskans Hurt in Action," *The Columbus Telegram* (Columbus, Nebraska), 29 June 1944, 1; "Final Day Sees 49 of 52 Accepted, Included Two from Here," *The Missoulian* (Missoula, Montana), 22 March 1941, 1; Cogdill lived in Missoula, Montana, when inducted in March 1941.
116 Wilkinson letter, 31 May 2005.
117 Schultz, *85th Division in WWII*, 89.

118 Davies, "Operations of Co I, 337th Inf Regt, Castellonorato, Italy 11–15 May 1944," 14–15; 337th Inf Regt Operation Report, May 1944.
119 756th Commander's Narrative for 11 May to 11 June 1944, 7.
120 Ibid.
121 85th Inf Div, *Minturno to the Apennines*, 17–18.
122 US Army, *Fifth Army History: Part V*, 68; 85th Inf Div, Report of Operations, May 1944.
123 Redle interview, 13 March 2004.
124 756th Commander's Narrative for 11 May to 11 June 1944, 7.
125 Fazendin, *756th at Cassino*, 192.

Chapter 13

1 756th Commander's Narrative for 11 May to 11 June 1944, 7.
2 The conclusions about this incident are an interpretation of the circumstances and events by the author. Lewis recalled the difficulty in which Rogers had been placed, and Redle reported Coulter threatened to relieve Rogers if this mission wasn't carried out. In his May Commander's Narrative, Rogers listed misgivings over the Castellonorato recon mission and displeasure over unnecessarily losing tanks during the earlier ill-fated recon mission to San Croce. The first mission to San Croce was carried out within the hour. The second mission to Castellonorato was delayed nearly six hours by Rogers requesting clarification and making preparations. The author concludes Rogers artfully "stalled" to prevent needless losses—not an uncommon practice by junior officers dealing with senior officers making unreasonable requests. This conduct, of course, was never admitted.
3 337th Inf Regt Operation Report, May 1944.
4 Shultz, *85th Division in WWII*, 90; 85th Inf Div, *Minturno to the Apennines*, 16.
5 756th Commander's Narrative for 11 May to 11 June 1944, 8; A Co, B Co, and C Co/756th Morning Reports, 20 May 1944, "Record of Events."
6 756th Commander's Narrative for 11 May to 11 June 1944, 8.
7 Ibid.; B Co/756th Unit Journal, "Actions of 2nd Platoon, 11 May to 10 June": Newman reports his 2nd Platoon consisted of only two tanks at this time: his and Sgt Gilkerson's.
8 Fazendin, *756th at Cassino*, 164–65: Redle recollection; 756th Commander's Narrative for 11 May to 11 June 1944, 8; B Company Unit Journal, 16 May 1944; B Co/756th Unit Journal "Commander's Narrative 11 May to 10 June 1944."
9 337th Inf Regt Operation Report, May 1944.
10 85th Inf Div, *Minturno to the Apennines*, 17–18; Schultz, *85th Division in WWII*, 90; 85th Inf Div, Report of Operations, May 1944.
11 756th Commander's Narrative for 11 May to 11 June 1944, 8.
12 Ibid, Sketch No. 2: Identified as "Point M" on this map; B Company Unit Journal, 16 May 1944.
13 B Co/756th Unit Journal, "Actions of 2nd Platoon, 11 May to 10 June."
14 Ibid.
15 756th Commander's Narrative for 11 May to 11 June 1944, 8.
16 Schultz, *85th Division in WWII*, 90.
17 B Co/756th Morning Report 19 May 1944: It is not known exactly how Harris broke his hand.
18 B Co/756th Unit Journal, "Actions of 2nd Platoon, 11 May to 10 June."
19 B Co/756th Morning Report, 15 May 1944; Redle letter 28 June 2009. Redle remembers Harley as a fine and courageous officer but his departure was caused, in part, by a personality conflict with S/Sgt Oric Johannesen. Redle didn't recall the particulars—only that neither man seemed to like the other.
20 B Co/756th Unit Journal, "Actions of 2nd Platoon, 11 May to 10 June."
21 B Company Unit Journal, 16 May 1944.
22 US Army, *Fifth Army History: Part V*, 70.
23 337th Inf Regt Operation Report, May 1944.
24 756th Commander's Narrative for 11 May to 11 June 1944, 8.
25 Ibid., 8–9; Bridge location identified as "Point P" on map.
26 Ibid., 7–9.

27 Ibid. Identified as "Point I" on Rogers's map.
28 Ibid., 9.
29 Ibid.
30 B Company Unit Journal, 16 May 1944; B Co/756th Unit Journal, "Actions of 2nd Platoon, 11 May to 10 June"; B Company Journal; B Co/756th Unit Journal "Commander's Narrative 11 May to 10 June 1944."
31 Fazendin, *756th at Cassino*, 165: Redle recollection.
32 756th Commander's Narrative for 11 May to 11 June 1944, 9; B Co/756th Unit Journal "Commander's Narrative 11 May to 10 June 1944"; Fazendin, *756th at Cassino*, 165: Redle recollection; B Company Unit Journal, 16 May 1944; A Co, B Co, and HQ Co/756th Morning Reports, 20 May 1944, "Records of Events."
33 B Co/756th Unit Journal, "Actions of 2nd Platoon, 11 May to 10 June."
34 337th Inf Regt Operation Report, May 1944.
35 US Army, *Fifth Army History: Part V*, 70.
36 337th Inf Regt Operation Report, May 1944.
37 US Army, *Fifth Army History: Part V*, 70; Fisher, *Cassino to the Alps*, 84–85.
38 756th Commander's Narrative for 11 May to 11 June 1944, 9.
39 Ibid.
40 B Company Unit Journal, 17 May 1944; B Co/756th Unit Journal, "Actions of 2nd Platoon, 11 May to 10 June."
41 US Army, *Fifth Army History: Part V*, 70.
42 Bernhard "Life in the Service"; 756th Unit History, 1944: This driver was T/4 Fabio Pinada.
43 756th Commander's Narrative for 11 May to 11 June 1944, 9.
44 85th Inf Div, *Minturno to the Apennines*, 19–20.
45 337th Inf Regt Operation Report, May 1944.
46 US Army, *Fifth Army History: Part V*, 70; 85th Inf Div, *Minturno to the Apennines*, 20–22; Schultz, *85th Division in WWII*, 90–91.
47 Schultz, *85th Division in WWII*, 77, 90–91; US Army, *Fifth Army History: Part V*, 70; 85th Inf Div, *Minturno to the Apennines*, 17–18; 85th Inf Div, Report of Operations, May 1944.
48 337th Inf Regt Operation Report, May 1944; Schultz, *85th Division in WWII*, 90–91.
49 756th Commander's Narrative for 11 May to 11 June 1944, 9: "Point Q" on sketch #2; B Company Unit Journal, 17 May 1944; B Co and C Co/756th Morning Report, 20 May 1944, "Record of Events."
50 756th Commander's Narrative for 11 May to 11 June 1944, 9.
51 US Army, *Fifth Army History: Part V*, 70; HQ staff, 85th Inf Div, *Minturno to the Apennines*, 20–22; 85th Inf Div, Report of Operations, May 1944.
52 85th Inf Div, *Minturno to the Apennines*, 20–21.
53 Fisher, *Cassino to the Alps*, 79.
54 Ibid., 85–86.
55 Ibid.; Schultz, *85th Division in WWII*, 91–93; 85th Inf Div, *Minturno to the Apennines*, 20–22; A, B, C, and HQ Cos/756th Morning Reports 20 May 1944, Record of events for 18 May 1944.
56 Delaney, *Blue Devils*, 82; Böhmler, *Cassino: A German View*, 268–69; CMH "Rome-Arno," 17–18.
57 Duane Schultz, "Bombing the Abbey," *WWII History* magazine, December 2018, 15.
58 B Company Unit Journal, 18 May 1944; Bernhard "Life in the Service."
59 Donley diary, 18 May 1944.
60 Ibid.
61 756th Commander's Narrative for 11 May to 11 June 1944, 10.
62 Ibid.; Mudd, "History 756th," 39.
63 Fazendin, *756th at Cassino*, 165–166: Redle recollection.
64 756th Commander's Narrative for 11 May to 11 June 1944, 10–11; A, B, C, and HQ Cos/756th Morning Reports, 20 May 1944, "Record of Events"; Fazendin, *756th at Cassino*, 193: Lewis recollection; Donley diary, 19 May 1944; Lewis, personal papers, 756th HQ attachments document dated 8 May 1945.
65 756th Commander's Narrative for 11 May to 11 June 1944, 10–11.
66 These varied between the 1926 models with a spine ridge top, and 1935 models without the spine. Some French units also wore American M1 helmets.

67 Mudd, "History 756th," 39; Fazendin, *756th at Cassino*, 152: Redle recollection.
68 Fazendin, *756th at Cassino*, 166: Redle recollection; 756th Commander's Narrative for 11 May to 11 June 1944, 10–11.
69 756th Commander's Narrative for 11 May to 11 June 1944, 10–11; Lewis, personal papers, 756th HQ attachments document dated 8 May 1945.
70 Bernhard "Life in the Service"; Fazendin, *756th at Cassino*, 193: Lewis recollection.
71 756th Commander's Narrative for 11 May to 11 June 1944, 10–11; A, C, and HQ Cos/756th Morning Report, 20 May 1944, "Record of Events."
72 Donley interview, 16 September 2005.
73 Ibid.
74 B Company Unit Journal, 20 May 1944.
75 Fazendin, *756th at Cassino*, 166: Redle recollection.

Chapter 14

1 Blumenson, *Mark Clark*, 205.
2 US Army, *Fifth Army History: Part V*, 89.
3 Paul Gaujac, *Le Corps Expéditionnaire Français en Italie,* (Paris, France : Histoire & Collections, 2003), 38. French name: 6ème Régiment de Tirailleurs Marocains. This was Col Cherriere's unit. https://fr.wikipedia.org/wiki/6e_r%C3%A9giment_de_tirailleurs_marocains
4 Table of Organization at https://custermen.com/ItalyWW2/ArmyOrg/FrenchOrg.htm
5 US Army, *Fifth Army History: Part V*, 91.
6 Fazendin, *756th at Cassino*, 166: Redle recollection; Mudd, "History 756th," 39.
7 Redle letter, 25 January 2004.
8 B Co/756th Unit Journal, 21 May 1944.
9 Fazendin, *756th at Cassino*, 194: Lewis recollection.
10 Ibid., 152: Redle recollection.
11 B Co/756th Unit Journal, 21 May 1944: location was 603053.
12 B Co/756th Unit Journal "Commander's Narrative 11 May to 10 June 1944."
13 B Co/756th Morning Report, 21 May 1944.
14 Redle letter, 25 January 2004.
15 B Co/756th Unit Journal, 21 May 1944.
16 Fazendin, *756th at Cassino*, 167: Redle recollection.
17 , B Co/756th Unit Journal, 2nd Lt Bert Gilden, "Critical Resume of Important Actions of the 1st Platoon, Company B, 756th Tank Battalion, for period May 17 to June 10, 1944." Gilden gives coordinates for Taverna as 599130.
18 B Co/756th Unit Journal, 21 May 1944.
19 PaK is the abbreviation for *PanzerAbwehrKanone*. The PaK 40 was the most common German towed AT gun of the war.
20 B Co/756th Unit Journal, "Actions of 1st Platoon, May 17 to June 10, 1944."
21 Ibid.; B Co/756th Unit Journal, 21 May 1944.
22 B Co/756th Unit Journal, 21 May 1944: arrived at 1815.
23 B Co/756th Morning Report, 22 May 1944; US World War II Hospital Admission Card Files, 1942–1954: Durham was sent first to the 313th Clearing Station and then 45th General Hospital and did not return to duty until 19 June 1944.
24 B Co/756th Unit Journal, "Actions of 1st Platoon, May 17 to June 10, 1944."
25 Redle letter to Harry Yeide, 30 January 2008.
26 B Co/756th Unit Journal "Commander's Narrative 11 May to 10 June 1944"; Fazendin, *756th at Cassino*, 166–67: Redle recollection; Mudd, "History 756th," 43.
27 Redle letter 6 January 2005.
28 Redle letter dated 24 June 1994 in Lewis personal documents; Redle letter, 25 January 2004.
29 First name not provided.

30 B Co/756th Unit Journal, 22 May 1944.
31 http://lenola.shapcott-family.com/page6.html: Lenola served as a German command center and also had a field hospital. Allied planes bombed the town on 23 January 1944 in support of the Anzio landings. Fifty-eight civilians (including thirteen children) died in that attack. Many more were left wounded.
32 Sgt Grate had previously been in the 1st Platoon. Evidently, he was moved to the 2nd Platoon ahead of this action.
33 B Co/756th Unit Journal, "Actions of 2nd Platoon, 11 May to 10 June"; Redle letter, 30 October 2000.
34 US World War II Hospital Admission Card Files, 1942–1954.
35 B Co/756th Unit Journal, "Actions of 2nd Platoon, 11 May to 10 June"; Fazendin, *756th at Cassino,* 168: Redle recollection; Redle letter, 25 January 2004.
36 B Co/756th Unit Journal, "Actions of 2nd Platoon, 11 May to 10 June."
37 Ibid.
38 B Co/756th Morning Reports, 22 and 23 May 1944: Pfc Francis Payne LWA, evacuated to 313th Collection Station; S/Sgt Hamilton A. Smith, minor head and hand wounds, remained on duty; T/4 Henry Sanislow, minor head wounds, remained on duty; Pvt William H. Buisset, minor hand wound, remained on duty. Sanislow was Smith's driver (Sanislow interview, 15 September, 2006). It is unclear to which crew Buisset belonged, but the 21-year-old suffered from a minor shell fragment wound to the forehead according to US World War II Hospital Admission Card Files, 1942–1954.
39 B Co/756th Unit Journal, "Actions of 2nd Platoon, 11 May to 10 June."
40 US Army, *Fifth Army History: Part V*, 92–93.
41 Ibid., 88–93.
42 B Co/756th Unit Journal, 22 May 1944.
43 Sanislow interview, 15 September 2006.
44 Bernhard, "Life in the Service," Fazendin, *756th at Cassino*, 193–98: Lewis recollection; 756th Commander's Narrative for May 11 to June 11, 1944, 11–13: The rest of the 756th Tank Battalion was assigned to *Group Bonjour* with B Company, 755th Tank Battalion attached; US Army, *Fifth Army History: Part V*, 92–93.
45 Lewis, personal papers, 756th HQ attachments document dated 8 May 1945.
46 756th Commander's Narrative for 11 May to 11 June 1944, 13–14; Donley Diary, 22 May 1944.
47 756th Commander's Narrative for 11 May to 11 June 1944, 14; A Co/756th Morning Report, 23 May 1944.
48 756th Commander's Narrative for 11 May to 11 June 1944, 33.
49 Yeide, *The Infantry's Armor*, 84–85.
50 756th Commander's Narrative for 11 May to 11 June 1944, 33.
51 Yeide, *The Infantry's Armor*, 84–85.
52 Rick Atkinson, *The Day of Battle: The War in Sicily and Italy, 1943–1944* (New York, New York: Henry Holt and Company, LLC., 2007), 557–58; http://lenola.shapcott-family.com/page6.html, last accessed 20 January 2021.
53 http://lenola.shapcott-family.com/page6.html, last accessed 20 January 2021. Alberto Moravio based his novel "La Ciociara" on these events. Sophia Lauren starred in the 1960 film adaption renamed "Two Women" and won the Academy Award for Best Actress for her performance.
54 Fazendin, *756th at Cassino*, 164: George B. Wilkerson was the A Company crewman nearly shot.
55 Ibid., 194: Lewis recollection.
56 Anderson phone conversation, 20 June 2009; Anderson said this French-Canadian officer was killed in action a few days later and that he recovered the officer's 1911-based 9mm pistol model from his belt.
57 Fisher, *Cassino to the Alps*, 91–92.
58 US Army, *Fifth Army History: Part V*, 94–95.
59 Ibid.
60 B Co/756th Unit Journal, 22 May 1944.
61 Donley diary, 23 May 1944; B Co/756th Unit Journal, 23 May 1944.
62 Fazendin, *756th at Cassino*, 169: Redle recollection; Redle letter, 28 June 2009.
63 B Co/756th Unit Journal, 23 May 1944; 756th Commander's Narrative for 11 May to 11 June 1944, 14.
64 Fazendin, *756th at Cassino*, 169: Redle recollection; B Co/756th Unit Journal, S/Sgt Oric Johannesen, "Resume of Action on the 23rd and 24th of May 1944."

65 B Co/756th Unit Journal, "Resume of Action on the 23rd and 24th of May 1944."
66 C Co/756th Morning Report, 24 May 1944; HQ Co/756th Morning Report, 20 May 1944, "Record of Events"; Sv Co/756th Morning Report, 23 May 1944. C Co arrived in Lenola at 1500, HQ Co arrived at 1700, but Service Co remained in Itri.
67 756th Commander's Narrative for 11 May to 11 June 1944, 14; B Co/756th Morning Report, 23 May 1944.
68 B Co/756th Unit Journal, "Resume of Action on the 23rd and 24th of May 1944."
69 Fazendin, *756th at Cassino*, 169: Redle recollection.
70 B Co/756th Unit Journal, 24 May 1944: B Company CP location recorded as 557108. This was about a half-mile southeast of Lenola, tucked on the northwest foot of San Martino Hill.
71 Ibid., 23 May 1944: Tanks #6, #8, and #23 were salvaged. Tank #23 is an unusual number for a tank, and may have been a spare. Normally the company tanks were numbered 1–17.
72 Advance halted at position 511138. This is another draw and a likely place the Germans would have blasted holes in the roadway.
73 B Co/756th Unit Journal, "Resume of Action on the 23rd and 24th of May 1944."
74 Ibid.; B Co/756th Unit Journal, 24 May 1944, and 756th Commander's Narrative for 11 May to 11 June 1944, 14, reports one platoon from C Company relieved the tanks and arrived at 1700. Rogers needed French permission to do so—which also added to the delay.
75 756th Commander's Narrative for 11 May to 11 June 1944, 14; B Co/756th Unit Journal, 2nd Lt Andrew Orient, "Narrative of Actions of Third Platoon of Company B, 756th Tank Battalion, 11 May to 10 June."
76 B Co/756th Unit Journal, 24 May 1944.
77 Guild phone conversation, 11 February 2004.
78 Ibid.
79 Fazendin, *756th at Cassino*, 168: Redle recollection.
80 Donley diary, 25 May 1944.
81 Fazendin, *756th at Cassino*, 169: Redle recollection.
82 Ibid., 194: Lewis recollection.
83 Ibid., 168: Redle recollection.
84 Ibid.
85 Ibid., 138: Redle recollection.
86 Ibid., 168: Redle recollection.
87 Steven J. Zaloga, *Anzio 1944: The Beleaguered Beachhead* (Oxford, UK: Osprey Publishing, 2005), 84–85; Schultz, *85th Division in WWII*, 99–100.
88 Böhmler, *Monte Cassino: A German View*, 275.
89 Fisher, *Cassino to the Alps*, 98–99.
90 Clayton D. Laurie, *The U.S. Army Campaigns of World War II: Rome-Arno* (CMH Pub 72-20) (U.S. Army Center of Military History, 1994), 19.
91 Laurie, *Rome-Arno*, 20; Zaloga, *Anzio 1944*, 85–87; Parker, *Monte Cassino*, 160: Clark remained resentful that his American forces failed to capture the abbey at Monte Cassino.
92 US Army, *Fifth Army History: Part V*, 94–95.
93 Ibid.
94 756th Commander's Narrative for 11 May to 11 June 1944, 14–15.
95 B Co/756th Unit Journal, 25 May 1944.
96 B Co/756th Morning Report, 25 May 1944.
97 Ibid., 24 May 1944.
98 Ibid., 25 May 1944.
99 IDPF for Andrew D. Orient IDPF; A Co/756th Morning Report, 11 February 1944: Orient was wounded on this date.
100 B Co/756th Unit Journal, "Narrative of Action, 3rd Platoon, 11 May to 10 June"; B Co/756th Unit Journal, 26 May 1944.
101 US Army, *Fifth Army History: Part V*, 94–95.
102 B Co/756th Unit Journal, "Narrative of Action, 3rd Platoon, 11 May to 10 June."
103 756th Commander's Narrative for 11 May to 11 June 1944, 15.
104 Ibid., 15–16.

105 B Co/756th Unit Journal, "Narrative of Action, 3rd Platoon, 11 May to 10 June"; B Co/756th Morning Report, 27 May 1944.
106 756th Commander's Narrative for 11 May to 11 June 1944, 15–16; C Co/756th Morning Report, 27 May 1944: "Record of Events"; HQ Co/756th Morning Report, 27 May 1944; Donley diary, 27 May 1944.
107 756th Commander's Narrative for 11 May to 11 June 1944, 16–18.
108 B Co/756th Unit Journal, 28 May 1944; B Co/756th Unit Journal, "Narrative of Action, 3rd Platoon, 11 May to 10 June."
109 B Co/756th Unit Journal, "Actions of 1st Platoon, May 17 to June 10, 1944."
110 Rogers mistakenly identifies this location as north of Guilano, but obviously meant Prossedi when compared to his reports of B Company's actions the following day.
111 756th Commander's Narrative for 11 May to 11 June 1944, 17–18.
112 Ibid.
113 B Co/756th Unit Journal, 29 May 1944; 756th Commander's Narrative for 11 May to 11 June 1944, 18.
114 B Co/756th Unit Journal, "Narrative of Action, 3rd Platoon, 11 May to 10 June"; 756th Commander's Narrative for 11 May to 11 June 1944, 18. Orient's platoon was under the command of Col Cherrière during this engagement.
115 B Co/756th Unit Journal, 29 May 1944: Location was 380260. 756th Commander's Narrative for 11 May to 11 June 1944, 18. B Company (less 3rd Platoon) was under the command of Col Maullet while operating from Prossedi.
116 B Co/756th Unit Journal, "Actions of 1st Platoon, May 17 to June 10, 1944."
117 "Maullet" is the surname and spelling provided by Lt Col Rogers in his commander's narrative. His first name is unknown.
118 B Co/756th Unit Journal, "Actions of 1st Platoon, May 17 to June 10, 1944." B Co/756th Unit Journal "Commander's Narrative 11 May to 10 June 1944"; 756th Commander's Narrative for 11 May to 11 June 1944, 18–19; B Co/756th Morning Report, 29 May 1944; B Co/756th Unit Journal, 30 May 1944.
119 B Co/756th Unit Journal, "Actions of 2nd Platoon, 11 May to 10 June."
120 Ibid.
121 B Co/756th Unit Journal, "Narrative of Action, 3rd Platoon, 11 May to 10 June"; This was Col Cherriere's regiment. Orient names a "Major La Gouvell" as the battalion commander. His first name is unknown.
122 Ibid.; B Co/756th Unit Journal, 29 May 1944, reports the Mark IV as "destroyed" but doesn't record how. The German crew may have destroyed it rather than leave it intact, or the Goum troops may have destroyed it upon taking the cemetery.
123 Fazendin, *756th at Cassino*, 167: Redle recollection.
124 Offerman, "My Dad Was A Tanker," 23.
125 Fazendin, *756th at Cassino*, 167: Redle recollection.
126 US World War II Hospital Admission Card Files, 1942–1954.
127 Offerman, "My Dad Was A Tanker," 23.
128 US World War II Hospital Admission Card Files, 1942–1954.
129 IDPF for Leak H. Smitherman; B Co/756th Morning Report, 31 May 1944; B Co/756th Unit Journal, 30 May 1944.
130 B Co/756th Morning Report, 4 June 1944.
131 Ibid., 13 June 1944; IDPF for Harold M. Behymer: born 10 June 1919. Behymer was unmarried but left behind a grieving mother, father, and brother.
132 Redle letter, 28 June 2009.
133 Ibid.
134 Ibid.
135 B Co/756th Unit Journal, "Narrative of Action, 3rd Platoon, 11 May to 10 June."
136 US World War II Hospital Admission Card Files, 1942–1954; B Co/756th Morning Report, 4 June 1944.
137 Redle letter, 25 January 2004; Fazendin, *756th at Cassino*, 168: Redle recollection; US World War II Hospital Admission Card Files, 1942–1954.
138 756th Commander's Narrative for 11 May to 11 June 1944, 18.
139 Ibid., 18–19.
140 B Co/756th Morning Report, 31 May 1944; B Co/756th Unit Journal, 31 May 1944.

141 B Co/756th Unit Journal, 31 May 1944.
142 B Co/756th Unit Journal, "Narrative of Action, 3rd Platoon, 11 May to 10 June"; Lewis, personal papers, 756th HQ attachments document dated 8 May 1945; B Co/756th Morning Report, 31 May 1944: Technically, the 756th was detached from the US 2nd Armored Group with the CEF, and attached to the 1st Armored Group with the U.S. II Corps.
143 756th Commander's Narrative for 11 May to 11 June 1944, 19–20.
144 Ibid.; Fazendin, *756th at Cassino*, 169: Redle recollection.
145 756th Commander's Narrative for 11 May to 11 June 1944, 19–20.
146 C Co/756th Morning Report, 31 May 1944; HQ Co/756th Morning Report, 31 May 1944.
147 B Co/756th Unit Journal, 31 May 1944; B Co/756th Morning Report, 31 May 1944.
148 756th Commander's Narrative for 11 May to 11 June 1944, 19–20.
149 Ibid.

Chapter 15

1 Mark W. Clark, *Calculated Risk* (New York, New York: Harper and Brothers Publishing, 1950), 2.
2 Fisher, *Cassino to the Alps*, 190.
3 Ibid., 190–92.
4 Lewis, personal papers, 756th HQ attachments document dated 8 May 1945.
5 Thad A. Broom, ed., *Howitzer* (West Point, NY: United States Corps of Cadets, 1930), 136.
6 Yeide, *The Infantry's Armor*, 81.
7 756th Commander's Narrative for 11 May to 11 June 1944, 20–21.
8 Donald G. Taggart, *The History of the Third Infantry Division in World War II* (Reprint, Nashville, Tennessee: The Battery Press, 1987), 178.
9 Fazendin, *756th at Cassino*, 169: Redle recollection.
10 Donley diary, 1 June 1944.
11 756th Commander's Narrative for 11 May to 11 June 1944, 20–21; B Co/756th Morning Report, 1 June 1944; Lewis, personal papers, 756th HQ attachments document dated 8 May 1945; Yeide, *The Infantry's Armor*, 81.
12 756th Commander's Narrative for 11 May to 11 June 1944, 19–20. Major Dolvin was also with Lewis's tanks while at Carpineto.
13 B Co/756th Morning Report, 1 June 1944.
14 Redle interview, 13 March 2004.
15 US World War II Hospital Admission Card Files, 1942–1954.
16 Smitherman IDPF.
17 Donley diary, 1 June 1944.
18 These were likely "*Sprengbombe Dickwandig* 2 kg" anti-personnel munitions with a 30-foot blast radius. Each had "wings" set to rotate a certain number of times, which, in turn, armed each bomb to explode before striking the ground—thus maximizing the blast effect.
19 Fazendin, *756th at Cassino*, 169: Redle recollection.
20 756th Commander's Narrative for 11 May to 11 June 1944, 20–21.
21 B Co/756th Unit Journal, 2 June 1944; B Co/756th Morning Report, 2 June 1944: The B Co Morning Report improperly identifies the location as five miles NW of Valmontone. Should be five miles SW of Valmontone.
22 756th Commander's Narrative for 11 May to 11 June 1944, 21; B Co/756th Unit Journal, 2 June 1944.
23 Rogers records Sloan told him to report to the 350th Inf Regt, but Col Champeny commanded the 351st.
24 B Co/756th Unit Journal, "Actions of 1st Platoon, May 17 to June 10, 1944."
25 756th Commander's Narrative for 11 May to 11 June 1944, 20–21.
26 Taggart, *Third Infantry Division*, 181; Nathan W. White, *From Fedala to Berchtesgaden: A History of the Seventh United States Infantry in WWII* (Providence, RI: Bickford Engraving & Electrotype Co., 1947), 121.
27 Fisher, *Cassino to the Alps*, 196–197.
28 Ibid.; 88th Inf Div G-3 Operations Report 1–30 June 1944, 2 June 1944 (RG 407 E 427 Box 10855); Delaney, *Blue Devils*, 89–90.

29 B Co/756th Unit Journal, "Actions of 1st Platoon, May 17 to June 10, 1944."
30 351st Inf Regt Operations Report for June 1944 transcribed at https://www.351inf.com/opsreports/June-1944.
31 Ibid.
32 756th Commander's Narrative for 11 May to 11 June 1944, 21–22; B Co/756th Unit Journal, 2 June 1944; B Co/756th Unit Journal "Commander's Narrative 11 May to 10 June 1944." B Company gives the time as 0500 but Rogers's 0700 time seems to fit in better with other events.
33 B Co/756th Unit Journal, "Actions of 1st Platoon, May 17 to June 10, 1944"; B Co/756th Unit Journal, "Narrative of Action, 3rd Platoon, 11 May to 10 June"; B Co/756th Unit Journal, "Actions of 2nd Platoon, 11 May to 10 June."
34 B Co/756th Unit Journal, "Narrative of Action, 3rd Platoon, 11 May to 10 June."
35 Fazendin, *756th at Cassino*, 169–70: Redle recollection.
36 Ibid., 170; 756th Commander's Narrative for 11 May to 11 June 1944, 21–22; B Co/756th Unit Journal, "Actions of 2nd Platoon, 11 May to 10 June."
37 Fazendin, *756th at Cassino*, 169–70: Redle recollection.
38 756th Commander's Narrative for 11 May to 11 June 1944, 21–22.
39 Fazendin, *756th at Cassino*, 170: Redle recollection; B Co/756th Unit Journal "Commander's Narrative 11 May to 10 June 1944."
40 Fazendin, *756th at Cassino*, 170: Redle recollection.
41 Ibid.; B Co/756th Unit Journal "Commander's Narrative 11 May to 10 June 1944."
42 B Co/756th Unit Journal, "Narrative of Action, 3rd Platoon, 11 May to 10 June."
43 351st Inf Regt Operations Report, June 1944.
44 Fazendin, *756th at Cassino*, 170: Redle recollection.
45 88th Inf Div G-3 Unit Journal, 2 June 1944 (1100 entry): Identified alternately as "Hill 413." Coordinates listed as 033528.
46 B Co/756th Unit Journal, "Narrative of Action, 3rd Platoon, 11 May to 10 June."
47 351st Inf Regt Operations Report, June 1944.
48 88th Inf Div G-3 Unit Journal, 2 June 1944 (1305 entry).
49 351st Inf Regt Operations Report, June 1944: Infantry reported at Torraccio Mezza Selva (coordinates 040560) by 1455. Again, the 351st, misidentifies their tank support as 752nd when it was the 756th; B Co/756th Unit Journal "Commander's Narrative 11 May to 10 June 1944"; 756th Commander's Narrative for 11 May to 11 June 1944, 21–22: Rogers puts the time at 1600, a half hour earlier.
50 B Co/756th Unit Journal, "Actions of 1st Platoon, May 17 to June 10, 1944": Gilden's three tank platoon may have been the first to cross the highway. Gilden was down to three tanks as one developed mechanical trouble and another had been commandeered earlier by Lt Col Rogers.
51 756th Commander's Narrative for 11 May to 11 June 1944, 21–22, near "Point Q" on Rogers's map, or "La Torre" on 1944 maps; B Co/756th Unit Journal, "Actions of 2nd Platoon, 11 May to 10 June."
52 B Co/756th Unit Journal, "Narrative of Action, 3rd Platoon, 11 May to 10 June."
53 351st Inf Regt Operations Report, June 1944.
54 Fazendin, *756th at Cassino*, 170: Redle recollection.
55 Headquarters 351st Inf Regt., *History of 351st Inf Reg in World War II*. 1945, Booklet downloaded from https://www.351inf.com/collections
56 Delaney, *Blue Devils*, 89; 88th Inf Div G-3 Operations Report, 1–30 June 1944, (2 June 1944 entry): Both the G-3 Operations report and the official Blue Devils history mistakenly list the 752nd as attached to the division on 2 June. They were not, the 752nd was in fact fighting with FSSF troops moving east from Artena to Colleferro, according to the 752nd Tank Bn official history. The 752nd joined the 351st the following day, 3 June, according to the same history. (United States Army. *752nd Tank Bn*. 1945. (PDF version downloaded from Bangor Public Library), World War Regimental Histories. Book 60. http://digicom.bpl.lib.me.us/ww_reg_his/60)
57 Fisher, *Cassino to the Alps*, 196–97; 351st Inf Reg Operations Report, June 1944.
58 This was likely an overloaded German Sd.Kfz. Seven half-track personnel carrier.
59 Redle interview, 16 September 2005.
60 B Co/756th Unit Journal, "Actions of 1st Platoon, May 17 to June 10, 1944"; B Co/756th Unit Journal "Commander's Narrative 11 May to 10 June 1944"; Gilden records an 88mm crew. Redle records a 75mm

crew. Fazendin, *756th at Cassino*, 170–71: Redle recollection; 756th Commander's Narrative for 11 May to 11 June 1944, 21–22. There is ambiguity on where exactly this event took place, but the likely spot was the road to the north leading down from Palestrina to Highway 7 at San Cesareo.

61 Hamilton H. Howze, *A Cavalryman's Story: Memoirs of a Twentieth Century General* (Washington, D.C.: Smithsonian Institute Press, 1996), 112–13.

62 Fazendin, *756th at Cassino*, 198: Lewis recollection; Lewis, personal papers, 756th HQ attachments document dated 8 May 1945.

63 Fazendin, *756th at Cassino*, 198–99: Lewis recollection.

64 756th Commander's Narrative for 11 May to 11 June 1944, 21–22.

65 Ibid., 22.

66 Ibid.

67 Fazendin, *756th at Cassino*, 199: Lewis recollection.

68 Yeide, *The Infantry's Armor*, 89. The light tanks had been attached earlier, but detached prior to 3 June.

69 Robert W. Jones, Jr., "Race to Rome" (From Veritas, Vol. 2, No. 2, 2006) at https://arsof-history.org/articles/v2n2_race_to_rome_page_1.html (Jones cites General Hamilton Howze, U.S. Army War College Senior Officers Debriefing Program, 14 October 1972); Yeide, *The Infantry's Armor*, 89; George F. Howe, *Old Ironsides: The Battle History of the 1st Armored Division* (Washington, D.C.: Combat Forces Press, 1957; Reprint, Nashville, Tennessee: The Battery Press, 1979), 338.

70 756th Commander's Narrative for 11 May to 11 June 1944, 22–23; Howe, *Old Ironsides*, 338.

71 Howze, *A Cavalryman's Story*, 112; Broom, ed, *Howitzer, 1930*, 136: Howze was from El Paso, Texas.

72 756th Commander's Narrative for 11 May to 11 June 1944, 22: Location of road junction was at 997585.

73 Ibid. Lt Col Frank M. Izenour commanded the 1st Bn, 7th Inf Regt.

74 Ibid.

75 Fazendin, *756th at Cassino*, 200: Lewis recollection.

76 756th Commander's Narrative for 11 May to 11 June 1944, 22–23.

77 Ibid.; B Co/756th Unit Journal "Commander's Narrative 11 May to 10 June 1944"; White, *Fedala to Berchtesgaden*, 122.

78 756th Commander's Narrative for 11 May to 11 June 1944, 23.

79 Fisher, *Cassino to the Alps*, 206; Howe, *Old Ironsides*, 339.

80 Howze, *A Cavalryman's Story*, 113.

81 756th Commander's Narrative for 11 May to 11 June 1944, 23.

82 Fazendin, *756th at Cassino*, 200: Lewis recollection.

83 Howe, *Old Ironsides*, 338.

84 Howze, *A Cavalryman's Story*, 113; Fazendin, *756th at Cassino*, 171–73: Redle recollection.

85 Howze, *A Cavalryman's Story*, 113.

86 756th Commander's Narrative for 11 May to 11 June 1944, 23.

87 B Co/756th Unit Journal "Commander's Narrative 11 May to 10 June 1944."

88 Fazendin, *756th at Cassino*, 171–72: Redle recollection: This is Redle's description of the terrain roughly three miles east of Tor Carbone.

89 Howe, *Old Ironsides*, 338; Howze, *A Cavalryman's Story*, 114.

90 This intersection seems to match a location roughly a mile-and-a-half east of Tor Carbone.

91 Fazendin, *756th at Cassino*, 201–02: Lewis recollection: Early into the mission, Lewis had to relieve a lieutenant for placing his tanks "in a draw" with a poor field of fire. An approaching German jeep escaped as a result. The platoon sergeant, placed in charge, subsequently corrected the lieutenant's mistake.

92 Fazendin, *756th at Cassino*, 172: Redle recollection.

93 Howze, *A Cavalryman's Story*, 114.

94 Ibid.: His name was Corporal Scully.

95 Ibid., 113: This brigadier general was probably Kendall because of the close proximity of the 88th Inf Div. Howze does not give his name but describes him with irritation as "some footloose brigadier general who lopped off one of my attached infantry companies."

96 Ibid., 114: Howze does not name the outfit, nor were they formally attached, but they were likely TDs from the 701st Tank Destroyer Battalion.

97 Ibid.

98 Ibid.
99 Howe, *Old Ironsides*, 338–39.
100 Ibid., 338.
101 B Co/756th Morning Report, 3 June 1944.
102 B Co/756th Unit Journal, "Actions of 2nd Platoon, 11 May to 10 June."
103 B Co/756th Unit Journal "Commander's Narrative 11 May to 10 June 1944"; Redle does not specifically name the route, but the yardages given and his physical descriptions of the location match Via Prenestina.
104 Ibid.; White, *Fedala to Berchtesgaden*, 122.
105 Fazendin, *756th at Cassino*, 172: Redle recollection.
106 B Co/756th Unit Journal "Commander's Narrative 11 May to 10 June 1944."
107 B Co/756th Unit Journal, "Actions of 2nd Platoon, 11 May to 10 June."
108 Ibid.; 756th Commander's Narrative for 11 May to 11 June 1944, 23.
109 White, *Fedala to Berchtesgaden*, 122; Fazendin, *756th at Cassino*, 172: Redle recollection.
110 B Co/756th Unit Journal "Commander's Narrative 11 May to 10 June 1944"; 756th Commander's Narrative for 11 May to 11 June 1944, 23; B Co/756th Unit Journal, "Actions of 2nd Platoon, 11 May to 10 June"; B Co/756th Unit Journal, 3 June 1944: The B Co Morning Report, 3 June 1944, claims roadblocks were established on Via Collatina, but this is not supported by Rogers, Redle, or Newman's reports—each of which put B Company at point "B" on Via Presentina for the remainder of the evening.
111 Fazendin, *756th at Cassino*, 172: Redle recollection; White, *Fedala to Berchtesgaden*, 122.
112 B Co/756th Unit Journal, "Actions of 2nd Platoon, 11 May to 10 June."
113 756th Commander's Narrative for 11 May to 11 June 1944, 23. A Company's roadblock positions are identified as "C" and "D" positions on Rogers's Commander's Narrative map. These are on Via Collatina at the 877683 and 879685 locations.
114 Howze, *A Cavalryman's Story*, 114: The exact location of this column was not given. Howze writes Rogers's tanks also secured a bridge across the Aniene river further to the north, but Rogers does not record this detail in his commander's narrative for 3 June and the 756th Unit Journal from this period is missing. An Aniene bridge was secured the following day (4 June) by 756th D Company tanks. Howze may be referring to that event.
115 756th Commander's Narrative for 11 May to 11 June 1944, 23: Rogers lists the following vehicles taken as of 2200 when he visited the location: twelve German heavy trucks, one dual purpose 88mm gun, three staff cars, one ambulance, four motorcycles, three or four light duty personnel carriers, and two or three quarter-ton Volkswagens.
116 756th Commander's Narrative for 11 May to 11 June 1944, 23.
117 Fazendin, *756th at Cassino*, 202–03: Lewis recollection.
118 White, *Fedala to Berchtesgaden*, 122.
119 Fazendin, *756th at Cassino*, 203: Lewis recollection.
120 Position "E" on Rogers's map.
121 Fazendin, *756th at Cassino*, 172: Redle recollection; Redle interview, 13 March 2004.
122 Fazendin, *756th at Cassino*, 173: Redle recollection.
123 Ibid.
124 Howze, *A Cavalryman's Story*, 115.
125 B Co/756th Unit Journal, 3 June 1944.
126 The 756th Unit History, 1944, lists nobody killed, wounded or captured for 3 June 1944.
127 B Co/756th Morning Report, 3 June 1944; B Co/756th Morning Report, 9 June 1944. The details are unknown. Stomach flu was not uncommon.
128 Yeide, *The Infantry's Armor*, 89; Fazendin, *756th at Cassino*, 200: Lewis recollection.
129 Redle letter, 28 June 2008.
130 Howe, *Old Ironsides*, 339.
131 Howze, *A Cavalryman's Story*, 114.
132 Ibid., 113–115.
133 Clinton B. Conger, "First Special Service Force, Which Trained Here, is Now Dealing Nazis Misery; Holds Unique Record," *The Independent-Record* (Helena, Montana), 22 August 1944, 2; NARA photos.
134 Howze, *A Cavalryman's Story*, 115.
135 Ibid., 115.

Chapter 16

1 Bret Werner, *First Special Service Force 1942–44* (Oxford, UK: Osprey Publishing Ltd., 2006), 10–11.
2 Ibid., 5–6.
3 Ibid., 3; Clinton B. Conger, "First Special Service Force, Which Trained Here, is Now Dealing Nazis Misery; Holds Unique Record," *The Independent-Record* (Helena, Montana), 22 August 1944, 2.
4 Known as a V-42 knife.
5 Werner, *First Special Service Force*, 11.
6 Ibid., 3.
7 Ibid., 6–7.
8 Ibid., 10–11.
9 Joseph A. Springer, *The Black Devil Brigade: The True Story of the First Special Service Force* (Pacifica California: Pacifica Military History, 2001), 229–30.
10 Werner, *First Special Service Force*, 14–15.
11 Ibid., 15.
12 Ibid., 16–20.
13 Ibid., 21–23; Clinton B. Conger, "First Special Service Force, Which Trained Here, is Now Dealing Nazis Misery; Holds Unique Record," *The Independent-Record* (Helena, Montana), 22 August 1944, 2.
14 Werner, *First Special Service Force*, 24–25.
15 Ibid., 24; Clinton B. Conger, "First Special Service Force, Which Trained Here, is Now Dealing Nazis Misery; Holds Unique Record," *The Independent-Record* (Helena, Montana), 22 August 1944, 2; Seymour Korman, "First General in Rome Describes Battle on the Tiber" *Chicago Tribune* (Chicago, Illinois), 10 June 1944, 5.
16 Zaloga, *Anzio 1944*, 89–90; US Army, *Fifth Army History, Part V*, 155; Fisher, *Cassino to the Alps*, 205–06, 210. Clark was privy to Ultra Secret intelligence and should have been well aware the orders for the German Army to vacate and spare Rome destruction came directly from Hitler. Nevertheless, Clark's push to secure the Tiber bridges demonstrates a complete lack of trust in German promises.
17 Fisher, *Cassino to the Alps*, 218–19.
18 B Co/756th Unit Journal, "Narrative of Action, 3rd Platoon, 11 May to 10 June"; B Co/756th Unit Journal, 4 June 1944: arrived 0200.
19 Fazendin, *756th at Cassino*, 173: Redle recollection.
20 Frank W. Mielcarski draft card, United States Army WWII Draft Cards 1940-1947; US Army, *Fifth Army History, Part V*, 149: Both the 2nd and 3rd Regiments moved into Tor Sapienza at 0400 hours, 4 June.
21 756th Commander's Narrative for 11 May to 11 June 1944, 23–25; Lewis, personal papers, 756th HQ attachments document dated 8 May 1945.
22 Fazendin, *756th at Cassino*, 173: Redle recollection.
23 US Army, *Fifth Army History, Part V*, 158; Howe, *Old Ironsides*, 343–44.
24 Laurie, *Rome-Arno*, 2.
25 Springer, *Black Devil Brigade*, 224–26; Werner, *First Special Service Force*, 24; Seymour Korman, "First General in Rome Describes Battle on the Tiber" *Chicago Tribune* (Chicago, Illinois), 10 June 1944, 5. Fredericks stands by the time of 0620.
26 US Army, *Fifth Army History, Part V*, 158; Fisher, *Cassino to the Alps*, 211–16; Howze, *A Cavalryman's Story*, 115–16; *Mark Clark*, 214; Howe, *Old Ironsides*, 344: The two knocked out tanks were from H Co, 13th Armored Regt.
27 Seymour Korman, "First General in Rome Describes Battle on the Tiber" *Chicago Tribune* (Chicago, Illinois), 10 June 1944, 5; *Mark Clark*, 214.
28 Fisher, *Cassino to the Alps*, 215–16.
29 Howe, *Old Ironsides*, 344.
30 Blumenson, *Mark Clark*, 215.
31 Fisher, *Cassino to the Alps*, 215–16.
32 Ibid.
33 Blumenson, *Mark Clark*, 215.
34 Howze, *A Cavalryman's Story*, 116; Springer, *Black Devil Brigade*, 267.
35 756th Commander's Narrative for 11 May to 11 June 1944, 23–24.

36 Fazendin, *756th at Cassino*, 173: Redle recollection.
37 756th Commander's Narrative for 11 May to 11 June 1944, 24.
38 Ibid.; Fazendin, *756th at Cassino*, 173 and 203–04: Redle and Lewis recollections; Cheryl Esposito, *The 756th Tank Battalion in the European Theatre* (Privately printed, 1999), 17: Deenihan recollection; Redle interview, 13 March 2004. French Lewis and other 756th members were convinced the strafing planes were flown by the Tuskegee Airmen. The particular unit responsible is not important as these types of "friendly fire" incidents plagued all Allied air units—especially bomber units.
39 756th Commander's Narrative for 11 May to 11 June 1944, 24; B Co/756th Unit Journal, "Narrative of Action, 3rd Platoon, 11 May to 10 June"; B Co/756th Unit Journal "Commander's Narrative 11 May to 10 June 1944."
40 756th Commander's Narrative for 11 May to 11 June 1944, 24; Howze, *A Cavalryman's Story*, 115; Redle interview 13 March 2004. The tankers never did find out why they kept getting strafed by Allied planes. Either a miscommunication occurred over proper smoke colors or perhaps the smoke color used washed out in the sunlight.
41 US Army, *Fifth Army History, Part V*, 158–59.
42 Fisher, *Cassino to the Alps*, 216–18.
43 Ibid., 214–15; US Army, *Fifth Army History, Part V*, 158–59.
44 Zaloga, *Anzio 1944*, 90.
45 Howze, *A Cavalryman's Story*, 116.
46 Ibid., 115–16.
47 FSSF 1st Bn/2nd Regt was commanded at this time by Maj Edward H. Thomas, and the FSSF 2nd Bn/2nd Regt was commanded by Maj Stanley C. Waters.
48 756th Commander's Narrative for 11 May to 11 June 1944, 24; Redle interview 13 March 2004; Lewis, personal papers, 756th HQ attachments document dated 8 May 1945; Fazendin, *756th at Cassino*, 204: Lewis recollection.
49 756th Commander's Narrative for 11 May to 11 June 1944, 24–25.
50 B Co/756th Unit Journal "Commander's Narrative 11 May to 10 June 1944"; Fazendin, *756th at Cassino*, 173–74: Redle recollection.
51 B Co/756th Unit Journal, "Narrative of Action, 3rd Platoon, 11 May to 10 June."
52 756th Commander's Narrative for 11 May to 11 June 1944, 24–25.
53 Ibid., 32: "Clockwork" is Rogers's description; Fisher, *Cassino to the Alps*, 216; Yeide, *The Infantry's Armor*, 90–91; B Co/756th Unit Journal "Commander's Narrative 11 May to 10 June 1944"; Fazendin, *756th at Cassino*, 204: Lewis recollection.
54 B Co/756th Unit Journal, "Narrative of Action, 3rd Platoon, 11 May to 10 June."
55 Howze, *A Cavalryman's Story*, 116.
56 Fazendin, *756th at Cassino*, 174: Redle recollection.
57 Ibid., 173–75; Howze, *A Cavalryman's Story*, 116; Fisher, *Cassino to the Alps*, 216–18. The 1943 US Army maps do not show a "barracks" in the immediate area. The location was likely a series of school buildings along the Via Prenestina and 500 yards south of the railroad tracks.
58 Springer, *Black Devil Brigade*, 226–27: S/Sgt W. E. Murray died of the chest wound. Pvt J. J. Constantine was killed by the headshot. Another Forceman named Ed Bechtel was the third man hit and seemingly survived. This detail comes from the account of S/Sgt John Dawson of 6th Company, 2nd Battalion, 2nd Regiment, who pulled all three men clear of the advancing tanks. Dawson convinced a medic to mercifully administer a morphine shot to Constantine—even though the man was doomed.
59 Fazendin, *756th at Cassino*, 174–75: Redle recollection.
60 Redle interview, 16 September 2005.
61 756th Commander's Narrative for 11 May to 11 June 1944, 25.
62 Redle letter to Harry Yeide, 30 January 2008: "Exceptional" is Redle's description. Fazendin, *756th at Cassino*, 174: Redle recollection. The identity of this fearless movie photographer and whether he or the film footage even survived is unknown.
63 Fazendin, *756th at Cassino*, 174: Redle recollection.
64 Redle letter, 2 May 2002; US World War II Hospital Admission Card Files, 1942–1954; IDPF for Joe K. Wright; B Co/756th Unit Journal, 4 June 1944.

65 US World War II Hospital Admission Card Files, 1942–1954; Fazendin, *756th at Cassino*, 173–75: Redle recollection.
66 US World War II Hospital Admission Card Files, 1942–1954.
67 Ibid.: Some speculation is involved here. The record does not clearly establish Hulin was a member of Stout's crew, but the circumstances (gunshot to leg outside the tank) suggests he was. Cardullo had been left alone according to S/Sgt Oliver's Silver Star Citation. It was not uncommon for wounded tankers to insist their comrades leave to save themselves. It's possible, too, that because Hulin and Stout were also wounded, they may not have been able to carry Cardullo.
68 B Co/756th Unit Journal, "Actions of 2nd Platoon, 11 May to 10 June"; B Co/756th Unit Journal, 4 June 1944; Redle letter, 3 January 2001.
69 Fazendin, *756th at Cassino*, 174: Redle recollection.
70 Oliver Silver Star citation, (GO #175 HQ 3rd Inf Div dated 8 August 1944); B Co/756th Unit Journal "Commander's Narrative 11 May to 10 June 1944"; Redle letter, 5 October 2000; B Co/756th Unit Journal, "Narrative of Action, 3rd Platoon, 11 May to 10 June"; Redle interview, 16 September 2005; Fazendin, *756th at Cassino*, 174: Redle recollection. Some credited Bulen for also destroying a second tank. The others were likely knocked out by the supporting TDs.
71 Oliver Silver Star citation (GO #175 HQ 3rd Inf Div dated 8 August 1944).
72 Ibid.
73 Fazendin, *756th at Cassino*, 175: Redle recollection.
74 B Co/756th Unit Journal "Commander's Narrative 11 May to 10 June 1944."
75 Oliver Silver Star citation (GO #175 HQ 3rd Inf Div dated 8 August 1944).
76 B Co/756th Unit Journal "Commander's Narrative 11 May to 10 June 1944"; B Co/756th Unit Journal, "Actions of 2nd Platoon, 11 May to 10 June."
77 Fazendin, *756th at Cassino*, 174–75 and 177–78: Redle recollection.
78 Ibid.
79 Howze, *A Cavalryman's Story*, 116.
80 B Co/756th Unit Journal "Commander's Narrative 11 May to 10 June 1944."
81 756th Commander's Narrative for 11 May to 11 June 1944, 25; Fazendin, *756th at Cassino*, 204: Lewis recollection.
82 B Co/756th Unit Journal "Commander's Narrative 11 May to 10 June 1944."
83 Fazendin, *756th at Cassino*, 175: Redle recollection.
84 Ibid., 175 and 177: Redle identifies the route a Highway 6, but that road was nearly a mile to the south. He likely meant the Via Prenestina, which was much closer.
85 Fazendin, *756th at Cassino*, 174–75: Redle recollection.
86 Fisher, *Cassino to the Alps*, 216; Howze, *A Cavalryman's Story*, 116: Howze writes Col Marshall was killed by a 20mm projectile through the forehead—which must have been a horrific and gruesome event for those with him.
87 Howze, *A Cavalryman's Story*, 116–17; Fisher, *Cassino to the Alps*, 216–18.
88 Fisher, *Cassino to the Alps*, 216; US Army, *Fifth Army History, Part V*, 158–59.
89 Howze, *A Cavalryman's Story*, 116–17: Howze places the time his tanks entered the city proper as 1830.
90 Springer, *Black Devil Brigade*, 226–27; Daniel De Luce, "Roman Populace in Warm Greetings For Fifth Army Forces" *Corsicana Semi-Weekly Light* (Corsicana, Texas), 6 June 1944, 1 and 14.
91 US Army, *Fifth Army History, Part V*, 158–59.
92 Böhmler, *Monte Cassino: A German View*, 285.
93 756th Commander's Narrative for 11 May to 11 June 1944, 25.
94 Fazendin, *756th at Cassino*, 204: Lewis recollection.
95 Laurie, *Rome-Arno*, 2; Zaloga, *Anzio 1944*, 90; Delaney, *Blue Devils*, 91–94.
96 Seymour Korman, "First General in Rome Describes Battle on the Tiber" *Chicago Tribune* (Chicago, Illinois), 10 June 1944, 5; Fisher, *Cassino to the Alps*, 218; Howze, *A Cavalryman's Story*, 117–18: Howze describes the incident in his book with this dash of sardonic humor: "They shot through the shoulder an unattached engineer colonel who had been giving me unsought-for advice all day, thus saving me the trouble."
97 B Co/756th Unit Journal, 4 June 1944; B Co/756th Unit Journal, "Narrative of Action, 3rd Platoon, 11 May to 10 June"; B Co/756th Unit Journal, 4 June 1944: Bivouac location was a half-mile east of town.

98 B Co/756th Morning Report, 13 June 1944.
99 US World War II Hospital Admission Card Files, 1942–1954; B Co/756th Morning Reports 12, 13, and 23 June 1944. The 22-year-old Hulin never returned to B Company.
100 B Co/756th Morning Report, 4 June 1944; B Co/756th Unit Journal, 4 June 1944.
101 Fazendin, *756th at Cassino*, 174: Redle recollection.
102 IDPF, Wright.
103 Redle letter, 2 May 2002.
104 Fazendin, *756th at Cassino*, 178: Redle recollection; B Co/756th Unit Journal, 5 June 1944.
105 B Co/756th Morning Report, 3 June 1944.
106 Redle letter, 28 June 2009: Redle described Newman as a fine platoon leader and stated he never heard any complaints about him from the men or supporting infantry.
107 756th Commander's Narrative for 11 May to 11 June 1944, 25–26; Donley diary, 5 June 1944; Lewis, personal papers, 756th HQ attachments document dated 8 May 1945; Bernhard "Life in the Service."
108 US Army, *Fifth Army History, Part V*, 166–67; Clark, *Calculated Risk*, 365–66.
109 Blumenson, *Mark Clark*, 215–16; Delaney, *Blue Devils*, 97.
110 US Army, *Fifth Army History, Part V*, 166–67; Fisher, *Cassino to the Alps*, 222.
111 US Army, *Fifth Army History, Part V*, 166–67; Springer, *Black Devil Brigade*, 228.
112 Clark, *Calculated Risk*, 352.
113 Zaloga, *Anzio 1944*, 91.
114 Blumenson, *Mark Clark*, 217–18.
115 Lewis, personal papers, 756th HQ attachments document dated 8 May 1945.
116 Fazendin, *756th at Cassino*, 178 and 205: Redle and Lewis recollections.
117 Guild phone conversation, 11 February 2004.
118 756th Commander's Narrative for 11 May to 11 June 1944, 26; B Co/756th Morning Report, 5 June 1944; B Co/756th Unit Journal, 6 June 1944; Donley diary, 6 June 1944.
119 Delaney, *Blue Devils*, 89, 92–93; US Army, *Fifth Army History, Part V*, 157–58.
120 Fisher, *Cassino to the Alps*, 215. Both Howze and Cairns became generals in the 1950s and were staunch proponents for the integration of helicopters in US Army cavalry operations. Ironically, Maj Gen Cairns died in a helicopter crash in 1958. General Howze retired in 1965 and passed away in 1998 at age 89.
121 Werner, *First Special Service Force*, 24; Springer, *Black Devil Brigade*, 224–26.
122 Ankrum, *Dogfaces Who Smiled Through Tears*, 533–34.

Chapter 17

1 91st Cavalry Reconnaissance Squadron After Action Reports, May 1944 through May 1945, "Report of Operations, dated 19 July 1944," at http://usacac.army.mil/organizations/cace/carl
2 756th Commander's Narrative for 11 May to 11 June 1944, 26; B Co/756th Morning Report, 6 June 1944.
3 B Co/756th Unit Journal, 6 June 1944.
4 Ibid.
5 Charles A. Ellis, US Select Military Registers, 1862–1985, (www.ancestry.com); Charles A. Ellis memorial at www.findagrave.com/memorial/63098731/charle-a-ellis
6 Fazendin, *756th at Cassino*, 178: Redle recollection.
7 Zaloga, *Anzio 1944*, 90.
8 "Battle Experiences of Cavalry are Told," *Lebanon Daily News* (Lebanon, Pennsylvania), 22 September 1944, 3; "SAIC Ellis, San Antonio, Retires July 31" biography dated 23 July 1954, obtained from the Fort Sam Houston Museum.
9 "Hero to Aid Sale of Bonds", *Press and Sun-Bulletin*, Binghamton, New York, 29 May 1945, 5.
10 91st Cavalry Reconnaissance Squadron Operations Reports, 1 November 1943 to 20 February 1945 (Colonel T. Q. Donaldson Summary, dated 28 February 1945) at http://usacac.army.mil/organizations/cace/carl
11 Fazendin, *756th at Cassino*, 205: Lewis recollection; B Co/756th Morning Report, 6 June 1944.
12 88th Inf Div G-3 Report for 6 June 1944 with overlay.
13 91st Cav Operations Reports, 1 November 1943–20 February 1945, (Donaldson Summary).

14 Ibid.
15 756th Commander's Narrative for 11 May to 11 June 1944, 26; Yeide, *The Infantry's Armor*, 92; 88th Inf Div G-3 Report, 6 June 1944.
16 Fisher, *Cassino to the Alps*, 229 and 236.
17 88th Inf Div G-3 Report, 7 June 1944, directive signed by Sloan to Task Force Ellis.
18 91st Cav After Action Reports, May 1944–February 1945, Report of Operations, dated 19 July 1944: A Captain Watson commanded the "red" (A) column, and a Captain Day commanded the "blue" (B) column.
19 756th Commander's Narrative for 11 May to 11 June 1944, 26.
20 Ibid.
21 Donley diary, 6 June 1944.
22 Ibid.
23 91st Cav After Action Reports, May 1944–February 1945, Report of Operations, dated 19 July 1944; 756th Commander's Narrative for 11 May to 11 June 1944, 26: The 117th Reconnaissance Squadron admitted to making the observation error.
24 91st Cav After Action Reports, May 1944–February 1945, Report of Operations, dated 19 July 1944.
25 756th Commander's Narrative for 11 May to 11 June 1944, 26–27: Identified as Point "D" on Rogers's sketch 3(c) map.
26 Fazendin, *756th at Cassino*, 205–06: Lewis recollection.
27 756th Commander's Narrative for 11 May to 11 June 1944, 27.
28 Fazendin, *756th at Cassino*, 178–79: Redle recollection.
29 B Co/756th Unit Journal, 6 June 1944.
30 Fazendin, *756th at Cassino*, 179: Redle recollection.
31 756th Commander's Narrative for 11 May to 11 June 1944, 27.
32 Point "F" on Rogers's sketch 3(c) map.
33 Fazendin, *756th at Cassino*, 206: Lewis recollection; 756th Commander's Narrative for 11 May to 11 June 1944, 27–28.
34 Bernhard, "Life in the Service"; 91st Cav Operations Reports, 1 November 1943–20 February 1945 (Donaldson Summary).
35 756th Commander's Narrative for 11 May to 11 June 1944, 27–28; Donley diary, 7 June 1944.
36 Fazendin, *756th at Cassino*, 206: Lewis recollection; Bernhard, "Life in the Service."
37 B Co/756th Unit Journal "Commander's Narrative 11 May to 10 June 1944."
38 B Co/756th Unit Journal, 7 June 1944.
39 Fazendin, *756th at Cassino*, 179: Redle recollection; B Co/756th Morning Report, 7 June 1944; 756th Commander's Narrative for 11 May to 11 June 1944, 28; 91st Cav Operations Reports, 1 November 1943–20 February 1945 (Donaldson Summary).
40 B Co/756th Unit Journal, "Narrative of Action, 3rd Platoon, 11 May to 10 June"; B Co/756th Unit Journal, "Actions of 2nd Platoon, 11 May to 10 June."
41 756th Commander's Narrative for 11 May to 11 June 1944, 28.
42 Ibid., 27–28.
43 Ibid., 29: Rogers labeled these columns "left" and "right" but the 91st Cavalry continued referring to them as "blue" and "red." Blue was the left, and red was the right.
44 Donley diary, 8 June 1944.
45 B Co/756th Unit Journal, 8 June 1944.
46 91st Cav After Action Reports, May 1944–February 1945, Report of Operations, dated 19 July 1944.
47 B Co/756th Unit Journal, "Narrative of Action, 3rd Platoon, 11 May to 10 June."
48 Ibid.
49 B Co/756th Unit Journal, "Actions of 1st Platoon, May 17 to June 10, 1944."
50 Ibid.
51 88th Inf Div G-3 reports, directions from Sloan to Task Force Ellis dated 8 June 1944.
52 91st Cav Operations Reports, 1 November 1943–20 February 1945 (Donaldson Summary).
53 91st Cav After Action Reports, May 1944–February 1945, Report of Operations, dated 19 July 1944.
54 B Co/756th Morning Report, 8 June 1944.
55 756th Commander's Narrative for 11 May to 11 June 1944, 29.

56 91st Cav Operations Reports, 1 November 1943–20 February 1945 (Donaldson Summary).
57 88th Inf Div G-3 reports, directions from Sloan to Task Force Ellis dated 8 June 1944. The line technically ran from Orte to a road junction east of Soriano at the 5830 grid-line.
58 756th Commander's Narrative for 11 May to 11 June 1944, 29–30.
59 B Co/756th Unit Journal, "Actions of 2nd Platoon, 11 May to 10 June."
60 Ibid.
61 756th Commander's Narrative for 11 May to 11 June 1944, 29–30.
62 B Co/756th Morning Report, 12 June 1944; "Knox Man Wounded in Italian Drive" *The Knoxville News-Sentinel* (Knoxville, Tennessee), 23 June 1944, 3; "Lt Newman Reported Wounded in Italy" *The Knoxville Journal* (Knoxville, Tennessee), 24 June 1944, 10; B Co/756th Unit Journal, "Actions of 2nd Platoon, 11 May to 10 June"; B Co/756th Unit Journal "Commander's Narrative 11 May to 10 June 1944."
63 B Co/756th Unit Journal "Commander's Narrative 11 May to 10 June 1944."
64 Fazendin, *756th at Cassino*, 179: Redle recollection.
65 B Co/756th Unit Journal "Commander's Narrative 11 May to 10 June 1944"; B Co/756th Unit Journal, "Narrative of Action, 3rd Platoon, 11 May to 10 June."
66 756th Commander's Narrative for 11 May to 11 June 1944, 30; Fazendin, *756th at Cassino*, 179: Redle recollection; B Co/756th Unit Journal, "Actions of 2nd Platoon, 11 May to 10 June"; B Co/756th Unit Journal "Commander's Narrative 11 May to 10 June 1944."
67 Fazendin, *756th at Cassino*, 179: Redle recollection.
68 B Co/756th Unit Journal "Commander's Narrative 11 May to 10 June 1944."
69 B Co/756th Unit Journal, "Narrative of Action, 3rd Platoon, 11 May to 10 June"; B Co/756th Unit Journal, 9 June 1944.
70 B Co/756th Unit Journal, "Actions of 2nd Platoon, 11 May to 10 June"; Fazendin, *756th at Cassino*, 179: Redle recollection.
71 Lewis, personal papers, 756th HQ attachments document dated 8 May 1945; 756th Commander's Narrative for 11 May to 11 June 1944, 30.
72 B Co/756th Morning Report, 10 June 1944; 756th Commander's Narrative for 11 May to 11 June 1944, 29–30.
73 Ibid.
74 B Co/756th Unit Journal, 10 June 1944.
75 B Co/756th Morning Report, 9 June 1944.
76 B Co/756th Unit Journal, 8 June 1944.
77 Perdue phone conversation, 31 January 2004: Sheffield was from Texas.
78 B Co/756th Morning Report, 10 June 1944; B Co/756th Morning Report, 13 June 1944.
79 756th Commander's Narrative for 11 May to 11 June 1944, 30.
80 Fazendin, *756th at Cassino*, 206: Lewis recollection.

Chapter 18

1 Fazendin, *756th at Cassino*, 206: Lewis recollection; Bernhard, "Life in the Service."
2 Donley diary, 11 June 1944.
3 Fazendin, *756th at Cassino*, 179–80: Redle recollection.
4 Donley diary, 11 June 1944.
5 B Co/756th Morning Report, 11 June 1944; B Co/756th Unit Journal, 11 June 1944.
6 756th Commander's Narrative for 11 May to 11 June 1944, 30.
7 B Co/756th Unit Journal, 11 June 1944.
8 Donley diary, 28 May 1944.
9 Ibid., 10 and 12 June 1944.
10 756th Commander's Narrative for 11 May to 11 June 1944, 30.
11 Donley diary, 13 June 1944.
12 756th Commander's Narrative for 11 May to 11 June 1944, 30.
13 Bernhard, "Life in the Service."

14 Fazendin, *756th at Cassino*, 206: Lewis recollection.
15 B Co/756th Morning Report, 13 June 1944: The replacements were: Pfc Simon Bramblett and Pvts George F. Fick, Norman W. Keller, Paul H. Kreuziger, Max M. Kristal, Frank J. Mandalski, James Mariani, John D. Mekus, William T. Payne, William F. Pennetta, Ray H. Sipe, and Edward C. Skinner—all assigned and joined from Personnel Center #1.
16 B Co/756th Morning Report, 15 June 1944; B Co/756th Unit Journal, 15 June 1944.
17 Anderson interview, 19–21 September 2002; Anderson, phone conversation, 20 June 2009: After the war, Roy Anderson asked Dave Redle if he ever got into trouble for this incident. Dave laughed and said "not much."
18 Redle letter, 13 February 2001; Redle letter, 24 June 2002. These reports are kept at the Eisenhower Presidential Library and provided much detail for this book.
19 Lt Anthony Melfi letter to wife dated 10 November 1944.
20 Redle interview, 19 January 2002.
21 Perdue phone conversation, 31 January 2004.
22 Guild phone conversation, 11 February 2004.
23 Lt Anthony Melfi letter to wife dated 10 November 1944.
24 R & R is short for "rest and relaxation."
25 Donley diary, 15 June 1944; Fazendin, *756th at Cassino*, 206–07: Lewis recollection.
26 Donley diary, 16 June 1944.
27 Bernhard, "Life in the Service."
28 Offerman, "My Dad Was A Tanker," 24–25.
29 Redle interview, 13 March 2004; Fazendin, *756th at Cassino*, 180: Redle recollection.
30 Fazendin, *756th at Cassino*, 207: Lewis recollection.
31 Not everyone in the 135th Inf Regt had a poor opinion of Sweeting. Homer Ankrum called him "One of best tank-infantry tacticians of the war." (Ankrum, *Dogfaces Who Smiled Through Tears*, 533.) Sweeting was, without question, a very creative, aggressive, and driven officer. Wars are won by such men willing to push the limits.
32 Lewis, personal papers, 756th HQ attachments document dated 8 May 1945.
33 Ibid.; B Co Unit Journal, 18 June 1944.
34 Esposito, *756th in Europe*, 250: Long recollection.
35 Fazendin, *756th at Cassino*, 207: Lewis recollection.
36 Donley diary, 17 June 1944.
37 Ibid., 18 June 1944.
38 Bernhard, "Life in the Service."
39 B Co/756th Morning Report, 18 June 1944: Pvt Filimon Aragon, Pvt John W. Jarrett, and Pvt Raymond R. Reid were listed as AWOL as of 2000.
40 Ibid., 19 June 1944.
41 B Co Unit Journal, 19 June 1944.
42 Ibid.; Fazendin, *756th at Cassino*, 181: Redle recollection.
43 Donley diary, 19 June 1944.
44 B Co/756th Morning Report, 20 June 1944; B Co Unit Journal, 20 June 1944.
45 Donley diary, 20 June 1944.
46 B Co Unit Journal, 20 June 1944.
47 Donley diary, 20 June 1944.
48 Redle interview 13 March 2004; Lewis, personal papers, 756th HQ attachments document dated 8 May 1945.
49 B Co/756th Morning Report, 21 June 1944; Donley diary, 21 and 23 June 1944; B Co Unit Journal, 21 June 1944.
50 Fazendin, *756th at Cassino*, 181: Redle recollection.
51 B Co/756th Morning Report, 23 June 1944.
52 B Co Unit Journal, 23 June 1944; IDPF, Cardullo: Cardullo's family lived in Connecticut but his home address was listed in Albany, New York.
53 Redle letter, 29 April 2003.
54 B Co/756th Morning Report, 24 June 1944.

Index

References to maps are in *italics*.